Basics of
Social Research

Qualitative and Quantitative Approaches

THIRD EDITION

W. Lawrence Neuman

University of Wisconsin–Whitewater

PEARSON

Boston   Columbus   Indianapolis   New York   San Francisco
Upper Saddle River   Amsterdam   Cape Town   Dubai   London
Madrid   Milan   Munich   Paris   Montreal   Toronto   Delhi
Mexico City   Sao Paulo   Sydney   Hong Kong   Seoul
Singapore   Taipei   Tokyo

Editorial Director: Craig Campanella
Editor in Chief: Dickson Musslewhite
Publisher: Karen Hanson
Editorial Assistant: Christine Dore
Director of Marketing: Brandy Dawson
Executive Marketing Manager: Kelly May
Marketing Assistant: Janeli Bitor
Director of Production: Lisa Iarkowski
Senior Managing Editor: Karen Carter

Associate Managing Editor: Liz Napolitano
Senior Operations Supervisor: Megan Cochran
Cover Designer: Joel Gendron
Media Director: Brian Hyland
Supplements Editor: Mayda Bosco
Full-Service Project Management and
    Composition: Amy L. Saucier, Laserwords
Printer/Binder: R. R. Donnelley VA
Cover Printer: R. R. Donnelley VA

Credits and acknowledgments borrowed from other sources and reproduced, with permission, in this textbook appear on the appropriate page within text or on page 426.

Many of the designations by manufacturers and sellers to distinguish their products are claimed as trademarks. Where those designations appear in this book, and the publisher was aware of a trademark claim, the designations have been printed in initial caps or all caps.

Library of Congress Cataloging-in-Publication Data

Neuman, William Lawrence,
    Basics of social research : qualitative and quantitative approaches /
W. Lawrence Neuman.—3rd ed.
        p. cm.
    Includes bibliographical references and indexes.
    1. Sociology—Research—Methodology. 2. Social
sciences—Research—Methodology. I. Title.
    HM571.N48 2012
    301.072—dc23

                                2011018011

10 9 8 7 6 5 4 3 2 1

www.pearsonhighered.com

ISBN-10: 0-205-76261-1
ISBN-13: 978-0-205-76261-3

CONTENTS

I have found that many students approach a first course on social research with anxiety and trepidation. Sometimes this is because they associate the course with mathematics and statistics with which they had an unpleasant past experience. Other times, it is because they struggled in natural science courses that used experiments and abstract concepts. More often, they do not know what to expect but feel it is beyond them. They may wonder why they must take the course and think it only for advanced students preparing to become professors or research experts.

The purpose of *Basics of Social Research* is to introduce you to social research and presents "what researchers do and why" in a nonthreatening manner. It captures both the excitement and importance of doing "real" research. The "nuts and bolts" of methods to complete a study requires disciplined thinking and has rigor. It will help build these basic livelong skills that have many practical uses. With a little patience and time, learning social research methods is within easy reach of all undergraduate students.

First, you need to overcome the anxiety and see what doing social research is actually about. You will probably find it fascinating. A course in social research methodology differs from most social science courses that examine content topics, such as inequality, crime, racial divisions, gender relations, urban society, and so forth. It applies to all content areas. A course on research is relevant, both in preparing you to think in a more systematic way about content areas, and in revealing how content knowledge was created in the first place.

This book aims to be easy to understand and accessible. Accessible does not mean it is "Mickey Mouse" or "fluff." Indeed, doing proper research is a serious activity. Often how well a study was conducted has important consequences. Also, to do research you confront significant ethical issues. Study findings shape policy decisions and service delivery concerns. Ultimately social research yields new knowledge. It influences what we as a society know about most issues of importance. Just as the actual daily work of a nurse, social worker, police officer, teacher, physician, or counselor involves serious issues with real implications for people's lives, so does social research.

Basics of Social Research has three goals. First, it seeks to show you that social research is simultaneously an important enterprise and one that is open to you—you *can* understand it. Second, it uses many examples from "real research" in published studies. This shows you the origins of the findings and information you read in class textbooks or hear about in the media. Last, it gives you a foundation for further learning about doing research. You will soon see that doing social research requires dedication, creativity, and mature judgment.

It is important to nix a misconception: social research is not a matter of simply following a cookbook-like set of procedures or looking up the correct formula without really thinking. It is a creative process that requires you to have personal integrity and make moral choices. It includes core values—such as a strong commitment to free and open inquiry into vital questions about the social world.

This book is a shortened version of a larger, in-depth textbook on social research that I first wrote 20 years ago. I wrote this book to provide you with a more streamlined, less complex introduction to social research. It reflects what my students taught me over the 30 years that I have been helping undergraduates understand and appreciate social research methods.

From the first time I learned about and began teaching social research methods, I have been committed to the value of both quantitative and qualitative approaches to research. I believe each approach offers a distinct and complementary perspective to understanding the social world. Both are equally important and necessary to expand human understanding. Revisions in this edition include updated examples from the recent literature, rewording for greater clarity, a more student-centered focus, and a reorganization of material to make the presentation smoother.

Instructor's Manual and Test Bank (ISBN 0205762638: The Instructor's Manual and Test Bank has been prepared to assist teachers in their efforts to prepare lectures and evaluate student learning. For each chapter of the text, the Instructor's Manual offers different types of resources, including detailed chapter summaries and outlines, learning objectives, discussion questions, classroom activities and much more.

Also included in this manual is a test bank offering multiple-choice, true/false, fill-in-the-blank, and/or essay questions for each chapter. The Instructor's Manual and Test Bank is available to adopters at www.pearsonhighered.com.

MyTest (ISBN 0205762999): The Test Bank is also available online through Pearson's computerized testing system, MyTest. MyTest allows instructors to create their own personalized exams, to edit any of the existing test questions, and to add new questions. Other special features of this program include random generation of test questions, creation of alternative versions of the same test, scrambling question sequence, and test preview before printing. Search and sort features allow you to locate questions quickly and to arrange them in whatever order you prefer. The test bank can be accessed from anywhere with a free MyTest user account. There is no need to download a program or file to your computer.

PowerPoint Presentations (ISBN 0205225373): Lecture PowerPoints are available for this text. The Lecture PowerPoint slides outline each chapter to help you convey sociological principles in a visual and exciting way. They are available to adopters at www.pearsonhighered.com.

MySearchLab: MySearchLab provides a host of tools for students to master a writing or research project. It provides online access to reliable content for internet research projects, including thousands of academic journal articles, numerous periodicals, U.S. census data, online libraries of primary and secondary sources, daily news feeds, and articles from the EBSCO ContentSelect database, a complete online handbook for grammar and usage support. MySearchLab also includes step-by-step tutorials to help students understand and avoid plagiarism, and AutoCite, which helps students correctly cite sources.

Doing Social Research

INTRODUCTION

Social research is all around us. Educators, government officials, business managers, human service providers, and health care professionals make frequent use of social research findings. Many people use social research to raise children, reduce crime, improve health, sell products, or just understand life. Daily broadcast news programs, magazines, newspapers, and websites disseminate research results.

Research findings can affect our lives and public policies. For example, I recently read about a study that looked at the "summer slide" or decline in children's reading and spelling skills over the summer. The decline is greatest among low-income students who lose about two months of school learning each summer. At a time when many schools are cutting summer programs to save money, the study found that simply giving low-income children access to books at spring fairs and letting them pick books that most interested them reduced the summer reading gap. Low-income children given twelve books and who read them over three summers far outpaced those who did not. They gained as much as if they had attended summer school each summer.[1]

This book is about *social research.* In simple terms, research is a way to find answers to questions. Professors, professional researchers, practitioners, and students in many fields conduct research studies to answer questions and learn about social life. You probably already have some notion of what social research entails. First, let me end some possible misconceptions. When I asked students in my classes what they think social research entails, they gave the following answers:

- It is based on facts alone; there is no theory or personal judgment.
- Only experts with a Ph.D. degree or college professors read it or do it.
- It means going to the library and finding a lot of magazine articles or books on a topic.
- It is when someone hangs around a group and observes.
- It means conducting a controlled experiment.
- Social research is drawing a sample of people and giving them questionnaires to complete.
- It is looking up lots of statistical tables and information from official government reports.
- To do it, one must use computers to create statistics, charts, and graphs.

The first two answers are wrong, and the others describe only part of what constitutes social research. It is unwise to confuse one part with the whole.

We do social research to learn something new about the social world; or to carefully document our guesses, hunches, theories, or beliefs about it; or to better understand how the social world works. In research we combine theories and ideas with facts in a careful, systematic way and this requires creativity. To do a study, we must organize, plan carefully, and select appropriate techniques to address a specific question. We want to treat the people in a study in ethical and moral ways. Once we complete a study, it is time to communicate the results to others in a complete and accurate way.

In the process of social research we combine principles, outlooks, and ideas (i.e., methodology) with a collection of specific practices, techniques, and strategies (i.e., a method of inquiry) to produce knowledge. It is an exciting process of discovery, but it requires persistence, personal integrity, tolerance for ambiguity, interaction with others, and pride in doing quality work.

Reading this book will not transform you into an expert researcher, but it can teach you to be a better consumer of research results, help you to understand how the research enterprise works, and prepare you to conduct your own small-scale studies. After studying this book, you will be aware of what research can and cannot do, and why conducting research properly is important.

ALTERNATIVES TO SOCIAL RESEARCH

Unless you are very unusual, little of what you know about the social life comes from having done social research. Most likely, your knowledge comes from an alternative to social research. It comes from what your parents and others (e.g., friends, teachers) told you. It comes from your personal experiences as well as from books and magazines you have read. You also learned aspects of social life from the movies and television you have watched. You may also use plain old "common sense."

As you saw above, social research is more than a set of techniques; it is a process. Compared to most processes in daily life, it is much more structured, organized, and systematic. Your knowledge about social life from the alternatives to social research is often correct; however, the knowledge from research studies is more likely to be true and to have fewer errors. The research-based knowledge is not perfect, but compared to the alternatives it has fewer flaws and avoids common mistakes. Let us review the alternatives before examining social research.

Authority

Parents, teachers, and experts as well as books, television, and other media have provided you with knowledge about social life. When you accept something as true because someone in a position of authority says it is true, or because it appears in an authoritative outlet, you are relying on authority as a basis for knowledge. Relying on the wisdom of authorities is a quick, simple, and cheap way to learn something. Many authorities spend time and effort to learn something, and you benefit from their experience and work.

Nonetheless, relying on authority has limitations. First, it is easy to overestimate the expertise of others. History is full of past experts who now look misinformed. For example, some "experts" of the past measured intelligence by counting bumps on the skull; other "experts" used bloodletting to try to cure diseases. Their errors seem obvious now; however, can we be certain that today's experts will not become tomorrow's fools? Second, authorities may not agree, and not all authorities are equally dependable. Whom should you believe if authorities disagree? Third, authorities may speak on fields about which they know little about. An expert who is highly informed about one area may use his or her authority in an unrelated area. Also, using the halo effect (discussed later), legitimate expertise in one area might spill into illegitimate authority in a totally different area. Have you ever seen television commercials where a movie star uses his or her fame to convince you to buy a car?

An additional issue is the misuse of authority. Sometimes organizations or individuals try to give an appearance of authority so they can convince others to agree to something that they might not otherwise agree to. A related situation occurs when a person with little training and expertise is named as a "senior fellow" or "adjunct scholar" in a "think tank" with an impressive name, such as the Center for the Study of X or the Institute on Y Research. Some think tanks are legitimate research centers, but many are mere fronts that wealthy special-interest groups create to engage in advocacy politics. Think tanks can make anyone a "scholar" to facilitate the mass media accepting him or her as an authority on an issue. In reality, the person may not have any real expertise.[2] Also, too much reliance on authorities can be dangerous to a democratic society. Experts may promote strengthening their own power and position. When you accept the authority of experts, but do not know how they arrived at their knowledge, the ability to evaluate what the experts say is lost as is control of your destiny.

Tradition

Many people rely on tradition for knowledge. Tradition is a special case of authority—the authority of the past. Tradition means you accept something as being true because "it's the way things have always been." For example, my father-in-law says that drinking a shot of whiskey cures a cold. When I asked about his statement, he said that he had learned it from his father when he was a child, and it had come down from past generations. Tradition was the basis of the knowledge for the cure. Here is an example from the social world: Many people believe that children who are raised at home by their mothers grow up to be better adjusted and have fewer personal problems than those raised in other settings. People "know" this, but how did they learn it? Most accept it because they believe (rightly or wrongly) that it was true in the past or is the way things have always been done. Some traditional social knowledge begins as simple prejudice. You might rely on tradition without being fully aware of it with a belief such as "People from that side of the tracks will never amount to anything" or "You never can trust that type of person" or "That's the way men (or women) are." Even if traditional knowledge was once true, it may have grown distorted as it was passed on and may no longer be true. People may cling to traditional knowledge without understanding; they simply assume that because something may have worked or been true in the past, it will continue to be true.

Common Sense

Everyday reasoning or common sense provides knowledge about the social world. This is relying on what everyone knows and what "just makes sense." For example, it "just makes sense" that murder rates are higher in areas that do not have the death penalty because it is common sense that people are less likely to kill if they face execution for doing so. Unfortunately, this and other widely held commonsense beliefs, such

as that poor youth are more likely to commit deviant acts than those from the middle class or that most Catholics do not use birth control, are not true.

Common sense, valuable in daily living, nonetheless allows logical fallacies to slip into thinking. For example, the so-called gambler's fallacy says: "If I have a long string of losses playing a lottery, the next time I play, my chances of winning will be better." In terms of probability and the facts, this is false. Also, common sense contains contradictory ideas that often go unnoticed because people use the ideas at different times, such as "opposites attract" and "birds of a feather flock together." Common sense can originate in tradition. It is useful and sometimes correct, but it also contains errors, misinformation, contradiction, and prejudice.

Media Distortion

Television shows, movies, and newspaper and magazine articles are important sources of information. For example, most people have little contact with criminals but learn about crime by watching television shows and movies. However, the television portrayals of crime, and of many other things, do not accurately reflect social reality. The writers who create or "adapt" images from life for television shows and movie scripts distort reality. This is due to ignorance, or relying on authority, tradition, and common sense. Distortion also occurs because their primary goal is to entertain, not to represent reality accurately. Although many newspaper journalists try to present a realistic picture of the world, they must write stories quickly with limited information and within editorial guidelines.

Unfortunately, the mass media tend to perpetuate a culture's misconceptions and myths. For example, the media show that most people who receive welfare are Black (actually, most are White), that most people who are mentally ill are violent and dangerous (only a small percentage actually are), and that most people who are elderly are senile and in nursing homes (a tiny minority are). Also, mass media "hype" can create a belief that a serious problem exists when it may not (see Example Box 1.1). Visual images mislead more easily than other forms of "lying"; this means that stories or stereotypes that appear on film and television can have a powerful effect on people. For example, television repeatedly shows low-income, inner-city, African American youth using illegal drugs. Eventually, most people "know" that urban Blacks use illegal drugs at a higher rate than other groups

in the United States, even though this notion is false. Another example is how media coverage shaped public perceptions of the organization Habitat for Humanity. Media coverage of the organization grew and presented the Habitat as "a solution to government failure" in housing. This coincided with a political era of intensified ideological criticisms of the welfare state and growing neoliberal anti-government rhetoric nearly twenty years after the Habitat organization began. Most mass media presentations of the Habitat organization were slanted and made a part of political ideological debates and often did not accurately present the organization's views or its work (see Hackworth, 2009).

Advocacy groups use the media to win public support for their cause.[3] They mount public relations campaigns to sway public thinking about issues and scientific findings. This makes it difficult for the public to evaluate research findings. For example, nearly all scientific studies confirm the global warming thesis (i.e., pollutants from industrialization and massive deforestation are raising the earth's temperature and will cause dramatic climate change). The scientific evidence is growing and getting stronger each year. Yet, the media has given equal attention to a few dissenters who question global warming. This creates a perception that "no one really knows" or that scientists are undecided. Media sources fail to mention that the dissenters are less than 2 percent of all scientists, or that heavily polluting industries have paid for almost all studies by the dissenters, then spent millions of dollars to publicize the dissenter's findings. Polluting industries had financial and public relations objectives. They wanted to deflect criticism and delay environmental regulations, not to advance knowledge and understanding.

Media outlets regularly offer horoscopes and report on supernatural powers, ESP (extrasensory perception), UFOs (unidentified flying objects), and ghosts. Although scientific studies have long shown such phenomena to be bogus, between 25 and 50 percent of the U.S. public

---

1.1 EXAMPLE BOX
Is Road Rage a Media Myth?

Americans hear a lot about *road rage*. *Newsweek* magazine, *Time* magazine, and newspapers in most major cities have carried headlines about it. Leading national political officials have held public hearings on it, and the federal government gives millions of dollars in grants to law enforcement and transportation departments to reduce it. Today, even psychologists specialize in this disorder.

The term *road rage* first appeared in 1988, and by 1997, the print media were carrying over 4,000 articles per year on it. Despite media attention about "aggressive driving" and "anger behind the wheel," there is no scientific evidence for road rage. The term is not precisely defined and can refer to anything from gunshots from cars, use of hand gestures, running bicyclists off the road, tailgating, and even anger over auto repair bills! All the data on crashes and accidents show declines during the period when road rage reached an epidemic.

Perhaps media reports fueled perceptions of road rage. After hearing or reading about road rage and having a label for the behavior, people began to notice rude driving behavior and engaged in *selective observation*. We will not know for sure until it is properly studied, but the amount of such behavior may be unchanged. It may turn out that the national epidemic of road rage is a widely held myth stimulated by reports in the mass media. (For more information, see Michael Fumento, "Road Rage versus Reality," *Atlantic Monthly* [August 1998].)

accepts them as true. In fact, the percentage of people with such beliefs has been growing over time as the entertainment media give the bogus phenomenon great prominence.[4]

Personal Experience

If something happens to us, if we personally see it or experience it, we tend to accept it as true. Personal experience, or "seeing is believing," is a powerful source of knowledge. Unfortunately, personal experience can mislead. Something similar to an optical illusion or mirage can occur. What appears true may be due to a distortion in judgment. The power of immediacy and direct personal contact can be intense. Even knowing that, we fall for illusions. Most people will believe what they see or personally experience rather than what carefully designed research has discovered. Unfortunately, the least informed people are more likely to believe they do not need to examine research (see Expansion Box 1.1).

Four errors in personal experience reinforce each other and can occur in other areas, as well. They are a basis for misleading people through propaganda, cons or fraud, magic, stereotyping, and some advertising—overgeneralization, selective observation, premature closure, and halo effect.

A frequent problem is *overgeneralization*; it happens when some evidence supports your belief, but you falsely assume that it applies to most situations, too. Limited generalization may be appropriate; under certain conditions, a small amount of evidence can explain a larger situation. The problem is that we generalize far beyond what is justified by the evidence. For example, over the years, I have known five blind people. All of them were very friendly. Can I conclude that all blind people are friendly? Do the five people with whom I happened to have personal experience represent all blind people?

The second error, *selective observation*, occurs when we take special notice of some people or events and tend to seek out evidence that

EXPANSION BOX
Illusory Superiority

Numerous social psychological studies tell us that we have a cognitive bias to overestimate the degree to which we are informed and have desirable qualities, and to underestimate our ignorance and negative qualities. This happens in many areas, including rating our IQ or intelligence, how well we do on academic tests, and possessing desirable personality traits (e.g., being friendly and considerate). In a famous 1999 study Justin Kruger and David Dunning found that less skilled people tend to make poor decisions and reach false conclusions. Also, the incompetence of such people denies them the capacity to see the mistake. Often, low-skilled people have illusory superiority, which is a false belief that the low-skilled person has abilities far higher than they actually are. By contrast, highly skilled people tend to underrate their abilities. In short, the least informed, less competent people are overconfident and rate their ability higher than well-informed and highly competent people! This creates a self-reinforcing cycle. Because people with more knowledge and skill tend to underestimate their knowledge and abilities, they work extra hard to improve. By contrast, the less informed, low-skilled people tend to overestimate their knowledge and abilities, so they see little need to seek more information or try to improve. The illusory superiority effect appears stronger in highly individualistic cultures (e.g., the United States) than collectivist cultures (e.g., East Asia). Illusory superiority also reinforces the tendency of less-informed people to not use rigorous scientific methods for gaining knowledge. They believe, falsely, that they already know a lot, so they have little need to learn about doing research studies or their findings.[5]

confirms what we already believe and ignore contradictory information. We often focus on or observe particular cases or situations, especially when they fit preconceived ideas. We are sensitive to features that confirm our thinking but overlook features that contradict it. For example, I believe tall people are excellent singers. This may be because of stereotypes, what my mother told me, or whatever. I observe tall people and, without awareness, pay particular attention to their singing. I look at a chorus or top vocalist and notice those who are tall. Without realizing it, I notice and remember people and situations that reinforce my preconceived ideas. Psychologists found that people tend to "seek out" and distort their memories to make them more consistent with what they already think.[6]

A third error is *premature closure*. It often operates with and reinforces the first two errors. Premature closure occurs when we feel we have the answer and do not need to listen, seek information, or raise questions any longer. Unfortunately, most of us are a little lazy or get a little sloppy. We take a few pieces of evidence or look at events for a short while and then think we have it figured out. We look for evidence to confirm or reject an idea, and after getting a small amount of evidence we stop and "jump to conclusions." For example, I want to learn whether people in my town support Mary Smith or Jon Van Horn for mayor. I ask 20 people; 16 say they favor Mary, two are undecided, and only two favor Jon, so I stop there and believe Mary will win. Perhaps if I had asked 200 scientifically selected people I would find that a majority actually favor Jon.

Another common error is the *halo effect*; it is when we overgeneralize from a highly positive or prestigious source and let its strong reputation or prestige "rub off" onto other areas. For example, I pick up a report by a person from a prestigious university, say Harvard or Cambridge University. I assume that the author is smart and talented and that the report will be excellent. I do not make this assumption about a report by someone from Unknown University. I form an opinion and prejudge the report and may not approach it by considering its own merits alone. How the various alternatives to social research might address the issue of laundry is shown in Table 1.1.

TABLE 1.1   Alternatives to Social Research

Alternative Explanation to Social Research	Example Issue: In the division of household tasks by gender, why do women tend to do the laundry?
Authority	Experts say that as children, females are taught to make, select, mend, and clean clothing as part of a female focus on physical appearance and on caring for children or others in a family. Women do the laundry based on their childhood preparation.
Tradition	Women have done the laundry for centuries, so it is a continuation of what has happened for a long time.
Common Sense	Men just are not as concerned about clothing as much as women, so it only makes sense that women do the laundry more often.
Media Myth	Television commercials show women often doing laundry and enjoying it, so they do laundry because they think it's fun.
Personal Experience	My mother and the mothers of all my friends did the laundry. My female friends did it for their boyfriends, but never the other way around. It just feels natural for the woman to do it.

HOW SCIENCE WORKS

Social research builds on some aspects of the alternative ways of knowing but it differs because social research relies on science. It embraces a scientific worldview and follows scientific processes to create and evaluate knowledge.

Science

If you hear the term *science*, you might think of test tubes, computers, rocket ships, and people in white lab coats. These outward trappings are a part of science, especially natural science (i.e., astronomy, biology, chemistry, geology, and physics), that deals with the physical and material world (e.g., plants, chemicals, rocks, stars, and electricity). The social sciences, such as anthropology, psychology, political science, and sociology, involve the study of people—their beliefs, behavior, interactions, institutions, and so forth. People are slower to think of these fields when hearing the word *science*.

Science is a social institution and a way to produce knowledge. Unfortunately, many people are ill informed about it. A National Science Foundation study found that between one-fifth and one-third adults could correctly explain the basics of science in 2010, a proportion that has changed little over the past 20 years.[7]

All scientists use specialized techniques to gather data, and then use the data to support or reject theories. *Data* are the empirical evidence or information that one gathers carefully according to rules or procedures. Social science data can be *quantitative* (i.e., expressed as numbers) or *qualitative* (i.e., expressed as words, visual images, sounds, or objects).

Empirical evidence refers to observations that we experience through the senses—touch, sight, hearing, smell, and taste. This may sound confusing because researchers cannot directly observe many aspects of the social world about which they seek answers (e.g., intelligence, attitudes, opinions, feelings, emotions, power, authority, etc.). Social researchers have created many specialized techniques to indirectly measure such aspects of the social world.

The Scientific Community

Science comes to life through the operation of the scientific community, which sustains the assumptions, attitudes, and techniques of science. The *scientific community* is a collection of people who practice science and a set of norms, behaviors, and attitudes that bind them together. It is a professional community—a group of interacting people who share ethical principles, beliefs and values, techniques and training, and career paths. For the most part, the scientific community includes both the natural and social sciences.[8]

Many people outside the core scientific community use scientific research techniques. A wide range of practitioners and technicians apply the research principles and techniques developed and refined in science. Many use techniques (e.g., a survey) without a deep knowledge of social scientific research. Yet, anyone who uses the techniques or results of science can do so better if they also understand the principles and processes of the scientific community.

The boundaries of the scientific community and its membership are imprecise, without a membership card or master roster. Many people treat a Ph.D. degree in a scientific field as an informal "entry ticket" to membership in the scientific community. The Ph.D., which stands for doctorate of philosophy, is an advanced graduate degree beyond the master's that prepares one to conduct independent research. Some researchers do not have Ph.D.s and not all those who receive Ph.D.s enter occupations in which they conduct research. They enter many occupations and may have other responsibilities (e.g., teaching, administration, consulting, clinical practice, advising, etc.). In fact, about one-half of the people who receive scientific Ph.D.s do not follow careers as active researchers.

At the core of the scientific community are researchers who conduct studies on a full-time or part-time basis, usually with the help of assistants. Many research assistants are graduate students, and some are undergraduates. Working as a research assistant is the way that most scientists gain a real grasp on the details of doing research. Colleges and universities employ most members of the scientific community's core. Some scientists work for the government or private industry in organizations such as the National Opinion Research Center and the Rand Corporation. Most, however, work at the approximately 200 research universities and institutes located in a dozen advanced industrialized countries. Thus, the scientific community is scattered geographically, but its members closely cooperate and communicate across long distances.

You may wonder, How big is the scientific community? This is not an easy question to answer. Using the broadest definition (including all scientists and those in science-related professions, such as engineers and medical doctors), it is about 15 percent of the labor force in advanced industrialized countries. A better way to look at the scientific community is to examine the basic unit of the larger community: the discipline (e.g., sociology, biology, psychology, etc.). Scientists are most familiar with a particular discipline because knowledge is specialized. Compared to other fields with advanced training, the numbers are very small. For example, each year, about 500 people receive Ph.D.s in sociology, 16,000 receive medical degrees, and 38,000 receive law degrees.

A discipline such as sociology may have about 8,000 active researchers worldwide. Most researchers complete only three or four studies in their careers, whereas a small number of active researchers conduct many dozens of studies. In a specialty or topic area (e.g., study of the death penalty, social movements, divorce), only about 100 researchers are very active and conduct over half of all research studies. Although research results represent what we know and it affects the lives of many millions of people, only a small number of people actually produce most new scientific knowledge.

The Scientific Method and Attitude

You may be wondering how the scientific method fits into this discussion of science. The *scientific method* is not one single thing; it refers to the ideas, rules, techniques, and approaches that the scientific community uses. The method arises from a loose consensus within the community of scientists. It includes a way of looking at the world that places a high value on professionalism, craftsmanship, ethical integrity, creativity, rigorous standards, and diligence. It also includes strong professional norms such as honesty and uprightness in doing research, great candor and openness about how one conducted a study, and a focus on the merits of the research itself and not on any characteristics of individuals who conducted the study.

Journal Articles in Science

Consider what happens once a researcher finishes a study. He or she writes a detailed description of the study and the results as a research report or a paper using a special format. Often, he or she also gives an oral presentation of the paper before other researchers at a conference or a meeting of a professional association, seeking comments and suggestions. Next, the researcher sends several copies to the editor of a scholarly journal. Each editor, a respected researcher chosen by other scientists to oversee the journal, removes the title page, the only place the author's name appears, and sends the article to several reviewers. The reviewers are respected scientists who have conducted studies in the same specialty area or topic. The reviewers do not know who did the study, and the author of the paper does not know who the reviewers are. This reinforces the scientific principle of judging a study on its merits alone. Reviewers evaluate the research based on its clarity, originality, standards of good research methods, and advancing knowledge. They return their evaluations to the editor, who decides to reject the paper, ask the author to revise and resubmit it, or accept it for publication. It is a very careful, cautious method to ensure quality control.

A majority of active researchers regularly read the most highly respected scholarly journals in a field. Such journals receive far more reports of studies than they can publish. They accept only 10–15 percent of submitted manuscripts. Even lower-ranked journals regularly reject half of the submissions. After several experienced researchers screened the article based on its merits alone, publication represents the study's tentative acceptance by the scientific community as a valid contribution to knowledge. Unlike the authors of articles for the popular magazines found on newsstands, scientists are not paid for publishing in scholarly journals. In fact, they may have to pay a small fee to help defray costs to have their papers considered. Social scientists are happy to make their research available to their peers (i.e., other scientists and researchers) because a scholarly journal article communicates results of a study to which a researcher might have devoted years of his or her life. Publication is how researchers gain respect and visibility among professional peers. Reviewers are not paid for reviewing papers in the evaluation process. They consider it an honor to be asked to conduct the reviews and to carry out one of the responsibilities of being in the scientific community. The scientific community imparts great respect to researchers who publish many articles in the foremost scholarly journals. Such researchers are directly contributing to the scientific community's primary goal—advancing new knowledge.

You may never publish an article in a scholarly journal, but you will probably read many such articles. They are a vital part of the system of scientific research. Researchers actively read what appears in the journals to learn about new research findings and how researchers conducted studies. Eventually, the new knowledge will be disseminated in college textbooks, news reports, or public talks.

STEPS IN THE RESEARCH PROCESS

Social research proceeds in a sequence of steps, although different approaches to research vary the steps somewhat. Most studies follow the seven steps discussed here. First, select a *topic*—a general area of study or an issue, such as domestic abuse, homelessness, or powerful corporate elites. A topic is too broad for conducting a study. The crucial next step is to narrow down the topic, or *focus* the topic into a specific research question for a study (e.g., "Are people who marry younger more likely to engage in physical abuse of a spouse under conditions of high stress than those who marry older?"). After learning about a topic and narrowing the focus, review past research, or the *literature,* on a topic or question. It is at this stage that a possible answer to the research question, or hypothesis, and theory can be important.

After specifying a research question and reviewing the literature, designing a detailed plan of how to carry out the study comes next. In this step, decisions are made about the many practical details of doing the study (e.g., whether to use a survey or qualitative observation in the field, how many research participants to use, etc.). It is only after completing the design stage that *gathering the data* or evidence occurs (e.g., ask people questions, record answers, etc.). Once data have been collected, the next step is to examine or *analyze the data* looking for patterns, and giving meaning to or *interpreting* the data (e.g., "People who marry young and grew up in families with abuse have higher rates of physical domestic abuse than those with different family histories"). The last step is to *inform others* in a report that describes the study's background, how it was conducted, and what was discovered.

The seven-step process shown in Figure 1.1 is oversimplified. In practice, you will rarely complete one step totally then leave it behind to move to the next step. Rather, the process is interactive and the steps blend into each other. What you do in a later step may stimulate you to reconsider and slightly adjust your thinking in a previous one. The process is not strictly one-way and may flow back and forth before reaching an end. The seven steps are for one research project; it is one cycle of going through the steps in a single study on a specific topic.

FIGURE I.I   Steps in the Research Process

The ongoing enterprise of science builds on prior research and adds to a larger, collectively created body of knowledge. One study is only a small part of the larger whole of science. A single researcher might work on multiple research projects at once, or several researchers may collaborate on one project. Likewise, a researcher may report one study in one scholarly article, or in several articles, or in a book. Sometimes a single article reports on several smaller studies.

DIMENSIONS OF RESEARCH

Tim and Sharon graduated from college three years ago and met for lunch. Tim asked Sharon, "So, how is your new job as a researcher for Social Data, Inc.? What are you doing?" Sharon answered, "Right now I'm working on an applied research project examining day care quality in which we're doing a cross-sectional survey to get descriptive data for an evaluation study." Sharon's reply touched on four dimensions of social research. Social research comes in several shapes and sizes. The dimensions are a way to dissect the features of a study.

Before you begin a study, you must decide how you are going to conduct the research. To make the decision, you need to understand the advantages and disadvantages of a study's dimensions. The various features of a study correspond to each of four dimensions of research. Phrasing the dimensions as questions, they are as follows:

- How will you use study results?
- What is the primary purpose of your study?
- How will you incorporate time into the study?
- Which specific data collection technique and study design will you use?

The four dimensions overlap and some tend to go together (e.g., use of study results and a data collection technique). Once you learn the dimensions, you will see how particular research questions are more compatible with certain ways of designing a study and collecting data than with others. In addition, you will find it easier to read and understand the research reports by others because you will be able to quickly place or map a study onto each of the four dimensions.

Use of Research

There are two primary uses of study findings. One use is to advance understanding of the fundamental nature of social life and knowledge over the long term. Researchers who emphasize this use usually adopt a detached, pure science or academic orientation. A second use is to apply study results to solve specific, immediate problems or issues. Researchers who concentrate on this use tend to be activists, managers, or practitioners. They are pragmatic and interventionist oriented. The two uses are not rigidly separate. Across the two uses, researchers cooperate and maintain friendly relations. An individual researcher might focus on one or the other use at different career stages.

Basic Research.   *Basic social research* advances fundamental knowledge about the social world. It focuses on developing, testing, and supporting theories that explain how the social world operates, why social relations operate as they do, and how society changes. Basic research is the source of most new scientific ideas and ways of thinking about the world. Nonscientists often criticize basic research and ask, "What good is it?" Because results lack an immediate, practical application, they consider basic research to be a waste of time and money; basic research nonetheless provides a foundation for knowledge that advances understanding in many areas of study and across many issues over the long run. Basic research is the source of most of the tools, methods, theories, and ideas we have about the underlying causes of how people act or think. It provides most of the significant breakthroughs that truly advance knowledge,

Basic research requires the painstaking study of broad questions that have a potential to shift the way we think about a wide range of issues. It can influence thinking and studies across the next 50 years or century. Practical applications from basic research may be apparent years later, only after many accumulated advances in basic knowledge build over time. Frequently, basic research has practical application in unrelated or unexpected areas. For example, in 1984, Alec Jeffreys, a geneticist at the University of Leicester in England, was engaged in basic research studying the evolution of genes. As an indirect, accidental side effect of a new technique he developed, he discovered a way to produce what is now called human DNA "fingerprints" or unique markings of the DNA of individuals. This was not his intent. He even said he would have never thought of the technique if DNA fingerprints had been his goal. Within 10 years applied uses of the technique were developed. Today, DNA analysis is a widely used technique in criminal investigations.

Applied Research.   *Applied social research* addresses a specific concern or offers solutions to a practical problem that an employer, club, agency, social movement, or organization identified. In applied social research, building or testing theory or connecting results to a larger theory is a secondary concern. Clear, practical results that can be put to use are primary, so there is limited interest in developing a long-term general understanding. Most applied studies are small in scale and offer practical results we can use in the near term (i.e., next month or next year). For example, the student government of University X wants to know whether the number of University X students who are arrested for driving while intoxicated or involved in auto accidents will decline if it sponsors alcohol-free parties next year. Applied research would be most applicable for this situation.

People employed in businesses, government offices, health care facilities, social service agencies, political organizations, media organizations, recreational programs, and educational institutions often conduct applied research and use results in decision making. Applied research helps with decisions such as the following: Should an agency start a new program to reduce the wait time before a client receives benefits? Should a police force adopt a new type of response to reduce spousal abuse? Should a political candidate emphasize his or her stand on the environment instead of the economy? Should a company market a skin care product to mature adults instead of teenagers?

The scientific community is the primary consumer of basic research, while practitioners such as teachers, counselors, and social workers, or decision makers such as managers, agency administrators, and public officials are major consumers of applied research.

In applied research someone other than the researcher who conducted the study often uses the results. Applied research results are less likely to enter the public domain in publications and may be available to only a few decision makers or practitioners. This means that applied research findings are not widely disseminated and not closely evaluated by the larger scientific community.

Some decision makers who use applied research findings may not use them wisely. Sometimes managers or politicians ignore serious problems with a study's methodology and cautions made by the researchers. The manager or politician may only want to use study results to justify cutting a disliked program or advancing desired programs. Applied research frequently has immediate implications and involves controversial issues. This can generate conflict. One famous researcher, William Whyte (1984), encountered conflict over findings in his applied research on a factory in Oklahoma and on restaurants in Chicago. In the first case, the management was more interested in defeating a union than in learning about employment relations; in the other, restaurant owners really sought to make the industry look good and did not want findings on the specific details of its operations made public.

Applied and basic research orientations toward research methodology differ (see Table 1.2). Basic researchers emphasize adhering to the highest methodological standards. They try to conduct near-perfect research. Applied researchers typically make more tradeoffs between scientific rigor and quick, usable results. Tradeoffs are never an excuse for doing sloppy research. Applied researchers try to squeeze research into the constraints of an applied setting and balance rigor against practical needs. Such balancing requires an in-depth knowledge of research and an awareness of the consequences of compromising standards.

Types of Applied Research.   There are many specific types of applied research. Here, we look at three major types: evaluation, action, and social impact assessment.

Evaluation Research Study.   **Evaluation research** is applied research designed to find out whether a program, a new way of doing something, a marketing campaign, a policy, and so forth, is effective—in other words, "Does it work?" Evaluation research is the most widely used type

TABLE 1.2   Basic and Applied Social Research Compared

Basic	Applied
1. Research is intrinsically satisfying and judgments are by other sociologists.	1. Research is part of a job and is judged by sponsors who are outside the discipline of sociology.
2. Research problems and research participants are selected with a great deal of freedom.	2. Research problems are "narrowly constrained" to the demands of employers or sponsors.
3. Research is judged by absolute norms of scientific rigor, and the highest standards of scholarship are sought.	3. The rigor and standards of scholarship depend on the uses of results. Research can be "quick and dirty" or may match high scientific standards.
4. The primary concern is with the internal logic and rigor of research design.	4. The primary concern is with the ability to generalize findings to areas of interest to sponsors.
5. The driving goal is to contribute to basic, theoretical knowledge.	5. The driving goal is to have practical payoffs or uses for results.
6. Success comes when results appear in a scholarly journal and have an impact on others in the scientific community.	6. Success comes when results are used by sponsors in decision making.

Source: Based on Freeman and Rossi (1984:572–573).

of applied research.[9] Large bureaucratic organizations (e.g., businesses, schools, hospitals, government, large nonprofit agencies) often sponsor evaluation research studies to demonstrate the effectiveness of what they are doing. If you conduct evaluation research, you do not use techniques different from those of other social research. The difference lies in the fact that decision makers, who may not be researchers themselves, define the scope and purpose of the research, and their objective is to use results in a practical situation.[10]

Evaluation research questions might include: Does a Socratic teaching technique improve learning over lecturing? Does a law-enforcement program of mandatory arrest reduce spousal abuse? Does a flextime program increase employee productivity? Evaluation researchers measure the effectiveness of a program, policy, or way of doing something and often use several research techniques (e.g., survey and field). If you can use it, the experimental technique is usually preferred. Practitioners involved with running a policy or program may conduct a evaluation research study for their own information, or an outside decision maker may request a study.

Ethical and political conflicts frequently arise in evaluation research because of opposing interests in the findings. Research findings can affect who gets or keeps a job, they can build or reduce political popularity, or they may promote one or another program. People who are displeased because the findings do not support their personal goals may look for fault in the researcher or research methods. Sometimes outside decision makers may place limits on the research—restricting what you can study or specifying that they are narrowly interested in one specific outcome only. This can create an ethical dilemma for a serious, critically thinking researcher.

Limitations of evaluation research include the following: research reports rarely go through a rigorous peer review process, data are infrequently publicly available for others to inspect or learn from, and the focus is often very narrow and fails to examine the full process by which a program affects people's lives. In addition, decision makers may selectively use to suit their purposes or ignore evaluation findings with which they disagree.

Action Research Study. **Action research** is applied research that treats knowledge as a form of power. In it the line between creating knowledge and using knowledge for social–political improvement is abolished. Among the several types of action research, most share the following five characteristics:

1. You actively involve research participants in the research process (e. g., study design, data collection).
2. You incorporate the everyday experiences and knowledge of ordinary people into the study.
3. You examine issues of exploitation, oppression, power, or inequality in the study.
4. You seek to raise consciousness and increase awareness of issues with the study.
5. You directly link the study to a plan or program of social–political action.

Most often, a person involved in a social movement, political cause, or issue advocacy engages in action research. People from a range of political positions can conduct it. Action research can have an insurgent orientation with a goal to empower the powerless, fight oppression and injustice, and reduce inequality. Wealthy and powerful groups or organizations also sponsor and conduct action research. They seek to defend their status, position, and privileges in society.

Most action researchers are explicitly political, not value neutral. Because the primary goal is to affect sociopolitical conditions, publishing results in formal reports, articles, or books is a secondary concern. Most action researchers also believe that knowledge develops from direct experience, particularly the experience of engaging in social–political action.

For example, most feminist research is action research. It has a dual mission: to create social change by transforming gender relations and to contribute to the advancement of knowledge. A feminist researcher who studies sexual harassment might recommend policy changes to reduce it. The researcher will also inform potential victims so they can protect themselves and defend their rights. At times, researchers will explain study results in a public hearing to try to modify new policies or laws. For example, the authors of a study on domestic violence (Cherlin et al., 2004) testified in the United States Senate. The study findings and the testimony helped to alter marriage promotion provisions in a 2005 welfare reform law.[11]

Social Impact Assessment Research Study. In a **social impact assessment (SIA) study,** you estimate the likely consequences of a planned intervention or intentional change to occur in the future. It may be part of a larger environmental impact statement required by government agencies and used for planning and making choices among alternative policies. In an SIA you forecast how aspects of the social environment may change and suggest ways to mitigate changes likely to be adverse from the point of view of an affected population. The *impacts* in a social impact assessment are the difference between a forecast of the future with the project and without the project. For example, you could conduct a SIA to estimate the ability of a local hospital to respond to an earthquake, determine how housing availability for the elderly will change if a major new highway is built, or assess the impact on college admissions if a new group of students can receive interest-free loans.

Researchers who conduct SIAs often examine a wide range of social outcomes and work in an interdisciplinary research team. They measure outcomes including "quality of life" issues, such as access to health care, illegal drug and alcohol use, employment opportunities, schooling quality, teen pregnancy rates, commuting time and traffic congestion, availability of parks and recreation facilities, shopping choices, viable cultural institutions, crime rates, interracial tensions, or social isolation. There is an international professional association for SIA research that advances SIA techniques and promotes SIA by governments, corporations, and other organizations.

Social impact assessments are rarely required, but a few governments mandate them. For example, in New South Wales, Australia, a registered club or hotel cannot increase the number of poker machines unless the Liquor Administration Board in the Department Gaming and Racing approves an SIA for the club or hotel. The SIA enables the board to assess the likely local community impact from increasing the number of poker machines. The format includes a matrix that allows the board to identify the social and economic impacts, positive and negative, financial or nonfinancial, quantified or qualitative. In New Zealand, the Gambling Act of 2003 requires an SIA before expanding gambling. In one 2004 study in New Zealand for the Auckland City Council, it noted that 90 percent of New Zealand's adults gamble, 10 percent gamble regularly (once a week or more often), and about 1 percent are problem gamblers, although this varies by age, income, and ethnicity. The SIA recommended limiting the locations of new gambling venues, monitoring their usage, and tracing the amount of gambling revenues that are returned to the community in various ways (e.g., clubs, trusts, etc.). It contained a matrix with social (e.g., arrests, divorce, domestic violence), economic (e.g., unemployment, bankruptcy, tourism expansion), and cultural impacts (e.g., time away from other leisure activities) listed by their effect on all gamblers, problem gamblers, the local community, and the region.[12]

Purpose of a Study

If you ask someone why he or she is conducting a study, you might get a range of responses: "My boss told me to," "It was a class assignment,"

"I was curious," "My roommate thought it would be a good idea." There are almost as many reasons to do research as there are researchers. Yet, the purposes of social research may be organized into three groups based on what the researcher is trying to accomplish—explore a new topic, describe a social phenomenon, or explain why something occurs. Studies may have multiple purposes (e.g., both to explore and to describe), but one of three major purposes is usually dominant (see Expansion Box 1.2).

To Explore.   Perhaps you have explored a new topic or issue in order to learn about it. If the issue was new or no one has written about it yet, you began at the beginning. In *exploratory research*, a researcher examines a new area to formulate questions that he or she can address more specifically in future research. A researcher may need to conduct an exploratory study in order to know enough to design and execute a second, more systematic and extensive study and it may be the first stage in a sequence of studies.

Exploratory research frequently addresses the "what?" question—"What is this social activity really about?"—and it rarely yields definitive answers. Compared to the other two purposes of research, exploratory research tends to rely more on qualitative data and is less likely to use a specific theory. If you conduct an exploratory study, you may get frustrated because there are few guidelines to follow and everything is potentially important. Exploratory research lacks well-defined steps and the direction of inquiry changes frequently. It is especially important to be creative, open-minded, and flexible; adopt an investigative stance; and explore diverse sources of information.

Exploratory Study Example. The use of the Internet for advertising illegal sexual services appeared a little over a decade ago and has rapidly grown, but few studies examined prostitution solicitation over the Internet by male prostitutes. We know little about differences in Internet advertising for sex, and even less by males seeking female customers. Lee-Gonyea, Castle, and Gonyea (2009) conducted

---

| **1.2** | EXPANSION BOX |
| | **Purpose of Research** |

Exploratory	Descriptive	Explanatory
■ Become familiar with the basic facts, setting, and concerns.	■ Provide a detailed, highly accurate picture.	■ Test a theory's predictions or principle.
■ Create a general mental picture of conditions.	■ Locate new data that contradict past data.	■ Elaborate and enrich a theory's explanation.
■ Formulate and focus questions for future research.	■ Create a set of categories or classify types.	■ Extend a theory to new issues or topics.
■ Generate new ideas, conjectures, or hypotheses.	■ Clarify a sequence of steps or stages.	■ Support or refute an explanation or prediction.
■ Determine the feasibility of conducting research.	■ Document a causal process or mechanism.	■ Link issues or topics with a general principle.
■ Develop techniques for measuring and locating future data.	■ Report on the background or context of a situation.	■ Determine which of several explanations is best.

an exploratory study of online prostitution by examining 83 websites that advertised male escorts. They examined the websites to learn the type of male escort being advertised (independent or agency), the clientele of the escort services, the location of the escort, information about the escorts (e.g., physical descriptions, personal interests), information on how to communicate with the escort, costs of services, and type of payment accepted. The researchers learned that over half of escorts were independent. About 17% sought only female clients, 29% only male clients, and 37% males or females. The remaining websites (about 15%) listed couples or a mix of males and females. Most listed sexual services and most (85%) included a photograph of the escort. A little over one-half listed prices for services, but only about 20 percent included payment method (e.g., cash, credit card, PayPal). Sites for female customers tended to be less graphic and explicit in nature than those for males, presenting male escorts in subtle ways to suggest women were simply arranging a date.

To Describe.   **Descriptive research** is appropriate when you have basic information about social phenomenon and are ready to describe it in greater depth. You want to present a systematic picture with specific details of a situation, activity, social setting, or relationship. Descriptive research focuses on "how?" and "who?" questions: "How did it happen?" "Who is involved?" A great deal of social research is descriptive. Descriptive researchers use most data-gathering techniques—surveys, field research, content analysis, and historical-comparative research. Only experimental research is less often used. Much of the social research found in scholarly journals or used for making policy decisions is descriptive.

Descriptive and exploratory research often blur together in practice. In descriptive research, you start with a well-defined issue or question then design a study to describe it accurately. Your study offers a detailed picture of the issue.

The results may indicate the percentage of people who hold a particular view or engage in specific behaviors.

Descriptive Study Example.   Responses to religious diversity fall into two categories: pluralism and exclusivism. Pluralists believe that all (or at least many) religions are legitimate whereas exclusivists regard one theistic system as true and see others as false. Trinitapoli (2007) conducted secondary data analysis (explained later in this chapter) by examining survey data and qualitative interviews to answer three descriptive research questions: How prevalent are exclusivist religious beliefs among American adolescents? What denominational and social factors are associated with religious exclusivism? and How do adolescents reconcile exclusivist religious beliefs with today's pluralistic culture? She found that about 20 percent of all adolescents are exclusivists. Committed exclusivist beliefs are most common among Mormon (53 percent) and evangelical respondents (33 percent). Adolescents that believed in exclusive truth softened claims to truth with respect to other religions while maintaining a belief in the authenticity of their own religion. With the exception of some statements of unease about Muslims, data failed to reveal obvious bigotry or intolerance. Trinitapoli suggests that the adolescents did not express exclusivist religious beliefs freely in public but still held such beliefs. The exclusivists articulate their beliefs carefully so others do not view them intolerant or prejudiced in a larger culture that is pluralistic and tolerant.

To Explain.   When you encounter an issue that is well recognized and have a description of it, you might wonder why things are the way they are. **Explanatory research** identifies the sources of social behaviors, beliefs, conditions, and events; it documents causes, tests theories, and provides reasons. It builds on exploratory and descriptive research and often asks the "why?" question (e.g., "Why does this occur in this way?"). Explanatory studies often test theories or examine whether a theory can explain new situations or activities.

Explanatory Study Example. Many past studies have shown people living in urban areas tend to be more tolerant of diverse lifestyles, racial-ethnic groups, and opinions than people living in rural areas or small towns. More recently, Richard Florida (2002, 2005) argued that a "creative class" of young, highly educated professionals are attracted to cosmopolitan, open urban environments. Sharp and Joslyn (2008) conducted an explanatory study on tolerance in U.S. cities. They asked whether some cities have a subculture that supports "new" or nonconventional politics. One key feature to sustain such a subculture is a concentration of the "creative class." The theory suggests we can explain differences in racial tolerance among U.S. cities by whether the city has a new political culture. Creative class theory suggested, holding other factors constant, high concentrations of creative class members could build and sustain a tolerant "new political culture" in a city compared to the political culture of cities with few creative class members. The researchers examined survey data for 27 cities that measured concentration of creative class members and several social and racial attitudes. Based on the survey responses of Whites, they found "dramatic evidence that creative class and new political culture cities constitute distinctive cultural contexts. . . . Whites living in such contexts can presumably experience a higher level of minority-group presence without the racial threat dynamic taking hold than can Whites living in cities with traditional subcultures" (p. 589). In short, a high concentration of creative class members supports a new political culture and this explains why White racial attitudes differ across U.S. cities.

Time Dimension in Research

Different research questions and studies incorporate time in several ways. Some studies are like a "snapshot" of a single, fixed time point (i.e., cross-sectional studies), whereas others provide a "moving picture" that lets you follow events, people, or social relations across time (i.e., longitudinal studies). Both quantitative and qualitative approaches use cross-sectional or longitudinal studies. In this section, we look at five ways researchers incorporate time into a study (see Figure 1.2).

Cross-Sectional Research. Most social research studies are *cross-sectional*; they examine a single point in time. Advantages of cross-sectional research are that it is the simplest and least costly alternative. Its disadvantage is that it cannot capture social processes or change. Exploratory, descriptive, and explanatory studies use cross-cultural research. The example studies you read about earlier for these three purposes of research were all cross-sectional.

Longitudinal Research. Researchers using *longitudinal research* examine features of people or other units at more than one time. It is usually more complex and costly than cross-sectional research, but it is also more powerful and informative. Let us now look at the three main types of longitudinal research: time series, panel, and cohort.

Time-Series Study. A *time-series study* is longitudinal research in which a researcher gathers the same type of information across two or more time periods. This allows the researcher to observe stability or change in the features of the units and to track conditions over time. The specific individuals may change but the overall pattern is clear. For example, there has been a nationwide survey of a large sample of incoming freshman students since 1966. Since it began, over 11 million students at more than 1,800 colleges participated. The fall 2003 survey of 276,449 students found many facts and trends, such as only 34 percent of entering freshmen studied six or more hours per week. This was the lowest level since the question was asked in 1987 (when it was 47 percent).

FIGURE 1.2   The Time Dimension in Social Research

CROSS-SECTIONAL: Observe a collection of people at one time.

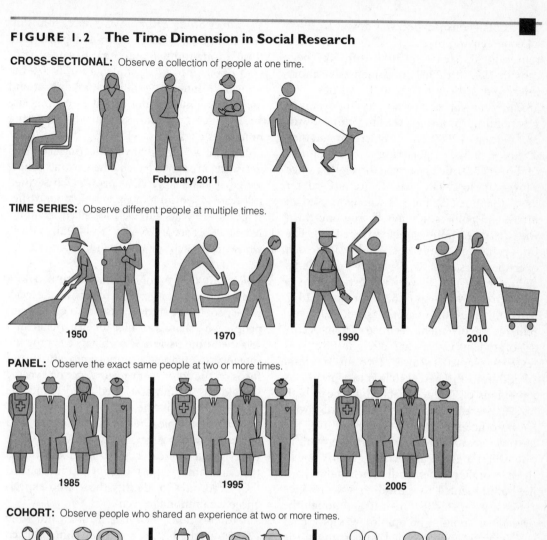

February 2011

TIME SERIES: Observe different people at multiple times.

1950   1970   1990   2010

PANEL: Observe the exact same people at two or more times.

1985   1995   2005

COHORT: Observe people who shared an experience at two or more times.

Married in 1962   1982   2002

CASE STUDY: Observe a small set intensely across time.

2006 → 2011

Yet, alcohol consumption was down. In 2003, 44.8 percent reported drinking beer, which represented a steady decline from 73.7 percent in 1982. In 2003, freshmen were more interested in keeping up with politics. The 33.9 percent who said it was very important to stay politically informed was up from a low of 28.1 percent in 2000, and 22.5 percent said they discussed politics regularly, up from 19.4 percent in 2002 (which had been the highest since a low point in 1993). These figures are still far lower than the 60.3 percent who expressed an interest in politics in 1966, or the one-third who discussed politics regularly in 1968. The importance of family has steadily increased over the years, with 74.8 percent of students calling it essential or very important. This is up from the low point of 58.8 percent in 1977 when the question was first asked. However, religious involvement declined. The percentage of students who attended religious services regularly was at its lowest level in 35 years. In addition, the percent claiming "none" as a religious preference reached a record high of 17.6 percent, compared to a record low of 6.6 percent in 1966. Another trend over the past two decades has been a steady growth in opposition to the death penalty. Nearly one in three incoming students advocated ending capital punishment. This is the highest score since 1980 (when it was 33.2 percent), although the percent withholding an opinion was far higher earlier in time; it exceeded 60 percent in the 1970s.[13]

Panel Study.   The **panel study** is a powerful type of longitudinal research in which the researcher observes exactly the same people, group, or organization across multiple time points. Panel research is formidable to conduct and very costly. Tracking people over time is often difficult because some people die or cannot be located. Nevertheless, the results of a well-designed panel study are very valuable. Even short-term panel studies can clearly show the impact of a particular life event.

Panel Study Example. Oesterle, Johnson, and Mortimer (2004) examined panel data from a longitudinal study that began in 1988 with 1,000 ninth-grade students enrolled in the St. Paul, Minnesota, public school district and looked at volunteering activities during late adolescence and young adulthood, covering nine years from age 18–19 (1992) to age 26–27 (2000). They found that volunteering at an earlier stage strongly affected whether one volunteered at a later stage. Also, people who devoted full time to working or parenting at an earlier stage (18–19 years old) were less likely to volunteer at a later stage (26–27 years old) than those whose major activity was attending school.

Cohort Study.   A **cohort study** is similar to a panel study, but rather than observing the exact same people, the study focuses on a category of people who share a similar life experience in a specified time period. Researchers examine the category as a whole for important features and focus on the cohort, or category, not on specific individuals. Commonly used cohorts include all people born in the same year (called *birth cohorts*), all people hired at the same time, and all people who graduate in a given year. Unlike panel studies, researchers do not have to find the exact same people for cohort studies; rather, they need only to identify those who experienced a common life event.

Cohort Study Example. Bratter and King (2008) studied U.S. marriage cohorts (i.e., all people married in a certain year or set of adjoining years), to compare marriage stability among interracial and same-racial group marriage partners. They used data from a 2002 national sample of people ages 15–44, looking at people who were ever married and who had valid information on the race of their first spouse (1,606 males and 4,070 females). The authors looked at whether the marriage was intact or ended at a later time point. They examined six cohorts (earlier than 1980, 1980–84, 1985–89, 1990–94, 1995–99, after 2000). Comparisons across cohorts showed that interracial couples had higher divorce rates. However, this was not the case for all interracial couples or equal over time. Interracial couples marrying before the 1980s did not have higher divorce rates. They found that compared to White/White couples, White female/Black male, and White female/Asian male marriages had higher divorce rates, but marriages involving nonWhite females and White males and Hispanics and non-Hispanic persons had similar or lower risks of divorce.

Case Studies.   Most cross-sectional and longitudinal studies examine the features of many people or units, or an entire population. Typically, we measure several significant features of numerous units or cases, and then analyze the features across the many cases or units. Such studies are called cross-case analysis or population-oriented research. In contrast, *case-study research* examines one or a handful of cases over a duration of time with detailed, varied, and extensive data, usually qualitative data. Such studies are called with-case analysis or case-oriented research. Instead of looking at several features across numerous cases, in *case study* we examine numerous diverse features of the case or few cases in great depth. Rather than trying to gather all cases, or a sample of cases from an entire population, we carefully select one or a few cases that permit examining an issue in great depth. Unlike a longitudinal study in which we gather data on many units or cases then look for general patterns across them, in the case study we closely follow the unfolding or development of many complex features of one or a few cases across time, and situate the case or few cases within a specific historical and cultural context.[14]

Case Study Example. Rhomberg (2010) conducted a case study of one labor strike. His study of a strike of newspaper workers in Detroit opened up new theoretical insights. To study the strike, he provides extensive historical and other background. As is common in case study research, Rhomberg examined a very large amount of diverse qualitative data. As he reported (p. 1855):

> The case study relies on data collected from approximately 100 interviews. . . . I also collected hundreds of news stories . . . as well as reports from other major and local news, business, and professional media. Other archival sources include the trial transcript, exhibits, and decisions in the principal unfair labor practice complaints issued by the National Labor Relations Board (NLRB), along with legal records arising from other litigation. Finally, I obtained copies of documents from organizational and individuals' personal files, such as collective bargaining agreements, internal communications, flyers, public information, and videotape recorded by security forces and local television media.

The primary contributions of Rhomberg's case study were to describe the case of one strike, to provide new insights into how labor relations changed over the past thirty years, and to introduce new theoretical concepts for studying issues like a new type of labor strike.

Data Collection Techniques and Study Designs

Social researchers use one or more specific techniques to collect qualitative and quantitative data. This section is a brief overview of the major techniques and designs. You will read about them in greater depth in later chapters. Some data collection techniques and study designs are more effective at addressing specific kinds of questions or topics. It takes skill, practice, and creativity to match a research question to an appropriate data collection technique and design. The techniques and designs fall into two categories based on whether the data are quantitative or qualitative. Most quantitative studies look at a large number of cases, people, or units, and measure features about them in the form of numbers. By contrast, qualitative studies usually involve qualitative data and examine many diverse features of a small number of cases across time. Ideally, we mix qualitative and quantitative approaches in the same study, building on the strengths of each; however, this is often difficult to accomplish in practice.

Quantitative Data Collection Techniques and Designs.   Techniques for quantitative data collection include experiments, surveys, content analyses, and existing statistics.

Experiments.   **Experimental research** closely follows the logic and principles found in natural science research; researchers create situations and examine their effects on participants. A researcher conducts experiments in laboratories or in real life with a relatively small number of people and a well-focused research question. Experiments are most effective for explanatory research. In the typical experiment, the researcher divides the research participants into two or more groups. He or she then treats both groups identically, except that one group but not the other is given a condition he or she is interested in: the "treatment." The researcher measures the reactions of both groups precisely. By controlling the setting for both groups and giving only one group the treatment, the researcher can conclude that any differences occurring in the reactions of the groups are due to the treatment alone.

Surveys.   In **survey research** we ask people questions in a written questionnaire (mailed or handed to people) or during an interview and then record answers. We do not manipulate a situation or condition; we simply ask many people numerous questions in a short time period. Typically, we summarize answers to questions in percentages, tables, or graphs. We can use survey techniques in descriptive or explanatory research. Surveys give us a picture of what many people think or report doing. Survey researchers often use a sample or a smaller group of selected people (e.g., 150 students), but generalize results to a larger group (e.g., 5,000 students) from which the smaller group was selected. Survey research is very widely used in many fields of study and in applied research.

Content Analyses.   A **content analysis** is a technique for examining information, or content, in written or symbolic material (e.g., pictures, movies, song lyrics, etc.). In content analysis, we first identify a body of material to analyze (e.g., books, newspapers, films, etc.) and then create a system for recording specific aspects of it. The system might include counting how often certain words or themes occur. Finally, we record what was found in the material. We often measure information in the content as numbers and present it as tables or graphs. This technique lets us discover features in the content of large amounts of material that might otherwise go unnoticed. We can use content analysis for exploratory and explanatory research, but we primarily use it in descriptive research.

Existing Statistics.   In **existing statistics research**, we locate previously collected information, often in the form of government reports or previously conducted surveys, then reorganize or combine the information in new ways to address a research question. Locating sources can be time consuming, so we need to consider carefully the meaning of what we find. Frequently, we do not know whether the information of interest is available when we begin a study. Sometimes, the existing quantitative information consists of stored surveys or other data that we reexamine using various statistical procedures. We can use existing statistics research for exploratory, descriptive, or explanatory purposes, but it is most frequently used for descriptive research. **Secondary data analysis** is a type of existing statistics study using data from a past study. Many large, complex studies, usually surveys, generate a great quantity of data. The data are available to researchers other than those who designed and collected it in the initial study. The other researchers use various statistical techniques to analyze the data during which they can discover new patterns or test other theories.

Qualitative Data Collection Techniques and Designs. Techniques for qualitative data collection include field research and historical-comparative research.

Field Research. Most field research studies are case studies examining a small group of people over a length of time (e.g., weeks, months, years). In a ***field research*** study, we begin with a loosely formulated idea or topic, select a social group or natural setting for study, gain access and adopt a social role in the setting, and observe in detail. We get to know personally the people being studied. Often, we conduct open-ended and informal interviews, and take detailed notes on a daily basis. After leaving the field site, we carefully reread the notes and prepare written reports. We can use field research for exploratory and descriptive studies; it is rarely used for explanatory research.

Historical-Comparative Research. In ***historical-comparative research*** we examine aspects of social life in a past historical era or across different cultures. With this technique we may focus on one historical period or several, compare one or more cultures, or mix historical periods and cultures. Like field research, we combine theory building/testing with data collection and begin with a loosely formulated question that is refined during the research process. We often gather a wide array of evidence, including existing statistics and documents (e.g., novels, official reports, books, newspapers, diaries, photographs, and maps) for study. In addition, we may make direct observations and conduct interviews. Historical-comparative research can be exploratory, descriptive, or explanatory and can blend types.

CONCLUSION

This chapter gave you an overview of social research. You saw how social research differs from the ordinary ways of learning–knowing about the social world, how doing research is based on science and the scientific community, and about several types of social research based on its dimensions (e.g., its purpose, the technique used to gather data, etc.). The dimensions of research loosely overlap with each other. The dimensions of social research are a kind of "road map" to help you make your way through the terrain of social research. In the next chapter, we turn to social theory. You read about it a little in this chapter. In the next chapter, you will learn how theory and research methods work together and about several types of theory.

Key Terms

action research
applied social research
basic social research
case study
cohort study
content analysis
cross-sectional research
data
descriptive research
empirical evidence
evaluation research
existing statistics research
experimental research
explanatory research
exploratory research
field research
halo effect
historical-comparative research
longitudinal research
overgeneralization
panel study
premature closure
qualitative data

quantitative data
scientific community
scientific method
secondary data analysis
selective observation
social impact assessment study
social research
survey research
time-series study

Endnotes

1. See Parker-Pope, Tara. "Summer Must-Read for Kids? Any Book," *New York Times*, August 2, 2010.
2. See Rampton and Stauber (2001:247–277 and 305–306).
3. See Best (2001:15) on advocates and media.
4. See National Science Board (2002:735–739).
5. See Kruger and Dunning (1999). Also see Brown (2007), DeAngelis (2003), Dunning, Johnson, Ehrlinger, and Kruger (2003), and Hoorens (1993).
6. Schacter (2001) provides a summary of memory issues.
7. National Science Board (2002:739); National Science Board (2010, Appendix Table 7.13)
8. Discussions of the scientific community can be found in Cole and Gordon (1995), Crane (1972), Hagstrom (1965), Merton (1973), Mulkay (1991), and Ziman (1999).
9. See Patton (2001) and Weiss (1997) for a more detailed discussion of recent advances in evaluation research.
10. Beck (1995) provides a useful overview.
11. See Herring and Ebner (2005) on the use of domestic violence study findings.
12. See Adams (2004) for more information on the Auckland City study.
13. See the website at www.gseis.ucla.edu/heri/heri .html.
14. Bennett and Elman (2006) call studies cross-case or within-case analysis, and Mahoney (2008), population-oriented or case-oriented research. Also see George and Bennett (2005) on the case-study method generally.

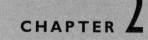

Theory and Social Research

When they begin college, many students move and live away from home for the first time. Even if they attended multiracial high schools, most of the students had lived in same-race close living situations prior to attending college. Depending on the colleges, they could be assigned a roommate in a college residence hall or dormitory. The students who get same-race roommates probably do not change their views on race, but you may wonder whether students assigned to a roommate from a different racial group change their views. Social scientists approach this type of question by looking to theories to explain how, why, or under what conditions a person's views on race change. A widely tested social psychological theory, the "contact hypothesis," says when someone has regular, close interpersonal contact with someone of a different "outgroup" (i.e., a different racial group from their own in the United States), the person is likely to modify views about out-group members. Negative stereotypes fade and positive feelings grow toward the out-group compared to the situation prior to close contact. How much this happens depends on certain conditions about the contact, such as whether the people involved are equals and whether the contact is cooperative versus competitive. The contact hypothesis is a small-scale social theory (also called middle-range, discussed later in this chapter), a type of theory often used in a research study.

What comes to mind when you hear the word *theory*? Theory is one of the least understood terms for students learning social science. My students' eyelids droop if I begin a class by saying, "Today we are going to examine the theory of . . .". Many students feel that theory is irrelevant to "real life." It floats high among the clouds. Some of my students have called it "a tangled maze of jargon."

Contrary to these views, theory is essential to expand understanding and it has a vital role in research. Its use varies by type of research, but most social science studies use theory in some way. In simple terms, a research study joins theory—which is like a story that explains how the social world operates—with data—carefully observed aspects of the social world that are relevant to the theory.

WHAT IS SOCIAL THEORY?

The purpose of social theory is to explain or answer why the social world has certain patterns, operations, or events. There are several ways to explain (see later in this chapter). We explain in daily life, as in why people's attitudes about people of a different race change. Theory is not exotic; we constantly use theory when we think about how the world works, or what makes something happen (e.g., why U.S. divorce rates dropped in recent years, why students from certain neighborhoods tend to do better in school than those from other neighborhoods). Our everyday theories are simply incomplete, limited, and fragmented versions of full social theories. Some social theories explain in a form that is similar to everyday life explanations whereas others explain in a form that is different. What distinguishes a theoretical explanation is less its form than that theory uses a collection of carefully considered concepts, has logical consistency, and is embedded within a larger arrangement of similar explanations.

In Chapter 1, I defined *social theory* as a system of interconnected abstractions or ideas. The system condenses and organizes knowledge. In this way, social theory is a compact way to expand understanding of the social world. Theories move understanding from one specific situation (e.g., students from neighborhood X in Nashville, Tennessee, get better grades in 10th grade than students from neighborhood Y) toward general understanding and knowledge (e.g., students living in neighborhoods with conditions A, B, and C tend to do better in school than those growing up in neighborhoods that lack A, B, and C).

Sometimes classes on social theory focus on the history of social thought, which mixes the history of famous past thinkers with social theory. Great classical social theorists (e.g., Durkheim, Freud, Marx, Tönnies, Weber) generated many innovative ideas that expanded our understanding of the social world. They created original theories that laid the foundation for subsequent generations of thinkers. We still study the classical theorists because they provided numerous creative and interrelated ideas. Their ideas significantly shifted how we understand the social world. We continue to discuss them because geniuses who generate many original, insightful ideas that fundamentally advance understanding are rare. The ideas of past thinkers contain many theories on specific issues and are sources of current theories.

Many laypeople confuse theory with a wild hunch or speculative guess. They may say, "It's only a theory" or ask, "What's your theory about it?" This everyday use of the term *theory* often creates confusion. Everyday guessing differs from serious social theory in several ways. Unlike a carefree guess we might toss out without much thought, dozens of serious professionals have built and debated social theory over many years. They securitize the theory for logical consistency and continue to evaluate and seek evidence for its key parts. They examine whether the theory applies to specific situations. Over time, they advance the parts of the theory on which there is much agreement and evidence. They refine and build on these parts. At the same time, they trim off or drop parts of theory that no longer fit well into its overall picture of the world, or parts for which the evidence is weak or contradictory.

You have probably heard the distinction between theory and fact. Life is rarely so simple and clear. What many people consider to be a "fact" (e.g., light a match in a gasoline-filled room and it will explode) is what many scientists call a theory (e.g., a theory of how combining certain quantities of particular chemicals with oxygen and a certain level of intense heat greatly increases the odds of an explosive force). Facts and theories can blur together because a theory contains concepts that divide up the empirical world into parts, pointing to what types of evidence or data (i.e., facts) are important for it. Facts and theories are less opposites than the complementary parts of an overall explanation.

Because most research involves some form of theory, the question is less *whether* you use theory than *how* you use it in a study. Being clear and explicit about theory will make it easier to read research reports and to conduct a study. It is very difficult to conduct a solid, logically tight study if you are vague and unclear about the theory within it. Once you are aware of how theory fits into the research process, you will find the studies of others easier to understand and can design better studies.

Many people use everyday theories without labeling them as such. For example, newspaper articles or television reports on social issues usually contain unstated social theories embedded within them. A news report on the difficulty of implementing a school desegregation plan contains an implicit theory about race relations. Likewise, political leaders frequently express social theories when they discuss public issues. A politician who claims that inadequate education causes people to be poor or who says that a decline in traditional moral values is the cause of crime is expressing a type of simple theory. Compared to the theories of social scientists, such laypersons' theories are usually less systematic, clearly formulated, or logically tight. Many everyday theories are more difficult than scientific theory to test and evaluate with empirical evidence. A common substitute for theory is blame analysis. Do not confuse social theory with blame analysis, a topic we look at next.

Blame Analysis is Not Theory

Blame analysis is a counterfeit argument that some people present as if it were a theoretical explanation. In it, people substitute attributing blame for a causal explanation. Blame belongs to the realm of making a moral, legal, or ideological claim. Blame implies an intention, negligence, or responsibility for an event or situation (usually unfavorable). Blame analysis focuses on the question of who is responsible instead of the social theory question of why did it occur or what makes events happen as they do. Blame analysis assumes there is a culprit or source on which we can fix responsibility. The goal of blame analysis is to identify a responsible party, not to expand understanding. In practice, blame analysis often exempts or shields certain people or ideas, such as the injured party, members of a sympathetic audience, or a sacred value or principle. Limits in blame analysis make even its search for a responsible party restricted. Blame analysis is rarely broad or inclusive; it fails to provide a complete picture. A focus on finding a responsible party and limits on the picture it provides means that blame analysis often hampers the development of a full explanation.

The mass media, politicians, and many public commentators frequently use blame analysis in place of theoretical analysis. Blame analysis spreads misunderstanding because it confuses blame with cause. It offers a particular account (or story of what occurred) instead of a full, logical explanation. Usually blame analysis first presents an unfavorable event or situation—such as a bank robbery, a group being paid less than other equally qualified people, or terrible traffic congestion in an area. Next, it identifies one or more "likely suspects" or responsible parties. It then provides selective evidence that focuses on one of the responsible parties, often shielding other parties or contributing sources. Unlike a theoretical explanation, it does not explore all potential causes or examine systematically collected empirical evidence, both for and against many competing causes.[1]

THE PARTS OF THEORY

Concepts

All theories contain many concepts, and concepts are the building blocks of theory.[2] A *concept* is an idea expressed as a symbol or as one or more words. In natural science concepts are expressed as symbols, such as Greek letters (e.g., α). or formulas (e.g., $s = d/t$; s = speed, d = distance, t = time). In social science, concepts are expressed as words. Some people are intimidated or nervous about the exotic symbols or formulas of natural science; however, the ordinary words used in specialized ways in social science can create confusion. The distinction between concepts expressed as symbols or as words is not a big one. After all, words are symbols too. Words are symbols we learn as language.

Let us take a concept with which you are already familiar: height. I can say the word *height* or write it down; the spoken sounds and written words are part of the English language. The combination of letters in the word symbolizes, or stands for, the idea in our heads of a *height*. Chinese or Arabic characters, the French word *hauteur,* the German word *höhe,* the Spanish word *altura*—all symbolize the same idea. In a sense, a language is merely an agreement among people to use sounds or written characters to represent ideas in their heads. We learned the connection between ideas and sounds or writing at some point in our lives. In this way, you can think of learning concepts and theory as being like learning a language.[3]

Concepts are everywhere, and you use them all the time. Height is a simple concept from your daily experience. Think about it, what does height mean? You may find it easy to use the concept of *height,* but you may find describing the concept itself more difficult. Height represents an abstract idea about a physical relationship. It is a characteristic of a physical object, the distance from top to bottom. All people, buildings, trees, mountains, books, and so forth have a height. We can measure height or compare it. A height of zero is possible, and height can increase or decrease over time. As with many words, we use the word in several ways. Height is used in the expressions *the height of the battle, the height of the summer,* and *the height of fashion.*

The word *height* refers to an abstract idea that we associate with a sound and written form. Nothing in the sounds or writing that make up the word are inherent in the idea it represents. The connection between an idea and its sounds or written form is arbitrary, but it is still very useful. The sounds and writing allow us to express the abstract idea to one another by using the symbol alone.

Concepts have two parts: a *symbol* (a written form or a word) and a *definition*. We learn definitions in many ways. I learned the word *height* and its definition from my parents. I learned it as I learned to speak and was socialized to the culture. My parents never gave me a dictionary definition. I learned the concept of height through a diffuse, nonverbal, informal process. My parents showed me many examples; I observed and listened to other people use the word; I sometimes used the word incorrectly and was corrected; and I used it correctly and was understood. Eventually, I mastered the concept and used it successfully in daily life, and later in school or work settings.

This example shows how we learn and share concepts in everyday language. Suppose my parents had isolated me from television and other people. They then taught me that the word for the idea *height* was *zodged*. I would have had difficulty communicating with other people. This illustrates that people must share the words and definitions for concepts if the concepts are to be of value. Concepts may begin in one person's mind, or one person might invent an entirely new esoteric concept and keep it private, but the usefulness of concepts rests in our ability to share them with other people.

Concepts are pervasive in daily life, but most layperson concepts have vague and unclear definitions. Ordinary or lay concepts tend to be shaped by the values, misconceptions, or experiences of the people living in a specific culture. These concepts tend to be more culturally limited and less precise than those in social science. Social scientists develop new concepts (e.g., family system, gender role, socialization, self-worth,

frustration, and displaced aggression) from many origins: personal experience, creative thought, or observation. They also borrow concepts from daily life, analyze, refine, and redefine the concepts, then connect them to other concepts to build a larger theory. The flow between social scientific and lay concepts also goes the other way. Many terms of daily life—such as *sexism, lifestyle, peer group, urban sprawl,* and *social class*—began as precise, technical concepts in social theory. Over time, the terms diffused into the culture, appearing in daily conversations and mass media. As they diffused, their origin was lost and their meaning became less precise.

We can use a simple nonverbal process (e.g., pointing to an object or event, mimicking a behavior) to define simple, concrete concepts such as *book* or *height.* Most social science concepts are more complex and abstract. We define them with formal, dictionary-type definitions that build on other concepts. It may seem odd to use concepts to define other concepts, but we do this all the time. Often we combine simple, easy-to-see concepts from ordinary experience to create "higher level" or abstract concepts. For example, I defined *height* as a distance between top and bottom. *Top, bottom,* and *distance* are concepts. *Height* is more abstract than *top* or *bottom.* Abstract concepts refer to aspects of the world we may not directly experience, but organize thinking and extend understanding.

In daily conversations, we can get away with being loose and sloppy with concepts. Social theory requires more logical and precise definition than in daily discourse. Definitions help us link theory with research. A valuable goal of high-quality research, and especially exploratory research, is to sharpen, clarify, and refine concepts. Weak, contradictory, or unclear definitions of concepts impede the advance of systematic thinking and scientific knowledge.

Concept Clusters. We rarely use concepts in isolation. Concepts form interconnected groups, or ***concept clusters***. This is true for concepts in everyday language as well as for those in social theory. Theories have collections of linked concepts that are consistent and mutually reinforcing. Together, they form a web of meaning. For example, to discuss a concept such as *urban decay,* I need a set of associated concepts (e.g., *urban expansion, economic growth, urbanization, suburbs, center city, revitalization, mass transit,* and *racial minorities*).

Some concepts take on a range of values, quantities, or amounts. Examples of these kinds of concepts are *amount of income, temperature, density of population, years of schooling,* and *degree of violence.* These are variable concepts, or just *variables* (discussed in a later chapter). Other concepts express types of nonvariable phenomena (e.g., *bureaucracy, family, revolution, homeless,* and *cold*). Theories use both variable and nonvariable concepts.

Classification Concepts. Some concepts are simple; they have a single dimension and vary along a continuum. Others are complex; they have multiple dimensions or many subparts. We can break complex concepts into a set of simple, or single-dimension, concepts. For example, Rueschemeyer, Stephens, and Stephens (1992:43–44) stated that democracy has three dimensions: (1) regular, free elections with universal suffrage; (2) an elected legislative body that controls government; and (3) freedom of expression and association. The authors recognized that each dimension varies by degree. They combined the dimensions to create a set of types of regimes. Regimes very low on all three dimensions are totalitarian, those high on all three are democracies, and those with other mixes are either authoritarian or liberal oligarchies.

Classifications are partway between a single concept and a theory.[4] They help to organize abstract, complex concepts. To create a new classification, we logically specify and combine characteristics of simpler concepts. One well-known type of classification is the ***ideal type***. Ideal types are pure, abstract models that define the essence of the phenomenon in question. They are mental pictures that tell us the central aspects of a concept. Ideal types are broader, more abstract concepts that bring together several narrower, more concrete concepts.

Ideal types are not theoretical explanations because they do not tell why or how something occurs. They are smaller than theories, but important. We use them to build a theory. Qualitative researchers often use ideal types to see how well observable phenomena match up to the ideal model. For example, Max Weber developed an ideal type of the concept *bureaucracy.* Many people use Weber's ideal type (see Example Box 2.1). It distinguishes a bureaucracy from other organizational forms (e.g., social movements, kingdoms, etc.). It also clarifies critical features of a kind of organization that people once found nebulous and hard to think about. No real-life organization perfectly

---

EXAMPLE BOX

2.1 **Max Weber's Ideal Type of Bureaucracy**

- It is a continuous organization governed by a system of rules.
- Conduct is governed by detached, impersonal rules.
- There is division of labor, in which different offices are assigned different spheres of competence.
- Hierarchical authority relations prevail; that is, lower offices are under control of higher ones.
- Administrative actions, rules, and so on are in writing and maintained in files.
- Individuals do not own and cannot buy or sell their offices.
- Officials receive salaries rather than receiving direct payment from clients in order to ensure loyalty to the organization.
- Property of the organization is separate from personal property of officeholders.

Source: Based on Chafetz (1978:72)

matches the ideal type, but the model helps us think about and study bureaucracy.

Scope. Concepts vary by scope. Some are highly abstract, some are in the middle, and some are at a concrete level (i.e., they are easy to experience directly with the senses, such as sight or touch). More abstract concepts have wider scope; that is, they can be used for a much broader range of specific time points and situations. More concrete concepts are easy to recognize but apply to fewer situations. The concepts *skin pigmentation, casting a ballot in an election,* and *age based on the date on a birth certificate* are less abstract and more concrete than the concepts *racial group, democracy,* and *maturity.* Theories with many abstract concepts apply to a wider range of social phenomena than those with concrete concepts. An example of a theoretical relationship is: Increased size creates centralization, which in turn creates greater formalization. *Size, centralization,* and *formalization* are very abstract concepts. They can refer to features of a group, organization, or society. We can translate this to say that as an organization or group gets bigger, authority and power relations within it become centralized and concentrated in a small elite. The elite will tend to rely more on written policies, rules, or laws to control and organize others in the group or organization. Thinking explicitly about the scope of concepts makes a theory stronger and easier to communicate to others than leaving the concept's scope unexamined.

Assumptions

Concepts contain built-in *assumptions*. They are statements about the nature of things that are not observable or testable. Assumptions are a necessary starting point. We define concepts and build theories based on the assumptions we make about the nature of human beings, social reality, or a particular phenomenon. Assumptions often remain hidden or unstated. One way to deepen our understanding of a concept is to identify explicitly the assumptions on which it rests.

For example, the concept *book* assumes a system of writing, people who can read, and the existence of paper. Without such assumptions, the idea of a *book* makes little sense. A social science concept such as *racial prejudice* rests on several assumptions. These include people who make distinctions among individuals based on their racial heritage, attach specific motivations and characteristics to membership in a racial group, and make judgments about the goodness of specific motivations and characteristics. If race became irrelevant, people would cease to distinguish among individuals on the basis of race, to attach specific characteristics to a racial group, and to make judgments about characteristics. If that occurred, the concept of *racial prejudice* would cease to be useful for research. All concepts contain assumptions about social relations or how people behave.

Relationships

Theories contain concepts and assumptions. They also specify how assumptions and concepts relate to one another. Theories tell us whether two concepts are related or not, and if related, how the concepts relate to one another. In addition to telling us that there is a relationship among concepts, theory offers reasons for why the relationship exists.

Let us begin with a relationship: Economic distress among the White population caused an increase in mob violence against African Americans. It contains several concepts: economic distress, White and African American racial categories, and mob violence. The theory might state why and under what conditions mob violence will or will not occur. We can empirically test or evaluate the relationship, which is called a *hypothesis.* A hypothesis is a relationship among two or more variables (explained more in Chapter 3). After many careful tests of a hypothesis with data confirming it, we start to treat it as a *proposition.* A proposition is a relationship in a theory in which we have some confidence and upon which we build other relationships and develop new hypotheses.

THE ASPECTS OF THEORY

Theory can be baffling at first because it comes in many shapes and sizes. To simplify, we can categorize a theory by examining its four aspects: (1) the direction of reasoning used, (2) the level of social reality explained, (3) the form of explanation employed, and (4) the board framework of assumptions and concepts in which it is embedded. Fortunately, we do not have to consider all the possible combinations of a theory's direction, level, explanation, and framework. Only about half a dozen of the combinations are operative.

Direction of Theorizing

We can build and test theory by beginning with theory or abstract ideas. We logically connect the ideas to empirical evidence, and then test the ideas against the data or evidence. Alternatively, we can begin with specific empirical evidence, and then generalize, building toward abstract ideas based on the evidence. In practice, we are flexible and may use both directions in a study (see Figure 2.1).

Deductive.   In a *deductive approach* to theory, we begin with theory or an abstract relationship among concepts, and then move toward concrete empirical evidence. In short, we have ideas about how the world operates and test our ideas against "hard data."

Example of the Deductive Approach. Ayers, Hofstetter, Schnakenberg, and Kolody (2009) adopted a deductive approach to study immigration attitudes. The researchers wanted to explain why people support various positions on immigration policy. One theory says economic cost–benefit factors affect how people think about immigration. It says people will tolerate

FIGURE 2.1   Deductive and Inductive Theorizing

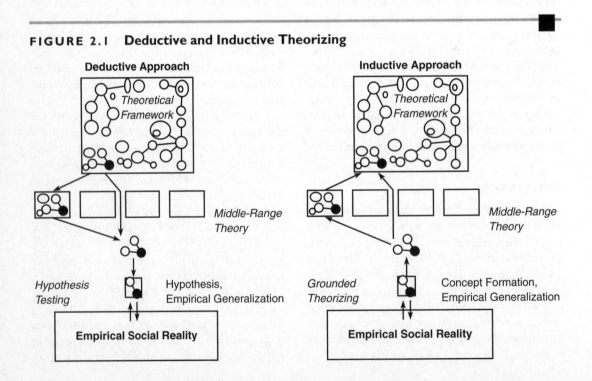

or accept greater immigration if they see an economic benefit (e.g., new investments, more taxes paid, a bigger pool of low-cost and talented workers to hire) and oppose immigration if they see it as a cost (e.g., more job competition, higher taxes, more crime). The researchers contrast the cost–benefit theory with an ideological theory of immigration. Ideological theory says that racism, among other political and social beliefs, affects how people think about immigration. It says people focus on immigrants' minority status and on the race/ethnicity of migrants. People who are racially prejudiced or who dislike a racial or ethnic category will oppose migration by people of a specific race or ethnicity irrespective of economic benefits. Thus, Ayers et al. began with abstract ideas from two theories. Based on these ideas, they designed a study to provide evidence or data. The data were in the form of answers to questions from a telephone survey given by 549 randomly selected San Diego County, California, Anglo residents. The researchers examined economic factors and reasons, racial beliefs and attitudes, and social background characteristics relative to immigration policy issues. After

analyzing the data, Ayers and colleagues' main conclusion was that "Attitudes about immigration may be motivated more by racial resentments than other considerations" (p. 593).

Inductive. We can begin with detailed empirical observations and move toward abstract generalizations; this is an ***inductive approach***. We may begin with only a topic and a few vague concepts. As we observe and examine the evidence, we develop and refine the concepts to create empirical generalizations (discussed later in this chapter), and then identify preliminary theoretical relationships. Because we build theory from the ground up, this is called ***grounded theory***. Theory follows from an inductive approach, building ideas and theoretical generalizations based on a close examination of the data (see Expansion Box 2.1). Grounded theory flows from attempts to explain, interpret, and render meaning from data.

Example of Inductive Approach. Hein and Moore (2009) used an inductive approach

---

2.1	EXPANSION BOX
	What Is Grounded Theory?

Grounded theory is a widely used approach in qualitative research. It is not the only approach and it is not used by all qualitative researchers. *Grounded theory* is "a qualitative research method that uses a systematic set of procedures to develop an inductively derived theory about a phenomenon" (Strauss and Corbin, 1990:24). The purpose of grounded theory is to build a theory that is faithful to the evidence. It is a method for discovering new theory. In it, the researcher compares unlike phenomena with a view toward learning similarities. He or she sees micro-level events as the foundation for a more macro-level explanation. Grounded theory shares several goals with more positivist-oriented theory. It seeks theory that is comparable with the evidence that is precise and rigorous, capable of replication, and generalizable. A grounded theory approach pursues

generalizations by making comparisons across social situations.

Qualitative researchers use alternatives to grounded theory. Some qualitative researchers offer an in-depth depiction that is true to an informant's worldview. They excavate a single social situation to elucidate the micro processes that sustain stable social interaction. The goal of other researchers is to provide a very exacting depiction of events or a setting. They analyze specific events or settings in order to gain insight into the larger dynamics of a society. Still other researchers apply an existing theory to analyze specific settings that they have placed in a macro-level historical context. They show connections among micro-level events and between micro-level situations and larger social forces for the purpose of reconstructing the theory and informing social action.

to study intergroup relations. Their inductive approach suggested modifying the contact hypothesis that states members of racial-ethnic groups will develop positive social relations if members of one group have frequent and cooperative contact with members of a different racial-ethnic group. The researchers conducted one- to three-hour face-to-face interviews with 28 Southeast Asian refugees, age 18–51, in Illinois, Minnesota, and Wisconsin. They asked open-ended questions about their experiences as refugees and contact with other racial-ethnic groups, specifically whether they talked to White and Black peers about ancestral history. All of the Southeast Asian refugees had personal and family stories about past struggles in Asia and entry into the United States. The refugees reported that only a few Whites were able to tell stories of their ancestors' migration from Europe. Most blacks had only vague stories about slave conditions and used their ancestor stories to express anger at Whites more than to relate personal or family experiences with transition. From the interviews, Hein and Moore learned that the Southeast Asian refugees felt much closer to peers of different racial-ethnic groups who were able to tell ancestral stories. From an inductive analysis, they suggest a modification to the contact hypothesis: shared storytelling of significant parallel life events across racial-ethnic lines will bridge intergroup relations and help build empathy toward out-group members.

Range of Theory

Some theories are highly specific, with concrete concepts of limited scope. At the opposite end are whole systems of many theories that are extremely abstract. As part of efforts to build, verify, and test theory, we often connect theoretical statements of various ranges together, like a series of different-sized boxes that fit into one another or a set of Russian dolls. Recognizing a theory's range helps us to sort out the different uses or kinds of theory. We next examine three points along the range of theories: empirical generalizations, middle-range theories, and theoretical frameworks.

Empirical Generalization. An empirical generalization is the least abstract theoretical statement and has a very narrow range. It is a simple statement about a pattern or generalization among two or more concrete concepts. An example of empirical generalization is, "More men than women choose engineering as a college major." This statement summarizes a pattern between gender and choice of college major and is easy to test or observe. It is a generalization because the pattern operates across time and social contexts.

Empirical Generalization Examples. A generalization from the study about adolescent religion in Chapter 1 is that few adolescents are religious exclusives, and even if they have exclusive beliefs, they rarely express the beliefs in public. An empirical generalization from the deductive study about immigration is that highly prejudiced people will oppose immigration by members of racial-ethnic groups against whom they are prejudiced.

Middle-Range Theory. Middle-range theories are slightly more abstract than empirical generalizations. A middle-range theory focuses on a specific substantive topic area (e.g., domestic violence, military coups, student volunteering), includes a multiple empirical generalization, and builds a theoretical explanation (see "Forms of Explanation," later in this chapter). As Merton (1967:39) stated, "Middle-range theory is principally used in sociology to guide empirical inquiry."

Middle-Range Theory Example. The study discussed in Chapter 1 about cities and the creative class used middle-range theory. The theory explained levels of racial tolerance in various cities by different political climates, and stated that a concentration of creative class members in a city helped create a more tolerant city political climate. The theory is more abstract than an empirical generalization and focuses on a specific topic: racial tolerance in U.S. cities.

Theoretical Framework. A theoretical framework (also called a paradigm or theoretical system) is more abstract than a middle-range theory. Figure 2.1 shows inductive and deductive approaches to theorizing. Few researchers use a theoretical framework directly in empirical research. A researcher may test parts of a theory on a topic and occasionally contrast parts of the theories from different frameworks. Example Box 2.2 illustrates range with the three levels of abstraction.

EXAMPLE BOX

2.2 Levels of Theory in Three Studies: Kalmijn's "Shifting Boundaries" Ayers et al.'s "Immigration" and Hein and Moore's "Race Relations Stories"

Theoretical Framework

Kalmijn Structural functionalism says that the processes of industrialization and urbanization change human society from a traditional to a modern form. In this process of modernization, social institutions and practices evolve. This evolution includes those that fill the social system's basic needs, socialize people to cultural values, and regulate social behavior. Modern institutions (such as formal schooling) have superseded the institutions that filled needs and maintained the social order in traditional society (such as religion). We expect society's need for members to select a mate, form a family, and socialize offspring to shift the major institution of traditional society (religion) to the central institution in modern society (formal schooling).

Ayers et al. Conflict theory says that established social, political, and legal institutions protect members of society who occupy dominant or privileged positions. People with power or privilege due to their wealth socioeconomic status, race, gender, and so forth have great influence over institutions, and the institutions tend to protect the powerful while containing or suppressing the activities of people in subordinate positions (i.e., low wealth socioeconomic status, minority racial-ethnic group, etc.). Suppression and control is greatest if the subordinate position could challenge the hierarchy of dominance. Conflict between the dominant and subordinate social groups is reflected in how major institutions operate, especially institutions or policies charged with maintaining order and formal social control. Immigration policy controls the inflow of people into a society. We expect that immigration policy will block entry of the types of

people perceived to be a potential threat to those with racial-ethnic or economic power.

Hein and Moore Interaction theory holds that face-to-face contact among people is the foundation of people's beliefs and actions. We form perceptions of other people and groups based on our symbolic and actual relations and interactions with others. Once formed, our perceptions and attitudes become self-reinforcing, affecting subsequent interactions. Negative perceptions of out-group members (i.e., a group to which we are not a member) can be changed based on social interaction.

Middle-Range Substantive Theory

Kalmijn A theory of intermarriage patterns notes that young adults in modern society spend less time in small, local settings where family, religion, and community all have a strong influence. Instead, young adults spend increasing amounts of time in school settings. In these settings, especially in college, they have opportunities to meet other unmarried people. In modern society, education has become a major socialization agent. It affects future earnings, moral beliefs and values, and leisure interests. Thus, young adults select marriage partners less on the basis of shared religious or local ties and more on the basis of common educational levels.

Ayers et al. A theory of group-position and racial-ethnic attitudes sees group competition over material rewards, power, and status as explaining intergroup attitudes. Members of a dominant racial-ethnic group who hold negative attitudes toward another racial-ethnic group or feel threatened by it will support laws and public policies that block,

(Continued)

control, or suppress that group and prevent it from growing in size or power. Members of a dominant racial-ethnic group lacking negative attitudes will be neutral or support policies that allow the other racial-ethnic group to grow in size or power.

Hein and Moore   The contact hypothesis says when someone has regular, close interpersonal contact with someone of a different out-group, the person is likely to modify views about out-group members. Negative stereotypes fade and positive feelings grow toward the out-group compared to the situation prior to close contact. Close interpersonal contact has a larger effect when contact is sustained among co-equals and is cooperative. Peers sharing personal life-history stories can be another way to create positive interpersonal contact.

Empirical Generalization

Kalmijn   Americans once married others with similar religious beliefs and affiliation. This practice is being replaced by marriage to others with similar levels of education.

Ayers et al.   Anglos who have racial-ethnic prejudice against Latinos will more strongly support immigration policies that block or greatly restrict immigration from Mexico than nonprejudiced Anglos.

Hein and Moore   Peers in out-groups who are able to exchange intimate life-stories of migration to the United States with Southeast Asian refugees will be viewed more positively by the refugees than peers who are unable to share such stories.

Sociology and other social sciences have several major theoretical frameworks.[5] The frameworks are orientations or sweeping ways of looking at the social world. They provide collections of assumptions, concepts, and forms of explanation. Frameworks include theories for many substantive areas (e.g., theories of crime, theories of the family, etc.). Thus, there can be a structural functional theory, an exchange theory, and a conflict theory of the family. Theories within the same framework share assumptions and major concepts. Some frameworks are oriented more to micro-level phenomena; others focus more on macro-level phenomena (see "Levels of Theory," next). Expansion Box 2.2 shows four major frameworks in sociology and briefly describes the key concepts and assumptions of each.

Levels of Theory

We can divide social theories into three broad groupings by the level of social reality on which they focus. Most people think about the micro level of reality (i.e., the individuals with whom they have face-to-face interactions and conversations day to day). *Micro-level theory* deals with small slices of time, space, or numbers of people. The concepts are usually not very abstract.

Brase and Richmond (2004) used a micro-level theory about doctor–patient interactions and perceptions. The theory stated that physician attire affects doctor–patient interactions. It suggested that a patient makes judgments about a physician's abilities based on attire and that a patient's trust-openness toward a physician is also affected. It said that perceptions of physician authority increased with traditional professional formal attire over informal attire, but that trust-openness was influenced in the opposite direction as authority. Thirty-eight male and 40 female research participants rated their perceptions of same- and opposite-gender models who were identified as being medical doctors, but who were wearing different attire. Findings showed that a white coat and formal attire are clearly superior to casual attire in establishing

2.2	EXPANSION BOX
	Major Theoretical Frameworks in Sociology

Structural Functionalism

Major Concepts.   System, equilibrium, dysfunction, division of labor

Key Assumptions.   Society is a system of interdependent parts that is in equilibrium or balance. Over time, society has evolved from a simple to a complex type, which has highly specialized parts. The parts of society fulfill different needs or functions of the social system. A basic consensus on values or a value system holds society together.

Exchange Theory (also Rational Choice)

Major Concepts. Opportunities, rewards, approval, balance, credit

Key Assumptions.   Human interactions are similar to economic transactions. People give and receive resources (symbolic, social approval, or material) and try to maximize their rewards while avoiding pain, expense, and embarrassment. Exchange relations tend to be balanced. If they are unbalanced, persons with credit can dominate others.

Symbolic Interactionism

Major Concepts.   Self, reference group, role-playing, perception

Key Assumptions.   People transmit and receive symbolic communication when they socially interact. People create perceptions of each other and social settings. People largely act on their perceptions. How people think about themselves and others is based on their interactions.

Conflict Theory

Major Concepts.   Power, exploitation, struggle, inequality, alienation

Key Assumptions.   Society is made up of groups that have opposing interests. Coercion and attempts to gain power are ever-present aspects of human relations. Those in power attempt to hold on to their power by spreading myths or by using violence if necessary.

---

physician authority, but it did not reduce trust-openness as expected.

Meso-level theory links macro and micro levels and operates at an intermediate level. Theories of organizations, social movements, and communities are often at this level.

Roscigno and Danaher (2001) used meso-level theory in a study on the 1930s labor movement among southern textile workers. The researchers used a theory of movement subculture and political opportunity to explain growing labor movement strength and increased strike activity among workers in one industry in a region of the United States across several years. They expected strike activity to grow as the result of a strong movement subculture that carried a message of injustice and a "political opportunity" or the expectation among people

that collective action at a particular time would produce positive results. Their study showed that a technological innovation (i.e., the spread of new radio stations with songs and discussions of working conditions and unfair treatment) contributed to the growth of a subculture of movement solidarity among the textile workers and fostered self-identity as a worker who had common interests with the other textile workers. The technological innovation and events in the political environment (i.e., union organizers and speeches by the President of the United States) also created a political opportunity for the workers. The workers believed that collection action (i.e., strike) was necessary to achieve justice and would produce gains because other workers and government authorities would support their actions.

Macro-level theory concerns the operation of larger aggregates such as social institutions, entire cultural systems, and whole societies. It uses more concepts that are abstract. For example, Mahoney (2003) used macro-level theory to study a puzzle about the countries of Spanish America, specifically 15 countries that had been mainland territories of the Spanish colonial empire. He observed that their relative ranking, from most to least developed in 1900, remained unchanged in 2000; that is, the least developed country in 1900 (Bolivia) remained the least developed a century later. This stability contrasts with dramatic changes and improvements in the region during the twentieth century. Mahoney noted that the richest, most central colonies at the height of the Spanish empire in the seventeenth century were later the poorest countries at the end of the nineteenth century, while marginal, backwater, poor colonies were the most developed, richest countries. Mahoney's data included maps, national economic and population statistics, and several hundred historical studies on the specific countries. He concluded that the most central, prosperous Spanish colonies were located where natural resources were abundant (for extraction and shipment to Europe) and large indigenous populations existed (to work as coerced labor). In these colonies, local elites arose and created rigid racial-ethnic stratification systems that concentrated economic-political power and excluded broad parts of society. The systems continued into the nineteenth century when new political events, trade patterns, and economic conditions appeared. In the 1700–1850 era, liberal-minded elites who were open to new ideas did not succeed in them. In contrast, colonies at the fringe of the Spanish empire in South America were less encumbered by rigid systems. New elites arose who were better able to innovate and adapt, so there was a "great reversal" of positions. After this historical "turning point" some countries got a substantial head start toward social-economic development. These countries built political-economic systems and institutions that propelled them forward; that is, they "locked into" a path that brought increasing returns through the twentieth century. Mahoney's theory covers several centuries, fifteen countries, and large-scale issues of socioeconomic development of a nation.

Forms of Explanation

Prediction and Explanation. A theory's primary purpose is to explain. Many people confuse prediction with explanation. There are two meanings or uses of the term *explanation*. Researchers focus on *theoretical explanation*, a logical argument that tells why something occurs. It refers to a general rule or principle. A researcher's theoretical argument makes connections among concepts. The second type of explanation, *ordinary explanation*, makes something clear or describes something in a way that illustrates it and makes it intelligible. For example, a good teacher "explains" in the ordinary sense. The two types of explanation can blend together. This occurs when a researcher explains (i.e., makes intelligible) his or her explanation (i.e., a logical argument involving theory).

Prediction is a statement that something will occur. It is easier to predict than to explain, and an explanation has more logical power than prediction because good explanations also predict. An explanation rarely predicts more than one outcome, but the same outcome may be predicted by opposing explanations. Although it is less powerful than explanation, many people are entranced by the dramatic visibility of a prediction.

A gambling example illustrates the difference between explanation and prediction. If I enter a casino and consistently and accurately predict the next card to appear or the next number on a roulette wheel, it will be sensational. I may win a lot of money, at least until the casino officials realize I am always winning and expel me. Yet, my method of making the predictions is more interesting than the fact that I can do so. Telling you what I do to predict the next card is more fascinating than being able to predict.

Here is another example. You know that the sun "rises" each morning. You can predict that at some time, every morning, whether or not clouds obscure it, the sun will rise. But why is this so? One explanation is that the Great Turtle carries the sun across the sky on its back. Another explanation is that a god sets his arrow ablaze, which appears to us as the sun, and shoots it across the sky. Few people today believe these ancient explanations. The explanation you probably accept involves a theory about the rotation of Earth and the position of the sun, the star of our solar system. In this explanation, the sun only appears to rise. The sun does not move; its apparent movement depends on Earth's rotation. We are on a planet that both spins on its axis and orbits around a star millions of miles away in space. All three explanations make the same prediction: The sun rises each morning. As you can see, a weak explanation can produce an accurate prediction. A good explanation depends on a well-developed theory and is confirmed in research by empirical observations.

Causal Explanation. *Causal explanation* is the most common type and centers on a cause–effect relationship. We use it all the time in everyday language, although everyday versions tend to be sloppy and ambiguous. For example, you may say that poverty causes crime or that looseness in morals causes an increase in the divorce rate. This does not tell how or why the causal process works. Researchers try to be more precise and exact when discussing causal relations.

Philosophers have long debated the idea of cause. Some people argue that causality occurs in the empirical world, but it cannot be proved. Causality is "out there" in objective reality, and researchers can only try to find evidence for it. Others argue that causality is only an idea that exists in the human mind, a mental construction, not something "real" in the world. This second position holds that causality is only a convenient way of thinking about the world. Without entering into a lengthy philosophical debate, many researchers pursue causal relationships.

Researchers use two basic types of causal explanations. One type is common in qualitative studies with a few cases, or in case studies that explain a specific historical event (e.g., the beginning of a war). This type is based on logic and depends on identifying necessary and/or sufficient causes. A necessary cause is something that must be present, if it is not present, then the effect will not follow (e.g., oxygen is necessary for fire). A sufficient cause is something that is enough to trigger the effect, but it may not always do so and alternatives may trigger the same effect. The spark of a match is sufficient to trigger a fire under some conditions (e.g., enough oxygen, dry combustible material, no strong wind to blow out the spark). Conditions other than a spark from a match may also be sufficient to trigger fire (e.g., intense heat, gasoline under pressure).

A second type of causal explanation is common in quantitative studies with many cases and in experiments. This population-based causality focuses on regularities or patterns. It offers explanations for aggregates, not particular individuals or cases. Aggregates are collections of many individuals, cases, or other units (e.g., businesses, schools, families, clubs, cities, nations, etc.). Thus, it cannot explain why Josephine decided to major in nursing rather than engineering, but it can explain why in certain cultures far more females than males choose nursing over engineering as a college major. The explanation states the odds or the tendency for events to occur, rather than saying that one event absolutely, always follows another. In this type of causal explanation, there may be multiple causes of a single outcome, and a researcher may try to parse out the relative impact of each of several causes.

Three things are needed to establish causality: temporal order, association, and elimination of plausible alternatives. An implicit fourth condition is an assumption that a causal relationship makes sense or fits with broad assumptions or a theoretical framework. We next examine the three conditions.

The *temporal order* condition means that a cause must come before an effect. This commonsense assumption establishes the direction of causality: from the cause toward the effect. You may ask, How can the cause come after what it is to affect? It cannot, but temporal order is only one of the conditions needed for causality. Temporal order is necessary but not sufficient to infer causality. Sometimes people make the mistake of talking about "cause" on the basis of temporal order alone. For example, a professional baseball player pitches no-hit games when he kisses his wife just before a game. The kissing occurred before the no-hit games. Does that mean the kissing is the cause of the pitching performance? It is very unlikely. As another example, race riots occurred in four separate cities in 1968, one day after an intense wave of sunspots. The temporal ordering does not establish a causal link between sunspots and race riots. After all, all prior human history occurred before some specific event. The temporal order condition simply eliminates from consideration potential causes that occurred later in time.

It is not always easy to establish temporal order. With cross-sectional research, temporal order is tricky. For example, we find that people who have a lot of education are also less prejudiced than others. Does more education cause a reduction in prejudice? Or do highly prejudiced people avoid education or lack the motivation, self-discipline, and intelligence needed to succeed in school? Here is another example. The students who get high grades in my class say I am an excellent teacher. Does getting high grades make them happy, so they return the favor by saying that I am an excellent teacher (i.e., high grades cause a positive evaluation)? Or am I doing a great job, so students study hard and learn a lot, which the grades reflect (i.e., their learning causes them to get high grades)? It is a chicken-or-egg problem. We can resolve

the time issue by bringing in other information or designing a study to test for temporal order.

Simple causal relations are unidirectional, operating in a single direction from the cause to the effect. Most studies examine unidirectional relations. More complex theories specify reciprocal-effect causal relations—that is, a mutual causal relationship or simultaneous causality. For example, studying a lot causes a student to get good grades, but getting good grades also motivates the student to continue to study. Theories often have reciprocal or feedback relationships, but these are difficult to test. Some researchers call unidirectional relations nonrecursive and reciprocal-effect relations recursive.

We also need an ***association*** for causality. Two phenomena are associated if they occur together in a patterned way or appear to act together. People sometimes confuse correlation with association. *Correlation* has a specific technical meaning, whereas *association* is a more general idea. A correlation coefficient is a statistical measure that indicates the amount of association, but there are many ways to measure association. Figure 2.2 shows 38 people from a lower-income neighborhood and 35 people from an upper-income neighborhood. Can you see an association between race and income level?

More people mistake association for causality than confuse it with temporal order. For example, when I was in college, I got high grades on the exams I took on Fridays but low grades on those I took on Mondays. There was an association between the day of the week and the exam grade, but it did not mean that the day of the week caused the exam grade. Instead, the reason was that I worked 20 hours each weekend and was very tired on Mondays. As another example, the number of children born in India increased until the late 1960s, then slowed in the 1970s. The number of U.S.-made cars driven in the United States increased until the late 1960s, then slowed in the 1970s. The number of Indian children born and the number of U.S. cars driven are associated: They vary together or increase and decrease at the same time. Yet there is no causal connection. By coincidence, the Indian government instituted a birth control program that slowed the number of births at the same time that Americans were buying more imported cars.

If we cannot find an association, a causal relationship is unlikely. This is why we attempt to find correlations and other measures of association. Yet, we can find an association without causality. The association eliminates potential causes that are not associated, but it cannot definitely identify a cause. It is a necessary but not a sufficient condition. In other words, we need association for causality, but it is not enough alone.

In causal relations for large numbers of cases (i.e., population-based causal relations), the association does not have to be perfect (i.e., every time one variable is present, the other also is) to show causality. In the example involving exam grades and days of the week, there is an association if on 10 Fridays I got seven As, two Bs, and one C, whereas my exam grades on 10 Mondays were six Ds, two Cs, and two Bs. An association exists, but the days of the week

and the exam grades are not perfectly associated. The race and income-level association shown in Figure 2.2 is also an imperfect association.

Eliminating alternatives means that we need to show that an effect or outcome is due to the causal variable and not to something else. It is also called *no spuriousness* because an apparent causal relationship that is actually due to an alternative but unrecognized cause is called a spurious relationship, which is discussed in Chapter 4.

Although we can observe temporal order and associations, we cannot easily observe the elimination of alternatives. Eliminating alternatives is an ideal we only strive for because eliminating all possible alternatives with total certainty is impossible. We try to eliminate alternatives in three ways: building controls for alternatives into a study design, measuring control variables (i.e., factors that are potential alternative causes), and using logic and in-depth knowledge of cases to identify and rule out possible alternative causes (see Expansion Box 2.3).

Causal explanations are usually in a linear form or state cause and effect in a straight line: *A* causes *B*, *B* causes *C*, *C* causes *D*. Most studies

FIGURE 2.2   Association of Income and Race

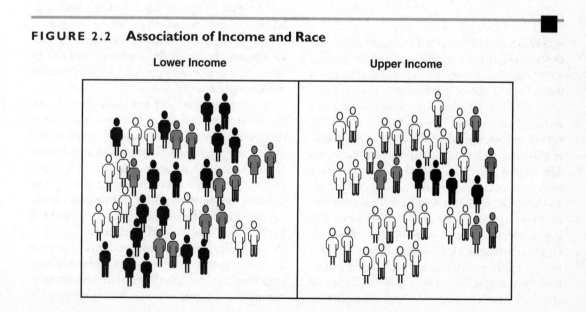

EXPANSION BOX

2.3

3 Ways to Eliminate Alternative Causes in Causal Explanations

1. *Design Controls.* In experimental studies, build controls for potential alternative causes into the study design itself by controlling the situation and physical conditions. Isolate the main cause from the influence of all competing alternatives, then examine its impact on the outcome of interest.

2. *Control Variables.* In quantitative studies that have numerous cases, such as in surveys or existing statistics research, identify and measure all major alternative causes, gathering data on them as well as on the main causes and outcome. These potential alternative causes are control variables. During data analysis, evaluate the impact of the causal variables and control variables on the outcome of interest.

3. *Logical Controls.* In qualitative field research and historical-comparative studies with a limited number of cases, use an intimate familiarity and detailed data about specific cases to logically consider and evaluate possible alternative causes. Trace through each step in a causal process and specify the operation of a causal mechanism or specific combination of factors that join to produce an outcome.

you read about in this chapter already use causal explanation. The study by Brase and Richmond (2004) on doctor–patient interactions discussed earlier used a causal explanation. The explanation was that physician attire caused certain patient perceptions. The study by Ayers et al. (2009) on immigration attitudes used a causal explanation. The explanation was that a person's racial beliefs caused him or her to take certain positions on immigration policy issues. In the study on South American development, Mahoney (2003) used a causal explanation. The explanation was that a combination of natural resources and large indigenous populations caused a rigid racial-ethnic stratification system and concentrated local elite power. Countries that had such rigid systems and concentrated

power blocked change, or caused a lack of development for several hundred years.

A good causal explanation identifies a causal relationship and specifies a causal mechanism. A simple causal explanation is: X causes Y or Y occurs because of X, where X and Y are concepts (e.g., early marriage and divorce). Sometimes we state causality in a predictive form: If X occurs, then Y follows. We can state causality in many ways: X leads to Y, X produces Y, X influences Y, X is related to Y, the greater X the higher Y.

Here is a simple causal theory: A rise in unemployment causes an increase in child abuse. The outcome we want to explain is an increase in the occurrence of child abuse. We explain it by a rise in unemployment (i.e., we explain the increase in child abuse by identifying its cause). A complete explanation also requires elaborating the causal mechanism. The theory says that when people lose their jobs, they feel a loss of self-worth. Once they lose self-worth, they are easily frustrated, upset, and angry. Frustrated people often express their anger by directing it toward those with whom they have close personal contact (e.g., friends, spouse, children, etc.). This is especially true if they do not understand the source of the anger or cannot direct the anger toward its true cause (e.g., an employer, government policy, or "economic forces"). The anger often comes out as physical aggression toward those who are less able to defend themselves or fight back (e.g., physically weak people and children).

The unemployment and child abuse example illustrates a chain of causes and a causal mechanism. We can test different parts of the chain. We might test whether unemployment rates and child abuse occur together, or whether frustrated people become violent toward the people close to them. A typical research strategy is to divide a larger theory into parts and test various relationships against the data.

Relationships between variables can be positive or negative. We imply a positive relationship if we say nothing. A **positive relationship** means that a higher value on the causal variable goes with a higher value on the outcome variable. For example, the more education a person has, the longer his or her life expectancy is. A *negative relationship* means that a higher value on the causal variable goes with a lower value on the outcome variable. For example, the more frequently a couple attends religious services, the lower the chances of their divorcing each other. In diagrams, a plus sign (+) signifies a positive relationship and a negative sign (−) signifies a negative relationship.

Structural Explanation. Unlike a causal explanation, which is similar to a string of balls lined up that hit one another causing each to bounce in turn, a structural explanation is similar to a wheel with spokes from a central idea or a spider web in which each strand forms part of the whole. To make a structural explanation we use metaphors or analogies so that relationships "make sense." The concepts and relations within a theory form a mutually reinforcing system. In structural explanations, we specify a sequence of phases or identify essential parts and linkages that form an interlocked whole. We next look at three theories using a *structural explanation:* network, sequential, and functional theories.

1. *Network theories* explain a situation or outcome by outlining a system of interconnected people, organizations, or units (i.e., the network). The theory identifies situations or outcomes that occur or do not occur due to the positions in the network. The theories often describe the shape and density of a network, discuss the centrality of various positions in the network, and examine direct and indirect connections. The theory may also outline how a network began or changes over time (see Example Box 2.3 for an example of network theory).

2. *Sequence theories* explain by outlining a set of steps that occur across time. The theory identifies separate steps in a process, the ordering of steps, the direction or flow among steps across time, and frequently indicates the duration of steps. The theories describe whether alternative steps can occur, and what happens if a step is missed or delayed.[6]

Sequential Theory Example. The panel study on volunteerism by Oesterle, Johnson, and Mortimer (2004) discussed in Chapter 1 employs sequence theory. The authors used a "life course" perspective in which the impact of an event happening at one phase of a person's life differs what it would have been if the same happened at other phases, and early events generally shape events in later phases. The authors noted that the transition to adulthood is a critical stage when a person learns new social roles and adult expectations. They found that the amounts and types of volunteer activity in the last stage they observed (age 26–27) was strongly influenced by such activities at prior stages of a person's life (age 18–19). People who volunteered at an early stage tended to volunteer at later stages. Those who did not volunteer at an early stage or who devoted full time to working or parenting at other prior stages (18–19 years old) were less likely to volunteer at a later stage (26–27 years old). Thus, later events flowed from an interconnected process in which earlier stages set a course or direction that pointed to specific events in a later stage.

3. *Functional theories* explain a situation or event by locating it within a larger, ongoing, balanced social system, often using biological metaphors. To explain often means identifying the function of an institution, social relationship, or activity within a larger system or discussing the need it fulfills for the maintaining the system.[7] Functional explanations are in this form: "*L* occurs because it serves needs in the system *M*." Functional theory assumes that a system will stay in equilibrium and continue over time. A functional theory of social change says that, over time, a social system moves through developmental stages, becoming increasingly differentiated and more complex.

2.3 EXAMPLE BOX
Example of Network Theory

Many studies examine social networks and map network structures as a way to explain social life. Entwisle, Faust, Rindfuss, and Kaneda (2007) studied networks in villages in a region of Thailand. The authors found that the networks connecting people, through kinship or other social ties, varied by village: "Networks are sparse in some, dense in others; porous in some, less so in others. Moreover, this variability matters" (p. 1524). The networks had many consequences for relations with nearby villages, for the economic activities in a village, for whether people migrated out of a village, and so forth. Network structure shaped the flow of activities and degree of intra village cooperation. To illustrate these findings, the authors provide a diagram with six households. Solid lines indicate people related as brother or sister, and dotted lines indicate those helping with the rice harvest. They show that households a, b, d and e work together. There is no direct family connection between a and d, or between b and e, but they cooperate due to their indirect connections in the network through d. A key network impact was on social cohesion. As the authors noted, "Networks in which actors have more ties, on average, are more cohesive than those in which actors have fewer ties. . . . The more cohesive a network, the more likely that information can travel through social ties to all members and that activities can be coordinated among network members" (p. 1508). In other words, networks influenced how activities in a village occur. More important, dense overall networks with many inter-connections were more socially cohesive than loose networks. *Cohesion* meant that people shared information, cooperated, and accomplished tasks faster and with fewer difficulties compared to people in villages that have sparse networks (*American Journal of Sociology*, 2007:1515).

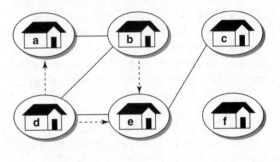

—— Siblings

--➤ People Helping with Rice Harvest

Source: Networks and Contexts: Variation in the Structure of Social Ties, by Barbara Entwisle, Katherine Faust, Ronald Rindfuss, and Toshiko Kaneda. American Journal of Sociology. Volume 112 Issue 5 (March 2007):1495–1533. (page 1505).

It evolves a specialized division of labor and develops greater individualism. These developments create greater efficiency for the system as a whole. Specialization and individualism create temporary disruptions. The traditional ways of doing things weaken, but new social relations emerge. The system generates new ways to fulfill functions or satisfy its needs.

Functional Theory Example. Kalmijn (1991) explained a shift in how people in the United States select marriage partners with a version of functional theory, secularization theory. Secularization theory holds that ongoing historical processes of industrialization and urbanization shape the development of society. During these modernization processes, people rely less on traditional ways of doing things. Religious beliefs and local community ties weaken, as does the family's control over young adults. People no longer live their entire lives in small, homogeneous communities. Young adults become more independent from their parents and from the religious organizations that formerly played a critical role in selecting marriage partners.

Society has a basic need to organize the way people select marriage partners and find partners with whom they share fundamental values. In modern society, people spend time away from small local settings in school settings. In these school settings, especially in college, they meet other unmarried people. Education is a major socialization agent in modern society. Increasingly, it affects a person's future earnings, moral beliefs and values, and ways of spending leisure time. This explains why there has been a trend in the United States for people to marry less within the same religion and increasingly to marry persons with a similar level of education. In traditional societies, the family and religious organization served the function of socializing people to moral values and linking them to potential marriage partners who held similar values. In modern society, educational institutions largely fulfill this function for the social system.

Interpretive Explanation.   The purpose of an *interpretive explanation* is to foster understanding and sometimes to build empathy. In interpretive theory we attempt to discover the meaning of an event or practice by placing it within a specific social context. We want to comprehend or mentally grasp the operation of the social world, as well as get a "feel for" something or to see the world as another person does. Because each person's subjective worldview shapes how he or she acts, we attempt to discern others' reasoning and view of things. The process is similar to decoding a text or work of literature. Meaning comes from the context of a cultural symbol system.

Edelman, Fuller, and Mara-Drita (2001) used an interpretative explanation to study how companies adopted policies related to diversity issues in the early 1990s—that is, affirmative action and equal opportunity. They examined what managers said (i.e., their rhetoric) about diversity concerns. Rhetoric included statements about diversity made by professional managers, business school professors, and consultants in professional workshops, meetings, specialized magazines, and electronic forums. Edelman et al. found that managers converted legal ideas, terms, and concepts into ones that fit into their organizational setting. The professional managers converted vague legal mandates and terms based on ideas about racial discrimination and ending injustice by interjecting their own views, values, training, and interests. They produced ideas and procedures slightly different from the original legal mandates. Management rhetoric changed legal ideas about specific actions to end racial-ethnic or gender discrimination into a "new idea" for effective corporate management. The "new idea" was that corporations benefit from a culturally diverse workforce. Simply put, diversity is good for company profits. Managers consolidated studies and discussions on how to improve corporate operations around the new idea—a socially heterogeneous workforce is more creative, productive, and profitable.

From the data, the researchers built a theory of "managerialization of law." It says that professional managers operate in a corporate environment and do not simply accept the ideas and mandates created in the external government–legal environment and then impose them directly onto the corporation. In fact, many corporate officials hold hostile views toward the legal ideas and requirements on affirmative action, seeing them as alien to a corporate environment. Managers convert or translate alien legal ideas into a form acceptable to a corporate-managerial point of view. They then use the converted ideas to move the corporation in a direction that will comply with the legal requirements.

Edelman et al.'s explanation is interpretive: they explain an outcome (i.e., corporations embracing programs and rhetoric favoring diversity) by looking at how the managers subjectively construct a way of looking at, thinking about, and talking about diversity. The central answer to explain why corporations embrace diversity is to describe how and why managers construct and apply an interpretation.

THE THREE MAJOR APPROACHES TO SOCIAL SCIENCE

Earlier in this chapter, we looked at small-scale parts of a theory (i.e., ideas or concepts). We then moved to middle-range and wider social theory, and arrived at major theoretical frameworks. Now, we move to a broader, more abstract level of the linkage between theory and research—the fundamental approaches to social science. These approaches involve *meta-methodological* issues (i.e., issues beyond methodology, or "supersized" methodological concerns). The approaches blur into the area of philosophy that considers the meaning of science. We cannot ignore them because they influence how we conduct social research studies, but we only briefly touch on the issues here.

About 50 years ago, a now famous philosopher of science, Thomas Kuhn, argued that science in a specific field develops over time based on researchers sharing core assumptions and a general approach on how to conduct research, or paradigm. A *paradigm* is an integrated set of assumptions, models of doing good research, and techniques for gathering and analyzing data. It organizes concepts, theoretical frameworks, and research methods.

Kuhn observed that paradigms hold a scientific field together for a long time, typically many decades or longer. Few researchers question the paradigm or operate outside of it. Most operate within the paradigm's boundaries and focus on accumulating new knowledge within the boundaries. On rare occasions, intellectual difficulties within the field increase, unexpected issues grow, and troubling concerns over proper research methods multiply. Slowly, many

members of a scientific field shift how they view their field's core assumptions and methods. Together they shift to a new paradigm. Once the new paradigm becomes fully established and widely adopted, the process of accumulating knowledge begins anew within the new paradigm's boundaries.

Kuhn's explanation described how most sciences operate most of the time. However, in a few fields of knowledge multiple or competing paradigms coexist. This is the case for several social science fields. Having multiple paradigms troubles some social scientists who believe multiple paradigms hinder the growth of knowledge. They view multiple paradigms as a sign that the social sciences are "immature" sciences and want all social scientists to embrace a single paradigm.

Other social scientists accept the coexistence of multiple paradigms. They recognize that multiple paradigms can be confusing and makes communicating among social scientists more complicated. Despite this, they argue that each paradigm provides valuable knowledge and insights. If we eliminate a paradigm, we limit what we can learn about the social world. These social scientists argue that no one definitely can say which paradigm is "best" or even if it is necessary to have a single paradigm. They hold that the multifaceted complexity of human social life and our historical stage in understanding it means we should retain multiple paradigms. We should not close off a paradigm that offers useful ways to study and learn about social life. Therefore, they argue we should retain a diversity of approaches.

In this section, we look at three social science paradigms or approaches. Each approach has been around for over 150 years and is embraced by a large group of well-respected social scientists. The approaches are unequal in terms of the number of followers, quantity of new studies, and types of issues addressed. Often, social scientists committed to one approach will disagree with those using a different approach, treating the alternative approaches as being less valuable or less "scientific" than their own approach. Although adherents to each approach use multiple research techniques, theories, and theoretical frameworks, researchers who adopt an approach tend to rely on certain research techniques, theories, and theoretical frameworks. The three approaches—positivism, interpretive, and critical—each has its own internal divisions, offshoots, and extensions, but here we focus on the core assumptions and ideas of each approach.

Positivist Approach

Positivism is the most widely practiced social science approach, especially in North America. *Positivism* sees social science research as fundamentally the same as natural science research; it assumes that social reality is comprised of objective facts. Value-free researchers can precisely measure and use statistics with the objective facts to test causal theories. Large-scale bureaucratic agencies, companies, and much of the public favor a positivist approach because it emphasizes objective measures or "hard facts" in the form of numbers. In this way, the approach both mimics natural science and appears to avoid ambiguity and political–moral controversies.

Positivists emphasize the principle of replication, even if in practice we only see a few studies replicated. *Replication* states to verify knowledge, we should repeat studies and get identical or very similar findings with a second, third, and additional replications. Positivists view replication as an ultimate test of valid knowledge, because different observers looking at the same objective facts should get the same results. We get the same results if we carefully specify concepts, precisely measure the facts, and follow clear standards of objective scientific research. As many independent researchers research similar findings, our confidence grows that we have accurately captured the workings of social reality. In this way, scientific knowledge advances. There are five possible reasons why

replication fails, (i.e., we repeat a study and do not get the same results):

1. The initial study was an unusual fluke, or based on a misguided understanding of the world.
2. Important conditions were present in the initial study, but we were unaware of their significance;
3. The initial study, or the repeat of it, was sloppy—it lacked careful, precise measures and analysis;
4. The initial study, or the repeat of it, was improperly conducted—we failed to follow the highest standards for procedures and techniques, or were not completely neutral and objective;
5. The repeated study was a rare, unusual fluke.

In the long term, over dozens of studies across many years of research, reasons 1 and 5 (i.e., the flukes) will disappear. The remaining reasons (2–4) are all due to poor-quality research or a failure to specify details and conditions fully (i.e., things we can improve with more careful, detailed research). Thus, the scientific process as a whole is self-correcting and improves or advances over time.

The positivist approach is deductive and **nomothetic**. Nomothetic means explanations using law or law-like principles. Positivists use both inductive and deductive inquiry, but a deductive process is preferred. It suggests we develop a general causal law or principle in theory, then use deductive logic to specify how it operates in particular situations in the social world. We empirically test predicted outcomes in specific settings using very precise measures. In this way, a general law or principle can cover many specific situations. For example, a general principle says that when two social groups are unequal and compete for scarce resources, in-group feelings and hostility toward the other groups intensify, and the competing groups tend to engage in conflict.

The principle applies to sports teams, countries, racial-ethnic groups, families, and other social groupings. Likewise, we can deduce that in cities with high levels of interracial inequality, when jobs become more scarce and economic competition increases, each group will express more hostility about other racial groups, and intergroup conflict (e.g., riots, demonstrations, violent attacks) will increase. Over time, we can make minor adjustments in our general principles based on many empirical tests of it, and gain confidence as empirical evidence accumulates supporting the general principle or law-like statement.

Most positivist studies are quantitative. Positivists see the experiment as the ideal way to do research, but also use other quantitative research techniques, such as surveys or existing statistics. Positivist researchers advocate value-free science, seek precise quantitative measures, test causal theories with statistics, and believe in the importance of replicating studies.

Interpretive Approach

The interpretive approach is also scientific; however, it has a somewhat different understanding of "scientific" from positivism. While a positivist sees no fundamental difference between social and natural science, interpretive researchers say that human social life differs qualitatively from phenomena of the natural world. Instead of just borrowing scientific principles from the natural sciences, we must develop a special type of science based on the uniqueness of humans. Only with a science designed for people will we capture what is unique and important in social life and conscious human interaction.

Interpretive researchers accept a version of the constructionist view of social reality. The constructionist view holds that social life rests less on objective, material reality than on what is in people's heads (i.e., our ideas, beliefs, and perceptions of reality). In other words, we socially interact and respond based as much, if

not more, on what we believe to be real than what is objectively real in the physical world. This means that to study and understand human social life, we must study how people construct subjective social reality.

We construct social reality as we grow up, interact, and live our daily lives. We continuously create ideas, relationships, symbols, and roles that we consider to be meaningful or important (e.g., intimate emotional attachments, religious or moral ideals, beliefs in patriotic values, racial-ethnic or gender differences, and artistic expressions). We relate to the objective, material reality both directly (e.g., "My automobile transports me from place to place") and through the filter of socially constructed beliefs and perceptions (e.g., "I and other people may see my automobile as a status symbol, as a cultural object, and as expressing an artistic style"). This means what positivists treat as an objective fact, an automobile, interpretive researchers see as the surface level of a more complex social life. Social response/meaning will vary depending on whether I am driving a new Mercedes Benz E550 (costing $92,000) or a 1985 rusted Honda Civic (costing $2,000). The difference involves more than the size, newness, and cost of the two automobiles; it involves socially created images and categories (e.g., luxury, prestige, and extravagance versus frugality or impoverishment).

Interpretive researchers are skeptical of the positivist attempts to produce precise quantitative measures of objective facts. This is because social reality is fluid and filled with shifting perceptions. We constantly construct, test, reinforce, or change beliefs, assumptions, and perceptions, which are embedded in daily social rituals, traditions, and institutions and become ongoing habits, practices, and procedures. To capture the fluid nature of socially constructed reality and social processes, interpretive researchers favor qualitative data. In addition, they favor interpretive over causal forms of explanation (see discussion earlier in this chapter).

Instead of a deductive–nomothetic approach, interpretative researchers favor inductive reasoning and an idiographic approach. *Idiographic* literally means specific description and emphasizes creating a highly detailed picture or description of a specific social setting, process, or type of relationship. The detailed picture or description will advance deep understanding.

Instead of replication as the ultimate test of knowledge, interpretative researchers emphasize *verstehen* or empathetic understanding. *Verstehen* is a desire to get inside the worldview of a person being studied and accurately represent how that person sees the world, feels about it, and acts within it. In other words, instead of replicating patterns among hard facts, we best advance knowledge if we truly grasp the inner world, subjective views, and personal perspective of the people we study. We need to "stand in another's shoes" and understand how and why people see, feel, and act as they do.

Critical Approach

The critical approach shares several features with an interpretive approach, but it blends an objective/materialist stance with a constructionist view of social reality. The critical approach emphasizes putting knowledge into action. The critical approach assumes the multilayered nature of social reality. On the surface level (i.e., what we easily see) is a great deal of illusion, myth, and distorted thinking. People are often misled, subjected to manipulated messages, or hold false ideas. Beneath the surface level at a deeper, often unseen level lies "real" objective reality. A vital task of social research is to strip away the surface layer of illusion or falsehood so we can see beyond the surface layer. We should not ignore the outer surface layer because it profoundly shapes much of human action, but it does not give us the full picture of social life. "Deep structures" or underlying social relations and conditions, such as power inequality and unequal opportunity, affect the operations of society and social institutions.

The critical approach holds that social research cannot be truly neutral or value free. People regularly use knowledge, including social scientific knowledge, to advance specific political–moral purposes. This connects the conduct of social research to advancing specific political–moral positions. The critical approach says that "value free" can be a cover for advancing specific purposes. Neutrality in research may mislead us if we do not recognize underlying power relations and inequalities. When we do a social science study, we have a choice: to assist those with power and authority in society, or to advance social justice and empower the powerless.

The critical approach favors action research. *Praxis* is the ultimate test of how good an explanation is in the critical approach. It blends theory and concrete action; theory informs us about the specific real-world actions we should take to advance social change, and we can use the experiences of engaging in action for social change to reformulate the theory. All three approaches see a mutual relationship between abstract theory and empirical evidence, but the critical approach goes further. It tries to dissolve the gap between abstract theory and the empirical experiences of having people use social theory to make changes in the empirical world, and learn from their attempts to use theory.

THE DYNAMIC DUO

Theory and research are interrelated. Only the naive, new researcher mistakenly believes that theory is irrelevant to research or that we just collect data in a study. To proceed without theory is to waste time collecting useless data and to fall into hazy, vague thinking, faulty logic, and imprecise concepts. Without theory, it is difficult to converge onto a crisp research issue or to generate a lucid account of a study's purpose. Without theory, we will be adrift when designing or conducting a research study.

Theory frames how we look at and think about a topic. It gives us concepts, provides basic assumptions, directs us to important questions, and suggests ways for us to make sense of data. Theory enables us to connect a single study to the immense base of knowledge to which other researchers contribute. To use an analogy, theory helps us see the forest instead of just a single tree. Theory increases our awareness of interconnections and of the broader significance of data (see Table 2.1).

Theory has a place in virtually all research, but its prominence varies. It is generally less central in applied descriptive research than in basic explanatory research. Its role in applied descriptive research may be indirect. The concepts are often more concrete, and the goal is not to create general knowledge. Nevertheless, researchers use theory in applied descriptive research to refine concepts, evaluate assumptions of a theory, and indirectly test hypotheses.

Theory does not remain fixed over time; it is provisional and open to revision. Theories grow into more accurate and comprehensive explanations about the makeup and operation of the social world in two ways. They advance as theorists toil to think clearly and logically, but this effort has limits. The way a theory makes significant progress is by interacting with research findings.

The scientific community expands and alters theories based on empirical results. In a deductive approach, theory guides the design of a study and the interpretation of results. We refute, extend, or modify theory based on the results. As we conduct empirical research to test a theory, we develop confidence that some parts of it are true. We may modify some propositions of a theory or reject them if several well-conducted studies have negative findings. A theory's core propositions and central tenets are more difficult to test and are refuted less often. In a slow process, we may decide to abandon or change a theory as the evidence against it mounts over time and cannot be logically reconciled.

The inductive approach follows a slightly different process. Inductive theorizing begins with a few assumptions and broad orienting concepts. Theory develops from the ground up as we gather and analyze the data. Theory emerges slowly, concept by concept in a specific area. The process is similar to a long pregnancy. Over time, the concepts and empirical generalizations emerge and mature. Soon, relationships become visible, and we weave together knowledge from different studies into more abstract theory.

CONCLUSION

In this chapter, you read about social theory—its parts, purposes, and types. The dichotomy between theory and research is artificial. The value of theory and its necessity for conducting good research should be clear. If we proceed without theory, we rarely conduct top-quality research and frequently find ourselves in a quandary. Likewise, theorists who proceed without linking theory to research or anchoring it to empirical reality can float off into incomprehensible speculation and conjecture.

TABLE 2.1 **Major Aspects and Types of Social Theory**

Aspect	Types of Social Theory
Direction	Inductive or deductive
Level	Micro, meso, or macro
Explanation	Causal, interpretive, or structural
Abstraction	Empirical generalization, middle range, framework, or paradigm

Key Terms

association
assumption
blame analysis
causal explanation
classification concept
concept cluster
deductive approach
empirical generalization
functional theory
grounded theory
ideal type
idiographic
inductive approach
macro-level theory
meso-level theory
micro-level theory
negative relationship
nomothetic
paradigm
positive relationship
praxis
prediction
proposition
replication
verstehen

Endnotes

1. See Felson (1991), Felson and Felson (1993), and Logan (1991) for a discussion of blame analysis.
2. For more detailed discussions of concepts, see Chafetz (1978:45–61), Hage (1972:9–85), Kaplan (1964:34–80), Mullins (1971:7–18), Reynolds (1971), and Stinchcombe (1968, 1973).
3. Turner (1980) discussed how sociological explanation and theorizing can be conceptualized as translation.
4. Classifications are discussed in Chafetz (1978: 63–73) and Hage (1972).
5. Introductions to alternative theoretical frameworks and social theories are provided in Craib (1984), Phillips (1985:44–59), and Skidmore (1979).
6. Sequential theory can be causal but does not have to be. Causal theories that specify necessary and sufficient conditions for causality sometimes overlap with sequential theory (see Mahoney, 2008).
7. See introduction to functional explanation in Chafetz (1978:22–25).

CHAPTER 3

Ethics in Social Research

WHAT ARE RESEARCH ETHICS?

In life, ethics guide behavior and decisions. Ethics tell us what is moral, right, or proper and what is not. They help identify boundaries between right and wrong, good and evil. Many professions (e.g., accountants, lawyers, medical doctors, journalists, police officers) and organizations (e.g., universities, hospitals, nonprofits, government agencies, newspapers, corporations) have ethical standards to guide behavior and decisions.

In social research, ethics guide us through a range of concerns, dilemmas, and conflicts that arise over the proper way to conduct a study. Ethics are not as simple as they may first appear, because there are few ethical absolutes and only broad principles. When we apply the principles, we must use judgment and some principles conflict with others when we use them to answer specific questions in practice.

Social researchers have a clear moral and professional obligation to behave in an ethical manner at all times, even if research participants or others in society are unaware of or unconcerned about ethics. Social researchers often must balance two values: the pursuit of knowledge and the rights of research participants or of others in society. We also must balance potential benefits—such as advancing the understanding of social life, improving decision making, or helping research participants—against potential costs—such as loss of dignity, self-esteem, privacy, or democratic freedoms.

Doing professional social research requires more than knowing the proper research techniques and design (e.g., sampling), it also requires being aware of ethical principles and applying them prudently. This is not always easy. For centuries, moral, legal, and political philosophers debated the kinds of issues researchers regularly face. It is difficult to appreciate fully the ethical dilemmas a researcher will encounter until after a research study begins, but waiting until the middle of a study is usually too late. This means we must prepare in advance and consider ethical concerns when designing a study. In addition, by developing sensitivity to ethical issues, we become alert to potential ethical concerns that can arise while conducting a study. Also, an ethical awareness helps us better understand the overall research process.

Ethics begin and end with the individual social researcher. A strong personal moral code by the researcher is the best defense against unethical behavior. Before, during, and after conducting a study, a researcher has opportunities to, and *should,* reflect on the ethics of research actions and consult his or her conscience. Ultimately, ethical research depends on the integrity of an individual researcher.

WHY BE ETHICAL?

Given that most social researchers are genuinely concerned about others, you might ask, Why would any researcher ever act in an ethically irresponsible manner? Most unethical behavior is due to a lack of awareness and pressures to take ethical shortcuts. Researchers face pressures to build a career, publish new findings, advance knowledge, gain prestige, impress family and friends, hold on to a job, and so forth. Ethical research will take longer to complete, cost more money, be more complicated, and be less likely to produce unambiguous results. Plus, there are many opportunities in research to act unethically, the odds of getting caught are small, and written ethical standards are vague, loose principles.

The scientific community demands ethical behavior without exceptions. The ethical researcher gets few rewards and wins no praise. The unethical researcher, if caught, faces public humiliation, a ruined career, and possible legal action. The best preparation for ethical behavior is to internalize sensitivity to ethical concerns, to adopt a serious professional role, and to interact regularly with other researchers.

Scientific Misconduct

The scientific community, research organizations, and agencies that fund research oppose a type of unethical behavior called scientific misconduct; it includes research fraud and plagiarism. *Scientific misconduct* occurs when a researcher falsifies or distorts the data or the methods of data collection, or plagiarizes the work of others. It also includes significant, unjustified departures from the generally accepted scientific practices for doing and reporting on research. *Research fraud* occurs when a researcher fakes or invents data that he or she did not really collect, or fails to honestly and fully report how he or she conducted a study. Although rare, it is a very serious violation. The most famous case of research fraud was that of Sir Cyril Burt, the father of British educational psychology. Burt died in 1971 as an esteemed researcher. He was famous for studies with twins that showed a genetic basis of intelligence. In 1976, it was discovered that he had falsified data and the names of coauthors. Unfortunately, the scientific community had been misled for nearly 30 years. More recently, in 2010 a Harvard University researcher studying the origin of morality resigned after he was accused of scientific fraud. *Plagiarism* occurs when a researcher "steals" the ideas or writings of another or uses them without citing the source. Plagiarism also includes stealing the work of another researcher, an assistant, or a student, and misrepresenting it as one's own. These are serious breaches of ethical standards.[1]

Unethical but Legal

Behavior may be unethical but legal (i.e., not break any law). A plagiarism case illustrates the distinction between legal and ethical behavior. The American Sociological Association documented that a 1988 book without any footnotes by a dean from Eastern New Mexico University contained large sections of a 1978 Ph.D. dissertation that a sociology professor at Tufts University wrote. Copying the dissertation was not

FIGURE 3.1   Typology of Legal and Moral Actions in Social Research

LEGAL	ETHICAL	
	Yes	No
Yes	Moral and Legal	Legal but Immoral
No	Illegal but Moral	Immoral and Illegal

illegal; it did not violate copyright law because the dissertation did not have a copyright filed with the U.S. government. Nevertheless, it was clearly *unethical* according to standards of professional behavior.[2] (See Figure 3.1 for relations between legal and moral actions.)

POWER RELATIONS

A professional researcher and the research participants or employee-assistants are in a relationship of unequal power and trust. An experimenter, survey director, or research investigator has power over participants and assistants, and in turn, they trust his or her judgment and authority. The researcher's credentials, training, professional role, and the prestige of science in society legitimate the power and expert authority. Some ethical issues involve an abuse of power and trust. The authority to conduct social research and to earn the trust of others is accompanied by an unyielding ethical responsibility to guide, protect, and oversee the interests of the people being studied.

When looking for ethical guidance, researchers can turn to a number of resources: professional colleagues, ethical advisory committees, institutional review boards at a college or institution, codes of ethics by professional associations (discussed later in this chapter), and books on research ethics. The scientific community firmly supports ethical behavior, even if an individual researcher is ultimately responsible to do what is ethical in specific situations.

ETHICAL ISSUES INVOLVING RESEARCH PARTICIPANTS

Have you ever been a participant in a research study? If so, how were you treated? More attention is focused on the possible negative study effects on research participants than any other ethical issue. Acting ethically requires that we balance the value of advancing knowledge against the value of noninterference in the lives of others. Either extreme causes problems. If research participants have absolute rights of noninterference, empirical research becomes impossible. Giving researchers absolute rights of inquiry could nullify participants' basic human rights. The moral question becomes: When, if ever, are we justified in risking physical harm or injury to those being studied, causing them great embarrassment or inconvenience, violating their privacy, or frightening them?

The law and codes of ethics recognize some clear prohibitions: Never cause unnecessary or irreversible harm to research participants; secure prior voluntary consent when possible; and never unnecessarily humiliate, degrade, or release harmful information about specific individuals that was collected for research purposes. In other words, always show respect for the research participant. These are minimal standards and are subject to interpretation (e.g., What does *unnecessary* mean in a specific situation?).

Origins of Research Participant Protection

Concern over the treatment of research participants arose after the revelation of gross violations of basic human rights in the name of science. The most notorious violations were "medical experiments" conducted on Jews and others in Nazi Germany, and similar "medical experiments" to test biological weapons by Japan in the 1940s. In these experiments, terrible tortures were committed. For example, people were placed in freezing water to see how long it took them to die, people were purposely starved to death, people were intentionally infected with horrible diseases, and limbs were severed from children and transplanted onto others.[3]

Human rights violations did stop after World War II. In a famous case of unethical research, the Tuskegee Syphilis Study, also known as *Bad Blood*, the President of the United States admitted wrongdoing and formally apologized in 1997 to the participant-victims. Until the 1970s, when a newspaper report caused a scandal to erupt, the U.S. Public Health Service sponsored a study in which poor, uneducated African American men in Alabama suffered and died of untreated syphilis, while researchers studied the severe physical disabilities that appear in advanced stages of the disease. The unethical study began in 1929, before penicillin was available to treat the disease, but it continued long after treatment was available. Despite their unethical treatment of the people, the researchers were able to publish their results for 40 years. The study ended in 1972, but a formal apology took another 25 years.[4]

Unfortunately, the Bad Blood scandal is not unique. During the Cold War era, the U.S. government periodically compromised ethical research principles for military and political goals. In 1995, reports revealed that the government authorized injecting unknowing people with radioactive material in the late 1940s. In the 1950s, the government warned Eastman Kodak and other film manufacturers about nuclear fallout from atomic tests to prevent fogged film, but it did not warn nearby citizens of health hazards. In the 1960s, the U.S. army gave unsuspecting soldiers LSD (a hallucinogenic drug), causing serious trauma. Today, researchers widely recognize these to be violations of two fundamental ethical principles: avoid physical harm and obtain informed consent.[5]

Physical Harm, Psychological Abuse, and Legal Jeopardy

Social research can harm a research participant in several ways: physical, psychological, and legal harm, as well as harm to a person's career, reputation, or income. Certain forms of harm are more likely in some types of research (e.g., in experiments versus field research). A researcher should be aware of all types of potential harm and to take specific actions to minimize the risk to participants at all times.

Physical Harm. Physical harm is rare, even in biomedical research, where the intervention into a person's life is much greater.[6] A straightforward ethical principle is that as researchers we should never cause physical harm. We must anticipate risks before beginning a study, including basic safety concerns (e.g., safe buildings, furniture, and equipment). We should screen out high-risk subjects (those with heart conditions, a history of mental breakdown or seizures, etc.) if the study involves great stress. We should anticipate possible sources of injury or physical attacks on research participants or assistants. It is the researcher's moral and legal responsibility to prevent injury due to participation in research and terminate a study immediately if physical safety of the participants cannot be guaranteed (see Zimbardo study in Example Box 3.1).

Psychological Abuse, Stress, or Loss of Self-Esteem. The risk of physical harm in social research is rare, but we can place people in highly stressful, embarrassing, anxiety-producing, or unpleasant situations. Social researchers want to learn about people's responses in real-life, high anxiety–producing situations, so they might place people in realistic situations of psychological discomfort or stress. Is it unethical to cause discomfort? The ethics of the famous Milgram obedience study are still debated (see Example Box 3.1). Some say that the precautions taken and the knowledge gained outweighed the stress and potential psychological harm that research participants experienced. Others believe that the extreme stress and the risk of permanent harm were too great. Such an experiment could not be conducted today because of heightened sensitivity to the ethical issues involved.

Social researchers have created high levels of anxiety or discomfort. They have exposed participants to gruesome photos; falsely told male students that they have strong feminine personality traits; falsely told students that they have failed a class; created a situation of high fear (e.g., smoke entering a room in which the door is locked); asked participants to harm others; placed people in situations where they face social pressure to deny their convictions; and had participants lie, cheat, or steal.[7] Researchers who study helping behavior often place participants in emergency situations to see whether they will lend assistance. For example, Piliavin, Rodin, and Piliavin (1969) studied helping behavior in subways by faking someone's collapse onto the floor. In the field experiment, the riders in the subway car were unaware of the experiment and did not volunteer to participate in it.

Only highly experienced researchers should consider doing a study that induces great anxiety or fear in research participants and they must take all necessary precautions to protect participants. They should take several specific precautions such as the following:

- Consult with others who have conducted similar studies and mental health professionals when planning the study.
- Screen out high-risk populations (e.g., those with emotional problems or heart conditions).
- Obtain written informed consent (to be discussed) before the research.
- Monitor conditions closely and arrange for emergency interventions or termination of the study if dangerous situations arise.
- Debrief the people immediately afterward (i.e., explain any deception and what actually happened in the study).

Researchers should never create *unnecessary* stress (i.e., beyond the minimal amount needed to create the desired effect) or stress that lacks a very clear, legitimate research purpose. Knowing what "minimal amount" means comes with experience. It is best to begin with too little stress, risking a finding of no effect, than to create too much. It is always wise to

Stanley Milgram's *obedience study* (Milgram, 1963, 1965, 1974) attempted to discover how the horrors of the Holocaust under the Nazis could have occurred by examining the strength of social pressure to obey authority. After signing "informed consent forms," research participants were assigned, in rigged random selection, to be a "teacher" while a confederate was the "pupil." The teacher was to test the pupil's memory of word lists and increase the electric shock level if the pupil made mistakes. The pupil was located in a nearby room, so the teacher could hear but not see the pupil. The shock apparatus was clearly labeled with increasing voltage. As the pupil made mistakes and the teacher turned switches, she or he also made noises as if in severe pain. The researcher was present and made comments such as "You must go on" to the teacher. Milgram reported, "Subjects were observed to sweat, tremble, stutter, bite their lips, groan and dig their fingernails into their flesh. These were characteristic rather than exceptional responses to the experiment" (Milgram, 1963:375). The percentage of research participants who would shock to dangerous levels was dramatically higher than expected. Ethical concerns arose over the use of deception and the extreme emotional stress experienced by research participants.

In Laud Humphreys's (Humphreys, 1975) *tearoom trade study* (a study of male homosexual encounters in public restrooms), about 100 men were observed engaging in sexual acts as Humphreys pretended to be a "watchqueen" (a voyeur and look-out). Research participants were followed to their cars, and their license numbers were secretly recorded. Names and addresses were obtained from police registers when Humphreys posed as a market researcher. One year later, in disguise, Humphreys used a deceptive story about a health survey to interview the research participants in their homes. Humphreys was careful to keep names in safety deposit boxes, and identifiers with research participants names were burned. He significantly advanced knowledge of homosexuals who frequent "tearooms" and overturned previous false beliefs about them. There has been controversy over the study: The research participants never consented; deception was used; and the names could have been used to blackmail subjects, to end marriages, or to initiate criminal prosecution.

In the *Zimbardo prison experiment* (Zimbardo, 1972, 1973; Zimbardo et al., 1973, 1974), male students were divided into two role-playing groups: guards and prisoners. Before the experiment, volunteer students were given personality tests, and only those in the "normal" range were chosen. Volunteers signed up for two weeks, and prisoners were told that they would be under surveillance and would have some civil rights suspended, but that no physical abuse was allowed. In a simulated prison in the basement of a Stanford University building, prisoners were deindividualized (dressed in standard uniforms and called only by their numbers) and guards were militarized (with uniforms, nightsticks, and reflective sunglasses). Guards were told to maintain a reasonable degree of order and served 8-hour shifts, while prisoners were locked up 24 hours per day. Unexpectedly, the volunteers became too caught up in their roles. Prisoners became passive and disorganized, while guards became aggressive, arbitrary, and dehumanizing. By the sixth day, Zimbardo called off the experiment for ethical reasons. The risk of permanent psychological harm, and even physical harm, was too great.

collaborate with other researchers when the risk to participants is high, because the involvement of several ethically sensitive researchers reduces the chances of making an ethical misjudgment.

Another risk from studies of great stress and anxiety in participants is the danger that researchers will develop a callous or manipulative attitude toward others. Researchers have reported feeling guilt and regret after conducting experiments that caused psychological harm to people. Studies that place participants in anxiety-producing situations may produce personal discomfort for the ethical researcher.

Legal Harm.   As researchers, we are responsible for protecting research participants from increased risk of arrest. If participation in a study increases the risk of arrest, few individuals will trust researchers or be willing to participate in future research. Potential legal harm is one criticism of Humphreys's 1975 tearoom trade study (see Example Box 3.1).

A related ethical issue arises when we learn of illegal activity when collecting research data. We must weigh the value of protecting the researcher–subject relationship and the benefits to future studies against potential serious harm to innocent people. We bear the cost of our decision. For example, in his field research on police, Van Maanen (1982:114–115) reported seeing police beat people and witnessing illegal acts and irregular procedures, but said, "On and following these troublesome incidents I followed police custom: I kept my mouth shut." When conducting field research on a mental institution, Taylor (1987) discovered the mistreatment and abuse of inmates by the staff. He had two choices: abandon the study and call for an immediate investigation, or keep quiet and continue with the study for several months, publicize the findings afterwards, and then advocate to end the abuse. After weighing the situation, he followed the latter course and is now an activist for the rights of mental institution inmates.

In some studies, observing illegal behavior may be central to the study. If we covertly observe and record illegal behavior, then supply the information to law-enforcement authorities, we are violating ethical standards regarding research participants and undermining future social research. At the same time, if we fail to report illegal behavior we are indirectly permitting criminal behavior. We could be charged as an accessory to a crime. We need to be clear about our professional role. Cooperation with law-enforcement officials raises the question, Are we professional social scientists who protect research participants in the process of seeking knowledge, or freelance undercover informants trying to "catch" criminals?

Other Harm to Participants

Research participants may face other types of harm. For example, a survey interview may create anxiety and discomfort if it asks people to recall unpleasant or traumatic events. An ethical researcher must be sensitive to any harm to participants, consider precautions, and weigh potential harm against potential benefits.

Another type of harm is a negative impact on the careers, reputations, or incomes of research participants. For example, a survey of employees reveals that the supervisor's performance is poor. As a consequence, the supervisor loses her job. Or, a study of homeless people living on the street shows that many engage in petty illegal acts to get food. As a consequence, a city government "cracks down" on the petty illegal acts and the homeless people can no longer eat. An ethical researcher considers the consequences for research participants and tries to avoid causing any harm simply because someone was a research participant. We must evaluate each case, weigh potential harm against potential benefits, and bear the responsibility for the decision.

Deception

Has anyone ever told you a half-truth or lie to get you to do something? How did you feel about it? Social researchers follow the ethical *principle of voluntary consent*: Never force anyone to participate in research, and do not lie to anyone unless it is necessary and the only way to accomplish a legitimate research purpose. Those who participate in social research should explicitly agree to participate. A person's right not to participate becomes a critical issue whenever we use deception, disguise the research, or use covert research methods.

We sometimes deceive or lie to participants in field and experimental research. We might slightly misrepresent actions or true intentions for legitimate methodological reasons. For example, if participants knew the true purpose, they would modify their behavior, making it impossible to learn of their real behavior. Another situation occurs when access to a research site would be impossible if we told the complete truth. Deception is never preferable if we can accomplish the same thing without using deception.

Experimental researchers often deceive subjects to prevent them from learning the hypothesis being tested and to reduce "reactive effects" (see Chapter 8). Deception might be acceptable if a researcher can show that it has a clear, specific methodological purpose, and even then, we should use it only to the minimal degree necessary. Researchers who use deception should always obtain informed consent, never misrepresent risks, and always explain the actual conditions to participants afterwards. You might ask, How can we obtain prior informed consent and still use deception? We can describe the basic procedures involved and conceal only specific information about hypotheses being tested.

Sometimes field researchers use covert observation to gain entry to field research settings. In studies of cults, small extremist political sects, illegal or deviant behavior, or behavior in a large public area, it may be impossible to conduct research if we announce and disclose our true purpose. If a covert stance is not essential, do not use it. If we are unsure whether covert access is necessary, then a strategy of gradual disclosure may be best. When in doubt, err in the direction of disclosing true identity and purpose. Covert research remains controversial, and many researchers feel that all covert research is always unethical. Even those who accept covert research as ethical in certain situations say that it should be used only when overt observation is impossible. Whenever possible, we should inform participants of the observation immediately afterwards and give them an opportunity to express concerns.

Deception and covert research may increase mistrust and cynicism as well as diminish public respect for social research. Misrepresentation in field research is analogous to being an undercover agent or government informer in nondemocratic societies. The use of deception has a long-term negative effect. It increases distrust among people who are frequently studied and makes doing social research more difficult in the long term.

Informed Consent

A fundamental ethical principle of social research is: Never coerce anyone into participating; participation *must* be voluntary at all times. Permission alone is not enough; people need to know what they are being asked to participate in so that they can make an informed decision. Participants can become aware of their rights and what they are getting involved in when they read and sign a statement giving ***informed consent***— an agreement by participants stating they are willing to be in a study and they know something about what the research procedure will involve.

3.1   EXPANSION BOX
Informed Consent

Informed consent statements contain the following:

1. A brief description of the purpose and procedure of the research, including the expected duration of the study

2. A statement of any risks or discomfort associated with participation

3. A guarantee of anonymity and the confidentiality of records

4. The identification of the researcher and of where to receive information about participants rights or questions about the study

5. A statement that participation is completely voluntary and can be terminated at any time without penalty

6. A statement of alternative procedures that may be used

7. A statement of any benefits or compensation provided to research participants and the number of participants involved

8. An offer to provide a summary of findings

Governments vary in the requirement for informed consent. The U.S. federal government does not require informed consent in all research involving human subjects. Nevertheless, we should get written informed consent unless there are good reasons for not obtaining it (e.g., covert field research, use of secondary data, etc.) as judged by an institutional review board (see later discussion).

Informed consent statements provide specific information (see Expansion Box 3.1). A general statement about the kinds of procedures or questions involved and the uses of the data are sufficient for informed consent. Studies suggest that participants who receive a full informed consent statement do not respond differently from those who do not. If anything, people who refused to sign such a statement were more likely to guess or answer "no response" to questions.

It is unethical to coerce people to participate, including offering them special benefits that they cannot otherwise attain. For example, it is unethical for a commanding officer to order a soldier to participate in a study, for a professor to require a student to be a research participant in order to pass a course, or for an employer to expect an employee to complete a survey as a condition of continued employment. It is unethical even if someone other than the researcher (e.g., an employer) coerces people (e.g., employees) to participate in research.

Full disclosure of the researcher's identity protects research participants against fraudulent research and protects legitimate researchers. Informed consent lessens the chance that a con artist in the guise of a researcher will defraud or abuse people. It also reduces the chance that someone will use a bogus researcher identity to market products or obtain personal information on people for unethical purposes.

Legally, a signed informed consent statement is optional for most survey, field, and secondary data research, but it is often mandatory for experimental research. Informed consent is impossible to obtain in existing statistics and documentary research. The general rule is: The

higher the risk of potential harm to research participants, the greater the need to obtain a written informed consent statement from them. In sum, there are many sound reasons to get informed consent and few reasons not to get it.

Special Populations and New Inequalities

Some populations or groups of research participants are not capable of giving true voluntary informed consent. *Special populations* are people who lack the necessary cognitive competency to give valid informed consent or people in a weak position who might cast aside their choice to refuse to participate in a study. Students, prison inmates, employees, military personnel, homeless people, welfare recipients, children, and the developmentally disabled may not be fully capable of making a decision, or they may agree to participate only because they see participation as a way to obtain a desired good—such as higher grades, early parole, promotions, or additional services. It is unethical to involve "incompetent" people (e.g., children, mentally disabled, etc.) in research unless we satisfy two minimal conditions: (1) a legal guardian grants written permission and (2) we follow all standard ethical principles to protect participants from harm. For example, we want to survey high school students to learn about their sexual behavior and drug/alcohol use. If the survey is conducted on school property, school officials must give official permission. For any research participant who is a legal minor (usually under 18 years old), written parental permission is needed. It is best to ask permission from each student, as well.

The use of coercion to participate can be a tricky issue, and it depends on the specifics of a situation. For example, a convicted criminal faces the alternative of imprisonment or participation in an experimental rehabilitation program. The convicted criminal may not believe in the benefits of the program, but we may believe that it will help the criminal. This is a case of coercion. As researchers we must honestly judge whether the benefits to the criminal and to society greatly outweigh the ethical prohibition on coercion. This is risky. History shows many cases in which a researcher believed he or she was doing something "for the good of" someone in a powerless position (e.g., prisoners, students, homosexuals), but it turned out that the "good" actually was for the researcher or a powerful organization in society, and it did more harm than good to the research participant.

You may have been in a social science class in which a teacher required you to participate as a participant in a research project. This is a special case of coercion and is usually ethical. Teachers have made three arguments in favor of requiring student participation: (1) it would be difficult and prohibitively expensive to get participants otherwise, (2) the knowledge created from research with students serving as research participants benefits future students and society, and (3) students will learn more about research by experiencing it directly in a realistic research setting. Of the three arguments, only the third justifies limited coercion. This limited coercion is acceptable only as long as it meets three conditions: it is attached to a clear educational objective, the students have a choice of research experience or an alternative activity, and all other ethical principles of research are followed.

Avoid Creating New Inequalities. Another type of harm occurs when one group of people is denied a service or benefit as a result of participating in a research project. For example, we find a new treatment for people with a terrible disease, such as acquired immune deficiency syndrome (AIDS). To determine the effects of the new treatment, half the group is randomly chosen to receive the treatment, while others receive nothing. The design may clearly show whether the treatment is effective, but participants in the group who receive no treatment may die. Of course, those receiving the treatment may also die, until more is known about whether it is effective. Is it ethical to deny people who have been randomly assigned to a study group the potentially

life-saving treatment? What if a clear, definitive test of whether a treatment is effective requires that one study group receive no treatment?

We can reduce creating a new inequality among research participants in three ways. First, the people who do not receive the "new, improved" treatment continue to receive the best previously acceptable treatment. In other words, instead of denying all assistance, they get the best treatment available prior to the new one being tested. This ensures that no one will suffer in absolute terms, even if they temporarily fall behind in relative terms. Second, we can use a *crossover design*, which is when a study group that gets no treatment in the first phase of the experiment becomes the group with the treatment in the second phase, and vice versa. Finally, we continuously monitor results. If it appears early in the study that the new treatment is highly effective, we should offer it to those in the control group. Also, in high-risk experiments with medical treatments or possible physical harm, researchers may use animal or other surrogates for humans.

Privacy, Anonymity, and Confidentiality

How would you feel if private details about your personal life were shared with the public without your knowledge? Because social researchers sometimes transgress the privacy of people in order to study social behavior, we must take several precautions to protect research participants' privacy.

Privacy. Survey researchers invade a person's privacy when they probe into beliefs, backgrounds, and behaviors in a way that reveals intimate private details. Experimental researchers sometimes use two-way mirrors or hidden microphones to "spy" on research participants. Even if people know they are being studied, they are unaware of what the experimenter is looking for. Field researchers may observe private aspects of behavior or eavesdrop on conversations.

In field research, privacy may be violated without advance warning. When Humphreys

(1975) served as a "watchqueen" in a public restroom where homosexual contacts took place, he observed very private behavior without informing research participants. When Piliavin and colleagues (1969) had people collapse on subways to study helping behavior, those in the subway car had the privacy of their ride violated. People have been studied in public places (e.g., in waiting rooms, walking down the street, in classrooms, etc.), but some "public" places are more private than others (consider, for example, the use of periscopes to observe people who thought they were alone in a public toilet stall).

Eavesdropping on conversations and observing people in quasi-private areas raises ethical concerns. To be ethical, we violate privacy only to the minimum degree necessary and only for legitimate research purposes. In addition, we take steps to protect the information on participants from public disclosure.

Anonymity. We protect privacy by not disclosing a participant's identity after information is gathered. This takes two forms that require us to separate an individual's identity from his or her responses: anonymity and confidentiality. *Anonymity* means that people remain anonymous or nameless. For example, a field researcher provides a social picture of a particular individual, but gives a fictitious name and location, and alters some characteristics. The research participant's identity is protected, and the individual remains unknown or anonymous. Survey and experimental researchers discard the names or addresses of research participants as soon as possible and refer to participants by a code number only to protect anonymity. If we use a mail survey and have a code on the questionnaire to determine which respondents failed to respond, we are not keeping respondents anonymous during that phase of the study. In panel studies, we track the same individuals over time, so we cannot uphold participant anonymity within the study. Likewise, in historical research we use specific names in historical or documentary research. We may do so if the original information was from public sources; if the sources were not publicly available, we must obtain written permission from the owner of the documents to use specific names.

It is difficult to protect research participant anonymity. In one study about a fictitious town, "Springdale," in *Small Town in Mass Society* (Vidich and Bensman, 1968), it was easy to identify the town and specific individuals in it. Town residents became upset about how the researchers portrayed them and staged a parade mocking the researchers. People often recognize the towns studied in community research. Yet, if we protect the identities of individuals with fictitious information, the gap between what we studied and what we report to others raises questions about what was found and what was made up. We may breach a promise of anonymity unknowingly in small samples. For example, let us say you conduct a survey of 100 college students and ask many questions on a questionnaire, including age, sex, religion, and hometown. The sample contains one 22-year-old Jewish male born in Stratford, Ontario. With this information, you could find out who the specific individual is and how he answered very personal questions, even though his name was not directly recorded on the questionnaire.

Confidentiality. Even if we cannot protect anonymity, we always should protect participant confidentiality. Anonymity means protecting the identity of specific individuals from being known. *Confidentiality* can include information with participant names attached, but we hold it in confidence or keep it secret from public disclosure. We release data in a way that does not permit linking specific individuals to responses and present data publicly only in an aggregate form (e.g., as percentages, statistical means, etc.).

We can provide anonymity without confidentiality, or vice versa, although they usually go together. Anonymity without confidentiality occurs if all the details about a specific individual are made public, but the individual's name is withheld. Confidentiality without anonymity occurs if detailed information is not made public, but a researcher privately links individual names to specific responses.

Researchers have used elaborate procedures to protect the identity of research participants from public disclosure: eliciting anonymous responses, using a third-party custodian who holds the key to coded lists, or using the random-response technique. Past abuses suggest that such measures may be necessary. For example, Diener and Crandall (1978:70) reported that during the 1950s, the U.S. State Department and the FBI requested research records on individuals who had been involved in the famous Kinsey sex study. The Kinsey Sex Institute refused to comply with the government. The institute threatened to destroy all records rather than release them. Eventually, the government agencies backed down. The moral duty and ethical code of social researchers obligated them to destroy the records rather than give them to government officials.

Confidentiality can sometimes protect research participants from legal or physical harm. In a study of illegal drug users in rural Ohio, Draus, Siegal, Carlson, Falck, and Wang (2005) took great care to protect the research participants. They conducted interviews in large multiuse buildings, avoided references to illegal drugs in written documents, did not mention names of drug dealers and locations, and did not affiliate with drug rehabilitation services, which had ties to law enforcement. They noted, "We intentionally avoided contact with local police, prosecutors, or parole officers" and "surveillance of the project by local law enforcement was a source of concern" (p. 169). In other situations, other principles may take precedence over protecting research participant confidentiality. For example, when studying patients in a mental hospital, a researcher discovers that a patient is preparing to kill an attendant. The researcher must weigh the benefit of confidentiality against the potential harm to the attendant.

Social researchers can pay high personal costs for being ethical. Although he was never accused or convicted of breaking any law and he closely followed the ethical principles of the American Sociological Association, Professor Rik Scarce spent 16 weeks in a Spokane jail for contempt of court after he refused to testify before a grand jury and break the confidentiality of research data. Scarce had been studying radical animal liberation groups and had already published one book on the topic. He had interviewed a research participant the police suspected of leading a group that broke into animal facilities and causing $150,000 in damage. Two judges refused to acknowledge the confidentiality of social research data and the advice of the social scientific community, and jailed Scarce for not handing over data.[8]

A special concern with anonymity and confidentiality arises when we study "captive" populations (e.g., students, prisoners, employees, patients, and soldiers). Gatekeepers, or those in positions of authority, may restrict access unless they receive information on research participants.[9] For example, a researcher studies drug use and sexual activity among high school students. School authorities agree to cooperate under two conditions: (1) students need parental permission to participate and (2) school officials get the names of all drug users and sexually active students in order to assist them with counseling and to inform the students' parents. An ethical researcher will refuse to continue rather than meet the second condition. Even though the officials claim to have the participants' best interests in mind, the privacy of participants will be violated and they could be in legal harm as a result of disclosure. If the school officials really want to assist the students and not use researchers as spies, they could develop an outreach program of their own.

Mandated Protections of Research Participants

Many national governments have regulations and laws to protect research participants and their rights. In the United States, legal restraint is found in rules and regulations issued by the U.S. Department of Health and Human Services Office for the Protection from Research Risks. Although this is only one federal agency, most researchers and other government agencies look to it for guidance. The National Research Act (1974) established the National Commission for the Protection of Human Subjects in Biomedical and Behavioral Research, which significantly expanded regulations and required informed consent in most social research. The responsibility for safeguarding ethical standards was assigned to research institutes and universities. The Department of Health and Human Services issued regulations in 1981, which are still in force. Federal regulations follow a biomedical model and protect subjects from physical harm. Other rules require **institutional review boards (IRBs)** at all research institutes, colleges, and universities to review all use of human research participants. An *IRB* is a committee of researchers and community members that oversees, monitors, and reviews the impact of research procedures on human participants and applies ethical guidelines by reviewing research procedures at a preliminary stage when first proposed. Some forms of research, educational tests, normal educational practice, most nonsensitive surveys, most observation of public behavior, and studies of existing data in which individuals cannot be identified are exempt from institutional review boards.

ETHICS AND THE SCIENTIFIC COMMUNITY

Physicians, attorneys, family counselors, social workers, and other professionals have a *code of ethics* and peer review boards or licensing regulations. The codes formalize professional standards and provide guidance when questions arise in practice. Social researchers do not provide a service for a fee, receive limited ethical training, and are rarely licensed. They incorporate ethical concerns into research because it is morally and socially responsible, and to protect social research from charges of insensitivity or abusing people. Professional social science associations have codes of ethics that identify proper and improper behavior. They represent a consensus of professionals on ethics. All researchers may not agree on all ethical issues, and ethical rules are subject to interpretation, but researchers are expected to uphold ethical standards as part of their membership in a professional community.

Codes of research ethics can be traced to the Nuremberg code adopted during the Nuremberg Military Tribunal on Nazi war crimes held by the Allied Powers immediately after World War II. The code, developed as a response to the cruelty of concentration camp experiments, outlines ethical principles and rights of human research participants. These include the following:

- Follow the principle of voluntary consent
- Avoid of unnecessary physical and mental suffering
- Avoid of any experiment where death or disabling injury is likely
- Terminate the research if its continuation is likely to cause injury, disability, or death
- Make certain that studies are only conducted by highly qualified people using the highest levels of skill and care
- Ensure that the results should be for the good of society and unattainable by any other method

The Nuremberg code dealt with the treatment of human research participants and focused on medical experimentation but it became the basis for the ethical codes in social research. Similar codes of human rights, such as the 1948 Universal Declaration of Human Rights by the United Nations and the 1964 Declaration of Helsinki, also have implications for social researchers. Expansion Box 3.2 lists some of the basic principles of ethical social research.

Professional social science associations have committees that review codes of ethics and hear about possible violations, but there is no formal policing of the codes. The penalty for a minor violation rarely goes beyond a letter of complaint. If laws have not been violated, the most extreme penalty is the negative publicity surrounding a well-documented and serious ethical violation. The publicity may result in the loss of employment, a refusal to publish the researcher's findings in scholarly journals, and a prohibition from receiving funding for research—in

3.2 Basic Principles of Ethical Social Research

- Ethical responsibility rests with the individual researcher.
- Do not exploit research participants or students for personal gain.
- Some form of informed consent is highly recommended or required.
- Honor all guarantees of privacy, confidentiality, and anonymity.
- Do not coerce or humiliate research participants.
- Use deception only if needed, and always accompany it with debriefing.
- Use the research method that is appropriate to a topic.
- Detect and remove undesirable consequences to research participants.
- Anticipate repercussions of the research or publication of results.
- Identify the sponsor who funded the research.
- Cooperate with host nations when doing comparative research.
- Release the details of the study design with the results.
- Make interpretations of results consistent with the data.
- Use high methodological standards and strive for accuracy.
- Do not conduct secret research.

other words, banishment from the community of professional researchers.

Codes of ethics do more than codify thinking and provide guidance; they also help universities and other institutions defend ethical research against abuses. For example, after interviewing 24 staff members and conducting observations, a researcher in 1994 documented that the staff at the Milwaukee Public Defenders Office were seriously overworked and could not effectively provide legal defense for poor people. Learning of the findings, top officials at the office contacted the university and demanded to know who on their staff had talked to the researcher, with implications that there might be reprisals. The university administration defended the researcher and refused to release the information, citing widely accepted codes that protect human research participants.[10]

ETHICS AND THE SPONSORS OF RESEARCH

Whistle-Blowing

You might find a job where you do research for a sponsor—an employer, a government agency, or a private firm that contracts others to conduct a study. Special ethical problems arise when a sponsor pays for research, especially applied research. Researchers may be asked to compromise ethical or professional research standards as a condition for receiving a contract or for continued employment. Researchers need to set ethical boundaries beyond which they will refuse the sponsor's demands. When confronted with an illegitimate demand from a sponsor, a researcher has three basic choices: loyalty to an organization or larger group, exiting from the situation, or voicing opposition.[11] These present themselves as caving in to the sponsor, quitting, or becoming a whistle-blower. A researcher must choose his or her own course of action, but it is best to consider ethical issues early in a relationship with a sponsor and to express concerns up front.

Whistle-blowing occurs when a researcher sees an ethical wrongdoing, and cannot stop it after informing superiors and exhausting internal avenues to resolve the issue, and then turns to outsiders and informs an external audience, agency, or the media. The whistle-blowing researcher must be convinced that the breach of ethics is serious and approved of in the organization. It is risky. The outsiders may or may not be interested in the problem or able to help. Outsiders often have their own priorities (making an organization look bad, sensationalizing the problem, etc.) that differ from ending the unethical behavior. Supervisors or managers often try to discredit or punish anyone who exposes problems and acts disloyal. Under the best of conditions, the issue may take a long time to resolve and create great emotional strain. By doing what is moral, a whistle-blower should be prepared to make sacrifices—loss of a job or no promotions, lowered pay, an undesirable transfer, abandonment by friends at work, or incurring legal costs. There is no guarantee that doing the ethical-moral thing will stop the unethical behavior or protect the honest researcher from retaliation.

Applied social researchers in sponsored research settings need to think seriously about their professional roles. They may want to maintain some independence from an employer and affirm their membership in a community of dedicated professionals. Many find a defense against sponsor pressures by participating in professional organizations (e.g., the Evaluation Research Society), maintaining regular contacts with researchers outside the sponsoring organization, and staying current with the best research practices. The researcher least likely to uphold ethical standards in a sponsored setting is someone who is isolated and professionally insecure. Whatever the situation, unethical behavior is never justified by the argument that "If I didn't do it, someone else would have."

Arriving at Particular Findings

How do you respond if a sponsor tells you, directly or indirectly, what results you should come up with before you do a study? An ethical researcher will refuse to participate if he or she is told to arrive at specific results as a precondition for doing research. Legitimate research is conducted without restrictions on the possible findings that a study might yield.

An example of pressure to arrive at particular findings is in the area of educational testing. Standardized tests to measure achievement by U.S. schoolchildren have come under criticism. For example, children in about 90 percent of school districts in the United States score "above average" on such tests. This was called the *Lake Wobegon effect* after the mythical town of Lake Wobegon, where, according to national radio show host Garrison Keillor, "all the children are above average." The main reason for this finding was that the researchers compared scores of current students with those of students many years ago. Many teachers, school principals, superintendents, and school boards pressured for results that would allow them to report to parents and voters that their school district was "above average."[12]

Limits on How to Conduct Studies. Is it ethically acceptable for a sponsor to limit research by defining what a researcher can study or by limiting the techniques used? Sponsors can legitimately set some conditions on research techniques used (e.g., survey versus experiment) and limit costs for research. However, we must follow generally accepted research methods. We should give a realistic appraisal of what can be accomplished for a given level of funding. The issue of limits is common in contract research, when a firm or government agency asks for work on a particular research project. There is often a tradeoff between quality and cost. Plus, once the research begins, a researcher may need to redesign the project, or costs may be higher. The contract procedure makes midstream changes difficult. A researcher may find that he or she is forced by the contract to use research procedures or methods that are less than ideal. The dilemma becomes: complete the contract and do low-quality research, or fail to fulfill the contract and lose money and future jobs.

We should refuse to continue a study if we cannot uphold generally accepted standards of research. If a sponsor demands a biased sample or leading survey questions, the ethical response is to refuse to cooperate. If a legitimate study shows a sponsor's pet idea or project to be a disaster, a common outcome is the end of employment or pressure to violate professional research standards. In the long run, the sponsor, the researcher, the scientific community, and society in general are harmed by the violation of sound research practice. We must decide if are we "hired hands" who always deliver to sponsors whatever they want, even if it is ethically wrong, or professionals. As professionals we are obligated to teach, guide, or even oppose sponsors in the service of higher moral principles.

We can ask, Why would sponsors want the social research conducted if they are not interested in using the findings or in the truth? The answer is that some sponsors are not interested in the truth and have little respect for the scientific process. They see social research only as a "cover" to legitimate a decision or practice that they plan to carry out. They are using research to justify their action or deflect criticism, abusing the researcher's professional status and undermining the integrity of science. They are being deceitful by trying to "cash in" on social research's reputation for honesty. When such a situation occurs, an ethical researcher has a moral responsibility to expose and stop the abuse.

Suppressing Findings

What happens if you conduct a study and the findings make the sponsor look bad, then the sponsor does not want to release the results? This is a common situation for many applied researchers. For example, a sociologist conducted a study for a state government lottery commission on the effects of state government–sponsored gambling. After she completed the report, but before releasing it to the public, the commission asked her to remove sections that outlined the many negative social effects of gambling and to eliminate her recommendations to create social services to help the anticipated increase of compulsive gamblers. The researcher was in a difficult position and faced two conflicting values: do what the sponsor requested and paid for, or reveal the truth to the public but then suffer the consequences.[13]

Government agencies may suppress scientific information that contradicts official policy or embarrasses high officials. Retaliation against social researchers employed by government agencies who make the information public also occurs. In 2004, leading scientists, Nobel laureates, leading medical experts, former federal agency directors, and university chairs and presidents signed a statement voicing concern over the misuse of science by the George W. Bush administration. Major accusations included suppressing research findings and stacking scientific advisory committees with ideologically committed advocates rather than impartial scientists. Other complaints included limiting the public release studies on auto-safety data, negative data about pharmaceuticals, and studies on pollution. These involved industries that were major political campaign supporters of the administration. Additional criticisms appeared over removing a government fact sheet citing studies that showed no relationship between abortions and breast cancer, removing study results about positive effects of condom use in pregnancy prevention, holding back information on positive aspects of stem cell research, and requiring researchers to revise their study findings on dangers of arctic oil drilling and endangered species so they would conform to the administration's political agenda.[14]

In sponsored research, we can negotiate conditions for releasing findings *prior to beginning* the study and sign a contract to that effect. It may be unwise to conduct the study without such a guarantee, although competing researchers who have fewer ethical scruples may do so. Alternatively, we can accept the sponsor's criticism and hostility and release the findings over the sponsor's objections. Most researchers prefer the first choice, since the second one may scare away future sponsors.

Social researchers sometimes self-censor or delay the release of findings. This is to protect the identity of informants, to maintain access to a research site, to hold onto their jobs, or to protect the personal safety of themselves or family members.[15] This type of censorship is not imposed by an outside power. It is done by someone who is close to the research and who is knowledgeable about possible consequences. Researchers shoulder the ultimate responsibility for their research. Often, they can draw on many different resources but they face many competing pressures, as well.

Concealing the True Sponsor

Is it ethical to keep the identity of a sponsor secret? For example, an abortion clinic funds a study on members of religious groups who oppose abortion, but it tells the researcher not to reveal to participants who is funding the study. The researcher must balance the ethical rule that it is best to reveal a sponsor's identity to participants against both the sponsor's desire for confidentiality and reduced cooperation by participants in the study. In general, an ethical researcher informs participants of the sponsor's identity unless there is a strong methodological reason for not doing so. When reporting or publishing results, the ethical mandate is very clear: We must always reveal the sponsor who provides funds for a study.

POLITICS OF RESEARCH

Ethics largely address moral concerns and standards of professional conduct in research that are under the researcher's control. Political concerns also affect social research, but many are beyond the control of researchers. The politics of research are actions by organized advocacy groups, powerful interests in society, governments, or politicians to restrict or control the direction of social research. Historically, the political influence over social research has included preventing researchers from conducting a study, cutting off or redirecting funds for research, harassing individual researchers, censoring the release of research findings, and using social research as a cover or guise for covert government intelligence/military actions. For example, U.S. Congress members targeted and eliminated funding for research projects that independent panels of scientists recommended because members of Congress did not like the topics. Also politically appointed officials have shifted research funds toward topics consistent with their political views while ending support for studies on topics that might contradict their views. Large corporations have threatened individual researchers with a lawsuit for delivering expert testimony in public

about research findings that revealed the corporation's past bad conduct. Until about a decade ago, social researchers who appeared to be independent were actually conducting covert U.S. government intelligence activities.[16]

Most uses of political or financial influence to control social research try to limit knowledge creation or restrict the autonomous scientific investigation of controversial topics. For example, a 2011 newspaper report indicated that research on the issues of gun violence, injury, and usage supported by the U.S. government has been nearly eliminated due to political pressure by the National Rifle Association and gun lobbyists. The report states " . . . the amount of money available today for studying the impact of firearms is a fraction of what it was in the mid-1990s, and the number of scientists toiling in the field has dwindled to just a handful as a result" (Luo, 2011). Major research centers, such as the Centers for Disease Control and Prevention and the National Institute for Justice, avoid funding such research because of political pressure. Researchers report, "it is often simply easier to avoid the topic" and most academic researchers have stopped conducting studies on the topics. When the factual scientific knowledge to inform public policies issues is limited, ideological–political forces can have greater sway in public debates.

Attempts at control seem motivated by a fear that researchers might discover something damaging if they have freedom of inquiry. This shows that free scientific inquiry is connected to fundamental political ideals of open public debate, democracy, and freedom of expression.

The three main reasons for blocking or steering research are as follows:

- People who defend or advance positions and knowledge originating in ideological, political, or religious beliefs, and fear that social research knowledge that contradicts their beliefs.

- Powerful interests want to protect or advance their political–financial position

3.3 EXPANSION BOX
What Is Public Sociology?

Michael Burawoy (2004, 2005) distinguished among four ideal types of social research: policy, professional, critical, and public. The aim of *public sociology* (or social science, more generally) is to enrich public debate over moral and political issues by infusing such debate with social theory and research. Public sociology frequently overlaps with action-oriented research. Burawoy argued that the place of social research in society centers on how one answers two questions: Knowledge for whom? and Knowledge for what? The first question focuses on the sources of research questions and how results are used. The second question looks at the source of research goals. Are they handed down by some external sponsor or agency or are they concerned with debates over larger societal political-moral issues? Public social science tries to generate a conversation or debate between researchers and public. By constrast, policy social science focuses on finding solutions to specific problems as defined by sponsors or clients. Both

rely on professional social science for theories, bodies of knowledge, and techniques for gathering and analyzing data. Critical social science, as was discussed in Chapter 2, emphasizes demystifying and raising questioning about basic conditions.

The primary audience for professional and critical social science are members of the scientific community, whereas the main audience for public and policy research are nonexperts and practitioners. Both critical and public social science seek to infuse a moral, value dimension into social research and they try to generate debates over moral-political values. Professional and policy social science are less concerned about debates over moral or value issues and may avoid them. Instead, their focus is more on being effective in providing advances to basic knowledge or specific solutions to practical problems. Both public and policy social science are applied research and have a relevance beyond the community of scientific researchers.

or privileges, and fear social research might show that their actions harm the public or some sectors of society.

- People who lack respect for the ideals of science to pursue truth/knowledge and view scientific research cynically (i.e., only as cover for advancing private interests) (see Expansion Box 3.3).

VALUE-FREE AND OBJECTIVE RESEARCH

You have undoubtedly heard about "value-free" research and the importance of being "objective" in research. This is not as simple at it might first appear for several reasons. First, there are different meanings of the terms *value free* and *objective*. Second, different approaches to social science (positivism, interpretative, critical)

hold different views on the issue. And last, even researchers who agree that social research should be value free and objective do not believe that it needs to be totally devoid of all values.

There are two basic ways the term *value free* is used: research free from any prior assumptions, theoretical stand, or values, and research free of influence from an individual researcher's personal prejudices/beliefs. Likewise, *objective* can mean focusing only on what is external or visible, or it can mean following clear and publicly accepted research procedures and not haphazard, personal ones.

The three approaches to social science that you read about in Chapter 2 hold different positions on the importance of value-free, objective research. Positivism puts a high value on such research. An interpretive approach seriously questions whether it is possible, since human values/beliefs pervade all aspects of human activities, including research. Instead of eliminating values and subjective dimension, it suggests a relativist stance—no single value position is better than any other. A critical approach also questions value-free research, and sees it as often being a cover for hidden interests and values.

Value free means free of everyone's values except those of science, and *objective* means following established rules or procedures without considering how they were created. In other words, a critical approach sees all research as containing some values, so those who claim to be value free are just hiding their values. Those who follow an interpretive and critical approach and reject value-free research do not embrace sloppy and haphazard research. They reject research that follows a particular researcher's whims or that has a foregone conclusion and automatically supports a specific value position. They believe that a researcher should make his or her own value position explicit, reflect carefully on reasons for doing a study and the procedures used, and communicate in a candid, clear manner exactly how the study was conducted. In this way, other researchers see the role of a researcher's values and judge for themselves whether the values unfairly influenced a study's findings.

Even highly positivist researchers who advocate value-free and objective studies admit a limited place for personal, moral values. A researcher's personal, moral position can enter when it comes to deciding what topic to study and how to disseminate findings. Being value free and objective only refers to conducting the study. This means that we can study the issues we believe to be important and after completing a study we can share the results with specific interest groups in addition to making them available to the scientific community.

CONCLUSION

In Chapter 1, we saw the distinctive contribution of science to society and how social research is a source of knowledge about the social world. Social science perspectives and research techniques can be powerful tools for understanding the world. Nevertheless, with that power to discover comes responsibility—a responsibility to yourself, a responsibility to your sponsors, a responsibility to the community of scientific researchers, and a responsibility to the larger society. These responsibilities can conflict with each other. Ultimately, you personally must decide to conduct research in an ethical manner, to uphold and defend the principles of the social science approach you adopt, and to demand ethical conduct by others. The truthfulness of knowledge produced by social research and its use or misuse depends on individual researchers like you, reflecting on their actions and on the serious role of social research in society. In the next chapter, we examine basic design approaches and issues that appear in both qualitative and quantitative research.

Key Terms

anonymity
confidentiality
crossover design
informed consent
institutional review board (IRB)
plagiarism
principle of voluntary consent
public sociology
research fraud
scientific misconduct
special populations
whistle-blowing

Endnotes

1. For a discussion of research fraud, see Broad and Wade (1982), Diener and Crandall (1978), and Weinstein (1979). Hearnshaw (1979) and Wade (1976) discuss the Cyril Burt case, and Wade (2010) on scientific fraud at Harvard in 2010.

Kusserow (1989) discusses the concept of scientific misconduct.

2. See Blum (1989) and D'Antonio (1989) for details on this case. Also see Goldner (1998) on legal versus scientific views of misconduct. Gibelman (2001) discusses several cases and the changing definition of misconduct.

3. See Lifton (1986) on Nazi experiments, and Williams and Wallace (1989) discuss Japanese experiments. Harris (2002) argues that the Japanese experiments were more horrific, but the United States did not prosecute the Japanese scientists as the Germans were because the U.S. military wanted the results to develop its own biological warfare program.

4. See Jones (1981) and Mitchell (1997) on "Bad Blood."

5. Diener and Crandall (1978:128) discuss examples.

6. A discussion of physical harm to research participants can be found in Kelman (1982), Reynolds (1979, 1982), and Warwick (1982).

7. For a discussion, see Diener and Crandall (1978: 21–22) and Kidder and Judd (1986:481–484).

8. See Monaghan (1993a, 1993b, 1993c).

9. Broadhead and Rist (1976) discuss gatekeepers.

10. See "UW Protects Dissertation Sources," *Capital Times* (Madison, Wisconsin), December 19, 1994, p. 4.

11. See Hirschman (1970) on loyalty, exit, or voice.

12. See Edward Fiske, "The Misleading Concept of 'Average' on Reading Test Changes, More Students Fall Below It," *New York Times* (July 12, 1989). Also see Koretz (1988) and Weiss and Gruber (1987).

13. See "State Sought, Got Author's Changes of Lottery Report," *Capital Times* (Madison, Wisconsin), July 28, 1989, p. 21.

14. Andrew Revkin, "Bush Aide Edited Climate Reports," *New York Times* (June 8, 2005). "White House Calls Editing Climate Files Part of Usual Review," *New York Times* (June 9, 2005). Union of Concerned Scientists, "Politics Trumps Science at U.S. Fish and Wildlife Service" (February 9, 2005). "Specific Examples of the Abuse of Science," www.ucsusa.org/global_environment/rsi/page.cfm?pageID=1398, downloaded August 3, 2005. "Summary of National Oceanic & Atmospheric Administration Fisheries Service Scientist Survey" by Union of Concerned Scientists (June 2005). E. Shogren, "Researchers Accuse Bush of Manipulating Science," *Los Angeles Times* (July 9, 2004). Jeffrey McCracker, "Government Bans Release of Auto-Safety Data," *Detroit Free Press* (August 19, 2004). Gardiner Harris, "Lawmaker Says FDA Held Back Drug Data," *New York Times* (September 10, 2004). James Glanz, "Scientists Say Administration Distorts Facts," *New York Times* (February 19, 2004). Dylan O. Krider, "The Politicization of Science in the Bush Administration," *Skeptic* Vol. 11, No. 2 (2004) at www.Skeptic.com. C. Orstein, "Politics Trumps Science in Condom Fact Sheet," *New York Times* (December 27, 2002). "Scientist Says Officials Ignored Advice on Water Levels," *Washington Post* (October 29, 2002).

15. See Adler and Adler (1993).

16. See Neuman, W. Lawrence. (2011) *Social Research methods: Qualitative and Quantitative Approaches.* Needham Heights MA: Allyn & Bacon, Neuman, W. Lawrence. (2011) Social Research methods: Qualitative and Quantitative Approaches. Needham Heights MA: Allyn & Bacon. Chapter 16) for a discussion of political issues in social research.

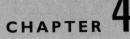

CHAPTER 4

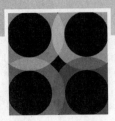

Reviewing the Scholarly Literature and Planning a Study

INTRODUCTION

Thus far, you read about the principles and types of research, discovered how theory and research complement one other, and saw how to conduct ethical studies. It is now time to examine the specifics of designing a study. Recall from Chapter 1 that you start with a general topic, narrow the topic into a specific research question, and then design a specific study to address the research question. In qualitative studies, the pattern varies somewhat because new questions can emerge during the research process.

Topics for study have many sources: previous studies, personal experiences, your discussions with friends and family, or something you saw on television or a film or you read about in a book, magazine, or newspaper. Often, it begins with something that arouses your curiosity, about which you hold deep commitments or strong feelings, or that you believe is wrong and want to change. Almost all social research topics involve patterns that operate in aggregates, and that you can empirically measure and observe. This rules out topics about one unique situation (e.g., why your boy/girlfriend dumped you yesterday, why your friend's little sister hates her schoolteacher), or one individual case (e.g., your own family), or something impossible to observe, even indirectly (e.g., unicorns, ghosts with supernatural powers, etc.). This may rule out some interesting topics, but it leaves tens of thousands for you to investigate.

Three things can help you learn the most effective type of study to pursue for a topic or question:

1. Reading studies that others have conducted on a topic
2. Grasping issues within qualitative and quantitative approaches to research design
3. Understanding how to use research techniques as well as their strengths and limitations

You will read about the first two of the three in this chapter, and the third item in subsequent chapters.

LITERATURE REVIEW

Reading the "literature" or studies published on a topic serves five important functions:

1. The literature can help you narrow down a broad topic. It shows how others conducted their studies, and this gives you a model of how narrowly focused a research question should be. It also shows you the kinds of study designs others have used, how to measure variables, and ways to analyze data.
2. The literature informs you about the "state of knowledge" on a topic. From the studies by others, you can learn "what we now know" collectively. You will see the key ideas, terms, and issues that surround a topic. You may consider replicating, testing, or extending what others already found.
3. The literature can stimulate creativity and curiosity. As you read many studies, you are likely to encounter some new, unexpected findings and fascinating information.
4. Even if you never get to conduct or publish your own research study, reading published studies offers you examples of what the final report on a study looks like, its major parts, its form, and its style of writing. You will develop skills to evaluate reports of studies and distinguish weak from strong reports.
5. A last reason is more practical. Just as your writing skills can improve if you attentively read top-quality writing, reading many reports of high-quality research enables you to grasp better the elements that go into conducting a research study.

You want to be organized as you locate and read the scholarly literature on a topic. In addition, it is wise to look ahead and prepare a written literature review. There are several types of reviews, but most often, the *literature review* is a carefully crafted summary of the recent studies on a topic with key findings and research methods. It carefully documents the sources in the review summary.

To prepare a literature review, first locate the relevant studies. You next read thoroughly to discover the major findings, central issues, and methods in each. You will want to take conscientious notes on what you read. While the reading is still fresh in your mind and with notes in front of you, begin to organize what you have learned. Write about the studies in a way that builds a context around a specific research question.

The literature review rests on the assumption that knowledge accumulates, and we can learn from and build on the work of others. Scientific research is a collective effort of many researchers. They share results with one another and pursue knowledge as a community. A few studies may be especially important and individual researchers may become famous, but a specific study is just one small part of the larger knowledge creation process. Today's studies build on those of yesterday.

Reviews vary in scope and depth. Some reviews are stronger at fulfilling one or another of four goals (see Expansion Box 4.1). It may take over a year to complete an extensive professional summary review of all the literature on a broad question but only a few weeks for highly focused review in a narrowly specialized area. To begin a review, decide on a topic, the amount of depth to go into, and the kind of review to conduct.

Where to Find Research Literature

Research reports appear in several written forms: periodicals, books, dissertations, government documents, or policy reports. Researchers also present papers on studies at the meetings of professional societies. For the most part, you can find research reports

4.1 EXPANSION BOX
Goals of Literature Review

1. *To demonstrate a familiarity with a body of knowledge and establish credibility.* A review tells a reader that the researcher knows the research in an area and knows the major issues. A good review increases a reader's confidence in the researcher's professional competence, ability, and background.

2. *To show the path of prior research and how a current project is linked to it.* A review outlines the direction of research on a question and shows the development of knowledge. A good review places a research project in a context and demonstrates its relevance by making connections to a body of knowledge.

3. *To integrate and summarize what is known in an area.* A review pulls together and synthesizes different results. A good review points out areas where prior studies agree, where they disagree, and where major questions remain. It collects what is known up to a point in time and indicates the direction for future research.

4. *To learn from others and stimulate new ideas.* A review tells what others have found so that a researcher can benefit from the efforts of others. A good review identifies blind alleys and suggests hypotheses for replication. It divulges procedures, techniques, and research designs worth copying so that a researcher can better focus hypotheses and gain new insights.

in a college or university library. This section is a simple "road map" on how to access the reports.

Periodicals   Social research results appear in newspapers, in popular magazines, on television or radio broadcasts, and in Internet news summaries. However, these are not full, complete reports of research that you need for a literature review. They are selected, condensed summaries written by journalists for a general audience. They lack essential details needed for a serious evaluation of the study. Textbooks and encyclopedias also present condensed summaries to introduce readers who are just starting to learn about a topic. These also lack essential details about a study required for you to evaluate it fully.

When preparing your first literature review, it is easy to be confused about the many types of periodicals. With skill, you will be able to distinguish among four types:

- Mass-market newspapers and magazines written for the general public
- Popularized social science magazines for the educated public
- Opinion magazines in which intellectuals debate and express views
- Scholarly, academic journals in which researchers present the findings of studies

Peer-reviewed empirical research findings appear in a complete form only in the last type of publication. Mass-market publications (e.g., *McLean's, Time, Newsweek, The Economist, The Nation, American Spectator,* and *Atlantic Monthly*) are sold at newsstands. They are designed to provide the public with news, opinion, and entertainment. A researcher might use them as a source on current events, but they do not include reports of research studies in the form that you need to prepare a literature review. Popularized social science magazines and professional publications (e.g., *Society, Contexts,* and *Psychology Today*) may be peer reviewed. They provide the interested, educated public a simplified version of key findings. They are not an outlet for original research findings. At best, they supplement to other sources in a literature review. Serious opinion magazines (e.g., *American Prospect, Commentary, Dissent,* and *Public Interest*) are carried by larger bookstores in major cities. Leading scholars may write articles for opinion

magazines about topics on which they may also conduct empirical research (e.g., welfare reform, prison expansion, voter turnout). The magazines differ in purpose, look, and scope from scholarly journals with research findings. Opinion magazines are an arena in which intellectuals debate current issues. They are not where social researchers present study findings to the scientific community.

Scholarly Journals. The scholarly journal (e.g., *American Sociological Review, Social Problems, Public Opinion Quarterly, Criminology,* and *Social Science Quarterly*) is the primary type of periodical for a literature review. It is filled with peer-reviewed research reports. You rarely find them outside of college and university libraries. Recall from Chapter 1 that researchers disseminate most findings of new studies in scholarly journals.

Some scholarly journals are specialized. Instead of research reports, they may have only book reviews that provide commentary and evaluations on new books (e.g., *Contemporary Sociology*). Alternatively, they may contain only literature review essays (e.g., *Annual Review of Sociology, Annual Review of Psychology,* and *Annual Review of Anthropology*) in which researchers give a "state of the field" essay for others. Literature review publications can be helpful if an article was recently published on a specific topic of interest. Many scholarly journals have a mix of articles—literature reviews, book reviews, reports on research studies, and theoretical essays.

No simple solution or "seal of approval" distinguishes scholarly journals from other periodicals, or instantly distinguishes the report on a research study from other types of articles. In the beginning, you will want to ask experienced researchers or professional librarians. Distinguishing among types of publications is an important skill to master. An excellent way to learn to distinguish among types of publications is to read many articles in scholarly journals.

The number of scholarly journals varies by field. Psychology has over 400 journals, whereas sociology has about 250. Political science and communication have fewer than sociology, anthropology-archaeology and social work have about 100. Urban studies and women's studies have about 50, and there are about a dozen journals in criminology. Each journal publishes from a few dozen to over 100 articles a year.

You can view many, but not all, scholarly journals via the Internet. A few Internet services provide full, exact copies of scholarly journal articles over the Internet. For example, JSTOR provides exact copies, but only for a small number of scholarly journals and only for past years. Other Internet services, such as EBSCO HOST, Sage Premier, or WILSON WEB, offer a full-text version of recent articles for some scholarly journals. Only a tiny handful of new Internet-only scholarly journals, called *e-journals,* present peer-reviewed research studies (e.g., *Sociological Research Online, Current Research in Social Psychology,* and *Journal of World Systems Research*). Eventually, the Internet format may replace print versions. However, for now, 98 percent of scholarly journals are available in print form and about three-fouths of these are available in a full-text version over the Internet. Access is limited to libraries that have paid for a special online subscription service.

Once you locate a scholarly journal that has research reports, you need to make sure that a particular article presents study results. Scholarly journals often have other types of articles. It is easier to identify quantitative studies because they usually have a methods or data section and charts, statistical formulas, and tables of numbers. Qualitative research articles are more difficult to identify, and many students confuse them with theoretical essays, literature review articles, idea-discussion essays, policy recommendations, book reviews, and legal case analyses. To distinguish among these types requires a good grasp of the varieties of research as well as experience in reading many articles.

Your college library has a section for scholarly journals and magazines, or, in some cases, mixes them with books. Look at a map of library facilities or ask a librarian to find this section. The most recent issues, which look like thin paperbacks or thick magazines, are often physically separate in a "current periodicals" section. Most libraries bind all issues of a volume together then add the volume to the permanent collection.

Libraries place scholarly journals from different fields together with popular magazines. All are periodicals, or *serials* in the jargon of librarians. Thus, you will find popular magazines (e.g., *Time, Road and Track, Cosmopolitan,* and *Atlantic Monthly*) next to journals for astronomy, chemistry, mathematics, literature, and philosophy as well as sociology, psychology, social work, and education. The "pure" academic fields usually have more journals than the "applied" or practical fields such as marketing or social work. You can find a list of journals in the library catalog system.

Scholarly journals are published as rarely as once a year or as frequently as weekly. Most appear four to six times a year. For example, *Sociological Quarterly* appears four times a year. To assist in locating articles, librarians and scholars created a system for tracking scholarly journals and their articles. Each issue of a journal has a date, volume number, and issue number. This information makes it easier to locate an article. Such information—along with details such as author, article title, and page numbers—is an article's **citation.** We use the information in bibliographies. When a journal is first published, it begins with volume 1, number 1, and the first article is on page 1. The journal continues increasing the numbers thereafter. Most journals follow a similar system, but there are enough exceptions that you must pay close attention to citation information. For most journals, one volume is one year. If you see a journal with volume 52, for example, it probably means that the journal has been in existence for 52 years. Most, but not all, journals begin their publishing cycle in January.

Most journals number pages by volume, not by issue. The first issue of a volume usually begins with page 1, and page numbering continues throughout the entire volume. For example, the first page of volume 52, issue 4 may be page 547. Most journals have an index for each volume and a table of contents for each issue. Issues contain as few as one or two articles, or as many as 50. Most have 8–18 articles. Articles may be 5–50 pages long. Articles often have **abstracts**. These are short summaries on the first page of the article, or for a few journals, the abstracts are grouped together at the beginning of the issue.

Many libraries do not retain physical, paper copies of old journals. To save space and costs, they retain only microfilm versions. There are hundreds of scholarly journals in most academic fields, with each costing $50 to $2,500 per year. Only the large research libraries subscribe to all of them. You may have to borrow a journal or photocopy of an article from a distant library through an *interlibrary loan service,* a system by which libraries lend books or materials to other libraries. Few libraries allow people to check out recent issues of scholarly journals. You should plan to use these in the library.

Once you find the periodicals section, wander down the aisles and skim what is on the shelves. You will see volumes containing many research reports. Each title of a scholarly journal has a call number like that of a regular library book. Libraries often arrange them alphabetically by title. Because journals change titles, it may create confusion if the library shelves the journal under its original title.

Citation Formats. An article's citation is the key to locating it. Suppose you want to read the study by Sharp and Joslyn on racial tolerance in U.S. cities discussed in Chapter 1. The citation for the article is: Elaine B. Sharp and Mark R. Joslyn, "Culture, Segregation, and Tolerance in Urban American," *Social Science Quarterly,* 2008, Vol. 89, No. 3, pp. 573–591. This tells you the article is in an issue of *Social Science Quarterly* that was published in 2008. The citation does not provide the month, but it gives the volume number, 89, issue number, 3, and the page numbers, 573–591.

There are many ways to cite the research literature. Formats for citing literature in the text itself vary. An internal citation format that uses an author's last name and date of publication in parentheses is very popular. The full citation appears in a separate bibliography, reference, or works cited section. There are several styles for full citations of journal articles, with books and other types of works each having a separate style. When citing articles, check with an instructor, journal, or other outlet for the desired format. Almost all include the following: names of authors, article title, journal name, and volume and page numbers. Beyond these basic elements, there is great variety. Some formats include the authors' first names. Others use initials only. Some include all the authors, while others give only the first one. Some include information on the issue or month of publication, others do not (see Figure 4.1).

Citation formats can get complex. Two major reference tools on the topic in social science are *Chicago Manual of Style,* which has nearly 80 pages on bibliographies and reference formats, and *American Psychological Association Publication Manual,* which devotes about 60 pages to the topic. In sociology, the *American Sociological Review* style, with two pages of style instructions, is widely followed.

Books. Books communicate information, provoke thought, and entertain. There are many types of books: picture books, textbooks, short story books, popular fiction or nonfiction, religious books, children's books, and others. Our concern here is with books with reports of original research or collections of research articles. Libraries shelve these books as they do with other types of books. You can find citation information on them (e.g., title, author, and publisher) in the library's catalog system.

FIGURE 4.1   Different Reference Citations for a Journal Article

The oldest journal of sociology in the United States, *American Journal of Sociology,* reports on a study of virginity pledges by Peter Bearman and Hannah Bückner. It appeared on pages 859 to 913 of the January 2001 issue (number 4) of the journal, which begins counting issues in March. It was in volume 106, or the journal's 106th year. Here are ways to cite the article. Two very popular styles are those of *American Sociological Review (ASR)* and *American Psychological Association (APA).*

ASR Style

Bearman, Peter and Hannah Bückner. 2001. "Promising the Future: Virginity Pledges and First Intercourse." *American Journal of Sociology* 106:859–912.

APA Style

Bearman, P., and Bückner, H. (2001). Promising the future: Virginity pledges and first intercourse. *American Journal of Sociology 106,* 859–912.

Other Styles

Bearman, P., and H. Bückner. "Promising the Future: Virginity Pledges and First Intercourse," *American Journal of Sociology* 106 (2001), 859–912.

Bearman, Peter and Hannah Bückner, 2001.
   "Promising the future: Virginity pledges and first Intercourse." *Am. J. of Sociol.* 106:859– 912.

Bearman, P. and Bückner, H. (2001). "Promising the Future: Virginity Pledges and First Intercourse." *American Journal of Sociology* 106 (January): 859–912.

Bearman, Peter and Hannah Bückner. 2001.
   "Promising the future: Virginity pledges and first Intercourse." *American Journal of Sociology* 106 (4):859–912.

Bearman, P. and H. Bückner. (2001). "Promising the future: Virginity pledges and first intercourse." *American Journal of Sociology* 106, 859–912.

Peter Bearman and Hannah Bückner, "Promising the Future: Virginity Pledges and First Intercourse," *American Journal of Sociology* 106, no. 4 (2001): 859–912.

It is difficult to distinguish a book that reports on social research from other books. You are most likely to find such books in a college or university library. Some publishers, such as university presses, specialize in publishing them. Nevertheless, there is no simple method for identifying one without reading it.

Some types of social research are more likely to appear in book form than others are. For example, studies by anthropologists and historians are more likely to be book-length reports than are studies by economists or psychologists. Yet, some anthropological and historical studies are articles, and some economic and psychological studies are books. In education, social work, sociology, and political science, the results of long, complex studies may appear both in two or three articles and in book form. Studies that involve detailed clinical or ethnographic descriptions and complex theoretical or philosophical discussions usually appear as books. Finally, an author who wants to communicate both to scholarly peers and to the educated public may write a book bridging a scholarly, academic style and a popular nonfiction style.

Locating original research studies in books is difficult. No single source lists them. Three types of books contain collections of articles or research reports. The first is for teaching purposes. Such books, called *readers,* may include original research reports. Usually, articles on a topic from scholarly journals are gathered and edited to be easier for nonspecialists to read and understand.

The second type is a collection of studies for scholars. It gathers journal articles or may contain original research or theoretical essays on a specific topic. Some collections have journal articles. A third type has original research reports organized around a specialized topic. The table of contents lists the titles and authors. Libraries shelve these collections with other books, and some library catalog systems include them.

Citations or references to books are shorter than article citations. They include the author's name, book title, year and place of publication, and publisher's name.

Dissertations. All graduate students who receive the Ph.D. degree are required to complete original research and report it in a dissertation thesis. Libraries of the university granting the Ph.D. degree shelve the dissertation in the library. About one-half of all dissertation research eventually is published as books or articles. Dissertations can be valuable sources of information. Some students who receive the master's degree also conduct original research and write a master's thesis, but fewer master's theses involve serious research. They are much more difficult to locate than unpublished dissertations. Specialized indexes list dissertations completed by students at accredited universities. For example, *Dissertation Abstracts International* lists dissertations with their authors, titles, and universities. This index is organized by topic and it contains an abstract of each dissertation. You can borrow most dissertations via interlibrary loan from the degree-granting university if the university permits this.

Government Documents. The federal government of the United States, the governments of other nations, state- or provincial-level governments, the United Nations, and other international agencies such as the World Bank sponsor studies and publish research reports. Many college and university libraries have these documents, usually in a special "government documents" section. It is difficult to find such reports in the library catalog system. To locate them, you must use specialized indexes, usually with the help of a librarian. Most college and university libraries hold only some of the government documents and reports.

Policy Reports and Presented Papers. Research institutes, think tanks, and policy centers (e.g., Brookings Institute, Institute for Research on Poverty, Rand Corporation, etc.) sponsor studies and publish research reports. You may examine these sources if you wish to conduct a thorough search of research studies. They are difficult to locate and obtain. A few major libraries purchase these and shelve them with books. It may be necessary to write directly to the institute or center and request a list of reports.

Each year, the professional associations in academic fields (e.g., sociology, political science, psychology) hold annual meetings. Thousands of researchers assemble to give, listen to, or discuss oral reports of recent studies. These oral reports are often available as written papers to those who attend the meeting. People who do not attend the meetings can see a listing of papers presented with its title, author, and author's place of employment. The papers may be listed in indexes or abstract services (to be discussed). You can write directly to the author and request a copy of the paper. Perhaps one-half of the papers will be published later as articles in scholarly journals.

How to Conduct a Systematic Literature Review

Define and Refine a Topic.   It is best to begin your literature review with a defined, focused review topic and a search plan. A good literature review topic should be almost as focused as a study research question. For example, "divorce" or "crime" is much too broad. More appropriate review topics are "the stability of families with stepchildren" or "economic inequality and crime rates across nations." For a context review for a study, the review topic should be a little broader than your specific study research question. You may not finalize on a specific research question until you have reviewed the literature. A literature review can bring focus and help you to narrow on a specific research question.

Design a Search.   After choosing a review topic, you can develop a search strategy. You will want to determine the type of review, its extensiveness, and the types of materials to include. As you plan, try to set the parameters of your search: How much time you can devote to the search, how far back in time you will look, how many research reports you can examine, how many libraries you will visit, and so forth.

It is important to be very systematic and well organized. You will need to decide how to record the bibliographic citation for each reference you find and how to record notes (e.g., in a notebook, on 3 × 5 cards, in a computer file). Many skilled researchers develop a schedule because several visits to a library or online service are necessary. In addition to a file for notes on located files, you may want to create a file folder or start a computer file in which you can place possible sources and ideas for new sources.

Locate Research Reports.   Locating research reports depends on the type of report or "outlet" of research being searched. You should use multiple search strategies to counteract the limitations of a single method.

Articles in Scholarly Journals.   As discussed earlier, social researchers publish results of most studies in scholarly journals, so they should be your main source. There are dozens of journals, most going back decades, and each has many articles. The task of searching for scholarly journal articles can be formidable. Luckily, specialized publications and online services make the task manageable.

You may have used an index for general publications, such as *Reader's Guide to Periodical Literature.* Many academic fields have "abstracts" or "indexes" for scholarly literature (e.g., *Psychological Abstracts, Social Sciences Index, Sociological Abstracts,* and *Gerontological Abstracts*). For education-related topics, the Educational Resources Information Center (ERIC) system is especially valuable. There are over 100 such publications. You can usually find them in the reference section of a library. Many abstracts or index services as well as ERIC are available via computer access, which speeds the search process.

Abstracts or indexes appear on a regular basis (monthly, six times a year, etc.). You can look up articles by author name or subject in them. The journals covered by the abstract or index are listed in it, often in the front. An index, such as the *Social Sciences Index,* lists only the citation, whereas an abstract, such as *Sociological Abstracts,* lists the citation and has a copy of the article's abstract. Abstracts do not give you all the findings and details of a research project. Researchers use abstracts to screen articles for relevance, and then locate the more relevant articles. Abstracts may also include papers presented at professional meetings.

An online literature search works on the same principle as using an abstract or an index. You can search by author, by article title, by subject, or by keyword. A *keyword* is an important term for a topic. It is likely to be part of a title. You will want to use six to eight keywords in most searches and consider several synonyms. The online search method can vary and most only look for a keyword in a title or abstract. If you choose too few words or very narrow terms, you will miss many relevant articles. If you choose too many words or very broad terms, you will get a huge number of irrelevant articles. The best way to learn the appropriate breadth and number of keywords is by trial and error.

It may sound as if all you have to do is to go find the index in the reference section of the library or on the Internet and look up a topic. Unfortunately, things are more complicated than that. To cover the studies across many years, you may have to look through many issues of the abstracts or indexes. Also, subject categories in indexes or online are broad. An issue of interest to you may fit into multiple subject areas. You have to check each one. For example, for the topic of illegal drug use in high schools, the following subject categories might contain relevant studies: drug addiction, drug abuse, substance abuse, drug laws, illegal drugs, high schools, adolescent deviance, delinquency, and secondary schools. Many of the articles located will not be relevant for your literature review. In addition, there is a 3- to 12-month time lag between the publication of an article and its appearance in the abstracts or indexes. Unless you are at a major research library, the most useful article may not be available in your library or through an online service. You may have to use an interlibrary loan service.

Several years ago, I conducted a study on how college students define *sexual harassment* (Neuman, 1992); in my literature search I used the following keywords: *sexual harassment, sexual assault, harassment, gender equity, gender fairness,* and *sex discrimination.* I later discovered a few important studies that lacked any of these keywords in their titles. I also tried the keywords *college student* and *rape*, but got huge numbers of unrelated articles that I could not even skim.

There are several online search services. All the computerized searching methods share a similar logic, but each has its own specific method of operation to learn. In my study, I looked for sources published in the previous seven years and used five online databases of scholarly literature: *Social Science Index, CARL (Colorado Area Research Library), Sociofile, Social Science Citation Index,* and *PsychLit.*

The same articles will appear in multiple scholarly literature databases, but each online database may identify a few new articles not present in the others. In addition, you will want to examine the bibliographies of the articles you locate. I discovered several excellent sources not listed in any of the online databases by studying the bibliographies of the relevant articles I had uncovered.

Based on a keyword or subject category search, you will want to skim article titles or abstracts. In my study, I quickly skimmed or scanned the titles or abstracts of over 200 articles. From these, I selected about 80 to read. I found about 49 of the 80 sources valuable, and they are in the bibliography of the published article.

Scholarly Books. Finding scholarly books on a specific topic can be difficult. The subject categories of library catalog systems are usually incomplete and too broad to be useful. Moreover, they list only the books in a particular library system, although you may be able to search other libraries for interlibrary loan books. Libraries organize books by call numbers based on subject matter. Again, the subject matter classifications may not reflect the subjects of interest to you or all the subjects discussed in a book. Once you learn the system for your library, you will find that most books on a topic will share the main parts of the call number. In addition, librarians can help you locate books from other libraries. For example, the *Library of Congress National Union Catalog* lists all books in the U.S. Library of Congress. Librarians have access to sources at other libraries, or you can use the Internet. There is no surefire way to locate relevant books. Use multiple search methods, including a look at journals that have book reviews and the bibliographies of articles.

Taking Notes

As you gather the relevant research literature, it is easy to feel overwhelmed by the quantity of information you find. The old-fashioned approach is to write notes onto index cards. You then shift and sort the note cards, place them in piles, and so forth as you look for connections among them or develop an outline for a report or paper. This method still works. Today, however, most people use word-processing software and gather photocopies or printed versions of many articles.

As you proceed, you may wish to create two kinds of files for your note cards or computer documents: a *Source File* and a *Content File*. Record *all* the bibliographic information for each source in the Source File, even though you may not use some and later erase them. Include the complete bibliographic citation, such as a page number or the name of a second author, or you will regret it later. It is far easier to erase a source you do not use than to try to locate bibliographic information later because you forgot one detail.

I recommend dividing the Source File into two parts: *Have File* and *Potential File*. The "Have File" is for sources that you have found and on which you have content notes. The "Potential File" is for leads and possible new sources that you have yet to track down or read. You can add to the Potential File anytime you come across a new source. Toward the end of writing a literature review, the Potential File will disappear and the Have File will become your bibliography.

Your note cards or computer documents go into the Content File. This file contains substantive information of interest from a source. These include major findings, details of methodology, definitions of concepts, or interesting quotes. If you directly quote from a source or take some specific information from a source, record the specific page number(s) on which the quote appears. Link the files by putting key source information, such as author and date, on each content file.

What to Record.   You will find it much easier to take all notes on the same type and size of paper or card, rather than having some notes on sheets of papers, others on cards, and so on. You must decide exactly what to record about an article, book, or other source. It is better to err in the direction of recording too much rather than too little. In general, record the hypotheses tested, how major concepts were measured, the main findings, the basic design of the research, the group or sample used, and ideas for future study (see Expansion Box 4.2). It is wise to examine the report's bibliography for sources that you might add to your search.

4.2   EXPANSION BOX
How to Read Journal Articles

1. Read with a clear purpose or goal in mind. Are you reading for basic knowledge or to apply it to a specific question?

2. Skim the article before reading it all. What can you learn from the title, abstract, summary and conclusions, and headings? What are the topic, major findings, method, and main conclusion?

3. Consider your own orientation. What is your bias toward the topic, the method, the publication source, and so on, that may color your reading?

4. Marshal external knowledge. What do you already know about the topic and the methods used? How credible is the publication source?

5. Evaluate as you read the article. What errors are present? Do findings follow the data? Is the article consistent with assumptions of the approach it takes?

6. Summarize information as an abstract with the topic, the methods used, and the findings. Assess the factual accuracy of findings and cite questions about the article.

Source: Based on Katzer, Cook, and Crouch (1991: 199–207)

Photocopying all relevant articles saves time recording notes. It also ensures that you will have an entire report and you can make notes on the photocopy. However, this practice has shortcomings. First, photocopying can be expensive for a large literature search. Second, be aware of and obey copyright laws. U.S. copyright laws permit photocopying for personal research use. Third, remember to record or photocopy the entire article, including all citation information. Fourth, organizing entire articles can be cumbersome, especially if you use several different parts of a single article. Finally, unless you highlight carefully or take good notes, you may not save time by photocopying and will have to reread the entire article later.

Organize Notes. After gathering a large number of references and notes, you need an organizing scheme. One approach is to group studies or specific findings by skimming notes and creating a mental map of how they fit together. You may wish to try several organizing schemes before settling on a final one. Organizing is a skill that improves with practice. You might place notes into piles representing common themes, or draw charts comparing what different reports say about an issue, noting agreements and disagreements.

In the process of organizing notes, you will find that some references and notes do not fit. You should discard them as irrelevant. Also, you may discover gaps or semi-relevant areas that you need to explore in more depth. This often necessitates return visits to the library.

There are many organizing schemes. The best one depends on the purpose of the review. Most researchers organize a review around a specific research question or the major, common findings of a field.

Writing the Review

A literature review requires planning and good, clear writing, which requires a lot of rewriting. Many people merge this step with organizing notes. All the rules of good writing (e.g., clear organizational structure, an introduction and conclusion, transitions between sections, etc.) apply to writing a literature review. Keep your purposes in mind when you write, and communicate clearly and effectively.

To prepare a good review, read articles and other literature critically. Recall that skepticism is a norm of science. It means that you should not accept what is written simply on the authority of its having been published. Question and evaluate what you read. The first hurdle to overcome is thinking something must be perfect just because it appears in a scholarly journal.

To critically read research reports, you need a set of skills that take time and practice to develop. Despite a peer-review procedure and high rejection rates, errors and sloppy logic slip in. Read carefully to see whether the introduction and title really fit with the rest of the article. Sometimes, titles, abstracts, and the introduction are misleading. They might not fully explain the research project's method and results. An article should be logically tight, and all the parts should fit together. Strong logical links should exist between parts of the argument. Weak articles make leaps in logic or omit transitional steps. Likewise, articles do not always make their theory or approach to research explicit. Be prepared to read the article more than once. (See Figure 4.2 on taking notes on an article.)

What a Good Review Looks Like

The author of a good review communicates the review's purpose by its organization. The *wrong* way to write a review is to list a series of research reports with a summary of the findings of each. This fails to communicate a sense of purpose. It reads as a set of notes strung together. Perhaps the reviewer got sloppy and skipped over the important organizing

FIGURE 4.2   Example of Notes on an Article

FULL CITATION ON BIBLIOGRAPHY (SOURCE FILE)

Goffman, Alice. 2009. "On the Run: Wanted Men in a Philadelphia Ghetto." *American Sociological Review* Vol. 74, No. 3, 339–357.

NOTE CARD (CONTENT FILE)

Goffman, 2009   **Topics:**   mass imprisonment, urban Black neighborhoods, surveillance, young Black males, policing, ethnography, theories of Foucault

With the world's highest rate of incarceration, many studies suggest the United States since the 1970s entered in an era of mass imprisonment. Imprisonment greatly affects African American males. A majority (60 percent of Black males) under age 30 who lack a high school degree have been to prison, it is 30 percent for those who have a high school degree. At the same time, the concentration of police officers has greatly increased. This ethnographic field research study in a low-income Black neighborhood of Philadelphia looks at how young Black men who have had some run-in with the law (an arrest, imprisonment, on parole) have their daily lives restricted.

Theory, Research Question, Hypothesis

The research question is on the everyday activities of low-income Black males. The author sees whether theories of Michel Foucault help explain the situation. Foucault argued that power and control in modern society is less based on direct fear of punishment than constant surveillance, and on a need to internalize control or self-discipline. The author explored whether this is the best explanation of daily life for poor Black men with criminal records.

Method

The author spent years becoming intimately acquainted with a specific poor Black neighborhood in Philadelphia. Although she was White and well educated, she befriended many residents and was treated as a sister within one local family. She conducted intensive observation of one area of the neighborhood between 2002 and 2003, closely following the lives of several young Black men. She also conducted interviews with local police officers, probations officers, and a judge, and followed up in the neighborhood for four years after the intensive observation.

Findings

The author found that surveillance was incomplete and partial. She suggests that Foucault's theory is incomplete and does not explain the young men's life in the ghetto. It was very easy for the young men to commit minor parole or other infractions that made them subject to arrest. A constant threat of arrest and re-imprisonment greatly influenced their lives and created a climate of fear. The young men learned stable, routine activities such as going to work, going to a hospital, or maintaining relations with friends and family increased their risk of being caught and arrested. The author provides a theoretical analogy to describe the exercise of state power over the men. She says the young men are more like semi-legal people who qualify for a sanction and must constantly try to avoid it. The analogy is being an undocumented immigrant or runaway slave, someone who can easily be caught and face punishment at any time.

step in writing the review. The *right* way to write a review is to organize common findings or arguments together. A well-accepted approach is to address the most important ideas first, to logically link statements or findings, and to note discrepancies or weaknesses in the research (see Example Box 4.1 for an example).

4.1 EXAMPLE BOX
Examples of Bad and Good Reviews

Example of Bad Review

Sexual harassment has many consequences. Adams, Kottke, and Padgitt (1983) found that some women students said they avoided taking a class or working with certain professors because of the risk of harassment. They also found that men and women students reacted differently. Their research was a survey of 1,000 men and women graduate and undergraduate students. Benson and Thomson's study in *Social Problems* (1982) lists many problems created by sexual harassment. In their excellent book, *The Lecherous Professor,* Dziech and Weiner (1990) give a long list of difficulties that victims have suffered.

Researchers study the topic in different ways. Hunter and McClelland (1991) conducted a study of undergraduates at a small liberal arts college. They had a sample of 300 students and students were given multiple vignettes that varied by the reaction of the victim and the situation. Jaschik and Fretz (1991) showed 90 women students at a mideastern university a videotape with a classic example of sexual harassment by a teaching assistant. Before it was labeled as *sexual harassment,* few women called it that. When asked whether it was sexual harassment, 98 percent agreed. Weber-Burdin and Rossi (1982) replicated a previous study on sexual harassment, only they used students at the University of Massachusetts. They had 59 students rate 40 hypothetical situations. Reilley, Carpenter, Dull, and Bartlett (1982) conducted a study of 250 female and 150 male undergraduates at the University of California at Santa Barbara. They also had a sample of 52 faculty. Both samples completed a questionnaire in which respondents were presented vignettes of sexual-harassing situations that they were to rate. Popovich and Colleagues (1986) created a nine-item scale of sexual harassment. They studied 209 undergraduates at a medium-sized university in groups of 15 to 25. They found disagreement and confusion among students.

Example of Better Review

The victims of sexual harassment suffer a range of consequences, from lowered self-esteem and loss of self-confidence to withdrawal from social interaction, changed career goals, and depression (Adams, Kottke, and Padgitt, 1983; Benson and Thomson, 1982; Dziech and Weiner, 1990). For example, Adams, Kottke, and Padgitt (1983) noted that 13 percent of women students said they avoided taking a class or working with certain professors because of the risk of harassment.

Research into campus sexual harassment has taken several approaches. In addition to survey research, many have experimented with vignettes or presented hypothetical scenarios (Hunter and McClelland, 1991; Jaschik and Fretz, 1991; Popovich et al., 1987; Reilley, Carpenter, Dull, and Barlett, 1982; Rossi and Anderson, 1982; Valentine-French and Radtke, 1989; Weber-Burdin and Rossi, 1982). Victim verbal responses and situational factors appear to affect whether observers label a behavior as harassment. There is confusion over the application of a sexual harassment label for inappropriate behavior. For example, Jaschik and Fretz (1991) found that only 3 percent of the women students shown a videotape with a classic example of sexual harassment by a teaching assistant initially labeled it as *sexual harassment.* Instead, they called it "sexist," "rude," "unprofessional," or "demeaning." When asked whether it was sexual harassment, 98 percent agreed. Roscoe and colleagues (1987) reported similar labeling difficulties.

USING THE INTERNET FOR SOCIAL RESEARCH

The Internet (see Expansion Box 4.3) has revolutionized how social researchers work. Just over decade ago, it was rarely used; today, most social researchers use the Internet regularly to help them review the literature, to communicate with other researchers, and to search for other information sources. The Internet continues to expand and change at an explosive rate.

4.3 EXPANSION BOX
The Internet

The Internet is not a single thing in one place. Rather, the Internet is a system or interconnected web of computers around the world. It is changing very rapidly. I cannot describe everything on the Internet; many large books attempt to do that. Plus, even if I tried, it would be out of date in six months. The Internet is changing, in a powerful way, how many people communicate and share information.

The Internet provides low-cost (often free), worldwide, fast communication among people with computers or between people with computers and information in the computers of organizations (e.g., universities, government agencies, businesses). There are special hardware and software requirements, but the Internet potentially can transmit electronic versions of text material, up to entire books, as well as photos, music, video, and other information.

To get onto the Internet, a person needs an account in a computer that is connected to the Internet. Most college mainframe computers are connected, many business or government computers are connected, and individuals with modems can purchase a connection from an Internet service provider that provides access over telephone lines, special DSL lines, or cable television lines. In addition to a microcomputer, the person needs only a little knowledge about using computers.

The Internet has been a mixed blessing for social research, but it has not proved to be the panacea that some people first thought it might be. It provides new and important ways to find information, but it remains one tool among others. It can quickly make some specific pieces of information accessible. The Internet is best thought of as a supplement rather than as a replacement for traditional library research. There are "up" and "down" sides to using the Internet for social research.

The Up Side

1. The Internet is easy, fast, and cheap. It is widely accessible and can be used from many locations. This near-free resource allows people to find source material from almost anywhere— local public libraries, homes, labs or classrooms, or anywhere a computer is connected to the Internet system. In addition, the Internet does not close; it operates 24 hours a day, seven days a week. With minimal training, most people can quickly perform searches and get information on their computer screens that would have required them to take a major trip to large research libraries a few years ago. Searching a vast quantity of information electronically has always been easier and faster than a manual search, and the Internet greatly expands the amount and variety of source material. More and more information (e.g., *Statistical Abstract of the United States*) is available on the Internet. In addition, once the information is located, a researcher can often store it electronically or print it at a local site.

2. The Internet has "links" that provide additional ways to find and connect to many other sources of information. Many websites, home pages, and other Internet resource pages have "hot links" that can call up information from related sites or sources simply by clicking on the link indicator (usually a button or a highlighted word or phrase). This provides "instant" access to cross-referenced material. Links make

embedding one source within a network of related sources easy.

3. The Internet speeds the flow of information around the globe and has a "democratizing" effect. It provides rapid transmission of information (e.g., text, news, data, video, and photos) across long distances and international borders. Instead of waiting a week for a report or having to send off for a foreign publication and wait for a month, the information is often available in seconds at no cost. There are virtually no limits on who can put material on the Internet, or on what appears on it. People who had difficulty publishing or disseminating their materials can now do so with ease.

4. The Internet provides a very wide range of information sources, some in formats that are more dynamic and interesting. Webpages can be more interesting than straight black and white text, as found in traditional academic journals. The Web transmits information in the form of bright colors, graphics, "action" images, audio (e.g., music, voices, and sounds), photos, and video clips. Authors and other creators of information can be creative in their presentations.

The Down Side

1. There is no quality control over what gets on the Internet. Unlike standard academic publications, there is no peer-review process, or any review for that matter. Anyone can put almost anything on a website. It may be poor quality, undocumented, highly biased, totally made up, or plain fraudulent. There is a lot of real "trash" out there! Once you find material, the real work is to distinguish the "trash" from valid information. You should treat a webpage with caution; it could contain the drivel of a "nut" or be valuable information. A less serious problem is that the "glitz" of bright colors, music, or moving images found in sites can distract an unsophisticated user. The "glitz" may attract you more

than serious content. Do not confuse glitz for high-caliber information. The Internet is better for short attention spans rather than the slow, deliberative, careful reading and study of content.

2. Many excellent sources and some of the most important resource materials (research studies and data) for social research are *not* available on the Internet (e.g., *Sociofile*, GSS datafiles, and recent journal articles). Much information is available only through special subscription services that can be expensive. Contrary to popular belief, the Internet has *not* made all information free and accessible. Often, what is free is limited, and fuller information is available only to those who pay. In fact, because some libraries redirected funds to buy computers for the Internet and cut the purchases for books and paper copies of documents, the Internet's overall impact may have actually reduced what is available for some users.

3. Finding sources on the Internet can be very difficult and time consuming. It is not easy to locate specific source materials. Also, different "search engines" can produce very different results. It is wise to use multiple search engines (e.g., Yahoo, Bing, and Google), since they work differently. Most search engines simply look for specific words in a short description of the webpage. This description may not reveal the full content of the source, just as a title does not fully tell what a book or article is about. In addition, search engines often come up with tens of thousands of sources, far too many for anyone to examine. The ones at the "top" may be there because they were recently added to the Internet or because their short description had several versions of the search word. The "best" or most relevant source might be buried as the 150th item found in a search. Also, one must often wade through a lot of advertisements to locate "real" information. There

are political, economic, and social biases in search engine results. For example, companies advertise with a search engine to become more popular.

4. Internet sources can be "unstable" and difficult to document. After one conducts a search on the Internet and locates webpages with information, it is important to note the specific "address" (usually it starts http://) where it resides. This address refers to an electronic file sitting in a computer somewhere. If the computer file moves, it may not be at the same address two months later. Unlike a journal article that will be stored on a shelf or on microfiche in hundreds of libraries for many decades to come and available for anyone to read, webpages can quickly vanish. This means it may be impossible to check someone's Web references, verify a quote in a document, or go back to original materials and read them for ideas. In addition, it is easy to copy, modify, or distort, then reproduce copies of a source. For example, a person could alter a text passage or a photo image then create a new webpage to disseminate the false information. This raises issues about copyright protection and the authenticity of source material.

The best sites on the Internet—ones that have useful and truthful information—tend to originate at universities, research institutes, or government agencies. They usually are more trustworthy for research purposes than ones that are individual home pages of unspecified origin or location, or that a commercial organization or a political/social issue advocacy group sponsors. In addition to moving or disappearing, many webpages or sources do not provide complete information to make citation easy. Better sources provide fuller or more complete information about the author, date, location, and so on.

As you prepare a review of the scholarly literature and more narrowly focus a topic, you should also think about how to design a study. The specifics of design can vary somewhat depending on whether your study will primarily employ a quantitative–deductive–positivist approach or a qualitative–inductive–interpretive/critical approach. The two approaches have a great deal in common and they mutually complement one another, but there are several places where "branches in the path" of designing a study diverge depending on the approach you adopt.

QUALITATIVE AND QUANTITATIVE RESEARCH ORIENTATIONS

Qualitative and quantitative research studies differ but they also complement each other. In both approaches to social research you systematically collect and analyze empirical data. In both approaches you carefully examine patterns in data to understand and explain social life. The nature of the data may differ. *Soft data,* in the form of impressions, words, sentences, photos, symbols, and so forth common in qualitative studies, dictate different research strategies and data collection techniques than *hard data,* in the form of numbers used in quantitative studies. Each approach to research rests on different assumptions about social life and may have different objectives. Such differences can make the use of certain research tools inappropriate or irrelevant. If you try to judge qualitative research by the standards of quantitative research, you may be very disappointed, and vice versa. It is best to appreciate the strengths each approach offers.

To appreciate the strengths of the two approaches, it is best to understand the distinct orientations of each. Qualitative researchers tend to rely on interpretive or critical social science, follow a nonlinear research path, and speak a language of "cases and contexts." They emphasize conducting detailed examinations of cases that arise in the natural flow of social life. They usually try to present authentic interpretations that are sensitive to specific social–historical contexts. Most quantitative researchers rely on a positivist approach to social science. They follow a linear research path, speak a language of "variables and hypotheses," and emphasize precisely measuring variables and testing hypotheses that are linked to general causal explanations.

A researcher who uses one approach alone may not always communicate well with those using the other, but the languages and orientations of each are mutually intelligible. It takes time and effort to understand both approaches and to see how they can be complementary.

Linear and Nonlinear Paths

You "follow a path" when you conduct a study. The path is a metaphor for the sequence of things to do: what you do first, what comes next, and where you are going. The path may be well worn and marked with clear signposts where many other researchers have trod. Alternatively, it may be a new path into unknown territory where few others have gone, lacking signs to mark the direction forward.

In general, in a quantitative study you will follow a linear path more than if you are doing qualitative research. A *linear research path* follows a fixed sequence of steps; it is like a staircase leading in one clear direction. It is a way of thinking and a way of looking at issues—the direct, narrow, straight path that is most common in western European and North American culture.

The path in a qualitative research study is more nonlinear and cyclical. Rather than moving in a straight line, a *nonlinear research path* makes successive passes through steps. It may move backward and sideways before moving on. It is more of a spiral, moving slowly upward but not directly. With each cycle or repetition, you collect new data and gain new insights.

People familiar with the direct, linear approach tend to become impatient with a less direct cyclical path. From a strict linear perspective, a diffuse cyclical path appears inefficient and sloppy. However, it can be highly effective for incorporating the whole of a complex situation and grasping subtle shades of meaning. Nonlinear pathways pull together divergent information and permit switching perspectives. It is never an excuse for doing poor-quality research. With its own kind of discipline and rigor, a nonlinear pathway borrows devices from the humanities (e.g., metaphor, analogy, theme, motif, and irony). It is oriented toward constructing meaning. A cyclical path is well suited for tasks such as translating languages, where delicate shades of meaning, subtle connotations, or contextual distinctions are critical.

Preplanned and Emergent Research Questions

Your first step when beginning the path to complete a research project is to select a topic. There is no formula for this task. Whether you are an experienced researcher or just beginning, the best guide is to conduct research on something that interests you.

All research begins with a topic but a topic is only a starting point. You must narrow it into a focused research question. Firebaugh (2008) argues a first rule of social research is that you must be ready to be surprised by the findings of a study. By this he means that intrinsic to the research enterprise is uncertainty of study outcome. In other words, whatever you may think at the start of a study, it could differ after you do the study and examine its empirical evidence. He provides a guide for selecting a research question. First, he says the question must be "researchable," and second it must be interesting. A researchable question is not too specific (Why has my brother Bob been unemployed for the past 12 months?) nor too general (Why is there crime?).

Depending on whether your study is qualitative and quantitative research, you will turn a topic to a focused research question for a specific study in different ways. In a qualitative research study, you will likely begin with semi-focused, broad research questions. You will probably combine focusing on a specific question with the process of deciding the details of study design. This occurs as you begin to gather data. The qualitative research approach is very flexible. It encourages slowly focusing the topic throughout a study. A limited amount of topic narrowing occurs in an early research planning stage. Narrowing or a redirection in the focus occurs after you have begun to collect and consider the data.

By contrast, in a quantitative research study you will narrow a topic into a focused question as a discrete planning step before finalizing the study design. Focusing the question is a step in the process of developing a testable hypothesis (to be discussed later) and the question will guide the design of a study before you collect any data.

Although focusing occurs later in the process, in many ways the qualitative research approach is more difficult because you begin data gathering with only a general topic and notions of what will be relevant. Focusing and refining continue with data collection and preliminary data analysis. You must adjust and sharpen the research question(s) during the study because you rarely know the most important issues or questions until you are immersed in the data. This requires you to focus as you actively reflect on and develop preliminary data interpretations. You must remain open to unanticipated data and constantly reevaluate the focus early in a study. You have to be prepared to change the direction of research and follow new lines of evidence.

Typical research questions for qualitative research include the following: How did a certain condition or social situation originate? How is the condition/situation maintained over time?

What are the processes by which a condition/situation changes, develops, or operates? A different type of question tries to confirm existing beliefs or assumptions. A last type of question tries to discover new ideas.

Before designing a quantitative research study, you focus on a specific research problem within a broad topic. For example, your personal experience might suggest labor unions as a topic. "Labor unions" is a topic, not a research question or a problem. In any large library, you will find hundreds of books and thousands of articles written by sociologists, historians, economists, management officials, political scientists, and others on unions. The books and articles focus on different aspects of the topic and adopt many perspectives on it. Before proceeding to design a research project, you must narrow and focus the topic. An example research question is, "How much did U.S. labor unions contribute to racial inequality by creating barriers to skilled jobs for African Americans in the post–World War II period?" When starting research on a topic, ask yourself questions such as, What is it about the topic that is of greatest interest? For a topic about which you know little, first get background knowledge by reading about it. Research questions refer to the relationships among a small number of variables. Identify a limited number of variables and specify the relationships among them.

A research question has one or a small number of causal relationships. Expansion Box 4.4 lists some ways to focus a topic into a research question. For example, the question, "What causes divorce?" is not a good research question. A better research question is, "Is age at marriage associated with divorce?" The second question suggests two specific variables: age at time of marriage and whether or not a marriage ended in divorce.

Another technique for focusing a research question is to specify the **universe**. The *universe* is the set of all units that the research covers,

EXPANSION BOX

4.4 Techniques for Narrowing a Topic into a Research Question

1. *Examine the literature.* Published articles are an excellent source of ideas for research questions. They are usually at an appropriate level of specificity and suggest research questions that focus on the following:

   a. Replicate a previous research project exactly or with slight variations.

   b. Explore unexpected findings discovered in previous research.

   c. Follow suggestions an author gives for future research at the end of an article.

   d. Extend an existing explanation or theory to a new topic or setting.

   e. Challenge findings or attempt to refute a relationship.

   f. Specify the intervening process and consider linking relations.

2. *Talk over ideas with others.*

   a. Ask people who are knowledgeable about the topic for questions about it that they have thought of.

   b. Seek out those who hold opinions that differ from yours on the topic and discuss possible research questions with them.

3. *Apply to a specific context.*

   a. Focus the topic onto a specific historical period or time period.

   b. Narrow the topic to a specific society or geographic unit.

   c. Consider which subgroups or categories of people/units are involved and whether there are differences among them.

4. *Define the aim or desired outcome of the study.*

   a. Will the research question be for an exploratory, explanatory, or descriptive study?

   b. Will the study involve applied or basic research?

or to which you can generalize findings. All research questions, hypotheses, and studies apply to some group or category of people, organizations, or other units. For example, your research question is about the effects of a new attendance policy on learning by high school students. The universe, in this case, is all high school students.

As you refine a topic into a research question and design a research project, you also need to consider practical limitations. Designing a perfect research project is an interesting academic exercise, but if you expect to carry out a research project, practical limitations will have an impact on its design.

Major limitations include time, costs, access to resources, approval by authorities, ethical concerns, and expertise. If you have 10 hours a week for five weeks to conduct a research project, but a study to address a research question will take five years, you must reformulate the research question more narrowly. Estimating the amount of time required is difficult. The research question, research techniques used, and the kind of data collected are relevant. Experienced researchers are the best source of good estimates.

Cost is another limitation. As with time, there are inventive ways to answer a question within limitations, but some questions are impossible to answer because of the expense involved. For example, addressing a research question about the attitudes of all sports fans toward their team mascot might require a great investment of time and money. Narrowing the research question to how students at two different colleges feel about their mascots might make it more manageable.

Access to resources is a common limitation. Resources can include the expertise of others, special equipment, or information. For example, a research question about burglary rates and family income in many different nations is almost impossible to answer. Information on burglary and income is not collected or available for most countries. Other research questions require the approval of authorities (e.g., to see medical records) or involve violating basic ethical principles (e.g., causing serious physical harm to a person to see the person's reaction). The expertise or background of the researcher is also a limitation. Answering some research questions involves the use of data collection techniques, statistical methods, knowledge of a foreign language, or special skills you may not have. Unless you can acquire the necessary training or can pay for another person's services, pursuing the research question may not be practical.

In summary, qualitative and quantitative research share a great deal but each has distinct design issues, such as taking a linear or nonlinear research path (see Table 4.1). Each approach to research has its own "language" and design issues. We consider the language and design issues of each approach next.

QUALITATIVE DESIGN ISSUES

The Language of Cases and Contexts

In qualitative research we tend to use a language of cases and contexts and examine social processes and cases in their social context. In a qualitative study, we focus on interpretations (i.e., how people create social understandings and meaning in specific settings). We try to see social life from multiple points of view and to explain how people construct identities. To do this, we rarely use variables or test hypotheses, or try to convert social life into numbers.

In qualitative approaches to social research, we see social life as being intrinsically qualitative. Qualitative data is not as imprecise or deficient; the data are highly meaningful. Instead of converting social life into variables or numbers, we borrow ideas from the people we study and place them within the context of a natural setting. We examine motifs, themes,

TABLE 4.1   Quantitative Research versus Qualitative Research

Quantitative Research	Qualitative Research
Test hypothesis that the researcher begins with.	Capture and discover meaning once the researcher becomes immersed in the data.
Concepts are in the form of distinct variables.	Concepts are in the form of themes, motifs, generalizations, and taxonomies.
Measures are systematically created before data collection and are standardized.	Measures are created in an ad hoc manner and are often specific to the individual setting or researcher.
Data are in the form of numbers from precise measurement.	Data are in the form of words and images from documents, observations, and transcripts.
Theory is largely causal and is often deductive.	Theory can be causal or noncausal and is often inductive.
Procedures are standard, and replication is assumed.	Research procedures are particular, and replication is very rare.
Analysis proceeds by using statistics, tables, or charts and discussing how what they show relates to hypotheses.	Analysis proceeds by extracting themes or generalizations from evidence and organizing data to present a coherent, consistent picture.

distinctions, and ideas instead of variables, and we adopt the inductive approach of *grounded theory*.

Some people who do not understand qualitative studies think that qualitative data are intangible and immaterial; the data are so fuzzy and elusive that nothing can be learned from them. This is not necessarily the case. Qualitative data are empirical. Qualitative data document real events. They are recordings of what people say (with words, gestures, and tone), observations of specific behaviors, studies of written documents, or examinations of visual images. These are all concrete aspects of the world. For example, a qualitative researcher might take and closely scrutinize photos or videotapes of people or social events. This empirical evidence is just as "hard" and physical as that used by quantitative researchers to measure attitudes, social pressure, intelligence, and the like.

Grounded Theory

We frequently develop theory during the data collection process of a qualitative study. This more inductive method builds theory from data or grounds theory in data. Moreover, conceptualization and operationalization (discussed in the next chapter) occur simultaneously with data collection and preliminary data analysis. It makes qualitative research flexible and lets data and theory interact. In qualitative research you want to remain open to the unexpected, change the direction or focus of a research project as needed, and may abandon an original research question in the middle of a project.

In qualitative research a common way to build theory is to make comparisons. For example, you observe an event (e.g., a police officer confronting a speeding motorist). You will immediately ponder questions and look for similarities and differences. You may ask, Does the police officer always radio in the car's license number before proceeding? After radioing the car's location, does the officer ask the motorist

to get out of the car sometimes, but in others casually walk up to the car and talk to the seated driver? When data collection and theorizing are interspersed, theoretical questions suggest future observations, so new data are tailored to answer theoretical questions that arise from thinking about previous data.

The Context Is Critical

We emphasize the social context for understanding thoughts and actions in qualitative studies. This is because the meaning of a social action or statement depends, in an important way, on the context in which it appears. Remove an event, social action, answer to a question, or conversation from the social context, or ignore the context, and you can seriously distort social meaning and significance.

Giving attention to context means that you will carefully note what came earlier and what surrounds the focus of study. The same events or behaviors might have different meanings in different cultures or historical eras. For example, instead of ignoring the context and counting votes across time or cultures, you are likely to ask, What does voting mean in the context? Who votes and who does not? What candidates or issues are or are not salient? How does the voting process occur? You may treat the same behavior (e.g., casting a vote for a presidential candidate) differently depending on the social context in which it occurs. You try to place parts of social life into a larger whole. Otherwise, the meaning of the part may be lost. For example, it is hard to understand what a baseball glove is without knowing something about the game of baseball. The whole of the game—innings, bats, curve balls, hits—gives meaning to each part, and each part without the whole has little meaning.

The Case and Process

In quantitative research, cases are usually the same as a unit of analysis, or the unit on which variables are measured (discussed later). In quantitative studies, we typically measure variables of hypotheses across many cases. For example, in a quantitative survey of 450 individuals, each individual is a case or unit on which you would measure variables. In qualitative studies, we tend to use a "case-oriented approach [that] places cases, not variables, center stage" (Ragin, 1992:5). We examine numerous aspects of one or a few cases. We include contingencies in "messy" natural settings (i.e., the co-occurrence of many specific factors and events in one place and time). This often makes explanations or interpretations complex. The explanation might be in the form of an unfolding plot or a narrative story about particular people or specific events. Rich detail and astute insight into the cases replace the sophisticated statistical analysis of precise measures across a huge number of units or cases found in quantitative research.

The passage of time is integral to qualitative research. When conducting qualitative research, we look at the sequence of events and pay very close attention to what happens first, second, third, and so on. Because we examine the same case, or a small set of cases, over time, we can see an issue evolve, a conflict emerge, or a social relationship develop. In historical research, the passage of time may involve years or decades. In field research, the passage of time is shorter. Nevertheless, in both, we note what is occurring at different points in time and recognize that *when* something occurs is often important.

Interpretation

Interpretation means to assign significance or a coherent meaning to something. You interpret data in both quantitative and qualitative research but in different ways. In a quantitative study, you assign meaning by rearranging, examining, and discussing the numbers. This often means using charts and statistics to explain how patterns in the data relate to a research question. In a qualitative study, you give meaning by rearranging, examining, and discussing textual or visual data. This is done to convey an authentic voice, and in a manner to remain true to the original understandings of the people being studied. In place of charts, statistics, and displays of numbers, you put an emphasis on extracting meaning from data that is "rich" or complex and filled with social meaning. This requires you to interpret, "translate," or make the originally gathered data understandable. The process of qualitative interpretation moves through the following three stages or levels:

1. *First-order interpretation.* This is the viewpoint of the people that are being studied. The goal is to grasp fully how they see the world and define situations and their meanings. A first-order interpretation contains the inner motives, personal reasons, and point of view of the people being studied.

2. *Second-order interpretation.* This refers to the researcher's own viewpoint. As you discover and document first-order interpretations, you will always be a step removed from the people being studied. Nonetheless, you try to get very close and "under the skin" of those being studied, although you are "on the outside looking in." Your perspective often brings a coherence or broader meaning to the specific data in context.

3. *Third-order interpretation.* This refers to the connections a researcher makes between the detailed understandings of specific people or events and abstract concepts, generalizations, or theories used to analyze the data. It refers to how you communicate with others outside the research setting. You share the insights and interpretations you acquired with a broader audience. In a sense, you translate the intimate understanding you have gained in the study to outsiders who may be very distant from the people, situations, and events under study.

QUANTITATIVE DESIGN ISSUES

The Language of Variables and Hypotheses

Variation and Variables. The **variable** is a central idea in quantitative research. Simply defined, a variable is a concept that varies. In a quantitative study, you should "speak" a language of variables and relationships among variables. In Chapter 2, you learned about two types of concepts: those that refer to a fixed phenomenon (e.g., the ideal type of bureaucracy) and those that vary in quantity, intensity, or amount (e.g., amount of education). The second type of concept and measures of the concepts are variables.

Variables take on two or more values. Once you begin to look for them, you will see variables everywhere. Gender is a variable; it can take on two values: male or female. Marital status is a variable; it can take on the values of single, married, divorced, or widowed. Type of crime committed is a variable; it can take on values of robbery, burglary, theft, murder, and so forth. Family income is a variable; it can take on values from zero to billions of dollars. A person's attitude toward abortion is a variable; it can range from strongly favoring legal abortion to strongly believing in antiabortion.

The values or the categories of a variable are its **attributes**. It is easy to confuse variables with attributes. Variables and attributes are related, but they have distinct purposes. The confusion arises because the attribute of one variable can itself become a separate variable with a slight change in definition. The distinction is between concepts themselves that vary and conditions within concepts that vary. For example, "male" is not a variable; it describes a category of gender and is an attribute of the variable "gender." Yet, a related idea, "degree of masculinity," is a variable. It describes the intensity or strength of attachment to attitudes, beliefs, and behaviors associated with the concept of *masculine* within a culture.

"Married" is not a variable; it is an attribute of the variable "marital status." Related ideas such as "number of years married" or "depth of commitment to a marriage" are variables. Likewise, "robbery" is not a variable; it is an attribute of the variable "type of crime." "Number of robberies," "robbery rate," "amount taken during a robbery," and "type of robbery" are all variables because they vary or take on a range of values.

As you saw in Chapter 2, concepts are the building blocks of theory; they organize thinking about the social world. Clear concepts with careful definitions are essential in theory. To conduct quantitative research you want to redefine most if not all concepts of interest into variables. As the examples of variables and attributes illustrate, slight changes in definition can change a nonvariable into a variable concept.

Types of Variables. Variables are classified into three basic types, depending on their location in a causal relationship. If you want to focus on causal relationships, it is best to begin with an effect then search for its causes. The variable that is the effect, result, or outcome of another variable is the **dependent variable**. Its name comes from its position of "depending on" the cause. The cause variable, or the one that identifies forces or conditions that act on something else, is the **independent variable**. It gets its name because it operates "independent of" prior causes that may act on it.

It is not always easy to determine whether a variable is independent or dependent. Two questions will help you identify the independent variable. First, does it come before or after other variables in time? Independent variables come before any other type. Second, if several variables occur at the same time, does one variable have an impact on another variable? Independent variables affect or they have an impact on other variables.

You will notice that most research topics are described and discussed in terms of the dependent variables. This is because dependent variables are what you wish to explain. For example, you examine the reasons for an increase in the crime rate in Dallas, Texas; your dependent variable would be the crime rate; it depends on or is caused by other variables (i.e., various social forces, factors, conditions in Dallas).

The most basic causal relationship requires only an independent and a dependent variable. A third type of variable, the *intervening variable*, appears in complex causal relations. It comes between the independent and dependent variables in time. Its role is to show the link or mechanism between the main variables of the relationship. Advances in knowledge depend not only on documenting cause-and-effect relationships but also on specifying the mechanisms that account for the causal relation. In a sense, the intervening variable acts as a dependent variable with respect to the independent variable and acts as an independent variable toward the dependent variable.

For example, French sociologist Emile Durkheim developed a theory of suicide that specified a causal relationship between marital status and suicide rates. Durkheim found evidence that married people are less likely to commit suicide than single people are. He believed that married people have greater social integration (i.e., feelings of social attachment or belonging to a group or family). He thought that a major cause of one type of suicide was that people had weak social integration. Thus, his theory can be restated as a three-variable relationship: a person's marital status (independent variable) causes greater social integration (intervening variable), which affects the likelihood of the person committing suicide (dependent variable). Specifying the chain of causality clarifies the linkages in a theory. It also helps when we want to test complex explanations.[1]

Only the simplest theories have only one dependent and one independent variable, whereas complex theories can contain dozens of variables with multiple independent,

intervening, and dependent variables. For example, a theory of criminal behavior (dependent variable) might include four independent variables: an individual's economic hardship, a person's opportunities to commit crime easily, belonging to a deviant subgroup of society that does not strongly disapprove of criminal behavior, and belief that punishment is unlikely to result from engaging in criminal acts. A multicause explanation usually specifies the independent variable that has the greatest causal effect. Thus, of the four independent variables, an explanation might state while both contribute to crime, membership in a deviant subgroup is more important than economic hardship to explain criminal behavior.

A complex theoretical explanation can link together a string of multiple intervening variables. Here is an example of such an explanation. Family disruption causes lower self-esteem among children, which causes depression, which causes poor grades in school, which causes reduced prospects for a good job, which causes a lower adult income. The chain of variables flows as follows: family disruption (independent), childhood self-esteem (intervening), depression (intervening), grades in school (intervening), job prospects (intervening), and adult income (dependent).

Two theories on the same topic may have different independent variables or predict different independent variables to be important. In addition, theories may agree about the independent and dependent variables but differ on the intervening variable or causal mechanism. For example, two theories say that family disruption causes lower adult income, but for different reasons. One theory holds that disruption encourages children to join deviant peer groups. In the groups, the children lack socialization to norms of work and thrift. Another theory emphasizes the impact of the disruption on childhood depression and poor academic performance. The children's depression and peer group directly affects job performance.

You usually can test only a small part of a complex causal chain in a single research study. For example, your study might examine four variables. You could take the four from a large, complex theory that contains 20 variables in total. Making the connections between your specific study and a larger theory explicit will strengthen and clarify your study and its contributions to knowledge. This applies especially for explanatory, basic research, which is the model for most quantitative research.

Causal Theory and Hypotheses

The Hypothesis and Causality.   A *hypothesis* is a proposition to test or a tentative statement that two variables are causally related. In some respects, hypotheses are your informed guesses about how the world works stated in a value-neutral form. A causal hypothesis has five characteristics (see Expansion Box 4.5). The first two define the minimum elements of a hypothesis. The third restates the hypothesis. For example, you can restate the hypothesis that attending religious services reduces the probability of divorce as a prediction: Couples who attend religious services frequently will have a lower divorce rate than do couples who rarely

EXPANSION BOX
4.5   Five Characteristics of Causal Hypothesis

1. It has at least two variables.

2. It expresses a causal or cause-effect relationship between the variables.

3. It can be expressed as a prediction or an expected future outcome.

4. It is logically linked to a research question and a theory.

5. It is falsifiable; that is, it is capable of being tested against empirical evidence and shown to be true or false.

attend religious services. You can test the prediction against empirical evidence. The fourth characteristic says that you should logically link the hypothesis to a research question and to a theory. You test hypotheses to answer the research question or to find empirical confirmation of a theory. The last characteristic requires you to test the hypothesis using empirical data. To be a scientific hypothesis means it must be testable. This means statements necessarily true because of logic, or questions impossible to answer through empirical observation (e.g., What is the "good life"? Is there a God?), cannot be scientific hypotheses.

Testing and Refining Hypotheses.   Knowledge does not advance based on one test of one hypothesis. In fact, you might get a distorted picture of the research process if you focus only on a single study that tests one hypothesis. Knowledge develops over time as many researchers throughout the scientific community test and retest many hypotheses. Knowledge grows slowly from shifting and winnowing through many tested hypotheses. Each hypothesis is an explanation of a dependent variable. If the data or evidence repeatedly fails to support some hypotheses, they will drop from consideration. The hypotheses that receive support will remain in contention. Theorists and researchers constantly create new hypotheses to challenge those that have received support. Figure 4.3 represents an example of the process of shifting through hypotheses over time.

Scientists tend to be a highly skeptical group. Empirical support for a hypothesis in one study is not sufficient for them to accept it. The principle of replication says repeated tests with consistent and repeated support are necessary before a hypothesis will gain broad acceptance. In addition to repeated tests, another way to strengthen confidence in a hypothesis is to test the related causal linkages in the theory from which it comes. Scientific knowledge grows from the combination of repeated empirical tests of a hypothesis, showing that evidence for a hypothesis is stronger

FIGURE 4.3   **How the Process of Hypothesis Testing Operates over Time**

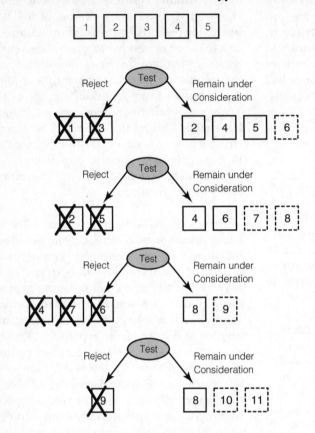

1970

There are five possible hypotheses.

1980

Two of the original five hypotheses
are rejected.
A new one is developed.

1990

Two hypotheses are rejected.
Two new ones are developed.

2000

Three hypotheses are rejected.
A new one is developed.

2010

One hypothesis is rejected.
Two new ones are developed.

than for competing explanations, and testing the linkages that connect one hypothesis to related ones in a broader explanation.

Types of Hypotheses.   You can think of hypotheses as links in a theoretical causal chain. Hypotheses take several forms and help you test both the direction and strength of relationships among variables. When a hypothesis "defeats" its competitors, or offers alternative explanations for a causal relation, it indirectly supports an explanation. A curious aspect of hypothesis testing is that evidence that is in support of a hypothesis is seen differently than evidence that negates it. The scientific community assigns greater significance to the negative evidence.

The idea that negative evidence is critical when the scientific community evaluates a hypothesis comes from the *logic of disconfirming hypotheses.*[2] This logic is associated with the writings of philosopher of science Karl Popper (1902–1994). He presented the idea of falsification and with it the use of null hypotheses (see later in this section). The central idea in falsification is that we can never prove a hypothesis; however, we can disprove it. If we have supporting evidence, the best we can say is that the hypothesis remains a possibility, or that it is still in the running. Negative evidence is more significant in building knowledge because it "tarnishes" or "soils" the hypothesis.

The reasoning behind the idea of falsification works as follows: a hypothesis makes predictions. Negative and disconfirming evidence shows that the hypothesis' predictions are wrong. Positive or confirming evidence for a hypothesis is less critical. This is because alternative hypotheses may make the same prediction. If we find confirming evidence for the prediction, it tells us that the hypothesis remains "in the running" but it does not necessarily elevate the explanation over its alternatives. We might have equal amounts of confirming evidence for many different alternative explanations.

Here is a simple example. You stand on a street corner with an open umbrella and claim that your umbrella protects you from elephants falling from the sky. You believe that the umbrella offers protection. Your hypothesis is that with the umbrella, no elephant will fall on you. This can be restated as a prediction—so long as you are under the open umbrella, you will be protected from falling elephants. You have supporting evidence. You have not had a single elephant fall on you in all the time you held the umbrella open. For each day that goes by, you accumulate more "evidence" in support of your explanation. Yet, such supporting evidence is weak; it is consistent with alternative explanations—such as elephants do not fall from the sky. Both explanations predict the same thing: you will be safe from falling elephants. Negative evidence—the elephant falls on you and the umbrella, crushing both—destroys the hypothesis for good.

You can test hypotheses in two ways: a straightforward way and a null hypothesis way. Many quantitative researchers, especially experimenters, frame hypotheses in terms of a ***null hypothesis*** based on the logic of the disconfirming hypotheses. They look for evidence that will allow them to accept or reject the null hypothesis. Most people talk about a hypothesis as a way to predict a relationship. The null hypothesis does the opposite. It predicts no relationship.

Here is an example. Sarah believes that students who live on campus in dormitories get higher grades than students who live far from campus and commute to college. Her null hypothesis is that there is no relationship between residence and grades. She matches a null hypothesis with a corresponding ***alternative hypothesis*** (also called experimental hypothesis). The alternative hypothesis says that a relationship exists. Sarah's alternative hypothesis would be that students' on-campus residence has a positive effect on grades.

You may feel that a null hypothesis approach is a backward way to test hypotheses. Null hypothesis thinking rests on the assumption that you want to find support for a relationship. The null hypothesis approach makes finding a relationship more demanding. If you use the approach, you only directly test the null hypothesis. If evidence supports it (i.e., it leads you to accept) the null hypothesis, you can conclude that the hypothesized relationship does not exist. Accepting the null hypothesis automatically means that the alternative hypothesis is false. On the other hand, if you find evidence to reject the null hypothesis, then the alternative hypothesis remains a possibility. You have not proven the alternative; rather, by testing null hypotheses around it, you keep the alternative hypothesis in contention. Adding the null hypothesis approach to having confirming evidence for the alternative hypothesis will help build confidence for the alternative hypothesis.

The null hypothesis approach shows that the scientific community is extremely cautious, because it considers a causal relationship to be false (i.e., not present) until many tests and mountains of evidence show it to be true. The scientific community is very hesitant to say anything with absolute certainty or state it has total empirical proof; it remains open to possibilities and cautious of the evidence. The logic is similar to the Anglo-American legal idea of innocent until proved guilty. We assume, or act as if, the null hypothesis is correct until *reasonable doubt* suggests otherwise. The null hypothesis approach is generally applied with specific statistical tests (e.g., *t*-test or *F*-test). Thus, if a statistical test tells you that the odds of the null hypothesis being false are 99 in 100, you can say reasonable doubt exists for the null hypothesis. This is the same as saying statistical tests allow you to "reject the null hypothesis at the .01 level of significance." (Statistical significance is discussed in Chapter 10.)

Aspects of Explanation

Clarity about Units and Levels of Analysis. It is easy to become confused at first about the ideas of units and levels of analysis. Nevertheless, they are essential for you to think clearly about a study and plan its details. All studies have both units and levels of analysis. However, when you read reports of studies, authors only occasionally explicitly label these two features. The levels and units of analysis in your study will depend on your topic and the research question.

Social reality has several levels. The level varies on a continuum from micro level (e.g., small groups or interactions among individuals) to macro level (e.g., rise and fall of civilizations or the structural aspects of a society). A *level of analysis* refers to the level of social reality in a theoretical explanation. The level of analysis can include a mix of the number of people, the amount of space, the scope of the activity, and the length of time. For example, an extreme micro-level analysis involves studying a minute of interaction between two people in the same small room. An extreme macro-level analysis involves studying five centuries of relations involving a billion people on four continents. Most social research studies operate at a level of analysis that lies between these two extremes.

The level of analysis delimits the kinds of assumptions, concepts, and theories that you can use. For example, I want to study the topic of dating among college students. I might use a micro-level analysis and develop an explanation that uses concepts that are at a micro level, such as interpersonal contact, mutual friendships, and common interests. I believe that students are likely to date someone with whom

they have had personal contact in a class, share friends in common, and share common interests. The topic and focus fit with a micro-level explanation. This is because the topic, concepts, and focus are at the level of face-to-face interactions among individuals. Another example topic is how inequality affects the forms of violent behavior in a society. I chose a more macro-level explanation because of the topic and the level of social reality at which it operates. The concepts I use are more macro-level ones. I examine the degree of inequality in a society (e.g., the distribution of wealth, property, income, and other resources) and look at patterns of societal violence (e.g., aggression against other societies, levels of crime and sexual assault, feuds among clans or families). The topic and research question suggest macro-level concepts and theories.

The *unit of analysis* refers to the type of unit you use when measuring concepts and variables. Common units in social science are the individual person, the group (e.g., family, friendship group), a community (e.g., town, neighborhood), the organization (e.g., business corporation, hospital, university), the social category (e.g., social class, gender, race), the social institution (e.g., religion, education system, the family), and the society (e.g., a nation, a tribe).

Numerous social science studies use the individual as the unit of analysis; however, it is by no means the only unit in social research. Different theories emphasize one or another unit of analysis, and different research techniques are associated with specific units of analysis. For example, the individual is usually the unit of analysis in survey and experimental research.

As an example, you conduct a survey in which you ask 150 students to rate their favorite football player. The individual is the unit of analysis in such a study. This is because you would measure the responses of each individual student. However, if you wanted to compare how much money 100 colleges have spent on their football programs over the past three years, the unit of analysis is the organization (i.e., the college). This is because you would record and compare the amount of spending by each college. In the first study, you measure and explain the activities of individuals (i.e., how they rate football players). In the second, you measure and explain the actions of organizations (i.e., allocate money on a football program).

You can use units of analysis other than individuals, groups, organizations, social categories, institutions, and societies. For example, you want to learn whether the speeches of three candidates for mayor contain specific themes. You use the content analysis technique and measure the themes in each speech of the candidates. In such a study, your unit of analysis is the speech. This is because you would examine and compare each speech for the themes it contains. You can also use geographic units of analysis. Perhaps you want to learn whether cities with higher percentages of teenagers also have a higher rate of vandalism than cities with low percentages of teenagers. In such a study, your unit of analysis is the city because you measure and compare city characteristics: the percentage of teenagers in the population of each city and the amount of vandalism that occurs in each.

Units of analysis tell you the data you will need to get and what you should be measuring in the data. The units of analysis also correspond loosely to the level of analysis from a theoretical explanation. Thus, social-psychological or micro levels of analysis best fit with the individual as a unit of analysis. Macro levels of analysis may fit with the social category or institution as a unit. Theories and explanations at the micro-level generally refer to features of individuals or interactions among individuals. Macro-level theories refer to social forces that operate across a society or relations among major parts of a society as a whole.

Thinking clearly about your levels and units of analysis is critical when you design a study. Being aware of them will help you to avoid making logical errors. For example, you want to study whether colleges in the North spend more on their football programs than do colleges in the South. This implies gathering information on colleges, its spending and its location. Your unit of analysis—the organization or, specifically, the college—flows from the research question and it directs you to collect data from each college.

At times, you have a choice and can choose among different units or levels of analysis for similar topics or research questions. For example, you want to study the topic of patriarchy and violent behavior. You could use the society as the unit of analysis and ask the research question, "Are patriarchal societies more violent?" For this research question, you would collect data on societies and classify each society by its degree of patriarchy and its level of violence. On the other hand, for the same topic you might ask a different research question, "Is the degree of patriarchy within a family associated with violence against a spouse?" For this research question your unit of analysis could be the group or the family, and a more micro-level of analysis would be appropriate. You could collect data on families by measuring the degree of patriarchy in the families and the level of violence that occurs between spouses in these families. You are able to address the same topic using different levels and units of analysis because patriarchy is a variable that can describe an entire society or the social relations within one family. Likewise, violence can be a characteristic of a society or an aspect of the interpersonal actions of one spouse toward the other.

Ecological Fallacy.   An *ecological fallacy* is a type of error that arises from a mismatch of units of analysis. It refers to a poor fit between the units for which you have empirical evidence and the units for which you want to make general statements. It is indicates imprecise reasoning or generalizing beyond what the evidence warrants. You make an ecological fallacy when you have data at *high* or *aggregated* units of analysis but make statements about *low* or *disaggregated* units. It is a fallacy because what happens in one unit of analysis does not always hold for a different unit of analysis. Thus, if you gather data for high or aggregated units (e.g., business corporations, entire countries, etc.) and then you make statements about low or disaggregated units (e.g., the behavior of individual people), you probably committed the ecological fallacy. To avoid this error, ensure that the unit of analysis in an explanation matches or is very close to the unit on which you collect data (see Example Box 4.2).

4.2   EXAMPLE BOX
The Ecological Fallacy

Researchers have criticized the famous study *Suicide* ([1897] 1951) by Emile Durkheim for the ecological fallacy of treating group data as though they were individual-level data. In the study, Durkheim compared the suicide rates of Protestant and Catholic districts in nineteenth-century western Europe and explained observed differences as due to differences between people's beliefs and practices in the two religions. He said that Protestants had a higher suicide rate than Catholics because they were more individualistic and had lower social integration. Durkheim and early researchers only had data by district. Since people tended to reside with others of the same religion, Durkheim used group-level data (i.e., region) for individuals.

Later researchers (van Poppel and Day, 1996) reexamined nineteenth-century suicide rates only with individual-level data that they discovered for some areas. They compared the death records and looked at the official reason of death and religion, but their results differed from Durkheim's. Apparently, local officials at that time recorded deaths differently for people of different religions. They recorded "unspecified" as a reason for death far more often for Catholics because of a strong moral prohibition against suicide among Catholics. Durkheim's larger theory may be correct, yet the evidence he had to test it was weak because he used data aggregated at the group level while trying to explain the actions of individuals.

Example.   Tomsville and Joansville each have a population of about 45,000 people. Tomsville has a high percentage of upper-income people. Over half of the households in the town have family incomes of over $200,000. The town also has more motorcycles registered in it than any other town of its size. In Tomsville there are 4,000 motorcycles. The town of Joansville has many poor people. Half its households live below the poverty line. It also has fewer motorcycles registered in it than any other town its size. In Joansville, there are only 100 motorcycles. You might look at the data on these two towns and falsely say, based on this information alone, that rich people are more likely to own motorcycles. In other words, your statement from the evidence is that you found a relationship between family income and motorcycle ownership. This is a fallacy because you do not know which families in Tomsville or Joansville own the motorcycles. You only know about the two variables—average income and number of motorcycles—for the towns as a whole. The unit of analysis for observing variables is the town as a whole. Perhaps all of the low- and middle-income families in Tomsville belong to a motorcycle club. They are the ones who own the motorcycles in Tomsville and not a single upper-income family belongs to the club or owns a motorcycle. Or perhaps in Joansville all 100 motorcycles are owned by poor families and none are owned by any middle- or upper-income families. If you want to make a statement about the relationship between ownership of motorcycles and family income, you must collect data on the families as a unit of analysis, not on the towns as a whole.

Reductionism.   Another error involving mismatched units of analysis and imprecise reasoning about evidence is **reductionism**. It is also called a *fallacy of nonequivalence* (see Example Box 4.3). This error occurs when you explain macro-level events using evidence only about specific individuals. It occurs when you observe a *lower* or *disaggregated* unit of analysis but then make statements about *higher* or *aggregated*

4.3	EXAMPLE BOX
	Error of Reductionism

Suppose you pick up a book and read the following:

American race relations changed dramatically during the Civil Rights Era of the 1960s. Attitudes among the majority, White population shifted to greater tolerance as laws and court rulings changed across the nation. Opportunities that had been legally and officially closed to all but the White population—in the areas of housing, jobs, schooling, voting rights, and so on— were opened to people of all races. From the Brown vs. Board of Education decision in 1955, to the Civil Rights Act of 1964, to the War on Poverty from 1966 to 1968, a new, dramatic outlook swept the country. This was the result of the vision, dedication, and actions of America's foremost civil rights leader, Dr. Martin Luther King Jr.

This says: *dependent variable* = major change in U.S. race relations over a 10- to 13-year period; *independent variable* = King's vision and actions.

If you know much about the civil rights era, you see a problem. The entire civil rights movement and its successes are attributed to a single individual. Yes, one individual does make a difference and helps build and guide a movement, but the *movement* is missing. The idea of a social–political movement as a causal force is reduced to its major leader. The distinct social phenomenon—a movement—is obscured. Lost are the actions of hundreds of thousands of people (marches, court cases, speeches, prayer meetings, sit-ins, rioting, petitions, beatings, etc.) involved in advancing a shared goal and the responses to them. The movement's ideology, popular mobilization, politics, organization, and strategy are absent. Related macro-level historical events and trends that may have influenced the movement (e.g., Vietnam War protest, mood shift with the killing of John F. Kennedy, African American separatist politics, African American migration to urban North) are also ignored.

This error is not unique to historical explanations. Many people think only in terms of individual actions and have an individualist bias, sometimes called *methodological individualism*. This is especially true in the extremely individualistic U.S. culture. The error is that it disregards units of analysis or forces beyond the individual. The *error of reductionism* shifts explanation to a much lower unit of analysis. One could continue to reduce from an individual's behavior to biological processes in a person, to micro-level neurochemical activities, to the subatomic level.

Most people live in "social worlds" focused on local, immediate settings and their interactions with a small set of others, so their everyday sense of reality encourages seeing social trends or events as individual actions or psychological processes. Often, they become blind to more abstract, macro-level entities—social forces, processes, organizations, institutions, movements, or structures. The idea that all social actions cannot be reduced to individuals alone is the core of sociology. In his classic work *Suicide*, Emile Durkheim fought methodological individualism and demonstrated that larger, unrecognized social forces explain even highly individual, private actions.

---

units. It is a mirror image of the mismatch error in an ecological fallacy. If you have data on how individuals behave but make statements about the dynamics of macro-level units, you could be committing the error of reductionism. It occurs because it is often easier to get data on concrete individuals. In addition, the operation of macro-level units is more abstract and nebulous. As with an ecological fallacy, avoid this error by ensuring that the unit of analysis in your explanation is very close to the one for which you have evidence.

If you fail to think precisely about the units of analysis and do not couple the data with the theory, you could easily commit an ecological fallacy or reductionism. In both, you are making a mistake about the data appropriate for a research question or seriously overgeneralizing from the data you have.

You can make assumptions about units of analysis other than the ones you study empirically. Thus, research on individuals rests on assumptions that individuals act within a set of social institutions. Many micro-level units together form macro-level units. The danger is that it is easy to slide into using the causes or behavior of micro units, such as individuals, to explain the actions of macro units, such as social institutions. It is important to remember that what happens among units at one level does not necessarily hold for different units of analysis. The discipline of sociology rests on the fundamental belief that a distinct level of social reality exists beyond the individual. Explanations of this level require that your data and theory go beyond the individual alone. You cannot reduce the causes, forces, structures, or processes that take place among macro units to individual motivations and behaviors.

Example.   Why did World War I occur? You may have heard that it was because a Serbian shot an archduke in the Austro-Hungarian Empire in 1914. This is an example of reductionism. Yes, the assassination was a factor, but you cannot reduce a macro-political event between nations—war—to a specific act of one individual. To see why not, think it through, why stop reducing at the individual. You could also say that the war occurred because the assassin's alarm clock worked and woke him up that morning. If it had not worked, there would have been no assassination. The reductionist logic tells you the alarm clock caused the war! The macro-level event, World War I, was much more complex. It was due to many social, political, and economic forces that came together at a point in history. The actions of specific individuals had a role, but only a minor one compared to these macro forces. Individuals do affect events. Eventually, in combination with larger-scale social forces and organizations, individuals

affect others and together they move nations to act, but individual actions alone are not the cause. Thus, it is likely that a major war would have broken out at about that time even if the assassination had not occurred. The assassination was one of many potential trigger events; its impact was possible because of preexisting conditions and subsequent actions by many others.

Spuriousness.   To say that a relationship between variables is *spurious* is to say it is false, or a mirage. Researchers get excited when they think they have found a spurious relationship. This is because they can show that what appears to be happening on the surface is in reality false; it is like a magic trick! Any association between two variables might be spurious, so you need to be cautious when you find that two variables are associated. Upon further investigation, the apparent association may not be the basis for a real causal relationship. It may be an illusion on the surface while the reality is more complex.

Spuriousness occurs when two variables appear to be associated, but the variables actually are not related. There is an "unseen" third factor, and it is the true cause. The unseen third or other variable causes both the independent and the dependent variable. This creates an apparent but illusionary relationship and accounts for the observed association. In terms of conditions for causality, the unseen factor is a more powerful alternative explanation.

You now understand that you should be wary of correlations or associations, but how can you tell whether a relationship is spurious? How do you find out what the mysterious "unseen" third factor is? You will need to use statistical techniques (discussed later in this book) to test whether an association is spurious. To use them, you need a theory, or at least a reasoned guess, about possible third factors.

Actually, spuriousness is based on commonsense logic that you use already. For example, you already know that there is an association between the use of air conditioners and ice cream cone consumption. If you measured the number of air conditioners in use and the number of ice cream cones sold for each day, you would find a strong correlation: more cones are sold on the days when more air conditioners are in use. However, you know that eating ice cream cones does not cause people to turn on air conditioners. Instead, a third factor causes both variables: hot days. You could verify the same thing through statistics by measuring the daily temperature as well as ice cream consumption and air conditioner use. In social research, opposing theories help identify which third factors could be relevant for many topics (e.g., the causes of crime or the reasons for war or child abuse).

Example 1.   Some people say that taking illegal drugs causes suicide, school dropouts, and violent acts. Advocates of the "drugs are the problem" position point to the positive correlations between taking drugs and being suicidal, dropping out of school, and engaging in violence. They argue that ending drug use will greatly reduce suicide, dropouts, and violence. Others argue that many people turn to drugs because of their emotional problems or high levels of disorder of their communities (e.g., high unemployment, unstable families, high

crime, few community services, and lack of civility). The people with emotional problems or who live in disordered communities are also more likely to commit suicide, drop out, and engage in violence. This means that reducing emotional problems and community disorder will cause illegal drug use, dropouts, suicides, and violence all to decline greatly. Reducing drug taking alone will have only a limited effect because it ignores the root causes. The "drugs are the problem" argument could be spurious because the initial relationship between taking illegal drugs and the problems is misleading. The emotional problems and community disorder are the true and often unseen causal variables.

Example 2.   In the United States and Canada, we observe an empirical association between students classified as being in a non-White racial category and the students scoring lower on academic tests (compared to students classified in a White category). The relationship between racial classification and test scores is illusionary, because the true cause of both the racial classification and the test scores is ignored (see Figure 4.4). In this case, the true cause operates

FIGURE 4.4   Example of a Spurious Relationship between Belonging to a Non-White "Race" and Getting Low Academic Test Scores

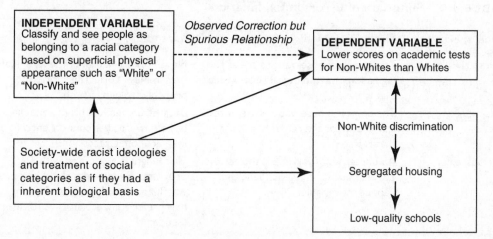

directly on the independent variable (racial classification) but indirectly through an intervening process on the dependent variable (test scores).

The true cause is a belief system that classifies people as belonging to racial groups and assigns great significance to superficial physical appearance, such as skin color, or what people call "race." Such a belief system also is the basis for prejudice and discriminatory behavior. In such a situation, people see one another as belonging to different races and treat one another differently because of it. They have different job opportunities and housing choices. Discriminated-against people who are in some racial categories find many limits in their job opportunities and housing choices. Majority groups and organizations separate or group together discriminated-against people in undesirable areas. This produces a concentration of low incomes, high unemployment, and poor housing in certain city areas or neighborhoods. Neighborhood location combines with unequal schooling. The lowest-quality schools are located in areas with the least desirable housing, low income, and high unemployment. The relationship between school quality and test scores is very strong, as is the relation between coming from a low-income family and test scores. This means students from families that live in low-income, undesirable housing areas with low-quality schools get lower test scores.

We now turn from the errors in causal explanation to avoid and more to other issues involving hypotheses. Table 4.2 provides a review of the major errors.

From the Research Question to Hypotheses

It may be difficult to narrow down a broad topic into a specific hypothesis to test in a study. However, the leap from a well-formulated research question to a hypothesis is a short one. A good research question contains hints about hypotheses. In addition, you can think of the hypothesis as providing a tentative answer to the research question (see Example Box 4.4).

Consider an example research question: "Is age at marriage associated with divorce?" The question contains two variables: "age at marriage" and "divorce." To develop a testable hypothesis from this question, you first might ask, "Which is the independent variable?" The independent variable is "age at marriage" because marriage logically precedes divorce. You then might ask, "What is the direction of the relationship?" The hypothesis could be "The lower the age at time of marriage, the greater the

TABLE 4.2   Summary of Errors in Explanation

Type of Error	Short Definition	Example
Ecological Fallacy	The empirical observations are at too high a level for the causal relationship that is stated.	New York has a high crime rate. Joan lives in New York. Therefore, she probably stole my watch.
Reductionism	The empirical observations are at too low a level for the causal relationship that is stated.	Because Steven lost his job and did not buy a new car, the country entered a long economic recession.
Spuriousness	An unseen third variable is the actual cause of both the independent and dependent variable.	Hair length is associated with TV programs. People with short hair prefer watching football; people with long hair prefer romance stories. (*Unseen:* Gender)

4.4	EXAMPLE BOX

Examples of Bad and Good Research Questions

Bad Research Questions

Not Empirically Testable, Nonscientific Questions
- Should abortion be legal?
- Is it right to have capital punishment?

General Topics, Not Research Questions
- Treatment of alcohol and drug abuse
- Sexuality and aging

Set of Variables, Not Questions
- Capital punishment and racial discrimination
- Urban decay and gangs

Too Vague, Ambiguous
- Do police affect delinquency?
- What can be done to prevent child abuse?

Need to Be Still More Specific
- Has the incidence of child abuse risen?
- How does poverty affect children?
- What problems do children who grow up in poverty experience that others do not?

Good Research Questions

Exploratory Questions
- Has the actual incidence of child abuse changed in Wisconsin in the past 10 years?

Descriptive Questions
- Is child abuse, violent or sexual, more common in families that have experienced a divorce than in intact, never-divorced families?
- Are the children raised in poverty households more likely to have medical, learning, and social-emotional adjustment difficulties than nonpoverty children?

Explanatory Questions
- Does the emotional instability created by experiencing a divorce increase the chances that divorced parents will physically abuse their children?
- Is a lack of sufficent funds for preventive treatment a major cause of more serious medical problems among children raised in families in poverty?

---

chances that the marriage will end in divorce." In this form, the hypothesis provides an answer to the research question. It also makes a prediction. Notice that you can reformulate and better focus the research question into, "Are couples who marry younger more likely to divorce?"

You can develop several hypotheses for one research question. Another hypothesis from the same research question could be, "The smaller the difference between the ages of the marriage partners at the time of marriage, the less likely that the marriage will end in divorce." In this case, you specify the variable "age at marriage" differently. Instead of thinking about age as chronological age of the people getting married from birth, it is the age gap between two marital partners. As you can see, turning a research question into hypotheses adds greater specificity. It may also force you to

think in a more focused and precise way about various aspects within your research question.

Hypotheses can specify that a relationship will hold up under some conditions but not others. For example, a hypothesis states: "The lower the age of the partners at time of marriage, the greater the chances that the marriage will end in divorce, unless it is a marriage between two members of a tightly knit traditional religious community in which early marriage is the norm." Here, a specific condition—membership in a tightly knit traditional religious community—elaborates on the simple two-variable relationship. Such elaboration tells you that the original relationship may hold under some conditions but not others. It might also reveal an unstated assumption of the original hypothesis, the marital partners were not members of a tightly knit religious community.

Formulating a research question and a hypothesis do not always proceed in fixed stages. You can formulate a tentative research question, then develop possible hypotheses, and then use the hypotheses to restate the research question more precisely in an interactive and creative process.

You may be wondering, Where does theory fit into the process of moving from a topic to a hypothesis I can test? Recall from Chapter 2 that theory takes many forms. You can use general theoretical issues as a source of topics. Theories provide concepts that you can turn into variables as well as the reasoning or mechanism that helps you to connect variables to form a research question. A hypothesis can both answer a research question and be an untested proposition from a theory. You can express a hypothesis at an abstract, conceptual level or restate it in a more concrete, measurable form. Examples of specific studies illustrate the parts of the research process. For examples of three quantitative studies, see Table 4.3; for two qualitative studies, see Table 4.4.

TABLE 4.3   Examples of Quantitative Studies

Study Citation (using ASA format style)	Mueller-Johnson, Katrin U. and Mandeep K. Dhami. 2010. "Effects of Offenders' Age and Health on Sentencing Decisions." *Journal of Social Psychology* 150:77–97.	Unnever, James D. and Francis T. Cullen. 2007. "The Racial Divide in Support for the Death Penalty: Does White Racism Matter?" *Social Forces* 85:1281–1301.	Lauzen, Martha M. and David M. Dozier. 2005. "Maintaining the Double Standard: Portrayals of Age and Gender in Popular Films." *Sex Roles* 52:437–446.
Methodological Technique	Experiment	Survey	Content analysis
Topic	Prison sentence recommended based on the age and health of a defendant	Support for capital punishment in the U.S. by White and Black adults	Age and gender stereotypes in U.S. mass media
Research Question	If a mock jury is presented with a male convicted of a crime (molesting a female child), will there be a leniency effect in the sentence the jury recommends based on the age and health status of the defendant?	How much of support for the death penalty by Whites is due to racist attitudes and is support for the death penalty among nonracist Whites similar to that of African Americans?	Do contemporary films show a double standard, in which males acquire greater status and leadership as they age, whereas females are not permitted to gain status and leadership with increased age?
Main Hypothesis Tested	Juries will recommend a lighter sentence for a defendant who is in poor health or who is old.	Significant support for the death penalty among Whites is due to those Whites with negative attitudes toward Blacks, who are more likely to receive the penalty.	As with past popular U.S. films and in other popular mass media, a double standard still exists.

Main Independent Variable(s)	Age and health status of defendant, also the severity of the crime.	Race, a set of questions measuring White racism, egalitarianism, and political orientation.	The age and gender of major film characters.
Main Dependent Variable(s)	Length of sentence recommended.	Support for capital punishment, and strength of that support.	Whether a character has a leadership role, high occupational status, and goals.
Unit of Analysis	Individual	Individual adult	The movie
Specific Units in the Study	40 university student participants, 16 men and 24 women with a mean age of 24.5 years.	Random sample of 1,555 U.S. adults from 48 states interviewed in 2000 as part of the National Election Survey	100 top-grossing domestic U.S. films in 2002
Universe	All juries	All adult Whites and Blacks in the United States	All films

TABLE 4.4   Examples of Qualitative Studies

Study Citation (using ASA format style)	Goffman, Alice. 2009. "On the Run: Wanted Men in a Philadelphia Ghetto." *American Sociological Review* 74:339–357.	Kane, Danielle and Jung Mee Park. 2009. "The Puzzle of Korean Christianity: Geopolitical Networks and Religious Conversion in Early 20th Century East Asia." *American Journal of Sociology* 115:365–405.
Methodological Technique	Field research	Historical–comparative research
Topic	Young men in Black ghettos	Christian religious beliefs in South Korea
Research Question	How has mass imprisonment and policing affected the daily activities of young men in poor Black urban neighborhoods?	Why did Christian beliefs spread in South Korea but not in Japan or China, which had similar East Asian cultural and religious traditions?
Grounded Theory	The power and control of the state over poor Black males in a ghetto in the era of mass incarceration is not mass surveillance as suggested by Foucault. Instead, it is to be placed in a semi-legal status and situation of constant fear of arrest. Constant fear of arrest for minor infractions followed by serious punishment cause them to alter their daily life activities and social relations.	Nationalist rituals took different forms in Japan, China, and Korea. Nationalist rituals in China and Japan associated patriotism with being anti-Christian because Christians were associated with unequal treaties. In Korea, Japanese colonialism allowed patriotism to reinforce Christian religious conversion.

(Continued)

TABLE 4.4 Continued

Social Process	Previously imprisoned young Black men easily commit minor legal infractions. They must avoid stable routine activities such as going to work, going to a hospital, attending a child's school events, or maintaining relations with friends and family because such activities increase their visibility and proximity to police, that in turn mean arrest and serious incarceration.	Religious conversion at the micro level occurs through social networks. Macro-level political identities associated with nationalist resistance to foreign domination can slow/counteract or accelerate/reinforce processes in the conversion networks.
Social Context or Field Site	A low-income Black neighborhood in Philadelphia in the early 2000s	China, Korea, and Japan in the 19th and 20th centuries

CONCLUSION

In this chapter, you read about how to lay the groundwork to begin a study. You saw how the qualitative and quantitative approaches to social research direct you to prepare for a study somewhat differently. In both approaches, you will narrow a topic into a more specific, focused research question. Yet, exactly how you go about focusing the topic may vary by whether you are following a quantitative or qualitative approach. The approach to research also suggests that you follow a slightly different sequence of decisions and timing for this process. The approach you use may depend on your topic, purpose, and intended use of study results, as well as the orientation toward social science that you adopt.

If you adopt a quantitative approach for a study, you will follow a linear path and move toward data that is precise and numerical. You are likely to use explicit and standardized research procedures. You should convert major features of your study in a language of variables and hypotheses. You will follow a somewhat deductive sequence of discrete steps that precede collecting any data: Narrow the topic to a more focused question, transform nebulous theoretical concepts into more exact variables, and develop one or more hypotheses to test. In actual practice, you may move back and forth. Nonetheless, the overall process will flow in a single, linear direction. Especially in a quantitative study, you will want to take special care to avoid logical errors in hypothesis development and causal explanation.

If you adopt a qualitative approach for a study, you will proceed along more of a nonlinear path. You will want to become intimate with the details of a natural setting or a particular cultural–historical context. Because you will have few standardized procedures or explicit steps, you may need to devise on-the-spot techniques for one situation or study. You will want to describe your study using a language of cases and contexts. Your study may require conducting a detailed investigation of particular cases or processes in a search for authenticity. You do not need to separate planning and design decisions into a distinct pre-data collection stage; rather, you can continue to refine a study design throughout early data collection. As you pursue an inductive qualitative style, you will slowly move toward a specific focus that arises from your ongoing learning from data. Grounded theory may emerge as you continuously reflect on the data.

Too often, the qualitative and quantitative distinction is overdrawn and presented as a rigid dichotomy. Adherents of one approach frequently judge the other based on the assumptions and standards of their own approach. Thus, a quantitative researcher may ask, What variables are you using and what hypothesis are you testing? Yet these questions may not be very relevant in a qualitative study. A qualitative researcher may balk when you turn human relations, thoughts, and feelings into hard, cold numbers.

Ideally, you will become a well-versed, prudent social researcher who understands and appreciates each approach on its own terms. You will be able to recognize the strengths and limitations of each. Keep in mind, the ultimate goal of social science is to develop a deeper understanding of and better explanations of the social world. These will come from an appreciation of what each approach to social research has to offer.

Key Terms

abstract
alternative hypothesis
attributes
citation
dependent variable
ecological fallacy
first-order interpretation
hypothesis
independent variable
intervening variable
level of analysis
linear research path
literature review
nonlinear research path
null hypothesis
reductionism
second-order interpretation
spuriousness
third-order interpretation
unit of analysis
universe
variable

Endnotes

1. For a discussion of the "logic of the disconfirming hypothesis," see Singleton, Straits, Straits, and McAllister (1988:456–460).
2. See Bailey (1987:43) for a discussion.

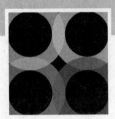

CHAPTER 5

Qualitative and Quantitative Measurement

WHY MEASURE?

Perhaps you have heard of the Stanford–Binet IQ test to measure intelligence, the Index of Dissimilarity to measure racial segregation, the poverty line to measure whether a person is poor, or Uniform Crime Reports to measure the amount of crime. Social researchers want to measure concepts and variables so they can test a hypothesis, evaluate an explanation, provide empirical support for a theory, or study an applied issue. This chapter explores how we measure the aspects of the social world—such as intelligence, segregation, poverty, crime, self-esteem, political power, alienation, or racial prejudice—for the purpose of research.

In quantitative research, we are far more concerned about measurement issues than for qualitative research. In a quantitative study, measurement is a special step in the research process. It occurs prior to data collection and has a distinct terminology. There are many specialized quantitative measurement techniques. Quantitative measurement follows a deductive approach. It starts with an abstract concept. We next create empirical measures that precisely and accurately capture the concept in a form that we can express in numbers.

In qualitative research, we approach measurement very differently. We have ways to capture and express concepts using alternatives to numbers. Often we follow an inductive approach. In qualitative studies, we may measure features of social life as one part of a broader process in which we create new concepts or theories at the same time. Instead of a separate step in the research process, we integrate measurement with data collecting and theorizing.

How we conceptualize and operationalize variables (conceptualizing and operationalizing are discussed later in this chapter) can significantly affect social issues beyond concerns of doing a study to advance knowledge. For example, psychologists debate the meaning and measurement of intelligence. Most of the intelligence tests used in schools, on job applications, and in making statements about racial or other inherited superiority measure only analytic reasoning (i.e., one's capacity to think abstractly and to infer logically). Yet, many argue that there are other types of intelligence in addition to analytic. Some say there is practical and creative intelligence. Others suggest more types, such as social–interpersonal, emotional, body–kinesthetic, musical, or spatial. If there are many forms of intelligence but people narrowly limit measurement to one type, it seriously restricts how schools identify and nurture learning; how larger society evaluates, promotes, and recognizes the contributions of people; and how a society values diverse human abilities.

Likewise, policymakers and researchers debate how to conceptualize and operationalize poverty. How we measure poverty can determine whether some people will get assistance from numerous social programs (e.g., subsidized housing, food aid, health care, childcare, etc.). For example, some say that people are poor only if they cannot afford the food required to prevent malnutrition. Others say that people are poor if they have an annual income that is less than one-half of the average (median) income. Still others say that people are poor if they earn below a "living wage" based on a judgment about the income needed to meet minimal community standards of health, safety, and decency in hygiene, housing, clothing, diet, transportation, and so forth. Decisions about how to measure a variable—poverty—can greatly influence the daily living conditions of millions of people.

We use many measures in our daily lives. For example, this morning I woke up and hopped onto a bathroom scale to see how well my diet is working. I glanced at a thermometer to find out whether to wear a coat. Next, I got into my car and checked the gas gauge to be sure I could make it to campus. As I drove, I watched the speedometer so I would not get a speeding ticket. By 8:00 A.M., I had measured weight, temperature, gasoline volume, and speed—all measures about the physical world. Such precise, well-developed measures, which we use in daily life, are fundamental in the natural sciences.

We also measure the nonphysical world in everyday life, but usually in less exact terms. We are measuring when we say that a restaurant is excellent, that Pablo is smart, that Karen has a negative attitude toward life, that Johnson is really prejudiced, or that the movie last night had a lot of violence in it. However, such everyday judgments as "really prejudiced" or "a lot of violence" are imprecise, vague measures.

Measurement also extends our senses. The astronomer or biologist uses the telescope or the microscope to extend natural vision. Scientific measurement is more sensitive, varies less with the specific observer, and yields more exact information than using our senses alone. You recognize that a thermometer gives more specific, precise information about temperature than touch can. Likewise, a good bathroom scale gives you more specific, consistent, and precise information about the weight of a 5-year-old girl than you get by lifting her and calling her "heavy" or "light." Social measures provide precise information about social reality.

In addition to extending human senses, measurement helps us observe what is otherwise invisible. It lets us observe things that were once unseen and unknown but our theories predicted. For example, you cannot see or feel magnetism with your natural senses. Magnetism comes from a theory about the physical world. We observe its effects indirectly; for instance, metal flecks move near a magnet. The magnet allows you to "see" or measure the magnetic fields. Natural scientists have invented thousands of measures to "see" very tiny things (molecules or insect organs) or very large things (huge geological landmasses or planets) that are not observable through ordinary senses. In addition, researchers are constantly creating new measures.

Some of the things we wish to measure are easy to see (e.g., age, sex, skin color, etc.), but many things cannot be directly observed (e.g., attitudes, ideologies, divorce rates, deviance, sex roles, etc.). Like the natural scientist who must create indirect measures of the "invisible" objects and forces of the physical world, social researchers devise measures for difficult-to-observe aspects of the social world.

QUANTITATIVE AND QUALITATIVE MEASUREMENT

All social researchers use careful, systematic methods to gather high-quality data. Yet, qualitative and quantitative research each approaches the measurement process differently based on type of data and study design. Their approaches to measurement differ in four ways (see Table 5.1).

TABLE 5.1   Measurement in Quantitative and Qualitative Social Research

Measurement Process Area	Measurement in Quantitative Research	Measurement in Qualitative Research
Measurement Design Timing	Before data collection	During data collection
Final Data Form	Numbers	Many diverse formats
Links of Construct to Data	Sequential	Interactive
Process Direction	Largely deductive	Largely inductive

1. *Timing.* In a quantitative study, we think about variables and convert them into specific actions during a separate planning stage that happens before gathering or analyzing data. Measurement for qualitative research occurs during the data collection process.

2. *Data Form.* In quantitative research, we develop techniques that can produce quantitative data (i.e., data in the form of numbers). We move from abstract ideas to specific data collection techniques to precise numerical information. The numerical information is an empirical representation of the abstract ideas. In contrast, data for qualitative research comes in the form of numbers, written or spoken words, actions, sounds, symbols, physical objects, or visual images (e.g., maps, photographs, videos, etc.). Rather than convert all data into a single, common medium, numbers, in qualitative research we develop many ongoing measurement processes that produce data in diverse shapes, sizes, and forms.

3. *Linkages.* In all research, data are empirical representations of ideas or concepts and the measurement process links data to concepts. In quantitative studies, we follow a clear sequence: contemplate and reflect on concepts, and then develop preplanned measurement techniques that can bridge between concepts and data before collecting data. In qualitative research, we also reflect on ideas before data collection, but we continue to reflect on, refine, and develop new concepts while gathering and examining data. In an interactive process, we simultaneously examine and evaluate the data and reconsider and adjust the concepts. Thus, a measurement process is created "on the fly" based on what we encounter in the data and with concepts that are continuously being readjusted.

4. *Direction.* In quantitative research, we primarily follow a deductive path. We start with abstract ideas, create ways to measure the ideas, and end with empirical data. For a qualitative study, we primarily follow an inductive route.

Often we start with empirical data, generate abstract ideas based on the data, align ideas with the data, and end with an interconnected mix of ideas and data.

PARTS OF THE MEASUREMENT PROCESS

As you measure a concept, you are linking an idea or construct[1] to a measure (i.e., a technique, process, or procedure). The measurement procedure enables you to capture or observe the abstract idea (e.g., prejudice) in empirical data (e.g., survey results, a person's statements). Although a quantitative study has sequence and structure, the measurement process is not rigid and inflexible. As you develop measurement procedures, you may reflect on and refine the constructs because the process of developing a way to measure ideas can clarify them. Likewise, as you apply a measurement procedure to gather data, you might adjust the measurement technique to better align with or capture details of the specific data. Although you have flexibility and develop concepts inductively in a qualitative study, you will still rely on concepts from before you started data collection.

In both qualitative and quantitative studies you use two processes to measure your ideas or constructs about how the social world operates: conceptualization and operationalization. To conceptualize you take a construct and refine it by creating a conceptual or theoretical definition for it. A *conceptual definition* is a definition in abstract, theoretical terms. It refers to other ideas or constructs. There is no magical way for you to create a precise conceptual definition for a concept. You must think carefully, observe closely, consult with others, read what others have said, and try possible alternative definitions.

Here is an example. How might you develop a conceptual definition of the construct *prejudice*? When beginning to develop a conceptual definition, you can rely on multiple sources—personal experience and deep thinking, discussions with other people, and the existing scholarly literature. You might reflect on what you know about prejudice, ask others what they think about it, and go to the library and look up its many definitions. As you gather definitions, the core idea should get clearer. Nonetheless, you will have many definitions and need to sort them out. Most definitions state that prejudice is an attitude about another group and involves a prejudgment, or judging prior to getting specific information.

As you think about the construct, you may notice that all the definitions refer to prejudice as an attitude. Usually it is an attitude about the members of another group. There are many forms of prejudice, but most are negative views about persons of a different racial-ethnic group. Prejudice could be about other kinds of groups (e.g., people of a religion, of a physical stature, or from a certain region). It is always about a collectivity or group to which someone does not belong. Many constructs have multiple dimensions or types. You may consider whether there could be several different types of prejudice—racial prejudice, religious prejudice, age prejudice, gender prejudice, nation prejudice, and so forth.

You read about units of analysis in the last chapter. You need to consider the units of analysis that best fit your definition of the construct. So far, you know that prejudice is an attitude. Individuals hold and express attitudes, but so might groups (e.g., families, clubs, churches, companies, media outlets). You need to decide, do you want your definition of prejudice to include only the attitudes of individuals, or should it include attitudes held by groups, organizations, and institutions as well? Can you say, the school or newspaper was prejudiced? You also need to distinguish the construct from closely related ones. For example, how is prejudice similar to or different from ideas such as discrimination, stereotype, or racism?

Conceptualization is the process of carefully thinking through a construct's meaning.

At this stage, you decided that *prejudice* means an inflexible negative attitude held by an individual and directed toward a racial or ethnic out-group. Prejudice can, but does not always, lead to behavior, such as treating people unequally (i.e., discrimination). It generally relies on a person's stereotypes of out-group members. Thus, your initial idea, "Prejudice is a negative feeling," has become a precisely defined construct.

Even with all the conceptualization, you will need to be even more specific. For example, if prejudice is a negative attitude about a race or an ethnic group to which one does not belong, you must specify what you mean by *race* or *ethnic group*. You cannot assume that everyone sees racial-ethnic categories the same. Likewise, it is possible for someone to have a positive prejudgment. If so, is that a kind of positive prejudice? The main point is that conceptualization requires you to be very clear and state what you mean in very explicit terms for other people to see.

Operationalization links a conceptual definition to a specific set of things you do (i.e., measurement techniques or procedures). It is the construct's **operational definition** (i.e., a definition in terms of the specific operations of actions). An operational definition could be a survey questionnaire, a method of observing events in a field setting, a way to measure symbolic content in the mass media, or any process that reflects, documents, or represents the abstract construct in a conceptual definition.

Usually there are multiple ways to measure a construct. Some are better or worse, and some are more or less practical, than other ways. The key is to fit a measure to your specific conceptual definition. You must do this within practical constraints (e.g., time, money, available research participants, etc.). Your measure is also limited to the research techniques you know or can learn. You can develop a brand new measure from scratch, or you can borrow a measure other researchers already use (see Expansion Box 5.1).

EXPANSION BOX

5.1   Five Suggestions for Coming Up with a Measure

1. *Remember the conceptual definition.* The underlying principle for any measure is to match it to the specific conceptual definition of the construct that will be used in the study.

2. *Keep an open mind.* Do not get locked into a single measure or type of measure. Be creative and constantly look for better measures.

3. *Borrow from others.* Do not be afraid to borrow from other researchers, as long as credit is given. Good ideas for measures can be found in other studies or modified from other measures.

4. *Anticipate difficulties.* Logical and practical problems often arise when trying to measure variables of interest. Sometimes a problem can be anticipated and avoided with careful forethought and planning.

5. *Do not forget your units of analysis.* Your measure should fit with the units of analysis of the study and permit you to generalize to the universe of interest.

Operationalization connects the language of abstract ideas with that of concrete empirical measures. The world of theory is filled with abstract concepts, assumptions, relationships, definitions, and causality. Empirical measures describe how particular people talk or act in a concrete setting or what specific events have occurred. A measurement procedure or technique is a set of specific operations that indicate the presence of an abstract idea in observable reality.

Quantitative Conceptualization and Operationalization

As stated earlier, quantitative research measurement flows in a straightforward sequence: first conceptualization, next comes operationalization, followed by applying the operational definition or using it to measure as you collect the data. There are several ways to link abstract ideas to measurement procedures in rigorous ways that will yield precise quantitative data.

Figure 5.1 illustrates the measurement process for two variables. The variables are linked together both at the level of abstract theory and at the level of a testable empirical hypothesis. There are three levels to consider: conceptual, operational, and empirical. At the most abstract level, you want to examine the causal relationship between two abstract constructs. This is your **conceptual hypothesis**. At the level of operational definitions, you want to test an **empirical hypothesis** to learn whether specific measures, or indicators, are associated. This is the level at which you use correlations, statistics, questionnaires, and the like. The third level is the concrete empirical world in which real people live and breathe, laugh and cry, fight and love.

If you logically link the operational definition or measures of a variable (e.g., questionnaires) to an abstract construct (e.g., racial prejudice), you can connect what happens in the concrete social world to the level of abstract theory.

The measurement process links three levels: abstract theory, specific measures or indicators, and the concrete social reality of human activity. If you adopt a deductive path, you move from the abstract to the concrete. First, you conceptualize a variable and assign it a clear conceptual definition. Next, you operationalize the variable; that is, you develop an operational definition for it. Last, you apply the operational definition in empirical reality or the concrete social world, and test empirical hypotheses. By using good measures of variables, you carefully build links between abstract ideas and empirical reality. This enables you to connect the results of empirical hypotheses back to conceptual hypotheses, and these are part of abstract theories that explain how the world works. In this way, measurement links abstract theory to empirical data.

FIGURE 5.1   Conceptualization and Operationalization

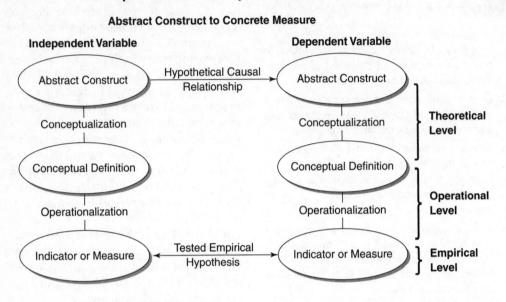

Abstract Construct to Concrete Measure

A hypothesis has at least two variables. You must apply the processes of conceptualization and operationalization to each variable. In the preceding example, prejudice is not a hypothesis. It is one variable. It could be a dependent variable caused by something else, or it could be an independent variable causing something else. It depends on your theoretical explanation.

To illustrate the measurement process, let us look at the explanatory, quantitative study you read about in Chapter 1 by Sharp and Joslyn on tolerance in U.S. cities. The researchers had two main variables in a causal hypothesis. Their independent variable was a subculture that supported "new" or "unconventional" politics. The presence of people with certain attitudes and a large number of the "creative class" in a city sustained such a subculture. Their dependent variable was racial tolerance. The *conceptual hypothesis* was that cities vary by subculture, with some subcultures supporting "new" or "unconventional" politics. In such cities, they hypothesized the subculture also encourages racial tolerance. The researchers relied on

another person's theory of the creative class and a theory of how certain subcultures support a "new" nontraditional political life in a city. The creative class includes certain occupations—scientists and professionals in architecture and design or in the entertainment industry. Sharp and Joslyn mention other features that sustain the subculture, including a high score on

> a creativity index consisting of the extent to which the workforce is in one of the "creative class" occupations noted above, the area's innovativeness (measured by patented innovations per capita), the share of the area's economic output that is from high-tech industry, and the prevalence of gays in the population. (2008:574)

We look at indexes later in this chapter. Other features sustaining a subculture of unconventional politics included many people who were not highly religious, who self-identified as political liberals, who had a college or graduate educations, and who were young to middle-age adults.

The researchers focused on 27 U.S. cities. They *operationalized* a supportive subculture using a combination of indicators: an average educational level, average population age, percentage of residents self-identifying as liberal on an ideology scale (scales are discussed later in this chapter), percent of people saying religion was not central to their lives, and the "creativity index" mentioned in the quote above. Thus, the researchers operationalized the subculture using data from the census and a survey of residents in the 27 cities. They operationalized the dependent variable with one survey question asked of Whites in the 27 cities. They asked how accepting the person would be if a family member married a Black person.

Sharp and Joslyn tested their hypothesis by examining the statistical relationship between a city's rank on measures of a subculture that sustains unconventional politics, especially the creativity index, and the percent of White residents who indicated racial tolerance. They found for their hypothesis that racial tolerance was highest in cities with a "new politics" subculture.

Qualitative Conceptualization and Operationalization

Conceptualization. The conceptualization process in a qualitative research study differs from that in quantitative research. Instead of refining abstract ideas into theoretical definitions early in the research process, in a qualitative study you refine rudimentary "working ideas" during the data collection and analysis process. You form coherent theoretical definitions as you struggle to "make sense" or organize the data and the preliminary ideas.

As you gather and analyze qualitative data, you will develop new concepts, formulate definitions for the concepts, and consider relationships among the concepts. Eventually, you want to link concepts to one another to create theoretical relationships. These may or may not be causal. In addition to using existing ideas, you construct new concepts as you examine the qualitative data (i.e., field notes, photos and maps, historical documents, etc.). Often, this involves asking theoretical questions about the data (e.g., Is this a case of class conflict? What is the sequence of events and could it be different? Why did this happen here and not somewhere else?).

In a qualitative study, you conceptualize by developing clear, explicit definitions of constructs. You form conceptual definitions out of rudimentary "working ideas" that you developed and used as you gathered and reflected on the data. The definitions are somewhat abstract and linked to other ideas, but usually they are tied closely to specific data. You might illustrate the concepts using the words and concrete actions of the people you have studied. In qualitative research, the data mold the conceptualization process.

Operationalization. In qualitative studies, operationalization differs from that in quantitative research, and it often precedes conceptualization. Instead of turning refined conceptual definitions into measurement operations, you operationalize by describing how specific observations and thoughts about the data contributed to your working ideas that became conceptual definitions and theoretical concepts. In short, operationalization in qualitative research is an after-the-fact description more than a before-the-fact preplanned technique. Almost in a reverse of the quantitative process, you gather data with or prior to full operationalization.

Just as quantitative operationalization does not follow a rigid deductive process, the process in a study is one of mutual interaction. You will often draw on ideas from other studies and go beyond the data of a specific research setting. Qualitative operationalization is a description of how you gathered and reflected on the data. In qualitative research, the ideas and empirical evidence are mutually interdependent.

The qualitative research study by Rhomberg (2010) on the Detroit newspaper strike that you read about in Chapter 1 illustrates how qualitative operationalization can occur. The qualitative study describes the five-and-a-half year strike that was among the most significant of the second half of the twentieth century. The central concept in the study is a "signal juncture."

Rhomberg developed the concept as he conducted the study. He connected the concept to other theoretical ideas, including the closely related idea of a "critical juncture." A critical juncture is when historical events come to a point, and can follow one of two future directions or paths. If one path is followed, it will "lock in" a set of political forces and patterns that will push a long series of future events, activities, and institutions in one direction instead of another. He says, "The signal juncture reveals moments in which one path has gained (or retains) the advantage" (p. 1855). The critical juncture is a crossroads, after which historical events take a certain direction. The signal juncture is the point during a critical juncture at which the major "players" or actors become fully aware of the stakes involved. It is when and how key actors recognize they are at a historic critical juncture that will lead to different future paths. They also see that one set of social–political forces has reached the "tipping point" and henceforth it will direct the direction of events.

Rhomberg operationalized signal juncture by providing readers with a highly detailed account of specific historical events. He discussed management and unionized labor relations throughout the twentieth century and outlined several systems or patterns of labor-management relations. He noted that a new, qualitatively different pattern of strikes and labor relations arose in the 1980s. The Detroit newspaper strike broke from this established pattern. The strike was far larger, more violent and radical, and widespread than any labor dispute in decades. This occurred due to specific features of the newspaper industry, labor relations in the city of Detroit, and the newspaper company involved. The union was very organized and had many supporters. The newspaper management was part of the country's largest chain and was very aggressive toward the union, refusing all union demands and spending over $40 million for private security forces. In the end, newspaper management won. The victory by management "set a new standard in labor relations nationwide and prefigured subsequent mass lockouts" (p. 1863).

Rhomberg (2010) provided readers with a close look at his data (e.g., interviews, transcripts, and written documents) and a description of how he came to assign specific meanings and significance to the data. The strike was a signal juncture because the highly unusual and strong union response threatened to redirect a major national pattern of labor relations that had become entrenched in the previous decade. The pattern appeared in legal rulings, strike activity, labor-management relations, economic trends, and political forces. The Detroit strike introduced new issues and was a "rival path" to the 1980s pattern. Thus, the Detroit strike represented a collision of two possible paths of labor relations. During the collision, the major parties directly involved (i.e., newspaper union and management) as well as many others (i.e., the national business community and labor union confederation) recognized the "signal" that the situation had reached a historic turning point. They saw that subsequent labor-management relations either would continue along the 1980s pattern, or it would diverge to follow a new path.

After showing readers how the signal juncture idea clarified events of the Detroit strike, Rhomberg next discussed how the idea also applies to other situations. He first operationalized the idea of a signal juncture (i.e., linked data with concept) in the Detroit strike study. Next, he showed how the abstract concept had a general applicability to many other historic turning points.

RELIABILITY AND VALIDITY

Reliability and validity are central issues in all measurement. Both concern how you connect concrete measures to abstract constructs. Reliability and validity are salient because social theory has ambiguous, diffuse constructs that are not directly observable. Perfect reliability and validity are virtually impossible to achieve. Rather, they are ideals for which all researchers strive.

All social researchers want reliable and valid measures because it helps to establish the truthfulness, credibility, and believability of findings. Both terms also have multiple meanings. Here, they refer to related, desirable aspects of measurement.

Reliability means dependability or consistency. It suggests that repeated, stable outcomes are the same under identical or similar conditions. The opposite of a reliable measure is one that yields erratic, unstable, or inconsistent outcomes.

Validity suggests truthfulness. It refers to matching a construct, or conceptual definition, with a specific measure. It tells us how well an idea about social reality "fits" with actual, empirical reality. The absence of validity indicates poor fit between a construct you use to describe, theorize, or analyze the social world and what occurs in the actual social world. In simple terms, validity addresses the question, How well does the social reality you measure in a study match the ideas you use to explain and understand it?

Both qualitative and quantitative researchers want reliable and valid measurement, but beyond an agreement on the basic ideas, each sees reliability and validity differently.

Reliability and Validity in Quantitative Research

Reliability.
As just stated, reliability means dependability. In a quantitative study, it means that the numerical measure does not vary because of characteristics of the measurement process or the measurement instrument itself. For example, I get on my bathroom scale and read my weight. I get off and get on again and again. My scale is reliable if it gives me the same weight each time—assuming, of course, that I am not eating, drinking, changing clothing, and so forth. An unreliable scale registers different weights each time, even when my "true" weight does not change. Another example is my car speedometer. If I drive along at a constant slow speed on a level surface, but the speedometer needle jumps from one end to the other, my speedometer is not a reliable indicator of how fast I am traveling.

How to Improve Reliability. It is rare to have perfect reliability. You can improve the reliability of measures in four ways: (1) clearly conceptualize constructs, (2) use a precise level of measurement, (3) use multiple indicators, and (4) use pilot-tests.

Clearly Conceptualize All Constructs. Reliability increases when you measure a single construct or subdimension of a construct. This means developing unambiguous, clear theoretical definitions. You should specify constructs to eliminate "noise" (i.e., distracting or interfering information) from other nearby constructs. Each measure should indicate one and only one concept. Otherwise, it is impossible to determine which concept is being "indicated." For example, the indicator of a pure chemical compound is more reliable than one in which the chemical is mixed with other material or dirt. In the latter case, it is difficult to separate the "noise" of other material from the pure chemical.

Increase the Level of Measurement. We discuss levels of measurement later. Indicators at higher or more precise levels of measurement are more likely to be reliable than less precise measures because the latter pick up less detailed information. If you measure more specific information, then it is less likely that you will capture something other than the construct of interest. The general principle is: Try to measure at the most precise level possible. However, it is more difficult to measure at higher levels of measurement. For example, if I have a choice of measuring prejudice as either high or low, or to use 10 categories from extremely low to extremely high, it would be better to measure it in 10 refined categories.

Use Multiple Indicators of a Variable.   A third way to increase reliability is to use multiple indicators, because two (or more) indicators of the same construct are better than one. Figure 5.2 illustrates the use of multiple indicators in hypothesis testing. Three indicators of the one independent variable construct are combined into an overall measure, *A,* and two indicators of a dependent variable are combined into a single measure, *B.*

For example, I create three indicators of the variable, racial-ethnic prejudice. My first indicator is an attitude question on a survey. I ask research participants their beliefs and feelings about many different racial and ethnic groups. For a second indicator, I observe research participants from various races and ethnic groups interacting together over the course of three days. I look for those who regularly either

(1) avoid eye contact, appear to be tense, and sound cool and distant; or (2) make eye contact, appear relaxed, and sound warm and friendly as they interact with people of their same or with people of a different racial-ethnic group. Last, I create an experiment. I ask research participants to read the grade transcripts, resumes, and interview reports on 30 applicants for five jobs—youth volunteer coordinator, office manager, janitor, clothing store clerk, and advertising account executive. The applicants have many qualifications, but I secretly manipulate their racial or ethnic group to see whether a research participant decides on the best applicant for the jobs based on an applicant's race and ethnicity.

Multiple indicators let you take measurements from a wider range of the content of a conceptual definition. You can measure different aspects of the construct, each with its own indicator. In addition, one indicator (e.g., one question on a questionnaire) may be imperfect, but several measures are less likely to have the same (systematic) error. Multiple indicator measures tend to be more stable than measures with one item.

Use Pretests, Pilot Studies, and Replication.   You can improve reliability by using a pretest or pilot version of a measure first. Develop one or more

FIGURE 5.2   Measurement Using Multiple Indicators

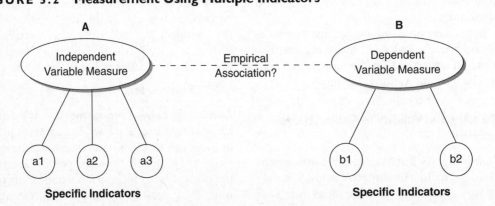

draft or preliminary versions of a measure and try them before applying the final version in a hypothesis-testing situation. This takes more time and effort.

The principle of using pilot-tests extends to replicating the measures other researchers have used. For example, I search the literature and find measures of prejudice from past research. I may want to build on and use a previous measure if it is a good one, citing the source, of course. In addition, I may want to add new indicators and compare them to the previous measure.

Validity.   *Validity* is an overused term. Sometimes, it means "true" or "correct." There are several general types of validity. Here, we are concerned with **measurement validity.** There are also several types of measurement validity. Nonmeasurement types of validity are discussed later.

When you say that an indicator is valid, it is valid for a particular purpose and definition. The same indicator can be valid for one purpose (i.e., a research question with units of analysis and universe) but less valid or invalid for others. For example, the measure of prejudice discussed here might be valid for measuring prejudice among teachers but invalid for measuring the prejudice of police officers.

At its core, measurement validity refers to how well the conceptual and operational definitions mesh with each other: The better the fit, the greater the measurement validity. Validity is more difficult to achieve than reliability. We cannot have absolute confidence about validity, but some measures are *more valid* than others. The reason we can never achieve absolute validity is that constructs are abstract ideas, whereas indicators refer to concrete observation. This is the gap between your mental pictures about the world and the specific things you do at particular times and places. Validity is part of a dynamic process that grows by accumulating evidence over time. Without it, all measurement becomes meaningless.

Three Types of Measurement Validity

Face Validity.   The easiest to achieve and the most basic kind of validity is **face validity**. It is a judgment by the scientific community that the indicator really measures the construct. It addresses the question, On the face of it, do most people believe that the definition and method of measurement fit? It is a consensus method. For example, few people would accept a measure of college student math ability using a question that asked students: $2 + 2 = ?$ This is not a valid measure of college-level math ability on the face of it. Recall that in the scientific community, aspects of research are scrutinized by others. See Table 5.2 for a summary of types of measurement validity.

Content Validity.   **Content validity** is a special type of face validity. It addresses the question, Is the full content of a definition represented in a measure? A conceptual definition holds ideas; it is a "space" containing ideas and concepts. Measures should represent all ideas or areas in the conceptual space. Content validity involves three steps. First, specify fully the entire content in a construct's definition. Next, sample from all areas of the definition. Finally, develop an indicator that taps all of the parts of the definition.

An example of content validity is my definition of *feminism* as a person's commitment to a set of beliefs creating full equality between men and women in areas of the arts,

---

TABLE 5.2   Summary of Measurement Validity Types

Validity (True Measure)
Face—in the judgment of others
Content—captures the entire meaning
Criterion—agrees with an external source
• Concurrent—agrees with a preexisting measure
• Predictive—agrees with future behavior

intellectual pursuits, family, work, politics, and authority relations. I create a measure of feminism in which I ask two survey questions: (1) Should men and women get equal pay for equal work? and (2) Should men and women share household tasks? My measure has low content validity because the two questions ask only about pay and household tasks. They ignore the other areas (intellectual pursuits, politics, authority relations, and other aspects of work and family). For a content-valid measure, I must either expand the measure or narrow the definition.

Criterion Validity. **Criterion validity** uses some standard or criterion to indicate a construct accurately. The validity of an indicator is verified by comparing it with another measure of the same construct that is widely accepted. There are two subtypes of this kind of validity: concurrent validity and predictive validity.

Concurrent Validity. To have **concurrent validity**, an indicator must be associated with a preexisting indicator that is judged to be valid (i.e., it has face validity). For example, you create a new test to measure intelligence. For it to be concurrently valid, it should be highly associated with existing IQ tests (assuming the same definition of intelligence is used). This means that most people who score high on the old measure should also score high on the new one, and vice versa. The two measures may not be perfectly associated, but if they measure the same or a similar construct, it is logical for them to yield similar results.

Predictive Validity. Criterion validity whereby an indicator predicts future events that are logically related to a construct is called **predictive validity**. You cannot use it for all measures. The measure and the action predicted must be distinct from but indicate the same construct. Do not confuse predictive measurement validity with prediction in hypothesis testing, where one variable predicts a different variable in the

future. For example, the Scholastic Assessment Test (SAT) that many U.S. high school students take measures scholastic aptitude—the ability of a student to perform in college. If the SAT has high predictive validity, then students who get high SAT scores will subsequently do well in college. If students with high scores perform the same as students with average or low scores, then the SAT has low predictive validity.

Another way to test predictive validity is to select a group of people who have specific characteristics and predict how they will score (very high or very low) vis-à-vis the construct. For example, I have a measure of political conservatism. I predict that members of conservative groups (e.g., John Birch Society, Conservative Caucus, Daughters of the American Revolution, Moral Majority) will score high on it, whereas members of liberal groups (e.g., Democratic Socialists, People for the American Way, Americans for Democratic Action) will score low. I "validate" the measure with the groups—that is, I pilot-test it by using it on members of the groups. It can then be used as a measure of political conservatism for the general public.

Reliability and Validity in Qualitative Research

Most qualitative researchers accept the principles of reliability and validity, but use the terms infrequently because of their close association with quantitative measurement. In addition, qualitative researchers apply the principles differently in practice.

Reliability. As stated earlier, *reliability* means dependability or consistency. Qualitative researchers use a variety of techniques (e.g., interviews, participation, photographs, document studies, etc.) to record their observations consistently. They want to be consistent (i.e., not vacillating and erratic) in how, over time, they make observations. One difficulty is that they often study processes that are not stable over time. Moreover, they emphasize the value of a changing or developing interaction between a researcher and the people or events he or she studies.

Qualitative researchers believe that the subject matter and a researcher's relationship to it should be a growing, evolving process. The metaphor for the relationship between a researcher and the data is one of an evolving relationship or living organism (e.g., a plant) that naturally matures. Most qualitative researchers resist the quantitative approach to reliability, which they see as a cold, fixed mechanical instrument that one repeatedly injects into or applies to some static, lifeless material.

Qualitative researchers consider a range of data sources and employ multiple measurement methods. They accept that different researchers or that the same researcher using alternative measures will get distinctive results. This is because qualitative researchers see data collection as an interactive process in which particular researchers operate in an evolving setting and the setting's context dictates using a unique mix of measures that cannot be repeated. The diverse measures and interactions with different researchers are beneficial because they can illuminate different facets or dimensions of a subject matter. Many qualitative researchers question the quantitative researcher's quest for standard, fixed measures. They fear that such measures ignore the benefits of having a variety of researchers with many approaches and may neglect key aspects of diversity that exist in the social world.

Validity.   *Validity* means truthful. It refers to the bridge between a construct and the data. Qualitative researchers are more interested in authenticity than validity. *Authenticity* means giving a fair, honest, and balanced account of social life from the viewpoint of someone who lives it. Qualitative researchers are less concerned with trying to match an abstract concept to empirical data and more concerned with providing a candid portrayal of social life that

is true to the experiences of people being studied. Most qualitative researchers concentrate on ways to capture an inside view and provide a detailed account of how those being studied feel about and understand events.

Qualitative researchers have developed several substitutes for the quantitative approach to validity. The substitutes emphasize conveying the insider's view to others. Historical researchers use internal and external criticisms (discussed in Chapter 12) to determine whether the evidence they have is real or they believe it to be. Qualitative researchers adhere to the core principle of validity, to be truthful (i.e., avoid false or distorted accounts). They try to create a tight fit between their understanding, ideas, and statements about the social world and what is actually occurring in it.

Relationship between Reliability and Validity

Reliability is needed for validity and is easier to achieve than validity. Although reliability is necessary to create a valid measure of a concept, it does not guarantee that a measure will be valid. It is not a sufficient condition for validity. A measure can produce the same result over and over (i.e., it has reliability), but may not measure the construct as defined (i.e., validity).

Here is an example of a reliable but invalid measure. I get on a scale and look at the weight indicated. The weight registered by the scale is the same each time I get on and off. I then go to another scale—an "official" one that measures true weight. It reports my weight as twice as great. The first scale yielded reliable (i.e., dependable) results but was not a valid measure of my weight.

A diagram might help you see the relationship between reliability and validity. Figure 5.3 illustrates the relationship between validity and reliability using the analogy of a target. The bull's-eye represents a perfect fit between the measure and the definition of the construct.

FIGURE 5.3   **Illustration of Relationship between Reliability and Validity**

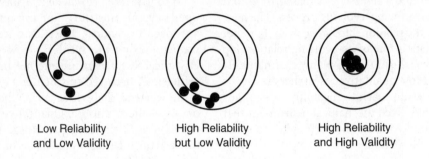

A Bull's-Eye = A Perfect Measure

Low Reliability
and Low Validity

High Reliability
but Low Validity

High Reliability
and High Validity

Source: Adapted version of Figure 5.2 An Analogy to Validity and Reliability, page 155 from Babbie, E. R. 1986.
The Practice of Social Research, Fourth Edition. Belmont, CA: Wadsworth Publishing Company.

Validity and *reliability* are usually complementary concepts, but they can conflict with each other. At times, as validity increases, reliability becomes more difficult to attain, and vice versa. This happens when you have a vague, abstract, and difficult to observe construct. Reliability is easiest to achieve when you measure something specific, concrete, and observable. A strain arises between having a highly abstract construct and applying specific, concrete procedures to observe and capture its true meaning. For example, the social science construct "alienation" is abstract, subjective, and impossible to see directly. It means a deep inner sense of loss of a person's humanity that diffuses across many aspects of one's life (e.g., social relations, sense of self, orientation toward nature). It suggests feeling an inner loss, being detached from people and human activity, and an inability to engage and connect with others or humanity generally. If you use six specific, concrete questions about alienation on a questionnaire to measure the construct, you may have a reliable measure. However, we can ask whether answering six specific questions can really capture the diffuse, subjective essence of the concept, alienation.

Other Uses of the Terms *Reliable* and *Valid*

Many words have multiple definitions, including *reliability* and *validity*. This creates confusion unless we distinguish among alternative uses of the same word.

Reliability.   We use *reliability* in everyday language. A reliable person is dependable, stable, and responsible. You can depend on and trust a reliable car. It means the person will behave in similar, predictable ways across times and conditions. We can say the same for the car. It always starts without any problem and operates consistently. In addition to measurement reliability, you may hear researchers say a study or its results are reliable. Study or results reliability means that other researchers can replicate the method of conducting a study or the results from it.

Internal Validity.   **Internal validity** means there are no errors internal to the design of the research project. The term is used to discuss experimental research and concerns possible errors or alternative explanations that may arise despite attempts to institute controls. High internal validity means there are few such errors. Low internal validity means that such errors are likely (you will learn more about internal validity in Chapter 8).

External Validity.   *External validity* also is a term from experimental research. It is the ability to generalize findings from a specific setting and small group to a broad range of settings and people. It addresses the question, If something happens in a laboratory or among a particular type of research participants (e.g., college students), can we generalize findings to the "real" (nonlaboratory) world or to the public (nonstudents)? High external validity means we can generalize results to many situations and people. Low external validity means that the results apply only to a very specific setting (you will learn more about external validity in Chapter 8).

Statistical Validity.   *Statistical validity* means that a researcher has used the correct statistical procedure and met the procedure's assumptions. Different statistical tests or procedures are appropriate for different conditions. All statistical procedures rely on assumptions about the mathematical properties of the numbers involved. Statistical results can be invalid and the results nonsense if you violate the procedure's assumptions. For example, to compute an average (actually the mean, which is discussed in Chapter 10), you cannot use information at the nominal level of measurement (to be discussed later in this chapter). For example, suppose I measure the race of a group of students. I assign each racial group a number: White = 1, African American = 2, Asian = 3, other = 4. It is nonsense to say that the "mean" race of a class of students is 1.9 (almost African American?). This is a misuse of the statistical procedure, and the results are invalid even if the computation is correct. Professional statisticians take great interest

in the degree to which statistical assumptions can be violated or bent (the technical term is *robustness*).

A GUIDE TO QUANTITATIVE MEASUREMENT

Thus far, you have learned about the principles of measurement, including reliability and validity. Quantitative researchers have developed specialized measurement procedures to help them create operational definitions that are reliable and valid measures. This section of the chapter is a brief guide to these ideas and a few of the measures.

Levels of Measurement

Levels of measurement is an abstract but important and widely used idea. Basically, it says that you have a variety of basic ways to measure a construct. Some are at a higher, more refined level with more detailed information, and other ways are lower, less precise with not as much detailed information. The level of measurement depends, in part, on how you conceptualize a construct—that is, assumptions about whether the construct has particular characteristics. The level of measurement will connect basic assumptions within a construct's definition and how you specifically measure the construct. The way in which you conceptualize a variable will restrict the levels of measurement, in turn, it has implications for how to measure variables and what types of statistical analysis you will be able to use.

Continuous and Discrete Variables.   We can first divide variables into two basic types: continuous or discrete. Quantitative research uses both types, but relies mostly on continuous variables. If qualitative research uses variables, most variables tend to be the discrete type.

Continuous variables have an infinite number of values or attributes that flow along a continuum. The values can be divided into many smaller increments; in mathematical theory, there are an infinite number of increments. Examples of continuous variables include temperature, age, income, crime rate, and amount of schooling.

Discrete variables have a relatively fixed set of separate values or variable attributes. Instead of a smooth continuum of values, discrete variables contain distinct categories. Examples of discrete variables include gender (male or female), religion (Protestant, Catholic, Jewish, Muslim, atheist), and marital status (single, married, divorced or separated, widowed). Whether a variable is continuous or discrete affects its level of measurement.

Four Levels of Measurement

Precision and Levels. The idea of levels of measurement expands on the difference between continuous and discrete variables. It also organizes types of variables for later statistical analysis. The four *levels of measurement* categorize the degree of precision of measurement.

How you conceptualize a construct can limit how precisely you will be able to measure it. For example, it is possible to reconceptualize some of the variables listed earlier as continuous into discrete variables. For example, temperature is usually a continuous variable (e.g., degrees, fractions of degrees), but it is also possible to measure it with discrete categories (e.g., hot or cold). Likewise, age is

usually a continuous variable (e.g., how old a person is in years, months, days, hours, and minutes), but we sometimes treat it as a few discrete categories (infancy, childhood, adolescence, young adulthood, middle age, old age).

While you can often reconceptualize continuous variables into discrete ones; it does not work the other way around. Most discrete variables cannot be reconceptualized as continuous variables. For example, sex, religion, and marital status cannot be conceptualized as continuous. However, you can conceptualize related constructs as continuous (e.g., femininity, degree of religiousness, commitment to a marital relationship, etc.).

The above discussion gives you a practical reason to conceptualize and measure variables at higher levels of measurement. You can always collapse higher levels of measurement to lower levels, but the reverse is not true. In other words, it is possible to measure a construct very precisely, gather very specific information, and then ignore some of the precision. But, it is not possible to measure a construct with less precision or with less specific information and then make it more precise later.

Distinguishing among the Four Levels. The four levels from lowest to greatest or highest precision are nominal, ordinal, interval, and ratio. Each level gives a different type of information (see Table 5.3).

TABLE 5.3   Characteristics of the Four Levels of Measurement

Level	Different Categories	Ranked	Distance between Categories Measured	True Zero
Nominal	Yes			
Ordinal	Yes	Yes		
Interval	Yes	Yes	Yes	
Ratio	Yes	Yes	Yes	Yes

- *Nominal* measures are discrete and indicate only that there is a difference among categories (e.g., religion: Protestant, Catholic, Jewish, Muslim; racial heritage: African, Asian, Caucasian, Hispanic, other).
- *Ordinal* measures are also discrete. They indicate a difference, *plus* the categories can be ordered or ranked (e.g., letter grades: A, B, C, D, F; opinion measures: strongly agree, agree, disagree, strongly disagree).
- *Interval* measures are continuous. They do everything the nominal and ordinal measures do, *plus* you can specify the amount of distance between categories (e.g., Fahrenheit or Celsius temperature: 5°, 45°, 90°; IQ scores: 95, 110, 125). Arbitrary zeroes may be used in interval measures; they are just there to help keep score.
- *Ratio* measures are also continuous. They do everything all the other levels do, *plus* there is a true zero. A true zero makes it possible to state relations in terms of proportion or ratios (e.g., money income: $10, $100, $500; years of formal schooling: 1 year, 10 years, 13 years).

In most practical situations, the distinction between interval and ratio levels makes little difference. The arbitrary zeroes used in some interval measures confuse many people, and people mistake the arbitrary zeroes for "true" zeroes. The zeroes look identical but have different meanings. An arbitrary zero is when the symbol for the number zero is placed on a continuum as a "place holder" but it does not carry the meaning of a true zero (i.e., nothing, or a dividing place between positive and negative numbers). Arbitrary zeroes appear in the measurement of temperature. For example, a rise in temperature from 30 to 60 Fahrenheit degrees is not really a doubling of the temperature, although the numbers double. This is because zero degrees is not the absence of all heat. You can see that the zero is arbitrary by comparing zero in a Celsius scale to the same actual temperature in Fahrenheit, where

the zero is valued at 32 degrees. Zero weight means the absence of weight; a zero in money means the absence of money. These are true and not arbitrary zeroes. Mathematical operations require the zero to be a true zero.

You can always covert a ratio-level measure into an interval, ordinal, or nominal level. You can also convert the interval level the ordinal or nominal level, but the process does not work in the opposite way!

When using the ordinal level, you generally want to use at least five ordinal categories and obtain many observations. This is because the distortion created by collapsing a continuous construct into a smaller number of ordered categories is minimized as the number of categories and the number of observations increase.

The ratio level of measurement is rarely used in the social sciences. For most purposes, it is indistinguishable from interval measurement. The only difference is that ratio measurement has a "true zero." In addition to the temperature example described above, another common example of arbitrary—not true—zeroes occurs when measuring attitudes where numbers are assigned to statements (e.g., 21 = disagree, 0 = no opinion, +1 = agree). True zeroes exist for variables such as income, age, or years of education. Examples of the four levels of measurement are shown in Table 5.4.

Specialized Measures: Scales and Indexes

Over the years, social researchers have created thousands of different scales and indexes to measure social variables. For example, they have developed scales and indexes to measure the degree of formalization in bureaucratic organizations, the prestige of occupations, the adjustment of people to a marriage, the intensity of group interaction, the level of social activity in a community, the degree to which a state's sexual assault laws reflect feminist values, and the level

TABLE 5.4   Examples of Levels of Measurement

Variable (Level of Measurement)	How Variable Measured
Religion (nominal)	Different religious denominations (Jewish, Catholic, Lutheran, Baptist) are not ranked, just different (unless one belief is conceptualized as closer to heaven).
Attendance (ordinal)	"How often do you attend religious services? (0) Never, (1) less than once a year, (3) several times a year, (4) about once a month, (5) two or three times a week, or (8) several times a week?" This might have been measured at a ratio level if the exact number of times a person attended was asked instead.
IQ Score (interval)	Most intelligence tests are organized with 100 as average, middle, or normal. Scores higher or lower indicate distance from the average. Someone with a score of 115 has somewhat above average measured intelligence for people who took the test, while 90 is slightly below. Scores of below 65 or above 140 are rare.
Age (ratio)	Age is measured by years of age. There is a true zero (birth). Note that a 40-year-old has lived twice as long as a 20-year-old.

of national socioeconomic development. There is no space in this book to discuss the thousands of scales and indexes. Instead, we can focus on principles of scale and index construction and explore a few major types.

Keep two things in mind. First, social science rests on the assumption that in some way we can measure, with greater or less accuracy, virtually every social phenomenon. Some constructs can be measured directly and yield precise numerical values (e.g., family income). Other constructs require the use of surrogates or proxies that indirectly measure a variable and may not be as precise (e.g., predisposition to commit a crime). In other words, there is some direct or indirect empirical manifestation of our constructs about the social world. Second, you can learn a lot from the measures used by other researchers. You are fortunate to have the work of thousands of researchers to draw on. It is not always necessary to start from scratch. You can use a past scale or index, or you can modify it for your own purposes.

Indexes and Scales.   You might find the terms *index* and *scale* confusing for good reason; they are often used interchangeably. One researcher's scale can be another's index. Both produce ordinal- or interval-level measures of a variable. To add to the confusion of terms, you can combine the techniques of scale and index construction in one measure. Scales and indexes give you more information about variables than very simple measures. They may also make it possible for you to assess the quality of measurement. Scales and indexes increase reliability and validity. They also aid in data reduction; that is, they condense and simplify the information that is collected (see Expansion Box 5.2).

Mutually Exclusive and Exhaustive Attributes.   Before discussing scales and indexes, it is important to review a few features of good measurement. The attributes of all measures, including nominal-level measures, should be mutually exclusive and exhaustive.

5.2   Scales and Indexes: Are They Different?

Social researchers do not use a consistent nomenclature to distinguish between them.

A *scale* is a measure in which a researcher captures the intensity, direction, level, or potency of a variable construct. It arranges responses or observations on a continuum. A scale can use a single indicator or multiple indicators. Most are at the ordinal level of measurement.

An *index* is a measure in which a researcher adds or combines several distinct indicators of a construct into a single score. This composite score is often a simple sum of the multiple indicators. It is used for content and convergent validity. Indexes are often measured at the interval or ratio level.

Researchers sometimes combine the features of scales and indexes in a single measure. This is common when a researcher has several indicators that are scales (i.e., that measure intensity or direction). He or she then adds these indicators together to yield a single score, thereby creating an index.

Mutually exclusive means that an individual or case fits into one and only one attribute of a variable. For example, you have a variable to measure type of religious belief—with the attribute being Christian, non-Christian, and Jewish. Such a measure is not mutually exclusive because Judaism is both a non-Christian religion and a Jewish religion. A Jewish person can fit into both the non-Christian and the Jewish categories. Here is another example. You have a variable measuring type of city. Its attributes are river port city, state capital, and interstate highway exit. This measure also is not mutually exclusive. One city could be all three (a river port state capital with an interstate exit), any one of the three, or none of the three.

Exhaustive attributes means that all cases fit into one of the attributes of a variable. When measuring religion, a measure with the attributes

Catholic, Protestant, and Jewish is not exclusive. People with Buddhist, Islamic, Hindu, or agnostic beliefs do not fit anywhere. Your measure's attributes should make certain that every possible situation is covered. For example, Catholic, Protestant, Jewish, or other is an exclusive and mutually exclusive set of attributes.

Unidimensionality. In addition to being mutually exclusive and exhaustive, scales and indexes should also be unidimensional. *Unidimensionality* means that all the items in a scale or index fit together, or measure a single construct. Unidimensionality was suggested in discussions of content and concurrent validity. Unidimensionality says: If you combine several specific pieces of information into a single score or measure, make certain that all the pieces work together and measure the same thing. There is a statistical measure called Cronbach's alpha to assess unidimensionality. Alpha ranges from a maximum of 1.0 for a perfect score to zero. To be considered a good measure, the alpha should be .70 or higher.

You may think there is an apparent contradiction between using a scale or index to combine several parts or subparts of a construct into one measure and the criteria of unidimensionality. You may wonder how a construct can have multiple parts yet all be a single thing or unidimensional. It is only an apparent contradiction because we can define constructs theoretically at different levels of abstraction. General, higher-level, or more abstract constructs can contain several subparts; each subpart is at a lower level of abstraction and is a part of the highly abstract construct's overall content.

For example, I define the construct "feminist ideology" as a general ideology about gender. Feminist ideology is a highly abstract and general construct. It includes specific beliefs and attitudes toward social, economic, political, family, and sexual relations. The ideology's five belief areas are parts of the single general construct. The parts are mutually reinforcing and together form a system of beliefs about the dignity, strength, and power of women.

If feminist ideology is unidimensional, then it suggests there is a unified belief system that varies from very antifeminist to very profeminist. We can test the validity of the measure that includes multiple indicators that tap the construct's subparts. If one belief area (e.g., sexual relations) is consistently distinct from the other areas in empirical tests, then we question its unidimensionality.

Another reason it is easy to become confused is because you can use a specific measure as an indicator of a unidimensional construct in one situation, and to indicate a part of a different construct in another situation. This is possible because you can use constructs that are at different levels of abstraction.

For example, a person's attitude toward gender equality with regard to pay is more specific and less abstract than feminist ideology (i.e., beliefs about gender relations throughout society). An attitude toward equal pay can be both a unidimensional construct in its own right and a subpart of the more general and abstract unidimensional construct, *ideology toward gender relations*.

INDEX CONSTRUCTION

The Purpose

You hear about indexes all the time. For example, U.S. newspapers report the Federal Bureau of Investigation (FBI) crime index and the consumer price index (CPI). The FBI index is the sum of police reports on seven so-called index crimes (criminal homicide, aggravated assault, forcible rape, robbery, burglary, larceny of $50 or more, and auto theft). It began with the Uniform Crime Report in 1930. The CPI, which is a measure of inflation, is created by totaling the cost of buying a list of goods and services (e.g., food, rent, and utilities) and comparing the total to the cost of buying the same list in the previous year. The U.S. Bureau of Labor Statistics has used the consumer price index since 1919; wage increases, union contracts, and Social Security payments

are based on it. An *index* is a combination of items into a single numerical score. Various components or subparts of a construct are each measured, then combined into one measure.

There are many types of indexes. For example, if you take an exam with 25 questions, the total number of questions correct is a kind of index. It is a composite measure in which each question measures a small piece of knowledge, and all the questions scored correct or incorrect are totaled to produce a single measure.

Indexes measure the most desirable place to live (based on unemployment, commuting time, crime rate, recreation opportunities, weather, etc.), the degree of crime (based on combining the occurrence of different specific crimes), the mental health of a person (based on the person's adjustment in various areas of life), and the like.

One way to demonstrate that indexes are not very complicated is to use one. Answer yes or no to the seven questions that follow on the characteristics of an occupation. Base your answers on your thoughts regarding the following four occupations: long-distance truck driver, medical doctor, accountant, and telephone operator. Score each answer 1 for yes and 0 for no.

1. Does it pay a good salary?
2. Is the job secure from layoffs or unemployment?
3. Is the work interesting and challenging?
4. Are its working conditions (e.g., hours, safety, time on the road) good?
5. Are there opportunities for career advancement and promotion?
6. Is it prestigious or looked up to by others?
7. Does it permit self-direction and the freedom to make decisions?

Total the seven answers for each of the four occupations. Which had the highest and which had the lowest score? The seven questions are my operational definition of the construct *good occupation*. Each question represents a subpart of my theoretical definition. A different theoretical definition would result in different questions, perhaps more than seven.

Creating indexes is so easy that it is important to be careful that every item in the index has face validity. You should exclude any items without face validity. You should also measure each part of the construct with at least one indicator. Of course, it is better to measure the parts of a construct with multiple indicators.

Weighting

An important issue in index construction is whether to weight items. Unless it is otherwise stated, assume that an index is unweighted. Likewise, unless you have a good theoretical reason for assigning different weights, use equal weights. An *unweighted index* gives each item equal weight. It involves adding up the items without modification, as if you multiplied each by 1 (or −1 for items that are negative).

In a weighted index, you value or weight some items more than others. The size of weights can come from theoretical assumptions, the theoretical definition, or a statistical technique such as factor analysis. Weighting changes the theoretical definition of the construct.

Weighting can produce different index scores, but in most cases, weighted and unweighted indexes yield similar results. Usually you are most concerned with the relationship between variables. In most cases, weighted and unweighted indexes will give similar results for the relationships between variables.

Missing Data

Missing data can be a serious problem when you construct an index. Validity and reliability are threatened whenever data for some cases are missing. There are ways to attempt to resolve the problem but none fully resolve it.

For example, I construct an index of the degree of societal development in 1985 for 50 nations. The index contains four items: life expectancy, percentage of homes with indoor plumbing, percentage of population that is literate, and number of telephones per 100 people. I locate a source of United Nations statistics for my information. The values for Belgium are 68 + 87 + 97 + 28; for Turkey, the scores are 55 + 36 + 49 + 3; for Finland, however, I discover that literacy data are unavailable. I check other sources of information, but none has the data because they were not collected. Therefore, I decide to drop Finland from the study.

Rates and Standardization

You have heard of crime rates, rates of population growth, and the unemployment rate. Some indexes and single-indicator measures are rates. Rates involve standardizing the value of an item to make comparisons possible. You often need to standardize the items in an index before you can combine them.

Standardization involves selecting a base and dividing a raw measure by the base. For example, City A had 10 murders and City B had 30 murders in the same year. In order to compare murders in the two cities, you need to standardize the raw number of murders by the city population. If the cities are the same size, City B is more dangerous. But City B may be safer if it is much larger. For example, if City A has 100,000 people and City B has 600,000, then the murder rate per 100,000 is 10 for City A and 5 for City B.

Standardization makes it possible to compare different units on a common base. The process of standardization, also called *norming*, removes the effect of relevant but different characteristics in order to make the important differences visible. For example, there are two classes of students. An art class has 12 smokers and a biology class has 22 smokers. A researcher can compare the rate or incidence of smokers by standardizing the number of smokers by the size of the classes. The art class has 32 students and the biology class has 143 students. One method of standardization that you already know is the use of percentages. When you use percentages you are standardizing measures to a common base of 100. In terms of percentages, it is easy to see that the art class has more than twice the rate of smokers (37.5 percent) than the biology class (15.4 percent).

A critical question in standardization is deciding what base to use (see Example Box 5.1). In the examples given, how did I know to use city size or class size as the base? The choice is not always obvious; it depends on the theoretical definition of a construct.

Different bases can produce different rates. For example, the unemployment rate can be defined as the number of people in the workforce who are out of work. The overall unemployment rate is:

$$\text{Unemployment rate} = \frac{\text{Number of unemployed people}}{\text{Total number of people working}}$$

We can divide the total population into subgroups to get rates for subgroups in the population, such as White males, African American females, African American males between the ages of 18 and 28, or people with college degrees. Rates for these subgroups may be more relevant to the theoretical definition or research problem. For example, a researcher believes that unemployment is an experience that affects an entire household or family and that the base should be households, not individuals. The rate will look like this:

$$\text{New unemployment rate} = \frac{\text{Number of households with at least one unemployed person}}{\text{Total number of households}}$$

Different conceptualizations suggest different bases and different ways to standardize. When combining several items into an index, it is best to standardize items on a common base.

5.1	EXAMPLE BOX

Standardization and Auto Deaths

More people died in automobile accidents in the state of Washington than in the state of Wyoming. Does that mean that Wyoming drivers are safer and more careful? In 2008, 521 people died in automobile accidents in Washington state, and 159 people died in Wyoming. You might think that in Washington you are (521/159 = 3.3) more than three times more likely to die in an automobile accident. But wait, many more people live in Washington state than Wyoming, so maybe that is why there are more accidents. You might want to standardize number of deaths based on each state's population size. Is the number of people in a state the correct base to use? Maybe a better base to use for standardizing is the number of drivers in the state rather than the total number of people. If one state had more people, but most of those people were below driving age or lived in an urban area with great mass transit so did not drive, then using the total number of people is not the best base. Luckily, there is even a better base, the number of miles driven in a state. The U.S. National Highway Traffic Safety Administration measures the vehicle miles driven by state. Once you standardize the number of auto deaths by number of miles driven in each state, you see that the auto death rate in Washington is 0.9, and in Wyoming it is 1.7. Despite having over three times more deaths, Washington is actually safer. In fact, Wyoming is among the more dangerous states (only Arkansas, Louisiana, Mississippi, Montana, South Carolina, and West Virginia have higher auto death rates). Washington is one of the nation's safer states (only Connecticut, Maine, Minnesota, New Jersey, and Rhode Island have lower auto death rates).

Source: Data are from the 2011 *U.S. Statistical Abstract of the United States,* Table 1103.

SCALES

The Purpose

Scaling, like index construction, creates an ordinal, interval, or ratio measure of a variable expressed as a numerical score. Scales are common in situations where a researcher wants to measure how an individual feels or thinks about something. Some call this the hardness or potency of feelings.

You can use scales for two related purposes. First, scales help in the conceptualization and operationalization processes. Scales show the fit between a set of indicators and a single construct. For example, you believe that there is a single ideological dimension that underlies people's judgments about specific policies (e.g., housing, education, foreign affairs, etc.). Scaling can help determine whether a single construct—for instance, "conservative/liberal ideology"—underlies the positions people take on specific policies. Second, scaling produces quantitative measures and you can use a scale with other variables to test hypotheses. This second purpose of scaling is our primary focus because it involves scales as a technique for measuring a variable.

Logic of Scaling

As stated before, scaling is based on the idea of measuring the intensity, hardness, or potency of a variable. Graphic rating scales are an elementary form of scaling. People indicate a rating by checking a point on a line that runs from one extreme to another. This type of scale is easy to construct and use. It conveys the idea of a continuum, and assigning numbers helps people think about quantities. A built-in assumption of scales is that people with the same subjective feeling mark the graphic scale at the same place.

Figure 5.4 is an example of a "feeling thermometer" scale that is used to find out how people feel about various groups in society (e.g., the

National Organization of Women, the Ku Klux Klan, labor unions, physicians, etc.). Political scientists have used this type of measure in the National Election Study since 1964 to measure attitudes toward candidates, social groups, and issues.

Commonly Used Scales

Likert Scale.   You have probably used *Likert scales;* they are widely used and very common in survey research. They were developed in the 1930s by Rensis Likert to provide an ordinal-level measure of a person's attitude. Likert scales usually ask people to indicate whether they agree or disagree with a statement. Other modifications are possible; people might be asked whether they approve or disapprove, or whether they believe something is "almost always true." Example Box 5.2 presents several examples of Likert scales.

Likert scales need a minimum of two categories, such as "agree" and "disagree." Using only two choices creates a crude measure and forces distinctions into only two categories. It is usually better to use four to eight categories. You can combine or collapse categories after the data are collected, but data collected with crude categories cannot be made more precise later.

FIGURE 5.4   "Feeling Thermometer" Graphic Rating Scale

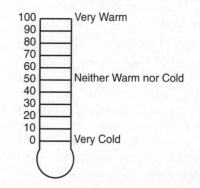

5.2

Examples of Types of Likert Scales

The Rosenberg Self-Esteem Scale

All in all, I am inclined to feel that I am a failure:

1. Almost always true

2. Often true

3. Sometimes true

4. Seldom true

5. Never true

A Student Evaluation of Instruction Scale

Overall, I rate the quality of instruction in this course as:

Excellent   Good   Average   Fair   Poor

A Market Research Mouthwash Rating Scale

Brand	Dislike Completely	Dislike Somewhat	Dislike a Little	Like a Little	Like Somewhat	Like Completely
X	_____	_____	_____	_____	_____	_____
Y	_____	_____	_____	_____	_____	_____

Work Group Supervisor Scale

My supervisor:

	Never	Seldom	Sometimes	Often	Always
Lets members know what is expected of them	1	2	3	4	5
Is friendly and approachable	1	2	3	4	5
Treats all unit members as equals	1	2	3	4	5

You can increase the number of categories at the end of a scale by adding "very strongly agree," "strongly agree," "somewhat agree," and so forth. Keep the number of choices to eight or nine at most. More distinctions than that are probably not meaningful, and people will become confused. The choices should be evenly balanced (e.g., "strongly agree," "agree" with "strongly disagree," "disagree").

Researchers have debated about whether to offer a neutral category (e.g., "don't know," "undecided," "no opinion") in addition to the directional categories (e.g., "disagree," "agree"). A neutral category implies an odd number of categories.

You can combine several Likert-scale questions into a composite index if they all measure a single construct. Consider the Jim

Crow Index of White racism that Unnever and Cullen (2007) used in their study of Whites' support for capital punishment was associated with anti-Black attitudes (see Example Box 5.3). As part of a larger survey, they asked four questions about group inequality. The answer to each question was a seven-point Likert scale with choices from strongly disagree to strongly agree. They created the index by adding the answers for each student to create scores that ranged from 4 to 28. They worded question number four in a reverse direction from the other questions. The reason for switching directions in this way is to avoid the problem of the *response set.* The response set, also called *response style* and *response bias,* is the tendency of some people to answer a large number of items in the same way (usually agreeing) out of laziness or a psychological predisposition. For example, if items are worded so that saying "strongly agree" always indicates self-esteem, we would not know whether a person who always strongly agreed had high self-esteem or simply had a tendency to agree with questions. The person might be answering "strongly agree" out of habit or a tendency to agree. Researchers

word statements in alternative directions, so that anyone who agrees all the time appears to answer inconsistently or to have a contradictory opinion.

Researchers often combine many Likert-scaled attitude indicators into an index. The scale and indexes have properties that are associated with improving reliability and validity. An index uses multiple indicators, which improves reliability. The use of multiple indicators that measure several aspects of a construct or opinion improves content validity. Finally, the index scores give a more precise quantitative measure of a person's opinion. For example, you can measure each person's opinion with a number from 10 to 40, instead of in four categories: "strongly agree," "agree," "disagree," and "strongly disagree."

Instead of scoring Likert items, as in the previous example, the scores -2, -1, $+1$, and $+2$ could be used. This scoring has an advantage in that a zero implies neutrality or complete ambiguity, whereas a high negative number means an attitude that opposes the opinion represented by a high positive number.

The numbers assigned to the response categories are arbitrary. Remember that the

---

5.3   EXAMPLE BOX
Indexes and Scales

In their study of whether White's racial prejudice influences their attitudes about capital punishment, Unnever and Cullen (2007) created two measures of White racism, one was traditional or Jim Crow racism. They created an index that summed answers to the following three scale questions:

1. Where would you rate Blacks on a scale of 1 to 7? (1 indicates hard-working, 7 means lazy, and 4 indicates Blacks are not closer to one end or the other end).

2. Where would you rate Blacks on a scale of 1 to 7? (1 indicates intelligent, 7 is unintelligent, and 4 indicates Blacks are not closer to one end or the other end).

3. Where would you rate Blacks on a scale of 1 to 7? (1 indicates trustworthy, 7 is untrustworthy, and 4 indicates Blacks are not closer to one end or the other end).

The Index = #1 answer + #2 answer + #3 answer. Thus, each person received an index score of between 3 and 21.

use of a zero does not give the scale or index a ratio level of measurement. Likert scale measures are at the ordinal level of measurement because responses indicate a ranking only. Instead of 1 to 4 or −2 to +2, the numbers 100, 70, 50, and 5 would have worked. Also, do not be fooled into thinking that the distances between the ordinal categories are intervals just because numbers are assigned. Although the number system has nice mathematical properties, the numbers are used for convenience only. The fundamental measurement is only ordinal.

The simplicity and ease of use of the Likert scale is its real strength. When several items are combined, more comprehensive multiple indicator measurement is possible. The scale has two limitations: Different combinations of several scale items can result in the same overall score or result, and the response set is a potential danger.

Bogardus Social Distance Scale.   The *Bogardus Social Distance Scale* measures the social distance separating ethnic or other groups from each other. It is used with one group to determine how much distance it feels toward a target or "out-group."

The scale has a simple logic. People respond to a series of ordered statements; those that are most threatening or most socially distant are at one end, and those that might be least threatening or socially intimate are at the other end. The logic of the scale assumes that a person who refuses contact or is uncomfortable with the socially distant items will refuse the socially closer items (see Example Box 5.4).

Researchers use the scale in several ways. For example, people are given a series of statements: People from Group X are entering your country, are in your town, work at your place of employment, live in your neighborhood, become your personal friends, and marry your brother or

---

5.4   EXAMPLE BOX
Replication of the Original Bogardus Social Distance Scale Study

In 1993, Kleg and Yamamoto (1998) replicated the original 1925 study by Emory Bogardus that first used the social distance scale. The original study had 110 subjects from the Pacific Coast. Participants included 107 White Americans of non-Jewish European ancestry, 1 Jewish White, 1 Chinese, and 1 Japanese (about 70 percent were female). In their 1993 replication, Kleg and Yamamoto selected 135 middle school teachers from an affluent school district in a Colorado metropolitan area. There were 119 non-Jewish Whites, 7 Jewish Whites, 6 African Americans, 1 American Indian, 1 Asian, and 1 unknown (65 percent were female). There were three minor deviations from the 1925 study. First, the original Bogardus respondents were given a list of 39 groups. Those in the replication had a list of 36 groups. The two lists shared 24 groups in common. Three target groups were renamed: Negroes in 1925 versus African Americans in 1993; Syrians versus Arabs; and German-Jews and Russian-Jews vs. Jews. Second, both studies contained

seven categories, but they were worded slightly differently (see below). Third, both studies had seven categories (called anchor points) printed left to right at the top. In the Bogardus original it said: "According to my first feeling reactions I would willingly admit members of each race (as a class, and not the best I have known, nor the worst members) to one or more of the classifications under which I have placed a cross (x)." In the 1993 replication it said: "Social distance means the degree that individuals desire to associate with others. This scale relates to a special form of social distance known as person to group distance. You are given a list of groups. Across from each group there are boxes identified by the labels at the top. Place an "x" in the boxes that indicate the degree of association you would desire to have with each group. Give your first reaction." The main finding was that although the average social distance declined a great deal over 68 years, the ranking of the 25 groups changed very little (see below).

Instructions

Original 1925 Study	1993 Replication
I would willingly admit members of each race:	*The degree of association I would desire to have with members of each group is:*
1. To close kinship by marriage	To marry into group
2. To my club as personal chums	To have as best friend
3. To my street as neighbors	To have as next-door neighbors
4. To employment in my occupation in my country	To work in the same office
5. To citizenship in my country	To have as speaking acquaintances only
6. As visitors only to my country	To have as visitors to my country
7. Would exclude from my country	To keep out of my country

Results

Group	1925 Original Mean Score	1925 Original Rank	1993 Replication Mean Score	1993 Replication Rank
English	1.27	1	1.17	2
Scottish	1.69	2	1.22	6
Irish	1.93	3	1.14	1
French	2.04	4	1.20	4
Dutch	2.12	5	1.25	9
Swedish	2.44	6	1.21	5
Danish	2.48	7	1.23	7
Norwegian	2.67	8	1.25	8
German	2.89	9	1.27	10
Spanish	3.28	10	1.29	11
Italian	3.98	11	1.19	3
Hindu	4.35	12	1.95	23
Polish	4.57	13	1.30	12
Russian	4.57	14	1.33	13
Native American	4.65	15	1.44	16
Jewish	4.83*	16	1.42	15
Greek	4.89	17	1.38	14
Arab	5.00*	18	2.21	24
Mexican	5.02	19	1.56	18
Black American	5.10*	20	1.55	17
Chinese	5.28	21	1.68	20
Japanese	5.30	22	1.62	19
Korean	5.55	23	1.72	21
Turk	5.80	24	1.77	22
Grand Mean	3.82		1.43	

*Slight change in name of group.

sister. People are asked whether they feel comfortable with the statement or if the contact is acceptable. It is also possible to ask whether they feel uncomfortable with the relationship. People may be asked to respond to all statements, or they may keep reading statements until they are not comfortable with a relationship. There is no set number of statements required; the number usually ranges from five to nine. The measure of social distance can be used as either an independent or a dependent variable.

You can use the Bogardus scale to see how distant people feel from one out-group versus another. In addition to studying racial-ethnic groups, it has been used to examine doctor–patient distance. For example, Gordon, Feldman, Tantillo, and Perrone (2004) found that college students reported different social distance toward people with different disabilities. Over 95 percent would be willing to be a friend with someone with arthritis, cancer, diabetes, or a heart condition. Fewer than 70 percent would ever consider being a friend to someone with mental retardation. The social distance scale is a convenient way to determine how close a respondent feels toward a social group. It has two potential limitations. First, a researcher needs to tailor the categories to a specific out-group and social setting. Second, it is not easy for a researcher to compare how a respondent feels toward several different groups unless the respondent completes a similar social distance scale for all out-groups at the same time. Of course, how a respondent completes the scale and the respondent's actual behavior in specific social situations may differ.

Semantic Differential.   **Semantic differential** provides an indirect measure of how a person feels about a concept, object, or other person. The technique measures subjective feelings toward something by using adjectives. This is because people communicate evaluations through adjectives in spoken and written language. Because most adjectives have polar opposites (e.g., *light–dark, hard–soft, slow–fast*), it uses polar opposite adjectives to create a rating measure or scale. The semantic differential captures the connotations associated with whatever is being evaluated and provides an indirect measure of it.

The semantic differential has been used for many purposes. In marketing research, it tells how consumers feel about a product; political advisers use it to discover what voters think about a candidate or issue; and therapists use it to determine how a client perceives him- or herself (see Example Box 5.5).

To use the semantic differential, you present research participants with a list of paired opposite adjectives with a continuum of 7 to 11 points between them. The participants mark the spot on the continuum between the adjectives that express their feelings. The adjectives can be very diverse and you should mix them (e.g., positive items should not be located mostly on either the right or the left side). Studies of a wide variety of adjectives in English found that they fall into three major classes of meaning: evaluation (*good–bad*), potency (*strong–weak*), and activity (*active–passive*). Of the three classes of meaning, evaluation is usually the most significant. The analysis of results is difficult, and you need to use statistical procedures to analyze a research participant's feelings toward the concept.

Results from a semantic differential tell you how one person perceives different concepts or how different people view the same concept. For example, political analysts might discover that young voters perceive their candidate as traditional, weak, and slow, and as halfway between good and bad. Elderly voters perceive the candidate as leaning toward strong, fast, and good, and as halfway between traditional and modern.

Guttman Scaling.   **Guttman scaling**, or cumulative scaling, differs from the previous scales or indexes in that you use it to evaluate data after they are collected. This means that you must design a study with the Guttman scaling technique in mind.

5.5 EXAMPLE BOX
Example of Using the Semantic Differential

As part of her undergraduate thesis, Daina Hawkes studied attitudes toward women with tattoos using the semantic differential (Hawkes, Senn, and Thorn, 2004). The researchers had 268 students at a medium-sized Canadian university complete a semantic differential form in response to several scenarios about a 22-year-old woman college student with a tattoo. They had five scenarios in which they varied the size of the tattoo (small versus large) and whether or not it was visible, and one with no details about the tattoo. The authors also varied features of the senario: weight problem or not; part-time job at restaurant, clothing store, or grocery store; boyfriend or not; average grades or failing grades. They used a semantic differential with 22 adjective pairs. They also had participants complete two scales: Feminist and Women's Movement scale and Neosexism scale. The semantic differential terms were selected to indicate three factors: evaluative, activity, and potency (strong/weak). Based on statistical analysis three adjectives were dropped. The 19 items used are listed below. Among other findings, the authors found that there were more negative feelings toward a woman with a visible tattoo.

Good	____	____	____	____	____	____	____	Bad*
Beautiful	____	____	____	____	____	____	____	Ugly
Clean	____	____	____	____	____	____	____	Dirty
Kind	____	____	____	____	____	____	____	Cruel*
Rich	____	____	____	____	____	____	____	Poor*
Honest	____	____	____	____	____	____	____	Dishonest*
Pleasant	____	____	____	____	____	____	____	Unpleasant*
Successful	____	____	____	____	____	____	____	Unsuccessful
Reputable	____	____	____	____	____	____	____	Disreputable
Safe	____	____	____	____	____	____	____	Dangerous
Gentle	____	____	____	____	____	____	____	Violent*
Feminine	____	____	____	____	____	____	____	Masculine
Weak	____	____	____	____	____	____	____	Powerful*
Passive	____	____	____	____	____	____	____	Active*
Cautious	____	____	____	____	____	____	____	Rash*
Soft	____	____	____	____	____	____	____	Hard
Weak	____	____	____	____	____	____	____	Strong
Mild	____	____	____	____	____	____	____	Intense
Delicate	____	____	____	____	____	____	____	Rugged*

*These items were presented in reverse order.

Guttman scaling begins with measuring a set of indicators or items. These can be questionnaire items, votes, or observed characteristics. Guttman scaling measures many different phenomena (e.g., patterns of crime or drug use, characteristics of societies or organizations, voting or political participation, psychological disorders). The indicators are usually measured in a simple yes/no or present/absent fashion. You can use from 3 to 20 indicators. You select items on the belief that there is a logical relationship among them. You then place the results into a Guttman scale and determine whether the items form a pattern that corresponds to the relationship. (See Example Box 5.6 for an example of a study using Guttman scaling.)

Once you measure a set of items, you then consider all possible combinations of responses for the items. For example, you measure the following three items: whether a child knows her age, her telephone number, and three local elected political officials. The little girl may know her age but no other answer, or all three, or only her age and telephone number. In fact, for three items there are eight possible combinations of answers or patterns of responses, from not knowing any through knowing all three. There is a mathematical way to compute the number of combinations (e.g., 2^3), but you can write down all the combinations of yes or no for three questions and see the eight possibilities.

5.6	EXAMPLE BOX

Guttman Scale Example

Crozat (1998) examined public responses to various forms of political protest. He looked at survey data on the public's acceptance of forms of protest in Great Britain, Germany, Italy, Netherlands, and the United States in 1974 and 1990. He found that the pattern of the public's acceptance formed a Guttman scale. Those who accepted more intense forms of protest (e.g., strikes and sit-ins) almost always accepted more modest forms (e.g., petitions or demonstrations), but not all who accepted modest forms accepted the more intense forms. In addition to showing the usefulness of the Guttman scale, Crozat also found that people in different nations saw protest similarly and the degree of Guttman scalability increased over time. Thus, the pattern of acceptance of protest activities was Guttman "scalable" in both time periods, but it more closely followed the Guttman pattern in 1990 than 1974.

FORM OF PROTEST

	Petitions	**Demonstrations**	**Boycotts**	**Strike**	**Sit-In**
Guttman Patterns					
	N	N	N	N	N
	Y	N	N	N	N
	Y	Y	N	N	N
	Y	Y	Y	N	N
	Y	Y	Y	Y	N
	Y	Y	Y	Y	Y
Other Patterns (examples only)					
	N	Y	N	Y	N
	Y	N	Y	Y	N
	Y	N	Y	N	N
	N	Y	Y	N	N
	Y	N	N	Y	Y

The logical relationship among items in Guttman scaling is hierarchical. Most people or cases have or agree to lower-order items. The smaller number of cases that have the higher-order items also have the lower-order ones, but not vice versa. In other words, the higher-order items build on the lower ones. The lower-order items are necessary for the appearance of the higher-order items.

An application of Guttman scaling, known as *scalogram analysis,* lets you test whether a hierarchical relationship exists among the items. For example, it is easier for a child to know her age than her telephone number, and to know her telephone number than the names of political leaders. The items are called *scalable,* or capable of forming a Guttman scale, if a hierarchical pattern exists.

You can divide the patterns of responses into two groups: scaled and errors (or nonscalable). The scaled patterns for the child's knowledge example would be as follows: not knowing any item, knowing only age, knowing only age plus phone number, knowing all three. Other combinations of answers (e.g., knowing the political leaders but not her age) are possible but are nonscalable. If a hierarchical relationship exists among the items, then most answers fit into the scalable patterns.

You can determine the strength or degree to which items can be scaled using statistics that measure whether the responses can be reproduced based on a hierarchical pattern. Most range from zero to 100 percent. A score of zero indicates a random pattern, or no hierarchical pattern. A score of 100 percent indicates that all responses to the answer fit the hierarchical or scaled pattern. Alternative statistics to measure scalability have also been suggested.

CONCLUSION

In this chapter, you learned about the principles and processes of measurement in quantitative and qualitative research. In both types of studies,

you conceptualize—or refine and clarify their ideas into conceptual definitions. In both types of studies, you also operationalize—or develop a set of techniques or processes that will link their conceptual definitions to empirical reality. Depending on whether you are conducting a qualitative or quantitative study, you may approach these processes differently, however. In a quantitative study, you are likely to take a more deductive path, whereas for a qualitative study it is a more inductive path. The goal remains the same: to establish unambiguous links between your abstract ideas and the empirical data.

You also learned about the principles of reliability and validity. Reliability refers to the dependability or consistency of a measure; validity refers to its truthfulness, or how well a construct and data for it fit together. Depending on whether you are doing quantitative or qualitative research, you may apply these principles differently. Nonetheless, in both quantitative and qualitative research, you try to measure in a consistent way, and seek a tight fit between the abstract ideas you use to understand social world and what occurs in the actual, empirical social world. In addition, you saw how to apply the principles of measurement when you create indexes and scales, and you read about some major scales they use.

Beyond the core ideas of reliability and validity, good measurement requires that you create clear definitions for concepts, use multiple indicators, and, as appropriate, weigh and standardize the data. These principles hold across all fields of study (e.g., family, criminology, inequality, race relations, etc.) and across the many research techniques (e.g., experiments, surveys, etc.).

As you are probably beginning to realize, research involves doing a good job in each phase of a study. Making serious mistakes or sloppiness in any one phase can do irreparable damage to the results, even if you conduct other phases of the research project in a flawless manner.

Key Terms

Bogardus Social Distance Scale
conceptual definition
conceptual hypothesis
conceptualization
concurrent validity
content validity
continuous variables
criterion validity
discrete variables
empirical hypothesis
exhaustive attributes
external validity
face validity
Guttman scaling
index
internal validity
interval-level measurement
levels of measurement
Likert scale
measurement validity
multiple indicators
mutually exclusive attributes
nominal-level measurement
operational definition

operationalization
ordinal-level measurement
predictive validity
ratio-level measurement
reliability
scale
semantic differential
standardization
unidimensionality
validity

Endnote

1. The terms *concept, construct,* and *idea* are used more or less interchangeably, but there are differences in meaning between them. An *idea* is any mental image, belief plan, or impression. It refers to any vague impression, opinion, or thought. A *concept* is a thought, a general notion, or a generalized idea about a class of objects. A *construct* is a thought that is systematically put together, an orderly arrangement of ideas, facts, and impressions. The term *construct* is used here because its emphasis is on taking vague concepts and turning them into systematically organized ideas.

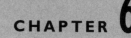

CHAPTER 6

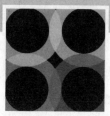

Qualitative and Quantitative Sampling

When you sample, you select some cases to examine in detail, then you use what you learn from them to understand a much larger set of cases. Most, but not all, social research studies use sampling. Depending on the study, how you conduct the sampling can differ. Most books on sampling emphasize its use in quantitative research and contain applied mathematics and quantitative examples. In quantitative studies, the primary purpose of sampling is to create a representative sample, that is, a *sample* (a selected small collection of cases or units) that closely reproduces features of interest in a larger collection of cases, called the *population*.

After sampling, you examine data in a sample in detail; if you sampled correctly, you can generalize accuracy to the entire population. To create representative samples in quantitative research you need to use very precise sampling procedures. These procedures rely on the mathematics of probabilities, hence they are called *probability sampling*.

In most quantitative studies, you want to see how many cases of a population fall into various categories of interest. For example, you might ask how many in the population of all Chicago's high school students fit into various categories (e.g., high-income family, single-parent family, illegal drug user, arrested for delinquent behavior, musically talented). The great thing about probability samples in quantitative research is their efficiency. They save a great deal of time and cost for the accuracy they deliver. A properly conducted probability sample may cost 1/1000 the cost and time of gathering information on an entire population yet yield virtually identical results. Let's say you wanted to learn about the 18 million people in the United States diagnosed with diabetes. From a well-designed probability sample of 1,800, you can take what you learned and generalize it to all 18 million. It is more efficient to study 1,800 people to learn about 18 million than to study all 18 million people.

Probability samples can be highly accurate. For large populations, a well-designed, carefully executed probability sample can be equally if not more accurate than trying to reach every case in the population. This confuses many people. The U.S. Census tries to get data on all approximately 300 million Americans. A careful probability sample of 30,000 has a very tiny and known error rate. Trying to locate every single person of 300 million allows systematic errors to slip in unless extraordinary efforts are undertaken and huge amounts of time and money are expended. By the way, the scientific community for many years recommended against the U.S. Census practice and recommended high-quality random samples, but political considerations overruled scientific ones.

Sampling proceeds differently and has different purposes in qualitative studies. In fact, using the word sampling creates confusion in qualitative research because the term is so closely associated with quantitative research. In qualitative studies, you rarely sample a small set of cases that is a mathematically accurate reproduction of the entire population so you can make statements about categories in the population. Instead, you sample to identify relevant categories at work in a few cases.

In quantitative sampling, you select cases/units that you treat the cases/units as carriers of aspects/features of the social world. A sample of cases/units "stands in" for the much larger population of cases/units. By contrast, the logic of the qualitative sample is to sample aspects/features of the social world. The aspects/features of your sample highlight or "shine light into" key dimensions or processes in a complex social life. You pick a few to provide clarity, insight, and understanding about issues or relationships in the social world. In qualitative sampling, your goal is to deepen understanding about a larger process, relationship, or social scene. A sample provides valuable information or aspects, and these aspects accentuate, enhance, or enrich key features or situations.

In a qualitative study, you sample to open up new theoretical insights, reveal distinctive aspects of people or social settings, or deepen understanding of complex situations, events, or relationships. However, we should not overdo the quantitative–qualitative distinction. In a few situations, a study that is primarily quantitative uses the qualitative–sampling strategy and vice versa. Nonetheless, most quantitative studies use probability or probabilitylike samples, and most qualitative studies use a nonprobability method and a nonrepresentative strategy.

NONPROBABILITY SAMPLING

Instead of probability sampling, qualitative researchers use nonprobability or **nonrandom samples**. This means they rarely determine the sample size in advance and have limited knowledge about the larger group or population from which the sample is taken. Unlike a quantitative researcher who uses a preplanned approach based on mathematical theory, in a qualitative study you select cases gradually, with the specific content of a case determining whether it is chosen. Table 6.1 shows a variety of nonprobability sampling techniques.

Convenience Sampling

In *convenience sampling* (also called accidental, availability, or haphazard) your primary criteria for selecting cases is that they are easy to reach, convenient, or readily available. This kind of sample may be legitimate for a few exploratory preliminary studies and some qualitative research studies when your purpose is something other than creating a representative sample. Unfortunately, it often produces very nonrepresentative samples. It is *not recommended* if you want to create an accurate sample to represent the population. When you haphazardly select cases that are convenient, you can easily get a sample that seriously misrepresents the population. Such samples are cheap and quick; however, the systematic errors that easily occur make them worse than no sample at all. The person-on-the-street interview conducted

TABLE 6.1   Types of Nonprobability Samples

Type of Sample	Principle
Convenience	Get any cases in any manner that is convenient.
Quota	Get a preset number of cases in each of several predetermined categories that will reflect the diversity of the population, using haphazard methods.
Purposive	Get all possible cases that fit particular criteria, using various methods.
Snowball	Get cases using referrals from one or a few cases, and then referrals from those cases, and so forth.
Deviant Case	Get cases that substantially differ from the dominant pattern (a special type of purposive sample).
Sequential	Get cases until there is no additional information or new characteristics (often used with other sampling methods).

by television programs is an example of a convenience sample. Television interviewers go out on the street with camera and microphone to talk to a few people who are convenient to interview. The people walking past a television studio in the middle of the day do not represent everyone (e.g., homemakers, people in rural areas, etc.). Likewise, television interviewers often select people who look "normal" to them and avoid people who are unattractive, poor, very old, or inarticulate. Another example of a convenience sample is that of a newspaper that asks readers to clip a questionnaire from the paper and mail it in. Not everyone reads the newspaper, has an interest in the topic, or will take the time to cut out the questionnaire and mail it. Some people will, and the number who do so may seem large (e.g., 5,000), but the sample cannot be used to generalize accurately to the population. Such convenience samples may have entertainment value, but they can give a distorted view and seriously misrepresent the population.

Quota Sampling

For many purposes, a well-designed *quota sample* is an acceptable nonprobability substitute method for producing a quasi-representative sample. In quota sampling, you first identify relevant categories among the population you are sampling to capture diversity among units (e.g., male and female; under age 30, ages 30–60, over age 60, etc.). Next, you determine how many cases to get for each category—this is your "quota." Thus, you fix a number of cases in various categories of the sample at the start (see Figure 6.1).

Quota sampling is an improvement because you are ensuring some variety in the sample. In convenience sampling, all those interviewed might be of the same age, sex, or race. But once you fix the categories and number of cases in each quota category, you use convenience sampling. For example, you interview the first five males under age 30 you encounter, even if all five just walked out of the campaign headquarters of a political candidate. Not only is

FIGURE 6.1 Quota Sampling

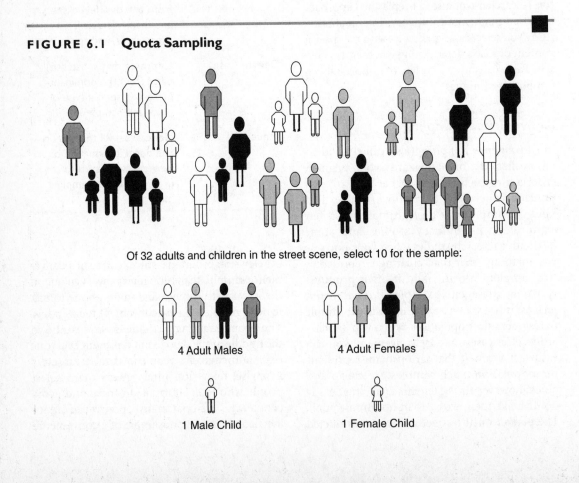

Of 32 adults and children in the street scene, select 10 for the sample:

4 Adult Males

4 Adult Females

1 Male Child

1 Female Child

misrepresentation possible because convenience sampling is used within the categories, but nothing prevents you from selecting people who "act friendly" or who want to be interviewed.

A case from the history of sampling illustrates the limitations of quota sampling. George Gallup's American Institute of Public Opinion, using quota sampling, successfully predicted the outcomes of the 1936, 1940, and 1944 U.S. presidential elections. But in 1948, Gallup predicted the wrong candidate. The incorrect prediction had several causes (e.g., many voters were undecided, interviewing stopped early), but a major reason was that the quota categories did not accurately represent all geographical areas and all people who actually cast a vote.

Purposive or Judgmental Sampling

Purposive sampling is a valuable kind of sampling for special situations. It is usually used in exploratory research or in field research. In this type of sampling the judgment of an expert or prior knowledge is used to select cases. It is not appropriate if it your goal is to get a representative sample, or if you want to pick the "average" or the "typical" case. In purposive sampling, the cases selected rarely represent the entire population.

Purposive sampling is most appropriate in the following three situations:

1. You use it to select unique cases that are especially informative. For example, you want to use content analysis to study magazines to find cultural themes. You select a specific popular women's magazine to study because it is trendsetting.
2. You may use purposive sampling to select members of a difficult-to-reach, specialized population. For example, you want to study prostitutes. It is impossible to list all prostitutes and sample randomly from the list. Instead, you use subjective information (e.g., locations where prostitutes solicit, social groups with whom prostitutes

associate, etc.) and experts (e.g., police who work on vice units, other prostitutes, etc.) to identify a "sample" of prostitutes for inclusion in the research project. You use many different methods to identify the cases because your goal is to locate as many cases as possible.

3. You want to identify particular types of cases for in-depth investigation. The purpose is less to generalize to a larger population than it is to gain a deeper understanding of specific types. For example, Gamson (1992) used purposive sampling in a focus group study of what working-class people think about politics. (Chapter 11 discusses focus groups.) Gamson wanted a total of 188 working-class people to participate in one of 37 focus groups. He sought respondents who had not completed college but who were diverse in terms of age, ethnicity, religion, interest in politics, and type of occupation. He recruited people from 35 neighborhoods in the Boston area by going to festivals, picnics, fairs, and flea markets and posting notices on many public bulletin boards. In addition to explaining the study, he paid the respondents well so as to attract people who would not traditionally participate in a study.

Snowball Sampling

Snowball sampling (also called *network, chain referral,* or *reputational sampling*) is a method for identifying and sampling (or selecting) the cases in a network. It uses the analogy of a snowball. It begins small but becomes larger as it is rolled on wet snow and picks up additional snow. Snowball sampling is a multistage technique. You begin with one or a few people or cases and spread out on the basis of links to the initial cases.

An important use of snowball sampling is to sample a network. We are often interested in an interconnected network of people or organizations. The network could be scientists around the world investigating the same problem, the elites of a medium-sized city, the members of an organized crime family, persons who sit on the boards of directors of major banks and corporations, or people on a college campus who have had sexual relations with each other. The crucial feature is that each person or unit is connected with another through a direct or indirect linkage. This does not mean that each person directly knows, interacts with, or is influenced by every other person in the network. Rather, it means that, taken as a whole, with direct and indirect links, they are within an interconnected web of linkages.

We can represent such a network by drawing a *sociogram*—a diagram of circles connected with lines. For example, Sally and Tim do not know each other directly, but each has a good friend, Susan, so they have an indirect connection. All three are part of the same friendship network. The circles represent each person or case, and the lines represent friendship or other linkages (see Figure 6.2).

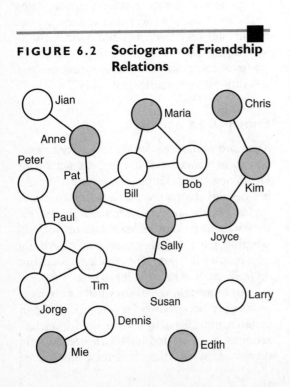

FIGURE 6.2   Sociogram of Friendship Relations

You can also use snowball sampling in combination with purposive sampling. This is what Kissane (2003) did in a descriptive field research study of low-income women in Philadelphia. The U.S. policy to provide aid and services to low-income people changed in 1996 to increase assistance (e.g., food pantries, domestic violence shelters, drug rehabilitation services, clothing distribution centers) delivered by nonpublic as opposed to government/public agencies. As frequently occurs, the policy change was made without a study of its consequences in advance. No one knew whether the affected low-income people would use the assistance provided by nonpublic agencies as much as that provided by public agencies. One year after the new policy, Kissane studied whether low-income women were equally likely to use nonpublic aid. She focused on the Kensington area of Philadelphia. It had a high (over 30 percent) poverty rate and was a predominately White (85 percent) section of the city.

First, Kissane (2003) identified nonpublic service providers by using telephone books, the Internet, referral literature, and walking down every street of the area until she identified 50 nonpublic social service providers. She observed that a previous study found low-income women in the area distrusted outsiders and intellectuals. Her snowball sample began asking service providers for the names of a few low-income women in the area. She then asked those women to refer her to others in a similar situation, and asked those respondents to refer her to still others. She identified 20 low-income women aged 21 to 50, most who had received public assistance. She conducted in-depth, open-ended interviews about their awareness and experience with nonpublic agencies. She learned that the women were less likely to get nonpublic than public assistance. Compared to public agencies, the women were less aware of nonpublic agencies. Nonpublic agencies created more social stigma, generated greater administrative hassles, were in worse locations, and involved more scheduling difficulties because of limited hours.

Deviant Case Sampling

You might use *deviant case sampling* (also called *extreme case sampling*) when you seek cases that differ from the dominant pattern or have features that differ from the predominant features of most other cases. Similar to purposive sampling, you use a variety of techniques to locate cases with specific characteristics. Deviant case sampling differs from purposive sampling in that your goal is to locate a collection of unusual, different, or peculiar cases that are not representative of the whole. You select the deviant cases because they are unusual, and you hope to learn more about the social life by considering cases that fall outside the general pattern or including what is beyond the main flow of events.

For example, you are interested in studying high school dropouts. Let us say that previous research suggested that a majority of dropouts from low-income, single-parent households have been geographically mobile, and they are disproportionately members of racial minority groups. The parent(s) and siblings tend to be high school dropouts. In addition, dropouts are more likely to have engaged in illegal behavior prior to dropping out. If you used deviant case sampling, you would seek majority-group dropouts without any prior evidence of illegal activities who are from stable two-parent, upper-middle-income families who are geographically stable and well educated.

Sequential Sampling

Sequential sampling is similar to purposive sampling with one difference. In purposive sampling, you try to find as many relevant cases as possible, until time, financial resources, or your energy is exhausted. You want to get every possible case. In sequential sampling, you continue to gather cases until the amount of new information or diversity of cases is filled. In economic terms, you gather information until

the marginal utility, or incremental benefit for additional cases, levels off or drops significantly. It requires that you continuously evaluate all the collected cases. For example, you locate and plan in-depth interviews with 60 widows who are over 75 years old and who have been widowed for 10 or more years. Depending on your purposes, getting an additional 20 widows whose life experiences, social backgrounds, and worldviews differ little from the first 60 widows may be unnecessary.

PROBABILITY SAMPLING

A specialized vocabulary or jargon has developed around terms used in probability sampling. Before examining probability sampling, it is important to review its language.

Populations, Elements, and Sampling Frames

You draw a sample from a larger pool of cases, or *elements*. A *sampling element* is the unit of analysis or case in a population. It can be a person, a group, an organization, a written document or symbolic message, or even a social action (e.g., an arrest, a divorce, or a kiss) that is being measured. The large pool is the *population,* which has an important role in sampling. Sometimes, the term *universe* is used interchangeably with *population*. To define the population, you specify the unit being sampled, the geographical location, and the temporal boundaries of populations. Consider the examples of populations in Example Box 6.1. All the examples include the elements to be sampled (e.g., people, businesses, hospital admissions, commercials, etc.) and geographical and time boundaries.

When sampling you start with an idea of the population (e.g., all people in a city) but define it more precisely. The term *target population* refers to the specific pool of cases that you want to study. The ratio of the size of the sample to

1. All persons aged 16 or older living in Singapore on December 2, 2009, who were not incarcerated in prison, asylums, and similar institutions

2. All business establishments employing more than 100 persons in Ontario Province, Canada, that operated in the month of July 2010

3. All admissions to public or private hospitals in the state of New Jersey between August 1, 1988, and July 31, 1993

4. All television commercials aired between 7:00 A.M. and 11:00 P.M. Eastern Standard Time on three major U.S. networks between November 1 and November 25, 2011

5. All currently practicing physicians in Australia who received medical degrees between January 1, 1960, and the present

6. All African American male heroin addicts in the Vancouver, British Columbia, or Seattle, Washington, metropolitan areas during 2009

the size of the target population is the *sampling ratio*. For example, the population has 50,000 people, and you draw a sample of 150 from it. Thus, the sampling ratio is 150/50,000 = 0.003, or 0.3 percent. If the population is 500 and you sample 100, then the sampling ratio is 100/500 = 0.20, or 20 percent.

A population is an abstract concept. You might ask, How can population be an abstract concept, when there are a given number of people at a certain time? Except for specific small populations, we can never truly freeze a population to measure it. For example, in a city at any given moment, some people are dying, some are boarding or getting off airplanes, and some are in cars driving across city boundaries. You must decide exactly who to count. Should you count a city resident who happens to be on vacation when the time is fixed? What about the tourist staying at a hotel in the city when the

time is fixed? Should you count adults, children, people in jails, those in hospitals? A population, even the population of all people over the age of 18 in the city limits of Kansas City, Missouri, at 12:01 A.M. on March 1, 2011, is an abstract concept. It exists in the mind but is impossible to pinpoint concretely.

Because a population is an abstract concept, except for small specialized populations (e.g., all the students in a classroom), you will need to estimate the population. As an abstract concept, the population needs an operational definition. This process is similar to developing operational definitions for constructs that are measured.

You operationalize a population by developing a specific list that closely approximates all the elements in the population. This list is a *sampling frame*. You can choose from many types of sampling frames: telephone directories, tax records, driver's license records, and so on. Listing the elements in a population sounds simple. It is often impossible because there is no good list of elements in a population.

A good sampling frame is crucial to good sampling. A mismatch between the sampling frame and the conceptually defined population can be a major source of error. Just as a mismatch between the theoretical and operational definitions of a variable creates invalid measurement, so a mismatch between the sampling frame and the population causes invalid sampling. You can minimize mismatches. For example, you would like to sample all people in a region of the United States, so you decide to get a list of everyone with a driver's license. But some people do not have driver's licenses, and the lists of those with licenses, even if updated regularly, quickly go out of date. Next, you try income tax records. But not everyone pays taxes; some people cheat and do not pay, others have no income and do not have to file, some have died or have not begun to pay taxes, and still others have entered or left the area since the last time taxes were due. You try telephone directories, but they are not much better; some people are not listed in a telephone directory, some people have unlisted numbers, and others have recently moved. With a few exceptions (e.g., a list of all students enrolled at a university), sampling frames are almost always inaccurate. A sampling frame can include some of those outside the target population (e.g., a telephone directory that lists people who have moved away) or might omit some of those inside it (e.g., those without landline telephones).

Any characteristic of a population (e.g., the percentage of city residents who smoke cigarettes, the average height of all women over the age of 21, the percent of people who believe in UFOs) is a population *parameter*. It is the true characteristic of the population. Parameters are determined when all elements in a population are measured. The parameter is never known with absolute accuracy for large populations (e.g., an entire nation), so researchers must estimate it on the basis of samples. They use information from the sample, called a *statistic*, to estimate population parameters (see Figure 6.3).

A famous case in the history of sampling illustrates the limitations of the technique. The *Literary Digest*, a major U.S. magazine, sent postcards to people before the 1920, 1924, 1928, and 1932 U.S. presidential elections. The magazine took the names for the sample from automobile registrations and telephone directories—the sampling frame. People returned the postcards indicating whom they would vote for. The magazine correctly predicted all four election outcomes. The magazine's success with predictions was well known, and in 1936, it increased the sample to 10 million. The magazine predicted a huge victory for Alf Landon over Franklin D. Roosevelt. But the *Literary Digest* was wrong; Franklin D. Roosevelt won by a landslide.

The prediction was wrong for several reasons, but the most important were mistakes in sampling. Although the magazine sampled a large number of people, its sampling frame did not accurately represent the target population (i.e., all voters). It excluded people without telephones or automobiles, a sizable percentage of the population in 1936, during the worst of the Great Depression of the 1930s. The frame excluded as much as 65 percent of the population and a segment of the voting population (lower income) that tended to favor Roosevelt. The magazine had been accurate in earlier elections because people with higher and lower incomes did not differ in how they voted. Also, during earlier elections, before the Depression, more lower-income people could afford to have telephones and automobiles.

You can learn two important lessons from the *Literary Digest* mistake. First, the sampling frame is crucial. Second, the size of a sample is less important than whether or not it accurately represents the population. A representative sample of 2,500 can give more accurate predictions about the U.S. population than a nonrepresentative sample of 1 million or 10 million.

FIGURE 6.3   A Model of the Logic of Sampling

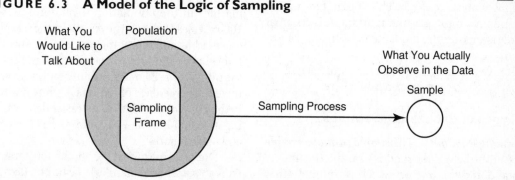

Why Random?

In applied mathematics, probability theory relies on random processes. The word random has several meanings. In daily life, it can mean unpredictable, unusual, unexpected, or haphazard. In mathematics, random has a specific meaning: a selection process without any pattern. In mathematical random processes, each element has an equal probability of being selected. We can mathematically calculate the probability of outcomes over many cases with great precision for true random processes.

Creating a probability sample that relies on random processes will require more time and effort than a nonrandom one. You must identify specific sampling elements (e.g., a person) to include in the sample. For example, if conducting a telephone survey, you need to try to reach the specific sampled person, by calling back four or five times, to get an accurate random sample.

Although they require more time and effort, random samples are most likely to yield a sample that truly represents the population. In addition, only with random sampling can you statistically calculate the relationship between the sample and the population—that is, the size of the *sampling error*. A nonstatistical definition of the sampling error is the deviation between sample results and a population parameter due to random processes.

Random sampling rests on a foundation of applied mathematics. This chapter focuses on the fundamentals of how sampling works, the difference between good and bad samples, how to draw a sample, and basic principles of sampling in social research. This does not mean that random sampling is unimportant. It is essential to first master the fundamentals. If you plan to pursue a career in which you will conduct quantitative studies, you should get more statistical background than space permits here.

Types of Probability Samples

Simple Random.   The *simple random sample* is both the easiest random sample to understand and the one on which we model other random samples. In simple random sampling, you develop an accurate sampling frame, select elements from the sampling frame according to a mathematically random procedure, and then locate the exact element that was selected for inclusion in the sample.

After numbering all elements in a sampling frame, you can use a list of random numbers to decide which elements to select. You will need as many random numbers as there are elements to be sampled. For example, for a sample of 100, you need 100 random numbers. You can get random numbers from a computer program that produces lists of random numbers or from a *random-number table*, a table of numbers chosen in a mathematically random way. Random-number tables are available in most statistics and research methods books and show numbers generated by a purely random process.

Once you select an element from the sampling frame, you might ask, Should I then return it to the sampling frame or do I keep it separate? The common answer is, do not return it. Unrestricted random sampling is random sampling with replacement—that is, replacing an element after sampling it so it can be selected again. In simple random sampling without replacement, you ignore elements already selected into the sample.

We can illustrate the logic of simple random sampling with an elementary example—sampling marbles from a jar. I have a large jar full of 5,000 marbles, some red and some white. The 5,000 marbles are my population. I want to estimate the parameter, the percentage of red marbles in the population. I randomly select 100 marbles (I close my eyes, shake the jar, pick one marble, and repeat the procedure 99 times). I now have a random sample of marbles. I count the number of red marbles in my sample to estimate the percentage of red versus white marbles in the population. This is a lot easier than counting all 5,000 marbles. My sample has 52 white and 48 red marbles.

Does this mean that the population parameter is 48 percent red marbles? Maybe not. Because of random chance, my specific sample might be off. I can check my results by dumping the 100 marbles back in the jar, mixing the marbles, and drawing a second random sample of 100 marbles. On the second try, my sample has 49 white marbles and 51 red ones. Now I have a problem. Which is correct? How good is this random sampling business if different samples from the same population can yield different results? I repeat the procedure over and over until I have drawn 130 different samples of 100 marbles each (see Example Box 6.2 for results). Most people might empty the jar and count all 5,000, but I want to see what is going on. The results of my 130 different samples reveal a clear pattern. The most common mix of red and white marbles is 50/50. Samples that are close to that split are more frequent than those with more uneven splits. The population parameter appears to be 50 percent white and 50 percent red marbles.

Mathematical proofs and empirical tests demonstrate that the pattern found in Example Box 6.2 always appears. The set of many random samples is my *sampling distribution*. It is a distribution of different samples that shows the frequency of different sample outcomes from many separate random samples. The pattern will appear if the sample size is 1,000 instead of 100; if there are 10 colors of marbles instead of 2; if the population has 100 marbles or 10 million marbles instead of 5,000; and if the population is people, automobiles, or colleges instead of marbles. In fact, the pattern will become clearer as more and more independent random samples are drawn from the population.

The pattern in the sampling distribution suggests that over many separate samples, the true population parameter (i.e., the 50/50 split in the preceding example) is more common than any other result. Some samples deviate from the population parameter, but they are less common. When many different random samples are plotted as in the graph in Example Box 6.2, then the sampling distribution looks like a normal or bell-shaped curve. Such a curve is theoretically important and is used throughout statistics.

The *central limit theorem* from mathematics tells us that as the number of different random samples in a sampling distribution increases toward infinity, the pattern of samples and the population parameter become more predictable. With a huge number of random samples, the sampling distribution forms a normal curve, and the midpoint of the curve approaches the population parameter as the number of samples increases.

Perhaps you want only one sample because you do not have the time or energy to draw many different samples. You are not alone. Few researchers draw many repeated samples. Although you draw only one random sample, the central limit theorem lets you generalize from one sample to the population. The theorem is about many samples, but it lets you calculate the probability of a particular sample being off from the population parameter.

Random sampling does not guarantee that every random sample perfectly represents the population. Instead, it means that most random samples will be close to the population parameter most of the time, and that you can calculate the probability of a particular sample being inaccurate. You can use information from the sample and the central limit theorem to estimate the chance that a particular sample is off or unrepresentative (i.e., the size of the sampling error). One way to do this is to combine sample information with knowledge of the central limit theorem to construct *confidence intervals*.

The confidence interval is a relatively simple but powerful idea. When television or newspaper polls are reported, you may hear about something called the margin of error being plus or minus 2 percentage points. This is a version of confidence intervals. A confidence interval is a range around a specific point used to estimate a population parameter. We use a range because the statistics of random processes do not let us predict an exact point. Nonetheless, they allow us to say with a high level of confidence (e.g., 95 percent) that the true population parameter lies within a certain range.

6.2 EXAMPLE BOX
Example of Sampling Distribution

Red	White	Number of Samples
42	58	1
43	57	1
45	55	2
46	54	4
47	53	8
48	52	12
49	51	21
50	50	31
51	49	20
52	48	13
53	47	9
54	46	5
55	45	2
57	43	1
	Total	130

Number of red and white marbles that were randomly drawn from a jar of 5,000 marbles with 100 drawn each time, repeated 130 times for 130 independent random samples.

Number of Samples

```
31                              *
30                              *
29                              *
28                              *
27                              *
26                              *
25                              *
24                              *
23                              *
22                           *  *
21                           *  *  *
20                           *  *  *
19                           *  *  *
18                           *  *  *
17                           *  *  *
16                           *  *  *
15                           *  *  *
14                           *  *  *
13                           *  *  *  *
12                        *  *  *  *  *
11                        *  *  *  *  *
10                        *  *  *  *  *
 9                     *  *  *  *  *  *  *
 8                  *  *  *  *  *  *  *  *
 7                  *  *  *  *  *  *  *  *
 6                  *  *  *  *  *  *  *  *
 5                  *  *  *  *  *  *  *  *  *
 4               *  *  *  *  *  *  *  *  *  *
 3               *  *  *  *  *  *  *  *  *  *
 2            *  *  *  *  *  *  *  *  *  *  *  *
 1      *  *     *  *  *  *  *  *  *  *  *  *  *     *
       42 43 44 45 46 47 48 49 50 51 52 53 54 55 56 57
              Number of Red Marbles in a Sample
```

The calculations for sampling errors or confidence intervals are beyond the level of this discussion, but they use the idea of the sampling distribution that lets you calculate the sampling error and confidence interval. For example, I cannot say, "There are precisely 2,500 red marbles in the jar based on a random sample." However, I can say, "I am 95 percent certain that the population parameter lies between 2,450 and 2,550." I can combine characteristics of the sample (e.g., its size, the variation in it) with the central limit theorem to predict specific ranges around the parameter with a great deal of confidence.

Systematic Sampling.   *Systematic sampling* is simple random sampling with a shortcut for random selection. Again, your first step is to number each element in the sampling frame. Instead of using a list of random numbers, you calculate a *sampling interval*. The interval becomes your quasi-random selection method. The sampling interval (i.e., 1 in *k*, where *k* is some number) tells you how to select elements from a sampling frame by skipping elements in the frame before selecting one for the sample. To use the interval, you should not always start at the beginning, but use a random process to pick a starting point, then use the interval. Continue to the beginning as if all numbered elements were in a circle. Stop when you return to your random starting point.

For instance, I want to sample 300 names from 900. After a random starting point, I select every third name of the 900 to get a sample of 300. My sampling interval is 3. Sampling intervals are easy to compute. I need the sample size and the population size (or sampling frame size as a best estimate). You can think of the sampling interval as the inverse of the sampling ratio. The sampling ratio for 300 names out of 900 is 300/900 = .333 = 33.3 percent. The sampling interval is 900/300 = 3.

In most cases, a simple random sample and a systematic sample yield virtually equivalent results. One important situation in which you cannot substitute systematic sampling for simple random sampling occurs when the elements in a sample are organized in some kind of cycle or pattern. For example, you arrange the sampling frame by married couples with the male first and the female second (see Table 6.2). Such a pattern easily produces an unrepresentative sample if you use systematic sampling. Your systematic sample can be nonrepresentative. If you had even-numbered sampling intervals, it would result in a sample with all husbands or all wives.

Table 6.3 illustrates simple random sampling and systematic sampling. Notice that different names were drawn in each sample. For example, H. Adams appears in both samples, but C. Droullard is only in the simple random sample. This is because it is rare for any two random samples to be identical.

The sampling frame contains 20 males and 20 females (gender is in parentheses after each name). The simple random sample yielded three males and seven females, and the systematic sample yielded five males and five females. Does

TABLE 6.2   Problems with Systematic Sampling of Cyclical Data

Case	
1	Husband
2[a]	Wife
3	Husband
4	Wife
5	Husband
6[a]	Wife
7	Husband
8	Wife
9	Husband
10[a]	Wife
11	Husband
12	Wife

Random start = 2; Sampling interval = 4.
[a]Selected into sample.

TABLE 6.3 How to Draw Simple Random and Systematic Samples

1. Number each case in the sampling frame in sequence. The list of 40 names is in alphabetical order, numbered from 1 to 40.

2. Decide on a sample size. We will draw two 25 percent (10-name) samples.

3. For a *simple random sample,* locate a random-number table (see excerpt). Before using random-number table, count the largest number of digits needed for the sample (e.g., with 40 names, two digits are needed; for 100 to 999, three digits; for 1,000 to 9,999, four digits). Begin anywhere on the random number table (we will begin in the upper left) and take a set of digits (we will take the last two). Mark the number on the sampling frame that corresponds to the chosen random number to indicate that the case is in the sample. If the number is too large (over 40), ignore it. If the number appears more than once (10 and 21 occurred twice in

the example), ignore the second occurrence. Continue until the number of cases in the sample (10 in our example) is reached.

4. For a *systematic sample,* begin with a random start. The easiest way to do this is to point blindly at the random number table, then take the closest number that appears on the sampling frame. In the example, 18 was chosen. Start with the random number, then count the sampling interval, or 4 in our example, to come to the first number. Mark it, and then count the sampling interval for the next number. Continue to the end of the list. Continue counting the sampling interval as if the beginning of the list was attached to the end of the list (like a circle). Keep counting until ending close to the start, or on the start if the sampling interval divides evenly into the total of the sampling frame.

No.	Name (Gender)	Simple Random	Systematic	No.	Name (Gender)	Simple Random	Systematic
01	Abrams, J. (M)			18	Green, C. (M)		START, Yes (10)
02	Adams, H. (F)	Yes	Yes (6)				
03	Anderson, H. (M)			19	Goodwanda, T. (F)	Yes	
04	Arminond, L. (M)			20	Harris, B. (M)		
05	Boorstein, A. (M)			21	Hjelmhaug, N. (M)	Yes[*]	
06	Breitsprecher, P. (M)	Yes	Yes (7)	22	Huang, J. (F)	Yes	Yes (1)
07	Brown, D. (F)			23	Ivono, V. (F)		
08	Cattelino, J. (F)			24	Jaquees, J. (M)		
09	Cidoni, S. (M)			25	Johnson, A. (F)		
10	Davis, L. (F)	Yes[*]	Yes (8)	26	Kennedy, M. (F)		Yes (2)
11	Droullard, C. (M)	Yes		27	Koschoreck, L. (F)		
12	Durette, R. (F)			28	Koykkar, J. (M)		
13	Elsnau, K. (F)	Yes		29	Kozlowski, C. (F)	Yes	
14	Falconer, T. (M)		Yes (9)	30	Laurent, J. (M)		Yes (3)
15	Fuerstenberg, J. (M)			31	Lee, R. (F)		
16	Fulton, P. (F)			32	Ling, C. (M)		
17	Gnewuch, S. (F)			33	McKinnon, K. (F)		

No.	Name (Gender)	Simple Random	Systematic	No.	Name (Gender)	Simple Random	Systematic
34	Min, H. (F)	Yes	Yes (4)	38	Oh, J. (M)		Yes (5)
35	Moini, A. (F)			39	Olson, J. (M)		
36	Navarre, H. (M)			40	Ortiz y Garcia, L. (F)		
37	O'Sullivan, C. (M)						

Excerpt from a Random-Number Table (for Simple Random Sample)

15010	18590	00102	42210	94174	22099
90122	38221	21529	00013	04734	60457
67256	13887	94119	11077	01061	27779
13761	23390	12947	21280	44506	36457
81994	66611	16597	44457	07621	51949
79180	25992	46178	23992	62108	43232
07984	47169	88094	82752	15318	11921

* Numbers that appeared twice in random numbers selected.

this mean that systematic sampling is more accurate? No. To check this, draw a new sample using different random numbers; try taking the first two digits and beginning at the end (e.g., 11 from 11921, then 43 from 43232). Also draw a new systematic sample with a different random start. The last time the random start was 18. Try a random start of 11. What did you find? How many of each sex?

Stratified Sampling. In *stratified sampling*, you first divide the population into subpopulations (strata) on the basis of supplementary information. After dividing the population into strata, you draw a random sample from each subpopulation. You can sample randomly within strata using simple random or systematic sampling. In stratified sampling, you control the relative size of each stratum, rather than letting random processes control it. This guarantees representativeness or fixes the proportion of different strata within a sample. Of course, the necessary supplemental information about strata is not always available.

In general, stratified sampling produces samples that are more representative of the population than simple random sampling. A simple example illustrates why this is so. Imagine a population that is 51 percent female and 49 percent male; the population parameter is a sex ratio of 51 to 49. With stratified sampling, you draw two random samples, one sample from all females and one from all males (e.g., for a sample of 1,000 draw 510 randomly from a list of males, and 490 from a list of females). Your final sample has a 51 to 49 percent sex ratio. Had you used simple random sampling, you would draw randomly from a list of males and females mixed. It would be possible for a random sample to be off from the true sex ratio in the population. Thus, you make fewer errors representing the population and have a smaller sampling error with stratified sampling.

The main situation in which we use stratified sampling is when a stratum of interest is a small percentage of a population and random processes could miss the stratum by chance. For example, you draw a sample of 200 from 20,000 college students. You get information from the college registrar indicating that 2 percent of the 20,000 students, or 400, are divorced women with children under the age of 5. Perhaps for your topic of interest, this group is very important to include in the sample. There would be four such students (2 percent of 200) in a representative sample, but you could miss them by chance in one simple random sample. With stratified sampling, you obtain a list of the 400 such students from the registrar and randomly

select four from it. This guarantees that the sample represents the population with regard to the important strata (see Example Box 6.3).

In special situations, you may want the proportion of a stratum in a sample to differ from its true proportion in the population. For example, the population contains 0.5 percent Aleuts, but you want to examine Aleuts in particular. You oversample so that Aleuts make up 10 percent of the sample. With this type of disproportionate stratified sample, you

---

6.3   EXAMPLE BOX
Illustration of Stratified Sampling

SAMPLE OF 100 STAFF OF GENERAL HOSPITAL, STRATIFIED BY POSITION

Position	Population N	Percent	Simple Random Sample n	Stratified Sample n	Errors Compared to the Population
Administrators	15	2.88	1	3	−2
Staff physicians	25	4.81	2	5	−3
Intern physicians	25	4.81	6	5	+1
Registered nurses	100	19.23	22	19	+3
Nurse assistants	100	19.23	21	19	+2
Medical technicians	75	14.42	9	14	+5
Orderlies	50	9.62	8	10	−2
Clerks	75	14.42	5	14	+1
Maintenance staff	30	5.77	3	6	−3
Cleaning staff	25	4.81	3	5	−2
Total	520	100.00	100	100	

Randomly select 3 of 15 administrators, 5 of 25 staff physicians, and so on.

Note: Traditionally, N symbolizes the number in the population and n represents the number in the sample.

The simple random sample overrepresents nurses, nursing assistants, and medical technicians, but underrepresents administrators, staff physicians, maintenance staff, and cleaning staff. The stratified sample gives an accurate representation of each type of position.

cannot generalize directly from the sample to the population without special adjustments.

In some situations, you want the proportion of a stratum or subgroup to differ from its true proportion in the population. For example, Davis and Smith (1992) reported that the 1987 General Social Survey (explained in a later chapter) oversampled African Americans. A random sample of the U.S. population yielded 191 Blacks. Davis and Smith conducted a separate sample of African Americans to increase the total number of Blacks to 544. The 191 Black respondents are about 13 percent of the random sample, roughly equal to the percentage of Blacks in the U.S. population. The 544 Blacks are 30 percent of the disproportionate sample. The researcher who wants to use the entire sample must adjust it to reduce the number of sampled African Americans before generalizing to the U.S. population. Disproportionate sampling helps if you want to focus on issues most relevant to a subpopulation. In this case, you can more accurately generalize to African Americans using the 544 respondents than using a sample of only 191. The larger sample is more likely to reflect diversity within the African American subpopulation.

Cluster Sampling. *Cluster sampling* addresses two problems: you lack a good sampling frame for a dispersed population and the cost to reach a sampled element is very high. For example, there is no single list of all automobile mechanics in North America. Even if you got an accurate sampling frame, it would cost too much for you to reach the sampled mechanics who are geographically spread out. Instead of using a single sampling frame, you can use a sampling design that involves multiple stages and clusters.

A *cluster* is a unit that contains final sampling elements but you can treat it temporarily as a sampling element itself. Here is how cluster sampling works, you first sample clusters, each of which contains elements, and then you draw a second sample from within the clusters selected in the first stage of sampling. In other words,

you randomly sample clusters, and then randomly sample elements from within the selected clusters. This has a big practical advantage. You can create a good sampling frame of clusters, even if it is impossible for you to create one for sampling elements. Once you get a sample of clusters, creating a sampling frame for elements within each cluster becomes more manageable. A second advantage for geographically dispersed populations is that elements within each cluster are physically closer to one another. This may produce a savings in locating or reaching each element.

You can draw several samples in stages in cluster sampling. In a three-stage sample, stage 1 is random sampling of big clusters; stage 2 is random sampling of small clusters within each selected big cluster; and the last stage is sampling of elements from within the sampled small clusters. For example, you want a sample of individuals from Mapleville. First, you randomly sample city blocks, then households within blocks, then individuals within households (see Example Box 6.4). Although there is no accurate list of all residents of Mapleville, there is an accurate list of blocks in the city. After selecting a random sample of blocks, you can count all households on the selected blocks to create a sample frame for each block. You can then use the list of households to draw a random sample at the stage of sampling households. Finally, you choose a specific individual within each sampled household.

Cluster sampling is usually less expensive than simple random sampling, but it is less accurate. Each stage in cluster sampling can introduce sampling errors. This means a multistage cluster sample has more sampling errors than a one-stage random sample.

If you use cluster sampling, you must decide the number of clusters and the number of elements within each cluster. For example, in a two-stage cluster sample of 240 people from Mapleville, you could randomly select 120 clusters and select 2 elements from each, or you could randomly select two clusters and select

EXAMPLE BOX

6.4 Illustration of Cluster Sampling

Goal: Draw a random sample of 240 people in Mapleville.

Step 1: Mapleville has 55 districts. Randomly select 6 districts.

1 2 3* 4 5 6 7 8 9 10 11 12 13 14 15* 16 17 18 19 20 21 22 23 24 25 26
27* 28 29 30 31* 32 33 34 35 36 37 38 39 40* 41 42 43 44 45 46 47 48
49 50 51 52 53 54* 55

* = Randomly selected.

Step 2: Divide the selected districts into blocks. Each district contains 20 blocks. Randomly select 4 blocks from the district.

Example of District 3 (selected in step 1):

1 2 3 4* 5 6 7 8 9 10* 11 12 13* 14 15 16 17* 18 19 20

* = Randomly selected.

Step 3: Divide blocks into households. Randomly select households.

Example of Block 4 of District 3 (selected in step 2):

Block 4 contains a mix of single-family homes, duplexes, and four-unit apartment buildings. It is bounded by Oak Street, River Road, South Avenue, and Greenview Drive. There are 45 households on the block. Randomly select 10 households from the 45.

1	#1 Oak Street	16	"	31*	"
2	#3 Oak Street	17*	#154 River Road	32*	"
3*	#5 Oak Street	18	#156 River Road	33	"
4	"	19*	#158 River Road	34	#156 Greenview Drive
5	"	20*	"	35*	"
6	"	21	#13 South Avenue	36	"
7	#7 Oak Street	22	"	37	"
8	"	23	#11 South Avenue	38	"
9*	#150 River Road	24	#9 South Avenue	39	#158 Greenview Drive
10*	"	25	#7 South Avenue	40	"
11	"	26	#5 South Avenue	41	"
12	"	27	#3 South Avenue	42	"
13	#152 River Road	28	#1 South Avenue	43	#160 Greenview Drive
14	"	29*	"	44	"
15	"	30	#152 Greenview Drive	45	"

* = Randomly selected.

Step 4: Select a respondent within each household.

Summary of cluster sampling:

1 person randomly selected per household
10 households randomly selected per block
4 blocks randomly selected per district
6 districts randomly selected in the city
1 × 10 × 4 × 6 = 240 people in sample

120 elements in each. Which is best? The general answer is that a design with more clusters is better. This is because elements within clusters (e.g., people living on the same block) tend to be similar to each other (e.g., people on the same block tend to be more alike than people living on different blocks). If you chose a few clusters, you would select many similar elements, which would be less representative of the total population. For example, Mapleville has 800 city blocks. You could select randomly two blocks, both happen to have wealthy people, and then randomly draw 120 people from each of the two blocks. This would be less representative of the city than a sample in which you randomly selected 120 city blocks and then randomly picked two individuals from each block.

When you sample from a large geographical area and must travel to each element for personal interviews or contact, cluster sampling significantly reduces travel costs. As usual, there is a tradeoff between accuracy and cost.

For example, Alan, Ricardo, and Barbara each plan to visit and personally interview a sample of 1,500 students who represent the population of all college students in North America. Alan obtains an accurate sampling frame of all students and uses simple random sampling. He travels to 1,000 different locations to interview one or two students at each. Ricardo draws a random sample of three colleges from a list of all 3,000 colleges, then visits the three and selects 500 students from each. Barbara draws a random sample of 300 colleges. She visits the 300 and selects five students at each. If travel costs average $250 per location, Alan's travel bill is $250,000, Ricardo's is $750, and Barbara's is $75,000. Alan's sample is highly accurate, but Barbara's is only slightly less accurate for one-third the cost. Ricardo's sample is the cheapest, but it is not representative at all.

Probability Proportionate to Size.   There are two methods of cluster sampling. The method just described is proportionate or unweighted cluster sampling. It is proportionate because the

size of each cluster (or number of elements at each stage) is the same. The more common situation is for the cluster groups to be of different sizes. When this is the case, you must adjust the probability or sampling ratio at various stages in sampling (see Example Box 6.5).

The foregoing cluster sampling example with Alan, Barbara, and Ricardo illustrates the problem with unweighted cluster sampling. Barbara drew a simple random sample of 300 colleges from a list of all 3,000 colleges, but she made a mistake—unless every college has an identical number of students. Her method gave each college an equal chance of being selected—a 300/3,000 or 10 percent chance. But colleges have different numbers of students, so each student does not have an equal chance to end up in her sample. Barbara listed every college and sampled from the list. A large university with 40,000 students and a small college with 400 students had an equal chance of being selected. But if she chose the large university, the chance of a given student at that college being selected was 5 in 40,000 (5/40,000 = 0.0125 percent), whereas a student at the small college had a 5 in 400 (5/400 = 1.25 percent) chance of being selected. The small-college student was 100 times more likely to be in her sample. The total probability of being selected for a student from the large university was 0.125 percent (10 × 0.0125), while it was 12.5 percent (10 × 1.25) for the small-college student. Barbara violated a principle of random sampling—that each element has an equal chance of being selected into the sample.

If Barbara uses **probability proportionate to size (PPS)** and samples correctly, then each final sampling element or student will have an equal probability of being selected. She does this by adjusting the chances of selecting a college in the first stage of sampling. She must give large colleges with more students a greater chance of being selected and small colleges a smaller chance. She adjusts the probability of selecting a college on the basis of the proportion of all students in the population who attend it.

Sampling has many terms for the different parts of samples or types of samples. A complex sample illustrates how researchers use them. Look at the 1980 sample for the best-known national U.S. survey in sociology, the General Social Survey.

The *population* is defined as all resident adults (18 years or older) in the U.S. for the *universe* of all Americans. The *target population* consists of all English-speaking adults who live in households, excluding those living in institutional settings such as college dormitories, nursing homes, or military quarters. The researchers estimated that 97.3 percent of all resident adults lived in households and that 97 percent of the household population spoke sufficient English to be interviewed.

The researchers used a complex multistage probability sample that is both a *cluster sample* and a *stratified sample*. First, they created a national *sampling frame* of all U.S. counties, independent cities, and Standard Metropolitan Statistical Areas (SMSAs), a Census Bureau designation for larger cities and surrounding areas. Each *sampling element* at this first level had about 4,000 households. They divided these elements into strata. The strata were the four major geographic regions as defined by the Census Bureau, divided into metropolitan and non-metropolitan areas. They then sampled from each strata using *probability proportionate to size (PPS)* random selection, based on the number of housing

units in each county or SMSA. This gave them a sample of 84 counties or SMSAs.

For the second stage, the researchers identified city blocks, census tracts, or the rural equivalent in each county or SMSA. Each *sampling element* (e.g., city block) had a minimum of 50 housing units. In order to get an accurate count of the number of housing units for some counties, a researcher counted addresses in the field. The researchers selected 6 or more blocks within each county or SMSA using PPS to yield 562 blocks.

In the third stage, the researchers used the household as a *sampling element*. They randomly selected households from the addresses in the block. After selecting an address, an interviewer contacted the household and chose an eligible respondent from it. The interviewer looked at a selection table for possible respondents and interviewed a type of respondent (e.g., second oldest) based on the table. In total, 1,934 people were contacted for interviews and 75.9 percent of interviews were completed. This gave a final sample size of 1,468. We can calculate the *sampling ratio* by dividing 1,468 by the total number of adults living in households, which was about 150 million, which is 0.01 percent. To check the representativeness of their sample, the researchers also compared characteristics of the sample to census results (see Davis and Smith, 1992:31–44).

Thus, a college with 40,000 students will be 100 times more likely to be selected than one with 400 students. (See Example Box 6.6 for another example.)

Random-Digit Dialing.   Random-digit dialing (RDD) is a sampling technique used in studies in which you contact the public by telephone. It differs from the traditional method of sampling for telephone interviews because a published list or telephone directory is not the sampling frame.

If your sampling frame is a telephone directory, you will miss three types of people: people without telephones or only cell phones, people who have recently moved, and people with unlisted numbers. Those without phones (e.g., the poor, the uneducated, and transients) are missed in any telephone interview study, but the proportion of the public with a telephone is nearly 95 percent in advanced industrialized nations. As the percentage of the public with telephones has increased, the percentage with unlisted numbers has also grown. Several kinds

6.6

EXAMPLE BOX
Cluster Sample Example

Vaquera and Kao (2005) studied displays of affection among adolescent couples in which the couple were either from the same or different racial groups. Their data were from a national longitudinal study of adolescent health given to students in grades 7 through 12 in 80 randomly selected U.S. high schools. There were over 90,000 students in these schools. After the schools were sampled, approximately 200 students were sampled for interviews from within those schools. Thus, the first cluster was the school, and students were sampled from within the school. Because the schools were not of the same size, ranging from 100 to 3,000 students, the authors adjusted using probabilities proportionate to size (PPS). They found that 53 percent of respondents had a relationship with someone of the opposite sex in the previous 18 months. Whites and Blacks were more likely to have same-race relationships (90 percent) compared to Asians and Hispanics (70 percent). The authors found that same- and mixed-race couples differed little in showing intimate affection, but the interracial couples were less likely to do so in public than the same-race couples.

of people have unlisted numbers: people who want to avoid collection agencies; the very wealthy; and those who want privacy and want to avoid obscene calls, salespeople, and prank calls. In some urban areas, the percentage of unlisted numbers is as high as 50 percent. In addition, people change their residences, so directories that are published annually or less often have numbers for people who have left and do not list those who have recently moved into an area. If you use RDD you randomly select telephone numbers, thereby avoiding the problems of telephone directories. The population is telephone numbers, not people with telephones. Random-digit dialing is not difficult, but it takes time and can frustrate the person doing the calling.

Here is how RDD works in the United States. Telephone numbers have three parts: a three-digit area code, a three-digit exchange number or central office code, and a four-digit number. For example, the area code for Madison, Wisconsin, is 608, and there are many exchanges within the area code (e.g., 221, 993, 767, 455); but not all of the 999 possible three-digit exchanges (from 001 to 999) are active. Likewise, not all of the 9,999 possible four-digit numbers in an exchange (from 0000 to 9999) are being used. Some numbers are reserved for future expansion, are disconnected, or are temporarily withdrawn after someone moves. Thus, a possible U.S. telephone number consists of an active area code, an active exchange number, and a four-digit number in an exchange.

In RDD, you identify active area codes and exchanges, and then randomly select four-digit numbers. A problem is that you can select any number in an exchange. This means that some selected numbers are out of service, disconnected, pay phones, or numbers for businesses; only some numbers are what you want—working residential or personal phone numbers. Until you call, it is not possible to know whether the number is a working number. This means spending a lot of time calling numbers that are disconnected, for businesses, and so forth.

Remember that the sampling element in RDD is the phone number, not the person or the household. Several families or individuals can share the same phone number, or each person may have a separate phone number or multiple phone numbers. This means that after you reach someone, a second stage of sampling is necessary, within household sampling, to select the person to be interviewed.

Example Box 6.5 presents an example of how the many sampling terms and ideas can be used together in a specific real-life situation.

Hidden Populations

In contrast to sampling the general population or visible and accessible people, sampling *hidden populations* (i.e., people who engage in concealed activities) is a recurrent issue in the studies of deviant or stigmatized behavior. It illustrates the creative application of sampling principles, mixing qualitative and quantitative styles of research and often using nonprobability techniques. Examples of hidden populations include illegal drug users, prostitutes, homosexuals, people with HIV/AIDS, homeless people, and others.

Two studies used a respondent-driven sampling method to study the hidden population of illegal drug users in the state of Ohio. Respondent driven sampling (RDS) is a version of snowball sampling and is appropriate when members of a hidden population are likely to maintain contact with one another. It begins by identifying an eligible case or participant. Researchers give this person, called a "seed," referral coupons to distribute among other eligible people who engage in the same activity. For each successful referral, the "seed" receives money. This process is repeated with several waves of new recruits until a point of saturation.

Wang et al. (2006) used a respondent-driven sampling method to recruit 249 illicit drug users in three rural Ohio counties to study substance abuse and health care needs. To be eligible for the sample, participants had to be over 18 years old, not be in drug abuse treatment, and have used cocaine or methamphetamines in the past month. After locating an eligible participant, the researchers paid him or her $50 to participate. The participant could earn an additional $10 by recruiting eligible peers. In a snowball process, each subsequent participant was also asked to make referrals. The authors identified 19 people to start. Only a little over half (11 of the 19) referred peers for the study who were eligible and participated. Over roughly 18 months, the researchers were able to identify 249 participants for their study. They compared the study sample with characteristics of estimates of the population using illegal drugs and found that the racial composition of the originally identified participants (White) led to overrepresentation of that racial category. Otherwise, it appeared that the

method was able to draw a reasonable sample of the hidden population.

In a similar study, Draus and associates (2005) conducted a field research study of illicit drug users in four rural Ohio counties using respondent-driven sampling. In the study by Draus et al., each interviewed drug-using participant was paid $50 for an initial two-hour interview and $35 for an hour-long follow-up interview. The participants received three referral coupons at the end of the initial interview and got $10 for each eligible participant they referred who completed an initial interview. No participant received more than three referral coupons. Sometimes this yielded no new participants, but at other times more than the three people with referral coupons were recruited. In one case, a young man heard about the study at a local tattoo parlor and called the study office in July 2003. He (participant 157) had been a powder cocaine user and in his interview said he knew many other drug users. He referred two new participants (participants 161 and 146) who came in about one month later. Participant 161 did not refer anyone new, but participant 146 referred four new people, and two of the four (154 and 148) referred still others. Participant 154 referred four new people and 146 referred one new person, and that one person (participant 158) referred four others. This sampling process that took place in different geographic locations produced 249 users of cocaine or methamphetamine between June 2002 and February 2004.

You are now familiar with several major types of probability samples (see Table 6.4) and supplementary techniques used with them (e.g., PPS, within-household, RDD, and RDS) that may be appropriate. In addition, you have seen how to combine nonprobability and probability sampling for special situations, such as hidden populations. Next, we turn to determining a sample size for probability samples.

How Large Should a Sample Be?

Students and people new to social research often ask, "How large does my sample have to

TABLE 6.4	Types of Probability Samples	
Type of Sample	**Technique**
Simple Random	Create a sampling frame for all cases, then select cases using a purely random process (e.g., random-number table or computer program).
Stratified	Create a sampling frame for each of several categories of cases, draw a random sample from each category, then combine the several samples.
Systematic	Create a sampling frame, calculate the sampling interval 1/k, choose a random starting place, then take every 1/k case.
Cluster	Create a sampling frame for larger cluster units, draw a random sample of the cluster units, create a sampling frame for cases within each selected cluster unit, then draw a random sample of cases, and so forth.

be?" The best answer is, "It depends." It depends on the kind of data analysis you plan, on how accurate the sample has to be for your purposes, and on population characteristics. As you have seen, a large sample size alone does not guarantee a representative sample. A large sample without random sampling or with a poor sampling frame is less representative than a smaller one with random sampling and an excellent sampling frame. Good samples for qualitative purposes can be very small.

We can approach the question of sample size in two ways. One way is to make assumptions about the population and use statistical equations about random sampling processes. The calculation of sample size by this method requires a statistical discussion that is beyond the level of this text. You must make assumptions about the degree of confidence (or number of errors) that is acceptable and the degree of variation in the population. A second and more frequently used way is a rule of thumb—a conventional or commonly accepted amount. Most researchers use it because they rarely have the information required by the statistical method and because it gives sample sizes close to those of the statistical method. Rules of thumb are not arbitrary but are based on past experience with samples that have met the requirements of the statistical method.

One principle of sample sizes is, the smaller the population, the bigger the sampling ratio has to be for an accurate sample (i.e., one with a high probability of yielding the same results as the entire population). Larger populations permit smaller sampling ratios for equally good samples. This is because as the population size grows, the returns in accuracy for sample size shrink.

For small populations (under 1,000), you need a large sampling ratio (about 30 percent). For example, a minimum sample size of about 300 is required for a high degree of accuracy. For moderately large populations (10,000), a smaller sampling ratio (about 10 percent) is needed to be equally accurate, or a sample size of around 1,000. For large populations (over 150,000), smaller sampling ratios (1 percent) are possible. Samples of about 1,500 can be equally accurate. To sample from very large populations (over 10 million), you can achieve accuracy using tiny sampling ratios (0.025 percent) or a sample of about 2,500. The size of the population ceases to be relevant once the sampling ratio is very small, and samples of about 2,500 are nearly as accurate for populations of 200 million as for 10 million. These are approximate sizes, and practical limitations (e.g., cost) also play a role.

A related principle is that for small samples, small increases in sample size can produce huge gains in accuracy. For big samples, small increases in sample size make little difference. Equal increases in sample size produce more of an increase in accuracy for small than for large samples.

Your decision about the best sample size depends on three things: (1) the degree of accuracy required, (2) the degree of variability or diversity in the population, and (3) the number of different variables examined simultaneously in data analysis. Everything else being equal, larger samples are needed if you want high accuracy, if the population has a great deal of variability or heterogeneity, or if you want to consider many variables in the data analysis simultaneously. Smaller samples are sufficient when less accuracy is acceptable, when the population is homogeneous, or when you only consider a few variables a time.

The analysis of data on subgroups also affects your decision about sample size. If you want to analyze subgroups in the population, you will need a larger sample. For example, I want to analyze four variables for males between the ages of 30 and 40 years old. If this sample is of the general public, then only a small proportion (e.g., 10 percent) of sample cases will be males in that age group. A rule of thumb is you want to have about 50 cases for each subgroup you analyze. Thus, if I want to analyze a group that is only 10 percent of the population, then I should have at least 10 × 50 or 500 cases in the sample to be sure I get enough for the subgroup analysis.

Drawing Inferences

A reason to sample is so you can draw inferences from the sample to the population. In fact, an entire subfield of statistical data analysis called *inferential statistics* focuses on drawing accurate inferences. When you do a study, you directly observe measures of variables using units in the sample. The sample stands for or it represents the population. You are not interested in a sample in itself; rather, you want to infer from the sample to the population. Thus, a gap exists between what you concretely have (a sample) and what is of real interest (a population) (see Figure 6.4).

In the last chapter, you saw how the logic of measurement could be stated in terms of a gap between abstract constructs and concrete indicators. Measures of concrete, observable data are approximations for abstract constructs. You use the approximations to estimate what is of real interest (i.e., constructs and causal laws). Conceptualization and operationalization bridge the gap in measurement just as the use of sampling frames, the sampling process, and inference bridge the gap in sampling.

You can put the logic of sampling and the logic of measurement together by directly observing measures of constructs and empirical relationships in samples (see Figure 6.4). You infer or generalize from what you can observe empirically in samples to the abstract causal laws and constructs in the population.

Validity and sampling error have similar functions. This can be illustrated by the analogy between the logic of sampling and the logic of measurement—that is, between what you empirically observe and what you discuss in more abstract terms. In measurement, you want valid indicators of constructs—that is, concrete indicators that accurately represent abstract constructs. In sampling, you want samples that have little sampling error—concrete collections of cases that accurately represent unseen and abstract populations. A valid measure deviates little from the construct it represents. A sample with little sampling error permits estimates that deviate little from population parameters.

All researchers try to reduce sampling errors. The calculation of the sampling error is not presented here, but it is based on two factors: the sample size and the amount of diversity in the sample. Everything else being equal, the larger the sample size, the smaller the sampling error. Likewise, the greater the homogeneity (or the less the diversity) in a sample, the smaller its sampling error.

Sampling error is also related to confidence intervals. If two samples are identical except that one is larger, the one with more cases will have a smaller sampling error and narrower confidence intervals. Likewise, if two samples are identical except that the cases in one are more similar to each other, the one with greater homogeneity

FIGURE 6.4   Model of the Logic of Sampling and of Measurement

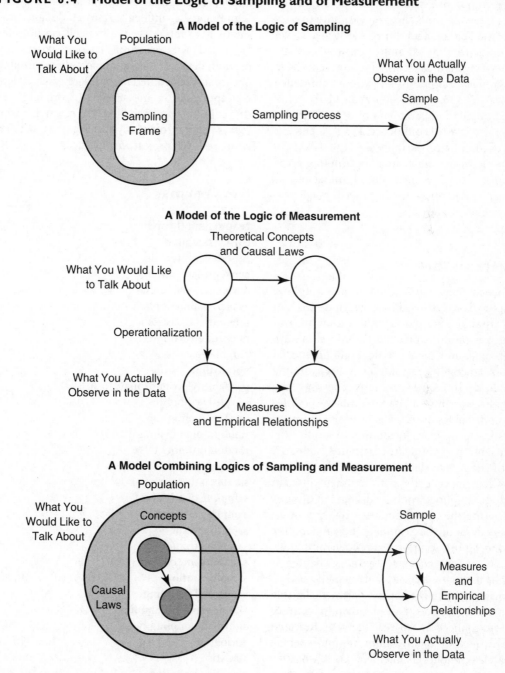

A Model of the Logic of Sampling

What You Would Like to Talk About

Population

Sampling Frame

Sampling Process

What You Actually Observe in the Data

Sample

A Model of the Logic of Measurement

Theoretical Concepts and Causal Laws

What You Would Like to Talk About

Operationalization

What You Actually Observe in the Data

Measures and Empirical Relationships

A Model Combining Logics of Sampling and Measurement

Population

What You Would Like to Talk About

Concepts

Causal Laws

Sample

Measures and Empirical Relationships

What You Actually Observe in the Data

will have a smaller sampling error and narrower confidence intervals. A narrow confidence interval means that you get more precise population parameter estimates for a given level of confidence. For example, you want to estimate average annual family income. You have two samples. Sample 1 gives you a confidence interval of $33,000–39,000 around the estimated population parameter of $36,000 for an 80 percent level of confidence. For a 95 percent level of confidence, the range is $21,000–45,000. A sample with a much smaller sampling error (because it is larger or is more homogeneous) might give a $35,000–37,000 range for a 95 percent confidence level.

CONCLUSION

In this chapter, you learned about sampling. Sampling is widely used in social research. You learned about types of sampling that are not based on random processes. Only some are acceptable, and their use depends on special circumstances. In general, probability sampling is preferred by quantitative researchers because it produces a sample that represents the population and enables the researcher to use powerful statistical techniques. In addition to simple random sampling, you learned about systematic, stratified, and cluster sampling. Although this book does not cover the statistical theory used in random sampling, from the discussion of sampling error, the central limit theorem, and sample size, it should be clear that random sampling produces more accurate and precise sampling.

Before moving on to the next chapter, it may be useful to restate a fundamental principle of social research: Do not compartmentalize the steps of the research process; rather, learn to see the interconnections between the steps. Research design, measurement, sampling, and specific research techniques are interdependent. Unfortunately, the constraints of presenting information in a textbook necessitate presenting the parts separately, in sequence. In practice, researchers think about data collection when they design research and develop measures for variables. Likewise, sampling issues influence research design, measurement of variables, and data collection strategies. As you will see in future chapters, good social research depends on simultaneously controlling quality at several different steps—research design, conceptualization, measurement, sampling, and data collection and handling. The researcher who makes major errors at any one stage may make an entire research project worthless.

Key Terms

central limit theorem
cluster sampling
confidence intervals
convenience sampling
deviant case sampling
hidden populations
inferential statistics
nonrandom sample
parameter
population
probability proportionate to size (PPS)
purposive sampling
quota sampling
random-digit dialing (RDD)
random-number table
random sample
sample
sampling distribution
sampling element
sampling error
sampling frame
sampling interval
sampling ratio
sequential sampling
simple random sampling
snowball sampling
sociogram
statistic
stratified sampling
systematic sampling
target population

Survey Research

Someone hands you a sheet of paper full of questions. The first reads: "I would like to learn your opinion of the Neuman research methods textbook. Would you say it is (a) well organized, (b) adequately organized, or (c) poorly organized?" You probably would not be shocked by this. It is a kind of survey, and most of us are accustomed to surveys by the time we reach adulthood.

The survey is the most widely used social science data-gathering technique. In fact, it might be too popular. Many people say, "Do a survey," to get information when they should ask, "What is the most appropriate way to get good data for this issue?" Widespread public familiarity with the survey technique and the ease of conducting a survey can be a drawback. Despite their wide use and popularity, without care, a survey can easily yield misleading results. Surveys can provide us with accurate, reliable, and valid data, but to do this they require serious effort and thought. Surveys have many uses and take many forms—phone interviews, Internet opinion polls, and paper questionnaires. All forms rely on the principles of the professional social research survey. In this chapter, you learn about survey research, as well as its limitations.

WHEN TO USE A SURVEY

Survey research developed within the positivist approach to social science (you read about positivism in Chapter 2). Following principles of positivism, survey research rests on the assumption that social reality is made up of stable, objective facts. Also, we can precisely measure features of social reality to convert it into quantitative data and then use statistics on the data to test causal relationships that exist in social reality.

To conduct a survey, you ask many people (called *respondents*) about their beliefs, opinions, characteristics, and past or present behavior. Surveys are appropriate when your research question is about self-reported beliefs or behaviors. If your variables can be measured by having people answer questions, then the survey is a good choice. It is usually more efficient to ask about many things at one time in a survey. You can measure many variables (often with multiple indicators) and test several hypotheses in a single survey.

Although the categories overlap, you can ask the following aspects of social life in a survey:

1. *Behavior.* How frequently do you brush your teeth? Did you vote in the last city election? When did you last visit a close relative?
2. *Attitudes/beliefs/opinions.* What kind of job do you think the mayor is doing? Do you think other people say many negative things about you when you are not there? What is the biggest problem facing the nation today?
3. *Characteristics.* Are you married, single, divorced, separated, or widowed? Do you belong to a union? What is your age?
4. *Expectations.* Do you plan to buy a new car in the next 12 months? How much schooling do you think your child will get? Do you think the population in this town will grow, shrink, or stay the same?
5. *Self-classification.* Do you consider yourself to be liberal, moderate, or conservative? Into which social class would you put your family? Would you say you are highly religious or not religious?
6. *Knowledge.* Who was elected mayor in the last election? About what percentage of the people in this city are non-White? Is it legal to own a personal copy of Karl Marx's *Communist Manifesto* in this country?

Be careful about using surveys to ask directly about explanations of social events or actions, the "why?" questions (e.g., Why do you think crime occurs?). Asking people directly does not always get a true reason or actual cause. Respondents are not always aware of the causal factors that shape beliefs or behavior. The "why?"

question is appropriate, however, if you want to discover a respondent's subjective understanding or the informal theory he or she uses. Knowing how people think is useful, but do not confuse a respondent's informal theory about what is occurring with the social science task of developing a causal theory that builds on the broad base of knowledge that is in the scientific literature.

An important limitation of the survey method is that its data is only about what a person or organization says. What a person says may differ from what he or she truly does or thinks. Pager and Quillian (2005) shed light on this issue when they compared telephone survey responses from Milwaukee-area employers about their willingness to hire ex-offenders of different races with an "audit." In the audit, a trained pair of young males with specific characteristics applied for 350 job openings. Employers agreed to hire 34 percent of White and 14 percent of Black applicants. The applicants had identical job experience and credentials and no criminal records. The same employers agreed to hire 17 percent of Whites and 5 percent of Blacks with identical job experience, credentials, and criminal records for illegal drug use. They conducted a phone survey of employers a few months later. Pager and Quillian found far more employers expressed a willingness to hire an ex-offender (67 percent). The data showed no differences in the offender's race in the telephone survey. Also, certain types of employers said they were more willing to hire an ex-offender, but in the audit all types of employers acted the same. The authors said, "Survey responses have very little connection to the actual behaviors exhibited by these employers" (p. 367).

THE LOGIC OF SURVEY RESEARCH

What Is a Survey?

When you conduct a survey, survey questions are measures of variables, and all respondents answer the same questions. You can use the answers to test multiple hypotheses and to

infer temporal order from questions about past behavior, experiences, or characteristics. For example, years of schooling or a respondent's race are prior to current attitudes. You can measure an association among variables with statistical techniques. Going back to the criteria for demonstrating causality, this gives you temporal order and associations. You also need to think of alternative explanations when planning a survey and measure variables that represent alternative explanations (i.e., control variables). Later, you can use statistics to examine their effects and to rule out alternative explanations. Survey research is often called *correlational*. This is because survey research has control variables instead of experimental controls. Control variables are substitutes for the control that experimenters have over a physical setting and events as they establish the temporal order of variables and rule out alternative explanations to establish a causal relationship (you will read about experiments in the next chapter). In survey research, you logically determine the temporal order of variables and examine the associations or correlations among variables, but to rule out alternative explanations you use control variables and examine the statistical relations among them.

Steps in Conducting a Survey

To conduct survey research, you follow a deductive approach to research. This means starting with a theoretical or applied research problem and ending with empirical measures and data analysis. Once you decide that the survey is an appropriate method, follow the steps outlined in Figure 7.1.

In the first phase, you develop an instrument—a survey questionnaire or interview schedule—that you use to measure variables. In a *questionnaire*, the respondents read the questions themselves and mark answers themselves. In an *interview schedule*, an interviewer reads questions to the respondent and then records the respondent's responses. To simplify the discussion, I will use only the term *questionnaires*.

FIGURE 7.1 **Steps in the Process of Survey Research**

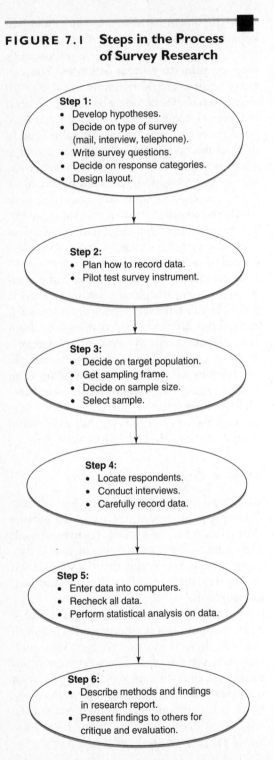

Step 1:
- Develop hypotheses.
- Decide on type of survey (mail, interview, telephone).
- Write survey questions.
- Decide on response categories.
- Design layout.

Step 2:
- Plan how to record data.
- Pilot test survey instrument.

Step 3:
- Decide on target population.
- Get sampling frame.
- Decide on sample size.
- Select sample.

Step 4:
- Locate respondents.
- Conduct interviews.
- Carefully record data.

Step 5:
- Enter data into computers.
- Recheck all data.
- Perform statistical analysis on data.

Step 6:
- Describe methods and findings in research report.
- Present findings to others for critique and evaluation.

To conduct a survey, you first conceptualize and operationalize all your variables as survey questions. You will want to write and rewrite questions for clarity and completeness. In addition, you must organize questions on the questionnaire based on the research question, the respondents, and the type of survey. (The types of surveys are discussed later.)

As you prepare a questionnaire, think ahead to how you will record and organize data for analysis. You should pilot-test the questionnaire with a small set of respondents similar to those in the final survey. If you use other people as interviewers, you must train them with the questionnaire. In the pilot-test you will ask respondents whether the questions were clear and explore their interpretations to see whether your intended meaning in the questions was clear. You draw a sample during this phase.

After the planning phase, you are ready to collect the data. This phase is usually shorter than the planning phase. You locate sampled respondents in person, by telephone, by mail, or on the Internet. You provide respondents with information and instructions on completing the questionnaire or interview. The questions follow. At this stage, it is a simple stimulus–response or question–answer pattern. You must accurately record answers or responses immediately. After all respondents completed the questionnaire and you have thanked them, you should organize the data and prepare them for statistical analysis.

Survey research can be simple and cheap or complex and expensive. A survey with 10 questions distributed by hand or completed online by 60 people is simple and cheap. A moderate-sized survey (e.g., 25 questions for 500 people contacted by phone) requires you to coordinate various people and several steps. A large-scale national sample (500 questions, 2,000 people interviewed face-to-face) involves a multimillion-dollar operation conducted by large professional organizations. In all cases, the administration of survey research requires excellent organization and accurate record keeping. You must keep track of each question, respondent, and questionnaire, and if you use interviewers, each interviewer as well.

In all surveys, you want to assign each sampled respondent an identification number that also appears on the questionnaire. You then can check each completed questionnaire against a list of sampled respondents. Next, you review responses on individual questionnaires, store original questionnaires, and transfer data from questionnaires into an electronic format for statistical analysis. Meticulous bookkeeping and labeling are essential. Otherwise, you may find that a lot of time, effort, and valuable data have been lost through sloppiness.

CONSTRUCTING THE QUESTIONNAIRE

Principles of Good Question Writing

The survey questions measure variables, with some variables measured by multiple questions. Instead of only considering each question in isolation, try to think of all the questions together in a survey. A good questionnaire forms an integrated whole. You want to weave questions together in a questionnaire so they flow smoothly. In addition to the survey questions, a questionnaire has introductory statements and instructions to add comfort and clarity and to reduce potential errors.

Three principles for writing effective survey questions are keep it clear, keep it simple, and keep the respondent's perspective in mind. Good survey questions can provide valid and reliable measures of variables. They also help respondents feel that they understand the question and that their answers are meaningful. Questions that fail to align with a respondent's viewpoint or ones that respondents find confusing will not be good measures of variables and may not produce valid, reliable data. Exercise extra care in writing questions if the respondents are very heterogeneous or

if they are from different life situations than your own.

As you write survey questions you face a dilemma. On the one hand, each respondent should read or hear exactly the same question. This ensures that all respondents are answering the same query, and allows you to merge all respondent data together. On the other hand, if respondents have diverse backgrounds or frames of reference, the exact same question may not be equally clear, relevant, and meaningful to all of them. In short, identical question wording does not equal identical meaning among all people. Yet, if you tailor question wording to each respondent, you cannot pool all data and easily make comparisons. If different respondents are answering different questions, you cannot know whether the question wording or the differences among respondents account for the variation in answers that are your data.

Question writing is more of an art than a science. It takes skill, practice, patience, and creativity. You can see the principles of question writing in the following 12 things you should try to avoid when writing survey questions. The list does not include every possible error, only the more frequent problems.

1. *Avoid jargon, slang, and abbreviations.* Jargon and technical terms come in many forms. Plumbers talk about *snakes,* lawyers about a contract of *uberrima fides,* psychologists about the *Oedipus complex.* Slang is a kind of jargon within a subculture—for example, the homeless talk about a *snowbird* and skiers about a *hotdog.* Also avoid abbreviations. *NATO* usually means North Atlantic Treaty Organization, but for a respondent, it might mean something else (National Auto Tourist Organization, Native Alaskan Trade Orbit, or North African Tea Office). You should avoid slang and jargon unless you are surveying a specialized population. Try to target the vocabulary and grammar to the respondents sampled. For the public, this is the language used on television or in the newspaper (about an eighth-grade reading vocabulary).

2. *Avoid ambiguity, confusion, and vagueness.* Ambiguity and vagueness plague most question writers. It is easy to make implicit assumptions without thinking of the respondents, and this often causes problems. For example, the question, "What is your income?" could mean weekly, monthly, or annual; family or personal; before taxes or after taxes; for this year or last year; from salary or from all sources. The confusion causes inconsistencies in how different respondents assign meaning to and answer the question. If you want before-tax annual family income for last year, you should explicitly ask for it.[1]

Another source of ambiguity is the use of indefinite words or response categories. For example, an answer to the question, "Do you jog regularly? Yes _____ No _____," hinges on the meaning of the word *regularly*. Some respondents may define *regularly* as every day, others as once a week. To reduce respondent confusion and get more information, you should be specific—ask whether a person jogs "about once a day," "a few times a week," "once a week," and so on. (See Example Box 7.1 on improving questions.)

As a general rule, to avoid ambiguous questions you must first think seriously about what

7.1 EXAMPLE BOX
Improving Unclear Questions

Here are three survey questions written by experienced professional researchers. They revised the original wording after a pilot test revealed that 15 percent of respondents asked for clarification or gave inadequate answers (e.g., don't know). As you can see, question wording is an art that may improve with practice, patience, and pilot testing.

Original Question	Problem	Revised Question
Do you exercise or play sports regularly?	What counts as exercise?	Do you do any sports or hobbies, physical activities, or exercise, including walking, on a regular basis?
What is the average number of days each week you have butter?	Does margarine count as butter?	The next question is just about butter—not including margarine. How many days a week do you have butter?
[Following question on eggs] What is the number of servings in a typical day?	How many eggs is a serving? What is a typical day?	On days when you eat eggs, how many eggs do you usually have?

	Responses to Question		Percentage Asking for Clarification	
	Original	*Revision*	*Original*	*Revision*
Exercise question (% saying "yes")	48%	60%	5%	0%
Butter question (% saying "none")	33%	55%	18%	13%
Egg question (% saying "one")	80%	33%	33%	0%

Source: Adapted from Fowler (1992).

you want to measure and then consider the circumstances of respondents. For example, if you want to ask about a respondent's employment, do you want information on the primary job or on all jobs, on full-time work only or both full- and part-time work, on jobs for pay only or on unpaid or volunteer jobs as well?

3. *Avoid emotional language.* Words have implicit connotative as well as explicit denotative meanings. Words with strong emotional connotations can color how respondents hear and answer survey questions. You want to use neutral language. Avoid words with emotional "baggage" because respondents may react to the emotionally laden words rather than to the issue. For example, the question, "What do you think about a policy to pay murderous terrorists who threaten to steal the freedoms of peace-loving people?" is full of emotional words (*murderous, freedoms, steal,* and *peace*).

4. *Avoid prestige bias.* Titles or positions in society (e.g., president, expert, etc.) carry prestige or status. Issues linked to people with high social status can color how respondents hear and answer survey questions. Avoid associating a statement with a prestigious person or group. Respondents may answer on the basis of their feelings toward the prestigious person or group rather than addressing the issue. For example, you ask, "Most doctors believe that cigarette smoke causes lung disease for non-smoking people near a smoker. Do you feel secondhand cigarette smoke is a health hazard?" People who want to agree with doctors are more likely to see it as a health hazard. Likewise, if you ask, "Do you support the Joint Chiefs of Staff's recent actions in Somalia?" Respondents who have never heard of Somalia or know nothing of the actions will answer based on how they feel about the Joint Chiefs of Staff.

5. *Avoid double-barreled questions.* Make each question about one and only one topic. A **double-barreled question** consists of two or more questions joined together. It makes a respondent's answer ambiguous. For example, you ask, "Does this company have pension and dental insurance benefits?" The respondent at a company with dental insurance benefits only, but no pension, could answer either yes or no. The response has an ambiguous meaning. If you want to ask about the joint occurrence of two things—for example, a company with both pension benefits and dental insurance—it is best to ask two separate questions, making each question about a single issue. You can always examine the answers of the two questions later to see whether the respondent works at a company with both, neither, or only pensions or only dental insurance.

6. *Do not confuse beliefs with reality.* This is similar to the warning about "why?" questions mentioned earlier. Do not confuse what a respondent believes with what you, as the researcher, want to measure. A respondent may think that a relationship exists between two variables. Yet, such a belief is not an empirical measurement of variables in a relationship. For example, you want to find out if students rate teachers higher if the teacher tells jokes in class. The two variables are "teacher tells jokes" and "rating the teacher." The *wrong* way to approach the issue is to ask students, "Do you rate a teacher higher if the teacher tells many jokes?" This question measures whether or not students *believe* that they rate teachers based on joke telling; it does not measure the empirical relationship. The *correct* way is to ask two separate questions: "How do you rate this teacher?" and "How many jokes does the teacher tell in class?" Then you can examine answers to the two questions to determine whether they are associated. People's beliefs about a relationship among variables are distinct from actual empirical relationships. People may be aware of a relationship and accurately assess it, or they may hold false beliefs about a relationship.

7. *Avoid leading questions.* Try to help respondents feel that all responses are legitimate. Do not let them become aware of an answer that you expect or want. A *leading* (or *loaded*)

question is one that leads the respondent to choose one response over another by its wording. There are many kinds of leading questions. For example, the question, "You don't smoke, do you?" leads respondents to state that they do not smoke. You can state loaded questions to elicit either a positive or negative answer. For example, "Should the mayor spend even more tax money trying to keep the streets in top shape?" would lead respondents to disagree. The question, "Should the mayor fix the pot-holed, dangerous streets in our city?" is loaded for agreement.

8. *Avoid asking questions that are beyond respondents' capabilities.* Asking something that few respondents know about will frustrate them and yield poor-quality responses. Respondents cannot always recall past details and may not know specific factual information. For example, asking an adult, "How did you feel about your brother when you were 6 years old?" is probably worthless. Asking respondents to make a choice about something they know nothing about (e.g., a technical issue in foreign affairs or an internal policy of an organization) may result in an answer, but one that is unreliable and meaningless. When many respondents are unlikely to know about an issue, use a full-filter question form (to be discussed).

Always try to phrase questions in the terms in which respondents think. For example, few respondents will be able to answer, "How many gallons of gasoline did you buy last year?" Yet, respondents may be able to answer a question about gasoline purchases for a typical week. You can then take that answer and multiply by 52 to estimate their annual purchases.[2]

9. *Avoid false premises.* Do not begin a question with a premise with which respondents may not agree, and then ask them about choices regarding it. Respondents who disagree with the premise will become frustrated and they will not know how to answer. For example, the question, "The post office is open too many hours. Do you want it to open four hours later or close four hours earlier each day?" leaves those to either oppose the premise or oppose both alternatives without a meaningful choice. A better question explicitly asks the respondent to assume a premise is true, then asks for a preference. For example, "Assuming the post office must reduce its operating hours, which would you find more convenient, opening four hours later or closing four hours earlier each day?" Answers to a hypothetical situation are not very reliable, but being explicit will reduce respondent frustration.

10. *Avoid asking about intentions in the distant future.* If you ask people about what they might do under hypothetical circumstances far in the future, you are probably wasting your time. Survey questions are poor predictors of behaviors far removed from a person's current situation or in the distant future. An example would be a question such as, "Suppose a new grocery store opened down the road in three years. Would you shop there?" It is best to ask about current or recent attitudes and behavior. Respondents answer specific, concrete questions that relate to their current or recent experiences more reliably than they do about hypothetical situations beyond their immediate experiences.

11. *Avoid double negatives.* Double negatives in ordinary language are grammatically incorrect and confusing. For example, "I ain't got no job" logically means that the respondent does have a job, but the second negative is used in this way for emphasis. Such blatant errors are rare, but more subtle forms of the double negative are also confusing. They arise when respondents are asked to agree or disagree with a statement. For example, respondents who *dis*agree with the statement, "Students should *not* be required to take a comprehensive exam to graduate" are logically stating a double negative because they *disagree* with *not* doing something.

12. *Avoid overlapping or unbalanced response categories.* Make response categories or choices

mutually exclusive, exhaustive, and balanced. *Mutually exclusive* means that response categories do not overlap. Overlapping categories that are numerical ranges (e.g., 5–10, 10–20, 20–30) can be easily corrected (e.g., 5–9, 10–19, 20–29). The ambiguous verbal choice is another type of overlapping response category—for example, "Are you satisfied with your job or are there things you don't like about it?" *Exhaustive* means that every respondent has a choice—a place to go. For example, asking respondents, "Are you working or unemployed?" leaves out respondents who are not working but do not consider themselves unemployed (e.g., full-time homemakers, people on vacation, students, people with disabilities, retired people, etc.).

Keep response categories *balanced*. A case of unbalanced choices is the question, "What kind of job is the mayor doing: outstanding, excellent, very good, or satisfactory?" Another type of unbalanced question omits information—for example, "Which of the five candidates running for mayor do you favor: Eugene Oswego or one of the others?" Researchers can balance responses by offering bipolar opposites. It is easy to see that the terms *honesty* and *dishonesty* have different meanings and connotations. Asking respondents to rate whether a mayor is highly, somewhat, or not very *honest* is not the same as asking them to rate the mayor's level of *dishonesty*. Unless there is a specific purpose for doing otherwise, it is better to offer respondents equal polar opposites at each end of a continuum.[3] For example, "Do you think the mayor is: very honest, somewhat honest, neither honest nor dishonest, somewhat dishonest, or very dishonest?" (see Table 7.1).

Aiding Respondent Recall

Often you will ask respondents to recall a past event or behavior, such as how many days did you watch television in the past three weeks? Or, when was the last time you saw a medical doctor? Recalling events accurately requires more time and effort than the five seconds that respondents typically take to answer survey questions. Also, a person's ability to recall accurately declines over time. Studies in hospitalization and crime victimization show that while most respondents can recall significant events that occurred in recent weeks, half are inaccurate a year later. Memory is affected by many factors—the topic, events occurring simultaneously and subsequently, the significance of an event for a person, situational conditions (question wording and interview style), and the respondent's need to have internal consistency.

The complexity of respondent recall does not mean that you cannot ask about past events; rather, you need to customize questions and interpret results cautiously. One technique is to provide respondents with special instructions and extra thinking time. You may also want to provide aids to respondent recall, such as a fixed time frame or location references. Rather than ask, "How often did you attend a sports event last winter?" you can ask, "I want to know how many sports events you attended last winter. Let's go month by month. Think back to December. Did you attend any live sports events for which you paid admission in December? Now, think back to January. Did you attend any sports events in January?"

Types of Questions and Response Categories

Threatening Questions. At times, you may want to ask about sensitive issues, ones that respondents may feel uncomfortable answering, or ones that can undermine their presentation of self. These include questions about sexual behavior, drug or alcohol use, mental health problems, abuse of a child or intimate other person, or deviant behavior. Respondents may be reluctant to answer the questions at all, or to answer them completely and truthfully. If you wish to ask such questions, it requires great

TABLE 7.1   Summary of Survey Question Writing Pitfalls

Things to Avoid	Not Good	A Possible Improvement
1. Jargon, slang, abbreviations	Did you drown in brew until you were totally blasted last night?	Last night, about how much beer did you drink?
2. Vagueness	Do you eat out often?	In a typical week, about how many meals do you eat away from home, at a restaurant, cafeteria, or other eating establishment?
3. Emotional language 4. Prestige bias	"The respected Grace Commission documents that a staggering $350 BILLION of our tax dollars are being completely wasted through poor procurement practices, bad management, sloppy bookkeeping, 'defective' contract management, personnel abuses and other wasteful practices. Is cutting pork barrel spending and eliminating government waste a top priority for you?"*	How important is it to you that Congress adopt measures to reduce government waste? Very Important Somewhat Important Neither Important or Unimportant Somewhat Unimportant Not Important At All
5. Double-barreled questions	Do you support or oppose raising social security benefits and increased spending for the military?	Do you support or oppose raising social security benefits? Do you support or oppose increasing spending on the military?
6. Beliefs as real	Do you think more educated people smoke less?	What is your education level? Do you smoke cigarettes?
7. Leading questions	Did you do your patriotic duty and vote in the last election for mayor?	Did you vote in last month's mayoral election?
8. Issues beyond respondent capabilities	Two years ago, how many hours did you watch TV every month?	In the past two weeks, about how many hours do you think you watched TV on a typical day?
9. False premises	When did you stop beating your girl/boyfriend?	Have you ever slapped, punched, or hit your girl/boyfriend?
10. Distant future intentions	After you graduate from college, get a job, and are settled, will you invest a lot of money in the stock market?	Do you have definite plans to put some money into the stock market within the coming two months?
11. Double negatives	Do you disagree with those who do not want to build a new city swimming pool?	There is a proposal to build a new city swimming pool. Do you agree or disagree with the proposal?
12. Unbalanced responses	Did you find the service at our hotel to be, Outstanding, Excellent, Superior, or Good?	Please rate the service at our hotel: Outstanding, Very Good, Adequate, or Poor.

*Actual question taken from a mail questionnaire that was sent to me in May 1998 by the National Republican Congressional Committee. It is also a double-barreled question.

care and you must be extra cautious about the results[4] (see Table 7.2).

Threatening questions are part of a larger issue of self-presentation and ego protection. Respondents usually want to try to present a favorable image of themselves to other people. They may be ashamed, embarrassed, or afraid to give truthful answers. They may find it emotionally painful to confront their own actions honestly, let alone admit them to someone else. They may underreport or self-censor reports of behavior or attitudes they wish to hide or that they believe violate social norms. One study (Tourangeau, Groves, and Redline 2010) suggests people who feel threatened are less likely to participate in surveys and if they do, to answer accurately. People also overreport positive behaviors or generally accepted beliefs (social desirability bias is discussed later).

People tend to underreport having an illness or disability (e.g., cancer, mental illness, venereal disease), engaging in illegal or deviant behavior (e.g., evading taxes, taking drugs, consuming alcohol, engaging in uncommon sexual practices), or revealing their financial status (e.g., income, savings, debts) (see Table 7.3).

TABLE 7.2   Threatening Questions and Sensitive Issues

Topic	Percentage Very Uneasy
Masturbation	56
Sexual intercourse	42
Use of marijuana or hashish	42
Use of stimulants and depressants	31
Getting drunk	29
Petting and kissing	20
Income	12
Gambling with friends	10
Drinking beer, wine, or liquor	10
Happiness and well-being	4
Education	3
Occupation	3
Social activities	2
General leisure	2
Sports activity	1

Source: Adapted from Bradburn and Sudman (1980:68).

TABLE 7.3   Over- (+) and Underreporting (−) Behavior on Surveys

	Percentage Distorted or Erroneous Answers		
	Face to Face	*Phone*	*Self-Administered*
Low Threat/Normative			
Registered to vote	+15	+17	+12
Voted in primary	+39	+31	+36
Have own library card	+19	+21	+18
High Threat			
Bankruptcy	−32	−29	−32
Drunk driving	−47	−46	−54

Source: Adapted from Bradburn and Sudman (1980:8).

Several survey techniques help increase getting truthful answers to threatening questions. Some techniques involve the context and wording of the question itself. You should ask potentially threatening questions only after a warm-up, when an interviewer has developed rapport and trust with the respondents, and respondents have been told that the interviewer wants honest answers. You can phrase the threatening question in an "enhanced way" by providing a context that makes it easier for respondents to give honest answers. For example, the following enhanced question was asked of heterosexual males: "In past surveys, many men have reported that at some point in their lives they had some type of sexual experience with another male. This could have happened before adolescence, during adolescence, or as an adult. Have you ever had sex with a male at some point in your life?" In contrast, a standard form of the question would have asked, "Have you ever had sex with another male?" Males who feel embarrassed or uncomfortable about reporting that they have engaged in same-sex sexual activity are more likely to answer the enhanced version of the question. Another technique is to embed a semi-threatening response within a set of more serious or threatening responses. This may make it seem less deviant or unusual. For example, you want to learn about whether respondents ever shoplifted. They might hesitate to admit shoplifting if you ask about it first, but answer if it appears after being asked four or five other questions about crimes such as armed robbery or burglary. They may answer to shoplifting honestly because it appears less serious, and therefore less threatening, in the context of other questions about more serious criminal behavior.

Socially Desirable Questions. *Social desirability bias* is when respondents distort answers to make their reports conform to social norms. People tend to overreport being cultured (i.e., reading, attending high-culture events), giving money to charity, having a good marriage, loving their children, and so forth. For example, one-third of people who reported in a survey that they gave money to a local charity really did not. Because a norm says that one should vote in elections, many people report voting when they did not. In the United States, people under the greatest pressure to vote (i.e., highly educated, politically partisan, highly religious people who had been contacted by an organization that urged them to vote) are the people most likely to say they voted when they actually did not.

As with threatening questions, you can reduce social desirability bias by phrasing questions in ways that make norm conformity or violation appear to be less objectionable and present a wide range of behavior as acceptable. You can also offer multiple-response categories that give respondents "face-saving" alternatives.

Knowledge Questions. Studies suggest that a large majority of the public cannot correctly answer elementary geography questions, identify major national leaders, or recognize important political documents (e.g., the Declaration of Independence). At times, you may want to learn whether respondents know about an issue or topic. However, knowledge questions can be threatening because respondents do not want to appear ignorant.

In addition, surveys about opinions can get a more accurate picture by first asking about factual information because people may offer opinions based on inaccurate factual knowledge. For example, overall taxes may have gone down but when asked, people have a false belief that the taxes have gone up. This happened in 2010. Survey data showed that after 95 percent of Americans had received a tax cut from the federal government, 24 percent reported that their taxes had increased, 53 percent said taxes stayed the same, and 12 percent said that taxes decreased. Many people expressed political opinions based on a belief that their taxes had gone up, but were doing so based on false information.[5] Of course, people behave based on perceptions, even when those perceptions are inaccurate but survey questions help to reveal whether the perceptions that guide people's behavior are based on accurate or false knowledge.

Respondents do not always accurately answer simple knowledge questions, such as asking the number of people living in a household. In some households, a marginal person—the boyfriend who left for a week, the adult daughter who left after an argument about her pregnancy, or the uncle who walked out after a dispute over money—may be reported as not living in a household, but he or she may not have another permanent residence and considered him- or herself to live there.[6] The inaccuracy is not due to ignorance but different perceptions of the situation. You ask John, a 45-year-old male, how many people are in his household, and he reports four people (John, his wife Sarah, son Jason, and daughter Emily). Then you talk to Emily, who says Julie also lives there and there are five people in the household. You find Julie (a 20-year-old) and ask her. She says she lives at home with John, Sarah, Jason, and Emily most of the time, but gets into frequent fights with her parents then moves in temporarily with several male or female friends. In her view, there are five people in the household.

It is a very good idea to pilot-test questions to check that questions are at an appropriate level of difficulty. Little is gained if 99 percent of respondents cannot answer the question. In addition, you may consider rewording knowledge questions so that respondents feel more comfortable saying they do not know the answer—for example, "How much, if anything, have you heard about. . . ."

Skip or Contingency Questions. You want to avoid asking questions that are irrelevant for a respondent. Yet, some questions apply only to specific respondents. A ***contingency*** ***question*** is a two- (or more) part question. The answer to the first part of the question determines which of two different questions a respondent next receives. Contingency questions select respondents for whom a second question is relevant. Sometimes they are called *screen* or *skip questions*. On the basis of the answer to the first question, the respondent or an interviewer goes to another question or skips certain questions (see Example Box 7.2). Contingency questions are a very valuable type of question that may not be utilized as much as they should be.

Open versus Closed Questions

Debates over advantages and disadvantages of open versus closed questions in survey research have raged for many years. An ***open-ended***

7.2 EXAMPLE BOX
Contingency Question Example

1. Did you complete an internship as part of your major?
   [ ] Yes _____ (GO TO QUESTION 2)
   [ ] No _____ (CONTINUE TO a)

   a. What are your plans immediately after graduating?
      __ (1) Further schooling (e.g., law school, graduate school)
      __ (2) Military service
      __ (3) Employment (go to b below)
      __ (4) Other (please specify, e.g., travel, raise a child) _____
      _____

   b. Have you previously worked for the same employer prior to graduating?
      __ Yes
      __ No

NOW GO TO QUESTION 2

(unstructured, free-response) *question* asks a question (e.g., "What is your favorite television program?") to which respondents can give any answer. A *closed-ended* (structured, fixed-response) *question* both asks a question and gives the respondent fixed responses from which to choose (e.g., "Is the president doing a very good, good, fair, or poor job, in your opinion?").

Each form has advantages and disadvantages (see Expansion Box 7.1). The crucial issue is not which form is best. Rather, it is under what conditions is a form most appropriate. Your choice to use an open- or closed-ended question will depend on the purpose and the practical limitations of a study. The demands of using open-ended questions, with interviewers writing verbatim answers or respondents providing elaborate answers that you must decipher and code in a time-consuming manner, often make them impractical.

Most large-scale surveys have closed-ended questions because they are quicker and easier for both respondents and researchers. Yet something important could be lost when an individual's beliefs and feelings are forced into a few fixed-answer categories. To learn how a respondent thinks, to discover what is really important to him or her, or to get an answer to a question with many possible answers (e.g., age), open questions may be best. At the same time, threatening or sensitive topics (e.g., sexual behavior, liquor consumption) may be more accurately measured with closed questions.

You can reduce disadvantages of a question form by mixing open-ended and closed-ended questions in a questionnaire. Mixing them also offers a change of pace and helps interviewers establish rapport. Periodic probes (i.e., follow-up questions by interviewers) with closed-ended questions can reveal a respondent's reasoning.

Having interviewers periodically use probes to ask about a respondent's thinking is a good way to check whether respondents understand the questions as you intended. However, probes are not substitutes for writing clear questions or creating a framework of understanding for the respondent. Unless carefully stated, probes might shape the respondent's answers or force answers when a respondent does not have an opinion or information. Yet, flexible or conversational interviewing in which interviewers use many probes can improve accuracy on questions about complex issues on which respondents do not clearly understand basic terms or about which they have difficulty expressing their thoughts. For example, to the question, "Did you do any work for money last week?" a respondent might hesitate then reply, "Yes." Then the interviewer probes, "Could you tell me exactly what work you did?" The respondent replies, "On Tuesday and Wednesday, I spent a couple hours helping my buddy John move into his new apartment. For that he gave me $40, but I didn't have any other job or get paid for doing anything else." If your intention was only to get reports of regular employment, the probe has revealed a misunderstanding. You may also use *partially open questions* (i.e., a set of fixed choices with a final open choice of "other"), which allows respondents to offer an answer that you did not include. Open-ended questions are especially valuable in early or exploratory stages of research. For large-scale surveys, you can use open questions in pilot-tests, and then develop closed-question responses from the answers respondents give to the open questions.

As you write closed questions you must make many decisions. How many response choices should be given? Should the questions have a middle or neutral choice? What should be the order of responses? What types of response choices should be used? How will the direction of a response be measured? Answers to these questions are not easy. For example, two response choices are too few, but more than five response choices are rarely effective. You want to measure meaningful distinctions and not collapse them. More specific responses

7.1   EXPANSION BOX
Closed versus Open Questions

Advantages of Closed

■ It is easier and quicker for respondents to answer.

■ The answers of different respondents are easier to compare.

■ Answers are easier to code and statistically analyze.

■ The response choices can clarify question meaning for respondents.

■ Respondents are more likely to answer about sensitive topics.

■ There are fewer irrelevant or confused answers to questions.

■ Less articulate or less literate respondents are not at a disadvantage.

■ Replication is easier.

Advantages of Open

■ They permit an unlimited number of possible answers.

■ Respondents can answer in detail and can qualify and clarify responses.

■ Unanticipated findings can be discovered.

■ They permit adequate answers to complex issues.

■ They permit creativity, self-expression, and richness of detail.

■ They reveal a respondent's logic, thinking process, and frame of reference.

Disadvantages of Closed

■ They can suggest ideas that the respondent would not otherwise have.

■ Respondents with no opinion or no knowledge can answer anyway.

■ Respondents can be frustrated because their desired answer is not a choice.

■ It is confusing if many (e.g., 20) response choices are offered.

■ Misinterpretation of a question can go unnoticed.

■ Distinctions between respondent answers may be blurred.

■ Clerical mistakes or marking the wrong response is possible.

■ They force respondents to give simplistic responses to complex issues.

■ They force people to make choices they would not make in the real world.

Disadvantages of Open

■ Different respondents give different degrees of detail in answers.

■ Responses may be irrelevant or buried in useless detail.

■ Comparisons and statistical analysis become very difficult.

■ Coding responses is difficult.

■ Articulate and highly literate respondents have an advantage.

■ Questions may be too general for respondents who lose direction.

■ Responses are written verbatim, which is difficult for interviewers.

■ A greater amount of respondent time, thought, and effort is necessary.

■ Respondents can be intimidated by questions.

■ Answers take up a lot of space in the questionnaire.

yield more information, but too many specifics create confusion. For example, if you rephrase the question, "Are you satisfied with your dentist?" (which has a yes/no answer) to "How satisfied are you with your dentist: very satisfied, somewhat satisfied, somewhat dissatisfied, or not satisfied at all?", you will obtain more information and give the respondent more choices.

Nonattitudes and the Middle Positions. Survey researchers have debated whether to include choices for neutral, middle, and nonattitudes (e.g., "not sure," "don't know," or "no opinion").[7] You can make two types of errors: accepting a middle choice or "nonattitude" response when respondents actually hold a nonneutral opinion, or forcing respondents to choose a position on an issue when they have no opinion about it.

Many people fear that respondents will pick the nonattitude answer to evade making a choice. Yet, it is usually best to offer a nonattitude choice in a survey. Many people express opinions on fictitious issues, objects, and events. By offering a nonattitude (middle or no opinion) choice, you can identify the people holding middle positions or those without opinions.

Three kinds of attitude questions can help you with the issue of nonattitudes: standard-format, quasi-filter, and full-filter questions (see Example Box 7.3). In the ***standard-format question***, you do not offer a "don't know"

7.3 EXAMPLE BOX
Standard-Format, Quasi-Filter, and Full-Filter Questions

Standard Format

Here is a question about an other country. Do you agree or disagree with this statement? "The Russian leaders are basically trying to get along with America."

Quasi-Filter

Here is a statement about an other country: "The Russian leaders are basically trying to get along with America." Do you agree, disagree, or have no opinion on that?

Full Filter

Here is a statement about an other country. Not everyone has an opinion on this. If you do not have an opinion, just say so. Here's the statement: "The Russian leaders are basically trying to get along with America." Do you have an opinion on that? If yes, do you agree or disagree?

Example of Results from Different Question Forms

	Standard Form (%)	Quasi-Filter (%)	Full Filter (%)
Agree	48.2	27.7	22.9
Disagree	38.2	29.5	20.9
No opinion	13.6[*]	42.8	56.3

[*]Volunteered
Source: Adapted from Schuman and Presser (1981:116–125). Standard format is from Fall 1978; quasi- and full-filter are from February 1977.

choice; a respondent must volunteer it. In a *quasi-filter question*, you offer respondents a "don't know" alternative. A *full-filter question* is a special type of contingency question. You first ask respondents whether they have an opinion, then you ask for the opinion of those who stated that they have an opinion.

Many respondents will answer a question if a "no opinion" choice is missing, even if they actually have no opinion. The same people will select "don't know" when it is offered, or if asked state that they do not have an opinion. Such respondents are called *floaters*—they "float" from giving a response to not knowing. The responses of such people are greatly affected by minor wording changes, so you want to screen them out by using quasi-filter or full-filter questions. Filtered questions do not eliminate all answers to nonexistent issues, but they reduce the problem.

Agree/Disagree, Rankings, or Ratings? If you want to measure values and attitudes, you might ask about the kind of responses to offer.[8] Should questionnaire items make a statement and then ask respondents whether they agree or disagree with it, or should it offer respondents specific alternatives? Should the questionnaire include a set of items and ask respondents to rate them (e.g., approve, disapprove), or should it give them a list of items and force them to rank-order items (e.g., from most favored to least favored)?

Current research suggests you should offer respondents explicit alternatives. For example, instead of asking, "Do you agree or disagree with the statement, 'Men are better suited to. . . .' ?", instead ask, "Do you think men are better suited, women are better suited, or both are equally suited?" Less well-educated respondents are more likely to agree with a statement, whereas forced-choice alternatives encourage thought and avoid the *response set* bias—a tendency of some respondents to agree and not really decide.

You create bias if question wording gives the respondents a reason for choosing one alternative over others. For example, you ask respondents whether they support or oppose a law on energy conservation. The results may change if respondents are asked, "Do you support the law or do you oppose it because the law would be difficult to enforce?" instead of simply asking, "Do you support or oppose the law?"

It is usually better to ask respondents to choose among alternatives by ranking instead of rating items along an imaginary continuum. This is because respondents can rate several items equally high, but will place them in a hierarchy if asked to rank them.[9]

For example, you ask about the most important public issue among a list of seven issues. Respondents rate crime, environment, taxes, and unemployment as important issues, and rate immigration, transportation, and the deficit as not important. However, if asked respondents to rank items, they say unemployment is the most important issue followed by environment, crime, taxes, transportation, immigration, and the deficit in that order. By having the respondents rank issues, you get more information.

Wording Issues

You face two wording issues in surveys. The first, discussed earlier, is to use simple vocabulary and grammar to minimize respondent confusion. Many respondents are confused about the meanings of words or their connotations. For example, respondents were asked whether they thought television news was impartial. It was found that large numbers of respondents had ignored the word *impartial*—a term the middle-class, educated researchers assumed everyone knew. Less than half the respondents had interpreted the word as intended with its proper meaning. Over one-fourth ignored it or had no idea of its meaning. Others gave it unusual meanings, and one-tenth thought it was directly opposite to its true meaning.

The second issue involves how specific words or phrases can influence respondents.

This is trickier because you do not always know in advance whether a word or phrase affects responses. The well-documented difference between *forbid* and *not allow* illustrates the wording issue. Both terms have the same meaning, but many more people say they will "not allow" something than "forbid" it. In general, less well-educated respondents are most influenced by minor wording differences. Sometimes a word has strong connotations or triggers an emotional reaction. For example, Smith (1987) found large differences (e.g., twice as much support) in U.S. survey responses depending on whether a question asked about spending "to help the poor" or "for welfare." During the 1970s and 1980s, hostile rhetoric by U.S. politicians and mass media modified the connotation of the word *welfare* to create a strong negative response (lazy people, wasteful and expensive programs, etc.). Smith suggested avoiding the term because it had become emotionally loaded.

In summary, you need to be vigilant when writing survey questions. Respondents may interpret the meaning of specific words or a question differently than intended, introducing bias into the survey. Some **wording effects** (e.g., the difference between *forbid* and *not allow*) have been around for decades, but other wording effects may appear at any time.[10]

Questionnaire Design Issues

Length of Survey or Questionnaire. How long should your questionnaire be or an interview last? The advantage of long questionnaires or interviews is that they are more cost effective. The cost for extra questions—once you have sampled and contacted a respondent—is small. There is no absolute proper length. The length depends on the survey format (to be discussed) and on the respondent's characteristics. A 5-minute telephone interview is rarely a problem and may be extended to 20 minutes. A few researchers stretched this to beyond 30 minutes. Mail questionnaires are more variable. A short (three- or four-page) questionnaire is appropriate for the general population. Some researchers have had success with questionnaires as long as 10 pages (about 100 items) with the general public, but responses drop significantly for longer questionnaires. For highly educated respondents and a salient topic, you might be able to use a 15-page questionnaire. Face-to-face interviews lasting an hour are not uncommon. In special situations, face-to-face interviews as long as three hours have been conducted.

Question Order or Sequence. You face three question sequence issues: organization of the overall questionnaire, question order effects, and context effects.

Organization of Questionnaire. In general, you want to sequence questions to minimize the discomfort and confusion of respondents. A questionnaire has opening, middle, and ending questions. After an introduction explaining the survey, it is best to make opening questions pleasant, interesting, and easy to answer. This helps a respondent feel comfortable about the questionnaire. Avoid asking many boring background questions or threatening questions first. Organize questions into common topics. Mixing questions on different topics causes confusion. Orient respondents by placing questions on the same topic together and introduce the section with a short introductory statement (e.g., "Now I would like to ask you questions about housing"). Make question topics flow smoothly and logically, and organize them to assist respondents' memory or comfort levels. Do not end with highly threatening questions, and always end with a "thank you."

Order Effects. The order in which you present questions might influence respondent answers. Such "order effects" appear to be strongest for people who lack strong views, for less educated respondents, and for older respondents or those with memory loss.[11] For example, support for an unmarried woman having an abortion rises if the question is preceded by a question about abortion being acceptable when a fetus has serious defects, but not when the question is by itself or before a question about fetus defects. A classic example of order effects is presented in Example Box 7.4.

Respondents may not perceive each survey item as isolated and separate. They respond to survey questions based on the set of issues and their order of presentation. A previous question can influence later ones in two ways: through content (i.e., the substantive issue) and through the respondent's response.

Respondents often interpret a question based on the question or issue that immediately preceded it. For example, you ask a student respondent, "Do you support greater educational contributions for university education?" If this question came after questions about payments by students or their families, such as, "How much do you think the average U.S. college student pays in tuition and fees?", the respondents may interpret "contribution" in the question to mean what students are to

pay. If you ask the same question after ones about nonstudent support for education, such as "What percent of public university operations do you think are provided by government grants and aid?", the respondents are likely to interpret the question to be about increasing government aid.

Answers to a previous question can also influence how a respondent interprets a question. This is because having already answered what is understood as one part an issue, the respondent assumes no overlap. For example, you ask a respondent who is married, "How is your spouse's health?" You next ask, "How is your family's health?" Most respondents will assume that the second question refers to family members other than the spouse (e.g., children, parents, other relatives) because they have already answered about the spouse. Now imagine you asked the same two questions but in the opposite order. This time the respondent would assume the question "How is your family's health?" includes the spouse.[12]

| **7.4** | EXAMPLE BOX
Question Order Effects |

Question 1

"Do you think that the United States should let Communist newspaper reporters from other countries come in here and send back to their papers the news as they see it?"

Question 2

"Do you think a Communist country like Russia should let American newspaper reporters come in and send back to America the news as they see it?"

	Percentage Saying Yes	
Heard First	Yes to #1 (Communist Reporter)	Yes to #2 (American Reporter)
#1	54%	75%
#2	64%	82%

The context created by answering the first question affects the answer to the second question.

Source: Adapted from Schuman and Presser (1981:29).

Context Effects.   In addition to the immediately preceding question or answer, respondents can be influenced by the context of several surrounding questions. As a practical matter, for the same topic you want to use a **funnel sequence** of questions—that is, ask more general questions before specific ones (e.g., ask about health in general before asking about specific diseases).

Sudman, Bradburn, and Schwarz (1996:90–91) showed the context effect by asking how much a respondent followed politics in three ways. When they asked the question alone, about 21 percent of respondents said they followed politics "now and then" or "hardly at all." When they asked the question after asking what the respondent's elected representative recently did, the percentage who said they did not follow nearly doubled, going to 39 percent. Apparently, the knowledge question about the elected representative caused many respondents to feel that they did not really know much. When a question about the amount of "public relations work" the elected representative provided to the area came between the two questions, 29 percent of respondents said they did not follow politics. This question gave respondents an excuse for not knowing the first question—they could blame their representative for their ignorance. Thus, the context made a difference.

Entire topics can create a context. Let us say you want to ask about three topics: child care, future schooling, and employment. The order of the topics might influence later ones. Perhaps the questions about child care influences how a respondent answers about schooling questions. Perhaps after answering questions about child care, the respondent began to think about difficulties managing child care. Because the respondent has child-care difficulties in mind when you next ask about future schooling, the respondent reports lower expectations of future schooling than if the schooling questions had come first.

If you want to see whether there are context effects, you can divide the number of respondents in half and give a random half of the respondents the topics in one order and the other half in the alternative order. You then can examine the results to see whether question order mattered. If question order effects are found, which order tells you what the respondents really think? The answer is that you cannot know for sure.

Several years ago, a class of my students conducted a telephone survey on two topics: concern about crime and attitudes toward a new anti-drunk-driving law. A random half of the respondents heard questions about the drunk-driving law first; the other half heard about crime first. I examined the results to see whether there was any **context effect**—a difference by topic order. I found that respondents who were asked about the drunk-driving law first expressed less fear about crime than did those who were asked about crime first. Likewise, they were more supportive of the drunk-driving law than were those who first heard about crime. The first topic created a context within which respondents answered questions on the second topic. After they were asked about crime in general and thought about violent crime, drunk driving may have appeared to be a less important issue. By contrast, after they were asked about drunk driving and thought about drunk driving as a crime, they may have expressed less concern about crime in general.

Context effects should remind you to always keep the respondent's point of view in mind and strive for unambiguous, clear meaning in survey questions. The more ambiguous a question's meaning, the stronger the context effects can be. Respondents will draw on the context as they interpret survey questions. Previous topics, past questions, or the question a respondent just heard can produce a context effect.

Format and Layout.   You need to decide two format or layout issues: the overall physical layout of the questionnaire and the format of questions and responses.

Questionnaire Layout. Layout is important, whether your questionnaire is for an interviewer or for the respondent. You want questionnaires to be clear, neat, and very easy to follow. A professional appearance with high-quality graphics, space between questions, and good layout improves accuracy and completeness and helps the questionnaire flow.

Give each question a number and put identifying information (e.g., name of organization) on questionnaires. Never cramp questions together or create a confusing appearance. Saving money on printing may ultimately cost you more in terms of lower validity due to a lower response rate or of confusion of interviewers and respondents. For interviews, make a ***cover sheet*** or face sheet for each interview for administrative use. On it put the time and date of the interview, the name of the interviewer, the respondent identification number, and the interviewer's comments and observations. Include interviewer instructions on the questionnaire and print instructions in a different style from the questions for the respondent. This is so an interviewer can easily distinguish between the questions for respondents and instructions.

Layout is especially critical for self-administrated, mail, and online questionnaires. This is because there is no friendly interviewer to interact with the respondent. Instead, you want the questionnaire's appearance to persuade and motivate a respondent. In mail surveys, include a polite, professional cover letter on letterhead stationery. It should identify the researcher and offer a telephone number for questions. Details matter. Respondents will be turned off if they receive a bulky brown envelope with bulk postage addressed to Occupant or if the questionnaire does not fit into the return envelope. Always end with "Thank you for your participation." In online surveys, it is best not to clutter a screen but place one or a few questions on each, with an easily identifiable "continue" or "next" button. Having a graphic indicator of how far the respondent is through the entire survey, such as a clock or chart, or a numerical indicator (5 of 15

questions, or 30% complete) helps respondents who are completing a Web survey. Offering a final open-ended comment box as well as a thank you is good practice on Web surveys. The general rule is you want to leave respondents with a positive feeling about the survey and a sense that you value their participation.

Question design matters. One study of college students asked how many hours they studied per day. Some students saw five answer choices ranging from 0.5 hour to more than 2.5 hours; others saw five answer choices ranging from less than 2.5 hours to more than 4.5 hours. Of students who saw the first set, 77 percent said they studied under 2.5 hours versus 31 percent of those receiving the second set. When the mail questionnaire and telephone interview were compared, 58 percent of students hearing the first set said under 2.5 hours, but there was no change among those hearing the second set. More than differences in response categories were involved, because when students were asked about hours of television watching per day with similar response categories, then the alternative response categories made no difference. What can we learn from this? Respondents without clear answers will rely on questionnaire response categories for guidance. Formats to answer that are more anonymous tend to yield more honest responses.[13]

Question Format. Survey researchers decide on a format for questions and responses. Should respondents circle responses, check boxes, fill in dots, or put an × on a blank line? The basic principle is to make responses unambiguous. Boxes or brackets to be checked and numbers to be circled are usually clearest. Also, listing responses down a page rather than across makes them easier to see (see Example Box 7.5). As mentioned before, use arrows and instructions for contingency questions. Visual aids are helpful. For example, thermometer-like drawings help respondents when you ask about how warm or cool they feel toward someone. A ***matrix question*** (or grid question) is a compact way to present a series of questions using

7.5 EXAMPLE BOX
Question Format Examples

Example of Horizontal versus Vertical Response Choices

Do you think it is too easy or too difficult to get a divorce, or is it about right?

■ Too Easy   ■ Too Difficult   ■ About Right

Do you think it is too easy or too difficult to get a divorce, or is it about right?

■ Too Easy

■ Too Difficult

■ About Right

Example of a Matrix Question Format

	Strongly Agree	Agree	Disagree	Strongly Disagree	Don't Know
The teacher talks too fast.	■	■	■	■	■
I learned a lot in this class.	■	■	■	■	■
The tests are very easy.	■	■	■	■	■
The teacher tells many jokes.	■	■	■	■	■
The teacher is organized.	■	■	■	■	■

Examples of Some Response Category Choices

Excellent, Good, Fair, Poor
Approve/Disapprove
Favor/Oppose
Strongly Agree, Agree, Somewhat Agree, Somewhat Disagree, Disagree, Strongly Disagree
Too Much, Too Little, About Right
Better, Worse, About the Same
Regularly, Often, Seldom, Never
Always, Most of Time, Some of Time, Rarely, Never
More Likely, Less Likely, No Difference
Very Interested, Interested, Not Interested

the same response categories. It saves space and makes it easier for the respondent or interviewer to note answers for the same response categories.

Nonresponse.   Have you ever refused to participate in a survey or left many questionnaire items blank? The failure to get a valid response from every sampled respondent weakens a survey. Every day people are asked to respond

to many requests from charities, marketing firms, candidate polls, and so forth. Asking for a person's time and attention to a survey can be burdensome. Charities and marketing firms tend to get low response rates, whereas government organizations get much higher cooperation rates. Nonresponse can be a major problem for survey research because if a high proportion of the sampled respondents do not respond, researchers may not be able to generalize results, especially if those who do not respond differ from those who do respond.

Public cooperation in survey research has declined over the past 30 years across many countries, with The Netherlands having the highest refusal rate, and with refusal rates as high as 30 percent in the United States.[14] There is both a growing group of "hard core" refusing people and a general decline in participation because many people feel there are too many surveys. Other reasons for refusal include a fear of crime and strangers, a more hectic lifestyle, a loss of privacy, and a rising distrust of authority or government. The misuse of the survey to sell products or persuade people, poorly designed questionnaires, and inadequate explanations of surveys to respondents also increase refusals for legitimate surveys.

You can improve rates by careful respondent screening, better sample-frame definition, and multilingual interviewers. Refuses decrease if respondents receive a letter in advance of an interview that includes the offer to reschedule an interview. Other ways to procure responses include offering small incentives (i.e., small gifts), adjusting interviewer behavior and statements (i.e., making eye contact, expressing sincerity, explaining the sampling or survey, emphasizing importance of the interview, clarifying promises of confidentiality, etc.). For interviews, you can increase response by having alternative interviewers (i.e., different demographic characteristics, age, race, gender, or ethnicity), using alternative interview methods (i.e., phone vs. face to face), or accepting an alternative respondent in the same household.

A critical area of nonresponse or refusal to participate occurs with the initial contact between an interviewer and a respondent. In a face-to-face or telephone interview, it is important to overcome hesitation or resistance and to reassure respondents. For mail or Web surveys, many researchers have used small incentives (e.g., a one-dollar bill, a gift card, or a contribution to a charity). It appears that prepaid incentives can increase respondent cooperation and they do not appear to have negative effects on survey composition or future participation. A huge literature exists on how to increase response rates for mail surveys with many details varied (e.g., postage stamp vs. prepaid postage, colored paper, etc.) (see Expansion Box 7.2). Heberlein and Baumgartner (1978, 1981) reported 71 factors

---

EXPANSION BOX

7.2 Ten Ways to Increase Mail Questionnaire Response

1. Address the questionnaire to specific person, not "Occupant," and send it first class.

2. Include a carefully written, dated cover letter on letterhead stationery. In it, request respondent cooperation, guarantee confidentiality, explain the purpose of the survey, and give the researcher's name and phone number.

3. *Always* include a postage-paid, addressed return envelope.

4. The questionnaire should have a neat, attractive layout and reasonable page length.

5. The questionnaire should be professionally printed and easy to read, with clear instructions.

6. Send two follow-up reminder letters to those not responding. The first should arrive about one week after sending the questionnaire, the second a week later. Gently ask for cooperation again and offer to send another questionnaire.

7. Do not send questionnaires during major holiday periods.

8. Do not put questions on the back page. Instead, leave a blank space and ask the respondent for general comments.

9. Sponsors that are local and are seen as legitimate (e.g., government agencies, universities, large firms, etc.) get a better response.

10. Include a small monetary inducement ($1) if possible.

that can affect mail questionnaire response rates. However, the tactics that increase response rates in paper surveys may not directly translate to Web surveys.[15] In general, mail surveys have higher response rates than Web surveys. More highly educated and younger respondents favor Web surveys over mail surveys compared to other respondents, and follow-up reminders are not as effective in Web surveys compared to mail surveys (see Shih and Fan, 2008).

TYPES OF SURVEYS: ADVANTAGES AND DISADVANTAGES

Mail and Self-Administered Questionnaires

Advantages. You can give questionnaires directly to respondents or mail them to respondents who read instructions and questions, then record their answers. This type of survey is inexpensive, and is easy for a a single researcher to conduct. With mail you can send questionnaires to a wide geographical area at a low cost. The respondent can complete the questionnaire when it is convenient and can check personal records if necessary. Mail questionnaires also offer anonymity and avoid interviewer bias. They can be effective, and response rates may be sufficient if you have an educated target population with a strong interest in the topic or the survey organization.

Disadvantages. Since many people do not complete and return questionnaires, the biggest problem with mail questionnaires is a low response rate. Most questionnaires are returned within two weeks, but others trickle in up to two months later. You can raise response rates by sending nonrespondents several reminder letters, but this adds to the time and cost of data collection. Also, you have no control over the conditions under which a mail questionnaire is completed. You do not know whether the questionnaire has been completed during a drinking party by a dozen laughing people or by an earnest respondent. Also, no one is present to clarify questions or to probe for more information when respondents give incomplete answers. It is possible that someone other than the sampled respondent (e.g., spouse, new resident, etc.) completed the questionnaire. Also different respondents can complete the questionnaire weeks apart or answer questions in a different order than what you intended. Incomplete questionnaires can also be a serious problem.

The mail questionnaire format limits the kinds of questions that you can use. Questions requiring visual aids (e.g., look at this picture and tell me what you see), open-ended questions, many contingency questions, and complex questions do poorly in mail questionnaires. Likewise, mail questionnaires are ill suited for the illiterate or near-illiterate, or those who do not read the dominant language (e.g., English). Questionnaires mailed to illiterate respondents are not likely to be returned; if they are completed and returned, the questions may be misunderstood, making the answers meaningless (see Table 7.4).

Web Surveys

Access to the Internet and e-mail has become widespread in the twenty-first century. Only 3 percent of the U.S. population had e-mail in 1994, but by 2010, 75 percent or more of the population in Canada, Germany, Japan, South Korea, the United Kingdom, and the United States had Internet connections (internetworldstats.com/top20.htm, downloaded February 15, 2011).

Advantages. Web-based surveys over the Internet or by e-mail are fast and inexpensive. They allow flexible design and can use visual images, or even audio or video in some Internet versions. Despite great flexibility, the basic principles for question writing and for paper questionnaire design generally apply.

TABLE 7.4   Types of Surveys and Their Features

Features	Mail Questionnaire	Web Survey	Telephone Interview	Face-to-Face Interview
Administrative Issues				
Cost	Cheap	Cheapest	Moderate	Expensive
Speed	Slowest	Fastest	Fast	Slow to moderate
Length (number of questions)	Moderate	Moderate	Short	Longest
Response rate	Lowest	Moderate	Moderate	Highest
Research Control				
Probes possible	No	No	Yes	Yes
Specific respondent	No	No	Yes	Yes
Question sequence	No	Yes	Yes	Yes
Only one respondent	No	No	Yes	Yes
Visual observation	No	No	No	Yes
Success with Different Questions				
Visual aids	Limited	Yes	None	Yes
Open-ended questions	Limited	Limited	Limited	Yes
Contingency questions	Limited	Yes	Yes	Yes
Complex questions	Limited	Yes	Limited	Yes
Sensitive questions	Some	Yes	Limited	Limited
Sources of Bias				
Social desirability	Some	Some	Some	Most
Interviewer bias	None	None	Some	Most
Respondent's reading skill	Yes	Yes	No	No

Disadvantages. Web surveys have three areas of concern: coverage, privacy and verification, and design issues. The first concern involves sampling and unequal Internet access or use. Despite high coverage rates, older, less-educated, low-income, and more rural people often lack good Internet access. In addition, many people have multiple e-mail addresses. This limits using email addresses for sampling purposes. Self-selection is a potential problem with Web surveys. For example, a marketing department could get very distorted results of the population of new car buyers. Perhaps half of the new car buyers for a model are over age 55, but 75 percent of respondents to a Web survey are under age 32 and only 8 percent are over age 55. Not only would the results be distorted by age but the relatively small percentage of over-55 respondents may not be representative of all over-55 potential new car buyers (e.g., they may be higher income or more educated).

A second concern is protecting respondent privacy and confidentiality. When possible, data should be encrypted and only secure websites used. It is best to remove nonessential respondent identification or linking information. It is also best to verify respondents and ensure that only the sampled respondent participate and do so only once. This may involve a system such as giving each respondent a unique PIN number to access the questionnaire.

A third concern involves the complexity of questionnaire design. Clear, simple design is best. It is also wise to check and verify the compatibility of Web software and hardware combinations. Web survey design is still improving, but it is best to provide screen-by-screen questions and make an entire question visible on the screen at one time in a consistent format. Simple check boxes or drop-down boxes for answer choices are best. Progress indicators such as a clock or chart appear to be very helpful. You want to keep the visual appearance of a screen consistent with easy readability. Provide clear instructions for all computer actions (e.g., use of drop-down screens) and simple "click here" instructions wherever possible. Also, make it easy for respondents to move back and forth across questions. Pretesting to avoid technical glitches is important when using a dedicated server. If the Web survey has many users, it may be necessary to use a dedicated server and obtain sufficient broadband to handle the demand.[16]

Telephone Interviews

Advantages. The telephone interview is a popular survey method because almost the entire population can be reached by telephone. The process is straightforward: an interviewer calls a respondent (usually at home), asks questions, and records answers. You can sample respondents from lists, telephone directories, or random digit dialing, and can quickly reach many people across long distances. A staff of interviewers can interview 1,500 respondents across a nation within a few days and, with several callbacks, get acceptable response rates (e.g., 80 percent). Although this method is more expensive than a mail questionnaire, the telephone interview is flexible. It has most of the strengths of face-to-face interviews but for about half the cost. Interviewers control the sequence of questions and can use some probes. A specific respondent is chosen and is likely to answer all the questions alone. You know when the questions were answered and can use contingency questions effectively, especially with computer-assisted telephone interviewing (CATI) (discussed later in this chapter).

Disadvantages. Higher cost and limited interview length are among the disadvantages of telephone interviews. In addition, respondents without a telephone are impossible to reach. The use of an interviewer reduces anonymity and introduces potential interviewer bias. Open-ended questions are difficult to use, and questions requiring visual aids are impossible. Interviewers can only note serious disruptions (e.g., background noise) and respondent tone of voice (e.g., anger or flippancy) or hesitancy.

Changing telephone technologies affects survey research by phone. Caller ID has been around since the mid-1980s and has gained in popularity. By 2006, over one-half of U.S. households had caller ID. There are few differences in willingness to participate in a survey between caller ID subscribers and non–caller ID users. Studies suggest that respondents with Caller ID are more likely to answer a recognized, legitimate survey organization than "unknown" or "out of area" types of identification. Caller ID can be an advantage to survey organizations if the name of the survey organization is well known.

People increasingly use cell phones instead of landline phones. Sampling cell phone numbers is possible, but it is more difficult, more costly, and has lower rates of survey partici-pation than landline phones. Also the demo-graphic characteristics of cell phone users differ from landline users, with lower income and younger people relying exclusively on cell phones more than middle-income people or older adults. For some topics, it appears that the landline versus cell phone difference is not important, but it may be for other survey topics.[17]

Face-to-Face Interviews

Advantages.   Face-to-face interviews have the highest response rates and permit the longest questionnaires. Interviewers also can observe the surroundings and can use nonverbal communication and visual aids. Well-trained interviewers can ask all types of questions, can ask complex questions, and can use extensive probes.

Disadvantages.   High cost is the biggest dis-advantage of face-to-face interviews. The train-ing, travel, supervision, and personnel costs for interviews can be high. Interviewer bias is also greatest in face-to-face interviews. The appear-ance, tone of voice, question wording, and so forth of the interviewer may affect the respon-dent. In addition, interviewer supervision is less than for telephone interviews, which supervi-sors monitor by listening in.[18]

INTERVIEWING

The Role of the Interviewer

Interviews are used to gather information and occur in many settings. Survey research inter-viewing is a specialized kind of interviewing. As with most interviewing, the goal is to obtain accurate information from another person.[19]

The survey interview is a special type of social relationship. Like other social relationships, it involves social roles, norms, and expectations.

The interview is a short-term, secondary social interaction between two strangers with the explicit purpose of one person's obtaining spe-cific information from the other. The social roles are those of the interviewer and the interviewee or respondent. Information is obtained in a structured conversation in which the interviewer asks prearranged questions and records answers, and the respondent answers. It differs in several ways from ordinary conversation (see Table 7.5).

An important problem for interviewers is that respondents are often not familiar with the survey respondents' role. As a result, the respon-dents substitute another role that may affect their responses. Some believe the interview is an intimate conversation or therapy session. Some see it as a bureaucratic exercise in completing forms. Some view it as a citizen referendum on policy choices. Some view it as a testing situa-tion. Some consider it a form of deceit in which interviewers are trying to trick or entrap respon-dents. Even in a well-designed, professional sur-vey, follow-up research found that only about half the respondents understand questions exactly as intended by researchers. Respondents reinterpreted questions to make them applicable to their idiosyncratic, personal situations or to make them easy to answer.[20]

The interviewer's role is a difficult one. Often an interviewer will explain the nature of survey research or give hints about social roles in an interview. The interviewer must obtain coop-eration and build rapport, yet remain neutral and objective. The interviewer encroaches on a respondent's time and privacy for information that may not directly benefit the respondent. An interviewer tries to reduce feelings of embarrass-ment, fear, and suspicion by a respondent so the respondent can feel comfortable revealing infor-mation. Good interviewers constantly monitor the pace and direction of the social interaction as well as the content of answers and the behav-ior of respondents.

The survey interviewer is nonjudgmental and does not reveal personal opinions, verbally or nonverbally (e.g., by a look of shock). If a

TABLE 7.5 **Differences between Ordinary Conversation and a Structured Survey Interview**

Ordinary Conversation	The Survey Interview
1. Questions and answers from each participant are relatively equally balanced.	1. Interviewer asks and respondent answers most of the time.
2. There is an open exchange of feelings and opinions.	2. Only the respondent reveals feelings and opinions.
3. Judgments are stated and attempts made to persuade the other of a particular points of view.	3. Interviewer is nonjudgmental and does not try to change respondent's opinions or beliefs.
4. A person can reveal deep inner feelings to gain sympathy or as a therapeutic release.	4. Interviewer tries to obtain direct answers to specific questions.
5. Ritual responses are common (e.g., "Uh huh," shaking head, "How are you?" "Fine").	5. Interviewer avoids making ritual responses that influence a respondent and also seeks genuine answers, not ritual responses.
6. The participants exchange information and correct the factual errors that they are aware of.	6. Respondent provides almost all information. Interviewer does not correct a respondent's factual errors.
7. Topics rise and fall and either person can introduce new topics. The focus can shift directions or digress to less relevant issues.	7. Interviewer controls the topic, direction, and pace. He or she keeps the respondent "on task," and irrelevant diversions are contained.
8. The emotional tone can shift from humor, to joy, to affection, to sadness, to anger, and so on.	8. Interviewer attempts to maintain a consistently warm but serious and objective tone throughout.
9. People can evade or ignore questions and give flippant or noncommittal answers.	9. Respondent should not evade questions and should give truthful, thoughtful answers.

Source: Adapted from Gorden (1980:19–25) and Sudman and Bradburn (1983:5–10).

respondent asks for an interviewer's opinion, he or she politely redirects the respondent and indicates that such questions are inappropriate. For example, if a respondent asks, "What do you think?" the interviewer may answer, "Here, we are interested in what *you* think; what I think doesn't matter." Likewise, if the respondent gives a shocking answer (e.g., "I was arrested three times for beating my infant daughter and burning her with cigarettes"), the interviewer does not show shock, surprise, or disdain but treats the answer in a matter-of-fact manner. He or she helps respondents feel that they can give any truthful answer.

You might ask, "If the survey interviewer must be neutral and objective, why not use a robot or machine?" Machine interviewing has not been successful because it lacks the human warmth, sense of trust, and rapport that an interviewer creates. An interviewer helps define the situation and ensures that respondents have the information sought, understand what is expected, give relevant and serious answers, and are motivated to cooperate.

Interviewers do more than interview respondents. Face-to-face interviewers spend only about 35 percent of their time interviewing. About 40 percent is spent in locating the correct respondent, 15 percent in traveling, and 10 percent in studying survey materials and dealing with administrative and recording details.[21]

Stages of an Interview

The survey research interview proceeds through several stages. It begins with an introduction and entry. The interviewer gets in the door, shows authorization, and reassures and secures cooperation from the respondent. He or she is prepared for reactions such as "How did you pick me?" "What good will this do?" "I don't know about this," "What's this about, anyway?" The interviewer can explain why the specific respondent is interviewed and not a substitute.

The main part of the interview consists of asking questions and recording answers. The interviewer uses the exact wording on the questionnaire—no added or omitted words and no rephrasing. He or she asks all applicable questions in order, without returning to or skipping questions unless the directions specify this. He or she goes at a comfortable pace and gives nondirective feedback to maintain interest.

In addition to asking questions, the interviewer accurately records answers. This is easy for closed-ended questions, where interviewers just mark the correct box. For open-ended questions, the interviewer's job is more difficult. He or she listens carefully, must have legible handwriting, and must record what is said verbatim without correcting grammar or slang. More important, the interviewer never summarizes or paraphrases. This causes a loss of information or distorts answers. For example, the respondent says, "I'm really concerned about my daughter's heart problem. She's only 10 years old and already she has trouble climbing stairs. I don't know what she'll do when she gets older. Heart surgery is too risky for her and it costs so much. She'll have to learn to live with it." If the interviewer writes, "concerned about daughter's health," much is lost.

The interviewer knows how and when to use probes. A *probe* is a neutral request to clarify an ambiguous answer, to complete an incomplete answer, or to obtain a relevant response. Interviewers recognize an irrelevant or inaccurate answer and use probes as needed.[22]

There are many types of probes. A three- to five-second pause is often effective. Nonverbal communication (e.g., tilt of head, raised eyebrows, or eye contact) also works well. The interviewer can repeat the question or repeat the reply and then pause. He or she can ask a neutral question, such as, "Any other reasons?" "Can you tell me more about that?" "How do you mean?" "Could you explain more for me?" (see Example Box 7.6).

The last stage is the exit. This is when the interviewer thanks the respondent and leaves. He or she then goes to a quiet, private place to edit the questionnaire and record other details such as the date, time, and place of the interview; a thumbnail sketch of the respondent and interview situation; the respondent's attitude (e.g., serious, angry, or laughing); and any unusual circumstances (e.g., "Telephone rang at question 27 and respondent talked for four minutes before the interview started again"). He or she notes anything disruptive that happened during the interview (e.g., "Teenage son entered room, sat at opposite end, turned on television with the volume loud, and watched a music video"). The interviewer also records personal feelings and anything that was suspected (e.g., "Respondent became nervous and fidgeted when questioned about his marriage").

Training Interviewers

For a small, simple study you can conduct the interviews yourself. However, a large-scale survey requires hiring multiple interviewers. Few people appreciate the difficulty of the interviewer's job. A professional-quality interview requires the careful selection of interviewers and extensive training. As with

Examples of Probes and Recording Full Responses to Closed Questions

Interviewer Question: What is your occupation?

Respondent Answer: I work at General Motors.
   Probe: What is your job at General Motors? What type of work do you do there?

Interviewer Question: How long have you been unemployed?

Respondent Answer: A long time.
   Probe: Could you tell me more specifically when your current period of unemployment began?

Interviewer Question: Considering the country as a whole, do you think we will have good times during the next year, or bad times, or what?

Respondent Answer: Maybe good, maybe bad, it depends, who knows?
   Probe: What do you expect to happen?

Record Response to a Closed Question

Interviewer Question: On a scale of 1 to 7, how do you feel about capital punishment or the death penalty, where 1 is strongly in favor of the death penalty, and 7 is strongly opposed to it?
   (Favor) 1 __   2 __   3 __   4 __   5 __   6 __   7 __ (Oppose)
Respondent Answer   About a 4. I think that all murderers, rapists, and violent criminals should get death, but I don't favor it for minor crimes like stealing a car.

---

any employment situation, adequate pay and good supervision are essential for consistent high-quality performance. Unfortunately, professional interviewing has not always paid well or provided regular employment. In the past, interviewers were largely drawn from a pool of middle-age women willing to accept irregular part-time work.

Good interviewers are pleasant, honest, accurate, mature, responsible, moderately intelligent, stable, and motivated. They have a non-threatening appearance, have experience with many different types of people, and possess poise and tact. Researchers may consider interviewers' physical appearance, age, race, sex, languages spoken, and even the sound of their voice.

It is fairly common for a professional interviewer to receive a week-long training course.

The course includes lectures and reading, observation of expert interviewers, mock interviews in the office and in the field that are recorded and critiqued, many practice interviews, and role-playing. The interviewers learn about survey research and the role of the interviewer. They become familiar with the questionnaire and the purpose of questions, although not with the answers expected.

The importance of carefully selecting and training interviewers was evident during the 2004 U.S. presidential election. Exit polls are quick, very short surveys conducted outside a polling place for people immediately after they voted. On Election Day of 2004 exit polls showed candidate John Kerry well ahead, but after final votes were counted he lost to his opponent, George W. Bush. A major cause of the mistake was that the research organization, paid $10 million by six major news organizations to conduct the exit polls, had hired many young, inexperienced interviewers and gave them only minimal training. Younger voters tended to support Kerry, whereas older voters tended to support Bush. The interviewers were less successful in gaining cooperation from older voters and felt more comfortable handing the questionnaire to someone of a similar age. As a result, exit poll participants did not reflect the composition of all voters and poll results showed greater support for Kerry than actually existed among all voters.[23]

Although interviewers work alone, in most large studies with many interviewers there is also an interviewer supervisor. Supervisors are familiar with the area, assist with problems, oversee the interviewers, and ensure that work is completed on time. For telephone interviewing, this includes helping with calls, checking when interviewers arrive and leave, and monitoring interview calls. In face-to-face interviews, supervisors check to find out whether the interview actually took place. This means calling back or sending a confirmation postcard to a sample of respondents. They can also check the response rate and incomplete questionnaires to see whether interviewers are obtaining cooperation, and they may reinterview a small subsample, analyze answers, or observe interviews to see whether interviewers are accurately asking questions and recording answers.

Interviewer Bias

You need to proscribe specific interviewer behavior to reduce bias. This goes beyond having interviewers read each question exactly as worded. Ideally, a particular interviewer's behavior has no effect on how a respondent answers, and responses do not differ from what they would be if asked by any other interviewer. Interviewer expectations can create significant bias. Interviewers who expect difficult

interviews have them, and those who expect certain answers are more likely to get them (see Example Box 7.7). Proper interviewer behavior and exact question reading may be difficult, but the issue is larger.

The social setting in which the interview occurs can affect answers, including the presence of other people. For example, students answer differently depending on whether they are asked questions at home or at school. In general, you do not want others present because they may affect respondent answers. It may not always make a difference, however, especially if the others are small children.[24]

An interviewer's visible characteristics, including age, race, and gender, can influence interviews and respondent answers. This is especially true for questions about issues related to race or gender. For example, African American and Hispanic American respondents express different policy positions on race- or ethnic-related issues depending on the apparent race or ethnicity of the interviewer. This occurs even with telephone interviews when a respondent has clues about the interviewer's race or ethnicity. In general, interviewers of the same racial-ethnic group get more accurate answers.[25] Gender also affects interviews both in terms of obvious issues, such as sexual behavior, as well as support for gender-related collective action or gender equality.[26] You will want to note the race and gender of both interviewers and respondents.

Computer-Assisted Telephone Interviewing

Advances in computer technology and lower computer prices have enabled professional survey research organizations to install *computer-assisted telephone interviewing (CATI)* systems.[27] With CATI, the interviewer sits in front of a computer and makes calls. Wearing a headset and microphone, the interviewer reads the questions from a computer screen that have

7.7 Interviewer Characteristics Can Affect Responses

Example of Interviewer Expectation Effects

Asked by Female Interviewer Whose Own	Female Respondent Reports That Husband Buys Most Furniture
Husband buys most furniture	89%
Husband does not buy most furniture	15%

Example of Race or Ethnic Appearance Effects

Interviewer	Percentage Answering Yes to:	
	"Do you think there are too many Jews in government jobs?"	*"Do you think that Jews have too much power?"*
Looked Jewish with Jewish-sounding name	11.7	5.8
Looked Jewish only	15.4	15.6
Non-Jewish appearance	21.2	24.3
Non-Jewish appearance and non-Jewish-sounding name	19.5	21.4

Note: Racial stereotypes held by respondents can affect how they respond in interviews.
Source: Adapted from Hyman (1975:115, 163).

been selected for the specific respondent who is called. The interviewer listens then enters the answer via the keyboard. Once he or she enters an answer, the computer shows the next question on the screen.

Computer-assisted telephone interviewing speeds interviewing and reduces interviewer errors. It also eliminates the separate step of entering information into a computer and speeds data processing. Of course, CATI requires an investment in computer equipment and some knowledge of computers. The CATI system is valuable for contingency questions because the computer can show the questions appropriate for a specific respondent; interviewers do not have to turn pages looking for the next question. In addition, the computer can check an answer immediately after the interviewer enters it. For example, if

an interviewer enters an answer that is impossible or clearly an error (e.g., an *H* instead of an *M* for "Male"), the computer will request another answer. Innovations with computers and Web surveys also help to gather data on sensitive issues (see Expansion Box 7.3).

Several companies have developed software programs for personal computers that help develop questionnaires and analyze survey data. They provide guides for writing questions, recording responses, analyzing data, and producing reports. The programs may speed the more mechanical aspects of survey research—such as typing questionnaires, organizing layout, and recording responses—but they cannot substitute for a good understanding of the survey method or an appreciation of its limitations. The researcher must still clearly conceptualize variables, prepare well-worded questions, design the

7.3 Computer-Aided Surveys and Sensitive Topics

The questioning format influences how respondents answer questions about sensitive topics. Formats that permit the greatest respondent anonymity, such as a self-administered questionnaire or the web survey, are more likely to elicit honest responses than ones that require interaction with another person, such as in a face-to-face interview or telephone interview. One of a series of computer-based technological innovations is called *computer-assisted self-administered interviews (CASAI)*. It appears to improve respondent comfort and honesty in answering questions on sensitive topics. In CASAI, respondents are "interviewed" with questions that are asked on a computer screen or heard over earphones. The respondents answer by moving a computer mouse or entering information using a computer keyboard. Even when a researcher is present in the same room, the respondent is semi-insulated from human contact and appears to feel comfortable answering questions about sensitive issues.

sequence and forms of questions and responses, and pilot-test questionnaires. Communicating unambiguously with respondents and eliciting credible responses remain the most important parts of survey research.

It is wise to ask others to review your questionnaire before using it in a survey. One recent study (Olson, 2010) found that having a group of experienced survey researchers review a questionnaire helped identify possible weaknesses and improved the final survey.

THE ETHICAL SURVEY

A major ethical issue in survey research is the invasion of privacy. You may intrude into a respondent's privacy by asking about intimate actions and personal beliefs. People have a right to privacy. Respondents decide when and to whom to reveal personal information. They are likely to provide such information when you ask for it in a comfortable context that includes mutual respect and trust. It is most likely when respondents believe you have a legitimate research purpose that requires serious answers. It is also most likely when they believe their answers will remain confidential. As a social researcher, you should treat all respondents with dignity and do what you can to reduce anxiety or discomfort. You are also responsible for protecting the confidentiality of data.

A second issue involves voluntary participation by respondents. Respondents agree to answer questions and can refuse to participate at any time. They give "informed consent" to participate in research either formally or informally. You depend on respondents' voluntary cooperation, so researchers need to ask well-developed questions in a sensitive way and be very sensitive to confidentiality.

A third ethical issue is the exploitation of surveys and pseudosurveys. Because of its popularity, some people have used surveys to mislead others. A *pseudosurvey* is when someone who has little or no real interest in learning information from a respondent uses the survey format to try to persuade someone to do something. Charlatans use the guise of conducting a survey to invade privacy, gain entry into homes, or "suggle" (sell in the guise of a survey). I personally experienced a type of pseudosurvey known as a "suppression poll" in an election campaign. In this situation, an unknown survey organization telephoned potential voters and asked whether the voter supported a given candidate. If the voter supported the candidate, the interviewer next asked whether the respondent would still support the candidate if he or she knew that the candidate had an unfavorable characteristic (e.g., had been arrested for drunk driving, used illegal drugs, raised the wages of convicted criminals in prison, etc.). The goal of the interview was not to measure candidate support; rather, it was to identify a candidate's supporters, and then attempt to suppress voting for that candidate. Although such polling is illegal, no one has been prosecuted for using this campaign tactic.

Another ethical issue is when people misuse survey results or use poorly designed or purposely rigged surveys. Why does this occur? People may demand answers from surveys that surveys cannot provide and not understand a survey's limitations. Those who design and prepare surveys may lack sufficient training to conduct a legitimate survey. Unfortunately, policy decisions are sometimes made based on careless or poorly designed surveys. They often result in waste or human hardship. This is why legitimate researchers conducting methodologically rigorous survey research are important.

The media report more surveys than other types of social research, yet sloppy reporting of survey results permits abuse.[28] Few people reading survey results may appreciate it, but researchers should include details about the survey (see Expansion Box 7.4) to reduce the misuse of survey research and increase questions about surveys that lack such information. Survey researchers urge the media to include such information, but it is rarely included. Over 88 percent of reports on surveys in the mass media fail to reveal the researcher who conducted the survey, and only 18 percent provide details on how the survey was conducted.[29] Currently, there are no quality-control standards to regulate the opinion polls or surveys reported in the U.S. media.

Since the late 1940s, professional researchers have made unsuccessful attempts to require adequate samples, interviewer training and supervision, satisfactory questionnaire design, public availability of results, and controls on the integrity of survey organizations.[30] Unfortunately, the media report both biased, misleading survey results and rigorous, professional survey results with little distinction. It is not surprising that the public becomes confused and distrusts surveys.

EXPANSION BOX

7.4 **Ten Items to Include When Reporting Survey Research**

1. The sampling frame used (e.g., telephone directories)
2. The dates on which the survey was conducted
3. The population that the sample represents (e.g., U.S. adults, Australian college students, housewives in Singapore)
4. The size of the sample for which information was collected
5. The sampling method (e.g., random)
6. The exact wording of the questions asked
7. The method of the survey (e.g., face to face, telephone)
8. The organizations that sponsored the survey (paid for it and conducted it)
9. The response rate or percentage of those contacted who actually completed the questionnaire
10. Any missing information or "don't know" responses when results on specific questions are reported

---

CONCLUSION

In this chapter, you learned about survey research. You also learned some principles of writing good survey questions. There are many things to avoid and to include when you write survey questions. You learned about the advantages and disadvantages of four types of survey research: mail, web, telephone interviews, and face-to-face interviews. You saw that interviewing, especially face-to-face interviewing, can be difficult.

This chapter focused on survey research, but you can use questionnaires to measure variables in other types of quantitative research (e.g., experiments). The survey, often called the sample survey because random sampling is usually used with it, is a distinct technique. It is a process of asking many people the same questions and examining their answers.

Although you try to minimize errors, survey data may contain them. Survey errors can compound each other. For example, errors can arise in sampling frames, from nonresponse, from question wording or order, and from interviewer bias. Do not let the existence of errors discourage you from using the survey method, however. Instead, learn to be very careful when designing survey research and be cautious about generalizing from the results of surveys.

Key Terms

closed-ended question
computer-assisted telephone interviewing (CATI)
context effect
contingency question
cover sheet
double-barreled question
floaters
full-filter question
funnel sequence
interview schedule
matrix question
open-ended question
order effects
partially open question
prestige bias
probe
quasi-filter question
response set
social desirability bias
standard-format question
threatening questions
wording effects

Endnotes

1. Sudman and Bradburn (1983:39) suggested that even simple questions (e.g., "What brand of soft drink do you usually buy?") can cause problems. Respondents who are highly loyal to one brand of traditional carbonated sodas can answer the question easily. Other respondents must implicitly address the following questions to answer the question as it was asked: (a) What time period is involved—the past month, the past year, the last 10 years? (b) What conditions count—at home, at restaurants, at sporting events? (c) Buying for oneself alone or for other family members? (d) What is a "soft drink"? Do lemonade, iced tea, mineral water, or fruit juices count? (e) Does "usually" mean a brand purchased as 51 percent or more of all soft drink purchases, or the brand purchased more frequently than any other? Respondents rarely stop and ask for clarification; they make assumptions about what the researcher means.

2. See Dykema and Schaeffer (2000) and Sudman et al. (1996:197–226).

3. See Ostrom and Gannon (1996).

4. See Bradburn (1983), Bradburn and Sudman (1980), and Sudman and Bradburn (1983) on threatening or sensitive questions. Backstrom and Hursh-Cesar (1981:219) and Warwick and Lininger (1975:150–151) provide useful suggestions as well.

5. See CBS News, cbsnews.com/8301-503544_162-6201911-503544.html, downloaded February 14, 2011. Also see Cooper, Michael. "From Obama, the Tax Cut Nobody Heard Of," *New York Times,* October 18, 2010.

6. See Martin (1999) and Tourangeau et al. (1997).

7. For a discussion of the "don't know," "no opinion," and middle positions in response categories, see Backstrom and Hursh-Cesar (1981:148–149), Bishop (1987), Bradburn and Sudman (1988:154), Brody (1986), Converse and Presser (1986:35–37), Duncan and Stenbeck (1988), and Sudman and Bradburn (1983:140–141).

8. The disagree/agree versus specific alternatives debate can be found in Bradburn and Sudman (1988:149–151), Converse and Presser (1986:38–39), and Schuman and Presser (1981:179–223).

9. The ranking versus ratings issue is discussed in Alwin and Krosnick (1985) and Krosnick and Alwin (1988). Also see Backstrom and Hursh-Cesar (1981:132–134) and Sudman and

Bradburn (1983:156–165) for formats of asking rating and ranking questions.

10. See Foddy (1993) and Presser (1990).

11. Studies by Krosnick (1992) and Narayan and Krosnick (1996) show that education reduces response-order (primacy or recency) effects, but Knäuper (1999) found that age is strongly associated with response-order effects.

12. This example comes from Strack (1992).

13. For a discussion, see Couper et al. (1998), de Heer (1999), Keeter et al. (2000), Sudman and Bradburn (1983:11), Tourangeau and Ye (2009). and "Surveys Proliferate, but Answers Dwindle," *New York Times,* October 5, 1990, p. 1. Smith (1995) and Sudman (1976:114–116) also discuss refusal rates.

14. See Dillman 2000:32–39 for more details.

15. Bailey (1987:153–168), Church (1993), Dillman (1978, 1983), Fox, Crask, and Kim (1988), Goyder (1982), Heberlein and Baumgartner (1978, 1981), Hubbard and Little (1988), Jones (1979), Porter and Whitcomb (2009), and Willimack, Schuman, Pennell, and Lepkowski (1995) discuss increasing return rates in surveys.

16. See Couper (2008) for an overview on designing Web surveys. Also see Kreuter, Presser, and Tourangeau (2008) on social desirability in Web surveys.

17. On cell phones and survey research, see Blumberg and Luke (2007), Keeter (2006), Keeter, Kennedy, Clark, Tompson, and Mokrzycki (2007), Link, Battaglia, Frankel, Osborn, and Mokdad (2007), and Tucker, Brick, and Meekins (2007). See Callegaro, McCutcheon, and Ludwig (2010) on Caller ID.

18. For a comparison among types of surveys, see Backstrom and Hursh-Cesar (1981:16–23), Bradburn and Sudman (1988:94–110), Dillman (1978:39–78), Fowler (1984:61–73), and Frey (1983:27–55).

19. For more on survey research interviewing, see Brenner, Brown, and Canter (1985), Cannell and Kahn (1968), Converse and Schuman (1974), Dijkstra and van der Zouwen (1982), Foddy (1993), Gorden (1980), Hyman (1975), and Moser and Kalton (1972:270–302).

20. See Turner and Martin (1984:262–269, 282).

21. From Moser and Kalton (1972:273).

22. The use of probes is discussed in Backstrom and Hursh-Cesar (1981:266–273), Gorden (1980:368–390), and Hyman (1975:236–241).

23. Report by Steinberg, Jacques. "Study Cites Human Failings in Election Day Poll System," *New York Times,* January 20, 2005.

24. See Bradburn and Sudman (1980), Pollner and Adams (1997), and Zane and Matsoukas (1979).

25. The race or ethnicity of interviewers is discussed in Anderson, Silver, and Abramson (1988), Bradburn (1983), Cotter, Cohen, and Coulter (1982), Davis (1997), Finkel, Guterbock, and Borg (1991), Gorden (1980:168–172), Reese, Danielson, Shoemaker, Chang, and Hsu (1986), Schaffer (1980), Schuman and Converse (1971), and Weeks and Moore (1981).

26. See Catania et al. (1996) and Kane and MacAulay (1993).

27. CATI is discussed in Bailey (1987:201–202), Bradburn and Sudman (1988:100–101), Frey (1983:24–25, 143–149), Groves and Kahn (1979:226), Groves and Mathiowetz (1984), and Karweit and Meyers (1983).

28. On reporting survey results in the media, see Channels (1993) and MacKeun (1984).

29. See Singer (1988).

30. From Turner and Martin (1984:62).

CHAPTER 8

Experimental Research

Experimental research builds on the principles of a positivist approach.[1] Natural scientists (e.g., chemists or biologists) and researchers in related applied fields (e.g., agriculture, engineering, and medicine) conduct experiments. You can also find experiments being conducted in education, criminal justice, journalism, marketing, nursing, political science, psychology, social work, and sociology to examine social issues and theories. The experiment provides us with powerful evidence about how one or two variables affect a dependent variable.

In commonsense language, when you *experiment* you modify one thing in a situation, then compare some outcome to what happened without the modification. For example, I try to start my car. To my surprise, it does not start. I "experiment" by cleaning off the battery connections because I have a simple hypothesis that it is causing the problem. I try to start it again. I had modified one thing (cleaned the connections) and compared the outcome (whether the car started) to the previous situation (it did not start). An experiment begins with a "hypothesis about causes." My hypothesis was that a buildup of crud on the battery connections was blocking the flow of electricity and the cause of the car not starting; so once I cleared off the crud, the car can start. This commonsense experiment is simple, but it illustrates three critical steps in an experiment: (1) start with a causal hypothesis, (2) modify one specific aspect of a situation that is closely connected to the cause, and (3) compare outcomes. Compared to other social research techniques, experimental research gives you the strongest tests of causal relationships because it is designed to meet all three conditions for causality (i.e., temporal order that independent precedes dependent variables, evidence of an association, and ruling out alternative causes).

EXPERIMENTS

Appropriate Technique?

Deciding what research technique best fits a specific research question can be a difficult decision. There is no ready-made, fixed match between technique and question. You must make an "informed judgment." The way to develop judgment skills is to learn the strengths and weaknesses of the various research techniques, read the methodology section of many published studies, assist an experienced social researcher, and acquire practical experience by conducting studies.

Compared to other research techniques, the experiment has advantages and limitations, and these help you see where it is most appropriate. The experiment is often artificial. It is a purposeful simplification of the complex social world. You probably think "artificial" means something negative, but Webster and Sell argue:

> The greatest benefits of experiments reside in the fact that they are artificial. That is, experiments allow observation in a situation that has been designed and created by investigators rather than one that occurs in nature. (2007:11)

Artificial means that the experimenter consciously controls the study situation. You control to incorporate theoretically relevant variables and to remove variables without a causal importance for a hypothesis. In this sense, artificial means you sharpen the focus and create narrowly targeted effects that are easier to see and measure than what happens in the natural world. You include the independent and dependent variable, but exclude irrelevant or **confounding variables** (i.e., variables not part of your hypothesis test). An analogy is the chemist who does not find pure sodium in the natural world. In a controlled laboratory setting, the chemist mixes pure sodium precisely with another pure chemical to study its effects. The controlled, sterile laboratory is artificial, pure sodium is artificial, and what the chemist mixes it with is artificial, yet the chemist produces new knowledge and compounds that have utility in the real world.

The logic of the social science experiment is powerful, but using it has practical and ethical limitations. In an experiment, you manipulate some aspects of the world then examine the outcomes; however, you cannot manipulate all areas of human life for the sake of science. You are limited to questions that have specific conditions you are able to manipulate and that fall within standards for ethical human research. Thus, you cannot conduct an experiment to directly answer questions such as, Do people who complete a college education increase their annual income more than people who do not attend college? Do children raised with younger siblings develop better leadership skills than only children? Do people who belong to more organizations vote more often in elections? You cannot assign some people to attend college and prevent others from attending so you can discover who earns more income later in life. You cannot induce couples to have either many children or a single child so you can examine how leadership skills develop in the children. You cannot compel people to join or quit organizations and then see whether they vote. Although you cannot manipulate every situation or variable you find of interest, you can be creative in simulating such interventions or conditions.

In general, experiments are usually best for issues with a narrow scope or scale. You often can assemble and conduct multiple experiments with limited resources in a short period, yet still test significant hypotheses. For example, you might replicate a study like that of Niven (see Example Box 8.1) in less than a month and at very low cost.

The experiment is usually most suited for micro-level (e.g., individual psychological or small-group phenomena) rather than for macro-level theoretical concerns. This is why social psychologists and political psychologists conduct experiments. Experiments cannot easily address questions involving macro-level conditions that operate across an entire society or over many years.

In an experiment, you isolate and target one or a few causal variables. Despite its strength to demonstrate a causal effect, experiments are not effective if you want to consider a dozen variables simultaneously. It is rarely appropriate for questions that require you to look at the impact of many variables together, or to assess conditions across a range of complex settings or numerous social groups.

Experiments provide focused tests of hypotheses, each experiment considering one or two variables in a specific setting. Knowledge advances slowly by compiling, comparing, and synthesizing the findings from numerous separate experiments. This knowledge-building strategy differs from that in other social research, such as the survey or field research, in which you can examine 15–20 variables simultaneously in one study across a range of social settings.

Convention also influences which research questions best align with the experimental method. There is a vast research literature that uses experiments to examine many topics. This facilitated rapid, smooth communication about those topics and the replication of experiments with minor adjustments. While it has advantages, it also can be a limitation. Researchers who specialize in such topics expect everyone else to use the experimental method and evaluate new studies by the standards of an experiment. They are slower to accept and assimilate new knowledge that comes from a nonexperimental study.

8.1 EXAMPLE BOX
News Reports and Death Penalty Views

Niven (2002) noted the overwhelming support (75–80 percent) in opinion polls for the death penalty among Americans in recent decades. However, if people have a choice between supporting the death penalty for a murder or a sentence of life imprisonment without parole (LIWP), their support for the death penalty drops by nearly one-half. Niven found that more than 90 percent of media stories on death penalty opinions report overwhelming public support for it, but very few stories report that many people would prefer LIWP as an alternative punishment for the same crimes. Niven hypothesized that support for the death penalty might change if people had exposure to media stories that told them about high levels of public support for the LIWP alternative. To test his hypothesis, he went to waiting areas in the Miami International Airport for more than a two-week period and recruited 564 participants for his study. He randomly assigned people to read one of three newspaper articles, which were his independent variable. One newspaper article told about overwhelming support for the death penalty, another reported public support for LIWP, and the third was unrelated to the death penalty issue and about airport expansion plans. He told respondents a cover story: that the study was about newspaper article writing style. Participants

completed a questionnaire about the clarity and organization of the article to disguise the purpose of the experiment. He also had a section on political beliefs under the premise that he wanted to know whether people with different political beliefs reacted the same way to the article. This section included his dependent variable, three questions about support or opposition for the death penalty for the crime of murder, preference for the death penalty or LIWP, and an estimate as to whether more or fewer states would adopt the death penalty in the future. His results showed no differences on the death penalty questions between participants who read about overwhelming death penalty support and the control group that read about airport expansion. More than 80 percent of both groups supported the death penalty, a little over one-half preferred it to LIWP, and most thought more states would adopt the death penalty in the future. People who read about LIWP showed much less support for the death penalty (62 percent), preferred LIWP over the death penalty (by a 57 to 43 percent margin), and predicted that fewer states would have the death penalty in the future. Thus, Nevin found support for his hypothesis that media stories that report on public support for the death penalty only perpetuate public opinion for it over the LIWP alternative.

You can also mix experimental and nonexperimental methods in a study. For example, you want to study attitudes toward people in wheelchairs. You could survey a thousand people on their views about people in wheelchairs. You could conduct a field research study and observe reactions to you in real-life settings while you are in a wheelchair. You can also design an experiment in which you interact with other people. Half the time while you are in a wheelchair, and half the time as you are standing or walking without using a wheelchair, and note responses in the two

situations. To test theories and develop a fuller understanding, you can combine knowledge from all types of studies (see Example Box 8.2).

A Short History of the Experiment

The social sciences, starting with psychology, borrowed the experimental method from the natural sciences. Psychology did not fully embrace the experiment until after 1900.[2] Wilhelm M. Wundt (1832–1920), a German psychologist and physiologist, introduced the

Transue (2007) combined experimental logic with survey research methods in one study and tested an abstract social science theory by applying it to a real public policy issue. His work contributed to a growing literature showing how a subtle emphasis on racial differences among Americans tends to accentuate divisions along racial lines regarding public issues.

According to social identity theory, we automatically categorize other people into in-groups (groups to which we belong) and out-groups (groups to which we do not belong). These groups form the basis of social boundaries and feelings of social distance from or closeness to other people. We also have multiple identities. A subset of the broader theory, self-categorization, says we recategorize others as members of in-groups or out-groups based on which of our identities is more active. Social boundaries and feelings of social distance depend on the most salient in-group. We feel closer to members of an in-group and further from people in salient out-groups. *Priming* is a process by which something happens to activate a particular identity. Once activated, this identity tends to have greater influence over subsequent behavior or thinking. Once reminded of an identity (i.e., it has been primed) it moves to the forefront of how we think about ourselves and therefore influences our behavior.

In most past studies on social identity theory, researchers used laboratory experiments with small convenience samples of students and tested the effect of a temporary, artificially created identity on a contrived issue. Transue (2007) sought more external validity. To obtain it, he used a large random sample of adults, an actual social identity, and a real public policy issue. His study used a telephone survey of a random sample of 405 White U.S. citizens in the Minneapolis metropolitan area in summer 1998 relying on random-digit dialing. Transue considered two actual identities, race and nation. He built on past studies that showed racially prejudiced Whites who had been primed or reminded of their race to be more likely to think in racist ways when they voted. The real policy issue he examined was support for paying taxes for public schools.

For the independent variable, social identity, Transue asked randomly assigned subsets of survey respondents one of two questions: "How close do you feel to your ethnic or racial group?" or "How close do you feel to other Americans?" This question primed or raised awareness of an identity. Later in the survey, he asked randomly assigned subsets of two questions about paying school taxes, "to improve education in public schools" or "to improve opportunities for minorities." This was the main dependent variable. Tansue hypothesized that Whites who were primed about their racial identity would reject paying taxes to help minorities more than Whites who were primed about their American national identity. He also thought that Whites primed about an American national identity would more strongly support taxes for public schools generally than those primed about their racial identity.

Transue found that Whites primed with a racial identity and asked about helping minorities had the least amount of support for paying school taxes. The most support came from Whites primed with an American national identity and asked about helping public schools generally. Transue also looked at the Whites who had identified more strongly with their racial-ethnic group and compared them with Whites having a weak or no racial identification. Consistent with social identity theory, he found that Whites with the strongest racial identity showed the most resistance to paying taxes to improve minority opportunities. In this study, a primed racial self-identity increased the salience of a person's racial in-group and heightened social boundaries associated with racial categories. A strong identity with one's racial in-group increased social distance for people in racial out-groups and lowered a desire to provide them with assistance.

experimental method into psychology. Germany was the center of graduate education in the late nineteenth and early twentieth century. By early 1900, universities in the United States and elsewhere were establishing psychology laboratories to conduct experimental research. The experiment displaced a more philosophical, introspective, integrative approach that was closer to the interpretive social science approach. For example, leading philosopher and psychologist William James (1842–1910) did not embrace the experimental method. Over the years, the experimental method became entrenched in some social science areas. The experiment's appeal was its objective, unbiased, scientific approach to studying social life.[3]

Experiments and Theory

Some social science experiments are empirically based and others theory directed.[4] The practical process of doing an experiment differs little, but the two have different purposes. Most studies are empirically based.

Your primary goal when conducting an empirically based experiment is to find out whether an independent variable has a significant effect on a specific dependent variable. You want to document and describe an effect (i.e., its size, direction, or form) by showing it empirically in a controlled setting. You later generalize to "real-life" conditions (see discussion of external validity later in this chapter). For example, Solomon Asch's famous experiment demonstrated the effect of conformity to group pressure by having eight students look at three lines. Once Asch demonstrated the power of group conformity, he generalized group conformity effects beyond his specific study of eight students looking at three lines to many groups of all sizes and all kinds of people engaged in real-life tasks. The study in Example Box 8.1 on reading news reports on death penalty opinions by Niven demonstrated a news report effect.

In a theory-directed experiment, you deductively convert an abstract model of how you think the world operates (i.e., your theory) into a specific study design with specific measures. Your experiment is a replica of the theoretical model. When generalizing from a theory-directed experiment, you generalize to the theory as a model of how the world operates. This is how you test the theory and learn whether the empirical evidence supports it. You want to find out whether a theory's predictions are close to the empirical findings. For this reason, you worry little about the experiment being highly artificial and unrealistic to the natural world. Your concern is whether the results match the theory. As Webster and Sell (2007:21) argue, "experimental results themselves are really not interesting except as they bear on a theory."

You use statistics to find out whether results match the theory. If the theory-predicted outcome is very unlikely (i.e., it has a low probability) but it occurs regularly in your experiment, then your confidence in the theory grows. Here is a simple example. A friend believes he can distinguish among six brands of diet colas (Diet Coke, Diet Coke Zero, Diet Pepsi, Pepsi One, Diet Rite, Tab). You have him drink 24 cups of soda over five days. Four cups are of each brand and their order is mixed. You serve it in colored cups so he cannot know which brand is in which cup. If he correctly identifies the brand 24 of the 24 times, you can be confident he can tell the difference. In testing a theory, like your friend is correct 100 percent of the time, your confidence in the theory grows. This is rare. However, if your friend was correct 90 percent of the time, you might think his evaluation was good but not perfect. If he was correct just 30 percent of the time, he is only a little better than chance guessing. Your confidence in his evaluation would be low. In theory-testing, confidence in an explanation varies by whether the results matching a theory's predictions far exceed what is expected by chance alone, and by whether it survives many repeated tests.

The study by Transue in Example Box 8.2 replicated tests of self-categorization theory that had survived many experimental tests.

He applied the priming effect to activate self-categorization so people selected an in-group identity, then he provided evidence that supported the theory. His study combined survey methods and a realistic policy issue. Another study on the contact hypothesis described later in this chapter (see Example Box 8.6) is also a theory-directed experiment, although applied in a real-life situation.

RANDOM ASSIGNMENT

In daily life, you are always making comparisons. Is this pair of shoes better-looking than that pair? Is this class more interesting than that class? Is this restaurant meal a better deal for the price than that one? When you compare you may recall the cliché, "Compare apples to apples, don't compare apples to oranges." It is not about fruit; it is about how to make comparisons. It means that a valid comparison depends on comparing items that are fundamentally alike. You compare one college course to another, not a college course to spending time at an amusement park.

In an experiment you can compare in the following three ways:[5]

1. *Within-participants.* You compare the same person over multiple points in time (e.g., before and after completing a training course). This is useful but you are often less interested in how one person changes than whether the treatment, or independent variable, has an impact on people more generally.

2. *Within-groups.* You compare one group of participants at two or more times (e.g., the group average of 15 people before and after a training course). You can also compare the same group of people across a series of treatments (e.g., three training programs in sequence) to see whether each treatment (training session) produces an effect (improvement in skill or knowledge).

3. *Between-groups.* You compare two different groups of participants, those who have and have not had the treatment (e.g., a group average of 15 who had the training course compared with 15 who did not have the course). To compare between groups, you can randomly assign participants to create similar groups.

Random assignment is a method for assigning cases (e.g., participants, organizations) to groups that allows you to make comparisons. It is a way to divide a collection of participants into two or more groups to increase your confidence that the groups do not differ in a systematic way. It is a purely mechanical method; the assignment is automatic. You cannot assign based on your or a participant's personal preference, or their features (i.e., you thought they acted friendly, someone wants to be in a group with a friend, put all people who arrived late in one group).

To compare between groups, you do not want the groups to differ with regard to variables that could be alternative explanations for a causal relationship. For example, you want to compare two groups to determine the causal effect of completing a firefighting training course on their ability to respond to a fire. You want the two groups to be similar in all respects except for taking the course. If the groups were identical except for the course, you can compare outcomes knowing that the course caused any differences you found. If the groups differed (e.g., one had experienced firefighters, or one group had much younger and more physically fit participants) you could not be certain that the training course was the only cause of any differences you observe.

Random assignment is random in a statistical or mathematical sense, not in an everyday sense. You may say *random* to mean unplanned, haphazard, or accidental. In probability theory, *random* is a process in which each case has an equal chance of being selected. With random selection, you can mathematically calculate the odds that a specific case appears in one group over another. For example, you have 50 people and use a random process (such as the toss of a coin) to place some in one (those that the coin indicates heads) or another group (the coin indicates tails). This way all participants have an equal chance of ending up in one or the other group.

The great thing about a mathematically random process is that over many separate random occurrences, very predictable things happen. The process is entirely due to chance, and you cannot predict a specific outcome at a specific time, but highly accurate predictions are possible across many situations.

Random assignment is *unbiased* because your desire to confirm a hypothesis, or a research participant's personal interests, do not enter into the selection process. *Unbiased* does not mean that groups are identical in each specific random assignment selection. It says something close to that: You can determine the probability of selecting a case mathematically, and, in the long run, across many separate selections, the groups are not different.

Random sampling, which you read about in Chapter 6, and random assignment both use the principle of randomness for selecting cases. To sample randomly, you use a random process to select a smaller subset of cases from a far larger collection of cases. To assign randomly, you use a random process to sort a collection of cases into two or more groups (see Figure 8.1). You can

FIGURE 8.1   Random Assignment and Random Sampling

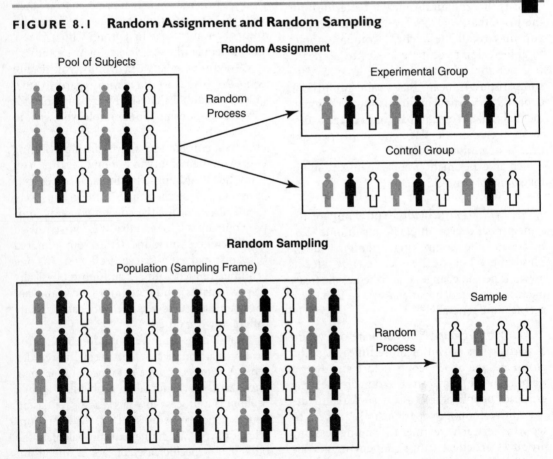

Note: Shading indicates various skin tones.

both sample and randomly assign. For example, you first randomly sample to obtain a small set of cases (e.g., 150 people out of 20,000), and next you use random assignment to divide the smaller set into three equal-sized groups (e.g., divide the 150 people into three groups of 50).

Random assignment is simple in practice. Start with a collection of cases (i.e., individuals, teams, companies, or whatever your unit of analysis), and then divide the collection into two or more groups using a random process, such as asking people to count off, tossing a coin, or throwing dice. If you wish to divide 32 people into two groups of 16 randomly, you could have each person write his or her name on a standard-sized slip of paper, and then put all slips in a hat, mix the slips with your eyes closed, and then with eyes still closed draw the first 16 names for group 1 and the second 16 for group 2. A specific situation can be unusual and the groups may differ. Though extremely unlikely, maybe all cases with one characteristic will end up in one group. For example, of 32 people with 16 males and 16 females, all the males end up in one group and all the females in another. Although possible by random chance,

it is extremely rare (see Figure 8.2 on random selection).

Matching versus Random Assignment

You may ask, if the purpose of random assignment is to produce two (or more) equivalent groups, would it not be easier to match the characteristics of cases in each group? Some researchers match cases on certain characteristics, such as age and sex. Matching is an alternative, but it is an infrequently used one because it has a problem: What are the relevant characteristics to match on, and can you locate exact matches? Individual cases differ in thousands of ways, and you cannot know which might be relevant.

For example, you want to compare two groups of 16 students. Group 1 has eight males, so we need eight males in group 2. Two males in group 1 are only children; the parents of one divorced when he was 12 years old; the other only child male comes from an intact family. One is tall, slender, and Jewish; the other is short, heavy, and Catholic. In order to match

---

FIGURE 8.2   How to Randomly Assign

Step 1: Begin with a collection of subjects.

Step 2: Devise a method to randomize that is purely mechanical (e.g., flip a coin).

Step 3: Assign subjects with "Heads" to one group 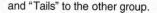 and "Tails" to the other group.

Control Group

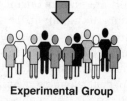

Experimental Group

Note: Shading indicates various skin tones.

groups, do we have to find a tall Jewish male only child from a divorced home and a short Catholic male only child from an intact home? The tall, slender, Jewish male only child is 22 years old, and he is a pre-med major. The short, heavy Catholic male is 20 years old and is an accounting major. Do we also need to find two males with the same age and career aspirations as well as the same family background, religion, and statute for group 2? True matching soon becomes an impossible task. Random assignment, over the long run with many assignments, produces groups with no real difference.

EXPERIMENTAL DESIGN LOGIC

The Language of Experiments

In experimental research, many studies call the participants *subjects*, although in recent years research participant is more common.

Parts of the Experiment.   The experiment has seven parts. Not all experiments have all these parts, and some have all seven parts plus others.

1. Treatment or independent variable
2. Dependent variable
3. Pretest
4. Posttest
5. Experimental group
6. Control group
7. Random assignment

In most experiments, you will create a situation or enter into an ongoing situation and do something to modify it. This is the *treatment* (or the stimulus or manipulation). The term is from medical practice in which a physician administers a treatment to patients. When treating a patient, the physician intervenes or does something to modify a physical or psychological condition.

The treatment is the independent variable or a combination of independent variables. In Niven's study (Example Box 8.1), the treatment was which of three news stories that participants received to read while in an airport waiting area. In Transue's study (Example Box 8.2), the treatment was which of two questions about identity participants heard in a telephone survey.

At times, experimenters go to great lengths to create treatments. Experimenters have created different false records, read different news stories, heard different survey questions, or shown different videos to groups (see Example Box 8.4). Others can be complex, such as putting participants into situations with elaborate equipment, staged physical settings, or contrived social situations. You saw this in the famous Milgram and Zimbardo experiments that you read about in Chapter 3. You want the treatment to have an impact and produce specific reactions, feelings, or behaviors (see section on experimental realism later in this chapter).

Dependent variables or outcomes in experimental research are the physical conditions, social behaviors, attitudes, feelings, or beliefs of participants that change in response to a treatment. You can measure dependent variables by paper-and-pencil indicators, observations, interviews, or physiological responses (e.g., heartbeat or sweating palms).

You may want to measure the dependent variable more than once during an experiment. The *pretest* is the measurement of the dependent variable prior to introduction of the treatment. The *posttest* is the measurement of the dependent variable after the treatment has been introduced into the experimental situation.

When you divide participants into two or more groups for purposes of comparison, only one will receive the treatment. The *experimental group* receives the treatment or is the one in which the treatment is present. The group that does not receive the treatment is the *control group*. When the independent variable has several values, you can have more than one experimental group.

Steps in Conducting an Experiment. Following the basic steps of the research process, you decide on a topic, narrow it into a testable research question, and then develop a hypothesis with variables. A crucial early step is to plan a specific experimental design (to be discussed). As you plan, you must know how many groups to create, how and when to create treatment conditions, how and the number of times to measure the dependent variable, and what the groups of participants will experience from the beginning to the end of the study. It is always a good idea to pilot-test the experiment (i.e., conduct it as a "dry run"). This helps you identify potential mishaps and flaws prior to conducting the actual experiment.

Your experiment begins after you locate volunteer participants and randomly assign them to groups. You want to give them precise, preplanned instructions. Next, you can measure the dependent variable in a pretest before the treatment. Then you expose one group only to the treatment (or a high level of it). Finally, you measure the dependent variable in a posttest. It is always wise to also interview participants about the experiment before they leave to learn their perspective and answer questions. You record measures of the dependent variable and examine the results for each group to see whether the data support your hypothesis.

Control in Experiments. Control is crucial in experimental research.[6] You want to control all aspects of the experimental situation in order to isolate the effects of the treatment. By controlling confounding variables you eliminate alternative explanations that could undermine your attempts to establish causality.

Experimenters sometimes use deception to control the experimental setting (see the section on the ethical experiment later in this chapter). ***Deception*** is when you intentionally mislead research participants through written or verbal instructions, the actions of others, or aspects of the setting. It may involve the use of a ***confederate***—someone who pretends to

be another research participant or bystander but who actually works for the researcher and deliberately misleads participants. Milgram's experiment used confederates.

Deception is used only to change what the participants see and hear and to shift slightly what they believe is occurring. It usually means you create a ***cover story***. A cover story is a false explanation of the study's purpose that you tell to participants to mislead them about its true purpose. The cover story helps to satisfy curiosity but reduces demand characteristics (see later in this chapter). Many studies use a cover story (see studies in Example Boxes 8.1, 8.4, and 8.6).

Types of Design

You combine the parts of an experiment (e.g., pretests, control groups, etc.) together to create an ***experimental design***. Some designs lack pretests, some do not have control groups, and others have several experimental groups. The widely used standard designs have names. You want to learn the standard designs for two reasons. First, when you read research reports, authors may give the name of a standard design instead of describing it. Second, the standard designs illustrate common ways to combine design parts. You can use them for experiments you conduct or create your own variations.

You can see the various designs with a simple example. Let us say that you want to learn whether wait staff (waiters and waitresses) receive more in tips if they first introduce themselves by first name and return to ask, "Is everything fine?" 8–10 minutes after delivering the food. The dependent variable is the size of the tip received. Your study occurs in two identical restaurants on different sides of a town that have had the same types of customers and average the same amount in tips.

Classical Experimental Design. All designs are variations of the ***classical experimental design***, the type of design discussed so far, which has random assignment, a pretest and a posttest, an experimental group, and a control group. *Example.* You give 40 newly hired wait staff an identical two-hour training session and instruct them to follow a script in which they are not to introduce themselves by first name and not to return during the meal to check on the customers. You next randomly divide them into two equal groups of 20 and send each group to the two restaurants to begin employment. You record the amount in tips for all participants for one month (pretest score). Next, you "retrain" the 20 participants at restaurant 1 (experimental group). You instruct them henceforth to introduce themselves to customers by first name and to check on the customers, asking, "Is everything fine?" 8–10 minutes after delivering the food (treatment). You remind the group at restaurant 2 (control group) to continue without an introduction or checking during the meal. Over the second month, you record the amount of tips for both groups (posttest score).

Preexperimental Designs. Some designs lack random assignment and are compromises or shortcuts. You can use these **preexperimental designs** in situations in which it is difficult to use the classical design. Inferring a causal relationship from them can be less clear than using the classical design.

One-Shot Case-Study Design. Also called the one-group posttest-only design, the **one-shot case-study design** has only one group, a treatment, and a posttest. Because there is only one group, there is no random assignment.

Example. You take a group of 40 newly hired wait staff and give all a two-hour training session in which you instruct them to introduce themselves to customers by first name and to check on the customers, asking, "Is everything fine?" 8–10 minutes after delivering the food (treatment). The participants begin employment, and you record the amount in tips for all for one month (posttest score).

One-Group Pretest–Posttest Design. This design has one group, a pretest, a treatment, and a posttest. It lacks a control group and random assignment.

Example. You take a group of 40 newly hired wait staff and give all a two-hour training session. You instruct them to follow a script in which they are not to introduce themselves by first name and not to return during the meal to check on the customers. All begin employment, and you record the amount in tips for all for one month (pretest score). Next, you "retrain" all 40 participants and instruct them henceforth to introduce themselves to customers by first name and to check on the customers, asking, "Is everything fine?" 8–10 minutes after delivering the food (treatment). Over the second month, you record the amount of tips for both groups (posttest score).

This is an improvement over the one-shot case study because you measure the dependent variable before and after the treatment. However, it lacks a control group. You cannot know whether something other than the treatment occurred between the pretest and the posttest to cause the outcome.

Static Group Comparison. Also called the posttest-only nonequivalent group design, a **static group comparison** has two groups, a posttest, and a treatment. It lacks random assignment and a pretest. A weakness is that any posttest outcome difference between the groups could be due to group differences prior to the experiment instead of to the treatment.

Example. You give 40 newly hired wait staff an identical two-hour training session and instruct all to follow a script in which they are not to introduce themselves by first name and not to return during the meal to check on the customers. They can choose one of the two restaurants in which to work, as long as each restaurant ends up with 20 people. All begin employment. After one month, you "retrain" the 20 participants at restaurant 1 (experimental group) and instruct them henceforth to introduce themselves to customers by first name and to check on the customers, asking, "Is everything fine?" 8–10 minutes after delivering the food (treatment). The group at restaurant 2 (control group) is "retrained" to continue without an introduction or checking during the meal. Over the second month, you record the amount of tips for both groups (posttest score).

Quasi-Experimental and Special Designs. These designs, like the classical design, make identifying a causal relationship more certain than do preexperimental designs. **Quasi-experimental designs** help to test for causal relationships in situations in which the classical design is difficult or inappropriate. They are *quasi* because they are "weaker" variations of the classical experimental design: some use randomization but no pretest; some use more than two groups; some substitute many observations of one group over time for a control group. In general, you have less control over the independent variable compared to the classical design (see Table 8.1).

Two-Group Posttest-Only Design. This is identical to the static group comparison, with one exception: you randomly assign. It has all the parts of the classical design except for a pretest. Random assignment reduces the chance that the groups differed before the treatment, but without a pretest, you cannot be as certain that the groups began the same on the dependent variable.

In a study using a two-group posttest-only design with random assignment, Rind and Strohmetz (1999) examined restaurant tips. The treatment was messages about an upcoming special written on the back of customers' checks. The participants were 81 dining parties eating at an upscale restaurant in New Jersey. The treatment was whether a female server wrote a message about an upcoming restaurant special on the back of a check and the dependent variable was the size of tips. They gave a server with two years' experience a randomly shuffled stack of cards. One half said No Message and half said Message. Just before she gave a customer his or her check, she randomly pulled a card from her pocket. If it said Message, she wrote about an upcoming special on the back of the customer's check. If it said No Message, she wrote nothing. The experimenters recorded the amount of the tip and the number of people at the table. They instructed the server to act the same toward all customers. They found that higher tips came from customers who received the message about upcoming specials.

Interrupted Time Series. In an **interrupted time-series design**, you measure the dependent

TABLE 8.1   A Comparison of the Classical Experimental Design

Design	Random Assignment	Pretest	Posttest	Control Group	Experimental Group
Classical	Yes	Yes	Yes	Yes	Yes
One-shot case study	No	No	Yes	No	Yes
One-group pretest/posttest	No	Yes	Yes	No	Yes
Static group comparison	No	No	Yes	Yes	Yes
Two-group posttest only	Yes	No	Yes	Yes	Yes
Time series designs	No	Yes	Yes	No	Yes

variable on one group over time and many multiple dependent variable measures before (pretests) and after a treatment (posttests).

Equivalent Time Series. An **equivalent time-series design** is similar to the one-group design interrupted time series. It extends over a time period but instead of a single treatment, it has a treatment several times. Like the interrupted time-series design, you measure the dependent variable several times before and after the treatments. The study on alcohol sales and suicide rates (see Example Box 8.3) illustrated equivalent time series.

Latin Square Designs. At times, you want to find out how several independent variables in different sequences or time orders influence the dependent variable. The **Latin square design** is created in this situation. For example, a geography instructor has three units to teach students: map reading, using a compass, and the longitude/latitude (LL) system. The units can be taught in any order, but the teacher wants to know which order most helps students learn. In one class, students first learn to read maps, then how to use a compass, then the LL system. In another class, using a compass comes first, then map reading, then the LL system.

8.3	EXAMPLE BOX

Interrupted Time Series, Alcohol Sales, and Suicide Rates

Governments face strong pressures by economic interests to modify laws to allow them to collect increased profits from alcohol sales. In most of western Canada, a public monopoly controlled alcohol sales and distribution through most of the twentieth century. Proponents of privatization point to its economic benefits, including selling previously government-owned retail outlets and the sale of licenses to merchandise alcohol. Others point to the impact of privatization on consumption and health. Studies of privatization of sales of alcoholic beverages indicate that privatization greatly expands alcohol availability and consumption.

Alberta moved to privatize alcohol sales in three stages: the opening of privately owned wine stores in 1985, the opening of privately owned cold beer stores and sale of spirits and wine in hotels in the rural areas in 1989–1990, and finally the privatization of all liquor stores in 1994. The number of alcohol outlets increased substantially, and consumption of spirits increased dramatically at a time when consumption was decreasing elsewhere in the country. Privatization in Alberta has been associated with an increase in criminal offenses, such as liquor store break-ins and less strict enforcement of underage purchase laws. Alberta also has some of the highest rates of drunk-driving fatalities in the

country. Many past studies also showed a strong relationship between suicide rates and alcohol consumption.

Zalcman and Mann (2007) used a three-stage interrupted time-series design to examine the influence of Alberta's privatization of alcohol sales on suicide rates between 1976 and 1999. They considered whether suicide rates changed after each privatization phase. They also compared Alberta's suicide levels to those for the same years in Ontario where alcohol sales remained a government monopoly.

The researchers found that the 1985 privatization of wine retailers increased suicide rates in Alberta by 51 percent for males and 35 percent for females. After the 1989–1990 privatization of spirits and wine a significant increase occurred in male and female suicide rates, estimated to be 17 percent and 52 percent, respectively. The 1994 privatization event significantly increased male suicide mortality rates, estimated at 19 percent, but not female suicide rates. Part of the increase was a short-term spurt but long-term suicide rates also rose. By tracing the rates both over time by comparing those in a "control group" or to those in Ontario, the authors provided evidence of the effect of alcohol privatization on increased suicides.

In a third class, the instructor first teaches the LL system, then compass usage, and ends with map reading. The teacher gives tests after each unit, and students take a comprehensive exam at the end of the term. The students were randomly assigned to classes, so the instructor can see whether presenting units in one sequence or another resulted in improved learning.

Solomon Four-Group Design.   You may believe that the pretest measure has an influence on the treatment or dependent variable. A pretest can sometimes sensitize participants to the treatment or improve their performance on the posttest (see the discussion of testing effect to come). Richard L. Solomon developed the **Solomon four-group design** to examine pretest effects. It combines the classical experimental design with the two-group posttest-only design and randomly assigns participants to one of four groups. For example, a mental health worker wants to learn whether a new training method will improve client coping skills. The worker measures coping skills with a 20-minute test of reactions to stressful events. However, clients might learn coping skills from taking the test itself, so the worker uses a Solomon four-group design. She first randomly divides clients into four groups. Two groups receive the pretest; one gets the new training method and the other gets the old method. Another two groups receive no pretest; one gets the new method and the other gets the old method. She administers the same posttest to all four groups and compares posttest results. If the two treatment (new method) groups have similar results, and the two control (old method) groups have similar results, then she knows pretest learning is not a problem. If the two groups with a pretest (one treatment, one control) differ from the two groups without a pretest, then she concludes that the pretest itself may have an effect on the dependent variable.

Factorial Designs.   Sometimes, you may be curious about the simultaneous effects of two or more independent variables. A **factorial design** uses two or more independent variables in combination. You can look at each combination of the categories in variables (sometimes called *factors*). When each variable contains several categories, the number of combinations grows quickly. In this type of design, the treatment is not each independent variable; rather, it is each combination of the variable categories. There is a shorthand way to discuss factorial design. A "two by three factorial design" is written 2×3. It means that there are two treatments, with two categories in one and three categories in the other. A $2 \times 3 \times 3$ design means that there are three independent variables, one with two categories and two with three categories each. Factorial designs allow you to measure and examine more of the world's complexity than other designs.

For example, Krysan and associates wanted to study race and class in neighborhood preferences. It was difficult to examine both racial and social class features of a neighborhood at the same time, so they used a factoral design (see Example Box 8.4). The three independent variables of their study were participant race (two categories: Black or White), neighborhood composition (three types: all White, all Black, racially mixed), and social class (five levels). The dependent variable was desirability of a neighborhood, rated 1 to 7. They had a $2 \times 3 \times 5$ factorial design (The authors also asked participants about the strength of their identity with their own racial group.)

In a factorial design, treatments can have two kinds of effects on the dependent variable: main effects and interaction effects. Only *main effects* are present in one-factor or single-treatment designs. In other words, you simply examine the impact of the treatment on the dependent variable. In a factorial design, specific combinations of independent variable categories can have an effect beyond a single factor effect. They are **interaction effects** because the categories in a combination interact to produce an effect beyond that of each variable alone.

8.4   EXAMPLE BOX
Factorial Experiment on Neighborhood Preferences

Krysan and associates (2009) created an experiment to study neighborhood preferences among Blacks and White adults in the United States. Past studies had looked at this issue; however, examining both racial and social class factors at the same time was very difficult, and telling whether people preferred a neighborhood for its social class or its racial features was not possible. The authors said, "At the core of our analysis are two research questions: (1) Are neighborhood preferences color blind or race conscious? (2) If preferences are race conscious, do they reflect a desire to be in a neighborhood with one's 'own kind' or to avoid being in a neighborhood with another racial group?" (p. 529). In 2004–2005, the authors selected more than 700 participants in the Detroit region and nearly 800 in the Chicago metropolitan area. To disentangle the class and race effects in neighborhoods, the authors showed participants videotaped neighborhoods that varied by social class and racial mix. They created thirteen videos in total. The neighborhoods varied by five social class levels and three racial mix levels.

> We selected different neighborhoods to convey the different social class levels, relying on this assumption that respondents infer social class based on features such as home and property size, upkeep of the houses, and other cues gleaned from observation. Each of the different neighborhoods had, in turn, three variants in terms of the race of the individuals shown: (1) all residents are White; (2) all residents are Black; (3) three residents are White and two residents are Black. (p. 537)

One video was a control without people. In each other video, five people (actors) appeared as residents engaged in ordinary activities. They noted,

> In each neighborhood, there was one scene in which three individuals were shown together talking in the driveway, in the front yard, at the mailbox, or surrounding a car that was being repaired. Residents wore short-sleeved shirts and no hats to increase the likelihood that the respondents could detect their racial/ethnic identity. Residents within each neighborhood social class level were matched on approximate age, gender, and style of dress (p. 537).

As a manipulation check, the authors showed videos to a small group of other participants prior to the actual study to verify that people saw the class and race composition of neighborhoods as intended. After viewing videos, the authors asked participants to rate each neighborhood on a seven-point Likert scale from very desirable to very undesirable. They said (p. 539), "Our dependent variables are the desirability ratings of the four neighborhoods, and thus our unit of analysis is the video. Given that each respondent saw and rated the same baseline video–an upper-working-class neighborhood with no residents–we include the ratings of this neighborhood as a respondent-level control." The authors used a factorial design with three independent variables: research participant race, neighborhood social class, and neighborhood racial mix. The authors randomly assigned participants to view different racial compositions in the same neighborhoods. Among their many findings, the authors note (p. 538), "Our fundamental conclusion is that race, per se, shapes how Whites and, to a lesser extent, Blacks view residential space. Residential preferences are not simply a reaction to class-based features of a neighborhood; they are shaped by the race of the people who live there."

Interaction effects are of special interest because they suggest that not only does an independent variable have an impact, but specific combinations have unique effects, or variables only have an impact under certain conditions.

Mueller-Johnson and Dhami (see Example Box 8.5 and Figure 8.3) created a trial-like situation and had participants serve on a mock jury. They presented various combinations of characteristics of offenders to see their impact

EXAMPLE BOX

8.5 Mock Jury and Interaction Effects by Age and Crime

Mueller-Johnson and Dhami (2010) created a mock jury. They formed a trial-like situation and had participants form a jury. The authors presented various combinations of characteristics of offenders to see how they impacted jury sentencing decisions. Sentencing was length of prison term. Their jurors were forty-seven students (thirty-six women and eleven men) from an English university. The authors varied the age, health, offense severity, and prior convictions of an offender to create a $2 \times 2 \times 2 \times 2$ factorial design. In past experiments, they had found main effects for health, prior convictions, and severity of offense. People in poor health received shorter sentences, and older (66- to 72-year-old) received shorter sentences than younger (21- to 26-year-old) offenders regardless of the number of prior convictions. Younger offenders with prior convictions and more severe offences received longer sentences. In the current study, they investigated child sex offenders. Prior offense was either no prior conviction or one for sexual contact with a child 4 years earlier, and offense severity was either once touching a 7-year-old girl's genitals over her clothing or touching naked genitalia ten times over the course of a year. The participants usually decided on a sentence in 15 minutes. The authors found interesting interaction effects among age, offense severity, and previous convictions. For those with a prior conviction, older offenders received a longer sentence than younger offenders with less serious offenses, but shorter sentences if the offense was more serious. In other words, the combination of a prior conviction and less serious offense for older offenders resulted in a longer sentence. This is consistent with the "dirty-old-man" stereotype.

on sentencing decisions. The authors varied the age, health, offense severity, and prior convictions of an offender to create a $2 \times 2 \times 2 \times 2$ factorial design. They found main effects for severity of crime, age, and prior conviction. People committing more severe crimes,

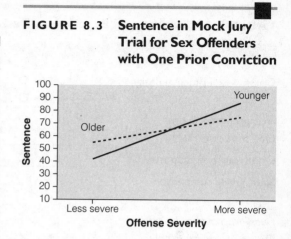

FIGURE 8.3 Sentence in Mock Jury Trial for Sex Offenders with One Prior Conviction

younger offenders, and those with prior convictions received longer sentences than people committing less serious crimes, older offenders, and no prior convictions. They also found a few interaction effects. One interaction effect was age and severity of crime for those with a past conviction.

Design Notation

Because you can design experiments in many ways, it is useful to learn a shorthand system for symbolizing experimental design called *design notation*.[7] The notation system can express a complex, paragraph-long description of the parts of an experiment in five or six symbols arranged in two lines. Once you learn design notation, you will find it easier to think about and compare designs. It uses the following symbols: O = observation of dependent variable; X = treatment, independent variable; R = random assignment. The Os are numbered with subscripts from left to right based on time order. Pretests are O_1, posttests O_2. When the independent variable has more than two levels, the Xs are numbered with subscripts to distinguish among them. Symbols are in time order from left to right. The R is first, followed by the pretest, the treatment, and then the posttest. We arrange symbols in rows, with each row representing a group of participants. For example,

TABLE 8.2 **Summary of Experiment Designs with Notation**

Name of Design	Design Notation
Classical experimental design	R ⟶ O X O R ⟶ O O
Preexperimental designs One-shot case study	X O
One-group pretest/posttest	O X O
Static group comparison	X O O
Quasi-experimental designs Two-group posttest only	R ⟶ X O O
Interrupted time series	O O O O X O O O
Equivalent time series	O X O X O X O X O
Latin square designs	O X_a O X_b O X_c O O X_b O X_a O X_c O R → O X_c O X_b O X_a O O X_a O X_c O X_b O O X_b O X_c O X_a O O X_c O X_a O X_b O
Solomon four-group design	O X O R O O X O O
Factorial designs	R X_1 Z_1 O X_1 Z_2 O X_2 Z_1 O X_2 Z_2 O

Note: Subscripts with letters indicate different treatment variables. Subscripts with numbers indicate different categories of the same treatment variable, such as male or female for gender.

an experiment with three groups has an R (if random assignment is used), followed by three rows of Os and Xs. The rows are on top of each other because the pretest, treatment, and posttest occur in each group at about the same time. Table 8.2 gives the notation for many standard experimental designs.

INTERNAL AND EXTERNAL VALIDITY

The Logic of Internal Validity

Internal validity is when the independent variable, and nothing else, influences the dependent variable. Anything other than the independent variables influencing the dependent variable threatens internal validity. These are confounding variables; they confound logic of an experiment to exclude everything except the relationship between the variables in your hypothesis. They threaten your ability to say that the treatment was the true causal factor that produced a change in the dependent variable. They come not from the natural relationship you are examining, but from the particular experimental arrangement by accident. For example, you clean a room before participants arrive for an experiment on the emotional effects of going without sleep, but the cleaning solution you used to wipe down tables and chairs causes irritability in many people. Your results show increased irritability among people who had little sleep. However, it is not because of sleep loss but an unintended side effect of your cleaning solution. You want to eliminate anything that might influence the dependent variable other than the treatment. To do this, you control experimental conditions with experimental designs. Next, we examine major threats to internal validity.

Threats to Internal Validity

The following are 12 threats to internal validity.[8]

1. **Selection Bias. Selection bias** can arise when you have more than one group of participants in an experiment. You want to compare the groups, but they differ or do not form equivalent groups. It is a problem in designs without random assignment. For example, you design a two-group experiment on aggressiveness. If you do not use randomization or it is not effective, the treatment group could by chance differ. You may have 60 research participants who are active in various campus activities. By chance your volunteers for the experimental group are on football, rugby, hockey, and wrestling teams, whereas volunteers in your control group are musicians, chess club members, ballet dancers, and painters. Another example is an experiment on the ability of people to dodge heavy traffic.

You would have selection bias if participants assigned to one group are from rural areas with little traffic experience, and in the other grew up in large cities. You can often detect selection bias by comparing pretest scores. If you see no group differences in the pretest scores, selection bias is probably not a problem.

2. **History.** This is when an event unrelated to the treatment occurs during the experiment and influences the dependent variable. **History effects** are more likely in experiments that continue over a long time. For example, halfway through a two-week experiment to evaluate feelings about pet dogs, a fire at a nearby dog kennel kills and injures many young puppies, with news reports showing injured animals and many local people crying over the incident.

3. **Maturation.** This is the threat that a biological, psychological, or emotional process within participants other than the treatment takes place during the experiment and influences the dependent variable. A **maturation effect** is more common in experiments over a long time. For example, during a day-long experiment on reasoning ability, participants become bored and sleepy and, as a result, score lower. Another example is an experiment on the styles of children's play between grades 1 and 6. Play styles are affected by physical, emotional, and maturation changes that occur as the children grow older, instead of or in addition to the effects of a treatment. Designs with a pretest and control group help us determine whether maturation or history effects are present because both experimental and control groups will show similar changes over time.

4. **Testing.** Sometimes, the pretest measure itself affects an experiment. This **testing effect** threatens internal validity because more than the treatment alone is affecting the dependent variable. The Solomon four-group design helps you detect testing effects. For example, your pretest measures how much participants know about geology and geography. The treatment is a series of videos about geology and geography during

two days. If participants remember the pretest questions and this affects what they learned (i.e., paid attention to in the videos) or how they answered questions on the posttest, a testing effect is present. If testing effects occur, you cannot say that the treatment alone affects the dependent variable. Both memory of the pretest and the treatment influenced the dependent variable.

5. *Instrumentation.* This threat is related to stability reliability. It occurs when the *instrument* or dependent variable measure changes during the experiment. For example, in a weight-loss experiment, the springs on the scale weaken during the experiment, giving lower readings in the posttest. Another example is your treatment of showing a video but the equipment breaks down when trying to show it to one group of participants.

6. *Experimental mortality. Experimental mortality*, or attrition, arises when some participants do not continue throughout the entire experiment. *Mortality* means death, but it does not necessarily mean that they died. If many participants leave partway through an experiment, you cannot know whether the results would have been different had they stayed. For example, you begin a weight-loss experiment with 60 people. At the end of the program, 40 remain, each of whom lost 5 pounds with no side effects. The 20 who left could have differed from the 30 who stayed, changing the results. Maybe the program was effective for those who left, and they withdrew after losing 25 pounds. Or, the program made them sick and forced them to quit. Or, they saw no improvement so they dropped out. You need to notice and report the number of participants at all stages of an experiment to detect this threat.

7. *Statistical Regression.* Not easy to grasp intuitively, *statistical regression* is a problem of extreme values or a tendency for random errors to move group results toward the average. It can occur in two ways.

One situation is when participants are unusual with regard to the dependent variable.

Because they are unusual, they do not respond further in one direction. For example, you want to see whether playing violent video games makes people more aggressive. Your participants are a group of convicts from a high-security prison. You give them a pretest, have them play 60 hours of extremely violent video games, then administer a posttest. To your surprise, there is no change. It could be that the convicts began as extremely aggressive. They were so aggressive that your treatment could not make them any more aggressive. By random chance alone, some may even appear less aggressive when measured in the posttest.[9]

A second situation involves problems with the measurement instrument. If your measure is such that most people score very high (at the ceiling) or very low (at the floor) on a variable, random chance alone tends to create a change between the pretest and the posttest. For example, you give 80 participants a simple math test, and 77 get perfect scores. You give a treatment designed to improve math scores. Because so many already had perfect scores, random errors could reduce the group average because the 77 who got perfect scores can move in only one direction—downward—and get answers wrong. Only three participants could show improvement. As a result, the group average could be lower in the posttest due to chance alone. You need to monitor the range of scores to detect statistical regression.

8. *Diffusion of Treatment or Contamination. Diffusion of treatment* is the threat that participants from different groups will communicate and learn about the other group's treatment. You can avoid it by isolating groups or having them promise not to reveal anything to other participants. For example, you have 80 participants who participate in a daylong experiment on ways to memorize words. You teach the treatment group a simple method, and tell the control group to use any technique they want to use. During a break, participants in the treatment group tell those in the control

group about the new method. After the break control group particpants start using it too. You might ask about possible diffusion in a postexperiment interview with participants to reduce this threat.

9. *Compensatory Behavior.* Experiments that provide something of value to one group of participants but not to another, and the difference becomes known, is *compensatory behavior.* The inequality between groups may create a desire to reduce differences, competitive rivalry between groups, or resentful demoralization. Such behavior can affect the dependent variable in addition to the treatment. For example, students in one school receive a treatment of longer lunch breaks to produce gains in learning. Once the inequality is known, stundents in a control group without long lunch breaks work extra hard to learn and overcome the inequality. Alternatively, the control group students could become demoralized by the unequal treatment and put less effort into learning. It is difficult to detect this threat unless you obtain outside information (see the discussion of diffusion of treatment).

10. *Experimenter Expectancy.* Experimenter behavior might threaten internal validity if the experimentor indirectly communicates a desired outcome.[10] Because of a strong belief in the hypothesis, even the most honest experimenter might unintentionally communicate desired findings. For example, you study participant reactions toward people with disabilities. You deeply believe that females are more sensitive than males toward people with disabilities. Through eye contact, tone of voice, pauses, nods of the head, and other nonverbal communication, you unconsciously encourage your female participants to report positive feelings toward people with disabilities. For males, your nonverbal behavior is the opposite.

The *double-blind experiment* controls for *experimenter expectancy.* In it, the only people who have direct contact with participants do not know the details of the hypothesis or

the treatment. It is *double* blind because both the participants and those in contact with them are blind to details of the experiment (see Figure 8.4). For example, you want to see if a new drug is effective. Using pills of three colors—green, yellow, and pink—you put the new drug in the yellow pill, an old drug in the pink one, and make the green pill a *placebo*—(e.g., a sugar pill without any effects). Assistants who give the pills and record the effects do not know which color contains the new drug. They just administer the pills and record results by color of pill. Only you know which colored pill contains the drug and examine the results, but you have no contact with the research participants. The double-blind design is nearly mandatory in medical research because experimenter expectancy effects are well recognized.

11. *Demand Characteristics.* A threat to internal validity related to reactivity (discussed in the next section of this chapter) is a *demand characteristic.* It is when participants pick up clues about the hypothesis or an experiment's purpose, then modify behavior to what they believe the study demands of them (i.e., support the hypothesis). Participants often do this to please the researcher. This is why you might use mild deception or create a cover story.

12. *Placebo effect.* The last type of threat to internal validity is the *placebo effect.* A placebo is an empty or nonactive treatment, such as a "sugar pill" in medical research. The effect occurs when you give some participants a placebo but they respond as if they received the real treatment. For example, you create an experiment on ways to stop smoking among heavy smokers. You give some participants a pill with an antinicotine drug to reduce their nicotine dependence. You give other participants a placebo (an empty pill). If participants who received the placebo also stop smoking, then merely participating in the experiment and taking something that they believed would help them quit smoking had an effect. The belief in the placebo alone affected the dependent

FIGURE 8.4   Double-Blind Experiment: An Illustration of Single-Blind, or Ordinary, and Double-Blind Experiments

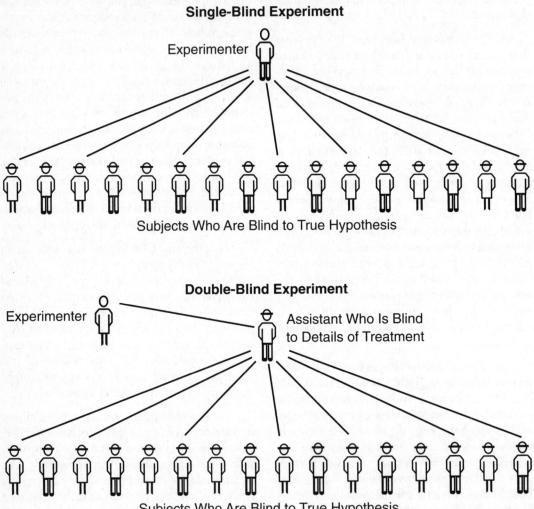

variable (see Table 8.3 for a summary of internal validity threats).

Pretests, pilot-tests, and experimental debriefing can help you verify measurement validity, experimental conditions, and experimental realism (experimental realism is discussed later in this chapter). These practices help you make certain that the variables and conditions of your experiment operate as intended and help rule out possible threats to internal validity. For example, you have a confederate act as if he or she is disabled and have preliminary research participants observe the confederate. As a check, you ask whether they believed the confederate was truly disabled or just acting.

TABLE 8.3   Internal Validity and External Validity Issues

Internal Validity	External Validity
Selection bias	Population generalization
History effect	
Testing effect	Naturalistic generalization
Maturation effect	
Instrumentation	Theoretical generalization
Experimental mortality	
Statistical regression effect	Mundane realism
Diffusion of treatment	Experimental realism
Compensatory behavior	
Experimenter expectancy	Hawthorne effect
Demand characteristics	
Placebo effect	

In the study on neighborhood preference (see Example Box 8.4), the researchers showed a small number of people videos of neighborhoods before using the videos in the study. This enabled them to verify that people recognized the racial mix and neighborhood's social class as the researchers intended. If you provide participants with written or oral instructions in an experiment, pretest them with a few preliminary participants. This lets you inquire about clarity of instructions and learn whether participants understood them as intended.

A "dry run" or pilot-test of the entire experimental procedure is very useful. During and after the pilot-test, you look for potential flaws, mishaps, or misunderstandings. You ask whether all parts of the experimental situation went smoothly and had their intended effects on participants. You may check to see whether participants paid attention and accepted your "cover story."

In experimental debriefing after a pilot-test or the actual experiment (unlike ethical debriefing that emphasizes removing a lie or deception)

you interview participants about details of the experiment. You ask what they thought was happening, whether they felt fully engaged and took the situation seriously, and ask about confusion, anxiety, or discomfort. You may look for compensatory behavior, demand characteristics, or diffusion of treatment in such interviews.

External Validity

Even if you eliminate all internal validity concerns, external validity remains an issue. *External validity* is your ability to generalize experimental findings. If a study lacks external validity, the findings may hold true only for a specific experiment but little beyond that. To build general theoretical knowledge in basic research and findings that relate to real-life problems in applied research, a study without external validity is of limited value.

External validity can involve several forms of generalization.[11] It addresses three questions about generalizing: Can you generalize from the specific collection of participants in an experiment to an entire population? Can you generalize from what occurs in a highly controlled and artificial experimental setting to most natural, "real-world" situations? Can you generalize from the empirical evidence of a specific experiment to a general model about relationships among variables? You can think of external validity as involving three forms of generalization that do not always overlap: population, naturalistic, and theoretical (see Figure 8.5).

Population Generalization.   This form of external validity asks whether you can accurately generalize from what was learned with a specific collection of people in one study to a universe or population of people. To generalize the findings, you should specify the universe to which you wish to generalize. For example, you conduct an experiment with 100 undergraduate volunteers from one course in one university. To whom can you generalize these findings? To all undergraduate students in all courses at

FIGURE 8.5 **Three Types of External Validity Generalization**

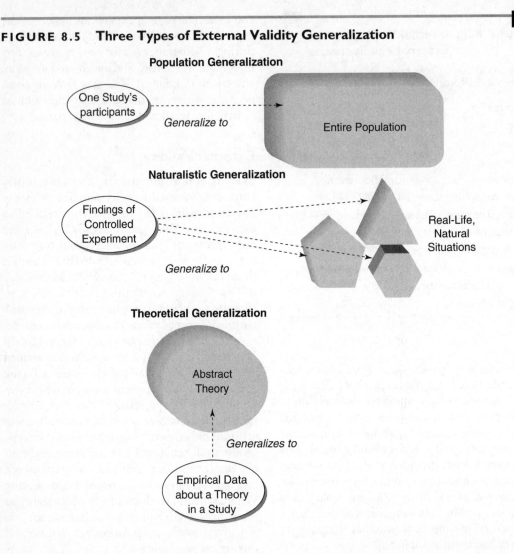

the same university during the same year? To all college students in the same country in the same decade? or to all humanity for all time? To improve the population generalization, you could draw a random sample and conduct the experiment on sampled participants.

Naturalistic Generalization. This is what most people first think of when hearing the term external validity. It asks whether you can generalize accurately from what you learned in an artificially created controlled laboratory-like setting to "real-life" natural settings. Naturalistic generalization involves two issues: mundane realism and reactivity.

Mundane realism asks, Is the experiment like the real world? For example, your study of learning has participants memorize four-letter nonsense syllables. Mundane realism would be stronger if you had them learn real-life factual information rather than nonsense syllables invented for an experiment alone.[12]

Reactivity is the effect of people reacting because they are aware that they are in a study.

Research participants might react differently in an experiment than in real life because they know someone is studying them. The *Hawthorne effect* is a specific kind of reactivity.[13] The name comes from a series of experiments by Elton Mayo at the Hawthorne, Illinois, plant of Westinghouse Electric during the 1920s and 1930s. Researchers modified many aspects of working conditions (e.g., lighting, time for breaks) and measured productivity. They discovered that productivity rose after each modification, no matter what it was. This curious result occurred because the workers did not respond to the treatment but to the additional attention they received from being part of the experiment and knowing that they were being watched. Later research questioned whether this had occurred, but the name is used for an effect from the attention of researchers.

The issue of reactivity is whether you can accurately generalize from activities that occur in a setting in which people are aware they are being studied to natural settings. Reactivity is most likely in a highly controlled experiment in which the research participants know an experimenter created the conditions and is observing their behaviors or responses.

Let us say that you conduct an experiment in a college classroom or laboratory in which the participants know they are participating in a study. You ask the participants to engage in some artificially created tasks (e.g., assemble a puzzle) or create artificial status using deception (e.g., tell participants that a confederate working for you has a genius IQ score). After working on the task, you ask participants to complete a questionnaire in which you have questions about their feelings about people with high IQ scores. To what settings in daily life might you generalize your study's findings? To all real-life workplace settings with people of varying intelligence levels, to all types of work tasks and all social statuses, to all attitudes about other people naturally formed in daily life and retained in everyday thoughts, behavior, or conversations? To improve the naturalistic generalization form of external validity in an experiment, you would conduct a field experiment (discussed below).

Theoretical Generalization. This asks whether you can accurately generalize from the concepts and relations in an abstract theory that we wish to test to a set of measures and arrangement of activities in a specific experiment. This is probably the most difficult type of generalization because it includes several other ideas: experimental realism, measurement validity, and control confounding variables (high internal validity). *Experimental realism* is the impact of an experimental treatment or setting on people; it occurs when participants are caught up in the experiment and are truly influenced by it. It is weak if they remain unaffected and it has little impact on them.

Field Experiments

You can conduct experiments under the controlled conditions of a laboratory or in real-life or field settings in which you have less control over the experimental conditions. The amount of control varies on a continuum. At one end is the highly controlled *laboratory experiment*. It takes place in a specialized setting or laboratory. At the opposite end is the *field experiment*. It takes place in the "field"—in natural settings such as a subway car, a liquor store, or a public sidewalk. Participants in field experiments are usually unaware that they are involved in an experiment and react in a natural way. For example, researchers have had a confederate fake a heart attack on a subway car to see how the bystanders react.[14]

Some field experiments, such as those by Transue on racial identity and school taxes, or Krysan and colleagues on neighborhood preference (see Example Box 8.2 and 8.4), presented participants with realistic choices. Others are "natural experiments" in which experiment-like situations arise without total researcher control, as with the Alberta privitization of alcohol sales (see Example Box 8.3). A related type of natural experiment in the field is when you take advantage of random assignment conditions of a key variable, as in the case of racial mixing of college roommates (see Example Box 8.6).

Degree of experimenter control is related to internal and external validity. Laboratory experiments tend to have greater internal validity but lower external validity. They are logically tighter and better controlled, but less generalizable. Field experiments tend to have greater external validity but lower internal validity. They are more generalizable but less controlled. Quasi-experimental designs are more common. For example, in the experiment involving college roommates, the roommate situation was very realistic and lasted several months. It had more external validity than putting people in a laboratory setting and then asking them what they would do hypothetically.

PRACTICAL CONSIDERATIONS

Every research technique has "tricks of the trade" that are pragmatic strategies learned from experience. They account for the difference between the successful studies of an experienced researcher and the difficulties a novice researcher faces. Three are discussed here.

8.6   EXAMPLE BOX
A Field Experiment on College Roommates

Contact hypothesis states that intimate, long-term contact with an out-group reduces prejudice. Shook and Fazio (2008) wanted "to assess the nature of interracial relationship and test the effect of intergroup contact" (p. 719). However, when we measure prejudice with self-report attitude measures, people often control prejudice reactions so they do not appear prejudicial even though they may harbor prejudicial attitudes. An indirect technique for measuring hidden or "automatic" racial prejudice measures the response time in seconds as a person sees visual images of people of different races matched with various adjectives (see Fazio et al., 1995). Speed of response indirectly measures racial prejudice because we respond more slowly as we try to hide true attitudes. To create a long-term field experiment, the authors took advantage of random assignment to college dormitory rooms and room shortage that prevented roommates from switching. The study had 136 White and 126 African American college freshmen. By random assignment, some had a same-race roommate, and others had a different race roommate. Roommate race was the independent variable. The authors had the students attend one session during the first two weeks and another during the last two weeks of the academic term. They asked students about several issues, including roommate satisfaction, activities with roommates, and social networks. The students also completed a questionnaire on racial attitudes and intergroup anxiety. In addition, the authors created a series of tasks asking students to respond to various images on a computer screen. After several such computer tasks to create a "cover story," a final task was to respond to images of faces matched with adjectives; one-half of the faces were African American and one-half White. This was the indirect measure of racial prejudice. Thus, the authors had multiple pretest and posttest measures of racial attitudes and interracial social interactions. As in past roommate studies, their results showed less social interaction and lower roommate satisfaction among the different race roommate pairs than same-race pairs. Over the academic term, satisfaction with same-race roommates declined slightly but for the different race roommates increased slightly. For roommates of a different race, intergroup anxiety declined and roommate social interactions increased over the three-month term. Both the direct and indirect measures of racial prejudice remained unchanged for same-race roommates. However, levels of prejudice declined significantly between the pretest and posttest for the students who had different race roommates, just as predicted by the contact hypothesis.

Planning and Pilot-Tests

All social research requires planning. During the planning phase, you anticipate alternative explanations or threats to internal validity, develop a well-organized system for recording data, and pilot-test any apparatus (e.g., computers, video cameras, tape recorders, etc.) used. After the pilot-tests, you interview participants to uncover aspects of the experiment that need refinement.

Instructions to Participants

Most experiments involve giving participants instructions that "set the stage." You must word instructions carefully and follow a prepared script so that all participants hear the exact same thing. This ensures reliability. The instructions are also important in creating a realistic cover story when deception is used.

Postexperiment Interviews

At the end of an experiment, you should interview participants, for three reasons. First, if you used deception, you must ethically *debrief* the research participants (i.e., explain the true purpose of the experiment and answer questions). Second, you can learn what participants thought and how their definitions of the situation affected their behavior. Finally, you can explain the importance of not revealing the true nature of the experiment to other potential participants.

EXPERIMENTAL RESULTS: MAKING COMPARISONS

Comparison is critical to all research. By carefully examining the results of experimental research, you can learn about possible threats to internal validity and treatment effects on the dependent variable. In each study discussed in this chapter, the researchers analyzed quantitative data to examine the effects of independent variables and consider potential internal validity concerns.

Figure 8.6 is an illustration of such comparisons based on the results of a series of five weight-loss experiments using the classical experimental design. In the example, the 30 research participants in the experimental group at Enrique's Slim Clinic lost an average of 50 pounds, whereas the 30 in the control group did not lose a single pound. Only one person dropped out during the experiment. Susan's Scientific Diet Plan had equally dramatic results, but 11 people in her experimental group dropped out. This suggests a problem with experimental mortality. People in the experimental group at Carl's Calorie Counters lost 11 pounds, compared to 2 pounds for the control group, but the control group and the experimental group began with an average of 31 pounds difference in weight. This suggests a problem with selection bias. Natalie's Nutrition Center had no experimental mortality or selection bias problems, but those in the experimental group lost no more weight than those in the control group. It appears that the treatment was not effective. Pauline's Pounds Off also avoided selection bias and experimental mortality problems. People in her experimental group lost 32 pounds, but so did those in the control group. This suggests that the maturation, history, or diffusion of treatment effects may have occurred. Thus, the treatment at Enrique's Slim Clinic appears to be the most effective one.

A WORD ON ETHICS

Ethical considerations are a significant issue in most experiments because experiments are often intrusive (i.e., interfere in ordinary activity). Experimental treatments may involve putting people in contrived social settings, asking them to engage in activities, or manipulating their feelings or behaviors. While doing this, you listen to what they say, observe their actions,

FIGURE 8.6   Comparisons of Results, Classical Experimental Design, and Weight-Loss Experiments

ENRIQUE'S SLIM CLINIC

	Pretest	Posttest
Experimental	190 (30)	140 (29)
Control group	189 (30)	189 (30)

NATALIE'S NUTRITION CENTER

	Pretest	Posttest
Experimental	190 (30)	188 (29)
Control group	192 (29)	189 (28)

SUSAN'S SCIENTIFIC DIET PLAN

	Pretest	Posttest
Experimental	190 (30)	141 (19)
Control group	189 (30)	189 (28)

PAULINE'S POUNDS OFF

	Pretest	Posttest
Experimental	190 (30)	158 (30)
Control group	191 (29)	159 (28)

CARL'S CALORIE COUNTERS

	Pretest	Posttest
Experimental	160 (30)	152 (29)
Control group	191 (29)	189 (29)

SYMBOLS FOR COMPARISON PURPOSES

	Pretest	Posttest
Experimental	A (A)	C (C)
Control group	B (B)	D (D)

COMPARISONS

	A–B	C–D	A–C	B–D	(A)–(C)	(B)–(D)
Enrique's	1	49	−50	0	−1	0
Susan's	1	48	−49	0	−11	0
Carl's	31	37	−8	−2	−1	0
Natalie's	2	1	−2	−3	−1	−1
Pauline's	1	1	−32	−32	0	−1

A–B   Do the two groups begin with the same weight? If not, selection bias may be possibly occurring.

C–D   Do the two groups end the same way? If not, the treatment may be ineffective, or there may be strong history, maturation, diffusion, or treatment effects.

A–C   Did the experimental group change? If not, treatment may be ineffective.

(A)–(C) and (B)–(D)   Did the number of participants in the experimental group or control group change? If a large drop occurs, experimental mortality may be a threat to internal validity.

INTERPRETATION

Enrique's: No internal validity threats evident, shows effects of treatment

Susan's: Experimental mortality threat likely problem

Carl's: Selection bias likely problem

Natalie's: No internal validity threat evident, shows no treatment effects

Pauline's: History, maturation, diffusion of treatment threats are a likely problem

Note: Numbers are average number of pounds. Numbers in parentheses ( ) are number of participants per group. Random assignment is made to the experimental or control group.

and record responses. Ethical requirements limit the amounts and types of allowable intrusion. You must never place research participants in physical danger. You should take precautions when you put them in embarrassing or anxiety-inducing situations. It is essential to continuously monitor and control experimental events to ensure safe and ethical study.[15]

Sometimes experiments use deception by temporarily misleading participants. Such dishonesty might be acceptable, but only if there is no other way to achieve a specific research goal. Even for a highly worthy goal, you may use limited deception only with restrictions. The amount and type of deception cannot exceed the minimum needed for the specific purpose. In addition, you must always debrief research participants as soon as possible, telling them that they had been temporarily deceived and explain the true situation to them.

CONCLUSION

In this chapter, you learned about experimental research. In most experimental designs, you will use random assignment to create two (or more) groups that you can treat as equivalent and hence compare. Experimental research provides precise and relatively unambiguous evidence for a causal relationship. It closely follows principles of a positivist approach to social science and produces quantitative results that we can analyze with statistics.

This chapter also examined how you can combine the parts of an experiment to produce different experimental designs. In addition to the classical experimental design, you learned about preexperimental and quasi-experimental designs and design notation.

You learned about threats to internal validity that are possible alternative explanations to the treatment. You also learned about external validity and how field experiments maximize naturalistic generalization in external validity.

The real strength of experimental research is its control and logical rigor in establishing evidence for causality. In general, experiments tend to be easier to replicate, less expensive, and less time consuming than the other techniques. Experimental research also has limitations. First, you cannot address some questions using experimental methods because control and experimental manipulation are impossible. Another limitation is that experiments usually test one or a few hypotheses at a time. This fragments knowledge and makes it necessary to synthesize results across many studies. External validity is a potential problem because many experiments rely on small nonrandom samples of college students.[16]

You learned how a careful examination and comparison of results can alert you to potential problems in research design. Finally, you saw some practical and ethical considerations in experiments.

In the next chapters, you will examine other research techniques. The logic of the nonexperimental methods differs from that of the experiment. Experimenters focus narrowly on a few hypotheses, target one or two independent variables operating on a single dependent variable, and usually examine small numbers of participants. By contrast, in other techniques we often test many hypotheses at once, measure many independent and dependent variables, and use a larger number of randomly sampled research participants.

Key Terms

classical experimental design
compensatory behavior
confederate
confounding variables
control group
cover story
debrief
deception
demand characteristics
design notation
diffusion of treatment

double-blind experiment
equivalent time-series design
experimental design
experimental group
experimental mortality
experimental realism
experimenter expectancy
external validity
factorial design
field experiment
Hawthorne effect
history effects
interaction effect
internal validity
interrupted time-series design
laboratory experiment
Latin square design
maturation effect
mundane realism
one-shot case-study design
placebo effect
posttest
preexperimental designs
pretest
quasi-experimental designs
random assignment
reactivity
selection bias
Solomon four-group design
static group comparison design
subjects
testing effect
treatment

Endnotes

1. Cook and Campbell (1979:9–36, 91–94) argued for a modification of a more rigid positivist approach to causality for experimental research. They suggested a "critical-realist" approach, which shares some features of the critical approach outlined in Chapter 4.

2. For discussions of the history of the experiment, see Danziger (1988), Gillespie (1988), Hornstein (1988), O'Donnell (1985), Scheibe (1988), and Webster and Sell (2007:6–9).

3. See Hornstein (1988:11).

4. See Willer and Walker (2007a, 2007b).

5. See Field and Hole (2003) for a review of different comparisons.

6. Cook and Campbell (1979:7–9) and Spector (1981:15–16) discuss control in experiment.

7. The notation for research design is discussed in Cook and Campbell (1979:95–96), Dooley (1984:132–137), and Spector (1981:27–28).

8. For additional discussions of threats to internal validity, see Cook and Campbell (1979:51–68), Kercher (1992), Spector (1981:24–27), Smith and Glass (1987), and Suls and Rosnow (1988).

9. This example is borrowed from Mitchell and Jolley (1988:97).

10. Experimenter expectancy is discussed in Aronson and Carlsmith (1968:66–70), Dooley (1984:151–153), and Mitchell and Jolley (1988:327–329).

11. For discussions of external validity, see Aronson and Carlsmith (1968:22–25), Cook and Campbell (1979:70–80), Lucas (2003), and Zelditch (2007).

12. For a discussion of external validity, see Lucas (2003), Mook (1983), Willer and Walker (2007b), and Vissersi et al. (2001).

13. The Hawthorne effect is described in Franke and Kaul (1978), Lang (1992), and Roethlisberger and Dickenson (1939). Also see the discussion in Cook and Campbell (1979:123–125) and Dooley (1984:155–156). Gillespie (1988, 1991) discussed the political context of the experiments and how it shaped them.

14. See Piliavin et al. (1969).

15. See Hegtvedt (2007) for a recent review of ethical issues in experiments.

16. See Graham (1992).

CHAPTER 9

Nonreactive Research and Secondary Analysis

NONREACTIVE MEASUREMENT

Both experiments and survey research are *reactive*; that is, the people you study are aware of that fact. In this chapter you learn about four *nonreactive research techniques*; that is, techniques in which the people you study are not aware that they are part of the study.

The first research technique, unobtrusive observation, is less a distinct technique than a loose collection of inventive nonreactive measures. Next, we look at content analysis. It builds on the fundamentals of quantitative research design and is a well-developed research technique. Existing statistics and secondary analysis, the last two techniques, refer to the collection of already existing information from government documents or previous surveys. With these studies, you examine the existing data in new ways to address new questions. Although when the data was initially collected it could have been reactive, you can address new questions without reactive effects.

Unobtrusive Observations

Nonreactive, unobtrusive observation begins when you notice something that indicates a variable of interest. With *unobtrusive measures* (i.e., measures that are not obtrusive or intrusive) you look for what people "naturally" or unintentionally leave behind publically as available evidence about their social behavior, thoughts, or actions. As an observant researcher, you infer from the evidence to behavior, thoughts, or actions, and do so nonreactively, that is, without disrupting or notifying the people being studied. Unnoticed observation can include closely watching and recording driving behavior or pedestrian behavior taking place in public, or observing details such as the number of signs on a street in different languages. For example, in a major U.S. city, you decide to map out the Chinese, Korean, and Latino commercial sections of the city based on number of store signs with those three languages per block in a 25-square-block area. Instead of business signs, you could use business names from phone directories as data (see Example Box 9.1).

Researchers have been creative in inventing indirect ways to measure social behavior using unobtrusive observation. The many possible unobtrusive measures have little in common except being nonreactive, so you can best learn them through examples. Some are *erosion measures* where you notice selective wear as a measure, and some are *accretion measures* where the measures are deposits of something left behind.[1]

Researchers have examined family portraits in different historical eras to see how gender relations within the family are reflected in seating patterns. Urban anthropologists have examined the contents of garbage dumps to learn about lifestyles from what is thrown away (e.g., liquor bottles indicate level of alcohol consumption). Based on garbage, people underreport their liquor consumption by 40–60 percent (Rathje and Murphy, 1992:71). Raento, Oulasvirta, and Eagle (2009) suggest that data from smartphones can provide data about everyday social behavior, such as location, usage for entertainment, communication or information seeking, and timing.

Researchers have studied the listening habits of drivers by checking what stations their radios are tuned to when cars are repaired. They have measured interest in different exhibits by noting worn tiles on the floor in different parts of a museum. They have studied differences in graffiti in male versus female high school restrooms to show gender differences in themes. Some have examined high school yearbooks to compare the high school activities of those who had psychological problems in later life versus those who did not (see Expansion Box 9.1).

To use data from unobtrusive observation, you follow the logic of quantitative

9.1   EXAMPLE BOX
Using Unobtrusive Data to Document the Decline of Dixie

Scholars have examined the decline of distinctive U.S. regions over the past half-century and the homogenization of culture (including food, customs, religion, accents). Several focused on the South, and its collective identity with a Confederate, regional separateness. Cooper and Knotts (2010) replicated a 1976 study on the decline of a Southern regional identification. The 1976 study examined business names in the telephone books of 100 U.S. cities to create two scores. The study calculated a "S score" as the percent of the word *Southern* in a business name compared to businesses with *American* in the name. If equal numbers of businesses in a town had *Southern* and *American* in the name (e.g., Southern Dental Associates, American Medical Clinic), it had a score of 1.0. The study calculated a "D score" as the number of businesses with the word *Dixie* in a business name compared to *American* (e.g., Dixie Gift and

Flower Shop, Real American Fried Chicken). Cooper and Knotts gathered data from an online "white pages" telephone directory of businesses. They calculated D and S scores for the same 100 cities as the 1976 study. They compared maps of D and S scores for 1976, and for similar studies in 1990 and 1999. They also examined other variables, percentage of Blacks in the city and population density. Overall, they found a great geographic continuity across time. However, they noticed a decline in the word *Dixie*, especially in cities with larger Black populations and urban areas. The data were unobtrusive. Researchers used already public and available information creatively to measure symbolic expression or identity of region for the business owners or customers. The data were nonreactive. The owners of the businesses were unaware that the store name was part of a research study.

measurement. First, conceptualize a construct. Next, link the construct to nonreactive empirical evidence, which is its measure. The operational definition of the variable includes observations that you systematically note and record. Because your measures indicate a construct indirectly, you need to rule out reasons for them other than the construct of interest. For example, to measure customer walking traffic in a store you measure dirt and wear on floor tiles. To use this as an unobtrusive measure, you must first clarify the meaning of customer traffic (e.g., Is the floor a path to another department? Does it indicate a good location for a visual display?). Next, you systematically measure dirt or wear on the tiles, compare it to that in other locations, and record results on a regular basis (e.g., every month). Finally, you rule out other reasons for the observations (e.g., the floor tile is of lower quality and

wears faster, or the location is near an outside entrance with a lot of dirt).

CONTENT ANALYSIS

What Is Content Analysis?

Content analysis is a research technique for gathering and analyzing the content of text. The *content* refers to words, pictures, symbols, ideas, themes, sounds, colors, or anything that communicates meaning or a message to people. The *text* is any written, visual, or audio medium of human communication. Text includes books, newspaper and magazine articles, advertisements, speeches, official documents, films and videotapes, commercials, webpages, cell phone text messages, musical lyrics, photographs, articles of clothing, and works of art.

Physical Traces

Erosion: Wear suggests greater use.
Example: A researcher examines children's toys at a day care that were purchased at the same time. Worn-out toys suggest greater interest by the children.

Accretion: Accumulation of physical evidence suggests behavior.
Example: A researcher examines the brands of aluminum beverage cans in trash or recycling bins in male and female dormitories. This indicates the brands and types of beverages favored by each sex.

Archives

Running Records: Regularly produced public records may reveal much.
Example: A researcher examines marriage records for the bride and groom's ages. Regional differences suggest that the preference for males marrying younger females is greater in certain areas of the country.

Other Records: Irregular or private records can reveal a lot.
Example: A researcher finds the number of reams of paper purchased by a college dean's office for

10 years when student enrollment was stable. A sizable increase suggests that bureaucratic paperwork has increased.

Observation

External Appearance: How people appear may indicate social factors.
Example: A researcher watches students to see whether they are more likely to wear their school's colors and symbols after the school team won or lost.

Count Behaviors: Counting how many people do something can be informative.
Example: A researcher counts the number of men and women who come to a full stop and those who come to a rolling stop at a stop sign. This suggests gender difference in driving behavior.

Time Duration: How long people take to do things may indicate their attention.
Example: A researcher measures how long men and women pause in front of the painting of a nude man and in front of a painting of a nude woman. Time may indicate embarrassment or interest in same or cross-sex nudity by each sex.

In content analysis, you use objective and systematic counting and recording procedures to produce a quantitative record of the text's content.[2] There are also qualitative or interpretive versions of content analysis, but in this chapter the emphasis is on quantitative data about a text's content.

Data in content analysis are nonreactive because an author or creator places the content of words, messages, or symbols in a text for the conscious or nonconscious purpose of communicating to a reader or receiver. This is done without an awareness that someone might come along later to study and analyze

content for research purposes. For example, I, as author of this book, wrote words and drew diagrams to communicate research methods content to you, the student. I wrote the book and the way you read it are without any knowledge or intention of its ever being content analyzed.

Through content analysis you can uncover or reveal both the explicit and hidden content (i.e., messages, meanings, etc.) in a communication medium. The technique lets you probe into and discover content in a different way from the ordinary way of reading a book or watching a television program.

Content analysis allows you to compare many texts and analyze the content with charts, statistics, and tables. It helps you to reveal difficult-to-see aspects of a text. For example, you might watch television commercials and feel that nonwhites rarely appear in commercials for expensive consumer goods (e.g., luxury cars, furs, jewelry, perfume, etc.). Through content analysis you can document—in objective, quantitative terms—whether your vague feelings based on unsystematic observation are true. The method of content analysis yields repeatable, precise data about the content within a text.

You use the basic processes of a quantitative research study in content analysis: random sampling, precise measurement, and operational definitions for abstract constructs. You convert aspects of content that represent abstract variables into numbers through a coding process. Once you have gathered the content analysis data, you analyze them with the same kinds of statistical analysis that an experimenter or survey researcher uses to analyze their quantitative data.

Topics Appropriate for Content Analysis

Researchers have examined many issues using content analysis: themes in popular songs and religious symbols in hymns, trends in the topics that newspapers cover and the ideological tone of newspaper editorials, and sex-role stereotypes in textbooks or feature films. Content analysis studies looked at the frequency that people of different races appeared on television, answers to open-ended survey questions, enemy propaganda during wartime, and symbolic expressions on the covers of popular magazines. For example, Kubrin (2005) looked at 403 rap songs popular in 1992 to 2002 and documented the presence and changes in themes of inner-city Black youth culture.

Generalizations you can make from content analysis are limited to the cultural communication itself. With content analysis, you cannot determine the truthfulness of an assertion or evaluate the aesthetic qualities of literature. The technique allows you to document and reveal patterns of content in text but it cannot tell you the content's significance. You need to look directly at the substance of the content and apply theory to interpret its meaning and relevance (see the "bad apple" theory in Example Box 9.2).

Content analysis is useful for three types of research questions. First, it is helpful for questions involving a large volume of text. With sampling and multiple coders, you can measure the content in large amounts of text (e.g., twenty years of newspaper articles in five cities). Second, it is helpful when you must study a topic "at a distance." For example, you can use content analysis to study 50-year-old historical documents, the writings of someone who has died, or broadcasts in a hostile foreign country. Finally, content analysis can reveal "hidden" or tacit messages in a text that are difficult to see with casual observation. Even the creator of the text or those who read it may not be aware of all its themes, biases, or characteristics. For example, authors of preschool picture books may not consciously intend to portray children in traditional stereotyped sex roles, but content analysis studies revealed a high degree of sex stereotyping.[3]

Measurement and Coding

Careful measurement is crucial in content analysis because you are converting diffuse and murky symbolic communication into precise, objective, quantitative data. To accomplish this, you must carefully design and document coding procedures to make replication possible. A *coding system* is a set of instructions or rules on how to systematically observe and record content from text. You tailor it to the specific type of communication medium being studied (e.g., television drama, novels, photos in magazine advertisements, etc.).

9.2

EXAMPLE BOX
Bad Apples and Media Coverage of Corporate Scandals

Bendiktsson (2010) used content analysis to examine how the mass media presents corporate scandals to the public by looking at a wave of five accounting scandals that rocked the U.S. in 2002. According to the "bad apple theory," journalists help the public understand broader issues but with a bias. They focus on particular acts of specific individuals rather than reveal the patterned behavior of large organizations, thereby deflecting criticism away from systematic corruption by powerful, wealthy corporations. Instead of revealing serious illegal behavior by large organizations, the media emphasizes the behavior of a few isolated individuals or "bad apples." In addition, Bendiktsson looked at media outlets in which news reports appeared, their ownership, editorial policy, and location. His data were articles that came from the 51 largest circulation newspapers during the period, January 1, 1999, to January 1, 2006. Using three databases, he identified 1,938 news articles on the accounting scandal (each article has over 100 words and excluded editorials). He found that while ownership (local versus large chain) had little impact on reporting, newspapers reported local companies more often than distant ones. A newspaper's political position, indicated by it endorsing a political candidate or political party on its editorial pages, significantly influenced how it reported corporate corruption. Newspapers that favored conservative candidates or the Republican Party were less likely to portray corporation corruption as systematic and serious, and more likely to emphasize the rare "bad apple" executive. Thus, the "bad apple" emphasis is less a widespread media bias than a bias found in media that favor a conservative, pro-business political position.

Units of Analysis. The unit of analysis can vary a great deal in content analysis. It can be a word, a phrase, a theme, a plot, a newspaper article, a character, and so forth. In addition to units of analysis, you can use other units in content analysis that may or may not be the same as units of analysis: recording units, context units, and enumeration units. There are few differences among them, and they are easily confused, but each has a distinct role. In simple projects, all three are the same.

What Do You Measure? In content analysis you use **structured observation**—systematic, careful observation based on written rules. The rules explain how to categorize and classify observations. As with other measurement, categories should be mutually exclusive and exhaustive. Written rules make replication possible and improve reliability. Although you may start with preliminary coding rules, you can conduct a pilot study and refine coding based on it. Coding systems identify four characteristics of text content: frequency, direction, intensity, and space.

Frequency. *Frequency* simply means counting whether or not something occurs and, if it occurs, how often. For example, how many elderly people appear on a television program within a given week? What percentage of all characters are they, or in what percentage of programs do they appear?

Direction. *Direction* is noting the direction of messages in the content along some continuum (e.g., positive or negative, supporting or opposed). For example, you devise a list of ways an elderly television character can act. Some are positive (e.g., friendly, wise, considerate) and some are negative (e.g., nasty, dull, selfish).

Intensity. *Intensity* is the strength or power of a message in a direction. For example, the characteristic of forgetfulness can be minor (e.g., not remembering to take your keys when leaving home, taking time to recall the name of someone you have not seen in years) or major (e.g., not remembering your name, not recognizing your children).

Space. You can record the size of a text message or the amount of space or volume allocated to it. *Space* in written text is measured by counting words, sentences, paragraphs, or space on a page (e.g., square inches). For video or audio text, you can measure space by the amount of time allocated. For example, a TV character may be present for a few seconds or continuously in every scene of a two-hour program.

Coding, Validity, and Reliability

Manifest Coding. To use **manifest coding** you carefully count the easy to identify, visible, surface content in a text. For example, you count the number of times a phrase or word (e.g., *red*) appears in written text, or whether a specific action (e.g., a kiss) appears in a photograph or video scene. The coding system lists terms or actions that are then located in the text. You can use a computer program to search for words or phrases in text and have a computer do the counting work. To do this, you learn about the computer program, develop a comprehensive list of relevant words or phrases, and put the text into a form that computers can read.[4]

Manifest coding is highly reliable because the phrase or word either is or is not present. Unfortunately, manifest coding does not take the connotations of words or phrases into account. The same word can take on different meanings depending on the context. The possibility that there are multiple meanings of a word limits the measurement validity of manifest coding.

For example, I read a book with a *red* cover that is a real *red* herring. Unfortunately, its publisher drowned in *red* ink because the editor could not deal with the *red* tape that occurs when a book is *red* hot. The book has a story about a *red* fire truck that stops at *red* lights only after the leaves turn *red*. There is also a group of *Reds* who carry *red* flags to the little *red* schoolhouse. They are opposed by *red*-blooded *red*necks who eat *red* meat and honor the *red*, white, and blue. The main character is a *red*-nosed matador who fights *red* foxes, not bulls, with his *red* cape. *Red*-lipped little *Red* Riding Hood is also in the book. She develops *red* eyes and becomes *red*-faced after eating a lot of *red* peppers in the *red*-light district. She is given a *red* mark on her backside by her angry mother, a *red*head.

Latent Coding. You use **latent coding** (also called *semantic analysis*) to look for the underlying, implicit meaning buried in the content of a text. For example, you read an entire paragraph and decide whether it contains erotic themes or a romantic mood. Your coding system has general rules to guide the interpretation of the text and for determining whether particular themes or moods are present.

Latent coding tends to be less reliable than manifest coding. It depends on a coder's knowledge of language and social meaning.[5] Training, practice, and written rules improve reliability, but still it is difficult to consistently identify themes, moods, and the like. Yet, the validity of latent coding can exceed that of manifest coding because people communicate meaning in many implicit ways that depend on context, not just in specific words. Often you can identify systematic cultural themes in text with latent coding (see Example Box 9.3).

If manifest and latent coding agree, the final result is strengthened; if they disagree, you may want to reexamine the operational and theoretical definitions.

9.3 EXAMPLE BOX
Content Analysis of Moral Messages about Eating Disorders and Obesity

Anorexia and overweight/obesity are medical categories related to body weight and eating but have different cultural and moral connotations. The culture presents being excessively heavy as connected to personal sloth and stupidity whereas being slender embodies moral virtue. To see how the mass media presents the two issues and shapes public understanding of them, Saguy and Gruys (2010) examined *New York Times* and *Newsweek* magazine articles published from 1995 to 2005. They looked at all news articles and opinion pieces that had the words "anorexia, anorexic, bulimia, bulimic" or "obese, obesity, overweight" in the heading or lead paragraph. They found 1,496 articles. Saguy and Gruys narrowed this number with three criteria. First, they eliminated the first two of every three articles in the *New York Times* list of articles on obesity/overweight because there were so many. Second, they eliminated articles under 300 words. Finally, they removed off-topic articles. This yielded a final sample of 174 articles on obesity and 64 on eating disorders from the *New York Times* and 88 articles on obesity and six on eating disorders from *Newsweek*. Saguy and Gruys describe how they coded articles: "Coding was done at the article level for over 200 variables for all of the articles in our sample. In initial 'practice' coding, three researchers coded the same articles and discussed differences as a way of arriving at shared agreement. Two coders coded 10 percent of the articles to test for intercoder reliability, which was

very high. The coefficient of reliability (the ratio of coding agreements to the total number of coding decisions) was over .95" (p. 237). They found that anorexia articles largely mentioned genetic factors and social constraints, directing attention away from individual blame. The articles generally described eating disorders as a disease or psychological problem. They rarely described individuals as responsible for curing the disorders. Instead, medical interventions were mentioned. In contrast, articles on overweight/obesity emphasized individual choices and bad decisions. They stressed the need for behavioral modification rather than medical interventions. In the media reports, anorexics were presented as victims of a terrible illness that was beyond their and their parents' control, while obesity was due to bad personal behaviors or parental neglect. "In contrast to reporting on eating disorders, even when articles mention more than one cause for overweight, individual blame usually predominates. . . . Moreover, while heaping the blame on individuals, news reports also draw upon and reproduce stereotypes of fat people as gluttonous, slothful, and ignorant, and of parents of fat children as neglectful and irresponsible." (p. 244). Thus, the media sources shaped public beliefs about the two eating problems very differently. In addition, the one problem was associated with white, middle-class young women as victims, whereas the other pointed to low-income minority people who individually made bad choices.

Intercoder Reliability. Content analysis often involves coding information from a very large number of units. One study might involve observing the content in dozens of books, hundreds of hours of television programming, or thousands of newspaper articles. In addition to coding the information personally, you may hire assistants to help with the coding. You teach coders the coding system and train them to fill out a recording sheet. Coders should understand

the variables, follow the coding system, and ask about ambiguities. You should record all decisions you make about how to treat a new specific coding situation after coding begins so that you will be consistent.

If you use several coders you must *always* check for consistency across coders. To do this, you ask coders to code the same text independently and then check for consistency across coders. You measure *intercoder reliability* with a statistical coefficient that tells the degree of consistency among coders. You *always* report the coefficient with the results of content analysis research. There are several intercoder reliability measures that range from 0 to 1, with 1.0 signifying perfect agreement among coders. An interreliability coefficient of .80 or better is generally required, although .70 may be acceptable for exploratory research. When the coding process stretches over a considerable time period (e.g., more than three months), you should also check reliability by having each coder independently code samples of text that were previously coded. You then check to see whether the coding is stable or changing. For example, you have six hours of television episodes coded in April and coded again in July without the coders looking at their original coding decisions. Large deviations in coding necessitate retraining and coding the text a second time.

Content Analysis with Visual Material.   Using content analysis to study visual "text," such as photographs, paintings, statues, buildings, clothing, and videos and film, is difficult. The "text" communicates messages or emotional content indirectly through images, symbols, and metaphors. Moreover, visual images often contain mixed messages at multiple levels of meaning.

To conduct content analysis on visual text, you must "read" the meaning(s) within visual text. This means interpreting signs and meanings attached to symbolic images. Such "reading" is not mechanical (i.e., image X always means G); it depends heavily on the cultural context because the meaning of an image is culture bound. For example, a red light does not inevitably mean "stop"; it means "stop" only in cultures where officials assign it that meaning. People construct cultural meanings that they attach to symbolic images, and the meanings can change over time. Some meanings are clearer and more firmly attached to symbols and images than others.

Most people share a common meaning for central symbols of the dominant culture, but some people may read a symbol differently. For example, one group of people may "read" a national flag to mean patriotism, duty to nation, and honor of tradition. For others, the same flag evokes fear, and they read it to indicate government oppression, abuse of power, and military aggression. When you conduct a content analysis of images, you need to be aware of divergent readings of symbols for people across different social situations or with divergent beliefs and experiences (see Example Box 9.4).

Social–political groups may invent or construct new symbols with attached meanings (e.g., a pink triangle came to mean gay pride). They may wrestle for control of the meaning of major existing symbols. For example, some people want to assign a Christian religious meaning to the Christmas tree; others want it to represent a celebration of tradition and family values without specific religious content; others see its origins as an anti-Christian pagan symbol; and still others want it to mean a festive holiday season for commercial reasons. Because the symbolic content of images is complex and multilayered, you usually must combine qualitative judgments about the images with quantitative data in content analysis.

How to Conduct Content Analysis Research

Question Formulation.   As in most social research, you begin with a research question. When the question involves variables that are messages or symbols present in text, content analysis may be appropriate. For example, I want to study how television news covered the issue of climate change/global warming. My construct "coverage" includes the amount of coverage, the prominence of the coverage, and whether the coverage favors one position over another. I could survey people about what they think of the news coverage, but a better strategy

9.4

Content Analysis of Visual Materials

Chavez (2001) conducted a content analysis of the covers of major U.S. magazines that dealt with the issue of immigration in the United States. Looking at the covers of 10 magazines from the mid-1970s to the mid-1990s, he classified the covers as displaying one of three major messages: affirmative, alarmist, or neutral and balanced. Beyond his classification and identifying trends in messages, he noted how the mix of people (i.e., race, gender, age, and dress) in the photographs and the recurrent use of major symbols, such as the Statute of Liberty or the U.S. flag, communicated messages. Chavez argued that magazine covers are a site, or location, where cultural meaning is created. Visual images on magazine covers have multiple levels of

meaning. Viewers construct specific meanings as they read the image and interpret it using their cultural knowledge. Collectively, the covers convey a worldview and express messages about a nation and its people. For example, a magazine cover that displayed the icon of the Statute of Liberty as strong and full of compassion (message: welcome immigrants) can be altered to have strong Asian facial features (message: Asian immigrants distorted the national culture and altered the nation's racial makeup), or holding a large stop sign (message: go away immigrants). Chavez observed that "images on magazines both refer to, and in the process, help to structure and construct contemporary 'American' identity" (p. 44).

---

is to examine the news programs directly using content analysis.

Units of Analysis.   You decide on the units of analysis (i.e., the amount of text that is assigned a code). For example, for a television news show, each story each day of the show is the unit of analysis.

Sampling.   You may use random sampling in content analysis. First, define the population and the sampling element. For example, the population might be all words, all sentences, all paragraphs, or all articles in certain types of documents over a specified period. Likewise, it could include each conversation, situation, scene, or episode of certain types of television programs over a specified time period. For example, I want to know how the news shows portrayed the climate change issue. My unit of analysis is a story on an evening news program. My population includes all "stories" in an evening news show between 1992 and 2012. I first identify what networks to consider (four national networks) and what constitutes

a news story (evening news, nationally shown) and define precisely what I mean by a "story." For instance, do special in-depth investigations count as stories? Is a visual image without commentary a story? Is there a minimum size (one minute) for a story? Second, I examine the four network news shows and find that the average evening news show has an average of eight stories, and shows run five days a week, 52 weeks per year. With a 20-year timeframe, my population contains over 166,400 stories (eight stories on four television network shows five nights a week for 52 weeks a year across 20 years = 166,400). My sampling frame is a list of all the stories. Next, I decide on the sample size and design. After looking at my budget and time, I decide to limit the sample size to 1,664 stories. Thus, the sampling ratio is 1 percent. I must choose a sampling design. I avoid systematic sampling because shows appear cyclically according to the calendar. Because each network is important and I want to cover all 20 years, I use stratified sampling. I stratify by network (four) and year (20), sampling 1,664/80 = 204 stories from each network for each year. I decide to sample by month of the year; this means I randomly select 17 stories (204/12 = 17) from each network for each month for each of 20 years.

Finally, I draw the random sample using a random-number table to select 17 numbers for the sample stories for each network, month, and year. I develop a sampling frame worksheet to keep track of my sampling procedure. It numbers each story and has the date and network. If the story is not about climate change, I indicate that; if it is about climate change, I need to code the data on a coding sheet (discussed in the next section).

Variables and Constructing Coding Categories. In my example, I am interested in the construct of climate change and global warming. I must define "climate change" in operational terms and express it as written rules for stories. For example, does a story that reports on the 1997 Kyoto Protocol (international treaty) count, does a politician denying the scientific evidence on climate change count, or does a story on melting icebergs count?

Because I am interested in any news on climate change, my measure indicates whether the story was a threat/warning or a statement that there is no problem due to it. I can do this with either latent or manifest coding. With manifest coding, I create a list of adjectives and phrases. If an event in a sampled story is referred to with one of the adjectives, then the direction is decided. For example, the terms *minor, benign, hoax,* or *controllable* are positive, whereas *dangerous, disaster, disruptive,* or *scientific consensus* are negative. For latent coding, I create rules to guide judgments. For example, I classify stories about business opposition to put controls on emissions from coal-fueled electrical power plants or rising sea levels as negative. By contrast, I classify the development and purchases of no-emission automobiles or a story on consumers seeing the carbon "footprint" or emissions created by each airplane flight they take as positive.

In addition to written rules for coding decisions, you create a ***recording sheet*** or *coding worksheet* on which to record information (see Table 9.1). Each unit should have a separate recording sheet. The sheets do not have to be pieces of paper; they can be file cards, or lines in a computer record or file. When you record a lot of information for each recording unit, you can use more than one sheet of paper. When planning a project, you should calculate the work required. For example, during my pilot-test, I find that it takes an average of 15 minutes to view, evaluate and code a three- to four-minute news story. This does not include sampling or locating stories. At this rate it will take nearly 420 hours. That is 10 weeks of nonstop work at 42 hours each week; I should consider hiring assistants as coders. See Table 9.1 for a coding worksheet on which is coded any climate change story of the 1,664 sampled stories.

Each coding worksheet has a place to record the identification number of the unit and spaces for information about each variable. I also put identifying information about the research project on the sheet in case I misplace it or it looks similar to other sheets I have. Finally, if I use multiple coders, the sheet indicates the coder to permit checking reliability and, if necessary, makes it possible to recode information for inaccurate coders. After completing all recording sheets and checking for accuracy, I can begin data analysis.

Inferences

The inferences you can or cannot legitimately derive from data is a critical issue in content analysis. Often, you would like to say that what you observed in the content of the text affects people's actions or behaviors. You can rarely do this. Content analysis only describes what is in the text. It cannot reveal the intentions of those who created the text or the effects of messages in the text on receivers. For example, content analysis shows that children's books contain sex stereotypes. That does not necessarily mean

TABLE 9.1   Coding Sheet for Study of News Stories on Climate Change

Blank Example

Professor Neuman, Sociology Department, Climate Change News Story Project Coder:_____
Story #_____ Network:_____ Date:_____ Length of time:_____

Aspect of climate change discussed

___ Rising world temperature ___ Ice caps or icebergs melting ____ Polar bears or wildlife dying ___ Flooding ___ Deserts growing ___ Food crops/forests dying ___ Ocean levels rising ___ Severe storms ___ Water shortages ___ Greenhouse gases ___ Carbon footprint ____ Emissions from industrial sources

Authority cited

___ Scientific organization ___ Individual scientist ___ Government agency ___ International agency ___ Nonscientist ___ Business or corporation ___ Business/trade association ____ Unknown source

Visual shown with story (check any/all)

___ Charts/graphs ___ Ice caps or icebergs melting ____ Polar bears or wildlife ___ Flooding ___ Deserts ___ Scientists ___ Politicians ___ Severe storms ___ Armed conflict

Direction

___ Climate change is real ____ Climate change is not true ___ Mixed/confusing evidence

Seriousness

___ Urgent immediate issue ____ Distant future or moderate issue ___ Minor concern or not a concern

Example of Completed Recording Sheet for One Story

Professor Neuman, Sociology Department, Climate Change News Story Project Coder: <u>Susan J.</u>
Story # <u> 223 </u> Network: <u> FOX </u> Date: <u>2/22/2001</u> Length of time: <u> 2.3 minutes </u>

Aspects of climate change discussed

___ Rising world temperature ___ Ice caps or icebergs melting ____ Polar bears or wildlife dying ___ Flooding ___ Deserts growing ___ Food crops/forests dying _X_ Ocean levels rising ___ Severe storms ___ Water shortages ___ Greenhouse gases ___ Carbon footprint ____ Emissions from industrial sources

Authority cited

___ Scientific organization ___ Individual scientist ___ Government agency ___ International agency _X_ Nonscientist ___ Business or corporation ___ Business/trade association ____ Unknown source

Visual shown with story (check any/all)

____Charts/graphs ___ Ice caps or icebergs melting ____ Polar bears or wildlife _X_ Flooding ___ Deserts ___ Scientists _X_ Politicians ___ Severe storms ___ Armed conflict

Direction

___ Climate change is real ____ Climate change is not true __X_ Mixed/confusing evidence

Seriousness

___ Urgent immediate issue __X_ Distant future or moderate issue ___ Minor concern or not a concern that the textbook authors are sexist. Nor does it mean the stereotypes within the text are shaping children's beliefs or behaviors. Such an inference requires a separate research project on how children's perceptions develop from what they read in books.

EXISTING STATISTICS/DOCUMENTS AND SECONDARY ANALYSIS

Appropriate Topics

Many government agencies, nonprofit organizations, hospitals, libraries, and companies collect mountains of information about the social world and make them available for research. Sometimes it is numerical information in the form of statistical documents (books, reports, etc.). Other information is in the form of published compilations available in a library or on computerized records. In either case, you can search through collections with a research question and variables in mind, and then reassemble the information in new ways to address the research question.

It is difficult to specify topics that are appropriate for existing statistics research because they are so wide-ranging and varied. Any topic on which information has been collected and is publicly available can be studied. In fact, existing statistics projects do not fit neatly into a deductive, linear model common in quantitative research because someone has already gathered the data. You need to locate and creatively think of how to reorganize the existing information into the variables for a research question.

In experiments, you control a situation and manipulate an independent variable. In a survey research study, you ask questions and learn about reported attitudes or behavior. In content analysis, you look into the content of messages in cultural communication. Existing statistics research differs, and involves information that large bureaucratic organizations routinely collect. They gather information for policy decisions or as a public service. They may not collect it for purposes directly related to a specific social research question. Thus, existing statistics research is appropriate when you test hypotheses using variables about social, economic, and political conditions, and for which information is already being routinely collected. These include descriptions of organizations (number of office locations, total spending in a year, number of employees, students, or patients) or the people in them (age or gender distribution, length of time employed, schooling completed). Often, organizations have collected such information over long time periods. For example, you might want to learn whether unemployment and crime rates are in association with one another in 150 cities over a 20-year time period. Such data can be found in existing statistical records from government labor agencies and law enforcement reports. It is also possible to combine data from Internet, census, and news sources around a specific research question (see Example Box 9.5).

Social Indicators

During the 1960s, some social scientists, dissatisfied with the information available to decision makers, spawned the "social indicators' movement" to develop indicators of social well-being. They wanted to combine information about social well-being with widely used indicators of economic performance (e.g., gross national product) to inform government and other policymaking officials. They hoped that systemic measures about the quality of social life could better inform public policy decisions.[6]

Today, there are books, articles, and reports on social indicators, and even a scholarly journal, *Social Indicators Research,* devoted to the creation and evaluation of social indicators. The U.S. Census Bureau produces a report, *Social Indicators,* and the United Nations has many measures of social well-being in different nations.

9.5   EXAMPLE BOX
Using Nonreactive, Existing Data to Study WalMart Expansion

WalMart is the world's biggest retailer and largest firm measured by employment, with 1.4 million employees in 7,800 stores. Its biggest enemies are not its business rivals, but antisprawl activists who resist new stores in their hometowns. Ingram, Yue, and Rao (2010) tested a theory that WalMart uses a low-cost "test for protest" approach. Protests are signals to WalMart of the high costs of obtaining regulatory approval and less positive shopper reception. When protests signal high costs, WalMart is likely to withdraw and try elsewhere. They noted that before placing a new store (often costing $10 million), WalMart files a planning document based on, for example, anticipated noise and traffic congestion (costing about $5,000) and pays local governments a fee ($2,000–10,000). Ingram et al. constructed a dataset from nonreactive, existing data sources. They located all proposed WalMart store openings from 1998 to 2005 and use the "place" as a unit of analysis. The U.S. Census identified 25,375 places in the United States in 2000 (town, village, unincorporated census area). Data on store openings came from WalMart's corporate website. Ingram et al. also gathered data from the website of Sprawl Busters and similar activist organizations. They searched media sources (LexisNexis and e America's News) for all mentions of store proposals and protests. In addition, they had census information and store information for each location. They found 1,599 new store proposals in 1,207 places; of them, 563 had protests and 1,040 resulted in store openings. Protests were successful 64 percent of the time. They found the WalMart strategy is to keep protests local and minimize the diffusion of the serious limiting regulations. When WalMart enters a community after a protest, it makes larger donations to community causes, what the author's call "goodwill-buying" actions. Ingram and colleagues' general conclusion is that community protests are shaping the geographic locations and behavior of the world's largest company.

A *social indicator* is any measure of social well-being used in policy. There are many specific indicators that are operationalizations of well-being. Social indicators include measures of the following areas: population, family structure, abuse and injury, housing, Social Security and welfare, health and nutrition, public safety, education and training, work, income, culture and leisure, social mobility, and public participation.

In the United States, the FBI's Uniform Crime Index is a social indicator. It indicates the amount of crime in U.S. society. Social indicators can measure negative aspects of social life, such as the infant mortality rate (the death rate of infants during the first year of life) or alcoholism, or they can indicate positive aspects, such as job satisfaction or the percentage of housing units with indoor plumbing. Social indicators often involve implicit value judgments (e.g.,

which crimes are serious or what constitutes a good quality of life; see Table 9.2).

Locating Data

Locating Existing Statistics. Government or international agencies and private sources collect the information that become existing statistics data. Because an enormous volume and variety of information exists, if you plan to conduct existing statistics research, it is wise to discuss your interests with an information professional—in this case, a reference librarian, who can point you in the direction of possible sources. The U.S. Census is a major source of data, but not the only one (see Expansion Box 9.2).

Many existing documents are "free"—that is, publicly available at libraries—but the time and effort it takes to search for specific information can be substantial. You can expect to spend

TABLE 9.2   Social Health Index of the United States

SIXTEEN SOCIAL INDICATORS USED TO CREATE SOCIAL HEALTH INDEX

Infant mortality	Health insurance coverage
Child poverty	Aging: poverty among the elderly
Child abuse	Suicide among the elderly
Teenage suicide	Homicide
Teenage drug abuse	Alcohol-related traffic fatalities
High school completion	Food stamp coverage
Unemployment	Affordable housing
Average wages	Income inequality

Social Health of States in 2008

RANK	SOCIAL HEALTH SCORE	RANK	SOCIAL HEALTH SCORE
1. Minnesota	75.0	26. Missouri	51.4
2. Iowa	71.1	27. Michigan	48.9
3. New Hampshire	67.2	28. Oregon	47.8
4. Nebraska	67.0	29. Rhode Island	46.8
5. Hawaii	63.1	30. Colorado	44.6
6. Vermont	62.7	31. New York	43.9
7. Connecticut	61.2	32. Georgia	43.7
8. North Dakota	61.1	33. Alaska	43.6
9. Utah	60.6	34. Nevada	42.6
10. New Jersey	59.9	35. California	41.7
11. Idaho	59.7	36. West Virginia	40.8
12. Virginia	59.7	37. Oklahoma	40.1
13. Pennsylvania	58.6	38. Montana	39.4
14. Maine	57.4	39. Alabama	38.8
15. Indiana	55.9	40. South Carolina	38.0
16. Kansas	55.9	41. Texas	37.8
17. Delaware	55.7	42. Louisiana	37.5
18. Illinois	55.2	43. Arkansas	36.4
19. Wisconsin	55.2	44. Kentucky	36.2
20. Maryland	54.9	45. Tennessee	35.5
21. South Dakota	54.4	46. Florida	34.3
22. Ohio	53.8	47. North Carolina	33.4
23. Wyoming	53.4	48. Arizona	32.8
24. Massachusetts	53.1	49. Mississippi	31.0
25. Washington	52.2	50. New Mexico	26.8

Source: From http://iisp.vassar.edu/socialhealth08.html. Institute for Innovation in Social Policy. Vassar College. Reprinted by permission.

EXPANSION BOX
The U.S. Census

Almost every country conducts a census, or a regular count of its population. For example, Australia has done so since 1881, Canada since 1871, and the United States since 1790. Most nations conduct a census every 5 or 10 years. In addition to the number of people, census officials collect information on topics such as housing conditions, ethnicity, religious affiliation, education, and so forth.

The census is a major source of high-quality existing statistical data, but it can be controversial. In Canada, an attempt to count the number of same-sex couples living together evoked public debate about whether the government should document the changes in society. In Great Britain, the Muslim minority welcomed questions about religion in the 2001 census because they felt that they had been officially ignored. In the United States, the measurement of race and ethnicity was hotly debated, so in the 2000 census, people could place themselves in multiple racial-ethnic categories.

The U.S. 2000 census also generated a serious public controversy because it missed thousands of people, most from low-income areas with concentrations of recent immigrants and racial minorities. Some double counting of people in high-income areas where many owned second homes also occurred. A contentious debate arose among politicians to end miscounts by using scientific sampling and adjusting the census. The politicians proved to be less concerned about improving the scientific accuracy of the census than retaining traditional census methods that would benefit their own political fortunes or help their constituencies because the government uses census data to draw voting districts and allocate public funds to areas.

many hours in libraries or on the Internet. After you locate the information, you must record it on computer files, cards, graphs, or recording sheets for later analysis. Some information is already available in a computer-file format. For example, instead of recording voting data from

books, a researcher could use a social science data archive at the University of Michigan (to be discussed).

There are so many sources that only a small sample of what is available is discussed here. The single-most valuable source of statistical information about the United States is the *Statistical Abstract of the United States* which has been published annually (with a few exceptions) since 1878. The *Statistical Abstract* is available in all public libraries and on the Internet. It is a selected compilation of the many official reports and statistical tables produced by U.S. government agencies. It contains statistical information from hundreds of more detailed government reports. You may want to examine more specific government documents. (The detail of what is available in government documents is mind-boggling. For example, you can learn that there were two African American females over the age of 75 in Tucumcari City, New Mexico, in 1980.)

The *Statistical Abstract* has over 1,400 charts, tables, and statistical lists from over 200 government and private agencies. It is hard to grasp all that it contains until you skim through the tables. The electronic version is also available as a two-volume set and summarizes similar information across many years; it is called *Historical Statistics of the U.S.: Colonial Times to 1970.*

Most governments publish similar statistical yearbooks. Australia's Bureau of Statistics produces *Yearbook Australia,* Statistics Canada produces *Canada Yearbook,* New Zealand's Department of Statistics publishes *New Zealand Official Yearbook,* and in the United Kingdom, the Central Statistics Office publishes *Annual Abstract of Statistics.*[7] Many nations publish books with historical statistics, as well.

Locating government statistical documents is an art in itself. Some publications exist solely to assist research. For example, the *American Statistics Index: A Comprehensive Guide* and *Index to the Statistical Publications of the U.S. Government and Statistics Sources: A Subject*

Guide to Data on Industrial, Business, Social Education, Financial and Other Topics for the U.S. and Internationally are two helpful guides for the United States.[8] The United Nations and international agencies such as the World Bank have their own publications with statistical information for various countries (e.g., literacy rates, percentage of the labor force working in agriculture, birth rates)—for example, the *Demographic Yearbook, UNESCO Statistical Yearbook,* and *United Nations Statistical Yearbook.*

In addition to government statistical documents, there are dozens of other publications. Many are produced for business purposes and can be obtained only for a high cost. They include information on consumer spending, the location of high-income neighborhoods, trends in the economy, and the like.[9]

Over a dozen publications list characteristics of businesses or their executives. You can find these in larger libraries. Three such publications are as follows:

> *Dun and Bradstreet Principal Industrial Businesses* is a guide to approximately 51,000 businesses in 135 countries with information on sales, number of employees, officers, and products.
>
> *Who Owns Whom* comes in volumes for nations or regions (e.g., North America, the United Kingdom, Ireland, and Australia). It lists parent companies, subsidiaries, and associated companies.
>
> *Standard and Poor's Register of Corporations, Directors and Executives* lists about 37,000 U.S. and Canadian companies. It has information on corporations, products, officers, industries, and sales figures.

Many biographical sources list famous people and provide background information on them. These are useful when you want to learn about the social background, career, or other characteristics of famous individuals. The publications are compiled by companies that send out questionnaires to people identified as "important" by some criteria. They are public sources of information, but they depend on the cooperation and accuracy of individuals who are selected.

Politics has its own specialized publications. There are two basic types. One has biographical information on contemporary politicians. The other type has information on voting, laws enacted, and the like. Here are three examples of political information publications for the United States:

> *Almanac of American Politics* is a biannual publication that includes photographs and a short biography of U.S. government officials. Committee appointments, voting records, and similar information are provided for members of Congress and leaders in the executive branch.
>
> *America Votes: A Handbook of Contemporary American Election Statistics* contains detailed voting information by county for most statewide and national offices. Primary election results are included down to the county level.
>
> *Vital Statistics on American Politics* provides dozens of tables on political behavior, such as the campaign spending of every candidate for Congress, their primary and final votes, ideological ratings by various political organizations, and a summary of voter registration regulations by state.

Secondary Survey Data.   Secondary analysis is a special case of existing statistics. In it you reanalyze previously collected survey or similar data that another researcher has gathered. It differs from most research (e.g., experiments, surveys, and content analysis), in which you devote a great deal of effort to collecting data, and only then turn to statistical analysis. Secondary analysis is relatively inexpensive; it permits comparisons across groups, nations, or time; it facilitates replication; and it permits asking about issues not thought of by the original researchers. It is also possible to combine existing statistics with data from an already conducted survey, or secondary data (see Example Box 9.6).

Large-scale data collection is expensive and difficult. The cost and time required for a major national survey that uses rigorous techniques might take a dozen people working for two years and cost nearly a million dollars. Fortunately, there are archives of past surveys that are open to researchers.

The Inter-University Consortium for Political and Social Research (ICPSR) at the University of Michigan is the world's major archive of social science data. Over 17,000 survey research and related sets of information are stored and made available to researchers at modest costs. Other centers hold survey data in the United States and other nations.[10]

There are many large-scale national surveys that are conducted on a regular basis, such as the National Election Survey (NES). Data from these surveys can be secondarily analyzed or

combined with other data to address new questions (see Example Box 9.7).

Perhaps the most widely used source of survey data for the United States is the *General Social Survey (GSS)*. The National Opinion Research Center at the University of Chicago has designed, organized, and conducted the survey about every other year since 1972. In recent years, it has covered other nations as well. GSS data are made publicly available for secondary analysis at a low cost (see Expansion Box 9.3).

Limitations

Despite the growth and popularity of secondary data analysis and existing statistics research, there are limitations in their use. Such techniques are not trouble-free just because a government agency or major research organization gathered the data. A serious danger is that the secondary data or existing statistics are inappropriate for your research question. Before proceeding, you

---

EXAMPLE BOX

9.6   **Combining Existing and Survey Data to Study Racially Imbalanced Incarceration**

Percival (2010) combined existing and secondary survey data to examine whether a community's political–ideological climate changes the racial-ethnic mix of who ends up going to prison. He specifically looked at whether racial-ethnic minority people in highly politically conservative communities were more likely to be incarcerated than those from less-conservative communities. Past studies linked ideological conservatism and rates of incarceration— conservative states generally have higher incarceration rates than liberal states even when crime rates are the same. Also past studies found that conservatives tended to blame street crime and other social ills on a racial (Black) underclass and appealed to antiminority beliefs among conservative Whites by enacting punitive crime policies. Percival gathered existing data on 56 of California's 58 counties (county is the unit of analysis) from three sources: (1) the Census Bureau on racial-ethnic composition;

(2) the California Department of Corrections and Rehabilitation's Data Analysis Unit (DAU) on crime, "county of commitment" and race-ethnicity of prisoners; and (3) previously collected survey data by county from the California Field Poll (1990–1999) that included a measure of ideology. He considered both the overall crime rate in each county and criminal involvement of each racial-ethnic group. From the statistical analysis, Percival found that "minority imprisonment rates are highly responsive to the local environment shaped by the politics of ideology and racial and ethnic diversity. Counties that are more ideologically conservative and those with greater diversity are more apt to incarcerate both Blacks and Hispanics" (p. 1079). In short, a minority person arrested in a highly politically conservative diverse area is more likely to be sent to jail than one who is arrested for the same crime in a less conservative area or one that is homogenous.

9.7 EXAMPLE BOX
Secondary Data Analysis on Being Rich and Happy

A very consistent research finding is the positive association between income and happiness. However, something called the Easterlin paradox adds complexity. Although the rich are happier than middle-income or poor people at any point in time, as an entire society gets richer and all incomes rise, happiness does not increase. This suggests that income level alone does not cause happiness; rather, it is income relative to other people that boosts happiness. Rich people enjoy higher consumption from higher incomes, but they also enjoy having more status by being richer than others. With rising societal income, everyone's absolute consumption rises, but the relative status effect on happiness continues. Status is relative to others. The others could be neighbors, extended family members, peers, or all strangers in larger society. Firebaugh and Schroeder (2009) hypothesized that living in a high-income neighborhood increases happiness because of neighborhood amenities; however, they asked whether status compared to nearby rich neighbors might reduce happiness if you are not as rich as they are. The authors conducted a secondary analysis with survey data collected in the National Election Study (NES). They matched individual respondent survey data with census data about the block in which the person lived and data on the county in which the block was located. They had income information at three levels: household, neighborhood, and county. Their sample had 1,266 individuals in 849 neighborhoods (census block groups) in 433 counties across the United States. The survey question on happiness was, "In general, how satisfying do you find the way you're spending your life these days? Would you call it completely satisfying, pretty satisfying, or not very satisfying?" The authors found that people living in higher income neighborhoods are happier, even if they have richer neighbors. However, the level of happiness is not as high if the entire neighborhood is located in a high-income county. Firebaugh and Schroeder conclude (p. 825), "Americans tend to be happiest when they live in a high-income neighborhood in a low-income region." The positive amenities of a high-income neighborhood and status from being part of a rich community promote happiness. The happiness effect is greatest if the community has a higher income relative to those of nearby communities because of the extra boost to happiness that comes from the status of being part of a high-income community relative to other communities.

need to consider units in the data (e.g., types of people, organizations), the time and place of data collection, the sampling methods used, and the specific issues or topics covered in the data. For example, a researcher wanting to examine racial-ethnic tensions between Latinos and Anglos in the United States uses secondary data that includes only the Pacific Northwest and New England states should reconsider the question or use other data.

A second danger is when you lack sufficient understanding of the substantive topic. Because the data are easily accessible, anyone who knows very little about a topic could make erroneous assumptions or false interpretations about results from it. Before using any data, you need to become well informed about the topic. For example, you use data on high school graduation rates in Germany without understanding the German secondary education system with its distinct academic and vocational tracks. This can cause you to make serious errors in interpreting results.

A third danger is to quote statistics in great detail to give an impression of scientific rigor. This can lead to the ***fallacy of misplaced concreteness***. It occurs when someone gives a false impression of precision by quoting statistics in greater detail than warranted and "overloading" the details. For example, existing statistics report that the population of Australia is 19,169,083, but it is better to say that it is a little over 19 million. One might calculate the percentage of

9.3 EXPANSION BOX
The General Social Survey

The General Social Survey (GSS) is the best-known set of survey data used by social researchers for secondary analysis. The mission of the GSS is "to make timely, high quality, scientifically relevant data available to the social science research community" (Davis and Smith, 1992:1). It is available in many computer-readable formats and is widely accessible for a low cost. Neither datasets nor codebooks are copyrighted. Users may copy or disseminate them without obtaining permission. You can find results using the GSS in over 2,000 research articles and books.

The National Opinion Research Center (NORC) has conducted the GSS almost every year since 1972. A typical year's survey contains a random sample of about 1,500 adult U.S. residents. A team of researchers selects some questions for inclusion, and individual researchers can recommend questions. They repeat some questions and topics each year, include some on a four- to six-year cycle, and add other topics in specific years. For example, in 1998, the special topic was job experiences and religion,

and in 2000, it was intergroup relations and multiculturalism.

Interviewers collect the data through face-to-face interviews. The NORC staff carefully selects interviewers and trains them in social science methodology and survey interviewing. About 120 to 140 interviewers work on the GSS each year. About 90 percent are women, and most are middle aged. The NORC recruits bilingual and minority interviewers. Interviewers with respondents are race-matched with respondents. Interviews are typically 90 minutes long and contain approximately 500 questions. The response rate has been 71 to 79 percent. The major reason for nonresponse is a refusal to participate.

The International Social Survey Program conducts similar surveys in other nations. Beginning with the German ALLBUS and British Social Attitudes Survey, participation has grown to include 33 nations. The goal is to conduct on a regular basis large-scale national general surveys in which some common questions are asked across cooperating nations.

divorced people as 15.65495 in a secondary data analysis of the 2000 General Social Survey, but it is better to report that about 15.7 percent of people are divorced.[11]

Units of Analysis and Variable Attributes. A common problem in existing statistics is finding the appropriate units of analysis. Many organizations publish statistics for aggregates, not the individual. For example, a table in a government document has information (e.g., unemployment rate, crime rate, etc.) for a state, but the unit of analysis for your research question is the individual (e.g., "Are unemployed people more likely to commit property crimes?"). The potential for committing the ecological fallacy is very real in this situation. It is less of a problem for secondary survey analysis because you

can obtain raw information on each respondent from archives.

A related problem involves the categories of variable attributes used in existing documents or survey questions. This is not a problem if the initial researcher gathered data in many highly refined categories. The problem arises when the original data were collected in broad categories or ones that do not match your needs. For example, you are interested in people of Asian heritage. If the racial-ethnic heritage categories in a document are "White," "Black," and "Other," you have a problem. The "Other" category includes people of Asian and other heritages. Sometimes information was collected in refined categories but is published only in broad categories. It takes special effort to discover whether more refined information was collected or is publicly available.

Validity.   Validity problems occur when your theoretical definition does not match that of the government agency or organization that collected the information. Official policies and procedures specify definitions for official statistics. For example, you define a *work injury* as including minor cuts, bruises, and sprains that occur while on the job, but the official definition in government reports only includes injuries that require a visit to a physician or hospital. Many work injuries, as you defined them, would not be in official statistics. Another example occurs when you define a person as *unemployed* if he or she wants work and would work if a job were available, must work part time now but is looking for full-time work, or has tried for a long time without success and has now given up looking for work. The official government definition, however, includes only those who are now actively seeking work (full or part time) as unemployed. The official statistics exclude those who stopped looking, who work part time out of necessity, who do not look because they believe no work is available, or who will not relocate hundreds of miles away for work. In both cases, your definition differs from that in official statistics.

Another validity problem arises when you use official statistics as a surrogate or proxy for a construct that really interests you. You do this out of necessity because you cannot collect original data on the issue. For example, you want to know how many people have been robbed, so you use police statistics on robbery arrests as a proxy. But the measure is not entirely valid. Many robberies are not reported to the police, and many reported robberies do not result in an arrest.

A third validity problem arises because you do not control how data are collected. Real people somewhere are responsible for collecting all information, even that in official government reports. You depend on them for collecting, organizing, reporting, and publishing data accurately. Systematic errors in data collection (e.g., census people who avoid poor neighborhoods and make up information, or people who put a false age on a driver's license); errors in organizing and reporting information (e.g., a police department that is sloppy about filing crime reports and loses data); and errors in publishing information (e.g., a typographical error in a table) can all reduce measurement validity.

Here is an example of such a problem in U.S. statistics on the number of people permanently laid off from their jobs. A university researcher reexamined the methods used to gather data by the government agency and found an error. Data on permanent job losses were from a survey of 50,000 people, but the government agency failed to adjust for a high survey nonresponse rate. The government report shows a 7 percent decline in the number of people laid off between 1993 and 1996, but once the data were corrected for survey nonresponses, there was actually no change.[12]

Reliability.   Problems with reliability can plague existing statistics research. Reliability problems develop when official definitions or the method of collecting information changes over time. Official definitions of work injury, disability, unemployment, and the like change periodically. Even if you learn of such changes, consistent measurement over time is impossible. For example, during the early 1980s, the government changed its ways of calculating the U.S. unemployment rate. Previously, the unemployment rate was calculated as the number of unemployed persons divided by the number in the civilian workforce. The new method divided the number of unemployed by the civilian workforce plus the number of people in the military. Likewise, when police departments computerize their records, there is an apparent increase in crimes reported, not because crime increases but due to improved record keeping.

Reliability can be a serious problem in official government statistics. This goes beyond recognized problems, such as the police stopping poorly dressed people more than well-dressed people, hence poorly dressed, lower-income people appear more often in arrest statistics. For example, the U.S. Bureau of Labor Statistics found a 0.6 percent increase in the female unemployment rate after it used gender-neutral measurement procedures. Until the mid-1990s, interviewers asked women only whether they had been "keeping house or something else." The women who answered "keeping house" were categorized as housewives, and not unemployed. This occurred even if the women had been seeking work. Once the survey asked women the same question as men, "Were you working or something else?", more women said they were not working but doing "something else," such as looking for work. This shows the importance of methodological details in how government statistics get created.

You can use official statistics for international comparisons but national governments collect data differently and the quality of data collection varies. For example, in 1994, the official unemployment rate reported for the United States was 7 percent, Japan's was 2.9 percent, and France's was 12 percent. If the nations defined and gathered data the same way, including discouraged workers and involuntary part-time worker rates, the rates would have been 9.3 percent for the United States, 9.6 percent for Japan, and 13.7 percent for France. To evaluate the quality of official government statistics, *The Economist* magazine asked a team of 20 leading statisticians to evaluate the statistics of 13 nations based on freedom from political interference, reliability, statistical methodology, and coverage of topics. The top five nations in order were Canada, Australia, Holland, France, and Sweden. The United States was tied for sixth with Britain and Germany. The United States spent more per person gathering its statistics than all nations except Australia and it released data the fastest. The quality of U.S. statistics suffered from being highly decentralized, having fewer statisticians employed than any nation, and politically motivated cutbacks on the range of data collected.[13]

Missing Data. A frequent problem that plagues existing statistics research is that of missing data. Sometimes, the data were collected but have been lost. More frequently, the data were never collected. The decision to collect official information is made within government agencies.

The decision to ask questions on a survey whose data are later made publicly available is made by a group of researchers. In both cases, those who decide what to collect may not collect what another researcher needs in order to address a research question. Government agencies start or stop collecting information for political, budgetary, or other reasons. For example, after many years of public complaints about racial profiling by police, the state law enforcement agency changed its computers, equipped all police cars with computers, and changed police procedures so that police recorded the race of the persons stopped. A few years later, a new political party came into office. The newly elected politicians were ideologically hostile to the concept of racial profiling so they ended the procedure of having police record the data. If you had wanted to study whether racial profiling was occurring in the state, you could no longer do so.

ISSUES OF INFERENCE AND THEORY TESTING

Inferences from Nonreactive Data

Your ability to infer causality or test a theory on the basis of nonreactive data is limited. It is difficult to use unobtrusive measures to establish temporal order and eliminate alternative explanations. In content analysis, you cannot generalize from the content to its effects on those who read the text, but can only use the correlation logic of survey research to show an association among variables. Unlike the case of survey research, you cannot ask respondents direct questions to measure variables, but must rely on the information available in the text.

Ethical Concerns

Ethical concerns are not at the forefront of most nonreactive research because the people being studied are not directly involved. The primary ethical concern is the privacy and confidentiality of using information gathered by someone else.

Another ethical issue is that official statistics are social and political products. Implicit theories and value assumptions guide which information is collected and the categories used when gathering it. As in the example about racial profiling mentioned above, government officials decide the data to be collected on a regular basis. Decisions about what data to collect can be influenced by political or ideological conflicts. By collecting certain data or defining one measure as official, such decisions can shape public policy outcomes differently than if alternative, but equally significant data or valid measures had been used.

Decisions about the data officially gathered affects public policy. For example, the collection of information on many social conditions (e.g., the number of patients who died while in public mental hospitals) was stimulated by political activity during the Great Depression of the 1930s. Previously, the conditions were not defined as sufficiently important to warrant public attention. Likewise, information on the percentage of nonwhite students enrolled in U.S. schools at various ages is available only since 1953, and for specific nonwhite races only since the 1970s. Earlier, such information was not salient for public policy.

The collection of official statistics stimulates new attention to a problem, and public concern about a problem stimulates the collection of new official statistics. For example, drunk driving became a bigger issue once law enforcement agencies began to record data of whether alcohol was a factor in an accident as well as the number of automobile accidents. By collecting or failing to collect certain data, government agencies can highlight or hide social conditions from public view.

Social–political values can shape decisions about which existing statistics to collect. Most official statistics are designed for top-down bureaucratic or administrative planning purposes. They may not conform to a research question, especially if the question comes from people who might question the values or direction chosen by bureaucratic decision makers. For example, a government agency measures

the number of tons of steel produced, miles of highway paved, and average number of people in a household. This information is useful for corporations that fabricate steel products, make tires for paved roads, or plan to sell food or consumer products. Officials may decide not to gather information on other conditions such as drinking-water quality, time needed to commute to work, stress related to a job, or number of children needing child care. In many countries, the gross national product (GNP) is treated as a critical measure of societal progress. But GNP ignores noneconomic aspects of social life (e.g., time spent playing with one's children) and types of work (e.g., housework) that are not paid. The information available reflects the outcome of political debate and the values of officials who decide which statistics to collect.[14]

CONCLUSION

In this chapter, you have learned about several types of nonreactive research techniques. They are ways to measure or observe aspects of social life without affecting those who are being studied. They result in objective, numerical data that you can analyze statistically to address research questions. You can use the techniques in conjunction with other types of quantitative or qualitative social research to address a large number of questions. As with any form of quantitative data, you need to be concerned with measurement issues. It is easy to take available information from a past survey or government document, but what it measures may not be the construct of interest to you.

Two potential problems in nonreactive research are limits on research questions that can be addressed and data validity. The availability of existing information restricts the questions you can address. If no organizations have collected the data of interest, you cannot address certain questions. Also, nonreactive variables often have weaker validity because they do not measure the construct of real interest to you. Although existing statistics and secondary data analysis are low-cost research techniques, your lack of control over and substantial knowledge of the data collection process may introduce a potential source of errors about which you need to be especially vigilant.

In the next chapter, we move from designing research projects and collecting data to analyzing data. The analysis techniques apply to the quantitative data you learned about in the previous chapters. So far, you have seen how to move from a topic, to a research design and measures, to collecting data. Next, you learn how to look at data and see what it can tell you about a hypothesis or research question.

Key Terms

accretion measures
coding
coding system
content analysis
erosion measures
fallacy of misplaced concreteness
General Social Survey (GSS)
latent coding
manifest coding
nonreactive
recording sheet
Statistical Abstract of the United States
structured observation
text
unobtrusive measures

Endnotes

1. See Webb, Campbell, Schwartz, Sechrest, and Grove (1981:7–11).
2. For definitions of content analysis, see Holsti (1968:597), Krippendorff (1980:21–24), Markoff, Shapiro, and Weitman (1974:5–6), Stone and Weber (1992), and Weber (1983, 1984, 1985:81, note 1).
3. Weitzman, Eifler, Hokada, and Ross (1972) is a classic in this type of research.
4. Stone and Weber (1992) and Weber (1984, 1985) summarized computerized content analysis techniques.

5. See Andren (1981:58–66) for a discussion of reliability. Coding categorization in content analysis is discussed in Holsti (1969:94–126).
6. A discussion of social indicators can be found in Carley (1981). Also see Bauer (1966), Duncan (1984:233–235), Juster and Land (1981), Land (1992), and Rossi and Gilmartin (1980).
7. Many non-English yearbooks are also produced; for example, *Statistiches Jahrbuch* for the Federal Republic of Germany, *Annuaire Statistique de la France* for France, *Year Book Australia* for Australia, and Denmark's *Statiskisk Ti Arsoversigt*. Japan produces an English version of its yearbook called the *Statistical Handbook of Japan*.
8. Guides exist for the publications of various governments—for example, the *Guide to British Government Publications, Australian Official Publications,* and *Irish Official Publications.* Similar publications exist for most nations.
9. See Churchill (1983:140–167) and Stewart (1984) for lists of business information sources.
10. Other major U.S. archives of survey data include the National Opinion Research Center, University of Chicago; the Survey Research Center, University of California–Berkeley; the Behavioral Sciences Laboratory, University of Cincinnati; Data and Program Library Service, University of Wisconsin–Madison; the Roper Center, University of Connecticut–Storrs; and the Institute for Research in Social Science, University of North Carolina–Chapel Hill. Also see Kiecolt and Nathan (1985) and Parcel (1992).
11. For a discussion of these issues, see Dale et al. (1988:27–31), Maier (1991), and Parcel (1992). Horn (1993:138) gives a good discussion with examples of the fallacy of misplaced concreteness.
12. See Stevenson (1996).
13. See *The Economist,* "The Good Statistics Guide" (September 11, 1993), "The Overlooked Housekeeper" (February 5, 1994), and "Fewer Damned Lies?" (March 30, 1996).
14. See Block and Burns (1986), Carr-Hill (1984), Hindess (1973), Horn (1993), Maier (1991), and Van den Berg and Van der Veer (1985).

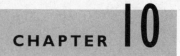

Analysis of Quantitative Data

If you read a research report or article based on quantitative data, you will see charts, graphs, and tables full of numbers. Do not be intimidated by them. The charts, graphs, and tables are there to give you, the reader, a condensed picture of the data. The charts and tables give you a view of the evidence that was collected. When you collect quantitative data, you will want to use similar techniques to help you see what is inside the data. By organizing and manipulating the data, they can reveal interesting details that are not easy to see otherwise. In this chapter, you learn the fundamentals of organizing and analyzing quantitative data. The analysis of quantitative data, or statistics, is a large, complex field of knowledge. This chapter covers only the most basic statistical concepts and data-handling techniques necessary to understand social research.

Data you collect using the techniques in the past chapters are in the form of numbers. The numbers represent values of variables and measure characteristics of subjects, respondents, or other cases. Initially, the numbers are in a raw form, on questionnaires, note pads, recording sheets, or paper. You need to organize them into a form that is suitable for computers and then create charts, tables, statistical tests, or graphs that will summarize their features in a way that allows you to interpret or give theoretical meaning to the data.

DEALING WITH DATA

Coding the Data

Before you examine quantitative data you collected in a study to test hypotheses and answer your research question, you must first organize them in a different form. You encountered the idea of coding data in the last chapter. Here, data *coding* means systematically reorganizing raw numerical data into a form usable by computer software. You must do this by applying consistent rules for how to transfer information from one form to another.

If you collected data in certain ways, such as a well-organized coding sheet, coding can be a simple clerical task. However, when the data are not well organized or not originally in the form of numbers, it gets complex. You must develop rules for assigning numbers to variable attributes. Each category of a variable and missing information needs a code. For example, you want to examine gender, so assign or code the males as 1 and the females as 2.

All of your rules and procedures for coding are put into a document called a *codebook*. In addition to describing the coding rules and procedure, it has information on the location of data for variables in a format usable by computer software. It is essential to create a well-organized, detailed codebook and make multiple copies of it. If you fail to write down the details of the coding procedure or misplace the codebook, you have lost the key to the data and may have to recode the data again, requiring many hours or even days of additional work.

You should think about a coding procedure and codebook before you collect any data. For example, you plan to conduct a survey. You should precode the questionnaire before collecting data. *Precoding* means placing the code categories (e.g., 1 for male, 2 for female) on the questionnaire.[1] Some survey researchers also place the location in the computer format on the questionnaire. If you do not precode a questionnaire, your first step after collecting data is to create a codebook. You need to give each respondent an identification number to keep track of them. Information on each respondent is a data record. Next, you transfer the information from each respondent questionnaire into a data record format that computer software can read.

Entering Data

Most computer programs for statistical analysis need the data in a grid format. In the grid, each row represents a data record (i.e., a respondent or case). A column or a set of columns represents specific variables. You should be able to go from a column and row location (e.g., row 8, column 5) back to the original data source (e.g., a questionnaire item on marital status for respondent 8). For example, you code survey data for three respondents in a computer-friendly format like that presented in Figure 10.1. Humans cannot easily read it, and without the codebook, it is worthless. It condenses answers to 50 survey questions for three respondents into three lines or rows. The raw data for many research projects look like this, except that there may be over 1,000 rows, and the lines may be over 100 columns long. For example, a 15-minute telephone survey of 250 students produces a grid of data that is 250 rows by 240 columns.

The codebook in Figure 10.1 tells that the first two numbers are identification numbers. Thus, the example data are for the first (01), second (02), and third (03) respondents. Notice the use of zeroes as place holders to reduce confusion between 1 and 01. The 1s are always in column 2; the 10s are in column 1. The codebook says that column 5 contains the variable "sex": Cases 1 and 2 are male and Case 3 is female. Column 4 tells us that Carlos interviewed Cases 1 and 2, and Sophia Case 3.

There are four ways for you to get raw quantitative data into a computer program:

1. **Code sheet.** Gather the information, then transfer it from the original source onto a grid format (code sheet). Next, type what is on the code sheet into a computer, line by line.
2. **Direct-entry method,** including *CATI.* As information is being collected, sit at a computer keyboard while listening to/observing the information and enter the information, or have a respondent/subject enter the information him- or herself. The computer must be preprogrammed to accept the information.
3. *Optical scan.* Gather the information, then enter it onto optical scan sheets (or have a respondent/subject enter the information)

by filling in the correct "dots." Next, use an optical scanner or reader to transfer the information into a computer.
4. *Bar code.* Gather the information and convert it into different widths of bars that are associated with specific numerical values, then use a bar-code reader to transfer the information into a computer.

Cleaning Data

Accuracy is extremely important when coding data. Errors you make when coding or entering data into a computer threaten the validity of measures and cause misleading results. You might have a perfect sample, perfect measures, and no errors in gathering data, but if you make errors in the coding process or in entering data into a computer, it can make your entire study worthless.

After you very carefully code, you want to verify the accuracy of coding, or "clean" the data. You might code a 10–15 percent random sample of the data a second time. If no coding errors appear, you can proceed; if you find errors, you must recheck all coding before moving forward.

Once your data are in the computer, you have two ways to check your coding. ***Possible code cleaning*** (or *wild code checking*) involves checking the categories of all variables for impossible codes. For example, respondent sex is coded 1 = Male, 2 = Female. Finding a 4 for a case in the field for the sex variable indicates a coding error. A second method, ***contingency cleaning*** (or *consistency checking*), involves cross-classifying two variables and looking for logically impossible combinations. For example, you cross-classify education by occupation. If you find a respondent never having passed the eighth grade and recorded as being a medical doctor, or if you find an 80-year-old woman listing a 10-year-old child as being her direct biological offspring, you better go back to check for a coding error.

You can modify data after it is in the computer but only in certain ways. You cannot use

■

FIGURE 10.1   Coded Data for Three Cases and Codebook

Exerpt from Survey Questionnaire

Respondent ID _____   Interviewer Name _____

Note the Respondent's Sex: ___ Male ___ Female

1. The first question is about the president of the United States. Do you Strongly Agree, Agree, Disagree, Strongly Disagree, or Have No Opinion about the following statement: The President of the United States is doing a great job.

   ___ Strong Agree ___ Agree ___ Disagree ___ Strong Disagree ___ No Opinion

2. How old are you? _____

Excerpt of Coded Data

```
                              Column
0000000000IIIIIIIIII2222222222223333333333444 ... etc. (tens)
1234567890123456789012345678901234567890I2 ... etc. (ones)
01 212736302 182738274 10239 18.82 3947461 ... etc.
02 213334821 124988154 21242 18.21 3984123 ... etc.
03 420123982 113727263 12345 17.36 1487645 ... etc.
etc.
```
Raw data for first three cases, columns 1 through 42.

Excerpt from Codebook

Column	Variable Name	Description
1-2	ID	Respondent identification number
3	BLANK	
4	Interviewer	Interviewer who collected the data:
		1 = Susan
		2 = Xia
		3 = Juan
		4 = Sophia
		5 = Clarence
5	Sex	Interviewer report of respondent's sex
		1 = Male, 2 = Female
6	PresJob	The president of the United States is doing a great job.
		1 = Strongly Agree
		2 = Agree
		3 = No Opinion
		4 = Disagree
		5 = Strongly Disagree
		Blank = missing information

more refined categories than you had when you collected the original data. You can, however, combine or group information into broader or less-refined categories. For example, you may group ratio-level income data that has over 1,000 different numbers into five ordinal categories. Also, you can combine information from several indicators to create a new variable or index score.

RESULTS WITH ONE VARIABLE

Frequency Distributions

The word *statistics* has at least two meanings: a record of collected numbers (e.g., numbers telling how many people live in a city) and a branch of applied mathematics for manipulating, describing, and summarizing the features of numbers. In social research you use both types of statistics. Here, we focus on the second type— ways to manipulate, describe, and summarize the features of numbers that are data from a study. There are multiple types of statistics, as a kind of applied mathematics. A simple, basic division is between descriptive and inferential statistics. We first consider descriptive statistics.

Descriptive statistics describe numerical data and can be categorized by the number of variables involved: univariate, bivariate, or multivariate (for one, two, and three or more variables). *Univariate statistics* describe one variable (*uni-* refers to one; *-variate* refers to variable). The easiest way to describe the numerical data of one variable is with a *frequency distribution*. You can use them with nominal-, ordinal-, interval-, or ratio-level data (recall the levels of measurement from Chapter 5) and they take many forms.

Think of this example. You have survey data for 400 respondents. You can summarize the information on the gender distribution of the respondents at a glance with a raw count or a percentage frequency distribution (see Figure 10.2). You can also present the same information in graphic form, such as a histogram, **bar chart**, and **pie chart**. Bar charts or graphs are used for discrete variables. They can have a vertical or horizontal orientation with a small space between the bars. The terminology is not exact, but histograms are usually upright bar graphs for interval or ratio data.

For interval- or ratio-level data, you often want to group information into categories for easier presentation (or you can use measures of central tendency, discussed next). The grouped categories should be mutually exclusive. You can plot interval- or ratio-level data in a *frequency polygon*. In it, you place the number of cases or frequency along the vertical axis, and the values of the variable or scores along the horizontal axis. A polygon appears when the dots are connected.

Measures of Central Tendency

Often you want to simplify and condense information. You may to want condense many numerical values across hundreds or thousands of cases of a variable, especially if it is measured at the interval or ratio level (e.g., education level, age, income) into a single number. You can do this with the measures of central tendency, or measures of the center of the frequency distribution: mean, median, and mode. They are often called *averages* (a less precise and less clear way of saying the same thing). Each measure of central tendency goes with data at a specific level of measurement (see Expansion Box 10.1).

The **mode** is the easiest measure to use. You can use it with nominal, ordinal, interval, or ratio data. It is simply the most common or frequently occurring number. For example, the mode of the following list is 5: 6 5 7 10 9 5 3 5. A distribution can have more than one mode. For example, the mode of this list is both 5 and 7: 5 6 1 2 5 7 4 7. If the list gets long, it is easy to spot the mode in a frequency distribution—just look for the most frequent score. There will always be at least one case with a score that is equal to the mode, unless every case is different.

FIGURE 10.2   Examples of Univariate Statistics

RAW COUNT FREQUENCY DISTRIBUTION		PERCENTAGE FREQUENCY DISTRIBUTION	
Gender	Frequency	Gender	Percentage
Male	100	Male	25%
Female	300	Female	75%
Total	400	Total	100%

BAR CHART OF SAME INFORMATION

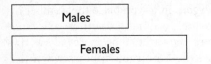

EXAMPLE OF GROUPED DATA FREQUENCY DISTRIBUTION

First Job Annual Income	N
Under $5,000	25
$5,000 to $9,999	50
$10,000 to $15,999	100
$16,000 to $19,999	150
$20,000 to $29,999	50
$30,000 and over	25
Total	400

EXAMPLE OF FREQUENCY POLYGON

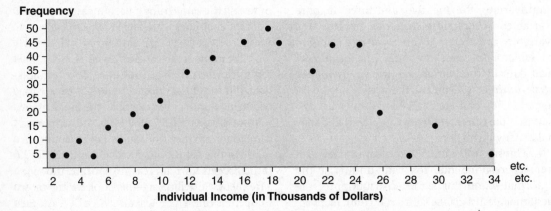

EXPANSION BOX

10.1

Measures of Central Tendency and Levels of Measurement

Level of Measurement	Measure of Central Tendency		
	Mode	Median	Mean
Nominal	Yes		
Ordinal	Yes	Yes	
Interval	Yes	Yes	Yes
Ratio	Yes	Yes	Yes

The **median** is more informative than the mode. It is the middle point and also the 50th percentile, or the point at which half the cases are above it and half below it. You can use it with ordinal-, interval-, or ratio-level data (but not nominal-level data). You can "eyeball" the mode, but computing a median requires a little more work. The easiest way is first to organize the scores from highest to lowest, then count to the middle. If there is an odd number of scores, it is simple. Seven people are waiting for a bus; their ages are: 12 17 20 27 30 55 80. The median age is 27. Note that the median does not change easily. If the 55-year-old and the 80-year-old both got on one bus, and the remaining people were joined by two 31-year-olds, the median remains unchanged. If there is an even number of scores, things are a bit more complicated. For example, six people at a bus stop have the following ages: 17 20 26 30 50 70. The median is somewhere between 26 and 30. Compute the median by adding the two middle scores together and dividing by 2, or 26 + 30 = 56/2 = 28. The median age is 28, even though no person is 28 years old. Note that there is no mode in the list of six ages because each person has a different age.

The **mean**, or arithmetic average, is the most widely used measure of central tendency. You *only* use it with interval- or ratio-level data.[2] Compute the mean by adding up all scores, then divide by the number of scores. For example, the mean age in the previous example is n is 17 + 20 + 26 + 30 + 31 + 31 = 213; 213/6 = 35.5. No one in the list is 35.5 years old, and the mean does not equal the median.

The mean is strongly affected by changes in extreme values (very large or very small). For example, the 50- and 70-year-old left and were replaced with two 31-year-olds. The distribution now looks like this: 17 20 26 30 31 31. The median is unchanged: 28. The mean is 17 + 20 + 26 + 30 + 31 + 31 = 155; 155/6 = 25.8. Thus, the mean dropped a great deal when a few extreme values were removed.

If the frequency distribution forms a "normal" or bell-shaped curve, the three measures of central tendency equal each other. If the distribution is a **skewed distribution** (i.e., more cases are in the upper or lower scores), then the three will not be equal. If most cases have lower scores with a few extreme high scores, the mean will be the highest, the median in the middle, and the mode the lowest. If most cases have higher scores with a few extreme low scores, the mean will be the lowest, the median in the middle, and the mode the highest. In general, the median is best for skewed distributions, although the mean is used in most other statistics (see Figure 10.3).

Measures of Variation

The measures of central tendency give you a one-number summary of a distribution of values for a collection of cases. While they are informative, they give only its *center*. Another characteristic of a distribution is its spread, dispersion, or variability around the center. Two distributions can have identical measures of central tendency but differ in their spread about the center. For example, seven people are at a bus stop in front of a bar. Their ages are 25 26 27 30 33 34 35. Both the median and the mean are 30. At a bus stop in front of an ice cream store, seven people have the identical median and mean, but their ages are 5 10 20 30 40 50 55. The ages of the group in front of the ice cream

FIGURE 10.3   Measures of Central Tendency

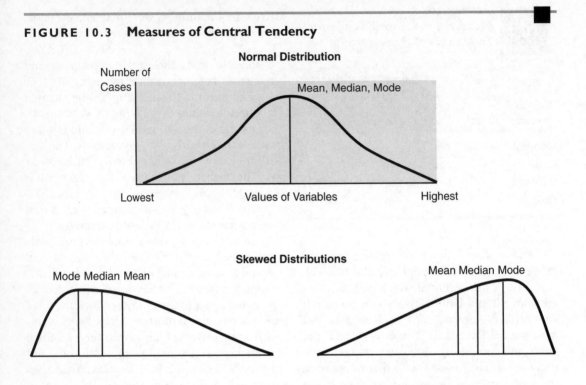

store are spread more from the center, or the distribution has more variability.

Variability has important social implications. For example, in city X, the median and mean family income is $35,600 per year, and it has zero variation. *Zero variation* means that every family has an income of exactly $35,600. City Y has the same median and mean family income, but 95 percent of its families have incomes of $12,000 per year and 5 percent have incomes of $300,000 per year. City X has perfect income equality, whereas there is great inequality in city Y. A researcher who does not know the variability of income in the two cities misses very important information.

You can measure variation in three ways: range, percentile, and standard deviation. *Range* is the simplest. It consists of the largest and smallest scores. For example, the range for the bus stop in front of the bar is from 25 to 35, or 35 − 25 = 10 years. If the 35-year-old got onto a bus and was replaced by a 60-year-old,

the range would change to 60 − 25 = 35 years. Range has limitations. For example, here are two groups of six with a range of 35 years: 30 30 30 30 30 65 and 20 45 46 48 50 55.

Percentiles tell you the score at a specific place within the distribution. One percentile you already learned is the median, the 50th percentile. Sometimes the 25th and 75th percentiles or the 10th and 90th percentiles are used to describe a distribution. For example, the 25th percentile is the score at which 25 percent of the distribution have either that score or a lower one. The computation of a percentile follows the same logic as the median. If I have 100 people and want to find the 25th percentile, I rank the scores and count up from the bottom until I reach number 25. If the total is not 100, I simply adjust the distribution to a percentage basis.

Standard deviation is the most comprehensive and widely used measure of dispersion, but difficult to compute by hand. The range and percentile are for ordinal-, interval-, and ratio-level data, but the standard deviation requires an interval or ratio level of measurement. It is based on the mean and gives an "average distance" between all scores and the mean. People rarely compute the standard deviation by hand for more than a handful of cases because computers do it in seconds.

The calculation of the standard deviation demonstrates its logic (see Figure 10.4). If you add up the absolute difference between each score and the mean (i.e., subtract each

---

FIGURE 10.4   The Standard Deviation

Steps in Computing the Standard Deviation
1. Compute the mean.
2. Subtract the mean from each score.
3. Square the resulting difference for each score.
4. Total up the squared differences to get the sum of squares.
5. Divide the sum of squares by the number of cases to get the variance.
6. Take the square root of the variance, which is the standard deviation.

Example of Computing the Standard Deviation
[8 respondents, variable = years of schooling]

Score	Score − Mean	Squared (Score − Mean)
15	15 − 12.5 = 2.5	6.25
12	12 − 12.5 = −0.5	.25
12	12 − 12.5 = −0.5	.25
10	10 − 12.5 = −2.5	6.25
16	16 − 12.5 = 3.5	12.25
18	18 − 12.5 = 5.5	30.25
8	8 − 12.5 = 4.5	20.25
9	9 − 12.5 = −3.5	12.25

Mean = 15 + 12 + 12 + 10 + 16 + 18 + 8 + 9 = 100, 100/8 = 12.5
Sum of squares = 6.25 + .25 + .25 + 6.25 + 12.25 + 30.25 + 20.25 + 12.25 = 88
Variance = Sum of squares/Number of cases = 88/8 = 11
Standard deviation = Square root of variance = $\sqrt{11}$ = 3.317 years.
Here is the standard deviation in the form of a formula with symbols.

Symbols:
X = SCORE of case   Σ = Sigma (Greek letter) for sum, add together
$\overline{X}$ = MEAN   N = Number of cases

Formula.[a]

$$\text{Standard deviation} = \sqrt{\frac{\Sigma(X - \overline{X})^2}{N}}$$

[a] is a slight difference in the formula depending on whether one is using data for the population or a sample to estimate there population parameter.

score from the mean), you will get zero. This is because the mean is equally distant from all scores. In the standard deviation, this difference is squared, so the scores that differ the most from the mean have the largest effect. These are then added (to create the sum of squares), then divided by the number of cases to get a type of average. Since the differences were squared, you need to take the square root to remove the squaring effect, and this gives you the standard deviation.

The primary use of the standard deviation, besides many advanced statistical measures, is to make comparisons. For example, you learn that the standard deviation for the schooling of parents of children in class A is 3.317 years; for class B, it is 0.812; and for class C, it is 6.239. The standard deviation tells you that the parents of children in class B are very similar in education level, whereas those for class C are very different. In fact, in class B, the schooling of an "average" parent is less than a year above or below the mean for all parents, so the parents are very homogeneous. In class C, however, the "average" parent is more than six years above or below the mean, so the parents are very heterogeneous.

You can use the standard deviation and the mean to create z-scores. Z-scores are very useful but underappreciated. With z-scores you can compare two or more distributions or groups. The **z-score,** also called a *standardized score,* expresses points or scores on a frequency distribution in terms of a number of standard deviations from the mean. Scores are in terms of their relative position within a distribution, not as absolute values.

For example, Katy, a sales manager in firm A, earns $80,000 per year, whereas Mike in firm B earns $58,000 per year. Despite the absolute income differences between them, the managers are paid equally relative to others in the same firm. Katy is paid more than two-thirds of other employees in her firm, and Mike is paid more than two-thirds of the employees in his firm. Although the $22,000 income difference

between Mike and Katy looks large and is real, when you compare Mike and Katy to others who work in the same company, they are at the same place.

Z-scores are easy to calculate from the mean and standard deviation (see Example Box 10.1). For example, an employer interviews students from Kings College and Queens College. She learns that the colleges are similar and that both grade on a 4.0 scale. Yet, the mean grade-point average at Kings College is 2.62 with a standard deviation of .50, whereas the mean grade-point average at Queens College is 3.24 with a standard deviation of .40. The employer suspects that grades at Queens College are inflated. Suzette from Kings College has a grade-point average of 3.62, and Jorge from Queens College has a grade-point average of 3.64. Both students took the same courses. The employer wants to adjust the grades for the grading practices of the two colleges (i.e., create standardized scores). She calculates z-scores by subtracting each student's score from the mean, then dividing by the standard deviation. For example, Suzette's z-score is $3.62 - 2.62 = 1.00/.50 = 2$, whereas Jorge's z-score is $3.64 - 3.24. = .40/.40 = 1$. Thus, the employer learns that Suzette is two standard deviations above the mean in her college, whereas Jorge is only one standard deviation above the mean for his college. Although Suzette's absolute grade-point average is lower than Jorge's, relative to the students in each of their colleges Suzette's grades are much higher than Jorge's.

RESULTS WITH TWO VARIABLES

A Bivariate Relationship

Univariate statistics describe a single variable in isolation. **Bivariate statistics** are much more valuable. They let you consider two variables together and describe the relationship between variables. Even simple hypotheses require two

10.1

EXAMPLE BOX

Calculating Z-Scores

Personally, I do not like the formula for z-scores, which is:

Z-score = (Score − Mean)/Standard Deviation,

or in symbols:

$$z = \frac{X - \overline{X}}{\delta}$$

where: X = score, $\overline{X}$ = mean, δ = standard deviation

I usually rely on a simple conceptual diagram that does the same thing and that shows what z-scores really do. Consider data on the ages of schoolchildren with a mean of 7 years and a standard deviation of 2 years. How do I compute the z-score of 5-year-old Miguel, or what if I know that Yashohda's z-score is a +2 and I need to know her age in years? First, I draw a little chart from −3 to +3 with zero in the middle. I will put the mean value at zero, because a z-score of zero is the mean and z-scores measure distance above or below it. I stop at 3 because virtually all cases fall within 3 standard deviations of the mean in most situations. The chart looks like this:

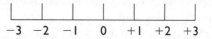

Now, I label the values of the mean and add or subtract standard deviations from it. One standard deviation above the mean (+1) when the mean is 7 and standard deviation is 2 years is just 7 + 2, or 9 years. For a −2 z-score, I put 3 years. This is because it is 2 standard deviations, of 2 years each (or 4 years), lower than the Mean of 7. My diagram now looks like this:

```
 I    3   5   7   9   II   13    age in years
 |____|___|___|___|___|____|
 −3  −2  −1   0  +1  +2   +3
```

It is easy to see that Miguel, who is 5 years old, has a z-score of −1, whereas Yashohda's z-score of +2 corresponds to 11 years old. I can read from z-score to age, or age to z-score. For fractions, such as a z-score of −1.5, I just apply the same fraction to age to get 4 years. Likewise, an age of 12 is a z-score of +2.5.

---

variables. Bivariate statistical analysis shows a *relationship* between variables—that is, things that appear together.

Statistical relationships are based on the ideas of covariation and independence. ***Covariation*** means that things go together, or are associated. To co-vary means to vary together; cases with certain values on a variable are likely to have certain values on the other variable. For example, people with higher values on an income variable also have higher values on the life expectancy variable. Likewise, those with lower incomes have lower life expectancy. You can say this in a shorthand way: income and life expectancy are related to one other, or they covary. We could also say that knowing one's income tells us one's probable life expectancy,

or that life expectancy depends on income. In everyday, nonprofessional speech people sometimes say "correlation" when they mean that two variables covary.

Independence is the opposite of covariation. It means there is no association or no relationship between variables. If two variables are independent, cases with certain values on one variable do not have any particular value on the other variable. For example, Rita wants to know whether number of siblings is related to life expectancy. If the variables are independent, then people with many brothers and sisters have the same life expectancy as those who are only children. In other words, knowing the number of brothers or sisters someone has tells Rita nothing about the person's life expectancy.

Most researchers state hypotheses in terms of a causal relationship or expected covariation; if they use the null hypothesis, the hypothesis is that there is independence. It is used in formal hypothesis testing and is frequently found in inferential statistics (to be discussed).

Three techniques help you to see whether a relationship exists between two variables: (1) a scattergram, or a graph or plot of the relationship; (2) cross-tabulation, or a percentaged table; and (3) measures of association, or statistical measures that express the degree of covariation in a single number (e.g., correlation coefficient).

Seeing the Relationship: The Scattergram

What Is a Scattergram (or Scatterplot)? A *scattergram* is a graph on which you plot each case or observation, where each axis represents the value of one variable. You use it for variables measured at the interval or ratio level, rarely for ordinal variables, and never if either variable is nominal. There is no fixed rule for which variable (independent or dependent) to place on the horizontal or vertical axis, but usually the independent variable (symbolized by the letter X) goes on the horizontal axis and the dependent variable (symbolized by Y) on the vertical axis. The lowest value for each should be the lower left corner and the highest value should be at the top or to the right.

How to Construct a Scattergram. Begin with the range of the two variables. Draw an axis with the values of each variable marked and write numbers on each axis (graph paper is helpful). Next, label each axis with the variable name and put a title at the top.

You are now ready for the data. For each case, find the value of each variable and mark the graph at a place corresponding to the two values. For example, you make a scattergram of years of schooling by number of children. You look at the first case to see years of schooling

(e.g., 12) and at the number of children (e.g., 3). Then you go to the place on the graph where 12 for the "schooling" variable and 3 for the "number of children" variable intersect and put a dot for the case. You then repeat the process for every other case. The scattergram in Figure 10.5 is a plot of data for 33 women. It shows a *negative relationship* between the years of education the woman completed and the number of children to which she gave birth.

What Can You Learn from the Scattergram? The scattergram shows you three aspects of a bivariate relationship: form, direction, and precision.

Form. Bivariate relationships can take three forms: independence, linear, and curvilinear. *Independence* or no relationship is the easiest to see. It looks like a random scatter with no pattern, or a straight line that is exactly parallel to the horizontal or vertical axis. A **linear relationship** means that a straight line can be visualized in the middle of a maze of cases running from one corner to another. A **curvilinear relationship** means that the center of a maze of cases would form a U curve, right side up or upside down, or an S curve.

Direction. Linear relationships can have a positive or negative direction. The plot of a *positive* relationship looks like a diagonal line from the lower left to the upper right. Higher values on X tend to go with higher values on Y, and vice versa. The income and life expectancy example described a positive linear relationship.

A *negative* relationship looks like a line from the upper left to the lower right. It means that higher values on one variable go with lower values on the other. For example, people with more education are less likely to have been arrested. If we look at a scattergram of data on a group of males where years of schooling (X axis) are plotted by number of arrests (Y axis), we see that most cases (or men) with many arrests are in the lower right, because most of them completed few years of schooling. Most cases with few arrests are in the upper left because most

FIGURE 10.5   Example of a Scattergram: Years of Education by Number of Natural Children for 33 Women

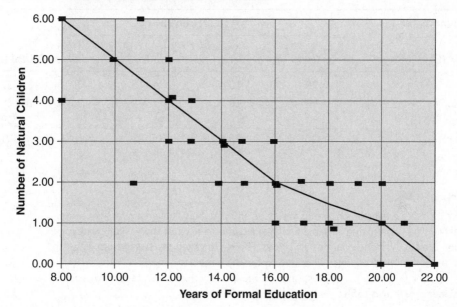

have had more schooling. The imaginary line for the relationship can have a shallow or a steep slope. More advanced statistics provide precise numerical measures of the line's slope.

Precision. Bivariate relationships differ in their degree of precision. *Precision* is the amount of spread in the points on the graph. A high level of precision occurs when the points hug the line that summarizes the relationship. A low level occurs when the points are widely spread around the line. You can "eyeball" a highly precise relationship or use advanced statistics to measure the precision of a relationship in a way that is analogous to the standard deviation for univariate statistics.

Bivariate Tables

What Is a Bivariate Table?   The bivariate contingency table presents the same information as a scattergram but in a more condensed form. In the table, you can use data measured at any level

of measurement, although interval and ratio data must be grouped if they have many values. The table is based on *cross-tabulation*; that is, the cases are organized in the table on the basis of two variables at the same time.

You can create a ***contingency table*** by crosstabulating two or more variables. It is "contingent" because the table distributes cases in each category of one variable into each category of a second (or additional) variable. As the table distributes cases into the categories of variables, it shows how the cases by category of one variable are "contingent upon" the categories of other variables.

Figure 10.6 is a raw count or frequency table. Its cells contain a count of the cases. It is easy to make but difficult to interpret a raw count table. This is because the rows or columns can have different totals.

To see a bivariate relationship, you need to convert raw count tables into a percentaged table. This allows you to compare percentages, and the

FIGURE 10.6   **Age Group by Attitude about Changing the Drinking Age, Raw Count Table**

Raw Count Table (a)	Age Group (b)				
Attitude (b)	*Under 30*	*30-45*	*46-60*	*61 and Older*	**Total (c)**
Agree	20	10	4	3	37
No opinion	3 (d)	10	10	2	25
Disagree	3	5	21	10	39
Total (c)	26	25	↑ 35	15	101
Missing cases (f) = 8.			(e)		

The Parts of a Table

(a) Give each table a *title,* which names variables and provides background information.

(b) Label the row and column variable and give a name to each of the variable categories.

(c) Include the totals of the columns and rows. These are called the **marginals.** They equal the univariate frequency distribution for the variable.

(d) Each number or place that corresponds to the intersection of a category for each variable is a **cell of a table.**

(e) The numbers with the labeled variable categories and the totals are called the **body of a table.**

(f) If there is missing information (cases in which a respondent refused to answer, ended interview, said "don't know," etc.), report the number of missing cases near the table to account for all original cases.

percentages adjust for, or standardize, differences in sizes of the totals for a row or column. You can percentage a table in three ways: by row, by column, and for the total. Only the first two are used in research to show relationships.

Is it best to percentage by row or column? Either can be appropriate. Let us first review the mechanics of creating a percentaged table. To calculate a *column percentage,* you compute each cell in the table as a percentage of its *column total.* This includes the total column or marginal for the column variable. For example, the first column total is 26 (there are 26 people under age 30), and the first cell of that column is 20 (there are 20 people under age 30 who agree). The percentage is 20/26 = 0.769 or 76.9 percent. Or, for the first number in

the marginal, 37/101 = 0.366 = 36.6 percent (see Table 10.1). Except for rounding, the total should equal 100 percent.

Computing row percentages follows a similar process. To calculate a *row percentage,* you compute each cell in the table as a percentage of its *row total.* For example, using the same cell with 20 in it, you now want to know what percentage it is of the row total of 37, or 20/37 = 0.541 = 54.1 percent. Percentaging by row or column gives you different percentages for a cell unless the marginals are the same.

The row and column percentages allow you to address different questions. The row percentage table answers the question, Among those who hold an attitude, what percentage come from each age group? It says of respondents

TABLE 10.1   Age Group by Attitude about Changing the Drinking Age, Percentaged Tables

Column-Percentaged Table

| Attitude | Age Group | | | | |
	Under 30	30–45	46–60	61 and Older	Total
Agree	76.9%	40%	11.4%	20%	36.6%
No opinion	11.5	40	28.6	13.3	24.8
Disagree	11.5	20	60	66.7	38.6
Total	99.9	100	100	100	100
(N)	(26)*	(25)*	(35)*	(15)*	(101)*
Missing cases = 8					

Row-Percentaged Table

| Attitude | Age Group | | | | | |
	Under 30	30–45	46–60	61 and Older	Total	(N)
Agree	54.1%	27%	10.8%	8.1%	100%	(37)*
No opinion	12	40	40	8	100	(25)*
Disagree	7.7	12.8	53.8	25.6	99.9	(39)*
Total	25.7	24.8	34.7	14.9	100.1	(101)*
Missing cases = 8						

*For percentaged tables, provide the number of cases or N on which percentages are computed in parentheses near the total of 100%. This makes it possible to go back and forth from a percentaged table to a raw count table and vice versa.

who agree, 54.1 percent are in the under-30 age group. The column percentage table addresses the question, Among those in each age group, what percentage hold different attitudes? It says that among those who are under age 30, 76.9 percent agree. From the row percentages, you learn that a little over half of those who agree are under 30 years old, whereas from column percentages, you learn that among the under-30 people, over three-quarters agree. One way of calculating percents tells you about people who have specific attitudes; the other way tells you about people in specific age groups.

Your hypothesis often suggests whether you want to look at row percentages or column percentages. Until you develop the skill to read tables and interpret their meaning quickly, you may want to calculate percentages both ways and practice interpreting, or figuring out, what each says. For example, my hypothesis is that a person's age affects his or her attitude. For this hypothesis, column percentages are most helpful. However, if my interest was in describing the age make-up of groups of people with different attitudes, then row percentages are appropriate.

Unfortunately, there is no "industry standard" for putting independent and dependent variables in a percentage table as a row or column, or for percentage by row and column. Most researchers place the independent variable as the column and percentage by column, but a large minority put the independent variable as the row and percentage by row.

Reading a Percentaged Table. Once you understand how to create a table, reading it and figuring out what it says are much easier. To read a table, first look at the title, the variable labels, and any background information. Next, look at the direction in which percentages have been computed—in rows or columns. Notice that the two percentaged tables (see Table 10.1) have the same title. This is because the same variables are used. It would have helped to note how the data were percentaged in the title, but this is rarely done. Sometimes, researchers present abbreviated tables and omit the 100 percent total or the marginals, which adds to the confusion. It is best to include all the parts of a table and clear labels.

Researchers read percentaged tables to make comparisons. Comparisons are made in the opposite direction from that in which percentages are computed. A rule of thumb is to compare across rows if the table is percentaged down (i.e., by column) and to compare up and down in columns if the table is percentaged across (i.e., by row).

For example, in row-percentaged Table 10.1, compare columns or age groups. Most of those who agree are in the youngest group, with the proportion declining as age increases. Most no-opinion people are in the middle-age groups, whereas those who disagree are older, especially in the 46-to-60 group. When reading column-percentaged (see Table 10.1) tables, compare across rows. For example, a majority of people in the youngest group agree. They are the only group in which most people agree. Only 11.5 percent disagree, compared to a majority in the two oldest groups.

It takes practice to see a relationship in a percentaged table. If there is no relationship in a table, the cell percentages look approximately equal across rows or columns. A linear relationship looks like larger percentages in the diagonal cells. If there is a curvilinear relationship, the largest percentages form a pattern across cells. For example, the largest cells might be the upper right, the bottom middle, and the upper left. It is easiest to see a relationship in a moderate-sized table (9–16 cells) where most cells have some cases (at least five cases are recommended) and the relationship is strong and precise.

You can use the principles of reading a scattergram to help you see relationships in a percentaged table. Imagine dividing a scattergram into 12 equal-sized sections. The cases in each section correspond to the number of cases in the cells of a table that you can superimpose onto the scattergram. Thus, a table is a condensed form of the scattergram. The bivariate relationship line in a scattergram corresponds to the diagonal cells in a percentaged table. Thus, a simple way to see strong relationships is to circle the largest percentage in each row (for row-percentaged tables) or column (for column-percentaged tables) and see if a line appears.

The circle-the-largest-cell rule for tables works—with one important caveat. The categories in the percentages table *must* be ordinal or interval and they *must* be in the same order as in a scattergram. In scattergrams the lowest variable categories begin at the bottom left. If you do not have categories in a table ordered the same way, the rule does not work.

For example, Table 10.2A looks like a positive relationship and Table 10.2B like a negative relationship. Both use the same data and are percentaged by row. The actual relationship is negative. Look closely—Table 10.2B has age categories ordered as in a scattergram. When in doubt, return to the basic difference between positive and negative relationships. A positive relationship means that as one variable increases, so does the other. A negative relationship means that as one variable increases, the other decreases.

TABLE 10.2A   Age by Schooling

Age	Years of Schooling				Total
	0–11	12	13–14	16 +	
Under 30	5%	25	30	40	100
30–45	15	25	40	20	100
46–60	35	45	12	8	100
61+	45	35	15	5	100

TABLE 10.2B   Age by Schooling

Age	Years of Schooling				Total
	0–11	12	13–14	16 +	
61+	45%	35	15	5	100
46–60	35	45	12	8	100
30–45	15	25	40	20	100
Under 30	5	25	30	40	100

Bivariate Tables without Percentages.   You can condense information in another kind of bivariate table, one that uses a measure of central tendency (usually the mean) instead of percentages. This is most common when one variable is nominal or ordinal and the other is at the interval or ratio level. You simply present the mean (or a similar measure) of the interval or ratio variable for each category of the nominal or ordinal variable. To do this, you divide all cases into the ordinal or nominal variable categories; then you calculate the mean for the cases in each of the variable categories. Table 10.3 shows the mean age of people in each of the attitude categories. The results suggest that the mean age of those who disagree is much higher than for those who agree or have no opinion.

Measures of Association

A *measure of association* is a single number that expresses the strength, and often the direction, of a relationship. It condenses information about a bivariate relationship into a single number. There are many measures of association. The correct one to use depends on the level of measurement.

Most measures of association go by letters of the Greek alphabet. Lambda (λ), gamma (γ), tau (τ), chi (squared) (χ), and rho (ρ) are commonly used measures. The emphasis here is on how to interpret the measures, not on their calculation. In order to understand each measure fully, you should complete a course in statistics.

A principle behind many measures of association is "proportionate reduction in error." This is how it works: if the association or relationship between two variables is strong, then you will make relatively few errors when predicting values of a second variable based on knowledge of the first. In other words, the proportion of errors you reduce will be large. If the variables are not associated, your prediction will be no better than pure chance, or knowing one variable will be no improvement over chance. Knowing the values of one variable will produce no reduction in errors when trying to predict the second variable. If income level and attendance at a classical music performance is strongly associated, knowing a person's income will improve predicting his or her attending a classical music performance. If the two variables are not associated, knowing income level would give you no better predictions than chance, or there would be no reduction in the number of

TABLE 10.3   Attitude about Changing the Drinking Age by Mean Age of Respondent

Drinking Age Attitude	Mean Age	(N)
Agree	26.2	(37)
No opinion	44.5	(25)
Disagree	61.9	(39)

Missing cases = 8.

errors you would make in predicting classical music attendance knowing a person's income.

In all measures of association, a large number suggests a stronger association. Expansion Box 10.2 describes five commonly used bivariate measures of association. Notice that most range from −1 to +1, with negative numbers indicating a negative relationship and positive numbers a positive relationship. A measure of 1.0 means a 100 percent reduction in errors, or perfect prediction.

10.2 EXPANSION BOX
Five Measures of Association

Lambda is used for nominal-level data. It is based on a reduction in errors based on the mode and ranges between 0 (independence) and 1.0 (perfect prediction or the strongest possible relationship).

Gamma is used for ordinal-level data. It is based on comparing pairs of variable categories and seeing whether a case has the same rank on each. Gamma ranges from −1.0 to +1.0, with 0 meaning no association.

Tau is also used for ordinal-level data. It is based on a different approach than gamma and takes care of a few problems that can occur with gamma. Actually, there are several statistics named tau (it is a popular Greek letter), and the one here is Kendall's tau. Kendall's tau ranges from −1.0 to +1.0, with 0 meaning no association.

Rho is also called Pearson's product moment correlation coefficient (named after the famous statistician Karl Pearson and based on a product moment statistical procedure). It is the most commonly used measure of correlation, the correlation statistic people mean if they use the term *correlation* without identifying it further. It can be used only for data measured at the interval or ratio level. Rho is used for the mean and standard deviation of the variables and tells how far cases are from a relationship (or regression) line in a scatterplot. Rho ranges from −1.0 to +1.0, with 0 meaning no association. If the value of rho is squared, sometimes called *R-squared*, it has a unique proportion reduction in error meaning. *R-squared* tells how the percentage in one variable (e.g., the dependent) is accounted for, or explained by, the other variable (e.g., the independent). Rho measures linear relationships only. It cannot measure nonlinear or curvilinear relationships. For example, a rho of zero can indicate either no relationship or a curvilinear relationship.

Chi-squared has two different uses. It can be used as a measure of association in descriptive statistics like the others listed here, or in inferential statistics. Inferential statistics are briefly described next. As a measure of association, chi-squared can be used for nominal and ordinal data. It has an upper limit of infinity and a lower limit of zero, meaning no association.

Summary of Measures of Association

Measure	Greek Symbol	Type of Data	High Association	Independence
Lambda	λ	Nominal	1.0	0
Gamma	γ	Ordinal	+1.0, −1.0	0
Tau (Kendall's)	τ	Ordinal	+1.0, −1.0	0
Rho	ρ	Interval, ratio	+1.0, −1.0	0
Chi-square	χ^2	Nominal, ordinal	Infinity	0

MORE THAN TWO VARIABLES

Statistical Control

If you can show an association or relationship between two variables, that is not sufficient to say that an independent variable clearly *causes* a dependent variable. In addition to showing the association and the temporal order of variables, you also must eliminate alternative explanations—explanations that could make the hypothesized relationship spurious. In experimental research, you do this by choosing a design that physically controls potential alternative explanations for results (i.e., that threaten internal validity).

In nonexperimental research, you control for alternative explanations by using statistics. You must first measure possible alternative explanations with **control variables**, then examine the control variables using multivariate tables and statistics. Examining the multivariate tables and statistics can help you decide whether a bivariate relationship is spurious. They also show the relative size of the effect of multiple independent variables on a dependent variable.

You control for alternative explanations in multivariate (more than two variables) analysis by introducing a third (or sometimes a fourth or fifth) variable. This third variable represents a possible alternative causal explanation for your dependent variable. For example, you have a bivariate table showing that taller teenagers like sports more than shorter ones do. But the bivariate relationship between height and attitude toward sports could be spurious. Perhaps teenage males are taller than females, and males tend to like sports more than females. To test whether the original relationship of height and interest is "real" or spurious and actually due to gender, you *control for* gender. In other words, you statistically remove the effects of gender on the relationship. Once you do this, you can see whether the bivariate relationship between height and attitude toward sports remains.

You control for a third variable by seeing whether the bivariate relationship persists within categories of the control variable. For example, you control for gender, and the relationship between height and sports attitude persists. This means that tall males and tall females both like sports more than short males and short females do. In other words, the control variable has no effect. When this is so, the bivariate relationship is real and not spurious.

If the bivariate relationship greatly weakens or disappears after you add the control variable, it indicates that the initial bivariate relationship is probably spurious. It means that tall males are no more likely than short males to like sports, and tall females are no more likely to like sports than short females. It suggests that the third variable, gender, and not height, is the true cause of differences in attitudes toward sports.

Statistical control is a central idea in many advanced statistical techniques. A measure of association, such as the correlation coefficient, only suggests a relationship. You need to be cautious in interpreting bivariate relationships until you have considered control variables because the relationship might be spurious.

The Elaboration Model of Percentaged Tables

Constructing Trivariate Tables. To "control for" or see whether an alternative explanation explains away a causal relationship and the bivariate relationship is spurious, you must first have operationalized alternative explanations as *control variables*. They are so named because they allow you to control for alternative explanation.

You can take control variables into consideration and see whether they influence the bivariate relationship by using trivariate or three-variable tables. Trivariate tables differ slightly from bivariate tables. In a way, they consist of multiple bivariate tables.

A trivariate table is a bivariate table of the independent and dependent variable, only for cases in each category of the control variable. These new tables are called **partials**. The number of partials depends on the number of categories in the control variable. Partial tables look like bivariate tables, but only use a subset of all cases. Only cases with a specific value on the control variable are in the partial. Thus, you can "break apart" a bivariate table to form partials, or combine partials to restore the initial bivariate table.

Trivariate tables have three limitations. First, they are difficult to interpret if a control variable has more than four categories. Second, control variables can be at any level of measurement, but interval or ratio control variables must be grouped (i.e., converted to an ordinal level), and how cases are grouped can affect the interpretation of effects. Finally, the total number of cases is a limiting factor. You keep dividing up the total number of cases among cells in partials. The number of cells in the partials equals the number of cells in the bivariate relationship multiplied by the number of categories in the control variable. For example, a control variable has three categories, and a bivariate table has 12 cells, so the partials have $3 \times 12 = 36$ cells. An average of five cases per cell is recommended, so the researcher will need $5 \times 36 = 180$ cases at minimum.

For three variables, three bivariate tables are logically possible. In the example, the combinations are (1) gender by attitude, (2) age group by attitude, and (3) gender by age group. You set up the partials based on the initial bivariate relationship. The independent variable in each is "age group" and the dependent variable is "attitude." "Gender" is the control variable. Thus, the trivariate table consists of a pair of partials, each showing the age–attitude relationship for a given gender.

Your hypothesis informs you as to the initial bivariate relationship and may suggest which variables provide alternative explanations (i.e., the control variables). Thus, the choice of the control variable is based on your original hypothesis, which may come from a theory.

The **elaboration paradigm** is a system for reading percentaged trivariate tables.[3] It describes the pattern that emerges when a control variable is introduced. The system has five patterns that describe how the partial tables compare to the initial bivariate table, or how the original bivariate relationship changes after you add the control variable (see Expansion Box 10.3). The examples of patterns presented here show strong cases (see Table 10.4). You need to use advanced statistics when the differences are not as obvious.

Multiple Regression Analysis

Multiple regression is a statistical technique whose calculation is beyond the level of this book. The appropriate statistics software can quickly compute it, but a background in statistics is needed to prevent making errors in its calculation and interpretation. It requires interval- or ratio-level data. I discuss it here for two reasons. First, it controls for many alternative explanations and variables simultaneously (it is rarely possible to use more than one control variable at a time using percentaged tables). Second, it is widely used in social science, and you are likely to encounter it when reading research reports or articles.

Multiple regression results tell the reader two things. First, the results have a measure called R-squared (R^2). It is a summary measure that tells how well a set of variables together "explain" a dependent variable. *Explain* means reduced errors when predicting the dependent variable scores on the basis of information about the independent variables. A good model with several independent variables might account for, or explain, a large percentage of variation in a dependent variable. For example, an R^2 of .50 means that knowing the independent and control variables improves the accuracy of predicting the dependent variable by 50 percent, or half as many errors are made as would be made without knowing about the variables.

Second, the regression results measure the direction and size of the effect of each variable on a dependent variable. It measures the effect

10.3   EXPANSION BOX
Five Patterns in the Elaboration Paradigm

1. The ***replication pattern*** is when the partials replicate or reproduce the same relationship that existed in the bivariate table before you considered the control variable. It means that the control variable has no effect.

2. The ***specification pattern*** is when one partial replicates the initial bivariate relationship but other partials do not. For example, you find a strong (negative) bivariate relationship between automobile accidents and college grades. You control for gender and discover that the relationship holds only for males (i.e., the strong negative relationship was in the partial for males, but not for females). This is specification because a researcher can specify the category of the control variable in which the initial relationship persists.

Note: The interpretation and explanation patterns both show a relationship in the bivariate table that disappears in the partials. The original relationship changes to statistical independence in the partials. You cannot distinguish interpretation from looking at the tables alone. The difference between them depends on the causal logic among variables, or location of the control variable in the causal order of variables. A control variable can be either between the original independent and dependent variables (i.e., the control variable is intervening), or before the original independent variable.

3. The ***interpretation pattern*** describes the situation in which the control variable intervenes between the original independent and dependent variables. For example, you examine a relationship between religious upbringing and abortion attitude. Political ideology is a control variable. You reason that religious upbringing affects current political ideology and abortion attitude. You theorize that political ideology is logically prior to an attitude about a specific issue, such as abortion. Thus, religious upbringing causes political ideology, which in turn has an impact on abortion attitude. The control variable is an intervening variable, which helps you interpret the meaning of the complete relationship.

4. The ***explanation pattern*** looks the same as interpretation but the control variable comes before the independent variable in the initial bivariate relationship. For example, the original relationship is between religious upbringing and abortion attitude, but now gender is the control variable. Gender comes before religious upbringing because it is usually fixed at birth. The explanation pattern changes how a researcher explains the results. It implies that the initial bivariate relationship is spurious.

5. The ***suppressor variable pattern*** occurs when the bivariate tables suggest independence but a relationship appears in one or both of the partials. For example, religious upbringing and abortion attitude are independent in a bivariate table. Once you add the control variable "region of the country," religious upbringing is associated with abortion attitude in the partial tables. The control variable is a suppressor variable because it suppressed the true relationship. The true relationship appears in the partials. In other words, there is a relationship between religious upbringing and abortion attitude in one region of the country but not in others; the relationship was hidden or being "suppressed" until you considered the region.

precisely and gives the effect's size a numerical value. For example, you can see how five independent or control variables simultaneously affect a dependent variable, with all variables controlling for the effects of one another. This is especially valuable for testing theories that state that multiple independent variables cause one dependent variable. The effect of an independent variable on the dependent variable in multiple regression is measured by a standardized regression coefficient or the Greek letter beta (β). It is similar to a correlation coefficient. In

TABLE 10.4   Summary of the Elaboration Paradigm

Pattern Name	Pattern Seen When Comparing Partials to the Original Bivariate Table
Replication	Same relationship in both partials as in bivariate table.
Specification	Bivariate relationship is only seen in one of the partial tables.
Interpretation	Bivariate relationship weakens greatly or disappears in the partial tables (control variable is intervening).
Explanation	Bivariate relationship weakens greatly or disappears in the partial tables (control variable is before independent variable).
Suppressor variable	No bivariate relationship; relationship appears in partial tables only.

EXAMPLES OF ELABORATION PATTERNS

Replication

Bivariate Table			Partials			
				Control = Low		Control = High
	Low	High		Low	High	Low	High
Low	85%	15%	Low	84%	16%	86%	14%
High	15%	85%	High	16%	84%	14%	86%

Interpretation or Explanation

Bivariate Table			Partials			
				Control = Low		Control = High
	Low	High		Low	High	Low	High
Low	85%	15%	Low	45%	55%	55%	45%
High	15%	85%	High	55%	45%	45%	55%

Specification

Bivariate Table			Partials			
				Control = Low		Control = High
	Low	High		Low	High	Low	High
Low	85%	85%	Low	95%	5%	50%	50%
High	15%	15%	High	5%	95%	50%	50%

Suppressor Variable

Bivariate Table			Partials			
				Control = Low		Control = High
	Low	High		Low	High	Low	High
Low	54%	46%	Low	84%	16%	14%	86%
High	46%	54%	High	16%	84%	86%	14%

fact, the beta coefficient for two variables will only equal the *r* correlation coefficient.

You can use the beta regression coefficient to determine whether control variables have an effect. For example, the bivariate correlation between *X* and *Y* is .75. Next, you statistically consider four control variables. If the beta remains at .75, it means that the four control variables have no effect. However, if the beta for *X* and *Y* gets smaller (e.g., drops to .20), it indicates that the control variables have an effect on the dependent variable.

One of the most interesting features of multiple regression is to tell you the relative size or impact of multiple independent and intervening variables on a dependent variable. Consider an example of regression analysis with age, income, education, and region as independent variables. The dependent variable is a score on a political ideology index. The multiple regression results show that income and religious attendance have large effects, education and region minor effects, and age no effect. All the independent variables together have a 38 percent accuracy in predicting a person's political ideology (see Table 10.5). The example suggests that high income, frequent religious attendance, and residence in the South are positively associated with conservative opinions, whereas having more education is associated with liberal opinions. The impact of income is more than twice the size of the impact of living in a Southern region. We have been examining descriptive statistics (see Expansion Box 10.4); next, we look at a different type: inferential statics.

INFERENTIAL STATISTICS

The Purpose of Inferential Statistics

Often you want to do more than describe; you want to test hypotheses, know whether sample results hold true in a population, and decide whether differences in results (e.g., between the mean scores of two groups) are big enough to indicate that a relationship truly exists. Inferential statistics use the mathematics of probability theory to test hypotheses formally, permit inferences from a sample to a population, and test whether descriptive results are likely to be due to random factors or to a real relationship. This section explains the basic ideas of inferential statistics but does not deal with inferential statistics in any detail. This area is more complex than descriptive statistics and serious students should complete a course in statistics to gain an understanding.

Inferential statistics rely on principles from probability sampling, in which you use a random process to select cases from the entire population. Inferential statistics are a precise way to talk about how confident you can be when inferring from the results in a sample to the population.

You have already encountered inferential statistics if you have read or heard about "statistical significance" or results "significant at the .05 level." You can use them to conduct various statistical tests (e.g., a *t*-test or an *F*-test). Statistical significance is also used in formal hypothesis testing, which is a precise way to decide whether to accept or to reject a null hypothesis.[4]

TABLE 10.5   Example of Multiple Regression Results

Dependent Variable Is Political Ideology Index (High Score Means Very Liberal)

Independent Variable	Standardized Regression Coefficients
Region = South	−.19
Age	.01
Income	−.44
Years of education	.23
Religious attendance	−.39
$R^2 = .38$	

10.4	EXPANSION BOX

Summary of Major Types of Descriptive Statistics

Type of Technique	Statistical Technique	Purpose
Univariate	Frequency distribution, measure of central tendency, standard deviation, z-score	Describe one variable.
Bivariate	Correlation, percentage table, chi-square	Describe a relationship or the association between two variables.
Multivariate	Elaboration paradigm, multiple regression	Describe relationships among several variables, or see how several independent variables have an effect on a dependent variable.

Statistical Significance

Statistical significance means that results are not likely to be due to chance factors. It indicates the probability of finding a relationship in the sample when there is none in the population. Because probability samples involve a random process, it is always possible that sample results will differ from a population parameter. You want to estimate the odds that sample results are due to a true population parameter or to chance factors of random sampling. Statistical significance uses probability theory and specific statistical tests to tell you whether random error in sampling could have produced the results (e.g., an association, a difference between two means, a regression coefficient).

Statistical significance only tells what is likely. It cannot prove anything with absolute certainty. It states that particular outcomes are more or less probable. Statistical significance is *not* the same as practical, substantive, or theoretical significance. Results can be statistically significant but theoretically meaningless or trivial. For example, two variables can have a statistically significant association due to coincidence, with no logical connection between them (e.g., length of fingernails and ability to speak French).

Levels of Significance

To simplify matters, we usually express statistical significance in terms of levels (e.g., a test is statistically significant at a specific level) rather than giving the specific probability. The *level of statistical significance* (usually .05, .01, or .001) is a way of talking about the likelihood that results are due to chance factors—that is, that a relationship appears in the sample when there is none in the population. If you say that results are significant at the .05 level, this means the following:

- Results like these are due to chance factors only 5 in 100 times.
- There is a 95 percent chance that the sample results are not due to chance factors alone, but reflect the population accurately.
- The odds of such results based on chance alone are .05, or 5 percent.
- One can be 95 percent confident that the results are due to a real relationship in the population, not chance factors.

These all say the same thing in different ways. This may sound like the discussion of sampling distributions and the central limit theorem in Chapter 6 on sampling. It is not an accident. Both are based on probability theory and link sample data to a population. Probability theory lets us predict what happens in the long run over many events when a random process is used. In other words, it allows precise prediction over many situations in the long run, but not for a specific situation. Since we have one sample and we want to infer to the population, probability theory helps us estimate the odds that our particular sample represents the population. We cannot know for certain unless we have the whole population, but probability theory lets us state our confidence—how likely it is that the sample shows one thing while something else is true in the population. For example, a sample shows that college men and women differ in how many hours they study. Is the result due to an unusual sample, and is there really no difference in the population, or does it reflect a true difference between the sexes in the population?

Type I and Type II Errors

The logic of statistical significance is based on stating whether chance factors produce results. You may ask, Why use the .05 level? It means a 5 percent chance that randomness could cause the results. Why not use a more certain standard—for example, a 1 in 1,000 probability of random chance? This gives a smaller chance that randomness versus a true relationship caused the results.

There are two answers. The simple answer is that the scientific community has informally agreed to use .05 as a rule of thumb for most purposes. Being 95 percent confident of results is the accepted standard for explaining the social world.

A second answer involves a tradeoff between making two types of logical errors. A *Type I error* occurs when you say that a relationship exists when in fact none exists. It means falsely rejecting a null hypothesis. A *Type II error* occurs when you say that a relationship does not exist, but in reality it does. It means falsely accepting a null hypothesis (see Expansion Box 10.5). Of course, you want to avoid both kinds of errors. You want to say that there is a relationship in the data only when it does exist and that there is no relationship only when there really is none, but you face a dilemma: As the odds of making one type of error decline, the odds of making the opposite error increase.

The idea of Type I and Type II errors may seem difficult at first, but the same logical dilemma appears in many other settings. For example, a judge can err by deciding that an accused person is guilty when in fact he or she is innocent. Or, the judge can err by deciding that a person is innocent when in fact he or she is guilty. The judge does not want to make either error. A judge does not want to jail the innocent or to free the guilty. The judge must render a judgment based on limited information and balance the two types of errors. Likewise, a physician has to decide whether to prescribe a new medication for a patient. The physician can err by thinking that the medication will be effective and has no side effects when, in fact, it

10.5	EXPANSION BOX		
	Type I and Type II Errors		

	True Situation in the World	
What the Researcher Says	*No Relationship*	*Causal Relationship*
No relationship	No error	Type II error
Causal relationship	Type I error	No error

has a serious side effect, such as causing blindness. Or, the physician can err by holding back an effective medication because of fear of serious side effects when in fact there are none. The physician does not want to make either error. By making the first error, the physician causes great harm to the patient and may even face a lawsuit. By making the second error, the physician does not help the patient get better. Again, a judgment must be made that balances two types of possible errors.

We can put the ideas of statistical significance and the two types of errors together. If you are overly cautious you set a very high level of significance. For example, you might use the .0001 level. You attribute the results to chance unless they are so rare that they would occur by chance only 1 in 10,000 times. Such a high standard means that you are most likely to err by saying results are due to chance when in fact they are not. You may falsely accept the null hypothesis when there is a causal relationship (a Type II error).

By contrast, if you are a risk-taker, you would set a very low level of significance, such as .10. Your results indicate a relationship would occur by chance 1 in 10 times. You are likely to err by saying that a causal relationship exists when, in fact, random factors (e.g., random sampling error) actually cause the results. You are likely to falsely reject the null hypothesis (Type I error). In sum, the .05 level is a compromise between Type I and Type II errors.

The statistical techniques of inferential statistics are precise and rely on the relationship between sampling error, sample size, and central limit theorem. The power of inferential statistics is their ability to let you state, with a very specific degree of certainty, that specific sample results are likely to be true in a population. For example, you conduct statistical tests and discover that a relationship is statistically significant at the .05 level. This allows you to say that the sample results are probably not due to chance factors. Indeed, there is a 95 percent chance that a true relationship exists in the social world.

Tests for inferential statistics have some restrictions. The data must come from a random sample, and the tests only take into account sampling errors. Nonsampling errors (e.g., a poor sampling frame or a poorly designed measure) are not considered. Do not be fooled into thinking that such tests offer easy, final answers. Many computer programs quickly do the calculation for inferential and descriptive statistics (see Expansion Box 10.6).

CONCLUSION

You have learned about organizing quantitative data to prepare them for analysis and about analyzing them (organizing data into charts or tables, or summarizing them with statistical measures). You can use statistical analysis to test hypotheses and answer research questions. The chapter explained how you must first code data and then analyze using univariate or bivariate statistics. Bivariate relationships might be spurious, so you will want to consider control variables and multivariate analysis. You also learned some basics about inferential statistics.

Beginning researchers sometimes feel their results should support a hypothesis. *There is nothing wrong with rejecting a hypothesis.* The goal of scientific research is to produce knowledge that truly reflects the social world, not to defend pet ideas or hypotheses. Hypotheses are informed theoretical guesses but based on limited knowledge. You need to test them. Excellent-quality research can find that a hypothesis is wrong, and poor-quality research can support a hypothesis. Good research depends on high-quality methodology, not on supporting a specific hypothesis.

Good research means guarding against possible errors or obstacles to true inferences from data to the social world. Errors can enter into the research process and affect results at many places: research design, measurement, data collection, coding, calculating statistics and constructing tables, or interpreting results. Even if you design, measure, collect, code, and calculate

10.6 EXPANSION BOX
Statistical Programs on Computers

Almost every social researcher who needs to calculate many statistics does so with a computer program, often using a basic spreadsheet program, such as Excel. Unfortunately, spreadsheets are designed for accounting and bookkeeping functions. They include statistics, but are clumsy and limited for that purpose. There are many computer programs designed for calculating general statistics. The marketplace can be confusing to a beginner, for products evolve rapidly with changing computer technology.

In recent years, the software has become less demanding for a user. The most popular programs in the social sciences are Minitab, Microcase, and SPSS (Statistical Package for the Social Sciences). Others include SAS (Statistical Analysis System), STATISTICA by StratSoft, and Strata. Many began as simple, low-cost programs for research purposes.

The most widely used program for statistics in the social sciences in SPSS. Its advantages are that social researchers used it extensively for over three decades, it includes many ways to manipulate quantitative data, and it contains most statistical measures. A disadvantage is that it can take a long time to learn because of its many options and complex statistics. Also, it is expensive to purchase unless the user gets an inexpensive, "stripped down" student version included with a textbook or workbook.

As computer technology makes using a statistics program easier, the danger increases that some people will use the programs, but not understand statistics or what the programs are doing. They can easily violate basic assumptions required by a statistical procedure, use the statistics improperly, and produce results that are pure nonsense but that look very technically sophisticated.

---

without error, another step in the research process remains. It is to interpret the tables, charts, and statistics, and to answer the question, What does it all mean? The only way to assign meaning to facts, charts, tables, or statistics is to use logic and theory.

Data, tables, or computer output cannot answer research questions. The facts do not speak for themselves. As a researcher, you must return to your theory (i.e., concepts, relationships among concepts, assumptions, theoretical definitions) and give the results meaning. Do not lock yourself into the ideas with which you began. There is room for creativity. You can generate new ideas by trying to figure out what results really say. It is important to be careful in designing and conducting research so that you can see the results as a reflection of the social world and not worry about whether they are produced by errors or artifacts of the research process itself.

Before we leave quantitative research, there is one last issue. Journalists, politicians,

and others increasingly use statistical results to make a point or bolster an argument. This has not produced greater accuracy and information in public debate. More often, it has increased confusion. It makes knowing what statistics can and cannot do more important. The cliché that you can prove anything with statistics is false; however, some people can and do *misuse* statistics. Through ignorance or conscious deceit, some people use statistics to advance pet ideas or manipulate others. The best way to protect yourself from being misled by statistics is not to ignore them or hide from the numbers. Rather, it is to understand the research process and statistics, think about what you hear, and ask questions.

We turn next to qualitative research. The logic and purpose of qualitative research differ from those of the quantitative, positivist approach of the past chapters. It is less concerned with numbers, hypotheses, and causality and more concerned with words, norms and values, and meanings.

Key Terms

bar chart
bivariate statistics
body of a table
cell of a table
code sheets
codebook
contingency cleaning
contingency table
control variable
covariation
cross-tabulation
curvilinear relationship
descriptive statistics
direct-entry method
elaboration paradigm
explanation pattern
frequency distribution
frequency polygon
independence
interpretation pattern
level of statistical significance
linear relationship
marginals
mean
median
mode
normal distribution
partials
percentile
pie chart
possible code cleaning
range
replication pattern
scattergram
skewed distribution
specification pattern
standard deviation
statistical significance
suppressor variable pattern
Type I error
Type II error
univariate statistics
z-score

Endnotes

1. Note that coding sex as 1 = Male, 2 = Female, or as 0 = Male, 1 = Female, or reversing the sex for numbers is arbitrary. The only reason numbers are used instead of letters (e.g., M and F) is because many computer programs work best with all numbers. Sometimes coding data as a zero can create confusion, so the number 1 is usually the lowest value.

2. There are other statistics to measure a special kind of mean for ordinal data and for other special situations, which are beyond the level of discussion in this book.

3. For a discussion of the elaboration paradigm and its history, see Babbie (1998:393–401) and Rosenberg (1968).

4. In formal hypothesis testing, researchers test the *null hypothesis*. They usually want to reject the null because rejection of the null indirectly supports the alternative hypothesis to the null, the one they deduced from theory as a tentative explanation.

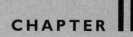

Field Research and Focus Group Research

This chapter and the two that follow shift from quantitative to qualitative research. This chapter describes field research, also called *ethnography* or *participant-observation research*. It is a type of qualitative research in which you, as a researcher, directly observe and participate in small-scale social settings in the present time and in your home culture. We also look at focus groups.

INTRODUCTION TO FIELD RESEARCH

Many students are excited by field research. It involves hanging out with some exotic group of people. There are no cold mathematics or complicated statistics, and no abstract deductive hypotheses. Instead, you interact directly, face-to-face with "real people" in a natural setting. Unlike many types of social research, in field research you talk with and directly observe the people you study. By observing and interacting over months or even years, you learn about them firsthand. You get to know their life histories, their hobbies and interests, and their habits, hopes, fears, and dreams. Meeting new people, developing friendships, and discovering new social worlds can be fun. It is also time consuming, emotionally draining, and sometimes physically dangerous.

Field research is appropriate when the research question involves learning about, understanding, or describing a group of interacting people. It is usually best when the question is, How do people do Y in the social world? or What is the social world of X like? You can use it when other methods (e.g., survey, experiments) are not practical, as in studying street gangs. You study people in the "field" location or setting. As a beginning field researcher, you will want to start with a relatively small group (30 or fewer) who interact with each other on a regular basis in a relatively fixed setting (e.g., a street corner, church, bar, beauty salon, baseball field, etc.).

In order to use consistent terminology, we can call the people you study in a field setting **members**. They are insiders or natives in the field and belong to a group, subculture, or social setting that you, the "outsider" field researcher, wants to penetrate and learn about.

Field researchers have explored a wide variety of social settings, subcultures, and aspects of social life[1] (see Figure 11.1). Places my students have conducted in successful short-term, small-scale field research studies include a beauty salon, day care center, bakery, bingo parlor, bowling alley, church, coffee shop, laundromat, police dispatch office, nursing home, tattoo parlor, and weight room.

Ethnography and Ethnomethodology

Two specialized extensions of field research, ethnography and ethnomethodology, build on the social constructionist perspective. Each has redefined how field research is conducted.

Ethnography comes from cultural anthropology.[2] It is mostly found in anthropology and sociology, but also used in communication studies, criminology, economics, education, geography, history, linguistics, marketing, medicine and nursing, and social work. *Ethno* means people or folk, and *graphy* refers to write or describe. Thus, **ethnography** means writing about/describing a people. It does this to understand better a people's way of life. The ethnographer is an outsider (i.e., a non-insider who does not belong to the community or culture that he or she studies). Yet, the ethnographer's goal is to learn from insiders, to gain the native point of view, and to understand deeply the culture or community. Ethnography is not a single technique but a collection of specific techniques and an approach to study human activity.

Ethnography assumes that people constantly make inferences. To infer means going beyond what we explicitly see or say outwardly in a situation to an implicit, inner meaning. Ethnography also assumes that people display

FIGURE 11.1   Examples of Field Research Sites/Topics

Small-Scale Settings

Passengers in an airplane
Bars or taverns
Battered women's shelters
Camera clubs
Laundromats
Social movement organizations
Social welfare offices
Television stations
Waiting rooms

Community Settings

Retirement communities
Small towns
Urban ethnic communities
Working-class neighborhoods

Children's Activities

Children's playgrounds
Little League baseball
Youth in schools
Junior high girl groups

Occupations

Airline attendants
Artists
Cocktail waitresses
Dog catchers

Door-to-door salespersons
Factory workers
Gamblers
Medical students
Female strippers
Police officers
Restaurant chefs
Social workers
Taxi drivers

Deviance and Criminal Activity

Body/genital piercing and branding
Cults
Drug dealers and addicts
Hippies
Nude beaches
Occult groups
Prostitutes
Street gangs, motorcycle gangs
Street people, homeless shelters

Medical Settings and Medical Events

Death
Emergency rooms
Intensive care units
Pregnancy and abortion
Support groups for Alzheimer's caregivers

their culture (i.e., what people think, ponder, or believe) through many behaviors (e.g., speech and actions) in specific social contexts. Displays of behavior do not give meaning in themselves; rather, people must infer or learn how to "read" meaning.

The center of ethnographic research is to be able to move from what you hear or observe explicitly to what a situation actually means for insiders. Ethnography can be difficult because the meaning you come away with depends on possessing a detailed knowledge of the immediate situational context and the broader social–cultural context. Another complication is that

different insiders might not all share the same meaning of an event or situation.

For example, a college student is invited to a "kegger." The student will infer certain things. It will be an informal party with other student-aged people and there will be beer at the party. To arrive at this inference, the student draws on prior knowledge about the local college culture. Cultural knowledge can include symbols, songs, sayings, facts, ways of behaving, values, customs, and objects (e.g., telephones, newspapers, etc.). We learn the culture by watching television, listening to parents, observing others, and the like.

Cultural knowledge includes both explicit knowledge (i.e., what we know and talk about directly) and tacit knowledge (i.e., what we rarely acknowledge but know about). For example, explicit knowledge includes easily recognized information such as college students, alcohol consumption patterns, and the social event (e.g., a "kegger"). Most college students can describe what happens at the event based on rumor or past participation. *Tacit knowledge* includes the unspoken cultural norms: quantity and types of beverages consumed at the kegger, types of people to be present (e.g., no young children or elderly grandparents), and the border between appropriate and inappropriate behavior (e.g., sexual comments or contact). Another example of tacit knowledge is the proper distance to stand from other people when you talk with them. People are generally unaware that they use this norm. They feel unease or discomfort when the norm is violated but find it difficult to pinpoint the source of their discomfort.

Ethnographers describe the explicit and tacit cultural knowledge that members use in a field setting. They create detailed descriptions of what they observe in setting and their interactions with members. They then conduct a careful analysis of the descriptions. They do this by relying on their detailed knowledge of the local culture and by disassembling and reassembling various aspects of the description, and looking at it from divergent viewpoints.

Ethnomethodology is a distinct approach developed in the 1960s. It is a method for the study of everyday commonsense knowledge and interactions of people. Some people consider it to be a distinct field of study unto itself, but others see it as a subfield within sociology. It is a radical or extreme form of field research that merges interactionist theory, phenomenological philosophy, a social constructionist orientation, and specific methodological techniques.

Ethnomethodologists study everyday common sense by observing its creation and use in ongoing social interactions that occur in natural settings. They use a specialized, highly detailed analysis of micro-situations (e.g., transcripts of short conversations or videotapes of social interactions). Compared to other field research, they are more concerned about method. They argue that knowledge about the social world depends greatly on the particular method used to study it.

Ethnomethodology assumes that social meaning is fragile and fluid, not fixed, stable, or solid. People are constantly creating and re-creating social meaning in ongoing interactions. One technique ethnomethodologists use is conversation analysis. They examine audio recording and/or transcription of each utterance, including pauses and the context of speech. The purpose is to uncover the implicit and explicit ways people understand and misunderstand, communicate and miscommunicate with each another.

Ethnomethodologists assume that people "accomplish" a commonsense understanding by applying many tacit social–cultural rules and see social interaction as an ongoing process of reality construction. People use their cultural knowledge and clues from a social context to interpret everyday events in a fluid, changing process. The goal of ethnomethodology is to examine how people in ordinary, everyday settings apply tacit rules to make sense of social life (e.g., to know whether or not someone is joking, to decide how to respond to a question) and how they construct a shared social reality.

By examining ordinary micro-level social interaction in great detail—minute by minute, over and over—ethnomethodologists try to identify the informal rules people use to construct social reality and commonsense understanding. They study how people apply existing rules and create new rules. For example, they argue that standardized tests or survey interviews are social interactions that reveal a person's ability to pick up implicit clues and apply commonsense understanding rather than being objective measures of fixed factual information.

The Logic of Field Research

Field research is not easy to define. It is an orientation toward doing social research more than a fixed set of techniques that you apply.[3] Field research is based on the principle of naturalism. *Naturalism* is found in the study of other phenomena (e.g., oceans, animals, plants, etc.) and involves observing ordinary events in natural settings, rather than in contrived, invented, or researcher-created settings. This means you conduct research "in the field" or outside an office, laboratory, or classroom. Removed from the safety, security, and predictability of such settings makes field research more uncertain and risky.

In field research, you examine social meanings and try to grasp multiple perspectives in a natural social setting. To do this, you try to empathize with and enter into the subjective meanings and social reality of members. Yet, you also need to be an outside observer. Doing field research requires you to switch perspectives and to view a setting from multiple points of view simultaneously. This can be complex and difficult, requiring sophisticated cognitive and emotional skills. In field research, you obtain information using multiple techniques and must be a resourceful, talented individual with ingenuity and an ability to think quickly "on your feet" while you are in the field (see Expansion Box 11.1).

Most field research is conducted by a single individual who works alone, although small teams also have been effective. In most field research, you are directly involved in and part of the social world that you study. This makes your personal characteristics (e.g., physical appearance, mannerisms, demeanor, and emotional condition) relevant to the research task. Your direct involvement in the field can also have an emotional impact on you. Field research can be fun and exciting, but it can also disrupt your personal life, threaten your physical security, or unsettle your emotional well-being. More than other types of social research, it can reshape your friendships, family life, self-identity, and personal values.

EXPANSION BOX
11.1   What Do Field Researchers Do?

A field researcher does the following:

1. Observes ordinary events and everyday activities as they happen in natural settings, in addition to any unusual occurrences
2. Becomes directly involved with the people being studied and personally experiences the process of daily social life in the field setting
3. Acquires an insider's point of view while maintaining the analytic perspective or distance of an outsider
4. Uses a variety of techniques and social skills in a flexible manner as the situation demands
5. Produces data in the form of extensive written notes, as well as diagrams, maps, or pictures to provide very detailed descriptions
6. Sees events holistically (e.g., as a whole unit, not in pieces) and individually in their social context
7. Understands and develops empathy for members in a field setting, and does not just record "cold" objective facts
8. Notices both explicit (recognized, conscious, spoken) and tacit (less recognized, implicit, unspoken) aspects of culture
9. Observes ongoing social processes without upsetting, disrupting, or imposing an outside point of view
10. Copes with high levels of personal stress, uncertainty, ethical dilemmas, and ambiguity

CONDUCTING A FIELD RESEARCH STUDY

Field research is less standardized or structured than the quantitative research techniques you read about in previous chapters. This makes it essential for you to be well organized and prepared before you enter the field. It also means that the steps of conducting a study are not rigidly predetermined but only serve as an approximate guide or road map (see Expansion Box 11.2).

Step 1: Prepare to Enter the Field

As you prepare to conduct field research, you want to be flexible, get organized, rehearse skills and build background, defocus attention, and become self-aware.

Be Flexible.   Flexibility is a key advantage of field research. This lets you shift direction and follow new leads as they develop. A good field researcher can quickly recognize and seize opportunities, "play it by ear," and rapidly adjust to changing social situations. In field research, you do not start with a fixed set of methods to apply or explicit hypotheses to test. Rather, you pick a technique based on its value for providing you with information. In the beginning, you should anticipate having little control over the data and little direction. After you become socialized to the setting, you can begin to focus the inquiry and assert some control over the data.

Get Organized.   Human and personal factors can play a role in any study, but they are central to field research studies. Field research studies often begin with chance occurrences or a personal interest. Field researchers start with personal experiences, such as working at a job, having a hobby, being a sports team member or devout religious believer, confronting a family tragedy, or being a patient or an activist. Your personal biography and experiences can play a large role in initiating a field research study.

Rehearse Skills and Build Background.   To conduct field research, you need the skills of careful looking and listening, good short-term memory, and regular writing. Before you enter the field, you practice observing the ordinary details of social situations and writing them down. Disciplined attention to details and short-term memory can improve with practice.

EXPANSION BOX

11.2   Steps in Conducting Field Research

1. Prepare to enter the field: Be flexible, Be organized, Rehearse skills and build background, Defocus attention, Be self-aware.

2. Choose a field site and gain access: Select a site, Deal with gatekeepers, Enter and gain access, Assume a social role, Adopt a level of involvement, Build rapport.

3. Apply Strategies: Negotiate, Normalize research, Decide on disclosure, Focus and sample, Assume the attitude of strangeness, Cope with stress.

4. Maintain Relations in the Field: Adjust and adapt, Use charm and nurture trust, Perform small favors, Avoid conflicts, Appear interested, Be an acceptable incompetent.

5. Gather and record data: Absorb and experience, Watch and learn, Record the data.

6. Exit the field site.

Likewise, keeping a daily diary or personal journal is good practice for writing field notes. As with all social research, you will want to read the scholarly literature to learn concepts, potential pitfalls, data collection methods, and techniques for resolving conflicts. In addition, you may find reading diaries, novels, journalistic accounts, and autobiographies useful for gaining familiarity with a setting and preparing yourself emotionally for field situations.

Defocus Attention.   Field research begins with a general topic or interest, not specific hypotheses. You do not want to lock onto initial misconceptions; instead, you want to be very open to discovering new ideas. Finding the "right questions" to ask about a field setting often takes time. As you first enter the field, try to erase preconceptions about it and defocus. *Defocusing* is the opposite of focusing. To focus, you restrict what you observe, limit your attention, and narrow the boundaries of your awareness to a specific issue or question and what is immediately relevant to it. To defocus, you release restrictions on what to observe, remove limits on attention, and loosen the boundaries of your awareness. You try to move beyond your usual, comfortable social niche to experience as much as possible in the field setting, yet always doing so without betraying a primary commitment to being a researcher.

Become Self-Aware.   Another preparation for field research is self-knowledge. You need to know yourself and reflect on personal experiences. Such an "inner search" or look into yourself is not always easy, but it is very helpful for field research. You can expect anxiety, self-doubt, frustration, and uncertainty in the field. Especially in the beginning, you may feel that you are collecting the wrong data and may suffer from emotional turmoil, isolation, and confusion.

You may feel doubly marginal: you are an outsider in the field setting and you are removed from friends, family, and other researchers.[4]

Field research requires a great deal of time. A study may require hundreds, if not thousands, of hours in direct observation and interaction, over several months or years, with nearly daily visits to a field setting. The researcher's emotional makeup, personal biography, and cultural experiences are highly relevant in field research. This suggests you should be aware of your personal values, commitments, and inner conflicts (see Example Box 11.1). You want to know "who you are." Fieldwork can have a great impact on your identity and outlook. The field experience has transformed many researchers personally. They adopted new values, interests, and moral commitments, or changed their religion or political ideology.[5]

| | . | EXAMPLE BOX
Field Research at a Country and Western Bar

Eliasoph (1998) conducted field research on several groups in a California community to understand how Americans avoid political expression. One was a social club. Eliasoph describes herself as an "urban, bi-coastal, bespectacled, Jewish, Ph.D. candidate from a long line of communists, atheists, liberals, book-readers, ideologues, and arguers" (p. 270). The social club's world was very foreign to her. The social club, the Buffalos, centered on country and western music at a bar, the Silverado Club. She describes it:

The Silverado huddled on a vast, rutted parking lot on what was once wetlands and now was a truck stop, a mile and a half from Amargo's [town name] nuclear battleship station. Occasional gulleys of salt water cattails poked through the wide flat miles of paved malls and gas stations. Giant four-wheeled-drive vehicles filled the parking lot, making my miniature Honda look like a toy. . . . Inside the windowless Silverado, initial blinding darkness gave way to a huge Confederate flag pinned up behind the bandstand, the standard collection of neon beer signs and beer mirrors, men in cowboys hats,

cowboys shirts and jeans, women in curly perms and tiered flounces of lace or denim skirts, or jeans, and belts with their names embroidered in glitter on the back. (1998:92)

Eliasoph introduced herself as a student. During her two years of research, she endured smoke-filled rooms as well as expensive beer and bottled-water prices; attended a wedding and many dance lessons; and participated in countless conversations and heard many abusive sexist/racist jokes. She listened, asked questions, observed, and took notes in the bathroom. When she returned home after hours with club members, it was to a university crowd who had little understanding of the world she was studying. For them, witty conversation was central and being bored was to be avoided. The club members used more nonverbal than verbal communication and being bored, or sitting and doing nothing, was just fine. The research forced Eliasoph to reexamine her own views and tastes, which she had taken for granted.

Step 2. Choose a Site and Gain Access

You do not follow fixed steps to conduct a field research study; nonetheless, some common concerns appear in the early stages. These include selecting a site and gaining access to the site, entering the field, learning the ropes, and developing rapport with members in the field.

Most field research examines a particular setting. In the early stages of a study, you need to select a site, deal with gatekeepers, enter and gain access to the setting, assume a social role, adopt a level of involvement, and build rapport with members.

Select a Site.   You hear about field research being conducted on a setting or *field site*, but this is a misleading term. A field site is a context in which events or activities occur. It is a socially defined territory with flexible and shifting invisible boundaries. The case, activity, or group you wish to study may span across several physical sites. For example, a college football team may interact on the playing field, in the locker room, in a dormitory, at a training camp, or at a local hangout. The team's field site includes all five locations. Selecting a field site is an important decision, and you should take notes on the site selection processes.

Your research question should guide you in site selection. Keep three factors in mind as you choose a field research site: richness of data, unfamiliarity, and suitability.[6] Some sites provide richer data than others. Sites that present a web of social relations, a variety of activities, and diverse events over time provide richer, more interesting data. It is easier if you are a beginning field researcher to study an unfamiliar setting. Although you may want to stay with what is familiar and comfortable, it is easier to see cultural events and social relations with a researcher's "eye" in a new site. A novice field researcher is easily overwhelmed or intimidated by an entirely new social setting. As you "case out" possible field sites, you also want to consider practical issues such as your time and

skills, serious conflicts among people in the site, your personal characteristics and feelings, and access to parts of a site.

Your ascriptive characteristics (age, race, gender, stature) can limit access to some sites. For example, an African American researcher cannot hope to study the Ku Klux Klan or neo-Nazis, although some researchers have successfully crossed ascriptive lines. In addition, a team with an "insider" (with local knowledge or one kind of ascriptive characteristic) and the "outsider" researcher can work together as a team.[7]

Gaining physical access to a site can be an issue. Field sites are on a continuum. Open and public areas (e.g., public restaurants, airport waiting areas, etc.) are at one end and closed, private settings (e.g., corporate inner offices, private clubs, activities in a person's home, etc.) are at the other. You may find that you are not welcome on the site, or face legal and political barriers to access. Laws and regulations in institutions (e.g., public schools, hospitals, prisons, etc.) can also restrict access.

Deal with Gatekeepers.   Most field sites have *gatekeepers*. They are people with the formal or informal authority to control access to a site.[8] The gatekeeper can be the thug on the corner, an administrator of a hospital, or the owner of a business. Informal public areas (e.g., sidewalks, public waiting rooms, etc.) rarely have gatekeepers, but formal organizations have authorities from whom you must obtain explicit permission. A gatekeeper is someone that members in the field obey, whether or not he or she has an official title. It may take time for you to discover who the gatekeeper is (see Example Box 11.2). You should expect to negotiate with gatekeepers and bargain for access.

It is ethically and politically astute to call on gatekeepers. Gatekeepers may not appreciate the need for conceptual distance or ethical balance. You will need to set nonnegotiable limits to protect research integrity. If a gatekeeper imposes many restrictions initially, often you can reopen negotiations later. Gatekeepers may forget their initial demands as trust develops.

11.2 Gatekeepers and Access

In his study of a crack-dealing gang, the Black Kings, in Chicago's low-income housing projects, Venkatesh (2008) had difficulty in gaining access. He describes in detail how he gained access and luckily came upon the sympathetic gang leader, J.T., who was the critical gatekeeper for both the gang's activities and the housing project. A graduate student of South Asian ancestry from middle-class California suburbs, Venkatesh naïvely entered the projects with a pile of survey questionnaires. He was not prepared for the extreme poverty, perils, and everyday reality of life in the dilapidated high-rise housing projects. Soon after he entered a building, a gang of menacing young men accosted him in a dark, dirty, urine-smelling stairwell. They mistook him for a Mexican-American (and member of rival gang, Latin Kings) and appeared ready to harm him, until J.T. arrived. As Venkatesh (2008:17-19) reports,

> *J.T. shot the young man a look, then turned to me. "You're not from Chicago," he said. "You should really not be walking through the projects. People get hurt."*

> *J.T. started tossing questions at me. . . . I spent most of the night sitting on the cold steps, trying to avoid protruding shards of metal. I would have liked to sleep also, but I was too nervous.*

The next afternoon Venkatesh returned with a six-pack of beer.

> *"Beer?" I said, tossing him a bottle. "You said I should hang out with folks if I want to know what their life was like." J.T. didn't answer. A few of the guys burst out laughing in disbelief. "He's crazy, I told you!" said one. "Nigger thinks he's going to hang out with us! I still think he's a Latin King." Finally J.T. spoke up. "All right, the brother wants to hang out," he said, unfazed. "Let him hang out." (p. 23)*

In gaining access to the site, Venkatesh made many missteps and mistakes, confronted serious physical danger, overcame uncertainty and fear, and had some fantastic good luck, particularly with the gatekeeper.

Many gatekeepers do not care about the findings, except insofar as they might provide evidence for someone to criticize them.

Dealing with gatekeepers is a recurrent issue as you enter new levels or areas of a field site. In addition, a gatekeeper can shape the direction of research. In some sites, gatekeeper approval creates a stigma that inhibits the cooperation of members. For example, prisoners may not be cooperative if they know that the prison warden gave approval to the researcher.

Enter and Gain Access. Entering and gaining access to a field site requires commonsense judgment and social skills. Most field sites have different levels or areas, and entry can be an issue for each. Access is more analogous to peeling away the layers of an onion than to opening a door. Moreover, bargains and promises of entry may not remain stable over time. You should have fallback plans or you may have to return later for renegotiation. Because your specific research focus may not emerge until later in the research process or may change, try not to get locked into rigid specifics by gatekeepers.

Assume a Social Role. You play many social roles in daily life—daughter/son, student, customer, sports fan—and maintain social relations with others. You choose some roles and others are given to you. Few of us have a choice but to occupy the role of son or daughter. Some roles are formal (e.g., bank teller, police chief, etc.); others are informal (flirt, elder statesperson, buddy, etc.). Every day you might switch roles, play multiple roles, and occupy a role in a particular way.

You occupy two kinds of roles in the field site; a social role (e.g., customer, patient, employee) and a researcher role (to be discussed in the next section). You may need to negotiate which preexisting social role field site members assign to you early in field site interactions. The role others assign to you and how you perform it can influence your access and success in developing trust and cooperation in the field. Some roles provide you with greater access than others. In better roles, you can observe and interact with all members, are free to move around, and can balance the requirements of researcher and member. At times, you might be able to introduce a new role or modify an existing one.

Your ascriptive features and physical appearance can restrict the social roles you can occupy. You can change some aspects of your appearance, such as dress or hairstyle, but not the ascriptive features such as age, race, gender, and attractiveness. Nevertheless, such factors may affect your ability to gain access or restrict roles available to you. For example, Gurney (1985) reported that being a female in a male-dominated setting required extra negotiations and "hassles." Nevertheless, her gender provided insights and created situations that would have been absent with a male researcher.

Almost any role will limit access to some parts of a field site. For example, the role of a bartender in a tavern limits knowledge of intimate customer behavior or presence at customer gatherings in other locations. You want to take care when choosing a role (or having it assigned) but should recognize that all roles involve tradeoffs.

Most social settings contain cliques, informal groups, hierarchies, and rivalries. A role can help you gain acceptance into or exclude you from a clique. It might help others treat you as a person in authority or as an underling. You need to be aware that by adopting a role, you may be forming allies and enemies who can assist or limit research.

Danger and high risk are features of some settings (e.g., police work, violent criminal gangs). You should be aware of risks to safety, assess the risks, and then decide what you are willing to do. Some observers argue that a field researcher must share in the risks and danger of a setting to understand it and its members. In addition to physical injury, you could face legal or financial risks based on actions in the field. Research into some settings (e.g., the severely mentally ill, trauma centers, war zones) may create emotional-psychological discomfort and damage a sense of inner well-being.

Adopt a Level of Involvement. Researcher roles are on a continuum and vary by degree of involvement with members in the field. At one end is a detached outsider observer; the opposite extreme is an intimately involved insider participant. Your level of involvement will vary by negotiations with members, specifics of the field setting, your personal comfort level, and your social role in the field site. You may move from outsider to insider levels with time in the field. Each level has its advantages and disadvantages.

Roles at the outsider end of the continuum reduce the time needed for acceptance, make overrapport less an issue, facilitate detachment that might help some members open up, and insulate your self-identity. Some field researchers reject the outsider observer role and argue that you can only acquire an understanding of members by engaging them and participating with them in the field setting.

Roles at the insider end of the continuum facilitate empathy and sharing of a member's lived experience. These roles help you to experience fully the intimate social world of a member. Nevertheless, a lack of distance from or overinvolvement with members has risks. Readers may question your study findings, gathering data is more difficult, their impact on the self can be dramatic, and you may lack the social distance required for serious data analysis.

Build Rapport.   You want to begin to build rapport with members as soon as you enter the field. At one level, it simply means getting along with members and takes time, tenacity, and openness. To do this, you forge a friendly relationship, share the same language, and learn to laugh and cry with members. It is a step toward obtaining an understanding of members and moving beyond understanding toward empathy—that is, seeing events from another's perspective.

It is not always easy to build rapport. The social world is not all in harmony, with warm, friendly, trusting people. A field site may contain fear, tension, and conflict. Members may be unpleasant, untrustworthy, or untruthful; they may do things that disturb or disgust you. You should prepare yourself for a range of events and relationships. You may find, however, that it is impossible to penetrate a setting or get really close to members. Settings where cooperation, sympathy, and collaboration are impossible require different techniques. Also, you accept what you hear or see at face value, but without being gullible.[9]

Step 3. Apply Strategies

Once in a field site, you will soon need to apply a range of strategies: negotiate, decide on how much to disclose, use personal charm and nurture social trust, sample and focus, and use the attitude of strangeness.

Negotiate.   You will negotiate and form new social relations throughout the fieldwork process.[10] You need to negotiate with members until you establish a stable relationship. It is part of the process as you gain access, build trust, obtain information, and contain resistance or hostility. Expect to negotiate and explain what you are doing over and over again in the field. Marginalized people, those engaged in illegal or illicit activities, and elites often require more intense negotiations to open access. For example, to gain access to deviant subcultures,

field researchers have used contacts from the researcher's private life, gone to social welfare or law enforcement agencies, advertised for volunteers, offered a service (e.g., counseling) in exchange for access, or gone to a location where deviants hang out and joined a group.

Normalize Research.   As a field researcher, you not only observe members in the field but the members are observing you as well. Field research is not an activity of the isolated researcher alone; rather, everyone in the field setting together creates a research outcome. In overt field research, many members will be uncomfortable at first with the presence of a researcher. Few may know about field research, and they may not distinguish among sociologists, psychologists, counselors, and social workers. They may see you as an outside critic, dangerous spy, a savior, or all-knowing expert.

It is important for you to ***normalize social research***—that is, help members to redefine social research from something unknown and threatening into something normal and acceptable. To do this, you might present your own biography, explain field research a little at a time, appear nonthreatening, or accept minor deviance in the setting (e.g., minor violations of official rules). You can normalize research by explaining it in terms members understand. Sometimes, members' excitement about being written up in a book is useful.

Decide on Disclosure.   In all social research, you need to decide how much to reveal to participants about yourself and the study. In field research, disclosing your personal life, hobbies, interests, and background can build trust and close relationships with members. In the process, you may lose privacy and have to direct the focus to events in the field. Disclosure ranges on a continuum. At one end is covert research, in which members are unaware that research is taking place. At the opposite end is a situation in which everyone knows all the specifics of the study. The degree and timing of disclosure depends on your judgment and particulars in the setting. Disclosure may unfold over time, as you feel more comfortable and secure.

You will want to disclose the study to gatekeepers and others unless there is a very good reason for not doing so. Even in these cases, you may disclose that you are a researcher, but you may pose as one who appears to be submissive, harmless, and interested in nonthreatening issues.

People explicitly and implicitly present themselves to others. We display who we are—the type of person we are or would like to be—through our physical appearance, what we say, and how we act. The presentation of self sends a symbolic message. It may be, "I'm a serious, hard-working student," "I'm a warm and caring person," "I'm a cool jock," or "I'm a rebel and party animal." Many selves are possible, and presentations of selves can differ depending on the occasion.

In field research, you want to be highly conscious of the presentation of self. For example, how should you dress in the field? The best guide is to respect both yourself and the members in the field. It is difficult to present a highly deceptive front or to present yourself in a way that deviates sharply from who you are ordinarily. Do not overdress in a manner that offends or stands out. Copying the dress of the people you study is not always necessary. A professor who studies street people does not have to dress or act like one; dressing and acting informally is sufficient. Likewise, more formal dress and professional demeanor are usually required when studying corporate executives or top officials.

Focus and Sample.   Once in the field, you first acquire a general picture. Only then can you gradually focus on a few specific issues (see Figure 11.2). You can only decide on specific research questions after experiencing the field firsthand. At first, everything may appear to be relevant; later, you can selectively focus your attention on specific questions and themes.

FIGURE 11.2   Focusing in Field Research

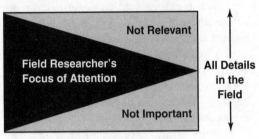

Field research sampling differs from that in survey research, although sometimes both use snowball sampling (you read about snowball sampling in Chapter 6). You may also wish to sample times, situations, types of events, locations, types of people, or contexts of interest. To sample times, observe a setting at various times of the day and days of the week. It is often best to overlap when sampling (e.g., to have sampling times from 7:00 A.M. to 9:00 A.M., from 8:00 A.M. to 10:00 A.M., from 9:00 A.M. to 11:00 A.M., etc.). You can sample locations by sitting or standing in different places to get a better sense of the whole site. For example, the peer-to-peer behavior of schoolteachers usually occurs in a faculty lounge, but it also occurs at a local bar or café where teachers gather or in a classroom temporarily used for a teacher meeting. To sample people, you want to focus attention or direct your interaction to different kinds of people (old-timers and newcomers, old and young, males and females, leaders and followers). As you identify the range of types of people in a field site, including people with diverse outlooks, you will want to interact with and learn about all the types.

You can also sample events or activities. For example, you might sample three kinds of events: routine, special, and unanticipated. Routine events (e.g., opening up a store for business) happen every day. You should not consider them unimportant simply because they are routine, but do not ignore them. Special events (e.g., annual office party) are announced and planned. They focus member attention and reveal aspects of social life not otherwise visible. Unanticipated events just happen to occur while you are present (e.g., unsupervised workers when the manager gets sick and cannot oversee workers at a store for a day). Try to pay attention and notice the full range of events and reflect on their meaning.

Assume the Attitude of Strangeness. It is hard to recognize what you are very close to. The everyday world you inhabit contains thousands of details. If you pay attention to everything all the time, you would suffer from severe information overload. What you do naturally is to ignore much of what is around you, engage in habitual thinking, and notice what stands out or is new. Unfortunately, this means you cease to see what is familiar to you and to treat your own way of living as being natural or normal. This "blindness" to what is familiar makes field research in familiar surroundings especially difficult.

By studying different cultures or subcultures, you will encounter assumptions and views about what is important or how to accomplish tasks that are divergent from what you consider normal or natural. A confrontation of cultures, or mini culture shock, can be a powerful analytic technique. Through it, you will find it easier to recognize assumptions or cultural elements that are otherwise invisible to you.

Field researchers use a version of the confrontation of cultures, the ***attitude of strangeness***, to gain these benefits. The attitude tells you to notice ordinary details and look at them through the eyes of a stranger. It also helps you to overcome the boredom of observing ordinary details. In addition, it reveals aspects of a setting that even field site members are not consciously aware.

Here is a simple example of how the attitude of strangeness reveals assumptions in a custom you may take for granted. How do you respond when someone gives you a gift? Do you

say "thank you" and praise the gift? Do you say the gift is unnecessary? This is not "natural" but a cultural custom. The attitude of strangeness can make the tacit culture visible—for example, that gift givers expect to hear "thank you" and "the gift is nice." They may feel offended or even become upset otherwise. Think of the reaction if you said nothing at all, or remarked, "Is that all?" when you received the gift.

In field research, you want to adopt both the attitude of strangeness and an insider's point of view. A stranger sees action or events as distinct or specific social processes, whereas to the insider, the same events or actions are unquestioned and seem natural. You need both views, as well as an ability to swiftly switch back and forth. The attitude of strangeness also encourages you to reconsider your own social world. Immersion in a different setting breaks old habits of thought and action. You may find reflection and introspection easier and more intense when encountering the unfamiliar, whether it is a different culture or a familiar culture seen through a stranger's eyes.

Cope with Stress. Fieldwork can be highly rewarding, exciting, and fulfilling, but it also can be difficult. New field researchers frequently face embarrassment, experience discomfort, and are overwhelmed by the fast flow of details in the field. For example, in her study of U.S. relocation camps for Japanese Americans during World War II, respected field researcher Rosalie Wax (1971) reported that she endured the discomfort of 120-degree Fahrenheit temperatures, filthy and dilapidated living conditions, dysentery, and mosquitoes. She felt isolated, she cried a lot, and she gained 30 pounds from compulsive eating. After months in the field, she thought she was a total failure; she was distrusted by members and got into fights with the camp administration.

Maintaining a "marginal" status in any social setting is stressful. In field research, you are often an outsider who is not fully involved, especially when you study a setting full of intense feelings (e.g., political campaigns, religious conversions, etc.). The loneliness and isolation of fieldwork may combine with a desire to develop rapport and empathy. This can cause overinvolvement. You may *go native* and abandon a professional researcher role to become a full member. Or you may feel guilt about learning intimate details as members drop their guard and overidentify with members.

A degree of emotional stress is inevitable in all field research. Instead of suppressing emotional responses, remain sensitive to your emotional reactions. Some ways to help you cope in the field include keeping a personal diary, emotional journal, or written record of inner feelings, or having a few sympathetic people outside the field site with whom you can confide.

Step 4. Maintaining Relations in the Field

There are many diverse strategies for maintaining relations in the field site. These include a need to adjust and adapt, use charm and nurture trust, perform small favors, avoid conflicts, appear interested, and become an acceptable incompetent.

Adjust and Adapt.   With time in the field site, you can develop and modify social relationships. Members who are cool at first may warm up later. Or, members who put on a front of initial friendliness may show fears and suspicions later. You are in a delicate position. Early in a study, when you are not yet fully aware of all in a field site, you should avoid rushing to form close relationships. This is because you do not yet have a full picture of the field site and members, and circumstances may change. On the other hand, if you develop close friends early on, you may develop vital allies in the field who can defend your presence to others and help you gain access.

As a field researcher, you need to monitor continuously how your actions or appearance affects members. For example, a physically attractive researcher who interacts with members of the opposite sex may encounter crushes, flirting, and jealousy. He or she develops an awareness of these field relations and learns to manage them.

In addition to developing social relationships, you must be capable of breaking off relationships as well. You may need to break off ties with one member to forge ties with others or to explore other aspects of the field site. As with the end of any friendly relationship, the emotional pain of social withdrawal can have an impact on you and on the member who you befriended. In field research, you must learn to balance social sensitivity and your research goals.

Use Charm and Nurture Trust.   To build rapport with members in a field site, you need social skills and personal charm. Trust, friendly feelings, and being liked by others can facilitate communication, and communication will help you to better understand the inner feelings of others. There is no magical way to do this. Showing a genuine concern for and an interest in others, being honest, and sharing your feelings can be effective. Yet, they are not foolproof. It depends on the specific setting and members. Your demeanor should always be nonthreatening. If possible, be warm and friendly, it can open many doors.

Many factors affect trust and rapport—how you present yourself; your role in the field; and the events that encourage, limit, or make achieving trust impossible. You do not gain trust once; it is a continuous process. You built up trust over time through many social nuances (e.g., sharing of personal experiences, storytelling, gestures, hints, facial expressions). Social trust is constantly re-created and needs regular "care and feeding." It is much easier to lose trust after you have built it up than to gain it in the first place.

Establishing trust is important, but it does not ensure that members will reveal all information to you. It may be limited to specific areas. For example, you might build up trust with someone regarding financial matters but not trust about intimate romantic behaviors, or vice versa. You may need to build trust anew in each area of inquiry.

You may wish to establish trust and rapport with everyone in a field site, but find that some members are not open or cooperative. Others may express an uncooperative attitude, hostility, or an overt unwillingness to participate. Do not expect to gain the cooperation of everyone. Sometimes the best you can hope for is a lukewarm relationship that only develops after prolonged persistence.

Rapport can help you to understand members, and understanding is a precondition for greater depth and analysis. It slowly develops in the field as you overcome an initial bewilderment with a new system of social meaning. Once you attain an understanding of the member's point of view, your next step is to learn how to think and act from the member's perspective. This is empathy, or adopting another's perspective. Empathy does not necessarily mean sympathy, agreement, or approval; it means being able to see and feel things as another does. Rapport helps create understanding and ultimately empathy, and empathy, in turn, will facilitate greater rapport.

Perform Small Favors. Exchange relationships develop in the field, in which small tokens or favors, including deference and respect, are exchanged. You may gain acceptance by helping out in small ways, offering to "lend a hand," running a quick errand, or doing "acts of kindness" expecting nothing in return. You may offer small favors but not burden members by asking for return favors. In his study of informal sidewalk vendors, Duneier (1999) used the small favor of watching tables for vendors when they have to leave a short time, such as going to the bathroom.

As you and members share more experiences and see each other repeatedly, members will recall the favors and may reciprocate by allowing you greater access. They may feel as if they "owe" you similar consideration and acts of kindness.

Avoid Conflicts. Fights, conflicts, and disagreements can erupt in the field, or you may study groups that adopt opposing positions. In such situations, you will feel pressure to take sides. You may be "tested" to see whether a side can trust you. In such occasions, you will want to stay on the neutral sidelines and walk a tightrope between opposing sides if you can. Once you align with one side, you will be cut off from access to the other side. In addition, after you align with one side, you will be seeing the situation only from one side's point of view.

Appear Interested. You will want to maintain an *appearance of interest* in the field. This simply means that you outwardly appear to be interested in and involved with field events by your statements and behaviors (e.g., facial expression, going for coffee, organizing a party, etc.) even if you are not truly interested. Once members see you acting bored or distracted, it can weaken field relationships. When you appear uninterested in field site activities, you are sending a message that the members are dull, boring people and you do not want to be there. This is hardly a way to build trust, intimacy, and strong social bonds. Putting up a temporary front of involvement is a common small deception you probably use in daily life because it is part of the social norm of being polite.

Of course, selective inattention (i.e., not staring or appearing not to notice) is also part of acting polite. If someone makes a social mistake (e.g., accidentally uses an incorrect word, passes gas, etc.), the polite thing to do is to ignore it. Selective inattention also works in field research. If you are alert, it gives you an opportunity to casually eavesdrop on conversations or observe events that are not meant to be known or seen by the public.

Be the Acceptable Incompetent. As a researcher, you are in the field to learn, not to be an expert. Depending on the setting, you want to be a friendly but somewhat naïve outsider, an *acceptable incompetent*. You want to present yourself as someone who is interested in learning about the social life of the field, but who is only partially competent (skilled or knowledgeable) in the setting. It is a strategy for encouraging members to accept you as a nonthreatening person. They will view you as someone who they need to guide or teach.

You probably know little about a specific field site or the local culture at first, and members might see you as a bit of a fool who can be easily hoodwinked or shortchanged. You might be the butt of jokes for your lack of adeptness in the setting. Do not let your ego get in the way; instead, use this social perception as a way to learn more about the field site and its members. Even when you become knowledgeable, you can display less than full information. This will help you to draw out a member's knowledge. In the field site, members are the experts and you should defer to their expertise. If you know more about something that they are talking about than they do, keep silent. Remember, you are primarily in the field to listen and learn from members, not to instruct, correct, or preach to them. Of course, you do not want to overdo this and appear so ignorant that they do not take you seriously.

Step 5. Gather and Record Data

This section looks at how to get good qualitative field data. Field data are what you experience, remember, and record in field notes.

Absorb and Experience.   You, as the researcher, are the measurement instrument for field data. As Lofland et al. (2006:3) observed, "In subjecting him- or herself to the lives of others and living and feeling those lives along with them, the researcher becomes the primary instrument or medium through which research is conducted." This has two implications. First, it puts pressure on you to be alert and sensitive to what happens in the field. You must be highly disciplined about recording data. Second, it has personal consequences. Doing research in the field involves your social relationships and personal feelings.

Your own subjective insights and feelings are "experiential data." Data in field research are not just "out there" in what other people say or do. The data are also your personal, subjective experiences in the field site. The experiences are valuable in themselves and for helping you to interpret events.

Instead of being completely neutral or objective and eliminating all your personal reactions to get good data, in field research your feelings are part of the data. Field research can heighten awareness of personal feelings. For example, you might be unaware of personal feelings about nudity until you go to a nudist colony for a study, or you have not thought about your feelings concerning personal possessions until you study a field site where others regularly "borrow" items from you. Your surprise, indignation, or questioning can become an opportunity for reflection and insight.

Watch and Listen.   A great deal of what you do in the field is to pay close attention, watch, and listen carefully. You use all senses, noticing what you can see, hear, smell, taste, or touch. You try to absorb all sources of information and scrutinize the physical setting so you can fully capture its atmosphere. As you observe ask yourself, What is the color of the floor, walls, and ceiling? How large is a room? Where are the windows and doors? How is the furniture arranged, and what is its condition (e.g., new or old, dirty or clean)? What type of lighting is there? Are there signs, paintings, or plants? What are the sounds or smells?

Why should you bother with such minor details? Think about it. You may have noticed that stores and restaurants often plan lighting, colors, and piped-in music to create a certain atmosphere. Maybe you know that used-car salespeople spray a new-car scent into cars. Perhaps you noticed bakeries in shopping malls intentionally send out the odor of freshly made cookies. Many realtors advise a fresh coat of paint and shampooing carpets to help sell a house. Many subtle, unconscious signals combine to influence human emotions and behavior.

If you are not noticing and recording such details of the field site, you will not be capturing everything that is affecting what occurs in a field site.

Observing in field research can be monotonous, tedious work. You need patience and an ability to concentrate on the particulars of everyday life. To understand a setting, the accumulated mountains of mundane, trivial, everyday minutia matter. Most people tend to overlook the constant flow of details, but to become a good field researcher you should notice and learn from it.

In addition to noticing physical surroundings, observe people and their actions, noting each person's observable physical characteristics: age, sex, race, and stature. This is because people generally interact differently depending on whether another person is 18, 40, or 70 years old; male or female; White or non-White; short and frail or tall, heavyset, and muscular. When noting such characteristics, include yourself. For example, an attitude of strangeness heightens sensitivity to a group's racial composition. Someone who ignores the racial composition of a group in a public setting that is 100 percent White in a multiracial society because he or she too is White is being blind to a potentially important dimension of that public setting.

Not everything you notice in the field will be significant, but you want to record all details because they could reveal something of significance. You may not know what is significant until later, and it is better to err by including everything than to ignore potentially significant details. For example, "The tall, White muscular 19-year-old male in a torn t-shirt and dirty jeans sprinted into the brightly lit room just as the short, overweight light-skinned Black woman in her sixties who was professionally dressed eased into a battered chair" says much more than "One person entered, another sat down."

You should note aspects of a person's physical appearance, such as neatness, dress, and hairstyle because they convey information that may influence social interactions. People spend a great deal of time and money selecting clothes, styling and combing hair, grooming with makeup, shaving, ironing clothes, and using deodorant or perfumes. These are part of their presentation of self. Even people who do not groom, shave, or wear deodorant present themselves and send messages by their appearance. No one dresses or looks "normal," and such statements suggest that you are not being sensitive to social signals.

In addition to appearance, actions can have significance. You want to notice where people sit or stand, the pace at which they walk, and their nonverbal communication. People express social information, feelings, and attitudes through nonverbal communication. These include gestures, facial expressions, and how one stands or sits (standing stiffly, sitting in a slouched position, etc.). People express relationships by how they position themselves in a group and the use of eye contact. You may read social communication by noting who stands close together, looks relaxed, and makes eye contact.

You also want to notice the context in which events occur: Who was present? Who just arrived or left the scene? Was the room hot and stuffy? Such details can help you assign meaning and understand why an event occurred. If you fail to notice details, they are lost, as is a full understanding of the event.

Serendipity and chance encounters can be important in field research. Many times, you do not know the relevance of what you are observing until later. This has two implications. First, keen observation and excellent notes are important at all times, even when it seems that "nothing is happening." Second, "wait time" and regularly reviewing field notes are important. In field research, you will spend a lot of time "waiting." Novice field researchers get frustrated with the amount of time they seem to "waste." It may be waiting for other people or waiting for events to occur. What novices need to learn is that "wait time" is a critical aspect of field research and can be valuable.

You need to learn the rhythms of the setting, learn to operate on other people's schedules, and learn to observe how events occur within the flow of time. "Wait time" does not need to be wasted time. It is time for reflection, for observing details, for nurturing social relations, for building rapport, and for becoming a familiar sight in the field setting. "Wait time" also displays your commitment and seriousness. Perhaps you are impatient to get in, do some research, finish it up, and get on with your "real life." For the people in the field site, this is their real lives. A good field researcher learns to subordinate personal desires and wants to the demands of life in the field site.

When in the field you will want to listen carefully to phrases, accents, and incorrect grammar. Listen to what people say as well as how they say it and what they do not state explicitly but imply. For example, people often use phrases such as "you know" or "of course" or "et cetera." You want to learn the meaning behind such phrases. You can try to hear everything, but listening is difficult when many conversations occur at once or when eavesdropping. Luckily, significant events and themes usually recur.

People who interact with each other over time often develop an insider's set of shared symbols and terminology. They will create new words or assign new meanings to ordinary words. New words or meanings arise from specific shared events, assumptions, or relationships. Knowing and using the language can signal membership in a distinct subculture.

In the field, you should begin with the premise that some words and symbols from your world might have different meanings for the people you are studying. Try to stay attuned to new words and the use of words in ways other than those with which you are familiar. They can be important source of insights and are a form of field data.

Record the Data. Information overload is common in field research. Doing field research and recording data can stretch a person's abilities, not matter how skilled he or she might be. The bulk of field research data are in the form of field notes. Full field notes can contain maps, diagrams, photographs, interviews, tape recordings, videotapes, memos, objects from the field, notes jotted in the field, and detailed notes you wrote away from the field. You can expect to fill many notebooks or the equivalent in computer memory. It is not unusual to devote as much or more time writing notes than being in the field site. Some researchers produce 40 single-spaced pages of notes for three hours of observation. With practice, you should produce several pages of notes for each hour in the field.

Writing field notes can be boring, tedious work that requires perseverance and self-discipline. Good field notes will contain extensive descriptive detail drawn from memory. If possible, always write notes before the day's thoughts and excitement begin to fade, without retelling events to other people. Pouring fresh memories into the notes with an intense immediacy often triggers an emotional release and it stimulates insightful reflection. At times, especially after a long, tiring day, writing may feel more like painful drudgery. Begin by allocating about a half hour to writing your field notes for each hour you spend in the field site.

You must keep notes neat and organized. They contain valuable information and you will return to them over and again. Once written, the notes are private. You should treat them with care and protect confidentiality. People in the field site have a right to remain anonymous. For this reason, most researchers use pseudonyms (false names) in the field notes. Field notes may be of interest to hostile parties, blackmailers, or legal officials. As a result, some researchers even write field notes in code.

Your state of mind, level of attention, and conditions in the field affect note taking. Begin with relatively short one- to three-hour periods in the field before writing notes.

Types of Field Notes. Field researchers take notes in many ways.[11] The recommendations here (also see Expansion Box 11.3) are suggestions. Full field notes have several types. Here I describe

11.3 EXPANSION BOX
Recommendations for Taking Field Notes

1. Record notes as soon as possible after each period in the field, and do not talk with others until observations are recorded.

2. Begin the record of each field visit with a new page, with the date and time noted.

3. Use jotted notes only as a temporary memory aid, with key words or terms, or the first and last things said.

4. Use wide margins to make it easy to add to notes at any time. Go back and add to the notes if you remember something later.

5. Plan to type notes and keep each level of notes separate so it will be easy to go back to them later.

6. Record events in the order in which they occurred, and note how long they last (e.g., a 15-minute wait, a one-hour ride).

7. Make notes as concrete, complete, and comprehensible as possible.

8. Use frequent paragraphs and quotation marks. Exact recall of phrases is best, with double quotes; use single quotes for paraphrasing.

9. Record small talk or routines that do not appear to be significant at the time; they may become important later.

10. "Let your feelings flow" and write quickly without worrying about spelling or "wild ideas." Assume that no one else will see the notes, but use pseudonyms.

11. Never substitute tape recordings completely for field notes.

12. Include diagrams or maps of the setting, and outline your own movements and those of others during the period of observation.

13. Include your own words and behavior in the notes. Also record emotional feelings and private thoughts in a separate section.

14. Avoid evaluative summarizing words. Instead of "The sink looked disgusting," say, "The sink was rust-stained and looked as if it had not been cleaned in a long time. Pieces of food and dirty dishes looked as if they had been piled in it for several days."

15. Reread notes periodically and record ideas generated by the rereading.

16. Always make one or more backup copies, keep them in a locked location, and store the copies in different places in case of fire.

---

six types: jotted, direct observation, inferences, analytic, personal journal, and interview notes. See Figure 11.3 for an example of the four major types. You usually will want to keep all the notes for an observation period together and to distinguish various types of notes by separate pages. Some researchers include inference notes with direct observation notes, but distinguish them by a visible device such as brackets or colored ink. The quantity of notes varies across types. For example, six hours in the field might result in one page of jotted notes, 40 pages of direct observation, five pages of researcher inference, and two pages total for methodological, theoretical, and personal notes.

1. *Jotted Notes.* It is nearly impossible to take good notes in the field. Even a known observer in a public setting looks strange when furiously writing. More important, when looking down and writing, you cannot see and hear what is happening. The attention you give to note writing reduces attention to observation, which is where it belongs. The specific setting will determine whether you can take notes in the field. You may be able to write, and members

FIGURE 11.3   Types of Field Notes

Direct Observation	Inference	Analytic	Personal Journal
Sunday, October 4. Kay's Kafe 3:00 pm. Large White male in mid-40s, overweight, enters. He wears worn brown suit. He is alone; sits at booth #2. Kay comes by, asks, "What'll it be?" Man says, "Coffee, black for now." She leaves and he lights cigarette and reads menu. 3:15 pm. Kay turns on radio.	Kay seems friendly today, humming. She becomes solemn and watchful. I think she puts on the radio when nervous.	Women are afraid of men who come in alone since the robbery.	It is raining. I am feeling comfortable with Kay but am bored today.

may expect it, or you may have to be secretive (e.g., go to the restroom).

The only notes you write in the field are *jotted notes*. They are very short memory triggers such as words, phrases, or drawings. You take them inconspicuously, perhaps scribbling on a convenient item (e.g., napkin, matchbook). Later you will incorporate them into your direct observation notes. They are never a substitute for the direct observation notes.

2. *Direct Observation Notes.* The primary source of field data are **direct observation notes**. You should write them immediately after leaving the field. You can add to them later. Organize the notes chronologically, and put the date, time, and location on each entry. These notes serve as a detailed description of everything you heard and saw in concrete, specific terms. To the extent possible, they are an exact recording of the particular words, phrases, or actions.

Your memory improves with practice and you will find that you can soon remember exact phrases. You should write verbatim statements with double quote marks to distinguish them from paraphrases. You should record dialogue accessories (nonverbal communication, props, tone, speed, volume, gestures) as well. Record what was actually said and do not clean it up; include ungrammatical speech, slang, and misstatements (e.g., write, "Uh, I'm goin' home, Sal," not "I am going home, Sally").

Your notes should have specific, concrete details, not summaries. For example, instead of "We talked about sports," write "Anthony argued with Sam and Jason. He said that the Cubs would win next week because they traded for a new shortstop, Chiappetta. He also said that the team was better than the Mets, who he thought had inferior infielders. He cited last week's game where the Cubs won against Boston by 8 to 3." When writing about an encounter or conversation, include details of the context—who was present, what happened, where did it occur, exactly when, and under what circumstances. Novice researchers may say they do not take notes because "nothing important happened." An experienced researcher knows even when "nothing happened" you can record a lot. For example, members may express feelings and organize experience into folk categories even in trivial conversations.

3. *Inference Notes.* You want to listen closely to what people say in the field so you can "climb into their skin" or "walk in their shoes." This involves a three-step process: (1) listen without applying analytical categories; (2) compare what you hear now to what you heard at other times and to what others say; and (3) apply your interpretation to infer what it means. In ordinary interaction, you do all three steps simultaneously and jump quickly to your own inferences. In field research, you want to look and listen without inferring or imposing an interpretation at first, and to put your observations without inferences into your direct observation field notes.

Recording observations without inferences does not mean you stop inferring. Rather, you record inferences in a separate section that you key to the direct observations. This separation has advantages. Although you may talk about social relationships, emotions, or the meanings of human actions, you never see those relations, emotions, or meaning directly. Instead, you infer them from the specific physical actions you see and words you hear. You apply background cultural knowledge, clues from the context, and an awareness of what occurred earlier to infer relations, emotions, or meanings. For example, you never see anger. You observe specific actions (red face, loud voice, wild gestures, obscenities, clenched hand) and use them to draw inferences (the person is angry).

We are all constantly inferring social meaning based on what we see and hear, but we do not always do so correctly. For example, my 5-year-old niece visited me and accompanied me to a store to buy a kite. The clerk at the cash register smiled and asked her whether she and her "Daddy" (looking at me) were going to fly the kite that day. The clerk had observed our interaction, then inferred a father/daughter, not an uncle/niece relationship. What she saw and heard was a male adult and a female child interact, but she inferred the social relationship incorrectly.

You want to keep inferred meaning separate from direct observation because the meanings of actions are not always self-evident. People may try to deceive others. For example, an unrelated couple register at a motel as Mr. and Mrs. Smith. More frequently, social behavior is ambiguous or multiple meanings are possible. For example, I see a White male and female, both in their late twenties, get out of a car and enter a restaurant together. They sit at a table, order a meal, and talk with serious expressions in hushed tones, sometimes leaning forward to hear each other. As they get up to leave, the man briefly hugs the woman, who has a sad facial expression and appears ready to cry. They then leave together. Did I witness a couple breaking up, two close friends discussing a third, two people trying to decide what to do because they have discovered that their spouses are having an affair with each other, or a brother and sister whose father just died? If you record an inferred meaning without separating it from direct observation, you lose the ability to assign other possible meanings to the direct observation.

4. *Analytic Memos.* You will make many decisions about how to proceed while in the field. You might plan some acts (e.g., to conduct an interview, to observe a particular activity, etc.) while others will happen spontaneously, almost "out of thin air." You will want to keep methodological notes to have a record of your plans, tactics, ethical and procedural decisions, and self-critiques of tactics.

Theory emerges in field research during data collection and when reviewing field notes. Theoretical notes are a running account of your attempts to give meaning to field events. You "think out loud" in the notes. In them, you might suggest new linkages between ideas, create hypotheses, propose conjectures, and develop new concepts. *Analytic memos* include your methodological and theoretical notes. They are collections of your thoughts, digressions into theory, and a record of your decisions. You can use them to elaborate and expand on ideas while still in the field. You can modify them or develop them into more complex theory by rereading and reflecting on the memos.

5. As discussed earlier, your personal feelings and emotional reactions are part of the data in field research. They color what you see or hear in the field. You should keep a section of notes that is like a personal diary. In it, record your personal life events and feelings ("I'm tense today, I wonder if it's because of the fight I had yesterday with . . ."; "I've got a headache on this gloomy, overcast day").

Personal notes provide you with a way to cope with stress; they are also a source of data about personal reactions. Use them to evaluate direct observation or inference notes when you read your notes later. For example, if you were in an especially good mood during observations, it might color what you observed in the field differently from when you feel a little depressed or are fighting a cold.

6. *Interview Notes.* If you conduct field interviews (to be discussed), keep the interview notes separate from other notes. In addition to recording questions and answers, you want to record information such as the date, place of interview, characteristics of interviewee, content of the interview, and so on. It helps you when rereading and making sense of the notes.

Maps, Diagrams and Artifacts. Many field researchers make maps and draw diagrams or pictures of the features of a field site. This serves two purposes: It helps to organize events in the field, and it helps you convey a field site to others. For example, you observe a restaurant counter with 15 stools. You might draw and number 15 circles to simplify recording (e.g., "Yosuke came in and sat on stool 12; Phoebe was already sitting at stool 10").

Three types of maps may be helpful: spatial, social, and temporal. The first helps you orient the data in space; the latter two are preliminary forms of data analysis. A spatial map locates people, equipment, and the like in terms of physical space to show where activities occur (Figure 11.4a). A social map shows the number or variety of people and the arrangements among them of power, influence, friendship, division of labor, and so on (Figure 11.4b). A temporal map shows the ebb and flow of people, goods, services, and communications in time (Figure 11.4c).

In addition to using maps, you may wish to gather artifacts. These are items from the field site that provide physical evidence (e.g., a brochure, a menu, a coffee cup, a t-shirt, a program or roster of participants, a party hat) and visible reminders of a specific site. You can use them to trigger a memory, illustrate a theme, or symbolize some activity or event.

Machine-Recorded Data. Photos, tape recorders, and videotapes can be helpful supplements in field research. However, they are never a substitute for field notes or your presence in the field. You cannot introduce them into all field sites, and you can only use them after you develop some rapport. Recorders and videotapes provide a close approximation to what has occurred. They are a permanent record that others can review, and can help you recall events and observe what does not happen, or nonresponses, which are easy to miss. Nevertheless, recording devices create disruption and an increased awareness of surveillance by people in the field. They can bring associated problems (e.g., ensure that batteries are fresh). Also, listening to or viewing videos can be time consuming. For example, it may take you over 100 hours to listen to 50 hours recorded in the field. Transcriptions are expensive and not always accurate; they cannot always convey subtle contextual meanings or mumbled words.

Step 6. Exit the Field Site

Researchers are often in a field site for weeks or years. In either case, at some point work in the field ends and you leave. Some researchers

FIGURE 11.4   Types of Maps Used in Field Research

A Spatial Map

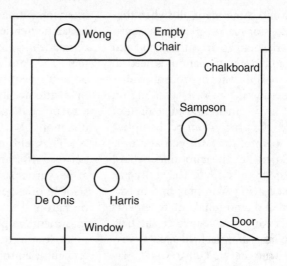

B Social Map

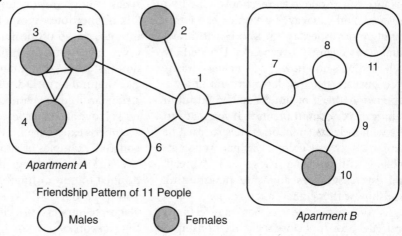

Apartment A

Friendship Pattern of 11 People

○ Males   ● Females

Apartment B

C Temporal Map

Day of Week, Buzz's Bar

	Mon	Tue	Wed	Thr	Fri	Sat
Open 10:00	Old Drunks	Old Drunks	Old Drunks	Old Drunks	Skip Work or Leave Early	Going to Fish
5:00	Football Watchers	Neighbors and Bridge Players	Softball Team (All-Male Night)	Young Crowd	Loud Music, Mixed Crowd	Loners and No Dates
Close 1:00						

suggest that the end comes naturally when theory building ceases or reaches a closure; others feel that fieldwork could go on without end and that a firm decision to cut off relations is needed.

You want to anticipate a process of disengaging and exiting the field. Depending on the intensity of involvement and the length of time in the field, the process can be disruptive or emotionally painful for both you and others. You may experience the emotional pain of breaking intimate friendships or feel guilty just before and after leaving. You may find breaking off personal and emotional entanglements to be difficult. If your involvement in the field was intense and long, and the field site was very different from your native culture, you may need a long adjustment period before you feel "at home" with your original life again.

Once you decide to leave, choose a method of exiting. You can leave by a quick exit (simply not return one day) or slowly withdraw, reducing involvement over weeks. Decide how to tell members and how much advance warning to give. In general, let members know a short period ahead of time. You should fulfill any bargains or commitments that you made to leave with a clean slate. Sometimes, a ritual or ceremony, such as a going-away party or shaking hands with everyone, helps signal the break. Feminist researchers advocate maintaining friendships with members after exiting.

As you leave, some members may feel hurt or rejected because a close social relationship is ending. They may react by trying to pull you back into the field and make you more of a member, or they may become angry and resentful. They may grow cool and distant because they are aware that you are an outsider.

THE FIELD RESEARCH INTERVIEW

Interviewing members in the field involves the unstructured, nondirective, in-depth interview, which differs from the formal survey research interview in many ways (see Table 11.1). Field research interviews go by many names: unstructured, depth, ethnographic, open ended, informal, and long. Generally, they involve one or more people being present, occur in the field, and are informal and nondirective (i.e., a member may take the interview in various directions).

The field interview is a joint production between you and the member. Members are active participants in the process with a mutual sharing of experiences. You might share your background to build trust and encourage the informant to open up, but do not force answers or use leading questions. You want to encourage and guide a process of mutual discovery.

In field interviews, members express themselves in the forms in which they normally speak, think, and organize reality. They may talk in anecdotes, meandering stories, wander into gossip, go off on tangents, and tell a few jokes. You want to retain everything—anecdotes, stories, gossip, tangents, and jokes—in their natural form. Do not repackage them into a standardized format. Focus on the member's perspective and experiences. To stay close to the member's experience, ask questions in terms of concrete examples or situations—for example, "What kinds of things happened before you decided to quit in June?" instead of "Why did you quit your job?" You want to elicit long, elaborate answers, not short, survey research–type responses.

Unlike one-time survey research interviews, field interviews occur in a series over time. You can start and stop it over the course of days or even months, interspacing it with "ordinary talk." You begin by building rapport. Avoid probing inner feelings or sensitive issues until you establish intimacy, and even then, expect apprehension. After several meetings, you may be able to probe into sensitive issues. In later interviews, you may return to topics and check past answers by restating them in a nonjudgmental tone and asking for verification—for example, "The last time we talked, you said that

TABLE I I.I   Survey Interviews versus Field Research Interviews

Typical Survey Interview	Typical Field Interview
1. It has a clear beginning and end.	1. The beginning and end are not clear. The interview can be picked up later.
2. The same standard questions are asked of all respondents in the same sequence.	2. The questions and the order in which they are asked are tailored to specific people and situations.
3. The interviewer appears neutral at all times.	3. The interviewer shows interest in responses, encourages elaboration.
4. The interviewer asks questions, and the respondent answers.	4. It is like a friendly conversational exchange, but with more interviewer questions.
5. It is almost always with one respondent alone.	5. It can occur in a group setting or with others in area, but varies.
6. It has a professional tone and businesslike focus; diversions are ignored.	6. It is interspersed with jokes, asides, stories, diversions, and anecdotes, which are recorded.
7. Closed-ended questions are common, with rare probes.	7. Open-ended questions are common, and probes are frequent.
8. The interviewer alone controls the pace and direction of interview.	8. The interviewer and member jointly control the pace and direction of the interview.
9. The social context in which the interview occurs is ignored and assumed to make little difference.	9. The social context of the interview is noted and seen as important for interpreting the meaning of responses.
10. The interviewer attempts to mold the framework communication pattern into a standard.	10. The interviewer adjusts to the member's norms and language usage.

Source: Based on Briggs (1986), Denzin (1989), Douglas (1985), Mishler (1986), Spradley (1979a).

you started taking things from the store after they reduced your pay. Is that right?"

The field interview is similar to a friendly conversation but differs slightly. It has an explicit purpose—you want to learn about the person and setting. You include explanations or requests that diverge from friendly conversations. For example, you may say, "I'd like to ask you about . . . ," or "Could you look at this and see if I've written it down right?" A typical conversation tends to have balance, with each participant asking and answering somewhat equally. In the field interview, you will ask more questions and express more ignorance and interest than you might in a typical conversation. You also may ask a member to elaborate or explain more often.

An *informant* in field research is a member with whom you develop a relationship and who tells about, or informs on, the field.[12] Who makes a good informant? The ideal informant has four characteristics:

1. The informant is familiar with the culture and is in a position to witness significant events makes a good informant. He or she lives and breathes the culture and engages in routines in the setting without thinking about them.
2. The informant is currently involved in the field. Ex-members who have reflected on the field may provide useful insights, but the longer they have been away from direct involvement, the more likely it is that they have reconstructed their recollections.
3. The informant can spend time with you. Interviewing may take many hours, and some members are simply not available for extensive interviewing.
4. Nonanalytic individuals make better informants. A nonanalytic informant is familiar with and uses native folk theory or pragmatic common sense. This is in contrast to the analytic member, who preanalyzes the setting, using categories from the media or education.

You might interview several types of informants. Contrasting types of informants who provide useful perspectives include rookies and old-timers, people in the center of events and those on the fringes of activity, people who recently changed status (e.g., through promotion) and those who are static, people who are frustrated or needy and those who are happy or secure, and the leader in charge and the subordinate who follows. You should expect mixed messages when you interview a range of informants.

Types of Questions in Field Interviews

A field interview can contain three types of questions: descriptive, structural, and contrast questions.[13] You can ask all concurrently, but each type is more frequently at a different stage in the process (see Figure 11.5). During the early stage, ask descriptive questions. Gradually add

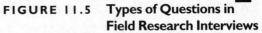

FIGURE 11.5 Types of Questions in Field Research Interviews

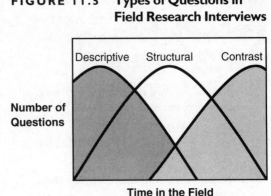

structural questions until, in the middle stage after you start analysis, structural questions become the majority. Begin to ask contrast questions in the middle and increase them until, by the end, you ask them more than the other types.

Descriptive questions help you explore the setting and learn about members. They can be about time and space—for example, "Where is the bathroom?" "When does the delivery truck arrive?" "What happened Monday night?" They can also be about people and activities: "Who is sitting by the window?" "What is your uncle like?" "What happens during the initiation ceremony?" They can be about objects: "When do you use a saber saw?" "Which tools do you carry with you on an emergency water leak job?" Questions that ask for examples or experiences are descriptive questions—for example, "Could you give me an example of a great date?" "What happened when you were a postal clerk?" Descriptive questions may ask about hypothetical situations: "If a student opened her book during the exam, how would you deal with it?" Another type of descriptive question asks members about terms they use in the field site: "What do you call a deputy sheriff?" (The answer is a "county Mountie.")

After you spent time in the field and have started to analyze data, you can ask more structural questions. They begin after you started to organize specific field events, situations, and conversations into categories. You use them to verify the categories you developed. For example, your observations of a highway truck-stop restaurant revealed that the employees informally classify customers who patronize the truck stop. In a preliminary analysis, you created a conceptual category, "type of customers." You may have started to recognize several types. As you talk to members, you start using structural questions to verify the types you think you have identified.

You can pose a structural question by asking whether a category includes elements in addition to those you already identified. For example, you might ask, "Are there any types of customers other than regulars, greasers, pit stoppers, and long haulers?" Another kind of structural question asks for confirmation: "Is a greaser a type of customer that you serve?" "Would you call a customer who . . . a greaser?" "Would a pit stopper ever eat a three-course dinner?"

The contrast question builds on the analysis that you verified using structural questions. These questions focus on similarities or differences between the elements in categories or distinguish categories. In them, you ask members to verify similarities and differences you believe exist: "You seem to have a number of different kinds of customers that come in here. I've heard you call some customers 'regulars' and others 'pit stoppers.' How are a regular and a pit stopper alike?" or "Is the difference between a long hauler and a greaser that the greaser doesn't tip?" or "Two types of customers just stop to use the restroom—entire families and a lone male. Do you call both pit stoppers?"

Data Quality

The Meaning of Quality.   In a quantitative study, high-quality data are reliable and valid; they give you precise, consistent measures of the "objective" truth. In qualitative field research, data quality differs because instead of assuming all members experience the same single, objective truth, the assumption is that members subjectively interpret events and actions as shaped by the social context, and they may do so differently. What a member takes to be true results from social interaction and interpretation. Thus, high-quality field research data captures such fluid processes and provides an understanding of the members' viewpoints.

In field research, you seek "rich" data. This means data that are diverse and detailed. To get them, you must gather many forms of data systematically over a prolonged period. The data have many sizes and shapes (e.g., memories, field notes, photos, conversations, artifacts). Quality data do not eliminate subjective views; rather, they purposely include subjective responses and experiences. High-quality field research data are detailed descriptions based on your immersion and authentic experiences in the social world of members.

The different notion of high-quality data in field research implies different ways to apply the general ideas of reliability and validity.

Reliability in Field Research.   Field data reliability has internal and external consistency. *Internal consistency* asks whether the data are plausible given all that is known about a person or event. It means common forms of human deception have been minimized. It asks, how well do the pieces fit together into a coherent picture of this person or event? For example, are a member's actions (e.g., Susan acts distrustful and a little fearful of her supervisor) consistent over time and across situations? *External consistency* situates data in a specific social context. It means verifying and cross-checking all observations against one other and integrating divergent sources of data. You ask, does it all fit into this specific context? What is said in one setting may differ in other contexts. For example, when asked, "Do you dance?" a member may say no in a public setting full of excellent dancers, but yes in a semiprivate setting with few dancers and different music. The context shaped the answer.

For external consistency ask, Can others verify what you observed? Does a wide range of evidence confirm it?

Reliability means consistency. In a field research study it includes both what you consistently observed happening or heard said, as well as what was not done or said but you expected or anticipated. Such omissions or null data can be significant but are difficult to detect. For example, you observed the cashier JoAnne end her shift. You observed that each time JoAnne did not count the money in a cash register drawer, but locked it then left. You noticed this omission because all other cashiers always counted money at the end of the shift before they locked the drawer.

In the field site, you depend on what members tell you. This makes the credibility of members and their statements part of reliability. To check member credibility, you must ask, Does the person have a reason to lie? Is she in a position to know that? What are the person's values and how might that shape what she says? Is he just saying that to please me? Is there anything that might limit his spontaneity? Take subjectivity and context into account as you evaluate credibility. A person's subjective perceptions influence his or her statements or actions. Statements and actions are colored by an individual's point of view and past experiences. Instead of evaluating each statement to see whether it is true, you may find statements useful in themselves. Even inaccurate statements and actions can be revealing.

Validity in Field Research. Validity in field research comes from your analysis and data as accurate representations of the social world in the field. Replication is not a major criterion for validity in field research, because the specific events in a particular setting are virtually impossible to replicate. Essential aspects of the field site may change over time: Events and context change, the members change, the field researcher differs, and so on.

The fluidity and subjective features of field research does not mean that validity is impossible. Rather, it shifts the nature of validity from that of quantitative research. There are four kinds of validity or ways to evaluate research accuracy: ecological validity, natural history, member validation, and competent insider performance.[14]

1. *Ecological validity* is the degree to which the social world you describe matches the world of members. It asks, Is the natural setting described relatively undisturbed by the researcher's presence or procedures? A study has ecological validity if events would likely have occurred without your presence.

2. **Natural history** is a detailed description of how you conducted the study. It is a full and candid disclosure of your actions, assumptions, and procedures for others to evaluate. A study is valid in terms of natural history if outsiders see and accept the field site and your actions.

3. *Member validation* occurs when you take field results back to members, who judge their adequacy. A study is "member valid" if many members recognize and understand your description as reflecting their intimate social world. Member validation has limitations because conflicting perspectives in a setting produce disagreement with your observations, and members may object when results do not portray their group in a favorable light. In addition, members may not recognize the description because it is not from their perspective or does not fit with their purposes.

4. *Competent insider performance* is the ability of a nonmember to interact effectively as a member or pass as one. This includes the ability to tell and understand insider jokes. A valid study gives enough of a flavor of the social life in the field and sufficient detail so that an outsider can act as a member. Its limitation is that it is not possible to know the social rules for every situation. Also, an outsider might be able to pass

simply because members are being polite and do not want to point out social mistakes.

ETHICAL DILEMMAS OF FIELD RESEARCH

Your direct, personal involvement in the social lives of other people during field research introduces ethical dilemmas. Dilemmas will arise when you are alone in the field and have little time to deliberate over ethics. Even if you are aware of general ethical issues before entering the field, situations arise unexpectedly. We look at five ethical issues in field research: covert research, confidentiality, involvement with illegal behavior, the powerful, and publishing reports.[15]

Covert Research.   The most debated issue is that of covert versus overt field research. Should you conduct secret or covert research and assume a false role, name, and identity, and consistently lie to members? Some in the research community support covert research and see it as necessary to enter into and gain a full knowledge of certain areas of life. Others oppose it absolutely and argue that it undermines a fundamental trust between social researchers and society. Although its moral status is questionable, you can only study certain field sites or activities with some degree of secrecy or deception. It is rarely easier than overt research because of the difficulties of maintaining a front and the constant fear of getting caught. The general principle is that covert research is never preferable.

Confidentiality.   You may learn intimate knowledge revealed in confidence and have a strong moral obligation to uphold the confidentiality of data. This includes keeping what you learn confidential from others in the field and disguising members' names in field notes. You may not be able to directly quote a person in a research report. One strategy is to find some public, documentary source that says the same thing and use the document (e.g., an old memo, a newspaper article, etc.) as the source of the information. A more serious ethical difficulty arises when you develop a close, personal friendship relationship with members. Based on deep trust, a member may share intimate secrets with you alone. Although this adds to your understanding of the person and field site, you cannot betray the confidence by referring to it explicitly in a report about the study.

Involvement with Illegal Behavior.   If you conduct field research on people who engage in illegal, immoral, or unethical behavior, you will learn of and might be indirectly involved in illegal activity. *Guilty knowledge* is of interest not only to law enforcement officials but also to other field site members.[16] You face a dilemma of building trust and rapport with the members, yet not becoming so involved as to violate your basic personal moral standards. One strategy is to be open about the issue and make an explicit arrangement with the deviant members.

The Powerful.   Many field research studies have been conducted on marginal, powerless people (e.g., street people, the poor, children, and low-level workers in bureaucracies), and elites and high officials have criticized the studies for having a bias in favor of the less powerful. The public often assumes that people with official authority and who are at the top of an organization are creditable and have a right to define events. This creates a tension between official, authoritative versions of events from elites or officials and the versions offered by field researchers who immerse themselves in the world of the disadvantaged. Field researchers often acquire an in-depth understanding of that side of social life that is a rarely heard perspective. Because field researchers are revealing, or "give a voice to" a perspective that is rarely heard or that differs from official versions, they are accused of bias. An ethical issue arises when the researcher's commitment to scientific evidence and documenting authentic life in the field site clashes with the official or widely held views on events or situations.

Publishing Field Reports. You may gain intimate knowledge about people and events in a field research study, and there is a right of privacy. This means you cannot always reveal all member secrets you learn without violating privacy or harming reputations. Yet, if you fail to make public what you learned in a report of the research, it will remain hidden. If you keep details hidden, you are not giving a complete and accurate account of the people and events. Others may question a report with critical details omitted.

Some researchers suggest asking members to look at a report to verify its accuracy and to approve of their portrayal in print. Yet, censorship or self-censorship can be a danger. A compromised position is to reveal truthful but unflattering material only if it is essential to your larger argument or to present an accurate total picture.

FOCUS GROUP RESEARCH

Focus group research is a qualitative technique in which you informally study a group-discussion setting.[17] In focus group research, you gather together 6–12 people in a room with a moderator to discuss a few issues. Most focus group sessions last about 90 minutes. The moderator is trained to be nondirective and to facilitate free, open discussion by all group members (i.e., not let one person dominate the discussion). Group members should be homogenous, but not include close friends or relatives. A typical study has four to six groups. Focus group topics can include public attitudes (e.g., race relations, workplace equality, homeless people), personal behaviors (e.g., dealing with a terminal disease, feelings about sexual orientation), a new product (e.g., breakfast cereal), or a political candidate (see Expansion Box 11.4).

EXPANSION BOX

11.4

Advantages and Limitations of Focus Groups

Advantages

- The natural setting allows people to express opinions/ideas freely.
- Open expression among members of marginalized social groups is encouraged.
- People tend to feel empowered, especially in action-oriented research projects.
- Survey researchers are provided a window into how people talk about survey topics.
- The interpretation of quantitative survey results is facilitated.
- Participants may query one another and explain their answers to each other.

Limitations

- A "polarization effect" exists (attitudes become more extreme after group discussion).
- Only one or a few topics can be discussed in a focus group session.
- A moderator may unknowingly limit open, free expression of group members.
- Focus group participants produce fewer ideas than in individual interviews.
- Focus group studies rarely report all the details of study design/procedure.
- Researchers cannot reconcile the differences that arise between individual-only and focus group-context responses.

In focus group settings, you need to provide clear instructions and carefully select participants. Although participants should be moderately homogenous, this does not always ensure openness and a willingness to share beliefs and opinions candidly. What people reveal in a focus group is influenced by the context. Context includes not only other participants, but also the broader social context (e.g., major news events and social trends), the institutional context (e.g.,

11.3	EXAMPLE BOX
	Focus Group Research on Disability Identity

Brown et al. (2009) used focus groups to explore how people with disabilities develop an understanding and self-identity of being disabled. They formed nine focus groups in three cities (Atlanta, Newark, and New Orleans), with three focus groups in each city. They recruited 58 people with disabilities using public radio, intermediary agencies (such as local employment providers and state agencies), and disability advocacy organizations. All participants were working or searching for work. Each group had 4–10 people with a facilitator and cofacilitator. Each focus group session lasted about 90 minutes. The authors tape-recorded, transcribed, and analyzed sessions. They used coding and analytic memo writing to analyze the session data. The types of questions introduced in the sessions included: What are employment services like in your state? How did you find out about employment services? Has anyone used multiple employment services? Many participants emphasized the difficulties they had in finding work because of inadequate public transportation, lack of assistive technology, and discrimination. A couple mentioned negative effects stigmas. The authors concluded that events that occurred as participants tried to become employed shaped their understanding of disability. The authors argued the multiple meanings of disability and several ways that a self-identity of being disabled is formed are both shaped by the context of seeking work and working.

location and sponsor of the focus group), and the status context (e.g., people of different social status or position). You should segment focus groups by status. For example, rather than mixing supervisors and their employees, each should be in different group. Likewise, it is unwise to mix teachers and their students together in the same focus groups. We do this because people often respond very differently when people of higher or lower status are present.

CONCLUSION

In this chapter, you learned about field research and the field research process (choosing a site and gaining access, relations in the field, observing and collecting data, and the field interview). Field researchers begin data analysis and theorizing during the data collection phase.

You can now appreciate the implications of saying that in field research, the researcher is directly involved with those being studied and is immersed in a natural setting. Doing field research usually has a greater impact on a researcher's emotions, personal life, and sense of self than doing other types of research. Field research is difficult to conduct, but it is a way to study parts of the social world that otherwise could not be studied.

Good field research requires a combination of skills. In addition to a strong sense of self, the best field researchers possess an incredible ability to listen and absorb details; tremendous patience; sensitivity and empathy for others; superb social skills; a talent to think very quickly "on one's feet"; the ability see subtle interconnections among people and/or events; and a superior ability to express oneself in writing.

Field research is strongest when you study a small group of people interacting in the present. It is valuable for micro-level or small-group face-to-face interaction. It is less effective when the concern is macro-level processes and social structures. It is nearly useless for events that occurred in the distant past or processes that stretch across decades. Historical–comparative research, discussed in the next chapter, is better suited to investigating these types of concerns.

Key Terms

acceptable incompetent
analytic memos
appearance of interest
attitude of strangeness
competent insider performance
defocusing
direct observation notes
ecological validity
ethnography
ethnomethodology
external consistency
field site
focus group
gatekeeper
go native
guilty knowledge
internal consistency
jotted notes
members
member validation
naturalism
normalize social research

Endnotes

1. For studies of these sites or topics, see Neuman (2000, 2003). On studies of children or schools, see Corsaro (1994), Corsaro and Molinari (2000), Eder (1995), Eder and Kinney (1995), Kelle (2000), and Merten (1999). On studies of homeless people, see Lankenau (1999), and on studies of female strippers, see Wood (2000).

2. Ethnography is described in Agar (1986), Franke (1983), Hammersley and Atkinson (1983), Sanday (1983), and Spradley (1979a:3–12, 1979b:3–16).

3. For a general discussion of field research and naturalism, see Adler and Adler (1993), Georges and Jones (1980), Holy (1984), and Pearsall (1970). For discussions of contrasting types of field research, see Clammer (1984), Gonor

(1977), Holstein and Gubrium (1994), Morse (1994), Schwandt (1994), and Strauss and Corbin (1994).

4. See Lofland (1976:13–23) and Shaffir, Stebbins, and Turowetz (1980:18–20) on feeling marginal.

5. See Adler and Adler (1987:67–78).

6. See Hammersley and Atkinson (1983:42–45) and Lofland et al. (2006:17–32).

7. See Neuman (2011:429) for examples and discussion.

8. For more on gatekeepers and access, see Beck (1970:11–29), Bogdan and Taylor (1975:30–32), and Wax (1971:367).

9. See Douglas (1976), Emerson (1981:367–368), and Johnson (1975:124–129) on the question of whether the researcher should always be patient, polite, and considerate.

10. Negotiation in the field is discussed in Gans (1982), Johnson (1975:58–59, 76–77), and Schatzman and Strauss (1973:22–23).

11. For more on ways to record and organize field data, see Bogdan and Taylor (1975:60–73), Hammersley and Atkinson (1983:144–173), and Kirk and Miller (1986: 49–59).

12. Field research informants are discussed in Dean and associates (1969), Kemp and Ellen (1984), Schatzman and Strauss (1973), Spradley (1979a:46–54), and Whyte (1982).

13. The types of questions are adapted from Spradley (1979a, 1979b).

14. For more on validity in field research, see Briggs (1986:24), Bogdan and Taylor (1975), Douglas (1976), Emerson (1981:361–363), and Sanjek (1990).

15. See Lofland and Lofland (1995:26, 63, 75, 168–177), Miles and Huberman (1994:288–297), and Punch (1986).

16. Fetterman (1989) discusses the idea of guilty knowledge.

17. For a discussion of focus groups, see Bischoping and Dykema (1999), Churchill (1983:179–184), Krueger (1988), Labaw (1980:54–58), and Morgan (1996).

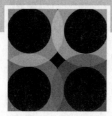

CHAPTER 12

Historical-Comparative Research

The nineteenth-century founders of the social sciences—such as Emile Durkheim, Karl Marx, and Max Weber—used the historical and comparative method to understand the great transformations wrought by the rise of industrialism. They used the method to arrive at many insights and concepts that still shape thinking today. The historical comparative method did not disappear in the nineteenth century. In the twenty-first century, social researchers use the method to study a wide range of topics. Although many studies focus on current conditions in a single country, social researchers use historical and/or comparative studies to explain and understand significant social changes of the late twentieth and early twenty-first centuries. Adams et al. (2005) called this a "third wave" of historical-comparative studies after a second-wave revival in the 1970s and 1980s.[1]

Historical-comparative (H-C) social research is a collection of techniques and approaches. Some of its techniques blend into traditional historical study. Others are extensions of quantitative research techniques. In this chapter, the focus is on the distinct form of H-C research that puts historical time and/or cross-cultural variation at the forefront.

Some students find H-C research studies difficult to grasp or uninteresting at first. Most often, this is because many H-C studies assume that readers possess knowledge of various countries and of history. If you know little except your own historical time and own society, H-C studies may not seem relevant. Yet, if you want to know what is going on and understand world events and the changes in society (e.g., an attack by terrorists, a nation going to war, the source of racism, large-scale immigration, violence based on religious hatred, urban decay), H-C research is very relevant. H-C research will help you make connections and see the bigger picture. The understanding you get from H-C research helps you to gain foresight of trends and events and to make sound everyday decisions as an active, aware citizen in the world today.

RESEARCH QUESTIONS APPROPRIATE FOR HISTORICAL-COMPARATIVE RESEARCH

Historical-comparative research is a powerful method when you want to address the "big questions": How or why did a major societal change (e.g., women gaining basic rights and more equality, the doubling of divorce rates, a large increase in the nations' homeless population) take place? What fundamental features are common to most societies? Why did the social arrangements we have today take the form they did here, but not in other societies? Will increasing globalization increase social inequality and reduce the standard of living for most people of the next generation?

H-C research is also well suited if you want to examine how several factors combine to produce a specific outcome (e.g., a civil war, rising immigration, major population shifts to different regions of the country). It is also appropriate when you are comparing an entire society to learn what is universal across all countries and what is special or unique.

Despite its real strength for addressing the "big questions" of explanatory theory, you also can use H-C research for some applied research questions. For example, when considering new ways to deliver health care to the elderly, looking at several other countries that do it successfully offers a deeper understanding and creative new alternatives. When developing a city plan to prepare for a major flood it is very instructive to look back at what happened 50 years ago when the last major, disastrous flood struck.

Much of H-C research is explanatory. It allows you to explain events or specific cases and to show how well a theory explains social processes and concepts in different cultural or historical contexts. You can also use the H-C method to reinterpret or challenge old explanations. By asking different questions, finding new evidence, or assembling evidence in different ways, H-C research helps to question old explanations or advance new ones.

Concept formation and theory building are strengths of H-C research. By looking at historical events or diverse cultural contexts, H-C research helps you generate new concepts and broaden existing concepts. H-C studies help you avoid a problem found in much social research: using concepts limited to a single historical time or to a single culture. H-C research helps you to compare across time or culture, but also ground concepts in the lived experiences of people in diverse cultural and historical contexts.[2]

By reading many H-C studies, you can expand your knowledge of the past and other cultures. This extends to better understanding the classical theorists as well. Without a broad knowledge of history and various cultures, many students struggle to understand general social theories. For example, you might read Karl Marx's *The Communist Manifesto*. Marx wrote it in the 1800s and discussed long-term trends and a macro-level theory of human history. In this work, Marx refers to conditions of feudal Europe 300 or 500 years earlier than when he was writing in the mid-1800s. In feudal Europe, serfs and peasants lived under conditions of deprivation and severe exploitation. Feudal societies were caste-based societies in which people were born into a social position with no real chance of moving up. Caste defined proper dress, marriage partners, and behavior. A system of peonage forced serfs or peasants to give half or more of what they produced to the landlords and nobles. These were people born into a position of privilege. There was only one Church, and it too had extensive landholdings. Tight familial ties linked the aristocracy, landowning class, and Church together. Most serfs and peasants toiled day and night, owned no land, lived in tiny hovels, and faced periodic food shortages. The landowning aristocrats had lavish feasts, lived in luxurious palaces or mansions, and played various games. Marx's theory grew out of trying to understand such conditions.

A modern reader might ask, Why did the serfs not run away from the landowning aristocrats or refuse to hand over what they produced if the exploitation was so bad? The answer requires an understanding of the daily life in that historical time. A serf or peasant was just little better than a slave and might suffer severe punishment, torture, or execution for refusing to hand over what was produced. Peasants and serfs who ran off had little chance to survive in European forests living on roots, berries, and hunting. No one would aid a fleeing serf refugee because the traditional societies did not embrace strangers, but feared them. Other landowners would not hire a fleeing serf. There were few towns or villages, and they lacked the open jobs of a modern wage economy. Travel would have been by foot on unpaved pathways or tiny one-lane dirt roads. Before regular mail service, telephones, or other communication, an illiterate serf had little way of knowing about life elsewhere. Knowing about life in feudal Europe would help you see where ideas in *The Communist Manifesto* originated. Lacking such knowledge, many of its ideas are difficult to appreciate.

The difficulty of understanding theory without a good background is not unique to the writings of Marx or nineteenth-century social theorists. Understanding and evaluating most macro-level explanations depends on having a broad-based knowledge of human cultures and history.

THE LOGIC OF HISTORICAL-COMPARATIVE RESEARCH

Although you might study the past as a historian or compare across countries using standard social science methods, a key question is, Is there a distinct H-C method with its own logic rooted in interpretative or critical science assumptions?

The Logic of Historical-Comparative Research and Quantitative Research

Quantitative versus Historical-Comparative Research. Some positivist-oriented researchers conduct studies on historical or comparative questions. A strict positivist researcher would reject the idea of a distinct H-C method. As you may recall, positivists measure variables, test hypotheses, analyze quantitative data, and replicate research to discover general laws that hold across time and societies. They see no fundamental difference between doing quantitative social research and studying historical-comparative questions. By contrast, researchers who adopt an interpretative or critical approach would argue that H-C research differs from a positivist approach. Many positivist-oriented social researchers criticize qualitative H-C studies for using a small number of cases and focusing on specific situations. They believe that qualitative H-C research is inadequate because it rarely produces probabilistic, universal causal generalizations that the positivists take as indicating a "true" (i.e., positivist) science.

The Logic of Historical-Comparative Research and Interpretive Research

A distinct qualitative from H-C research often involves case studies and qualitative data. Researchers examine in-depth a limited number of cases in which they emphasize social meaning and context. Case studies, even on one nation, can yield important information. Case studies can elaborate historical processes and specify concrete historical details about particular social relations in the past (see Example Box 12.1).

12.1 EXAMPLE BOX
Woman of the Klan

In *Women of the Klan,* Kathleen Blee (1991) noted that, prior to her research, no one had studied the estimated 500,000 women in the largest racist, right-wing movement in the United States. She suggested that this may have been due to an assumption that women were apolitical and passive. Her six years of research into the unknown members of a secret society over 60 years ago shows the ingenuity needed in historical-sociological research.

Blee focused on the state of Indiana, where as many as 32 percent of White Protestant women were members of the Ku Klux Klan at its peak in the 1920s. In addition to reviewing published studies on the Klan, her documentary investigation included newspapers, pamphlets, and unpublished reports. She conducted library research on primary and secondary materials at over half a dozen college, government, and historical libraries. The historical photographs, sketches, and maps in the book give readers a feel for the topic.

Finding information was difficult. Blee did not have access to membership lists. She identified Klan women by piecing together a few surviving rosters, locating newspaper obituaries that identified women as Klan members, scrutinizing public notices or anti-Klan documents for the names of Klan women, and interviewing surviving women of the Klan.

To locate survivors 60 years after the Klan was active, Blee had to be persistent and ingenious. She mailed a notice about her research to every local newspaper, church bulletin, advertising supplement, historical society, and public library in Indiana. She obtained 3 written recollections, 3 unrecorded interviews, and 15 recorded interviews. Most of her informants were over age 80. They recalled the Klan as an important part of their lives. Blee verified parts of their memories through newspaper and other documentary evidence.

Membership in the Klan remains controversial. In the interviews, Blee did not reveal her opinions about the Klan. Although she was tested, Blee remained neutral and did not denounce the Klan. She stated, "My own background in Indiana (where I lived from primary school through college) and white skin led informants to assume—lacking spoken evidence to the contrary—that I shared their worldview" (p. 5). She did not find Klan women brutal, ignorant, and full of hatred. Blee got an unexpected response to a question on why the women had joined the Klan. Most were puzzled by the question. To them it needed no explanation—it was just "a way of growing up" and "to get together and enjoy."

Extreme interpretive social researchers criticize qualitative H-C studies. They hold that the sole goal of social research is to acquire an empathic understanding of the people being studied. They would limit research to being strictly idiographic and only descriptive, rejecting a search for general causal patterns, systematic concepts, or abstract theoretical models that occurs in much H-C research.

Qualitative H-C research shares many features in common with field research. Both focus on culture, try to see events through the eyes of the people studied, reconstruct the lives of the people studied, and examine particular individuals or groups.

A Distinct Historical-Comparative Approach

The distinct H-C research method avoids the excesses of the positivist and extreme interpretive approaches. It combines sensitivity to specific historical or cultural contexts with theoretical generalization. The logic and goals of H-C research are closer to those of field research than to positivist approaches. The following discussion describes similarities between H-C research and field research, and six more unique features of historical-comparative research (see Table 12.1).

TABLE 12.1   Summary of a Comparison of Approaches to Research: The Qualitative versus Quantitative Distinction

Topic	Both Field and H-C	Quantitative
Researcher's perspective	Include as an intergral part of the research process	Remove from research process
Approach to data	Immersed in many details to acquire understanding	Precisely operationalize variables
Theory and data	Grounded theory, dialogue between data and concepts	Deductive theory compared with empirical data
Present findings	Translate a meaning system	Test hypotheses
Action/structure	People construct meaning but within structures	Social forces shape behavior
Laws/generalization	Limited generalizations that depend on context	Discover universal, context-free laws

Features of Distinct H-C Research Approach

Topic	Historical Comparative Researcher's Approach
Evidence	Reconstructs from fragments and incomplete evidence
Distortion	Guards against using own awareness of factors outside the social or historical context
Human role	Includes the consciousness of people in a context and uses their motives as causal factors
Causes	Sees cause as contingent on conditions, beneath the surface, and due to a combination of elements
Micro/macro	Compares whole cases and links the micro to macro levels or layers of social reality
Cross-contexts	Moves between concrete specifics in a context and across contexts for more abstract comparisons

Six Similarities between H-C and Field Research.   First, both H-C research and field research emphasize researcher interpretation and introduce the interpreter-researcher's location in time, place, and worldview into the way you do research. Unlike quantitative research, in neither H-C nor field research studies is your goal to find a single, unequivocal set of objective facts from which historical time or culture are erased.

Both H-C and field research recognize that you, as the researcher, have a historically and culturally shaped point of view. Moreover, the point of view is an unavoidable aspect of doing the study. Both types of research acknowledge that you live in a human culture and in the present time, and these factors will influence your relationship to the historical or comparative evidence.

For example, you will bring your cultural assumptions and background to a study. They will color how you see and understand the qualitative data about people or events. Whether your culture is Italian versus Indonesian versus Icelandic, how you see people or events is likely to vary somewhat based on your core cultural assumptions, values, and worldview. Likewise, how you see and understand people or events might differ if you live in 2012 versus in 1912 or in 1812.

Both types of research assume that someone who conducts a study can never escape the influence of his or her culture or a place in history. Your location in historical time and cultural-geographic place undoubtedly influences what you feel, see, and understand while conducting a study. Just because you have a point of view that is shaped by your historical and cultural situation does not mean that everything you think or see is seriously distorted or invalid. Rather, it means you should recognize and reflect on your historical and cultural situation explicitly as being an indispensible aspect of the study.

Second, in both field and H-C research you examine a great diversity of data. In both, the goal is to immerse yourself in a huge quantity of data as a means to gain an empathic understanding of events and people. In both types of research, you want to capture subjective feelings, all the while recognizing that people's everyday ordinary activities often signify deeper social meanings.

When doing field or H-C research, you will inquire, select, and focus on specific aspects of social life from the vast array of events, actions, symbols, and words. As you organize data and focus attention, you will use a set of evolving concepts. For example, you might examine a group's rituals and symbols that dramatize its culture (e.g., parades, clothing, placement of objects, etc.) and use them to investigate the motives, reasons, and justifications of the group members.

Third, in both field and H-C research you use *grounded theory*. Rather than start with specific hypotheses to test, theory will emerge during the process of collecting data. In both a study involves building new theory as much, if not more than, testing an existing theory.

Fourth, in both field and H-C research your meaning system will frequently differ from that of the people you study. Yet, your goal is to penetrate and understand their point of view. Once you have examined and mastered the life, language, and perspective of the people you are studying, your goal is to "translate" it for others who will read your research report.

Fifth, in both field and H-C research you focus on process and sequence. The passage of time and processes of social activity are essential to how people construct social reality. This is related to how both field and H-C research remain sensitive to the ever-present tension between agency—the active side of doing things that will change social reality—and structure—the fixed regularities and patterns that shape and constrain social life. In both types of research, you recognize that social reality is simultaneously what people create and what imposes restrictions on human choice.[3]

Sixth, historical and cross-cultural knowledge are incomplete and provisional; they are based on selective facts and limited questions. Neither deduces propositions or tests hypotheses in order to uncover universal fixed laws. Likewise, replication is unrealistic. This happens because each person conducting research brings a unique perspective and assembles a unique body of evidence.

Unique Features of Historical-Comparative Research. Despite its many similarities to field research, important features distinguish H-C research. Research on the past and on a different culture share much in common.

First, in H-C research you usually rely on limited and indirect evidence. Often, direct observation or involvement as in field research is impossible. This means you must reconstruct what occurred in the past or in a different culture from whatever evidence you have. The reconstruction process means you may not have absolute confidence in the accuracy of all the evidence. Historical evidence depends on the survival of data from the past, usually in the form of documents (e.g., letters and newspapers). This will limit you to what has not been destroyed and what has left a trace, record, or other evidence behind. To study a different culture, it often takes a decade or more to acquire true, in-depth cultural knowledge. If you conduct a study based on the experience of a few months or a year, your depth of culture knowledge will be limited.

In H-C research, you are always interpreting the evidence. Different people who look at the same evidence might ascribe different meanings to it. This means you must reflect on evidence. You can rarely understand it based on a quick or superficial glance. Instead, you immerse yourself fully in the evidence and absorb details about the context in which it exists. For example, to conduct a study on the family in the past or in a distant country, you need to be aware of the family's social context (e.g., the nature of work, forms of communication, transportation technology, etc.). This may require you to study maps and learn the laws in effect. You will want to know the condition of medical care and common social practices. For example, the meaning of "a visit by a family member" is affected by conditions such as roads of dirt and mud, the inability to call ahead of time, and the lives of people who work on a farm with animals that need constant watching.

It is easy for a reconstruction of the past or another culture to become distorted. Compared to the people you study, you may be more aware of events occurring prior to the time studied, events occurring in places other than the location studied, and events that occurred after the historical period. This awareness can give you a greater sense of coherence than the people who lived in the past or in an isolated social setting experienced. You need to guard against bringing your greater awareness to a reconstruction of the daily experiences of the people you are studying.

In H-C research, you want to recognize that people have a capacity to learn, make decisions, and act on what they learn to modify the course of events. This means that as you study people, you need to "know what they know, and what they do not know." For example, people in a city become aware of or gain consciousness of their own past history as becoming sick each summer by taking water from a nearby river. Because they know this, they change their future behavior to avoid the mistakes of the past. They change their water source in the summer. This conscious action alters the course of events (i.e., fewer people getting sick). Of course, people do not necessarily learn or act on what they have learned. Perhaps without scientific knowledge of pollution or contamination, they continue to get sick. Even if they do act to get another source of water, they will not necessarily be successful. Nevertheless, people's capacity to learn introduces indeterminacy into historical-comparative explanations.

When you conduct H-C research, you want to learn whether people viewed various courses of action as plausible. What the people you study saw as possible or impossible ways to achieve goals will have shaped their worldview and understandings. You need to ask whether they were conscious of certain things. For example, if an army knew an enemy attack was coming and so decided to cross a river in the middle of the night, the action "crossing the river" takes on a different meaning than in the situation where the army was not aware that the enemy was approaching.

When doing H-C research you integrate the micro (small-scale, face-to-face interaction) and macro (large-scale social structures) levels. You try to describe both levels and layers of reality and link them to each other. For example, you examine the details of individual biographies by reading diaries or letters to get a feel for the individuals: the food they ate, their recreational pursuits, their clothing, their sicknesses, their relations with friends, and so on. You then connect this micro-level view to macro-level processes: such as increased immigration, mechanization of production, proletarianization, tightened labor markets, and the like.

As you conduct H-C research, you shift between the details of specific contexts to make general comparisons. You closely examine specific contexts, noting similarities and differences, and then you generalize. When doing comparative research, you compare across cultural-geographic units (e.g., urban areas, nations, societies, etc.).[4] When doing historical research, you investigate past contexts, usually in one culture (e.g., periods, epochs, ages, eras, etc.), for sequence and compare across time. Of course, you can combine both to investigate multiple cultural contexts in one or more historical contexts. Yet, each period or society has its unique causal processes, meaning systems, and social relations, which may lack equivalent elements across the units. This produces a creative tension between the concrete specifics in a context and the abstract ideas you use to make linkages across contexts. For example, in his study of South America, Mahoney not only examined the economic development and trade of 15 countries over 150 years, but also learned about the lives, understandings, and experiences of elite groups within those 15 countries (see Example Box 12.2).

12.2 EXAMPLE BOX
Historical-Comparative Research

James Mahoney (2003) discovered a puzzle in Spanish America, specifically 15 countries that had been mainland territories of the Spanish colonial empire. He observed that their relative ranking, from most to least developed in 1900, remained unchanged in 2000; that is, the least developed country in 1900 (Bolivia) remained the least developed. This stability contrasts with dramatic changes and improvements in the region during the twentieth century. Going back to the height of the Spanish empire in the 1600s, Mahoney noted that the richest, most central colonies in that period later became the poorest countries. Many marginal, backwater, poor colonies had become the developed, richest countries of the late nineteenth century. To solve this puzzle, Mahoney used two qualitative data analysis tools: path dependency and qualitative comparative analysis (QCA) (both are discussed in Chapter 13). His data included maps, national economic and population statistics, and over 200 historical studies in English and Spanish on the specific countries. He concluded that the most central, prosperous Spanish colonies were located where natural resources were abundant (for extraction and shipment to Europe) and large indigenous populations existed (to work as coerced labor). Powerful local elites arose in these countries. They created rigid racial-ethnic stratification systems that concentrated economic–political power and excluded many sectors of society. These stratification systems continued into the nineteenth century when new political events, trade patterns, and economic conditions appeared. In the 1700–1850 era, liberal-minded elites who were open to new ideas did not succeed in them. In contrast, colonies on the fringe of Spain's South American empire in the 1600–1700s were less encumbered by rigid stratification systems. In them, new elites arose who could innovate and adapt. Thus, there was a "great reversal" of positions. After this historical "turning point" some countries got a substantial head start toward social-economic development in the late 1800s. These countries built political-economic systems and institutions that propelled them forward; that is, they "locked into" a particular direction or path that brought them increasing returns.

Many concepts are specific to a particular culture. They arise and "make sense" in a particular culture. Other concepts are transcultural; they hold across most cultures and are in some ways universal to all cultures. For example, "honor killing" exists in a few specific cultures. It indicates a strong cultural code or norm that justifies killing another person, or even his or her family members, when that person, or his or her family, brings great dishonor to a person, a family, or a community. The dishonor may be culturally specific, such as a person insults you or your ancestors, tells serious lies about you, steals something of value from you, or has sexual relations with you or a family member when your elders disapproved of it.

Similarly, some concepts are historically specific, or only apply in a specific historical era. For example, the "sworn loyalty" of a knight to his lord existed in the feudal era. A concept such as "private property" that we widely accept today did not always exist in the past. The expectation of romantic love between a male and female as the basis for marriage is specific to certain cultures and historical eras. Yet, other concepts may operate across time, or be transhistorical (e.g., economic inequality).

Using transcultural concepts in comparative analysis is analogous to the use of transhistorical ones in historical research.[5] In comparative research, you might translate the specifics of a cultural context into a general theoretical language to analyze events and communicate what you learned to others. The same takes place in historical research, you learn the historical specifics then might apply theoretical concepts that operate beyond the specific historical period so you can analyze events and communicate what you learned to others.

STEPS IN A HISTORICAL-COMPARATIVE RESEARCH PROJECT

In this section, we turn to the process of conducting study using H-C research. It does not involve strictly following a rigid sequence of steps. With only a few exceptions, it often uses a variety of techniques, many that are highly complex or specialized.

Conceptualizing the Object of Inquiry

To conduct a study using the H-C method, you want to begin by doing two things: (1) acquire foundation knowledge about a historical or culture setting, or data form, and (2) carefully conceptualize exactly what it is you will be studying.

These are mutually reinforcing, complementary tasks. You might begin with a few general questions, a loose model, or a set of preliminary concepts that you can apply to a setting or issue. However, your concepts are provisional. This is because you will want to refine them as you proceed with the study and gain depth of understanding about the particular historical era, culture, or type of evidence.

All concepts contain implicit assumptions and organizing categories that "package" your observations and guide your search through evidence. You want to become aware of the assumptions in provisional concepts and their guiding influence. This is because the assumptions, "packaging," and guidance might limit what you look for or consider evidence. For example, you are interested in studying high school graduation rates in a past historical era or across several countries. Perhaps you want to explain why more or fewer people graduate from high school over time or across countries. You should examine your assumptions about "high school" and "graduation." Rather than naïvely assume that your personal experience with high school in your culture and era is "normal" or universal, you should examine what these ideas might mean. Perhaps in a past era, most adolescents learned by becoming an apprentice or working on a farm, and high school was limited to a few who planned to become teachers, doctors, or lawyers. Perhaps high school taught ancient languages (Greek, Latin, or Confucian texts) and not the subjects that you learned. Perhaps high school was two years long and required living at the school year round, sleeping and eating there.

If you are not already very familiar with the historical era, comparative cultural setting, or a type of comparative data for your study, the first thing to do is acquire foundation knowledge. This could include taking one or more college courses on the historical period or cultural setting (e.g., the eighteenth-century American South, or German civilization). Reading textbooks is a helpful start, but beyond a basic course, you want to engage in an *orientation reading*. To do this, you read several general but serious book-length works to learn about a specific era or culture. It is best to ask someone who is already a specialist in the field or culture to recommend five or six books as a start. This will help you develop a general picture of the setting. Soon you can start to assemble organizing concepts, subdivide the main issue, and develop lists of further questions to ask.

For some cross-cultural studies, you will also need to learn another language. If not so well that you can read original sources in that language, at least well enough so you start to see how the language and culture operate together. You want to grasp the culturally specific concepts contained in the language.

In some types of comparative studies, you may analyze quantitative data from many countries. Before doing this, you will want to devote time and effort to learning exactly how the data were gathered and what the data measured in different countries. For example, you want to study high school graduation rates in 10 countries. Before doing this, you should read about what "high school" means in the different countries. How many years of schooling does high school involve? Do laws require compulsory attendance or is high school voluntary? Is there one type of high school or several types in a country? Are there separate high schools for different genders, races, or religions or one for everyone? Are the high schools public only, private only, or a mixture? Is high school free or very expensive to attend? Is high school open to all students, or only those who pass an entrance

test? Is the rate based on those who begin high school and complete it, or as a rate of all people of a certain age in the country who completed high school within a certain timeframe? Without understanding what high school graduation rates might mean in the 10 countries, you could easily make serious errors when analyzing the data about such rates across countries.

As with most serious social research, you will need a framework of assumptions, concepts, and theory to start an H-C study. Concepts and evidence interact to stimulate research. For example, Morgan and Prasad (2009) looked at why France and the United States adopted different systems of taxation. To conduct their study, they had to know about the history, government structure, and cultural conditions of the two countries, and about various forms of taxation (e.g., tax on purchases, tax on income, tax on property, etc.). In addition, they understood the ways different political beliefs and organized groups favored or opposed different forms of taxation influencing the enactment or collection of certain taxes (see Example Box 12.3).

Locating Evidence

After you have foundation knowledge and some preliminary concepts, you will want to begin locating and gathering evidence through extensive bibliographic work. As you begin, you may wish to narrow the scope of your study because doing H-C research can take a great amount of time. For historical research, you can use many library indexes, catalogs, and reference works that list what libraries contain. For comparative research, you will focus on specific nations or cultural units and on particular evidence about each. In H-C research, it is common to devote months to searching for sources in various libraries, traveling to specialized research libraries, and reading dozens of books and articles. As mentioned earlier, comparative research often involves learning one or more foreign languages, which can require a year or more of intense study.

**12.3   EXAMPLE BOX
Why Two Countries Tax People Very Differently**

Morgan and Prasad (2009) looked at why France and the United States adopted different systems of taxation. There are two major types of taxation: consumption taxes and income taxes. Consumption taxes tend be regressive (i.e., lower-income people pay more) but advance economic growth and avoid the political protests that income taxes generate. Governments that use them develop a bigger welfare state (i.e., more services and social programs for low- and middle-income familes). By contrast, income taxes can slow economic growth, generate political protest, and constrain the number and size of government services. To explain why a nation relies on one or the other, the authors compared how the national governments of France and the United States developed their taxing systems. Among advanced nations, the U.S. is near the highest in a reliance on a national income tax, while France is the lowest. Paradoxically, the U.S. has the most "free market" economy with the least government interference and a near absence of leftist political parties. By contrast, France has a very strong central government, extensive government involvement in the economy, and powerful leftist political parties who often win elections.

You would expect to see a progressive tax, like an income tax (tax the high-income people more) in France with a big government and leftist politics, not the U.S. Instead, France relies on a kind of national sales tax for most of its revenue. Before 1920, the U.S. shifted away from indirect consumption taxes to rely on income taxes. The authors explain the divergent paths of the two nations by examining the politics, economy, and government patterns in the two nations during the late nineteenth and early twentieth century. They show that protest movements to resist industrialization and a specific form of government centralization explain the taxation system and other features of the two nations today. They present a theory that goes beyond the two cases and conclude that we cannot explain major features of today's societies without knowing what occurred in the decades before World War I. The author's data consisted of rich historical details about the events and patterns in the two nations. They built a rigorous theoretical argument with the evidence while presenting and rejecting various alternative explanations. Their bibliography lists about 100 books and articles in English and French.

As you master the literature and take numerous detailed notes, you will be accomplishing many specific tasks:

- Create a bibliography list (on cards or on a computer) with complete citations of sources.
- Take notes that are neither too skimpy nor too extensive (i.e., more than a few sentences but less than dozens of pages of quotes).
- Leave spaces on note cards or documents so you can add analytic themes later on.
- Take all notes in the same format (e.g., on cards, paper, computer file, etc.).
- Develop a file of analytic themes or working hypotheses.

As you progress in the research, you will adjust initial concepts, questions, or focus based on what you discover in the evidence. As you gather evidence, you need to evaluate its quality.

Evaluating Quality of Evidence

You gather H-C evidence with two questions in mind: How relevant is the evidence to emerging research questions and evolving concepts? And, How accurate and strong is the evidence?

As the focus of your research shifts, evidence that was not relevant can become relevant and vice versa. In addition, some of the evidence may stimulate new avenues of inquiry or a search for additional confirming evidence. As you examine evidence, you want to look for three things in it: (1) the implicit conceptual frameworks, (2) particular details, and (3) empirical generalizations. You evaluate alternative interpretations of evidence and look for silences or cases where the evidence fails to address an event, topic, or issue. For example, when examining a group of leading male merchants in the 1890s, you find evidence and documents about them, but cannot find any evidence about their wives, families, or servants.

Organizing Evidence

You should begin to organize data as you gather evidence and locate new sources. Obviously, it is unwise to take notes madly and let them pile up haphazardly. You want to begin a preliminary analysis by noting low-level generalizations or themes. Next, you start to organize the evidence, using theoretical insights to stimulate new ways to organize data and new questions.

As data and theory interact, you can move beyond a surface examination of the evidence to develop new concepts. This occurs as you critically evaluate the evidence using theory. For example, you read a mass of evidence about a protest movement. From a preliminary analysis as you organize the evidence you notice a theme, the people active in protest regularly talk and interact with one other. As they talk and communicate about the protest, they develop new, shared cultural understandings. The shared understandings help bind people together. Soon they are interacting with one another in many ways unrelated to the protest itself (e.g., entertainment, shopping, etc.) based on their trust, familiarity, and shared experiences. They still hold values of the protest movement to oppose current conditions, but they created a distinct cultural area and system of support and interaction. You may examine theories of culture and movements, then formulate a new concept: "oppositional movement subculture." You can then use this concept to reexamine the evidence.

Synthesizing

As the evidence starts to accumulate, your next step is to synthesize. After most of the evidence is in, you will refine concepts, create new ones, and move toward a general explanatory model. Concrete events in the evidence can help to clarify and give meaning to the new concepts. You can look for patterns across time or units, drawing out similarities and differences with analogies. You can organize divergent events into sequences and group them together into categories or based on themes. Together, they help you create a larger picture. Eventually you will want to forge plausible explanations that subsume concepts and evidence into a coherent whole. To do this, you will review evidence, read and reread notes, and sort and resort notes into piles or files based on organizing schemes. All the while, you are looking for links or connections. You will want to examine the evidence in different ways and see it from various viewpoints. The next chapter on qualitative data analysis discusses this in more depth.

As you synthesize, you will be linking specific evidence to concepts, an abstract model of underlying relations, or causal mechanisms. You might use metaphors. For example, mass frustration leading to a revolution is "like an emotional roller coaster drop" in which things seem to be getting better, and then there is a sudden letdown after expectations have risen very fast.

Writing a Report

Assembling evidence, arguments, and conclusions into a report is a crucial step in all research, but more than in quantitative approaches, the careful crafting of evidence and explanation makes or breaks H-C research. You must distill mountains of evidence into clear exposition that you document with detailed examples and footnotes. You weave together the evidence and arguments to communicate a coherent, convincing picture or "tell a story" to readers.

DATA AND EVIDENCE IN HISTORICAL CONTEXT

Types of Historical Evidence

Historical studies have terms that need clarification. *History* can refer to events of the past (e.g., it is *history* that the French withdrew troops from Vietnam), a record of the past (e.g., a *history* of French involvement in Vietnam), and an academic field that studies the past (e.g., a department of *history*). *Historiography* is the method that historians use to do historical research or of gathering and analyzing historical evidence. *Historical sociology* is a part of historical-comparative social research.

Historical studies use four types of evidence or data: primary sources, secondary sources, running records, and recollections.[6] Traditional historians rely heavily on primary sources. In H-C research, you tend to use secondary sources or mix the data types.

Primary Sources. The letters, diaries, newspapers, movies, novels, articles of clothing, photographs, and so forth of those who lived in the past and have survived to the present are *primary sources*. You can find them in archives (a place where documents are stored), in private collections, in family closets, and in museums (see Expansion Box 12.1). Today's documents and objects (our letters, television programs, YouTube videos, clothing, or automobiles) will be primary sources for future historians. An example of a classic primary source is a bundle of yellowed letters written by a husband away at war to his wife found in an attic by a researcher. Professional historians specialize in the ways to locate, verify, and examine primary sources.

Published and unpublished written documents are the most important type of primary source. You can find them in their original form or preserved in microfiche or on film. They are often the only surviving record of the words, thoughts, and feelings of people in the past. Written documents are helpful for studying

societies and historical periods that have writing and many literate people. A frequent criticism of written sources is that elites or authorities in official organizations have written most of them. This criticism means it is easy to overlook the views of illiterate people, the poor or marginalized, or events outside official social institutions. For example, slaves in the United States were forbidden to read or write. This means finding written primary sources on the daily experience of slavery from the slave's point of view are rare and difficult to find.

Perhaps you have heard of Harriet Jacobs, who wrote *Incidents in the Life of a Slave Girl.* Born a slave in North Carolina in 1813, Ms. Jacobs had a very difficult life. Later she escaped, went into hiding, and fled to New York to work as a free woman for a well-known abolitionist. Ms. Jacobs began writing the book in 1853. Unable to get it published, she self-published it in 1861. Until the mid-1980s, scholars questioned the book's authorship. Today Ms. Jacobs is acclaimed for offering a powerful firsthand picture of the life of a female slave in America. Scholars have uncovered 900 primary sources related to her life, family, and writings.[7]

The written word on paper (e.g., letters, written ledgers, and newspapers) was the medium of communication prior to the spread of telecommunications, computers, and video technology. In fact, the switch to electronic communication (e.g., cell phone texts and conversations, Web pages, and television or radio broadcasts) may make the work of future historians difficult because electronic communication may not leave a permanent physical record.

Secondary Sources. Primary sources have realism and authenticity. Yet, the practical limitation of time can restrict research on many primary sources to a narrow timeframe or location. To get a broader picture, many H-C researchers rely on *secondary sources*. These are the writings of specialist historians who have devoted years to finding, collecting, and examining primary sources. To conduct an H-C study you might

12.1 EXPANSION BOX
Using Archival Data

The archive is the main source for primary histori-cal materials. Archives are accumulations of docu-mentary materials (papers, photos, letters, etc.) in private collections, museums, libraries, or formal archives.

Location and Access

Finding whether a collection exists on a topic, orga-nization, or individual can be a long, frustrating task of many letters, phone calls, and referrals. If the material on a person or topic does exist, it may be scattered in multiple locations. Gaining access may depend on an appeal to a family member's kindness for private collections or traveling to distant librar-ies and verifying one's reason for examining many dusty boxes of old letters. Also, the researcher may discover limited hours (e.g., an archive is open only four days a week from 10 A.M. to 5 P.M., but the researcher needs to inspect the material for 40 hours).

Sorting and Organization

Archive material may be unsorted or organized in a variety of ways. The organization may reflect crite-ria that are unrelated to the researcher's interests. For example, letters and papers may be in chrono-logical order, but the researcher is interested only in letters to four professional colleagues over three decades, not daily bills, family correspondence, and so on.

Technology and Control

Archival materials may be in their original form, on microforms, or, more rarely, in an electronic form. Researchers may be allowed only to take notes, not make copies, or they may be allowed only to see select parts of the whole collection. Researchers become frustrated with the limitations of having to read dusty papers in one specific room and being allowed only to take notes by pencil for the few hours a day the archive is open to the public.

Tracking and Tracing

One of the most difficult tasks in archival research is tracing common events or persons through the mate-rials. Even if all material is in one location, the same event or relationship may appear in several places in many forms. Researchers sort through mounds of paper to find bits of evidence here and there.

Drudgery, Luck, and Serendipity

Archival research is often painstaking slow. Spend-ing many hours pouring over partially legible docu-ments can be very tedious. Also, researchers will often discover holes in collections, gaps in a series of papers, or destroyed documents. Yet, careful read-ing and inspection of previously untouched material can yield startling new connections or ideas. The researcher may discover unexpected evidence that opens new lines of inquiry (see Elder et al., 1993, and Hill, 1993).

---

read a dozen books and articles. H-C schol-ars will examine many sources. For example, the bibliography of Mahoney's (2003) article described earlier in Example Box 12.2 had about 250 English and Spanish sources. Nearly all were secondary sources.

Running Records. ***Running records*** consist of files or existing statistical documents main-tained by organizations. An example of a run-ning record is a file in a country church that contains a record of every marriage and every death from 1910 to the present or a hospital's record of all admissions, medical treatments, and discharges covering a thirty-year time span.

Recollections. The words or writings of indi-viduals about their past lives or experiences based on memory are ***recollections***. These can be in the form of memoirs, autobiographies, or interviews. Because memory is imperfect, recollections can be distorted in ways that primary sources are not. For example, when Blee (1991) interviewed a woman in her late 80s about being a member of the Indiana Ku Klux Klan over 60 years earlier, she was aware that the woman's memory of events was not perfect (see Example Box 12.1). Blee's study included *oral history*. In this type of recollection, you conduct long, unstructured interviews with people about their lives or events in the past. It is especially valuable for people who are not part of elite groups or who are illiterate. The oral history technique began in the 1930s and now has a professional association, the Oral History Association, and scholarly journal, *Oral History Review,* devoted to this valuable technique.[8]

Research with Secondary Sources

Uses and Limitations. Most H-C researchers use secondary sources, but such sources have limitations and you need to exercise caution with them.[9] The limitations of secondary historical sources include problems of inaccurate historical accounts and an absence of studies in the area that interests you. You cannot test hypotheses in a rigorous positivist model with the sources because post facto (after-the-fact) explanations fail to meet positivist criteria of falsifiability. Nonetheless, historical research by others is valuable for developing general explanations and documenting the emergence and evolution of tendencies over time.

Potential Problems. The great volume of secondary sources, each having a maze of details and interpretations, requires that you transform a mountain of descriptive studies into an intelligible, condensed picture. You want to create a condensed picture that is consistent with the complexity and richness of the evidence. Often, you must integrate many detailed studies of a specific era, locale, or historical individuals.

Historians do not present theory-free, objective "facts." They implicitly frame raw data, categorize information, and shape evidence with concepts. The historian's concepts are a mixture drawn from journalism, the language

of historical actors, ideologies, philosophy, everyday language in the present, and social science. You may find them to be vague, applied inconsistently, and not mutually exclusive nor exhaustive. For example, a historian describes a group of people in a nineteenth-century town as upper class, but never defines the term and does not link it to any theory of social classes. The historian's implicit theories constrain the evidence. You might use a secondary source to search for evidence to support an explanation that is contrary to the explanation the historian implicitly used when writing the secondary source.

To conduct a study, historians will select certain information from all possible evidence. However, you rarely know exactly how the historian did this. Without knowing the selection process, you must rely on the historian's judgments, which can contain biases.[10] For example, a historian reads 10,000 pages of newspapers, letters, and diaries. He or she then boils down this raw information into a 100-page book with an explanation that is supported by summaries and selected quotes. You do not know whether the historian left out raw evidence relevant for your purposes.

The typical historian's research practice also introduces an individualist bias. The traditional historian's heavy reliance on primary sources and surviving artifacts combined with an atheoretical orientation often yields a focus on the particular actions of specific people. Such a particularistic, micro-level view directs attention away from broad integrating themes or patterns that are of interest in social research. The emphasis on specific individuals is a type of theoretical orientation.[11]

Traditional historians organize evidence as a *narrative history*. This can compound problems of undefined concepts and evidence selection. In the historical narrative, the author organizes material chronologically around a single coherent "story." Parts of the story are connected to other parts by the main story line and location in the sequence of events. Together, the parts form a unity or whole story.

Conjuncture and contingency are often used in historical narratives. Conjuncture means several things that come together in time or place to affect what occurs afterward. For example, A and B and C were all present, and that is why D resulted. Historians build conjuncture into the narrative history, making it difficult for H-C researchers using the historian's work as a secondary source to disentangle back to an original situation. Contingency means a historical event or pathway to future events depends on (i.e., was contingent upon) the presence of some other condition or situation being present. For example, if X plus Z occurred, then Y would occur, and if X plus Z had not occurred, something other than Y would have followed. The contingency creates a logical interdependency between earlier and later events. In simple terms, we cannot know for certain what would have happened if things had been different.

The historical narrative uses as its primary organizing tool—time order or position in a sequence of events—but this does not denote theoretical or historical causality. Thus, the narrative meets two of the three criteria for establishing causality: temporal order and association. Moreover, narrative writing frequently includes colorful anecdotes and details that tend to obscure causal processes. A historian will include events in the narrative to enrich the background or context and to spark interest in readers, but the events may have no causal significance for an outcome.

Historians also present events that have a delayed causal impact. An event's effect may be temporarily "on hold" with its causal impact occurring at some unspecified later time. For example, we learn about a couple divorcing, but the divorce may have relevance for the career direction of one person in the couple 10 years later.

Historical narratives rarely indicate in very explicit terms exactly how a combination or interaction operates, or the relative impact of different factors in a combination. For example,

a historian discusses three conditions (e.g., a serious flood, a bankruptcy of a company that employed many people, an influx of new immigrants) as causing an event (the closing of a local college in the town and exodus of educated people). Yet, rarely do readers know which of the three is most important or whether all three conditions had to occur for the outcome to take place. Perhaps, no two conditions alone, or no single condition alone, would create the same impact.[12] With the narrative organization of secondary sources, you must read through weak concepts, unknown selection criteria, and unclear casual logic. Theory may reside within the narrative but it remains implicit and hidden.

In addition, historians tend to follow a particular "school" of historiography. Various schools of historiography (e.g., diplomatic, demographic, ecological, psychological, Marxist, intellectual, etc.) have their own rules for seeking evidence and asking questions. Each gives priority to certain types of explanatory factors. As an H-C researcher, you will want to learn the approach or school of historiography that influenced a secondary source you are using so you can adjust for it.

Lastly, historians research and write a secondary source in a particular era. In different eras historians have access to different materials and tend to look at and emphasize different factors. A historian writing today may examine primary materials differently from those writing in the past, such as the 1920s, did.

Research with Primary Sources

When you rely on secondary sources for an H-C study, the historian is a major concern. When you use primary sources, a first concern is that only a fraction of everything written or used in the past has survived into the present. Moreover, what survived is a nonrandom sample of what once existed.

A second issue is that as you attempt to read primary sources, you try to do it though the eyes and assumptions of a contemporary who lived in the past. This means you must "bracket," or hold back, knowledge of subsequent events and modern values. For example, you read a primary source produced by a slaveholder in the 1820s. You "hold back" knowledge that the slave system of agriculture is doomed. Likewise, moralizing against slavery or faulting the writer for not seeing its evil will not get you "inside" the worldview of a slaveholder to see things from that viewpoint. As you are doing H-C research reading primary sources, you need to hold back moral judgments and become a temporary moral relativist so you can better grasp the position of the person who produced the primary source.

A third issue is that locating primary documents can be very time-consuming. You must search through specialized indexes and travel to archives or specialized libraries. Primary sources are often located in a dusty, out-of-the-way room full of stacked cardboard boxes containing masses of fading documents. These may be incomplete, unorganized, and in various stages of decay. Once you locate the documents or other primary sources, you evaluate them by subjecting them to external and internal criticism (see Figure 12.1).

External criticism means you evaluate the authenticity of a primary source itself to be certain that it is not a fake or a forgery. The criticism involves asking, Was this document created when it is claimed to have been, in the place where it was supposed to be, and by the person who claims to be its author? You may ask, Why was the document produced to begin with, and how did it survive?

Once the primary source passes the test as being authentic, you use *internal criticism*, an examination of its contents. To do this, you evaluate several issues: Did the author of the source directly witness what was recorded, or was it secondhand information? Was there one or multiple authors? You examine both the literal meaning of what is recorded and the subtle connotations or intentions. You want to note other events, sources, or people that the primary source mentions and ask whether they can be verified. You want to examine implicit assumptions or value positions present in the source. You may note how relevant conditions under which the source was produced (e.g., during wartime or under a totalitarian regime) may have influenced what the source contains. You consider the context of statements made within the source to distill their full meaning. In general, you will want to combine primary and secondary sources to build a full explanation (see Example Box 12.4).

FIGURE 12.1 Internal and External Criticism

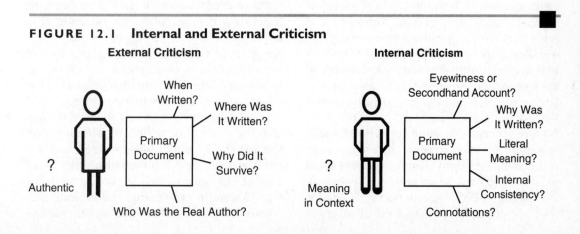

In an H-C study of Chinese migrant networks in Peru, Chicago, and Hawaii early in the twentieth century, McKeown (2001) used both primary and secondary historical sources and running records. He considered events over nearly a century and in three nations—everything from major international events and national laws to individual family biographies. He relied on secondary sources for major national or international events. Although his study was primarily historical and qualitative, he also examined quantitative data from running records and provided graphs, charts, and tables of statistics. His evidence also included geographic maps and photographs, quotes from 100-year-old telegrams, official government documents, original newspaper reports, and selections from personal letters in three languages. By comparing Chinese migrants over a long historical period and in divergent social–cultural settings, he could trace the formation and operation of transnational communities and social identities. He learned that networks with links back to villages in China and crossing several national borders helped to sustain a vibrant, interacting community. The network was held together by social relations from the village of origin, clan, family, business transactions, and shared language and customs. One of McKeown's major arguments is that a perspective based solely on nations can limit a researcher's ability to see a social community that is transnational and the hybrid of multiple cultures. Many aspects of the transnational community developed in reaction to specific interactions that occurred locally.

COMPARATIVE RESEARCH

Types of Comparative Research

Comparative research is more of a perspective or orientation to doing social research than a separate technique. Like other social research, it has strengths and limitations.

Strengths of Comparative Research. Comparative research tends to magnify methodological issues present in other forms of social research.[13] The comparative perspective exposes weaknesses in research design and helps you improve the quality of research. Although you use comparisons in all social research, identifying similarities and differences is the central focus of comparative research.

We generalize to some degree in all social research. A major strength of comparative research is its ability to identify aspects of social life that are general across units (e.g., cultures), and aspects limited to one unit alone. Ironically, positivist principles emphasize the discovery of general laws or patterns of social behavior that hold across all people and all societies, yet most positivist-oriented studies are only about one society, culture, or group. Few are comparative.

Comparative research encourages the development of broad or universal concepts that you can use in multiple cultural settings, and it can reveal cultural bias. It is more difficult to detect hidden biases, assumptions, and values until you apply a concept across cultures or settings. The range of events and behaviors in one culture is narrower than for all human behavior. This means social research that examines one culture only considers a limited range of all social activity. Implicit biases, assumptions, and values can be revealed when you conduct research on a broad range of cultural and social settings.

For example, two researchers, Hsi-Ping and Abdul, examine the relationship between the age at which a child is weaned and the onset of emotional problems. Hsi-Ping looks only at U.S. data, which show a range from 5 to 15 months at weaning, and indicate that emotional problems increase steadily as age of weaning increases. She concludes that late weaning causes emotional problems. Abdul looks at data from 10 cultures and discovers a range from 5 to 36 months at weaning. He finds that the rate of emotional problems rises with age of weaning until 18 months; it then peaks and falls to a lower level. Abdul arrives at conclusions that are more accurate: Emotional problems are likely for weaning between the ages of 6 and 18 months, but weaning either earlier or later reduces the chances of emotional problems. Hsi-Ping reached false conclusions about the relationship because of the narrow range of weaning age in the United States.

Another strength of comparative research is its ability to raise new questions and stimulate theory building. For example, Lamont (2000) compared samples of blue-collar and lower-white-collar workers in France and the United States. She drew random samples from telephone directories of Whites and Blacks in the suburbs of Paris and New York City and interviewed respondents for two hours. She looked at their justifications and forms of argument used to explain racial differences.

Lamont found that the arguments of racists and antiracists alike differed widely between France and the United States. The differences revealed how people used arguments and rationales that were closely tied to the dominant cultural themes of their society. For example, the United States has a long history of using biological inferiority to explain racial differences. This declined greatly but it still exists in racist and antiracist arguments in the United States. Such a rationale is absent in France. In the United States, the market has near-sacred status. Racist and antiracists in the United States frequently used the market and personal economic success in their arguments. In France, the market is not viewed as being a fair and efficient mechanism for allocating resources. The market factor was absent from racist and antiracist arguments in France. In France, cultural factors are viewed as very important, as are the fundamental human rights of all people.

The French racists and antiracists used cultural arguments, egalitarianism, and the universality of all humans much more than Americans. In fact, the idea of a fundamental equality among all human beings was nearly absent among the justifications given by people in the United States. The discrepancy Lamont found helps us see how specific beliefs and values embedded in the larger society and culture influence the people's basic understandings of social issues and relationships. The findings suggest new questions and theories about why and how people adopt various positions on race relations.

Limitations of Comparative Research. Compared to noncomparative research, research that includes a comparative perspective is often more difficult, more costly, and more time consuming to conduct. The types of data you can collect and problems with equivalence (discussed later) are also frequent limitations in comparative studies.

The number of cases is a common limitation of comparative studies. For example, you rarely can use random sampling in comparative research with the country as a unit of analysis. Sufficient information is not available for all of the approximately 200 nations in the world. Data are often unavailable for a nonrandom subset of all countries (poor countries, nondemocratic countries, etc.). In addition, there is a question of whether you treat all nations as equal units for sampling when they differ so widely. Some have over a billion people and others only 100,000. Although some quantitative cross-national studies have included over 150 countries, it is limited to a few variables. For example, Thorfason and Ingram (2010) had data on the rise of democracy in 187 countries across 185 years but were limited to four or five variables.

The number of cases available for comparative research suggests the research strategy you should use. If you have a small number of cases, you can go into greater depth and get a wider range of information for each case. This encourages you to see each case as unique, and it might limit generalizations you can make. If you have a large number of cases, you might use quantitative techniques, but a fundamental rule in quantitative research is that you need more cases than variables. If you want to examine 20 variables in five countries, you could not use quantitative techniques to test theory or determine relationships because you have more variables or characteristics than cases (see Chapter 13 for further discussion of this issue).

A third limitation is comparative research often allows you to apply or illustrate a theory, but not rigorously test it. Rigorous theory testing occurs in quantitative research but is rarely possible in comparative research. You can use comparative research to illustrate a theory or framework with cases to show its usefulness and plausibility rather than testing it, as occurs in quantitative research. Nonetheless, illustrating a theory or framework with comparative cases still provides valuable information and insights (see Example Box 12.5).

12.5   EXAMPLE BOX
Comparative Research on Gender Equity

Viterna and Fallon (2008) asked, When a country makes a major political change toward democracy, does the situation of women improve? They illustrated a theory about changing gender equality in situations of national change by comparing the transition to democracy in four countries and its impact on women's status. Their theoretical framework had four factors: (1) the context of the transition to democracy (how complete was it and were both genders critical to the change), (2) the legacy of women's previous mobilizations, (3) the role of political parties, and (4) international influences. They believed the four factors combined to shape opportunities for women's movements. Their four cases that had different outcomes were South Africa, Argentina, Ghana, and El Salvador. They chose the four cases because the cases demonstrated successes and failures in improving gender equity and differed from one another according to the four theoretical factors. To find the cases, Viterna and Fallon created tables ranking nations by the percentage of female parliamentarians across 10 years (1995–2005). Most African and Latin American countries showed gains for women. However, Ghana fell from 17th to 30th out of 40 African nations. El Salvador fell from 9th to 16th out of 21 Latin American nations. South Africa and Argentina, on the other hand, were new democracies that became regional leaders in placing women into political office. Viterna and Fallon next conducted a detailed analysis of their four theoretical factors in each country for the decade. They learned that gender equality advanced most when a large majority of the population welcomed the democratic transition. It also helped when the transition to democracy completely replaced the old regime and included beliefs inclusive of women's goals. Gender equality was more successful when women mobilized as distinct feminist movements in the pre-transition period, instead of women being simply a one part of a larger male-oriented political movement. The specific ideology of the ascendant political party had less an impact to advance gender equality than did the party's strength and whether it had incorporated women. Strong parties that had fully incorporated women advanced gender equality. When the international community (e.g., international or regional organizations) included women from the country and they actively pressured the post-transition government, equality advanced. Yet, if international organizations provided funding for women's causes, it did not advance gender equality as much when independent local, country-specific women's organizations were active. In summary, the authors compared factors among four countries to illustrate the importance of the factors as contributing to greater gender equality.

The Units Being Compared

Culture Versus Nation.   In most comparative research, you use the country or nation-state as a unit of analysis. The nation-state is the unit typically used to think about the divisions of humanity across the globe today. Although it is the predominant international unit in the current era, it is neither an inevitable nor a permanent one; in fact, it has been around for only about 300 years.

The nation-state means one government with sovereignty (i.e., military control and political authority) over populated territory. It usually integrates economic relations (e.g., currency, trade, etc.), transportation routes, and communication systems within territorial boundaries. The people of the territory tend to share a common language and customs. Most nation-states have a common educational system, legal system, and set of political symbols (e.g., flag, national anthem, etc.). The government claims to represent the interests of all people in the territory under its control.

Although you may first think of the nation-state as a unit of analysis and most data are collected on it as a unit, you may be more interested in culture. The nation-state is often used as a surrogate for culture. Culture refers to a common identity among people based on shared social relations, beliefs, and technology. Cultural differences in language, customs, traditions, and norms often follow national lines. In fact, sharing a common culture is a major factor that causes the formation of distinct nation-states. Culture is difficult to define as an observable unit but it may be more relevant for substantive questions and issues than the nation-state.

Nation-state boundaries do not necessarily match those of a culture. In some situations, a single culture spreads into several nation-states; in other cases, a single nation-state contains more than one culture. Over the centuries, boundaries among cultures have blurred. As wars, invasions, and conquests carved territory into colonies or nation-states, they destroyed, rearranged, or diffused distinct and vibrant human cultures. In the eighteenth and nineteenth centuries, European empires imposed arbitrary boundaries to merge several cultures to colonies that later became separate nations. Likewise, migrants or ethnic minorities within national borders do not always assimilate into a nation's dominant culture. People in one region of a nation-state may share a distinct culture from the dominant national culture, as demonstrated by their ethnic background, language, customs, religion, and identity (e.g., the province of Quebec in Canada). Having multiple cultures within a nation-state may become the basis for regional conflict, since ethnic and cultural identities are the basis for nationalism.

In sum, the distinction between culture and nation-state means that the nation-state is not always the best unit for doing comparative research. You should ask, what is the relevant comparative unit for my research question—the nation, the culture, a small region, or a subculture? For example, a research question is, Are income level and divorce related (i.e., are higher-income people less likely to divorce)? A group of people with a distinct culture, language, and religion live in one region of a nation. Among them, income and divorce are not related; elsewhere in the nation, however, where a different culture prevails, income and divorce are related. If you use the nation-state as the unit, the findings could be ambiguous and the explanation weak. Instead of assuming that each nation-state has a common culture, you may find that a unit smaller than the nation-state is more appropriate.

Galton's Problem.   Sir Francis Galton (1822–1911) identified a classic problem when comparing units. When you compare units or their characteristics, you want the units to be distinct and separate from one another. You do not want the units to blur into each other or to overlap. If the units are not different but are actually the subparts of a larger unit, then you will find spurious relationships. For example, you conduct a study of the 50 U.S. states, 6 Australian states, 10 Canadian provinces and 96 French departments, for

162 units total. You discover a strong association among the 162 units between speaking English and having the dollar as currency, or speaking French and using the euro as currency. Obviously, the association is due to the units (e.g., states, provinces, departments) being part of a bigger unit, the nation. The association you observe is due to units being parts of larger units and not to any real relationship among the language spoken and form of currency. Social geographers also encounter this because many social and cultural features diffuse across geographic space.

Galton's problem is an issue in comparative research because cultures rarely are separated by clear, fixed boundaries. Often it is hard to say where one culture ends and another begins. You may not be able to say one culture is completely independent and distinct from another because one culture's features may have diffused into another culture over time. Galton's problem occurs when the relationship between two variables in different units is actually due to having a common origin, and they are not truly distinct units (see Figure 12.2).

Galton's problem originated with regard to comparisons across cultures, but the same problem applies to making historical comparisons. You might ask whether units are really the same or different in different historical eras. For example, is the Cuba of 1872 the same country as the Cuba of 2012? Do 140 years since the end of Spanish colonialism, the rise of U.S. influence, independence, dictatorship, and a communist revolution fundamentally change the unit?

Data in Cross-Cultural Research

Comparative Field Research. In comparative research, you can use field research and participant observation in a culture other than your own. Anthropologists are specially trained and prepared to conduct this type of research. The interexchange of ideas and methods between anthropological and field research show that any differences between doing field research in your own or in another culture is only a matter

FIGURE 12.2   Galton's Problem
Galton's problem occurs when a researcher observes the same social relationship (represented by X) in different settings or societies (represented as A, B, and C) and falsely concludes that the social relationship arose independently in these different places. The researcher may believe he or she has discovered a relationship in three separate cases. But the actual reason for the occurrence of the social relation may be a shared or common origin that has diffused from one setting to others. This is a problem because the researcher who finds a relationship (e.g., a marriage pattern) in distinct settings or units of analysis (e.g., societies) may believe it arose independently in different units. This belief suggests that the relationship is a human universal. The researcher may be unaware that in fact it exists because people have shared the relationship across units.

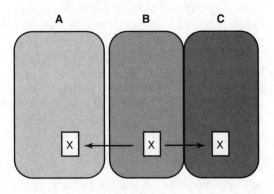

of degree. Doing field research in a different culture is usually more difficult and places more demands on you as the researcher.

Existing Sources of Qualitative Data. You can use secondary sources for comparative research. For example, you might conduct a comparative study of the Brazilian, Canadian, and Japanese educational systems. You can read studies by researchers from Brazil, Canada, and Japan and from elsewhere that describe the education systems in the three nations.

Humanity may have been 5,000 different cultures throughout its history. Of these, social researchers have studied about 1,000. A valuable source of ethnographic data on different cultures is the *Human Relations Area Files (HRAF)* and the related *Ethnographic Atlas.*[14] The HRAF is a collection of field research reports that bring together information from ethnographic studies on various cultures, most of which are primitive or small tribal groupings. The HRAF organizes extensive information on nearly 300 cultures by their social characteristics or practices (e.g., infant feeding, suicide, childbirth, etc.). The HRAF groups together information on a characteristic that comes from many different studies. This makes it easy for you to compare many cultures on the same characteristic. For example, you are interested in inheritance. You might learn that of 159 different cultures in which inheritance has been studied, 119 have a patrilineal form (father to son), 27 matrilineal (mother to daughter), and 13 mixed inheritance.

You can use the HRAF to study relationships among the characteristics of different cultures. For example, you want to find out whether sexual assault against women, or rape, is associated with patriarchy (i.e., the holding of power and authority by males). You can examine data in the HRAF to see whether the presence of sexual assault is associated with greater strength of patriarchy in a culture.

The HRAF has limitations, however. First, it depends on the quality of original research reports. The original reports vary by the initial researcher's length of time in the field, familiarity with the language, and prior experience, as well as how detailed and explicit the report is. Second, the initial researcher may have observed a limited range of behaviors or practices, and the depth of inquiry may not be equally strong for all behaviors or practices. Third, some of the HRAF classifications and categorizations of cultural characteristics are rough or unrefined because of limitations in the original research reports. Fourth, Western researchers have made

contact with and conducted field research only on a limited number of cultures prior to the cultures' having contact with the outside world. The cultures researchers studied are not a representative sample of all the human cultures. Lastly, Galton's problem (discussed earlier) can be an issue when studying the cultures in the HRAF.

Cross-National Survey Research. You read about survey research in Chapter 7. This section examines issues that arise when you apply the survey technique across cultures. The concerns and issues of doing a cross-cultural survey are the same in principle as those for doing a survey within one culture; however, they tend to be of greater magnitude and severity.

Doing survey research in a different culture requires that you possess an in-depth knowledge of its norms, practices, and customs. Without such an in-depth knowledge, it is easy to make serious errors in procedure and interpretation. Knowing another language is not enough. You need to be bicultural and thoroughly know the culture as well as have a solid knowledge of the survey method. Before planning a survey in a different culture, you will need substantial advance knowledge about the other culture. Close cooperation with people native to the other culture is essential.

You should make choices of the cultures or nations to include in a cross-cultural survey on both substantive (e.g., theoretical, research question) and practical grounds. You will have to tailor each step of survey research (question wording, data collection, sampling, interviewing, etc.) to the culture in which you will be conducting it. A critical issue is how the people from a culture experience the modern survey technique. In some cultures, the survey and interviewing are familiar; in others it may be a strange, frightening experience, analogous to a police interrogation.

The cultural context also influences sampling for a survey. You must consider whether accurate sampling frames are available, the quality of mail or telephone service, and transportation to remote rural areas. You need to be aware of many factors, such as how often people move, the types of dwellings in which people live, the number of people living in a dwelling, the telephone coverage, and typical rates of refusal. You need to tailor the sampling unit to the culture and consider how a culture defines basic units, such as the family. Depending on the local cultural setting, you may need to use special samples or methods for locating people to sample (e.g., snowball sampling).

Concerns with writing good survey questions that you read about in Chapter 7 are greatly magnified when you are writing them for the people of a different culture. You need to be very sensitive to question wording, questionnaire length, introductions, and topics included. You must become aware of local norms and of the topics that you can or cannot address in a survey. For example, open-ended questions about political issues, alcohol use, religion, or sexuality may be taboo. In addition to these cultural issues, translation and language equivalency often pose serious problems (see discussion of equivalence later in this chapter). Techniques such as back translation (discussed later) and the use of bilingual people are helpful, but it may be impossible to ask the exact same question in a different language or culture.

Interviewing can be complicated in cross-cultural situations. Selection and training of interviewers depends on the education, norms, and etiquette of the other culture. The interview situation raises issues such as specific cultural norms of privacy, ways to gain trust, beliefs about confidentiality, and differences in dialect. For example, in some cultures, the interviewer must spend a day in informal conversation and share a meal with respondents before achieving sufficient rapport to conduct a short survey interview. In other cultures, you must first secure permission from a local village authority or a religious leader before conducting interviews with village members.

Existing Sources of Quantitative Data.   Quantitative data are available for different nation-states. There are collections of quantitative data and existing statistics with information on many variables from a range of sources (e.g., newspaper articles, official government statistics, United Nations reports).

Existing cross-national statistical data is valuable but has many limitations. Some limitations are shared with other types of existing statistics. The theoretical definition of variables and the reliability of data collection can vary dramatically from nation to nation. Missing information is a frequent limitation. Intentional misinformation in the official data provided by some governments also can be a problem. Another limitation involves units on which data are collected. For example, during a 35-year period, new nations may come into existence and others change their names or change their borders.

Major data archives have existing statistical data in a form that computers can read, and you can conduct secondary analysis research using existing international statistical data. Although there are limitations with such data as discussed above, they can yield valuable insights. For example, Sutton (2004) conducted a quantitative study using existing statistical data on the relationship between unemployment and imprisonment in 15 nations between 1960 and 1990 (see Example Box 12.6).

EQUIVALENCE IN HISTORICAL-COMPARATIVE RESEARCH

The Importance of Equivalence

Equivalence is a critical issue in all research. It is the issue of whether you can make comparisons across divergent contexts. If you are from a specific historical era and culture, does this hinder your ability to correctly understand people who lived in a different historical era or are from a very different culture than yours? As you try to

12.6	EXAMPLE BOX

Imprisonment Rates Across 14 Countries

Many cross-national studies that use the nation as the unit of analysis rely on existing statistics data. For example, Sutton (2004) conducted a quantitative, statistical study on 15 nations between 1960 and 1990. Many researchers have long observed that imprisonment rates do not closely follow changes in crime rates. Sutton tested the Rusche and Kirchheimer thesis, which says that unemployment rates cause a rise in imprisonment rates because imprisonment is a government attempt to control a surplus of unemployed working-class males in the population who could be potentially unruly. Basically, prisons are filled when many workers are out of work and empty out when the economy is booming. Sutton gathered data from government statistical yearbooks of the 15 countries, from publications by international organizations such as the World Health Organization and the International Labor

Organization, and from prior social science studies that identified features of several nations, such as their unionization pattern, political party structure, and so forth. Sutton found only limited support for the original thesis, but he documented a strong effect from several other factors. He argued that the effect of unemployment on imprisonment was probably spurious (see the discussion of a spurious relationship in Chapters 2, 4, and 10 of this book). He found that specific features of the nation's politics and labor market structure appeared to be a cause of both specific unemployment patterns and different imprisonment policies. In short, when low-income people and workers were politically weak compared to wealthy people and corporate owners, there was a rise in both unemployment and imprisonment rates compared to times when low-income people and workers have greater political power.

make comparisons across time or culture, can you use the same concepts or methods to study them? Without equivalence, you cannot use the same concepts or measures. The general issue of equivalence in H-C research is that the two or more units you are comparing (different cultures or historical eras) must have enough in common to allow for comparison.

Types of Equivalence

The equivalence issue operates on two levels. First is research equivalence, or an ability to make comparisons across units in your research study. Second is findings communication equivalence, or an ability to communicate what you learned to other people.

When you conduct research in a very different era or culture, it is easy to misinterpret events, beliefs, and practices. Assuming that you achieved an accurate interpretation, you still need to conceptualize, measure, and study

events among different eras or cultures in a way that will allow comparison across time or place. To make comparisons, you need to find a degree of similarity or some features in common across the units. This is the central issue of H-C research equivalence.

Let us say you have fully grasped another culture and have been able to make comparisons. The next issue is to inform other people what you have learned in your study. To communicate, you need to find basic commonalities between what you have learned and the understandings of the people with whom you are trying to communicate. This is the central issue of findings communication equivalence.

We can divide H-C research equivalence into four subtypes: lexicon equivalence, contextual equivalence, conceptual equivalence, and measurement equivalence.

Lexicon Equivalence. At its simplest, ***lexicon equivalence*** is correctly translating the words and phrases between languages, or finding a word that means the same thing as a word in a different language. For example, in many languages and cultures there are different forms of address and pronouns. You use an informal form for intimates (e.g., close friends and family members) and subordinates (e.g., younger persons and lower-status people). You use a formal form for people in unknown or public settings, and for persons of higher social status. English has no directly equal linguistic forms of speech. However, the idea of close, informal personal relations and of formal public relations exists in English-speaking cultures. In other languages, switching pronouns and verb form when saying, "How are you today?" might indicate a change in social status or in the relationship between two people. In English, you would have to indicate such a change in another, perhaps nonverbal way. In cultures where age is an important status (e.g., Japan), many status-based words exist that are absent in English. Another example is that in some languages you cannot say, "my brother" without indicating whether you are speaking of an older or younger brother. There is no word for *brother*, only a different word for "my younger brother" or "my older brother." In English and in these other languages, the ideas of "brother in general" and "older brother" and "younger brother" exist, but the ways to express the ideas differ.

In comparative research, **back translation** is a technique used to achieve lexicon equivalence. In it, you translate a phrase or question from one language to another. Next, you have the question or phrase in the second language independently translated back to the first. You can then compare two versions in the first language for accuracy. For example, you have a phrase in English translated into Korean. You then have it independently translated from Korean back into English. You can compare the first and second English versions. If the versions differ, you need to adjust the wording. You repeat the back translation process multiple times until the two English versions are the same.

For example, in a study to compare knowledge of international issues by U.S. and Japanese college students, researchers developed a questionnaire in English. They next had a team of Japanese college faculty translate the questionnaire into Japanese. Based on recommendations of the translators, they made changes to the English questionnaire. When they used back translation, they still discovered 30 errors in translation with serious misinterpretations.[15]

Sometimes an idea in one language and culture lacks a word in a different language (e.g., there is no word for *trust* in Hindi, for *loyalty* in Turkish, for *privacy* in Chinese, or for *good quarrel* in Thai). This means translation may require you to provide complex explanations, or you may not be able to use certain concepts across cultures or languages easily (see discussion of conceptual equivalence later).

Lexicon equivalence is not limited to different languages in different cultures; it can be a significant issue in historical research with the same language as well. The meaning of the same word in the same language can change over time. The greater the distance in time, the greater are the chances that an expression has a different meaning or connotation. For example, today the word *weed* refers to unwanted plants or to marijuana, but in Shakespeare's era, the word meant clothing. Americans in the 1950s–1980s gave obscene sexual connotations to the slang phrases "you suck" or "it sucks" that people in the early twenty-first century widely use in public to indicate displeasure or disdain.

In addition, how a person says a word, phrase, or question can modify its meaning. Sometimes differences in context, tone of voice, or facial expression turn the same phrase from a polite request into an insult, a command, or a sarcastic remark. Issues of the same word, phrase, or question taking on different meanings depending on how you express them are only compounded when you cross to a different historical era, culture, or language.

Contextual Equivalence. The issue of *contextual equivalence* is closed related to lexicon equivalence. It is the issue of correctly applying terms or concepts across different social or historical contexts. You want to achieve equivalence—the same meaning—across different contexts to make comparisons. For example, in cultures with different dominant religions, a religious leader (e.g., priest, minister, or rabbi) can have different roles, training, and authority. In some contexts, a priest is always a full-time male professional who has wealth and respect. He is a highly esteemed, well-educated community leader who also wields political power. In other cultures, a priest is anyone who rises above others in a congregation on a temporary basis. The person's authority comes from his or her communication with the spirit world or with God, but he or she is without power or standing in the community. Priests in such a context may be less well educated and have lower incomes than others of the community have. Most people in the community may see a priest as a foolish but harmless person. If you ask about "priests" but fail to notice differences in the context, you could make serious errors in interpretations.

Context also applies across historical eras. For example, *attending college* has a different meaning today than in a historical context in which only the richest 1 percent of the population attended college, most colleges had fewer than 500 students, all were private all-male institutions that did not require a high school diploma for entry, and a college curriculum consisted of classical languages and moral training. Attending college 120 years ago was not the same as it is today; the historical context has altered the meaning of attending college.

Conceptual Equivalence. Your ability to use the same concept across divergent cultures or historical eras is *conceptual equivalence.* You, and other researchers, live in a specific culture and historical era. The concepts you and others know and use in research tend to come from experiences and knowledge of that particular culture and era. Current life conditions color these concepts, and they may not exist in or be appropriate when making comparisons to very different cultures or eras.

You can try to expand the concepts you use for comparison by learning about other cultures or eras. This creates a persistent tension between using concepts found in other cultures/eras or your own. It also raises the question, Can we use concepts that are simultaneously true reflections of life experiences in very different cultures or eras and make sense in our era and culture?

The issue of concept equivalence raises a larger issue, are there incompatible ideas or concepts across eras or cultures? Some social researchers believe it is not possible to create concepts that are accurate and valid representations of social life in cultural or historical settings that are fundamentally different. They hold what we must learn and use different concepts to study distinct eras or cultures, ones that are appropriate for those eras or cultures. Other social researchers believe that we should only use universal concepts that apply across all times and cultures. Still other social researchers recognize that some concepts may be universal but many are limited to one or a few eras and cultures, and we must make adjustments. For example, *social class* exists in many societies. Yet, the system of classes (i.e., income, wealth, job, education, status, relation to means of production), the number of classes, the connotations of being in a class, and class categories or boundaries differ across societies. This makes the study of social class across societies or eras difficult.

At times, the same concept, or a very similar concept, exists across cultures but in different forms or degrees of strength. For example, many cultures have two senses of self: an outer, public one and an inner, private and personal one. In some non-Western societies, the distinction between the outward, public presentation of self and the private, personal presentation and the definition of self is strong. What you reveal externally to outsiders may be culturally restricted and detached from your genuine internal feelings. Some languages also mark this linguistically. The idea of a self for display in public, non-family, or nonprivate situations exists in Western cultures as well, but it is weaker and less socially significant. In most Western cultures, the inner, private self is treated as being more real, and it is valued. The cultural ideal is to follow it. In some non-Western cultures, the external, "public self" takes precedent, and you hide and subordinate your inner, private self. Outward conformity by your outer, public self is the ideal and more highly valued than the expression of the private self. The concept of a distinction between a private/public self exists across different cultures, but its strength and practice varies.

At times, there is no direct cultural equivalent for a concept. For example, there is no direct Western conceptual equivalent for the Japanese *ie*. It is translated as family system. Outsiders created the translated idea of family system to explain Japanese behavior in terms that made sense to them. The *ie* includes a continuing line of familial descent going back generations and continuing into the future. Its meaning is closer to a European lineage "house" among the feudal nobility than the modern household or even an extended family. It includes ancestors, going back many generations, and future descendants, with branches created by noninheriting male offspring (or adopted sons). It can also include a religious identity and property-holding dimensions (as land or a business passed down for generations). It can include feelings of obligation to one's ancestors and feelings to uphold any commitments they may have made. The *ie* is also embedded in a web of hierarchical relationships with other *ie* and suggests social position or status in a community. No Western concept matches the meaning of the Japanese concept of *ie*.

Conceptual equivalence also applies to the study of different historical eras. For example, income or wealth have a different meaning in a historical era that was a noncash, agricultural society. In a society in which people grow their own food, make their own furniture and clothing, or barter goods and in which money is rarely used, income and wealth have different meanings. It makes little sense to measure wealth by money in the bank or income by number of dollars earned. Counting hogs, acres of land, pairs of shoes, servants, horse carriages, and the like for wealth may be more appropriate. Looking at a person's ability to procure on a regular basis adequate food, shelter, and clothing for self and family may be a better indicator of income level.

Measurement Equivalence. *Measurement equivalence* means measuring the same concept in different settings. If you locate or develop a concept that is appropriate across historical or cultural contexts, the question remains, how do you measure it? Must you use different measures for the different contexts to measure or capture the same concept? Perhaps you can measure education level with a survey in one culture, but the survey method may not be appropriate in a different culture.

To measure a concept you may have to examine different kinds of evidence or multiple sources of partial evidence in different contexts. When evidence exists in fragmentary forms, you might need to examine extensive quantities of indirect evidence in order to measure concepts. Making comparisons of the same concept (e.g., education level, income) when you have measured it with very different methods can be difficult. Can you compare being a "middle-income" family in one setting, measuring it by number of dollars, with being "middle income" in a different setting, measuring it by number of goats slaughtered in a year and ability to pay a dowry?

As with other forms of equivalence, there are no simple solutions to the measurement equivalence issue. The first step is to become sensitive to the issue and aware of possible misinterpretations. Once you are sensitive and aware, you then can explore how best to address the equivalence issues in a particular research study.

ETHICS

The ethical concerns you face in H-C research are similar to those of other nonreactive research techniques. The use of primary historical sources occasionally raises special ethical issues. First, it is difficult to replicate research based on primary material. This puts a burden on the integrity of the researcher to use honest selection criteria when identifying relevant evidence and when conducting an external or internal criticism of primary sources.

Second, the right to protect privacy may interfere with the right to gather evidence. A person's descendants may want to destroy or hide private papers or evidence of scandalous behavior. Ofen major political figures (e.g., presidents) want to hide embarrassing official documents.

In comparative research, you must be sensitive to cultural and political issues of cross-cultural interaction. You need to learn what a culture considers offensive. Sensitivity means showing respect for the traditions, customs, and meaning of privacy in a culture. For example, it may be taboo for a man to interview a married woman without her husband present. Local custom or law may forbid women researchers from entering important religious or political sites.

In general, when you visit another culture you want to establish good relations with the host country's government. You do not take data out of the country without giving something (e.g., results) in return. The military or political interests of your home nation or your personal values may conflict with official policy in the host nation. Host country officials or local people might suspect you of being a spy or you may be under pressure from your home country to gather covert information.

At times, a researcher's presence or findings caused diplomatic problems. For example, a foreign researcher examined health care practices in a country. He declared that official government policy was to ignore treating a serious illness. An international controversy followed. Perhaps you are highly sympathetic to a cause that the foreign government opposes. Unless you are careful, officials may bar you from entering the country, threaten you with arrest, or demand that you leave the country. If you plan to conduct research in a different country, it is essential to become aware of such issues and the potential consequences of conducting research.

CONCLUSION

In this chapter, you have learned principles for an inquiry into historical and comparative materials. The H-C approach is appropriate for addressing big questions about macro-level change, or for understanding social processes across time or are universal across several societies. You can conduct H-C research in several ways, but a distinct qualitative H-C approach is similar to that of field research in important respects.

Historical-comparative research involves adopting a distinct orientation toward social research more than it means applying specialized techniques. You may use some specialized techniques, such as the external criticism of primary documents, but the most vital feature is how you approach a question, probe data, and move toward explanations.

Historical-comparative research is more difficult to conduct than research that is neither historical nor comparative. Similar difficulties are present to a lesser degree in other types of social research. For example, issues of equivalence are present to a degree in all social research. In H-C research, however, the problems are not secondary concerns. Rather, they are often at the forefront of how you conduct research and determine whether you can answer a research question.

In the next chapter, you will see how you might analyze the qualitative research from field and H-C research.

Key Terms

back translation
conceptual equivalence
contextual equivalence
external criticism
Galton's problem
Human Relations Area Files (HRAF)
internal criticism
lexicon equivalence
measurement equivalence
oral history
orientation reading
primary sources
recollections
running records
secondary sources

Endnotes

1. See Mahoney (1999, 2004) for major works of historical-comparative research.
2. See Calhoun (1996), McDaniel (1978), Przeworski and Teune (1970), and Stinchcombe (1978) for additional discussion.
3. For additional discussion, see Sewell (1987).
4. See Naroll (1968) for a discussion of difficulties in creating distinctions. Also see Whiting (1968).
5. On transhistorical concepts, see Bendix (1963), Przeworski and Teune (1970), and Smelser (1976).
6. See Lowenthal (1985:187).
7. See Jacobs (1987). Yellin (2008) provides a collection of primary source documents. For more on Ms. Jacobs, see http://www.harrietjacobs.org/books.html (downloaded April 2, 2011).
8. A good beginning book is Ritchie (2003). See http://www.oralhistory.org/publications/
9. Bendix (1978:16) distinguished between the *judgments* of historians and the *selections* of sociologists.
10. Bonnell (1980:161), Finley (1977:132), and Goldthorpe (1977:189–190) discussed how historians use concepts. Selection in this context is discussed by Abrams (1982:194) and Ben-Yehuda (1983).
11. For introductions to how historians see their method, see Barzun and Graff (1970), Braudel (1980), Cantor and Schneider (1967), Novick (1988), or Shafer (1980).
12. See Abbott (1992), Gallie (1963), Gotham and Staples (1996), Griffin (1993), McLennan (1981:76–87), Runciman (1980), and Stone (1987:74–96).
13. On strengths and limitations of comparative research, see Anderson (1973), Holt and Turner (1970), Kohn (1987), Mahoney (2004), Ragin (1987), Smelser (1976), Vallier (1971a, 1971b), Walton (1973), and Whiting (1968).
14. For more on the *Human Relations Area File* and the *Ethnographic Atlas,* see Murdock (1967, 1971) and Whiting (1968).
15. See Cogan, Torney-Purta, and Anderson (1988:285).

CHAPTER 3

Analysis of Qualitative Data

Qualitative data are in the form of photos, written words, phrases, or symbols that describe or represent people, actions, and events in social life. To analyze qualitative data, you will rarely use precise statistical analysis, yet analyzing qualitative data is not based on vague impressions. It is as systematic and logically rigorous as the statistical analysis of quantitative data, but in a different way. Until the past two decades, researchers rarely explicitly described how they analyzed qualitative data. They used many different methods. More recently, methods to analyze qualitative data have become more explicit and several have gained wide acceptance.

This chapter has four parts. First, we compare qualitative and quantitative data analysis. Next, we look at coding and concept/theory building in the process of analyzing qualitative data. Third, we review some major analytic strategies for quantitative analysis and ways to link the analysis with theory. Lastly, we review other techniques for examining patterns in the qualitative data.

COMPARING METHODS OF DATA ANALYSIS

Similarities

First, in all data analysis, you carefully examine empirical information to reach a conclusion. To *infer* means to pass a judgment, use reasoning, and reach a conclusion based on evidence. In both quantitative and qualitative studies, you infer from the many empirical details of social life in your data to identify patterns or generalizations. You reach conclusions by reasoning, simplifying the complexity in the data, and abstracting from the data. Data analysis helps you use empirical evidence to anchor general statements about the social world.

Second, both qualitative and quantitative analyses are public methods or processes. You make accessible to other people how you systematically gathered data. In both, you collect large amounts of data, describe the data, and document how you did this. The degree to which the method is standardized and visible may vary, but in all research you reveal what you did.

Third, you use comparison in all data analysis. You compare features of the evidence you have gathered internally or with related external evidence. As you identify multiple processes, causes, properties, or mechanisms within the evidence, you seek patterns in it—similarities and differences, aspects that are alike and unalike.

Fourth, in both qualitative and quantitative research, you strive to avoid errors, false conclusions, and misleading inferences. You are always alert for possible fallacies or illusions as you sort through various explanations, discussions, and descriptions, and evaluate merits of rivals, seeking the more authentic, valid, true, or worthy among them.

Differences

Qualitative data analysis differs from quantitative analysis in four ways.

First, in quantitative research you choose from a specialized, standardized set of data analysis techniques. Quantitative analysis is highly developed and built on applied mathematics. Hypothesis testing and statistical methods vary little across studies that rely on numerical data. By contrast, qualitative data analysis is less standardized. The great variety in data types and techniques you use in qualitative research has a parallel in multiple approaches to data analysis.

Second, in quantitative research you begin data analysis only after you have collected all of the data and condensed them into a single format, that of numbers. You then manipulate the numbers to reveal patterns or relationships. When doing qualitative research, you start to look for patterns or relationships early in a research project while you are still collecting data. You use the results of early data analysis to guide subsequent data collection. Thus, analysis is less a distinct final stage of research than a dimension of research that stretches across all stages.

Third, the relationship between data and social theory differs in the two approaches. In quantitative research, you begin with a hypothesis about the social world, then manipulate numbers representing features of the social world to test the hypotheses. By contrast, in qualitative research you blend empirical evidence and abstract concepts together, creating new concepts and theory. Instead of testing a hypothesis, you illustrate or color in concepts with evidence that a theory, generalization, or interpretation is plausible.

Fourth, the approaches differ in the degree of abstraction, or distance from the details of social life. In all data analysis, you manipulate information to identify patterns and build generalizations. In quantitative research, information about features of social life is in a common abstract format of numbers. You then manipulate the numbers based on rules of statistics. The statistical results help reveal patterns in social life. Qualitative data are in many relatively imprecise, diffuse, and less-abstract context-based formats that remain closer to the concrete details of social life. In addition, qualitative data analysis does not draw on a large, standardized set of statistical procedures from mathematics. Because the information lacks a common abstract format, and there is no single standardized procedure for manipulating the multiformat information to reveal patterns, the process of manipulating information to reveal patterns remains closer to the original details of empirical evidence.

Explanations and Qualitative Data

Qualitative explanations take many forms and you do not have to choose between a rigid idiographic/nomothetic dichotomy—that is, between describing specifics and verifying universal laws. Instead, the explanations or generalizations you develop remain close to concrete data and contexts but go beyond simple summary descriptions of the data. Often you may use a low-level, less abstract theory that remains grounded in concrete details. You can develop explanations by creating new concepts or building new theories that offer a genuine picture of social life and deep understanding. Qualitative explanations tend to be rich in detail, sensitive to context, and capable of showing the complex processes or sequences of social life. The explanations may be causal, but this is not always the case. The goal is to develop an explanation that organizes specific details into a coherent picture, model, or set of interlocked concepts.

Instead of testing a hypothesis as being true or false, you see whether your qualitative explanation is highly unlikely or plausible based on the evidence. You might build a case and supply supportive evidence for one explanation's plausibility while eliminating other explanations because they are not consistent with the data. You eliminate an explanation by showing that it is contradicted by a wide array of evidence. The process is nuanced. Data might support more than one explanation; however, the data will not be consistent with *all* explanations. In addition to eliminating less plausible explanations, you help verify a sequence of events or steps in a process. This temporal ordering becomes a basis for finding associations and supporting causal arguments.

CODING AND CONCEPT FORMATION

The concepts you use in qualitative analysis are often nonvariable, or simple nominal-level variables. You draw on a range of general ideas, concepts, and themes. These are analytic tools to use as you move toward making generalizations.

Conceptualization

In quantitative research, you conceptualize and refine variables before you collect and analyze data. In qualitative research, you are continuously in a process of forming or refining concepts grounded in the data. Thus, concept formation is integral to qualitative data analysis and begins during the data collection process. Instead of a distinct pre–data collection step, conceptualization becomes a way to organize and make sense of the data as it is collected.

In a qualitative study, you organize detailed data into more abstract categories based on themes, concepts, or similar features. You develop new concepts, with conceptual definitions, and create themes to organize the overwhelming detailed specifics of the data. Eventually, you link theme and concepts to one other in terms of a sequence, as oppositional sets (*X* is the opposite of *Y*) or as sets of similar categories. You can later interweave these into theoretical statements.

You conceptualize, or form new concepts, as you repeatedly examine and ask yourself critical questions about the data (e.g., field notes, historical documents, secondary sources, etc.). The questions can arise from existing theories with an abstract vocabulary. For example, Is this a case of class conflict? Was role conflict present in that situation? Is this a social movement? The questions can come from seeking logical connections. For example, What was the sequence of events? How does the way it happened here compare to over there? Are these the same or different, general or specific cases? You can conceptualize (i.e., reflect upon, refine, and carefully define ideas) both as you gather data and as you code the qualitative data (coding is discussed later in this chapter).

In qualitative data analysis, you treat concepts and evidence as being mutually interdependent. This applies particularly to case study analysis. The cases are not pregiven empirical units or theoretical categories apart from data; they are defined by both data and theory. While analyzing a situation, you create and specify a case as you simultaneously organize data and apply ideas. Creating a case (i.e., *casing*) brings the data and theory together. Deciding what to treat as a case resolves the tension between specific observations and thoughts that arise from observations.

Coding Qualitative Data

In quantitative research, data coding is a phase after you have collected all data. You code by arranging the measures of variables, already in the form of numbers, into a machine-readable format to facilitate statistical analysis. Coding data has a different meaning in qualitative research. You code by organizing the raw data into conceptual categories (i.e., concepts and themes). Instead of a simple clerical task to prepare for statistical analysis as in quantitative research, qualitative data coding is an integral part of data analysis. Coding encourages higher-level thinking about the data and research questions. It moves you toward theoretical generalizations.

In a qualitative study, you engage in two simultaneous activities as you code: mechanical data reduction and analytic data categorization. Coding data is the hard work of reducing mountains of raw data into a manageable size. Beyond making a huge mass of data more manageable, coding is a way to impose order onto the data. In addition, coding allows you to retrieve relevant parts of the data. Coding huge amounts of qualitative data is no simple, easy task. Between the moments of thrill and inspiration, coding qualitative data, or "filework," is often wearisome and tedious.

The three forms of qualitative coding are open coding, axial coding, and selective coding. We examine each next.

Open Coding.   You perform ***open coding*** as a first pass through the collected data. As you review the data, you are identifying concepts and themes and assigning initial codes or labels to them. This is your first attempt to condense the mass of raw data into analytic categories. To code, you slowly examine field notes, historical sources, or other data looking for critical terms, key events, or shared themes. If you have pages of written data notes, you write a preliminary code or label at the edge of a page and might highlight relevant text with brightly colored ink. If your data is in electronic files, you can do something similar. In this process, you want to remain open to creating new themes and to changing initial codes in subsequent analysis. Having a general theoretical framework can help if you use it in a flexible manner.

During open coding, you are bringing concepts and themes buried deep inside the data to the surface. The concepts and themes are at a low level of abstraction. They come from your initial research question, concepts in the literature, terms used by people in the social setting you are studying, or new thoughts you have stimulated by this immersion in the data.

You can see an example of how to open-code based on LeMasters's (1975) field research study of a working-class tavern. He found that the topic of marriage came up in many conversations. If he reviewed his field notes, he could have open coded the field notes with the theme *marriage*. Following is an example of hypothetical field notes that could be open-coded with the theme *marriage*:

> I wore a tie to the bar on Thursday because I had been at a late meeting. Sam noticed it immediately and said. "Damn it, Doc. I wore one of them things once—when I got married—and look what happened to me! By God, the undertaker will have to put the next one on." I ordered a beer, then asked him, "Why did you get married?" He replied, "What the hell you goin' to do? You just can't go on shacking up with girls all your life—I did plenty of that when I was single" with a smile and wink. He paused to order another beer and light a cigarette, then continued, "A man, sooner or later, likes to have a home of his own, and some kids, and to have that, you have to get married. There's no way out of it—they got you hooked." I said, "Helen [his wife] seems like a nice person." He returned, "Oh, hell, she's

not a bad kid, but she's a goddamn woman and they get under my skin. They piss me off. If you go to a party, just when you start having fun, the wife says 'let's go home.'" (based on LeMasters, 1975:36–37)

You also can code qualitative data from historical research. For example, you study the Knights of Labor, a nineteenth-century movement for economic and political reform in the United States. In secondary sources you read about the activities of a local branch of the Knights movement in a specific town. As you read and take notes, you notice that the Prohibition Party was important in local elections and that members of the local Knights branch debated the issue of temperance. Initially you had not thought of prohibiting alcohol and your primary interest was in the internal structure, ideology, and growth of the Knights movement. Temperance is a new and unexpected idea. You could start to code notes with the label "temperance" and include it as a possible new theme.

Another example of coding comes from qualitative comparative research. Perhaps you are studying the families of university students in three countries, Mexico, Japan, and Spain. In each country, you talk with the parents, relatives, and neighbors of the students who left their hometown to attend a distant university. In the notes, you identify themes about gender roles, career choices, parental financial sacrifices, and family aspirations for upward social mobility. Your primary interest was on the parents' relationship to the university student. In the notes, you also notice sibling rivalry and parental discussions include not only the university student but also the student's siblings. You decide to add the family dynamics among siblings and parental relations to all their children as a new theme during coding.

When coding qualitative data, you have a choice. You can code every line of data or code entire paragraphs or code entire pages of notes. You will find that some raw data are not important to code. They become dross or left over and unused. The degree of detail when you code depends on your research question, the "richness" of the data, and your purposes.

Open-ended coding can extend beyond the raw data to analytic memos written as you collected data. You will want to continue to write analytic memos as you think about the codes (see the later discussion on analytic memo writing).

Axial Coding. This type of coding is a "second pass" through the data. During open coding, you focused on the raw qualitative data (e.g., field notes, historical documents, photos, open interview transcripts). You assigned codes for the concepts, themes, relationships, and so forth that you saw in a review of the data. In open coding, your primary focus was on the data. You were little concerned about connecting themes or elaborating on the concepts. By contrast, in *axial coding,* your primary focus is on the collection of codes and the initial, preliminary concepts or themes from the open-coding process. In this second pass, you focus on the initial concepts and themes more than on the raw data. Nonetheless, you can continue to review the data and add new concepts and themes. In this sense, a milder kind of open coding continues as you axial-code.

During this second pass through the data, new codes, themes, or concepts may emerge, and you should add them. You elaborate on and identify connections among themes or concepts as you review the codes. As you review your initial set of codes, your primary focus is on organizing the concepts and themes of the codes. While doing this, you identify a few key analytic axes, or central principles, around which you can connect and organize the concepts and themes. This is the source of the name "axial coding."

During axial coding, you are constantly considering causes and consequences, conditions and interactions, strategies and processes. You are looking for categories of concepts and sets of concepts and themes that cluster together. You ask yourself questions, Can I divide this concept into subtypes? Should I combine these three closely related concepts into a general one? Does it make sense to organize these themes into a time sequence (i.e., A, then B, then C) or by their physical location?

For example, in a field research study on working-class life in a tavern you divide the general theme of marriage into sequential subparts (e.g., engagement, weddings, or parenting). You mark all notes involving the parts of marriage and then relate marriage to other themes of sexuality, division of labor in household tasks, views on children, and so on. When a theme reappears in different areas of the field notes, you compare it to elsewhere to see connections and develop new themes (e.g., men and women have different attitudes toward marriage).

In the historical study on the Knights of Labor movement, you might look for themes related to temperance. You start looking for discussions of saloons, drinking alcohol, and drunkenness. You reexamine data to see whether alcohol was present at parties and picnics held by Knights of Labor chapters. You look for how the movement related to political parties that supported or opposed temperance. Based on the codes you elaborate on the temperance theme, you might add new codes such as drinking as a form of social recreation, drinking as a part of an immigrant-ethnic culture, and gender differences regarding drinking alcohol. You review the original data and add these new codes.

In the comparative research study of university students, you build on the theme of siblings in a family. You begin to look at how the student relates to his or her siblings, whether the parents invest in the education and careers for the children differently, and how the dynamic of being an only child or having multiple siblings influences the university student. You organize codes and add new ones to the sibling theme. You can begin to connect concepts related to the theme, including sibling rivalry, birth order of siblings, and gender of siblings.

Axial coding both stimulates thinking about linkages among the open-coding concepts and themes and introduces new codes, concepts, and questions. During the coding, you may decide to drop some themes or explore others in greater depth. In addition, it reinforces the connections between evidence and concepts as you consolidate codes, reevaluate themes, and return to the data for new evidence. The axial coding process helps you build a dense web of support in the data for increasingly interconnected themes and codes. This is analogous to the idea of multiple indicators in quantitative research. Multiple instances of concepts in the empirical evidence help to strengthen the connections between concepts and data.

Selective Coding.   This is a last pass through the data. By this phase you probably have identified the major themes for your study. *Selective coding* involves scanning the data using the central themes and concepts. You add an empirical grounding to themes and concepts and elaborate on them. You are looking selectively in the data for several strong examples that offer clear support for each concept and theme. You also seek data to compare and elaborate on major concepts and themes.

Selective coding occurs after data collection ended, after you have well-developed concepts and themes, and as you are finalizing concepts and themes into an overall analysis. In this phase, you organize the concepts and themes and build toward a few main generalizations or central themes. During selective coding, you may adjust the generalizations and central themes as you find multiple supporting instances of them in the data.

For example, in a study of working-class life in a tavern you decide to make gender relations a major theme. In selective coding, you go through the field notes and search for strong examples of male–female differences in talk about dating, engagements, weddings, divorce, extramarital affairs, or husband–wife relations. You then compare male and female attitudes about each area to your other major theme, marriage.

Likewise, in a study on the Knights of Labor you make the movement's failure to form alliances with other political groups a major theme. In selective coding, you look for codes that indicate a compromise and conflict between the Knights and political groups or parties, including temperance groups and the Prohibition Party. The array of concepts and themes related to temperance that you found in axial coding helps you document how the temperance issue facilitated or inhibited alliances.

In the comparative study of university students, you make sibling relations a central theme. You could then link it to concepts about each country's cultural norms about brother–sister cooperation/competition, proscribed behavior by sibling age and birth order, and parental favoritism of certain children over others. You then relate the sibling relations theme to your original interest in how a university student at a distant location relates to his or her family.

During the selective coding phase, you refine, reorganize, and elaborate on themes and concepts as you reexamine the data and select supporting evidence. For example, in the working-class tavern study, you reexamine the theme "opinions on marriage" and connect evidence about it to themes of gender relations and stages of the life cycle. You seek evidence on how marriage relates to gender relations and the life cycle. Likewise, in the Knights of Labor study, as you review evidence about the temperance theme, you form links to evidence on related themes, such are a failure to form alliances with other movements and growing internal divisions within the Knights movement based on ethnic and religious differences among members. In the comparative study on university students, you look for evidence on how the sibling theme relates to each society's dominant cultural norms about brother–sister interaction, proscribed sibling norms, and parental favoritism regarding their children. The three phases of coding work together to move you from a mass of raw data toward a final, integrated analysis (see Figure 13.1).

FIGURE 13.1   The Coding Process for Qualitative Data Analysis

Step 1: Open Coding

Carefully read and review all data notes, then create a code
that captures the idea, process, or theme in the data.

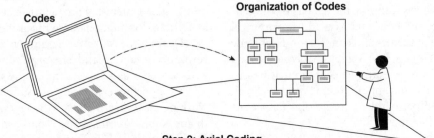

Step 2: Axial Coding

Organize all the codes created during open coding into a structure by separating
them into major or minor levels and showing relations among the codes.

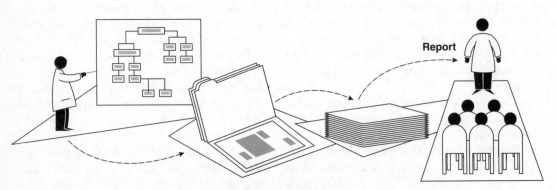

Step 3: Selective Coding

Take the organized codes from the axial coding process and review the codes in the original
data notes to select the best illustrations for entering them into a final report.

Analytic Memo Writing

You should to be a disciplined, compulsive note-taker to conduct qualitative research. You record data in notes, develop a research strategy in notes, and write notes about new concepts and themes. You must organize the notes into files and create files for various kinds of notes: a file of maps or diagrams, a file on methodological issues (e.g., locations of sources or ethical issues), a file on possible report outlines, a file of sources, a file on specific people or events, and so on.

The *analytic memo* is a special type of note. It is a memo of the ideas about the coding process and themes that you write to yourself. Each coded theme or concept forms the basis of a separate memo, and the memo has a discussion of the concept or theme. The analytic memos are also the beginning of generalizations and theoretical analysis.

Analytic memos link details in the concrete data or raw evidence to more abstract, theoretical thinking about the evidence (see Figure 13.2). They contain your reflections and thinking about the data and coding as well. You can continuously add to the memos and return to them as you pass through the data with each type of coding. They become a basis for data analysis in the research report. In fact, you might be able to rewrite parts of good-quality analytic memos into sections of a final research report.

The technology involved in writing analytic memos is simple: pen and paper, a few notebooks, computer files, and photocopies of notes. There are many ways to write analytic memos; develop your own style or method. You could make multiple copies of paper data notes, then cut them and insert selections into an analytic memo file. This works well if the data files are large and you keep analytic memos distinct within the file (e.g., on different-colored paper or placed at the beginning). You could link the electronic analytic memo files to the locations in data notes where a theme or concept discussed in the memo appears. This allows you to move quickly between the analytic memo and the data.

FIGURE 13.2   Analytic Memos and Other Files

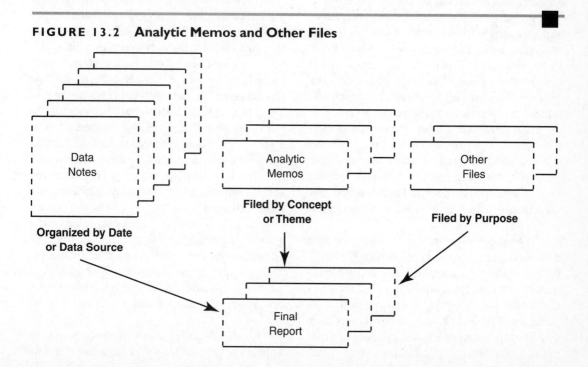

As you review and modify analytic memos, they may stimulate reflection and you might elaborate on the memos. You can also build on ideas in the memos by discussing ideas with colleagues and returning to the scholarly literature with new concepts and themes. You can use analytic memos to generate potential quasi-hypotheses during data collection and coding. You can add, modify, and drop the quasi-hypothesis as needed.

ANALYTIC STRATEGIES FOR QUALITATIVE DATA

Many qualitative researchers use the data coding and analytic memo writing techniques discussed in the previous sections. You can combine these techniques with a more specific analytic strategy. In this section, you learn about four strategies for analyzing the qualitative data: the narrative, ideal types, successive approximation, and the illustrative method.

Quantitative data analysis usually involves applying statistics to evaluate and display numerical information using formulas, charts, equations, and standard statistical tests. Qualitative data analysis is more diverse and less standardized. In the past, few qualitative researchers explained their methods of data analysis in depth. Recently have qualitative researchers begun to explain and outline exactly how they analyzed their data.

In general, *data analysis* is a search for patterns in data—recurrent behaviors, objects, belief systems, and relationships. Once you identify a pattern in the data, you can interpret it using themes, concepts, or theory, all the while remaining sensitive to the specific cultural–historical setting in which it occurred.

In qualitative research, you move from data that are documented, detailed descriptions of a historical event or social activity to data connected with concepts and themes. The concepts and themes help you build toward a broad interpretation of theoretical meaning or significance. The broad interpretation will include an organized, interrelated set of concepts and themes.

Data analysis is a process. You create connections from specific instances in particular data, to patterns across the data, to data-grounded concepts and themes, to generalizations that organize the concepts and themes. The four analytic strategies we examine next apply to the last two phases of the process. They are not mutually exclusive and you can combine them.

The Narrative

You encountered the narrative in the last chapter on H-C research. In field research, the **narrative** is also called a *natural history* or *realist tale* approach. The narrative is closer to a form of description than to abstract theory. In the narrative, you, as researcher–author, largely "disappear" from the analysis and present the concrete details in chronological order as if they were a "naturally unfolding" sequence of events. Your role is to "tell a story" of what you witnessed or what occurred.

A few scholars argue that a narrative should present data without analysis, or if a narrative has analysis, it is often "light" and subtle. In the narrative, you assemble the data into a descriptive picture or account of what occurred, but largely leave the data to "speak for themselves." You do little "repackaging" of data into concepts or themes. You interject little in the form of abstract theories or models. Your explanation resides less in abstract concepts and theories than in the way you combine and arrange a telling of specific details.

In the narrative, you try to reveal the social reality as experienced by members in a field setting, or you try to present the worldview and lived experience of specific historical actors at a particular point in time. Using little commentary, you convey an authentic feel for life's complexity as experienced by particular people in specific circumstances. You employ few abstract concepts and patterns for your reader.

As stated earlier, analysis in the narrative appears largely in how you organize the data for storytelling, giving attention to particular people, events, or facts. You may rely on literary devices—creatively selecting particular words, describing a setting's emotional atmosphere, showing "character development" of people in the study, and presenting events in a manner that maximizes their dramatic emphasis, intrigue, or suspense. In the narrative, you assemble specific details (i.e., the names, actions, and words of specific people and descriptions of particular events at specific times) that may be idiosyncratic if alone, but together they contribute to a complete picture or explanation (see Expansion Box 13.1).

There is a debate over the usefulness of the narrative strategy of data analysis. Positive features of the narrative are that it:

- Provides readers with rich, concrete details about people, situations, events or places.
- Demonstrates the temporal ordering of processes or specific events.
- Captures a high degree of complexity in people and situations.
- Conveys a nuanced understanding of how events mutually affect one other;
- Evokes an empathic or emotional connection to what the data reveal.

13.1 EXPANSION BOX
The Narrative

Many qualitative researchers, especially feminist researchers, use the narrative because they believe it best enables them to retain a richness and authenticity from their original data sources (i.e., individual personal stories or events in ethnographies, or specific historical events). In simple terms, the narrative is storytelling. In it, an author presents two or more events in temporal and causal sequences. Some narratives are complex, with elements such as (1) a summary statement of the entire story; (2) an orientation that identifies specific times, places, persons, and situations; (3) complicated actions or twists in the plot of "what happened"; (4) an evaluation or emotional assessment of the narrative's meaning or significance; (5) a resolution or what occurred after a dramatic high point that resolves a suspenseful climatic event; and (6) a coda or signal that the narrative is ending.

People frequently tell one another stories in daily life. They usually structure or organize their narratives into one of several recognized patterns, often recounting it with visual clues, gestures, or voice intonations for dramatic emphasis. The structure may include plot lines, core metaphors, and rhetorical devices that draw on familiar cultural and personal models to effectively communicate meanings to others.

The narrative is found in literature, artistic expressions, types of therapy, judicial inquiries, social or political histories, biographies and autobiographies, medical case histories, and journalistic accounts. As a way to organize, analyze, and present qualitative social science data, the narrative shares many features with other academic and cultural communication forms, but it differs from the positivist model for organizing and reporting on data. The positivist model emphasizes using impersonal, abstract, "neutral" language and a standardized analytic approach.

Many qualitative researchers argue that researchers who adopt the positivist model are simply using an alternative form of narrative, one with specialized conventions. These conventions encourage formal analytic models and abstract theories, but such models or theories are not necessarily superior to a storytelling narrative. Positivist data analysis and reporting conventions have two negative effects. First, they make it easier for researchers to lose sight of the concrete actual events and personal experiences that comprise social science data. Second, they make it more difficult for researchers to express ideas and build social theories in a format that most people find to be familiar and comfortable.

Negative features or limitations of the narrative include that it:

- Remains too complex, particular, and idiosyncratic.
- Repeats the contradictions, inconsistencies, and misinformation of the people studied.
- Fails to generalize and offer basic abstraction necessary for clear data organization.
- Inhibits use of shared concepts and general knowledge that can connect to other studies.
- Veils the researcher's analysis and limits an explicit examination of it by outsiders.
- Confuses creating reader emotional engagement with providing a scientific explanation.

Ideal Types

Max Weber developed the *ideal type*. It is a pure model or mental abstraction that facilitates recognizing, thinking about, and understanding social relations or processes at a deeper level. An ideal type is a pure standard you create. You can compare it to the data or "reality." It is primarily a device for comparison, because no reality ever perfectly fits an ideal type.

For example, you develop a mental model of the ideal democracy, serial killer, or college beer party. They are abstractions that exist only in your mind. You can create lists of their characteristics but they do not describe any specific democracy, serial killer, or beer party in reality. Although they never match any actual democracy, serial killer, or party, they are useful when you examine specific "real" cases because you can see how well a case measures up to the ideal.

You can use the ideal type strategy with the illustrative method (described later) and it also complements John Stuart Mill's method of agreement. With the method of agreement, you look for what is common across multiple cases. You may look for common causes in cases that have a common outcome. Let us say in a study of the Knights of Labor protest movement, you observe that other protest movements have failed (i.e., common outcome) and had similar

causes (e.g., internal divisions developed among movement members arising from deep-rooted prior values and identities, or an inability to build alliances with related movements that are equally large or powerful). Alone, the method of agreement implies comparing several cases.

You can also compare several cases against an ideal type. You might develop an ideal type of a social process (e.g., how a new protest movement develops, spreads quickly, but then collapses), and compare specific cases (e.g., five different protest movements from U.S. and Canadian history) to it. By comparing an ideal type with several cases you can better see areas where the ideal type receives consistent support. It also highlights shared features among the cases for you.

You can use ideal types in two ways: to contrast the impact of contexts and as an analogy.

Contrast Contexts. You can use an ideal type to interpret data in a way that highlights the context and cultural meanings. When you compare the ideal type to the specifics in each case, you can identify what is unique to a particular context and what is general and consistent with the ideal type across the diverse contexts. By using contrasting contexts, you learn to recognize particular manifestations of the general, abstract model in cultural or historical context.

Perhaps you have developed an ideal type of a protest movement and its process of rise, expansion, and fall. You identify 15 of such protest movements across history and in various countries. You examine the movements' protesting various causes in different countries and a century apart. Then you demonstrate how core features of the ideal type remain the same in diverse cultural–historical contexts. In this way, both the context (e.g., 1880s America, 1910s Canada, 1930s Mexico, 1950s France, and 1960s Japan) and the ideal type are parts of the analysis. When comparing contexts with the ideal type, you are trying less to discover a universal or "social law" than accentuate how the ideal type helps organize numerous details in what appear to be different specific and unique contexts.

Analogies.   A second way you can use the ideal type is as an analogy. An *analogy* is a statement that two objects, processes, or events are similar to each other. You probably use analogies to communicate ideas and facilitate logical comparisons. Analogies transmit information by referring to an already known or familiar experience. They are a shorthand way to highlight similarities and to facilitate understanding about a maze of specific details.

In an analogy, you identify something familiar or known then draw parallels between it and something new or something you are trying to explain. For example, when describing how a room went silent after person X spoke, you might say, "A chill like a cold gust of air" spread through the room. This does not mean that the room temperature dropped or people felt a breeze, but it succinctly expresses a type of rapid change in emotional tone. The analogy temporarily condenses and brings attention to certain details as it simultaneously pushes aside other, less relevant details.

You can use the ideal type in an analogy to describe a relationship buried deep within many specific details, making it easier to compare social processes across different cases or settings. For example, gender relations in society Y are such that women are "viewed like property and treated like slaves." This does not mean that the legal and social relations between genders are identical to those of slave owner and slave. It says that important similarities exist between the ideal type of a slave–master relationship and the gender relations of society Y. If people are familiar with the ideal type, using it in an analogy becomes a shortcut for you to advance an understanding (i.e., gender relations in society Y).

Analogies serve as a heuristic device (i.e., a device that helps one learn or see). They represent something complex and unknown in an idealized, abstract model. This makes them especially valuable when you want to discuss a pattern, a deep structure, or an underlying mechanism in a large amount of complex information. Ideal types do not provide a definitive test of an explanation but they guide the conceptual reconstruction of details into a format that facilitates comprehension.

Successive Approximation

Successive approximation is a process of repeated iterations or cycling through steps as you move toward a final analysis. After several iterations, you move from vague ideas and numerous concrete details in the data toward a compact analysis with a few main generalizations.

In successive approximation you cycle through a process that links data and concepts to one another. You might begin with a research question, a framework of assumptions, and several imprecise concepts. As you gather and probe into the data, you ask questions of the evidence. You try to see how well the concepts and the evidence fit one another. You examine how well the concepts reveal important features within the data, and how well the data fit within the concepts. You also create new concepts by abstracting from the evidence. Over time, you adjust concepts to fit the evidence better and collect additional evidence to address unresolved issues that appeared in an earlier stage. You then repeat the process, over and over again. At each stage, you realign concepts and data. Gradually the detailed data and abstract concepts shape one another. The term *successive* refers to the repeated process. The term *approximation* refers to modifying concepts to approximate the full details of the data. Through the repeated process of modifying abstract ideas and gathering specific data, they become increasingly aligned with one another. In this way abstract concepts become grounded or rooted in the concrete evidence. Although each pass through the data is provisional or incomplete, your analysis moves slowly toward abstract generalizations. Through this slow successive process, you arrive at abstract generalizations that remain true to the complexities and contingencies of the data.

For example, in an H-C study you believe that a 100-year historical era you are examining is not even or linear; rather, it is comprised of several discontinuous stages or steps. In short, instead of a constant and even flow, you believe the flow of events has distinct phases or periods and divide 100 years of history into periods. You break continuous time into discrete units or periods and you define the periods theoretically. A theory helps you identify what is significant, what is common within the periods, and what differs between the periods. However, you cannot determine the number or size of periods and the location breaks between them until after you have closely examined all the data.

In successful approximation, you might start with a general idea of four periods and what distinguishes them (years of political calm interrupted by year of intense conflict). After you review the data, you adjust the number of periods to five. You also adjust the length and the break points between periods. You then gather additional data and reexamine all the data using the second set of historical periods. You may return to your theory to reconsider what political claim and intensive violence really mean and how to recognize them. After reexamining the data, you adjust the periodization again. After several cycles, you end by identifying five periods of varying lengths across the 100 years.

The Illustrative Method

With the *illustrative method*, you illustrate or anchor a theory with empirical evidence. It is a way to apply a preexisting theory to a concrete historical situation or social setting. You reorganize data based on the theory. The preexisting theory provides you with *empty boxes*. These are conceptual categories empty of empirical content. You seek empirical evidence that can fill the boxes. Putting evidence into the boxes helps you support or reject the theory. If you find a great deal of strong evidence for a "box" it helps to

confirm the theory. If after looking for evidence, you find little to place into a conceptual box, you may conclude that the theory lacks support. Theories that you fill with evidence become useful devices for interpreting the social world. The theory can be in the form of a general model, an analogy, or a sequence of steps.

There are two ways to use the illustrative method. In the first, you show that the theoretical model illuminates or clarifies a specific case or single situation. You "fill in" a conceptual box with a great deal of complex, detailed evidence. By placing data into the existing conceptual box, the data become more understandable. In the second, you demonstrate a model by juxtaposing multiple cases (i.e., units or historical periods) to show that the theory helps clarify information on multiple cases. In this parallel demonstration method, you first outline a theoretical framework with "empty boxes." There are predicted or expected categories originating in the theory. You then locate cases to demonstrate how well the framework organizes data across cases. You saw this in the last chapter. Viterna and Fallon's study on democratization and gender equality (see previous chapter, Example Box 12.5; also see Expansion Box 13.2 for a summary of types).

EXPANSION BOX

13.2   A Summary of Four Strategies for Qualitative Data Analysis

1. *The narrative.* Tell a detailed story about a particular slice of social life.

2. *Ideal types.* Compare qualitative data with a pure model of social life.

3. *Successive approximation.* Repeatedly move back and forth between data and theory, until the gap between them shrinks or disappears.

4. *Illustrative method.* Fill the "empty boxes" of theory with qualitative data.

OTHER TECHNIQUES

There are several other qualitative data analysis techniques. Here is a brief look at a few other techniques to illustrate the variety.

Network Analysis

Social researchers have studied social networks long before the recent popularity of social network software, such as Facebook. They used network theory and gathered data on social networks with snowball sampling. In a study you may find it useful to "map" the network of connections among a set of people, organizations, events, or places. Sociograms and similar mapping techniques help you to see and display a complex set of interrelations. They also allow you to analyze relations of influence, communication, and power inside the network.

For example, at the airline, the pilot Harry gives orders to Sue, who is a flight attendant, Sue and Sam, another flight attendant, consult and help one another. Sam gets supplies from Sandra, on the ground crew. Sandra socializes with Mary, who works at the check-in counter. Studying networks helps you see and understand the structure of complex social relations.

Time Allocation Analysis

Time is an important resource. You can examine how people or organizations spend or invest time. This reveals implicit rules of conduct, power, and priorities. You can document the duration or amount of time people devote to various activities (e.g., housework, commuting, time on the Internet, time with family) to understand social life. An analysis of how people, groups, or organizations allocate the valuable resources they control (such as time, space, money, prestige) can reveal their true, as contrasted with officially professed, priorities. For example, someone says she hates housework, doesn't like television, and loves her children. You look at her time allocation and she spends four hours a week talking with her child, 20 hours watching television, and 22 hours doing housework. Often, people are unaware of or do not explicitly acknowledge the importance of an activity on which they spent time. For example, you notice that many people are required to wait before seeing a high government official. They may struggle to get an appointment, have to wait weeks to see the official, and then are allotted 10 minutes. A few other people see the official without having an appointment, go in immediately, and can spend an hour of the official's time. Studying the allocation of the official's time, a valued resource, shows both the official's power and who the official considers important. You can learn about social relations by analyzing amounts of time, waiting time, and how people feel about waiting.

Time can reveal many aspects of culture. You might document that people say that a certain celebration in a corporation is not important. Yet, you notice that everyone attends and spends two hours at the event. The collective allocation of two hours during a busy week for the celebration signals its latent or implicit importance in the culture of the corporation.

Flowchart and Time Sequence

In addition to the amount of time people devote to activities, you can analyze the ordering of events or decisions. The flow or sequence of events helps show causal relations. In addition to when events occur, you can create a decision tree or flowchart to outline the order of decisions or see how one event or decision relates to others. A decision tree is a visual mapping of when events or decisions occur and how they relate to one another. For example, you can outline an activity as simple as making a cake (see Figure 13.3). The mapping-out of steps, decisions, or events applies to many settings and activities.

Domain Analysis

Cognitive anthropologists study how people understand and organize material objects, events,

FIGURE 13.3 **Partial Flowchart of Cake Making**

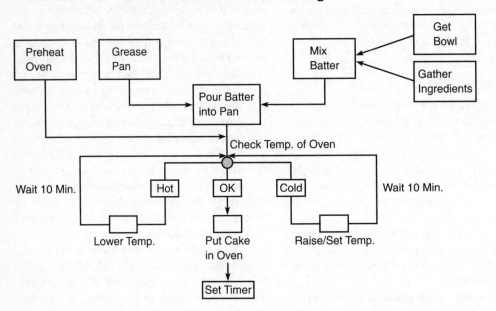

and experiences. They note that people make sense of reality based on cognitive categories and order events, material life, and ideas using cognitive categories. They try to discover and document cognitive categories, rules of behavior, and systems of thought that people use.

Cognitive anthropologists developed *domain analysis* to analyze data about culture.[1] It treats the *cultural domain* as the basic unit of a cultural setting. A domain is an organizing idea or concept that brings a unit to a setting. You analyze a cultural domain by using a cover term, included terms, and a semantic relationship. A *cover term* is simply the domain's name, *included terms* are the subtypes or parts of the domain, and a *semantic relationship* is the logical connection among included terms within the domain.

For example, a domain might be a witness in a judicial setting, such as a trial in a courtroom. The cover term for the domain is "witness." Three subtypes or included terms are defense witness, character witness, and expert witness. The semantic relationship is "is a kind of." Thus, the expert witness, character witness, and a defense witness are kinds of witnesses within the broader domain of witnesses. Other semantic relationships are listed in Example Box 13.1.

There are three types of domains: folk domains, mixed domains, and analytic domains.

1. *Folk domains* based on actual words and phrases used by members in a social setting (i.e., folk terms and folk concepts). You need to pay close attention to language and usage to record the words and phrases. By examining relations among folk terms or the language of historical actors, you can identify patterns in cultural meaning.

2. *Mixed domains* contain folk terms and concepts, but include your own ideas as well. For example, you might look at kinds of runners as named by the terminology of runners (e.g., long-distance, track, etc.), but

13.1   EXAMPLE BOX
Forms of Relationships in Cultural Domains

SEMANTIC RELATIONSHIP	EXAMPLE OF USE
Is a type of	A bus *is a type of* motor vehicle [types of vehicles].
Is a part of/is a place in	A tire *is a part of* a car [parts of cars].
Is a way to	Cheating *is a way to* get high grades in school [ways students get high grades].
Is used for	A train *is used for* transporting goods [ways to transport goods].
Is a reason for	High unemployment *is a reason for* public unrest [reasons for public unrest].
Is a stage of	The charge *is a stage of* a battle [stages of battle].
Is a result of/ is a cause of	A coal power plant *is a cause of* acid rain [causes of acid rain].
Is a place for	A town square *is a place for* a mob to gather [places where mobs gather].
Is a characteristic of	Wearing spiked, colored hair *is a characteristic of* punks [characteristics of punks].

you observe other types of people for whom no term exists in the usage of runners and you assign terms to them (e.g., infrequent visitors, newcomers, amateurs, etc.).

3. *Analytic domains* are organized around concepts that you, the researcher, or social theory provide. They are most helpful when the meanings in a setting are tacit, implicit, or unrecognized by participants. Folk terms may be authentic, but they are often poorly defined or contradictory. You may infer meaningful categories and patterns from your observations and artifacts, and then

you develop and assign conceptual terms to them.

To construct domains from data notes, first read your notes and look for domains (i.e., a social–cultural unit of interacting people). Next, identify a list of cover terms. For example, a witness in a judicial setting could be a cover term. Next, look for common semantic relationships (e.g., is a kind of place, is a kind of person, is a kind of feeling, etc.) to find included terms. Once you have several cover terms, organize the information from notes as included terms using the semantic relationship. Prepare a worksheet for each domain relationship. The worksheet contains the cover term, a list of included terms, and the semantic relationship (see Example Box 13.2 for an example worksheet).

You can now locate many examples from your notes. You proceed with the analysis until you have identified all relevant domains. You then organize the domains by comparing differences and similarities. Finally, you reorganize domains into typologies or taxonomies and reexamine the domains to create new, broader domains that include other domains as included terms (see Expansion Box 13.3 for a summary of domain analysis steps).

Multiple Sorting Procedure

Multiple sorting is a technique similar to domain analysis. It is especially useful in field research or oral history. We all have mental maps that we use to organize the objects, people, and activities of our lives. Multiple sorting helps you discover mental maps, or how people categorize their experiences or classify items into systems of "similar" and "different."

You can use multiple sorting to collect, verify, or analyze data. Here is how it works. First, give the people you are studying a list of terms, photos, places, names of people, and so on, and ask them to organize them into a limited number of categories or piles. They can use categories of their own devising. Once sorted,

13.2

EXAMPLE BOX
Example of Domain Analysis Worksheet

1. Semantic relationship: <u>Strict inclusion</u>
2. Form: <u>X (is a type of) Y</u>
3. Example: <u>An oak (is a type of) tree</u>

INCLUDED TERMS	SEMANTIC RELATIONSHIP	COVER TERM
laundromat, hotel lobby		
motor box, orchard,	is a type of	
flophouse, under bridge	──────────→	flop
box car, alley		
public toilet, steam grate		

INCLUDED TERMS	SEMANTIC RELATIONSHIP	COVER TERM
trusty, ranger		
bull cook, mopper,	is a type of	
head trusty, lockup	──────────→	jail inmate
bullet man, sweeper		
lawn man, inmate's barber		

you ask them about the criteria they used. For example, you go to a woman's home and ask her to sort movable nonfood objects in the kitchen—spices, cooking utensils, plates, and so forth. After she sorted everything, you record the organization and ask her about the criteria used (e.g., I use these for preparing holiday meals, this is what I use when I bake desserts, these are for eating fast food, etc.). You then shuffle the items and ask her to sort them a second time but in another way. The purpose of the sorting is to reveal a person's mental maps or inner organizational schemes. Perhaps the second time around, the woman sorts items by their cost, by whether she received them as a gift or she purchased them, or by sentimental association of the item (e.g., this is what I used

when my child was young, this is the pot I used to cook my husband's favorite meal before he died). Thus, multiple sorting is a vehicle you can use to see how people organize and understand their worlds.

Diagrams

Visual representations of data in the form of diagrams and charts help in three ways: they help you to organize ideas, to systematically examine and investigate relationships in the data, and to communicate your results to readers. There are many types of diagrams. These include flowcharts (discussed earlier in this chapter), spatial or temporal maps (discussed in Chapter 11), typologies (discussed in Chapter 3), or

13.3 Summary of Steps in Domain Analysis

Domain analysis formalizes six steps found in many types of qualitative data analysis:

1. Read and reread qualitative data notes that are full of details.
2. Mentally repackage the details into a few dozen organizing ideas.
3. Develop new ideas from the notes relying on subjective meanings or organizing ideas.
4. Look for relationships among the ideas and group them based on logical similarity.
5. Organize larger groups by comparing and contrasting the sets of ideas.
6. Reorganize and link the groups together into broader integrating themes.

sociograms (discussed in Chapter 6). You can also map social relations, draw organizational charts, and create grids of activities or events as a way to illustrate relations within qualitative data (see Figure 13.4).

SOFTWARE FOR QUALITATIVE DATA

Shortly after the invention of modern computers about 50 years ago, quantitative social researchers started using them to generate tables, graphs, and charts and calculate statistical measures as they analyzed numerical data. By contrast, computer software for analyzing qualitative data has been available only for the past 10 to 15 years.

The logic of computers for qualitative data can be seen with word processing. After you enter notes in a word-processing program, you can quickly search for words and phrases. If you found words in the notes, you could code the data notes. Word processing can also help you revise and move codes and parts of field notes.

New computer programs for qualitative data are being developed and existing programs are constantly being updated. They have detailed, program-specific user manuals and can take serious effort to learn. The review here only covers only the major approaches to qualitative data analysis at this time, not specific software programs. Because of the many ways to analyze qualitative data and types of data, the various software programs operate on different principles and allow you to examine different forms of qualitative data. The two dozen or so qualitative data analysis programs, such as Atlas.ti, Ethnograph, HyperRESEARCH, Kwalitan, MaxQDA, Nvivo, and QCA, make it confusing and take time to learn. Many are for text data. Others are for audio or video data, and some include photographic data.

Text retrieval programs in qualitative data analysis perform searches of text documents. What they do is similar to the searching function of word-processing software. The specialized text retrieval programs are faster and have the capability of finding close matches, slight misspellings, similar-sounding words, and synonyms. For example, if you look for the keyword *boat*, the program might also tell you whether any of the following appeared: *ship, battleship, frigate, rowboat, schooner, vessel, yacht, steamer, ocean liner, tug, canoe, skiff, cutter, aircraft carrier, dinghy, scow, galley, ark, cruiser, destroyer, flagship*, and *submarine*. In addition, some programs permit you to combine words or phases using logical terms (*and, or, not*) in what are called *Boolean searches*. For example, you can search long documents of notes for where *college student* and *drinking* and *smoking* occur within four sentences of one another and when the word *fraternity* is not present in a block of text. Boolean search uses *and* to seek the intersection of *college student* with either of two behaviors that are connected by the logical term *or*, whereas the logical search word *not* excludes situations in which the term *fraternity* appears.

Most qualitative software will show the keyword or phrase and the surrounding text. The

FIGURE 13.4   Examples of the Use of Diagrams in Qualitative Analysis

	EXAMPLE I			
Person	Worked before College	Part-Time Job in College	Pregnant Now	Had Own Car
John	Yes	Yes	N/A	No
Mary	Yes	DK	No	Yes\cr
Martin	No	Yes	N/A	Yes\cr
Yoshi	Yes	No	Yes	Yes

DK = don' t know, N/A = not applicable

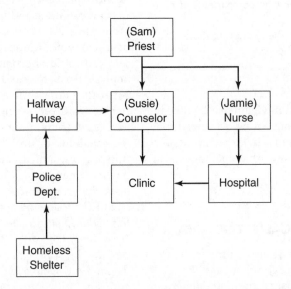

programs may also permit you to write separate memos or add short notes to the text. Some programs count the keywords found and give their location. Most create a very specific index for the text, based only on the terms of interest to you.

Text base managers are similar to text retrieval programs. The key difference is their ability to organize or sort information about search results. They allow you to sort notes by a key idea or to add factual information. For example, when the data are detailed notes on interviews, you can add information about the date and length of the interview, gender of the interviewee, location of the interview, and so on. You then can sort and organize each interview or part of the interview notes using a combination of keywords and added information.

In addition, some programs have hypertext capability. Hypertext lets you electronically link a term to other information. When you click the computer mouse on one term, it opens a new screen (one that has related information). You can identify codes, keywords, or topics and link them together. For example, in field research you want to examine Susan and the topic of hair (including haircuts, hairstyles, hair coloring, and hats or hair coverings). You can use hypertext to connect all places Susan's name appears to discussions of hair. By the mouse clicking on Susan's name, one block of text quickly jumps to another in the notes to see all places where Susan and the hair topic appear together.

Code-and-retrieve programs allow you to attach codes to lines, sentences, paragraphs, or blocks of text. The programs may permit multiple codes for the same data. In addition to attaching codes, the programs also help you to organize the codes. For example, a program can help you make outlines or "trees" of connections (e.g., trunks, branches, and twigs) among the codes, and among the data to which the codes refer. The program rearranges the qualitative data based on your codes and the relations among codes that you have specified.

Unlike most programs that facilitate coding or retrieving data in text, photo, audio or video forms, qualitative comparative analysis (QCA) is based on Boolean algebra. It facilitates case comparison, especially for data about macro-level phenomena. You input many details about a few cases and the program helps you examine logical relations among many aspects of the cases.

CONCLUSION

In this chapter, you learned the basics of analyzing qualitative data. In many respects, qualitative data are more difficult to analyze than data in the form of numbers. Numbers are uniform and have mathematical properties. You can use well-developed, standardized statistical procedures and widely available statistical software to analyze quantitative data. Qualitative data are much more varied and come in a variety of formats (e.g., photos, maps, text, transcripts, audio or video records, physical objects) that make analysis a challenge. Data analysis requires you to be creative and may involve more effort as you review (i.e., read text; view photos, maps, and videos; listen to audio) vast amounts of qualitative data over and over again. Most qualitative data is in the form of text notes. You must read and reread the notes, reflect on what you have read, and make comparisons using ingenuity, logic, and good judgment.

In most forms of qualitative data analysis you assign codes to data and write analytic memos. Both are labor-intensive efforts. You must review the data carefully and think about them seriously. This chapter also discussed various strategies for the analysis of qualitative data. They are a sample of the many ways to conduct qualitative data analysis.

This chapter ends the section of the book on research design, data collection, and data analysis. Social research is not finished until you have communicated your study findings to others. This involves preparing reports on a research project, which you will read about in the next chapter.

Key Terms

analytic domain
axial coding
cover term
domain analysis
empty boxes
folk domain
illustrative method
included term
mixed domain
narrative
open coding
selective coding
semantic relationship
successive approximation

Endnotes

1. See Spradley (1979a, 1979b).

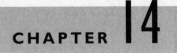

CHAPTER 14

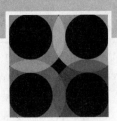

Writing the Research Report

In previous chapters, you saw how to design studies, gather data, and analyze the data. Yet, your research project is not complete until you have shared the results with others. A critical last step in the research process is to communicate publicly what you learned and how you conducted the study. It is usually in the form of a written report. In Chapter 1 you read that the scientific community emphasizes making public how researchers conducted studies and their findings. In this chapter, you learn about writing a research report.

THE RESEARCH REPORT

Why Write a Report?

After you finish a study or a significant phase of a large research project, it is time to communicate the findings to others through a research report. You can learn a lot about writing a research report by reading many reports and taking a course in scientific and technical writing.

A *research report* is a written document (or oral presentation based on a written document) that communicates the methods and findings of a study to others. More than a summary of findings, it is a record of the entire research process. You cannot wait until the research is done to start thinking about the report; you must think ahead to the report and keep careful records while conducting research. The report includes the reasons for initiating the study, a description of its steps, data presentation, and a discussion of how the data relate to the research question or topic.

The report is a vehicle for disseminating knowledge. It tells others what you, the researcher, did, and what you discovered. A research report plays a significant role in binding together the scientific community. It might fulfill a class or job assignment, meet an obligation to an organization that paid for the research, persuade a professional group about specific aspects of a problem, or inform the public about findings. Except in certain applied, action-oriented research, informing the public is rarely a primary purpose for communication of scientific results.

The Writing Process

Your Audience. Professional writers say: Always know for whom you are writing. This is because communication is most effective when you tailor it to a specific audience. You prepare a report differently depending on whether the primary audience is an instructor, students, professional social scientists, practitioners, or the public. No matter what the audience, your writing should be clear, accurate, and organized.

Instructors assign a report for various reasons and may place requirements on how it is written. In general, instructors look for writing that demonstrates clear, logical thinking and proper documentation. They want to see a solid grasp of substantive and methodological concepts. A good way to do this is to use technical terms properly and explicitly *when appropriate,* and not excessively or incorrectly.

When writing for students, you want to define technical terms and clearly label each part of the report. Your discussion should proceed in a clear, logical, step-by-step manner with many specific examples. Use straightforward language to explain how and why you conducted the various steps of the study. One strategy is to begin with the research question, then structure the report as an answer.

Scholars do not need definitions of technical terms or explanations of why you used a standard procedure (e.g., random sampling). They are interested in how the research connects to abstract theory or previous findings in the literature. They want a condensed, detailed description of research design. They pay close attention to how you measured variables and collected data. Scholars like a compact, tightly written, but extensive section on data analysis, with a meticulous discussion of results.

Practitioners prefer a short summary of how you conducted the study. They want to see results presented in a few simple charts and graphs. They like to see an outline of alternative paths of action implied by results with the practical outcomes of pursuing each path. You often must caution practitioners not to overgeneralize from the results of one study. It is best to place the details of your research design and full results in an appendix.

When writing for the public, use simple language, provide concrete examples, and focus on the practical implications of findings for specific problems. Do not include the details of research design or of results. Be careful not to make unsupported claims when writing for the public. Informing the public is an important service. It can help nonspecialists make better judgments about public issues.

Style and Tone.   Research reports have a narrow range of styles and a distinct tone. Their purpose is to communicate clearly and accurately the research method and findings.

Style refers to the types of words a writer chooses and the length and form of sentences or paragraphs used. *Tone* is a writer's attitude or relation toward the subject matter. For example, an informal, conversational style (e.g., colloquial words, idioms, clichés, and incomplete sentences) with a personal tone (e.g., these are my feelings) is appropriate for writing a letter to a close friend, but it is not appropriate for a research report. Research reports have a formal and succinct (saying a lot in few words) style. The tone expresses some distance from the subject matter; it is professional and serious. Field researchers will sometimes use an informal style and a personal tone, but this is the exception. Always avoid moralizing and flowery language. Your goal is to inform, not to be an advocate for a moral position or to entertain.

A research report should be accurate and clear. Check and recheck details (e.g., page references in citations) and fully disclose how you conducted the research. If readers detect carelessness in the writing, they may question the study itself. The study details can be complex, and complexity means that confusion is always a danger. It makes organized, clear writing essential. To achieve clear writing, think and rethink the research problem and design, explicitly define key terms, write with short declarative sentences, and limit your conclusions to what the evidence specifically supports.

Organizing Thoughts.   Writing does not happen magically or simply flow out as soon as you put pen to paper (or fingers to keyboard), although some people have such an illusion. Rather, it is hard work. You often must follow a sequence of steps that eventually result in a final product. Writing a research report is not radically different from other types of writing. Although some steps differ and the level of complexity may be greater, most of what you might do when writing a long letter, a poem, an instruction manual, or a short story applies to writing a research report.

First, you need something about which to write. The "something" in the research report includes the topic, research question, design and measures, data collection techniques, results, and implications. With so many parts to write about, good organization is essential. The most basic tool for organizing writing is the outline. Outlines help you ensure that you included all ideas and that the relationship among ideas is clear. Outlines are comprised of topics (words or phrases). Most of us are familiar with the basic form of an outline (see Figure 14.1).

Outlines can help you, but they can also become a barrier if you use them improperly. An outline is simply a tool to help you organize ideas. It helps you to:

- Put ideas in a sequence (e.g., what will be said first, second, and third)
- Group related ideas together (e.g., these are similar to each other but they differ from those)
- Separate the general, higher-level ideas from lower-level, specific ideas, and specific ideas from highly specific details

FIGURE 14.1   Form of an Outline

I. First major topic   One of the most important
  A. Subtopic of topic I   Second level of importance
    1. Subtopic of A   Third level of importance
      a. Subtopic of I   Fourth level of importance
      b. Subtopic of I   "
        (1) Subtopic of b   Fifth level of importance
        (2) Subtopic of b   "
          (a) Subtopic of (2)   Sixth level of importance
          (b) Subtopic of (2)   "
            i. Subtopic of (b)   Seventh level of importance
            ii. Subtopic of (b)   "
    2. Subtopic of A   Third level of importance
  B. Subtopic of topic I   Second level of importance
II. Second major topic   One of the most important

Some people feel that they need to have a complete outline before starting to write, and that once an outline is prepared, deviations from it are impossible. This is usually a mistake. Very few writers start with a complete outline and stick to it rigidly. Your initial outline may be sketchy, because until you write everything down, you cannot put all ideas in a sequence, group them together, or separate the general from the specific. For most writers, new ideas develop or become clearer during the process of writing itself.

A beginning outline may differ from the final outline by more than its degree of completeness. The process of writing not only reveals or clarifies ideas but it also stimulates new ideas, new connections among ideas, different ordering sequences, and new relations between general and specific ideas. In addition, during the process of writing you may be stimulated to reanalyze or reexamine the scholarly literature or findings. This does not mean you must begin all over again. Rather, you want to keep an open mind to new insights and be candid.

Back to the Library.   You should be familiar with the scholarly literature before beginning a study, but expect to return to it after you complete data collection and analysis. This is for three reasons:

- Time has passed between the beginning and the end of a research project, and new studies may have been published.
- After completing a study, you know better what is or is not central to it and you may have new questions in mind when you read studies in the literature.
- When writing the report, you may find that notes on the literature are not complete enough or a detail is missing in the citation of a reference source (see Example Box 14.1).

Your return visit to the library after data collection is less extensive and more selective or focused than that conducted at the beginning of research.

When writing the final research report, you will probably discard some notes and sources that you had gathered during the research project. This does not mean that the initial library work and literature review or the various memos and notes were a waste of time and effort. You

EXAMPLE BOX
Formats for Reference Lists, Using American Sociological Association Style

Books

First-Edition Books

Sanchez-Jankowski, Martin. 2008. *Cracks in the Pavement: Social Change and Resilience in Poor Neighborhoods.* Berkeley: University of California Press.

Glynn, Carroll J., Susan Herbst, Garrett J. O'Keefe, and Robert Y. Shapiro. 1999. *Public Opinion.* Boulder, CO: Westview Press.

Later Editions of Books

Castles, Stephen and Mark J. Miller. 2009. *The Age of Migration: International Population Movements in the Modern World, 4th ed.* New York: Guilford Press. [Abbreviations are 2d ed., 3d ed., Rev. ed., 2 vols.]

One Volume of Multivolume Book

Marx, Karl. [1887] 1967. *Capital: Critique of Political Economy, Volume 1, The Process of Capitalist Production.* Translated by Frederick Engles. Reprint. New York: International Publishers.

Translated Books

Durkheim, Emile. 1933. *The Division of Labor in Society.* Translated by George Simpson. New York: Free Press.

Weber, Max. 1958. *The Protestant Ethic and the Spirit of Capitalism.* Translated by Talcott Parsons. New York: Charles Scribner's Sons.

Edited Books

Della Porta, Donatella and Michael Keating, eds. 2008. *Approaches and Methodologies in the Social Sciences: A Pluralist Perspective.* New York: Cambridge University Press.

Republished Books

Mason, Edward S. [1957] 1964. *Economic Concentration and the Monopoly Problem.* Reprint. New York: Atheneum.

Articles from Books or Scholarly Journals

Hegtvedt, Karen A. 2007. "Ethics and experiments." In *Laboratory experiments in the social sciences,* edited by M. Webster, Jr. and J. Sell, pp. 141–172. New York: Academic Press.

Goffman, Alice. 2009. "On the run: Wanted men in a Philadelphia ghetto." *American Sociological Review* 74:338–357.

[Note: Omit issue number except when each issue is renumbered beginning with page 1. Then give volume(issue): pages—e.g., 84(2):709–733.]

Articles from Magazines and Newspapers

Janofsky, Michael. "Shortage of Housing for Poor Grows in the U.S." *New York Times* (April 29, 1998), p. A14.

Alterman, Eric. 2011. "The Liars' Network." *Nation* 292 (April 25, 2011):10–12.

[Note: It is not always necessary to include page numbers for newspapers.]

Book Reviews

Academic Journals

Bergen, Raquel Kennedy. 1998. Review of *A Woman Scorned: Acquaintance Rape on Trial,* by Peggy Reeves Sanday. *Contemporary Sociology* 27:98–99.

Popular Magazines

Wolfe, Alan. 2001. Review of *Heaven Below: Early Pentecostals and American Culture,* by Grant Wacker. *New Republic* 225 (September 10):59–62.

Government Documents

U.S. Bureau of Census. 2006. *Statistical Abstract of the United States, 125th ed.* Washington DC: U.S. Government Printing Office.

Doctoral Dissertations and Theses

Cooper, Marianne. 2008. "Doing Security in Insecure Times: Class and Family Life in Silicon Valley." Ph.D. dissertation, Department of Sociology, University of California, Berkeley.

Unpublished Papers, Policy Reports, and Presented Papers

Haines, Herbert H. 1980. "Ideological Distribution and Racial Flank Effects in Social Movements" Paper presented at the annual meeting of the American Sociological Association, August, New York City.

Internet Sources

[*Note:* The date retrieved is the date that the reader located and read the work on the Internet.]

Announcement or Personal Home Page

American Sociological Association. 2011. Journals and Publication. Retrieved April 6, 2011. http://www.asanet.org/journals/index.cfm

Online Journal Article

Hess, Stephen. 2010. "Nail Houses, Land Rights, and Frames of Injustice on China's Protest Landscape" *Studies on Asia: An Interdisciplinary Journal of Asian Studies* Series IV, Vol. 1, No. 1, Fall 2010. http://studiesonasia.illinoisstate.edu/seriesIV/documents/Steve_Hess.pdf. Retrieved April 2, 2011.

Sosteric, Mike, Mike Gismondi and Gina Ratkovic. 1998. "The University, Accountability, and Market Discipline in the Late 1990s." *Electronic Journal of Sociology* April 1988, Vol. 3. Retrieved January 16, 1999. http://www.sociology.org/content/vol003.003/sosteric.html.

Newspaper Article

Lee, Don. 1999. "State's Job Growth Hits Unexpected Cold Spell." *Los Angeles Times* (January 16). Retrieved January 16, 1999. http://www. latimes .com/HOME/BUSINESS/topstory.html.

Journal Abstract or Book Review

Stanbridge, Karen. 2005. Review of *The New Transnational Activism* by Sidney Tarrow. *Canadian Journal of Sociology Online.* Retrieved January 12, 2010.

should expect that some of the notes (e.g., 25 percent) taken before completion phase will become irrelevant. You do not want to include notes or references in a research report that are no longer relevant. If included, they will distract from the flow of ideas and reduce clarity.

Returning to the library to verify and expand references can focus ideas and help avoid plagiarism. **Plagiarism** is a serious form of cheating. Many universities expel students caught engaging in it. If a professional ever plagiarizes in a scholarly journal, it is a very serious offense. Take careful notes and identify the exact source of phrases or ideas to avoid unintentional plagiarism. Cite sources of both directly quoted words and paraphrased ideas. For direct quotes, include the exact location of the quote with page numbers in the citation.

Using another person's written words and failing to give credit is always wrong, but paraphrasing is less clear. **Paraphrasing** is not using another's exact words; it is restating another's ideas in your own words, condensing or rearranging at the same time. Most researchers regularly paraphrase. Good paraphrasing requires a solid understanding of what you are paraphrasing. It means more than replacing another's words with synonyms; paraphrasing is borrowing an idea, boiling it down to its essence, and giving credit to the source.

Steps in Writing

Writing is a process. The best way to learn to write is by writing. It takes time and effort, and it improves with practice. There is no single correct way to write, but some methods are associated with good writing. The process has three steps:

1. *Prewriting.* Prepare to write by arranging notes on the literature, making lists of ideas, outlining, completing bibliographic citations, and organizing comments on data analysis.
2. *Composing.* Get your ideas onto paper as a first draft by freewriting, drawing up the bibliography and footnotes, preparing data for presentation, and forming an introduction and conclusion.
3. *Rewriting.* Evaluate and polish the report by improving coherence, proofreading for mechanical errors, checking citations, and reviewing voice and usage.

Many people find that getting started is difficult. Beginning writers often jump to the second step and end there, which results in poor-quality writing. *Prewriting* means that a writer begins with a file folder full of notes, outlines, and lists. You must think about the form of the report and audience. Thinking time is important. It often occurs in spurts over weeks before the bulk of composing begins.

Some people become afflicted with a strange ailment called *writer's block* when they sit down to write. It is a temporary inability to write when the mind goes blank, the fingers freeze, and panic sets in. Writers from beginners through experts occasionally experience it. If you experience it, calm down and work on overcoming it.

Numerous writers begin to compose by freewriting—that is, they sit down and write down everything they can as quickly as it enters the mind. Freewriting establishes a link between a rapid flow of ideas in the mind and writing. When you freewrite, you do not stop to reread what you wrote, you do not ponder the best word, you do not worry about correct grammar, spelling, or punctuation. You just put ideas on paper as quickly as possible to get and keep the creative juices or ideas flowing. You can later clean up what you wrote.

Writing and thinking are closely intertwined. It is impossible to know where one ends and the other begins. This means that if you plan to sit and stare at the wall, the computer output, the sky, or whatever until all thoughts become totally clear before beginning to write, you may not get anything written. Writing itself can ignite the thinking process.

Rewriting.   Perhaps one in a million writers is a creative genius who can produce a first draft that communicates with astounding accuracy and clarity. For the rest of us mortals, writing means that rewriting—and rewriting again—is necessary. For example, Ernest Hemingway is reported to have rewritten the end of *Farewell to Arms* 39 times. It is not unusual for professionals to rewrite a research report 6–10 times.

Do not become discouraged. If anything, rewriting reduces the pressure; it means you can start writing soon and quickly get out a rough draft that you can polish later. Plan to rewrite a draft at least three or four times. A draft is a complete report, from beginning to end. It is not just a few rough notes or an outline.

Rewriting can help you express yourself with a greater clarity, smoothness, precision, and economy of words. When rewriting, focus on clear communication, not pompous or complicated language. Rewriting means slowly reading what you have written and, if necessary, reading out loud to see if it sounds right. It is a good idea to share your writing with others. Professional writers often have others read and criticize their writing. New writers soon learn that friendly, constructive criticism is very valuable. Sharing your writing with others may be difficult at first. It means exposing your written thoughts and encouraging criticism. Yet, the purpose of the criticism is to clarify writing, and the critic is doing you a favor.

Rewriting involves three processes: revising, editing, and proofing. *Revising* is inserting new ideas, adding supporting evidence, deleting or changing ideas, moving sentences around to clarify meaning, or strengthening transitions and links between ideas. *Editing* means cleaning up and tightening the more mechanical aspects of writing, such as spelling, grammar, usage, verb tense, sentence length, and paragraph organization. *Proofing* is a final review. At this final stage, you polish, check for minor errors, and review for clarity and smoothness of communication. Typically, it involves a few very minor adjustments or corrections.

When you begin to rewrite, go over the draft and revise it brutally to improve it. This is easier if some time passes between a draft and rewriting. A phrase that seemed satisfactory in a draft may look fuzzy or poorly connected after a week or two. With each rewrite, the amount of revising generally declines as you move toward a final draft (see Expansion Box 14.1).

14.1 EXPANSION BOX
Suggestions for Rewriting

1. *Mechanics.* Check grammar, spelling, punctuation, verb agreement, verb tense, and verb/subject separation with each rewrite. Remember that each time new text is added, new errors can creep in. Mistakes are not only distracting but they also weaken the confidence readers place in the ideas you express.

2. *Usage.* Reexamine terms, especially key terms, when rewriting to see whether you are using the exact word that expresses your intended meaning. Do not use technical terms or long words unnecessarily. Use the plain word that best expresses meaning. Get a thesaurus and use it. A *thesaurus* is an essential reference tool, like a dictionary, that contains words of similar meaning and can help you locate the exact word for a meaning you want to express. Precise thinking and expression requires precise language. Do not say *average* if you use the *mean.* Do not say *mankind* or *policeman* when you intend *people* or *police officer.* Do not use *principal* for *principle.*

3. *Voice.* Writers of research reports often make the mistake of using the passive instead of the active voice. It may appear more authoritative, but passive voice obscures the actor or subject of action. For example, the passive, *The relationship between grade in school and more definite career plans was confirmed by the data* is better stated as the active, *The data confirm the relationship between grade in school and more definite career plans.* The passive, *Respondent attitude toward abortion was recorded by an interviewer* reads easier in the active voice: *An interviewer recorded respondent attitude toward abortion.* Also avoid unnecessary qualifying language, such as *seems to* or *appears to.*

4. *Coherence.* Sequence, steps, and transitions should be logically tight. Try reading the entire report one paragraph at a time. Does the paragraph contain a unified idea? A topic sentence?

Is there a transition between paragraphs within the report?

5. *Repetition.* Remove repeated ideas, wordiness, and unnecessary phrases. Ideas are best stated once, forcefully, instead of repeatedly in an unclear way. When revising, eliminate deadwood (words that add nothing) and circumlocution (the use of several words when one more precise word will do). Directness is preferable to wordiness. The wordy phrase, *To summarize the above, it is our conclusion in light of the data that X has a positive effect of considerable magnitude on the occurrence of Y, notwithstanding the fact that Y occurs only on rare occasions,* is better stated, *In sum, we conclude that X has a large positive effect on Y, but Y occurs infrequently.*

6. *Structure.* Research reports should have a transparent organization. Move sections around as necessary to fit the organization better, and use headings and subheadings. A reader should be able to follow the logical structure of a report.

7. *Abstraction.* A good research report mixes abstract ideas and concrete examples. A long string of abstractions without the specifics is difficult to read. Likewise, a mass of specific concrete details without periodic generalization also loses readers.

8. *Metaphors.* Many writers use metaphors to express ideas. Phrases like *the cutting edge, the bottom line,* and *penetrating to the heart* are used to express ideas by borrowing images from other contexts. Metaphors can be an effective method of communication, but they need to be used sparingly and with care. A few well-chosen, consistently used, fresh metaphors can communicate ideas quickly and effectively; however, the excessive use of metaphors, especially overused metaphors (e.g., the *bottom line*), is a sloppy, unimaginative method of expression.

Even if you have not acquired keyboarding skills, it is a good idea to print out at least one draft word-processed copy before the final draft. It is usually easier to see errors and organization problems in a clean, printed draft. You should feel free to cut and paste, cross out words, or move phrases on the printed copy.

Good keyboarding skills and the ability to use a word processor are extremely valuable when writing reports and other documents. You will find that the time you invest into building keyboard skills and learning to use a word processor pays huge dividends later. Word processors not only make editing much easier but they also can check spelling, offer synonyms, and check grammar. You cannot rely on the word processing software to do all the work, but it makes writing easier. The speed and ease that a word processor offers is so dramatic that few people who become skilled at using one ever return to writing by hand.

One last suggestion: Rewrite your introduction and title after you have completed a near final draft so that they accurately reflect what you have said. Titles should be short and descriptive. They should communicate the topic and the major variables to readers. They can describe the type of research (e.g., "An experiment on . . .") but should not have unnecessary words or phrases (e.g., "An investigation into the . . .").

The Quantitative Research Report

The principles of good writing apply to all reports, but the parts of a report differ depending on whether your study is quantitative or qualitative. Before writing any report, read several reports on the similar kind of research for models.

The sections of a report on quantitative research roughly follow the sequence of steps of doing a quantitative research study.

Abstract or Executive Summary.   Quantitative research reports usually begin with a short summary or abstract. The size of an abstract varies; it can be as few as 50 words (this paragraph has 75 words) or as long as a full page. Most scholarly journal articles have abstracts that are printed on the first page of the article. The abstract includes information on the topic, the research problem, the basic findings, and any unusual research design or data collection features.

Reports of applied research for practitioners have a longer summary called the *executive summary*. It contains more detail than an article abstract and includes the implications of research and a report's major recommendations. Although it is longer than an abstract, an executive summary rarely exceeds four to six pages.

Abstracts and executive summaries serve several functions: For the less interested reader, they tell what is in a report; for readers looking for specific information, they help a reader determine whether the full report has relevant information. Readers use the abstract or summary to screen information and decide whether to read the entire report. It gives serious readers who intend to read the full report a quick mental picture of it. This makes reading the full report easier and faster.

Presenting the Problem.   The first section of the report defines the research problem. It can be placed in a section with titles such as "Introduction," "Problem Definition," "Literature Review," "Hypotheses," or "Background Assumptions." Although the subheadings vary, the contents include the main research question and a rationale for what you examine in the study. Here, you explain the significance of and provide a background to the research question. You can explain the study's significance by showing how different outcomes to it would lead to different applications or theoretical conclusions. Introductory sections frequently include a context literature review and link your study to broader theoretical issues. Introductory sections may also define key concepts and present conceptual hypotheses.

Describing the Methods.   The next section of the report describes exactly how you designed the study and collected the data. It goes by several names (e.g., "Methods," "Research Design," or "Data") and may be subdivided into other parts (e.g., "Measures," "Sampling," or "Manipulations"). It is the most important section for evaluating study methodology. The section answers several questions for the reader:

1. What type of study (e.g., experiment, survey) did you conduct?
2. Exactly how did you collect the data (e.g., study design, type of survey, time and location of data collection, experimental design used)?
3. How did you define and measure the variables? Are your measures reliable and valid?
4. What is the sample? How many participants or respondents are involved in the study? How did you select them?
5. How did you address or resolve any ethical issues or specific concerns of the design?

Results and Tables.   After describing how you collected the data, and the sampling and measurement methods you used, it is time to present the data. This section presents—it does not discuss, analyze, or interpret—the data. Some researchers combine the "Results" section with the next section, called "Discussion" or "Findings."

You have choices about how you will present the data. When analyzing the data, you probably examined dozens of univariate, bivariate, and multivariate tables and statistics as you tried to get a solid understanding of the data. You do not place every statistic or table you looked at in the final report. Rather, you select the minimum number of charts, tables, or statistics that will fully inform the reader. You rarely present the raw data itself. Data analysis techniques should summarize the data and test hypotheses (e.g., frequency distributions, tables with means and standard deviations, correlations, and other statistics).

You want to offer a complete picture of the data without overwhelming the reader—do not provide data in excessive detail or present irrelevant data. Readers can make their own interpretations. If you have detailed summary statistics of the data, place them in appendixes.

Discussion.   In the discussion section, you give the reader a concise, unambiguous interpretation of the data. The discussion is not a selective emphasis or partisan interpretation; rather, it is a candid review and elaboration of what appeared in the "Results" section. A "Discussion" section is separated from the "Results" section so that a reader can examine the data and arrive at different interpretations.

Beginning researchers often struggle to organize the "Discussion" section. The easiest approach is to organize the discussion according to the hypotheses you tested or research questions you asked. Discuss how the data relate to each hypothesis or question. In addition, you should discuss any unanticipated findings, possible alternative explanations of results, and weaknesses or limitations.

Drawing Conclusions.   Restate your research question and summarize major findings in the conclusion. The purpose of this section is to summarize the report. Often it is titled "Summary."

The only sections after the conclusion are the references and appendixes. The "References" section contains only sources that you referred to in the text or notes of the report. Appendixes, if used, usually contain additional information on methods of data collection (e.g., questionnaire wording) or results (e.g., detailed descriptive statistics). The footnotes or endnotes in quantitative research reports expand or elaborate on information in the text. You should use them sparingly to provide secondary information that clarifies the text but might distract from the flow of the reading.

The Qualitative Research Report

Compared to reports on quantitative research, a report on qualitative social research is usually more difficult to write. It has fewer rules and less structure. Nevertheless, the purpose is the same: clearly communicate the research process and findings on the data you collected.

Quantitative reports present hypotheses and evidence in a logically tight and condensed style. By contrast, qualitative reports tend to be longer. Book-length reports are common. The greater length is for five reasons:

1. The data in a qualitative report are more difficult to condense. Data are in the form of words, pictures, or sentences and you will include many quotes and examples.

2. In qualitative research, you may try to build a subjective sense of empathy and understanding among readers in addition to presenting factual evidence and analytic interpretations. Detailed descriptions of specific situations help readers better understand or get a feel for people and settings. You may try to transport the reader into the subjective worldview of a social setting.

3. You use less standardized techniques of gathering data, creating analytic categories, and organizing evidence in qualitative research. The techniques you applied may be particular to your study or setting. Thus, you must explain in great detail exactly what you did and why.

4. Exploring new settings or constructing new theory is a common goal in qualitative research. The development of new concepts and the examination of relationships among them will increase the length of reports. Theory flows out of evidence, and detailed descriptions demonstrate how you created interpretations.

5. In qualitative research you might use more varied and literary writing styles, which increases length. You have some freedom to employ literary devices to tell a story or recount a tale.

Field Research.   Field research reports rarely follow a fixed format with standard sections and theoretical generalizations. You do not separate the data from analysis and place it into a distinct section. Instead, you intertwine analysis or generalizations with the data. Data presentation takes the form of detailed descriptions with frequent concrete examples and quotes.

It is important to balance data presentation and analysis. You want to avoid an excessive separation of data from analysis, called the ***error of segregation***. This occurs when you separate data from analysis so much that readers no long see the connection between them.[1]

The tone of field research reports is less objective and formal, and more personal. You can write field research reports in the first person (i.e., using the pronoun *I*) because you were directly involved in the setting, interacted with the people studied, and were a measurement "instrument." Your decisions or indecisions, feelings, reactions, and personal experiences are "data" and a part of the field research process.

Field research reports often face greater skepticism than quantitative reports do. This makes it essential for you to assess an audience's demands for evidence and establish credibility. The key is to provide readers with enough evidence so that they believe the recounted events and accept your interpretations as plausible. They will accept a degree of selective observation in field research. The critical issue is whether other observers going to the same field site would have similar data and reach similar conclusions.

In field research, you face a data reduction dilemma when presenting evidence. The data are in the form of an enormous volume of field notes, but you cannot directly share all the observations or recorded conversations with the readers. For example, in their study of medical students, *Boys in White*, Becker, Geer, Hughes, and Strauss (1961) had about 5,000 pages of single-spaced field notes. Field researchers typically include only about 5 percent of field notes in a report as quotes. The remaining 95 percent is not wasted; there is just no room for it. Thus, you must select quotes carefully and indirectly convey the rest of the data to readers.

There is no fixed organization for a field research report, although a literature review often appears near the beginning. There are many acceptable organizational forms. Lofland (1976) suggests the following:

1. Introduction
   a. Most general aspects of situation
   b. Main contours of the general situation
   c. How you collected materials
   d. Details about the setting
   e. How the report is organized
2. The situation
   a. Analytic categories
   b. Contrast between this situation and other situations
   c. Development of the situation over time
3. Strategies
4. Summary and implications

Devices for organizing evidence and analysis also vary a great deal. For example, you can organize the report in terms of a *natural history,* an unfolding of events as you discovered them, or as a *chronology,* following the developmental cycle or career of an aspect of the setting or people in it. Another possibility is to organize the report as a ***zoom lens,*** beginning broadly and then focusing increasingly narrowly on a specific topic. Statements can move from universal statements about all cultures, to general statements about a specific culture, to statements about a particular cultural scene, to specific statements about one aspect of the cultural scene, to specific statements about specific incidents that occurred within one aspect in a particular scene.

You can organize the field research report around major themes that you identified in your study. You can choose between using abstract analytic themes and using themes from the categories used by research participants. The latter gives readers a vivid description of the setting and displays knowledge of the language, concepts, categories, and beliefs of those you are writting about.[2]

You want to discuss the research methods you used in the report, but its location and form vary. One technique is to interweave a description of the setting, the means of gaining access, the role of the researcher, and the member–researcher relationship into the discussion of evidence and analysis. This is intensified if the writer adopts what Van Maanen (1988:73) called a "confessional" style of writing.

If you use a chronological, zoom lens, or theme-based organization, you can place the data collection method near the beginning or the end. In book-length reports, methodological issues are often placed in a separate appendix.

Field research reports can contain transcriptions of tape recordings, maps, photographs, or charts illustrating analytic categories. This data supplements the discussion and appears near the discussion they complement. You can use creative formats that differ from the usual written text with examples from field notes. Harper's (1982) book contains many photographs with text. The photographs give a visual inventory of the settings described in the text and present the meanings of settings in terms of research participants. For example, field research articles have appeared in the form of all photographs, a script for a play, or a documentary film.[3]

Your direct, personal involvement in the intimate details of a social setting heightens ethical concerns. You want to write in a manner that protects the privacy of research participants and helps prevent the publication of a report from harming them. You can change their names and mask the exact location in a field report. Personal involvement in field research had led many researchers to include a short autobiography in the report. For example, in the appendix to *Street Corner Society,* the author, William Foote Whyte (1955), gave a detailed account of the occupations of his father and grandfather, his hobbies and interests, the jobs he held, how he ended up going to graduate school, and how his research was affected by his getting married.

Historical-Comparative Research. There is no single way to write a report on historical-comparative (H-C) research. Most frequently, you "tell a story" or describe details in general analytic categories. The writing usually goes beyond description to include generalizations and abstract concepts.

In H-C research, you rarely describe the methods in great detail. Having an explicit section of the report or an appendix that describes the research methodology is unusual. Occasionally, a book-length report will contain a bibliographic essay that discusses major sources used. More often, you have numerous detailed footnotes or endnotes that describe the sources and evidence. For example, a 20-page report on quantitative or field research typically has 5–10 notes, whereas an H-C research report of equal length may have 40–60 notes.

Historical-comparative reports can contain photographs, maps, diagrams, charts, or tables of statistics throughout the report. Place them in the section that discusses the evidence that relates to them. The charts, tables, and so forth supplement a discussion or give the reader a feel for the places and people you describe. Use them in conjunction with frequent quotes, because they are one among several types of evidence. H-C reports rarely summarize data to test specific hypotheses as in quantitative research. Instead, you try to build a web of meaning or descriptive detail. The way you organize the evidence itself conveys your interpretations and generalizations.

There are two basic modes of organizing H-C research reports: by topic and chronologically. You can mix the two types. For example, you can organize information chronologically within topics, or organize by topic within chronological periods. Occasionally, you may see H-C studies with other forms of organization—by place, by individual person, or by major events. If the report is truly comparative, you have additional options, such as making comparisons within topics. Expansion Box 14.2 provides a sample of some techniques used by historical-comparative researchers to organize evidence and analysis.

Some H-C researchers mimic the quantitative research report and use quantitative research techniques. They extend quantitative research rather than adopt a distinct historical-comparative research method. Their reports follow the model of a quantitative research report.

You learned about the narrative strategy of qualitative data analysis in Chapter 13. Researchers who use this strategy often adopt a narrative style of report writing. To do this, you organize the data chronologically and try to "tell a story" around specific individuals and events.

The Research Proposal

What Is the Proposal? A research *proposal* is a document that presents a plan for a project to professional reviewers for evaluation. It can be a supervised project submitted to instructors as part of an educational degree (e.g., a master's thesis or a Ph.D. dissertation) or it can be a research project that is proposed to a funding agency. Its purpose is to convince reviewers that you, the researcher, are capable of successfully conducting the proposed study. Reviewers have more confidence that you will successfully complete a planned study if your proposal is well written and organized, and if you demonstrate careful planning.

The proposal is similar to a research report, but you write it before beginning to do the research. A proposal describes the research problem and its importance, and gives a detailed account of the methods that you will use and why they are appropriate.

The proposal for quantitative research has most of the parts of a research report: a title, an abstract, a problem statement, a literature review, a methodology or design section, and a bibliography. It lacks results, discussion, and conclusion sections. The proposal includes a plan for data collection and analysis (e.g., types of statistics). It frequently includes a schedule of the steps to be undertaken and an estimate of the time required for each step.

14.2

1. *Sequence.* Historical-comparative researchers are sensitive to the temporal order of events and place a series of events in order to describe a process. For example, a researcher studying the passage of a law or the evolution of a social norm may break the process into a set of sequential steps.

2. *Comparison.* Comparing similarities and differences lies at the heart of comparative-historical research. Make comparisons explicit and identify both similarities and differences. For example, a researcher comparing the family in two historical periods or countries begins by listing shared and nonshared traits of a family in each setting.

3. *Contingency.* Researchers often discover that one event, action, or situation depends on or is conditioned by others. Outlining the linkages of how one event was contingent on others is critical. For example, a researcher examining the rise of local newspapers notes that it depended on the spread of literacy.

4. *Origins and consequences.* Historical-comparative researchers trace the origins of an event, action, organization, or social relationship back in time, or follow its consequences into subsequent time periods. For example, a researcher explaining the end of slavery traces its origins to many movements, speeches, laws, and actions in the preceding 50 years.

5. *Sensitivity to incompatible meaning.* Meanings change over time and vary across cultures. Historical-comparative researchers ask themselves whether a word or social category had the same meaning in the past as in the present or whether a word in one culture has a direct translation in another culture. For example, a college degree had a different meaning in a historical era when it was extremely expensive and less than 1 percent of the 18- to 22-year-old population received a degree compared

to the late twentieth century, when college became relatively accessible.

6. *Limited generalization.* Overgeneralization is always a potential problem in historical-comparative research. Few researchers seek rigid, fixed laws in historical-comparative explanation. They qualify statements or avoid strict determination. For example, instead of a blanket statement that the destruction of the native cultures in areas settled by European Whites was the inevitable consequence of advanced technological culture, a researcher may list the specific factors that combined to explain the destruction in particular social-historical settings.

7. *Association.* The concept of association is used in all forms of social research. As in other areas, historical-comparative researchers identify factors that appear together in time and place. For example, a researcher examining a city's nineteenth-century crime rate asks whether years of greater migration into the city are associated with higher crime rates and whether those arrested tended to be recent immigrants.

8. *Part and whole.* It is important to place events in their context. Writers of historical-comparative research sketch linkages between parts of a process, organization, or event and the larger context in which it is found. For example, a researcher studying a particular political ritual in an eighteenth-century setting describes how the ritual fit within the eighteenth-century political system.

9. *Analogy.* Analogies can be useful. The overuse of analogy or the use of an inappropriate analogy is dangerous. For example, a researcher examines feelings about divorce in country X and describes them as "like feelings about death" in country Y. This analogy requires a description of "feelings about death" in country Y.

(Continued)

14.2	EXPANSION BOX
	Continued

10. *Synthesis.* Historical-comparative researchers often synthesize many specific events and details into a comprehensive whole. Synthesis results from weaving together many smaller generalizations and interpretations into coherent main themes. For example, a researcher studying the French Revolution synthesizes specific generalizations about changes in social structure, international pressures, agricultural dislocation, shifting popular beliefs, and problems with government finances into a compact, coherent explanation. Researchers using the narrative form summarize the argument in an introduction or conclusion. It is a motif or theme embedded within the description. Thus, theoretical generalizations are intertwined with the evidence and appear to flow inductively out of the detailed evidence.

Proposals for qualitative research are more difficult to write. This is because the research process itself is less structured and preplanned. You can prepare a problem statement, literature review, and bibliography. You also can demonstrate your ability to complete a proposed qualitative project in two ways. First, you have a very clearly organized, well-written proposal. It contains an extensive discussion of the literature, the significance of the problem, and sources. This shows reviewers your familiarity with qualitative research and the appropriateness of the method for studying the problem. Second, the proposal describes a qualitative pilot study you conducted. This demonstrates your motivation, familiarity with research techniques, and ability to complete a report about unstructured research.

Proposals to Fund Research. The purpose of a research grant is to acquire the resources you need to complete a worthy study. If your primary goal is to use funding for personal benefit or prestige, to escape from other activities, or to build an "empire," you are not likely to be successful. The strategies of proposal writing and getting grants has become an industry called *grantsmanship*.

There are many sources of funding for research studies. Colleges, private foundations, and government agencies have programs to award grants to researchers. You might use the funds to purchase equipment, to pay your salary or that of others, for research supplies, for travel to collect data, or for help with the publication of results. The degree of competition for a grant varies a great deal, depending on the source. Some sources fund more than three out of four proposals they receive, others fund fewer than one in 20.

You need to investigate funding sources and ask questions: What types of projects have been funded—applied or basic research? What specific topics are supported? Are specific research techniques favored? What are the deadlines? What kind (e.g., length, degree of detail, etc.) of proposal is necessary? How large are most grants? What aspects (e.g., equipment, personnel, travel, etc.) are or are not funded? There are many sources of information on funding sources. Librarians or officials who are responsible for research grants at a college are good resource people. For example, private foundations are listed in an annual publication, *The Foundation Directory: The Guide to Federal Funding for Social Scientists,* which lists sources in the U.S. government. In the United States, there are many newsletters on funding sources and national computerized databases, which subscribers can search for funding sources. Some agencies periodically issue **requests for proposals (RFPs)** that ask for proposals to conduct research on a specific issue. You need to learn about funding sources because it is essential to send the proposal to an appropriate source in order to be successful.

You want to show a track record of past successes in the proposal, especially if you are going to be in charge of the project. The person in charge of a research project is the *principal investigator (PI)* or project director. Proposals usually include a curriculum vitae or academic résumé, letters of support from other researchers, and a record of past research. Reviewers feel safer investing funds in a project headed by someone who already has research experience than in a novice. The way to build a record is to complete pilot studies and small research projects, or by assisting an experienced researcher before you seek funding as a principal investigator.

The reviewers who evaluate a proposal will judge whether the proposal project is appropriate to the funding source's goals. Most funding sources have guidelines stating the kinds of projects they fund. For example, programs that fund basic research have the advancement of knowledge as a goal. Programs that fund applied research often have improvements in the delivery of services as a goal. Instructions specify page length, number of copies, deadlines, and the like. Follow all instructions exactly. Funding sources will not trust you to fully complete a proposed study if you are not even able to follow their instructions.

Proposals should be neat and professional looking. The instructions usually ask for a detailed plan for the use of time, services, and personnel. These should be clearly stated and realistic for the project. Excessively high or low estimates, unnecessary add-ons, or omitted essentials will lower how reviewers evaluate a proposal. Creating a budget for a proposed project is complicated and usually requires technical assistance. For example, pay rates, fringe benefit rates, and so on that must be charged may not be easy to obtain. It is best to consult a grants officer at a college or an experienced proposal writer. In addition, endorsements or clearances of regulations are often necessary (e.g., IRB approval). Proposals should also include specific plans for how you will disseminate results (e.g., publications, presentations before professional groups, etc.) and a plan for evaluating whether the project met its objectives.

The proposal is a kind of contract between you and the funding source. Funding agencies often require a final report. It has details on how you spent the funds, the findings, and an evaluation of whether the project met its objectives. Failure to spend funds properly, complete the project described in the proposal, or file a final report may result in you being barred from receiving future funds or you might face legal penalties and fines. A serious misuse of funds may even result in banning other researchers at the same university or company from receiving future funding.

The process of reviewing proposals after they are submitted to a funding source takes anywhere from a few weeks to almost a year, depending on the funding source. In most cases, reviewers rank a large group of proposals, and only highly ranked proposals receive funding. A proposal may undergo a peer review in which the reviewers know the proposer from the vitae in the proposal, but the proposer does not know the reviewers. Sometimes nonspecialists or non-researchers will review a proposal. Instructions on preparing a proposal indicate whether to write for specialists in a field or for an educated general audience.

If your proposal is funded, celebrate, but only for a short time. If your proposal is rejected, which is more likely, do not despair. Most proposals are rejected the first or second time they are submitted. Many funding sources provide written reviewer evaluations of the proposal. Always request them if they are provided. Sometimes, a courteous talk on the telephone with a person at the funding source will reveal the reasons for rejection. Strengthen and resubmit a proposal based on the reviewer's comments. Most funding sources accept repeated resubmissions of revised proposals. Revised proposals may be stronger in subsequent competitions.

If you submit a proposal to an appropriate funding source and follow all instructions, reviewers are more likely to rate it high when:

- It addresses an important research question. It builds on prior knowledge and represents a substantial advance of knowledge for basic research. It documents a major social problem and holds promise for solutions for applied research.
- It follows all instructions precisely, is well written, and is easy to follow with clear objectives.
- It completely describes research procedures and includes high standards of research methodology, and it applies research techniques appropriate to the research question.
- It includes specific plans for disseminating the results and evaluating whether the project has met its objectives.
- The project shows serious planning and has realistic budgets and schedules.
- You have the necessary experience or background to complete the project successfully.

CONCLUSION

Clearly communicating results is a vital part of the larger scientific enterprise, as are the ethics and politics of social research.

I end this chapter by urging you, as a consumer of social research or a new social researcher, to be self-aware. Be aware of the place of the researcher in society and of the societal context of social research itself. Social researchers, and sociologists in particular, bring a unique perspective to the larger society.

Key Terms

editing
error of segregation
executive summary
grantsmanship
paraphrasing
plagiarism
prewriting
principal investigator (PI)
request's for proposals (RFPs)
revising
rewriting
zoom lens

Endnotes

1. The error of segregation is discussed in Lofland and Lofland (1984:146).
2. See Van Maanen (1988:13).
3. See Becker and associates (1989), Dabbs (1982), and Jackson (1978).

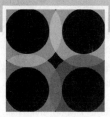

Following the definition, the number in parentheses indicates the chapter in which the term first appears in the text and is in the Key Terms section. Italicized terms refer to terms defined elsewhere in this glossary.

Abstract   A term with two meanings in literature reviews: a short summary of a scholarly journal article that usually appears at its beginning, and a reference tool for locating scholarly journal articles. (4)

Acceptable incompetent   When a field researcher pretends to be less skilled or knowledgeable in order to learn more about a *field site*. (11)

Accretion measures   *Nonreactive measures* of the residue of the activity of people or what they leave behind. (9)

Action research   A type of *applied social research* in which a researcher treats knowledge as a form of power and abolishes the division between creating knowledge and using knowledge to engage in political action. (1)

Alternative hypothesis   A *hypothesis* paired with a *null hypothesis* stating that the *independent variable* has an effect on a *dependent variable*. (4)

Analytic domain   In *domain analysis,* a type of domain a researcher develops using categories or terms he or she developed to understand a social setting. (13)

Analytic memo's   The written notes a qualitative researcher takes during data collection and afterward to develop concepts, themes, or preliminary generalizations. (11)

Anonymity   Research participants remain anonymous or nameless. (3)

Appearance of interest   A technique in *field research* in which researchers maintain relations in a *field site* by pretending to be interested and excited by the activities of those studied, even though they are actually uninterested or very bored. (11)

Applied social research   Research that attempts to solve a concrete problem or address a specific policy question and that has a direct, practical application. (1)

Association   A co-occurrence of two events, factors, characteristics, or activities, such that when one happens, the other is likely to occur as well. Many statistics measure this. (2)

Assumption   Parts of social theories that are not tested, but act as starting points or basic beliefs about the world. They are necessary to make other theoretical statements and to build social theory. (2)

Attitude of strangeness   A technique in *field research* in which researchers study a *field site* by mentally adjusting to "see" it for the first time or as an outsider. (11)

Attributes   The categories or levels of a *variable*. (4)

Axial coding   A second coding of *qualitative data* after *open coding*. The researcher organizes the codes, develops links among them, and discovers key analytic categories. (13)

Back translation   A technique in comparative research for checking *lexicon equivalence*. A researcher translates spoken or written text from an original language into a second language, then translates the same text in the second language back into the original language, then compares the two original language texts. (12)

Bar chart   A display of *quantitative data* for one variable in the form of rectangles where longer rectangles indicate more cases in a variable category. Usually, it is used with discrete data and there is a small space between rectangles. They can have a horizontal or vertical orientation. Also called bar graphs. (10)

Basic social research   Research designed to advance fundamental knowledge about the social world. (1)

Bivariate statistics   Statistical measures that involve two variables only. (10)

Blame analysis A counterfeit argument presented as if it were a theoretical explanation that substitutes attributing blame for a *causal explanation* and implies an intention or negligence, or responsibility for an event or situation. (2)

Body of a table The center part of a *contingency table*. It contains all the cells, but not the totals or labels. (10)

Bogardus Social Distance Scale A *scale* that measures the distance between two or more social groups by having members of one group express the point at which they feel comfortable with various types of social interaction or closeness with members of the other group(s). (5)

Case study Research, usually qualitative, on one or a small number of cases in which a researcher carefully examines a large number of details about each case. (1)

Causal explanation A statement in social theory about why events occur that is expressed in terms of causes and effects. They correspond to associations in the empirical world. (2)

Cell of a table A part of the *body of a table*. In a *contingency table*, it shows the distribution of cases into categories of variables as a specific number or percentage. (10)

Central limit theorem A lawlike mathematical relationship that states whenever many *random samples* are drawn from a *population* and plotted, a *normal distribution* is formed, and the center of such a distribution for a variable is equal to its *population parameter*. (6)

Citation Details of a scholarly journal article's location that helps people find it quickly. (4)

Classical experimental design An *experimental design* that has *random assignment*, a *control group*, an *experimental group*, and *pretests* and *posttests* for each group. (8)

Classification concept Complex, multidimensional concepts that have subtypes. They are parts of social theories between one simple concept and a full theoretical explanation. (2)

Closed-ended question A type of *survey research* question in which respondents must choose from a fixed set of answers. (7)

Cluster sampling A type of *random sample* that uses multiple stages and is often used to cover wide geographic areas in which aggregated units are randomly selected then *samples* are drawn from the sampled aggregated units, or clusters. (6)

Code sheets Paper with a printed grid on which a researcher records information so that it can be easily entered into a computer. It is an alternative to the *direct-entry method* and using optical-scan sheets. (10)

Codebook A document that describes the procedure for coding variables and their location in a format for computers. (10)

Coding The process of converting raw information or data into another form for analysis. In *content analysis,* it is a means for determining how to convert symbolic meanings in *text* into another form, usually numbers (see *Coding system*); in *quantitative data* analysis, it is a means for assigning numbers; and in *qualitative data* analysis, it is a series of steps for reading raw notes and assigning codes or conceptual terms (see *Axial coding, Open coding, Selective coding*). (9)

Coding system A set of instructions or rules used in *content analysis* to explain how to systematically convert the symbolic content from *text* into *quantitative data.* (9)

Cohort study A type of *longitudinal research* in which a researcher focuses on a category of people who share a similar life experience in a specified time period. (1)

Compensatory behavior A threat to internal validity that occurs when participants in the control group modify their behavior to make up for not getting the treatment. (8)

Competent insider performance A method field researchers use to demonstrate the authenticity and trustworthiness of a study by the researcher "passing" as a member of the group under study. (11)

Computer-assisted telephone interviewing (CATI) *Survey research* in which the interviewer sits before a computer screen and keyboard and uses the computer to read questions that are asked in a telephone interview, then enters answers directly into the computer. (7)

Concept cluster A collection of interrelated ideas that share common *assumptions,* belong to the same larger social theory, and refer to one another. (2)

Conceptual definition A careful, systematic definition of a construct that is explicitly written to clarify one's thinking. It is often linked to other concepts or theoretical statements. (5)

Conceptual equivalence In *historical-comparative research,* the issue of whether the same ideas or concepts occur or can be used to represent phenomena across divergent cultural or historical settings. (12)

Conceptual hypothesis A type of *hypothesis* in which the researcher expresses variables in abstract, conceptual terms and expresses the relationship among variables in a theoretical way. (5)

Conceptualization The process of developing clear, rigorous, systematic *conceptual definitions* for abstract ideas/concepts. (5)

Concurrent validity *Measurement validity* that relies on a preexisting and already accepted measure to verify the indicator of a construct. (5)

Confederate A person working for the experimenter who acts as another participant or in a role in front of participants to deceive them for an experiment's cover story. (8)

Confidence interval A range of values, usually a little higher and lower than a specific value found in a *sample,* within which a researcher has a specified and high degree of confidence that the *population parameter* lies. (6)

Confidentiality Information with participant names attached, but the researcher holds it in confidence or keeps it secret from the public. (3)

Confounding variable's In experimental research, variables or factors that are not part of the intended hypothesis being tests, but that have effects on variables of interest and threaten internal validity. (8)

Content analysis Research in which one examines patterns of symbolic meaning within written text, audio, visual, or other communication medium. (1) (9)

Content validity *Measurement validity* that requires that a measure represent all the aspects of the conceptual definition of a construct. (5)

Context effect An effect in *survey research* when an overall tone or set topics heard by a respondent affects how he or she interprets the meaning of subsequent questions. (7)

Contextual equivalence The issue in *historical-comparative research* of whether social roles, norms, or situations across different cultures or historical periods are equivalent or can be compared. (12)

Contingency cleaning Cleaning data using a computer in which the researcher looks at the combination

of categories for two variables for logically impossible cases. (10)

Contingency question A type of *survey research* question in which the respondent next goes to one or another later question based on his or her answer. (7)

Contingency table A table that shows the *cross-tabulation* of two or more variables. It usually shows *bivariate quantitative data* for variables in the form of percentages across rows or down columns for the categories of one variable. (10)

Continuous variable's Variables measured on a continuum in which an infinite number of finer gradations between variable *attributes* are possible. (5)

Control group The group that does not get the *treatment* in *experimental research.* (8)

Control variable A "third" variable that shows whether a *bivariate relationship* holds up to alternative explanations. It can occur before or between other variables. (10)

Convenience sampling A type of *nonrandom sample* in which the researcher selects anyone he or she happens to come across. (6)

Covariation The idea that two variables vary together, such that knowing the values in one variable provides information about values found in another variable. (10)

Cover sheet One or more pages at the beginning of a *questionnaire* with information about an interview or respondent. (7)

Cover story A type of deception in which the experimenter tells a false story to participants so they will act as wanted and do not know the true hypothesis.

Cover term In *domain analysis,* the name for a domain (i.e., a cultural setting or site in which people regularly interact and develop a set of shared understandings) or "miniculture" that can be analyzed. (13)

Criterion validity *Measurement validity* that relies on some independent, outside verification. (5)

Crossover design A design to reduce creating inequality; it is when a study group that gets no treatment in the first phase of the experiment becomes the group with the treatment in the second phase, and vice versa. (3)

Cross-sectional research Research in which a researcher examines a single point in time or takes a one-time snapshot approach. (1)

Cross-tabulation Placing data for two variables in a *contingency table* to show the number or percentage of cases at the intersection of categories of the two variables. (10)

Curvilinear relationship A relationship between two variables such that as the values of one variable increase, the values of the second show a changing pattern (e.g., first decrease then increase then decrease). It is not a *linear relationship*. (10)

Data The *empirical evidence* or information that a person gathers carefully according to established rules or procedures; it can be qualitative or quantitative. (1)

Debrief When a researcher gives a true explanation of the experiment to research participants after using *deception*. (8)

Deception When an experimenter lies to research participants about the true nature of an experiment or creates a false impression through his or her actions or the setting. (8)

Deductive approach An approach to inquiry or social theory in which one begins with abstract ideas and principles then works toward concrete, *empirical evidence* to test the ideas. (2)

Defocusing A technique early in *field research* when the researcher removes his or her past assumptions and preconceptions to become more open to events in a *field site*. (11)

Demand characteristics A type of *reactivity* in which the participants in *experimental research* pick up clues about the *hypothesis* and alter their behavior accordingly. (8)

Dependent variable The effect variable that is last and results from the causal variable(s) in a *causal explanation*. Also the variable that is measured in the *pretest* and *posttest* and that is the result of the *treatment* in *experimental research*. (4)

Descriptive research Research in which one "paints a picture" with words or numbers, presents a profile, outlines stages, or classifies types. (1)

Descriptive statistics A general type of simple statistics used by researchers to describe basic patterns in the data. (10)

Design notation The name of a symbol system used to discuss the parts of an experiment and to make diagrams of them. (8)

Deviant case sampling A type of *nonrandom sample*, especially used by qualitative researchers, in which a researcher selects unusual or nonconforming

cases purposely as a way to provide greater insight into social processes or a setting. (6)

Diffusion of treatment A threat to *internal validity* that occurs when the *treatment* "spills over" from the *experimental group*, and *control group* research participants modify their behavior because they learn of the *treatment*. (8)

Direct-entry method A method of entering data into a computer by typing data without code or optical scan sheets. (10)

Direct observation notes Notes taken in *field research* that attempt to include all details and specifics of what the researcher heard or saw in a *field site*. They are written in a way that permits multiple interpretations later. (11)

Discrete variables Variables in which the *attributes* can be measured only with a limited number of distinct, separate categories. (5)

Domain analysis A method of qualitative data analysis in which a researcher describes and reveals the structure of a cultural domain. (13)

Double-barreled question A problem in *survey research* question wording that occurs when two ideas are combined into one question, and it is unclear whether the answer is for the combination of both or one or the other question. (7)

Double-blind experiment A type of *experimental research* in which neither the research participants nor the person who directly deals with the research participants for the experimenter knows the specifics of the experiment. (8)

Ecological fallacy Something that appears to be a *causal explanation* but is not. It occurs because of confusion about *units of analysis*. A researcher has *empirical evidence* about an *association* for large-scale units or huge aggregates, but *overgeneralizes* to make theoretical statements about an *association* among small-scale units or individuals. (4)

Ecological validity A way to demonstrate the authenticity and trustworthiness of a *field research* study by showing that the researcher's descriptions of the field site matches those of the members from the site and that the researcher was not a major disturbance. (11)

Editing A step in the writing process that is part of *rewriting*, in which a writer cleans up and tightens the language and checks grammar, verb agreement, usage, sentence length, and paragraph organization to improve communication. (14)

Elaboration paradigm   A system for describing patterns evident among tables when a *bivariate contingency table* is compared with *partials* after the *control variable* has been added. (10)

Empirical evidence   The observations that people experience through their senses—touch, sight, hearing, smell, and taste; these can be direct or indirect. (1)

Empirical generalization   A quasi-theoretical statement that summarizes findings or regularities in *empirical evidence*. It uses few if any abstract concepts and only makes a statement about a recurring pattern that researchers observe. (2)

Empirical hypothesis   A type of *hypothesis* in which the researcher expresses variables in specific terms and expresses the *association* among the measured indicators of observable, *empirical evidence*. (5)

Empty boxes   A name for conceptual categories in an explanation that a researcher uses as part of the *illustrative method* of *qualitative data* analysis. (13)

Equivalent time-series design   An *experimental design* in which there are several repeated *pretests, posttests,* and *treatments* for one group often over a period of time. (8)

Erosion measures   *Nonreactive measures* of the wear or deterioration on surfaces due to the activity of people. (9)

Error of segregation   A mistake that can occur when writing qualitative research in which a writer separates concrete *empirical* details from abstract ideas. (14)

Ethnography   An approach to *field research* that emphasizes providing a very detailed description of a different culture from the viewpoint of an insider in that culture in order to permit a greater understanding of it. (11)

Ethnomethodology   An approach to social science that combines philosophy, social theory, and method to study. (11)

Evaluation research   A type of *applied research* in which one tries to determine how well a program or policy is working or reaching its goals and objectives. (1)

Executive summary   A summary of a research project's findings placed at the beginning of a report for an applied, nonspecialist audience. Usually a little longer than an *abstract*. (14)

Exhaustive attributes   The principle that response categories in a *scale* or other measure should provide a category for all possible responses (i.e., every possible response fits into some category). (5)

Existing statistics research   Research in which one examines numerical information from government documents or official reports to address new research questions. (1)

Experimental design   Arranging the parts of an experiment and putting them together. (8)

Experimental group   The group that receives the *treatment* in *experimental research*. (8)

Experimental mortality   Threats to internal validity due to participants failing to participate through the entire experiment. (8)

Experimental realism   External validity in which the experiment is made to feel realistic, so that experimental events have a real impact on participants.

Experimental research   Research in which one intervenes or does something to one group of people but not to another, then compares results for the two groups. (1)

Experimenter expectancy   A type of reactivity due to the experimenter indirectly making participants aware of the hypothesis or desired results. (8)

Explanation pattern   A pattern in the *elaboration paradigm* in which the *bivariate contingency table* shows a relationship, but the *partials* show no relationship and the *control variable* occurs prior to the *independent variable*. (10)

Explanatory research   Research that focuses on why events occur or tries to test and build social theory. (1)

Exploratory research   Research into an area that has not been studied and in which a researcher wants to develop initial ideas and a more focused research question. (1)

External consistency   A way to achieve *reliability* of data in *field research* in which the researcher cross-checks and verifies *qualitative data* using multiple sources of information. (11)

External criticism   In historical research, a way to check the authenticity of *primary sources* by accurately locating the place and time of its creation (e.g., it is not a forgery). (12)

External validity The ability to generalize from *experimental research* to settings or people that differ from the specific conditions of the study. (5) (8)

Face validity A type of *measurement validity* in which an indicator "makes sense" as a measure of a construct in the judgment of others, especially those in the scientific community. (5)

Factorial design A type of *experimental design* that considers the impact of several *independent variables* simultaneously. (8)

Fallacy of misplaced concreteness When a person uses too many digits in a quantitative measure in an attempt to create the impression that the data are accurate or the researcher is highly capable. (9)

Field experiment *Experimental research* that takes place in a natural setting. (8)

Field research A type of qualitative research in which a researcher directly observes the people being studied in a natural setting for an extended period. Often, the researcher combines intense observing with participation in the people's social activities. (1)

Field site One or more natural locations where a researcher conducts *field research*. (11)

First-order interpretation In qualitative research, what the people who are being studied actually feel and think. (4)

Floaters Respondents who lack a belief or opinion, but who give an answer anyway if asked in a *survey research* question. Often, their answers are inconsistent. (7)

Focus group A type of group interview in which an interviewer asks questions to the group and answers are given in an open discussion among the group members. (11)

Folk domain In *domain analysis,* a domain based on actual words, ideas, and phrases used by members in a social setting or historical actors in a specific era. (13)

Frequency distribution A table that shows the distribution of cases into the categories of one variable (i.e., the number or percent of cases in each category). (10)

Frequency polygon A graph of connected points showing the distribution of how many cases fall into each category of a variable. (10)

Full-filter question A type of *survey research* question in which respondents are first asked whether they have an opinion or know about a topic, then only

the respondents with an opinion or knowledge are asked a specific question on the topic. (7)

Functional theory A type of social theory based on biological analogies, in which the social world or its parts are seen as systems, with its parts serving the needs of the system. (2)

Funnel sequence A way to order *survey research* questions in a questionnaire from general to specific. (7)

Galton's problem In comparative research, the problem of finding correlations or *associations* among variables or characteristics in multiple cases or units, when the characteristics are actually diffused from a single unit or have a common origin. Thus, a researcher cannot really treat the multiple units (e.g., countries, cultures, etc.) as being wholly separate. (12)

Gatekeeper A person in an official or unofficial role who controls access to all or part of a *field site*. (11)

General Social Survey (GSS) A survey of a *random sample* of about 1,500 U.S. adults that has been conducted in most years between 1972 and the present and is available for many researchers to analyze. (9)

Go native What happens when a researcher in *field research* gets overly involved and loses all distance or objectivity and becomes like the people being studied. (11)

Grantsmanship The strategies and skills of locating appropriate funding sources and preparing high-quality proposals for research funding. (14)

Grounded theory Social theory that is rooted in observations of specific, concrete details. (2)

Guilty knowledge When a researcher in *field research* learns of illegal, unethical, or immoral actions by the people in the *field site* that are not widely known. (11)

Guttman scaling A *scale* that researchers use after data are collected to reveal whether a hierarchical pattern exists among responses, such that people who give responses at a "higher level" also tend to give "lower-level" ones. (5)

Halo effect An error often made when people use personal experience as an alternative to science for acquiring knowledge. It is when a person overgeneralizes from what he or she accepts as being highly positive or prestigious and lets its strong reputation or prestige "rub off" onto other areas. (1)

Hawthorne effect An effect of *reactivity* named after a famous case in which research participants reacted to the fact that they were in an experiment more than they reacted to the *treatment.* (8)

Hidden populations   People who engage in clandestine, deviant, or concealed activities and who are difficult to locate and study. (6)

Historical-comparative research   Research in which one examines different cultures or periods to better understand the social world. (1)

History effects   A threat to *internal validity* due to something that occurs and affects the *dependent variable* during an experiment, but which is unplanned and outside the control of the experimenter. (8)

Human Relations Area Files (HRAF)   An extensive catalog and comprehensive collection of *ethnographies* on many cultures (mostly preliterate) that permits a researcher to compare across cultural units. (12)

Hypothesis   The statement from a *causal explanation* or a *proposition* that has at least one *independent* and one *dependent variable,* but it has yet to be empirically tested. (4)

Ideal type   A pure model about an idea, process, or event. One develops it to think about it more clearly and systematically. It is used both as a method of *qualitative data* analysis and in *social theory* building. (2)

Idiographic   An approach that focuses on creating detailed descriptions of specific events in particular time periods and settings. It rarely goes beyond *empirical generalizations* to abstract social theory or *causal laws.* (2)

Illustrative method   A method of *qualitative data* analysis in which a researcher takes the concepts of a *social theory* or explanation and treats them as *empty boxes* to be filled with *empirical* examples and descriptions. (13)

Included term   In *domain analysis,* the subtypes or parts of the cultural domain that are within a *cover term* and have a *semantic relationship* to one another (13)

Independence   The absence of a *statistical relationship* between two variables (i.e., when knowing the values on one variable provides no information about the values that will be found on another variable). There is no *association* between them. (10)

Independent variable   The first variable that causes or produces the effect in a *causal explanation.* (4)

Index   The summing or combining of many separate measures of a construct or variable. (5)

Inductive approach   An approach to inquiry or social theory in which one begins with concrete empirical details, then works toward abstract ideas or general principles. (2)

Inferential statistics   A branch of applied mathematics or statistics based on a *random sample.* It lets a researcher make precise statements about the level of confidence he or she has in the results of a *sample* being equal to the *population parameter.* (6)

Informed consent   An agreement by participants stating they are willing to be in a study after they learn something about what the research procedure will involve. (3)

Institutional review board (IRB)   A committee of researchers and community members that oversees, monitors, and reviews the impact of research procedures on human participants and applies ethical guidelines by reviewing research procedures at a preliminary stage when first proposed. (3)

Interaction effect   The effect of two *independent variables* that operate simultaneously together. The effect of the variables together is greater than what would occur from a simple addition of the effects from each. The variables operate together on one another to create an extra "boost." (8)

Internal consistency   A way to achieve *reliability* of data in *field research* in which a researcher examines the data for plausibility and sees whether they form a coherent picture, given all that is known about a person or event, trying to avoid common forms of deception. (11)

Internal criticism   How historical researchers establish the authenticity and credibility of *primary sources* and determine its accuracy as an account of what occurred. (12)

Internal validity   The ability of experimenters to strengthen a *causal explanation*'s logical rigor by eliminating potential alternative explanations for an *association* between the *treatment* and the *dependent variable* through an *experimental design.* (5) (8)

Interpretation pattern   A pattern in the *elaboration paradigm* in which the *bivariate contingency table* shows a relationship, but the *partials* show no relationship and the *control variable* is intervening in the *causal explanation.* (10)

Interrupted time-series design An *experimental design* in which the *dependent variable* is measured periodically across many time points, and the *treatment* occurs in the midst of such measures, often only once. (8)

Interval-level measurement A *level of measurement* that identifies differences among variable *attributes,* ranks, and categories, and that measures distance between categories, but there is no true zero. (5)

Intervening variable A variable that is between the initial causal variable and the final effect variable in a *causal explanation.* (4)

Interview schedule The name of a *survey research questionnaire* when a telephone or face-to-face interview is used. (7)

Jotted notes In *field research,* what a researcher inconspicuously writes while in the *field site* on whatever is convenient in order to "jog the memory" later. (11)

Laboratory experiment *Experimental research* that takes place in an artificial setting over which the experimenter has great control. (8)

Latent coding A type of *content analysis* coding in which a researcher identifies subjective meaning such as general themes or motifs in a communication medium. (9)

Latin square design An *experimental design* used to examine whether the order or sequence in which research participants receive multiple versions of the *treatment* has an effect. (8)

Level of analysis A way to talk about the scope of a *social theory, causal explanation, proposition, hypothesis,* or theoretical statement. The range of phenomena it covers, or to which it applies, goes from social psychological (*micro level*) to organizational (*meso level*) to large-scale social structure (*macro level*). (4)

Level's of measurement A system that organizes the information in the measurement of variables into four general levels, from *nominal level* to *ratio level.* (5)

Level of statistical significance A set of numbers researchers use as a simple way to measure the degree to which a *statistical relationship* results from random factors rather than the existence of a true relationship among variables. (10)

Lexicon equivalence Finding equivalent words or phrases to express the identical meaning in different languages or in the translation from one language to another (see *Back translation*). (12)

Likert scale A *scale* often used in *survey research* in which people express attitudes or other responses in terms of several *ordinal-level* categories (e.g., agree, disagree) that are ranked along a continuum. (5)

Linear relationship An *association* between two variables that is positive or negative across the attributes or levels of the variables. When plotted in a *scattergram,* the basic pattern of the *association* forms a straight line, not a curve or other pattern. (10)

Linear research path Research that proceeds in a clear, logical, step-by-step straight line. It is more characteristic of a quantitative than a qualitative approach to social research. (4)

Literature review A systematic examination of previously published studies on a research question, issue, or method that a researcher undertakes and integrates together to prepare for conducting a study or to bring together and summarize the "state of the field." (4)

Longitudinal research Research in which the researcher examines the features of people or other units at multiple points in time. (1)

Macro-level theory Social theories and explanations about more abstract, large-scale, and broad-scope aspects of social reality, such as social change in major institutions (e.g., the family, education, etc.) in a whole nation across several decades. (2)

Manifest coding A type of *content analysis* coding in which a researcher first develops a list of specific words, phrases, or symbols, then finds them in a communication medium. (9)

Marginals The totals in a *contingency table,* outside the *body of a table.* (10)

Matrix question A type of *survey research* question in which a set of questions is listed in a compact form together, all questions sharing the same set of answer categories. (7)

Maturation effect A threat to *internal validity* in *experimental research* due to natural processes of growth, boredom, and so on, that occur to research participants during the experiment and affect the *dependent variable.* (8)

Mean A measure of central tendency for one variable that indicates the arithmetic average (i.e., the sum of all scores divided by the total number of scores). (10)

Measurement equivalence In *historical-comparative research,* creating or locating measures that will accurately represent the same construct or variable in divergent cultural or historical settings. (12)

Measurement validity How well an *empirical* indicator and the *conceptual definition* of the construct that the indicator is supposed to measure "fit" together. (5)

Median A measure of central tendency for one variable indicating the point or score at which half the cases are higher and half are lower. (10)

Members The insiders or native people in a *field site* who are being studied. (11)

Member validation A way to demonstrate the authenticity and trustworthiness of a *field research* study by having the people who were studied (i.e., members) read and confirm as being true that which the *researcher* has reported. (11)

Meso-level theory Social theories and explanations about the middle level of social reality between a broad and narrow scope, such as the development and operation of social organizations, communities, or social movements over a five-year period. (2)

Micro-level theory Social theories and explanations about the concrete, small-scale, and narrow level of reality, such as face-to-face interaction in small groups during a two-month period. (2)

Mixed domain In *domain analysis,* a domain that combines the words and categories of members under study with categories developed by a researcher for analysis. (13)

Mode A measure of central tendency for one variable that indicates the most frequent or common score. (10)

Multiple indicators Many procedures or instruments that indicate, or provide evidence of, the presence or level of a variable using *empirical evidence.* Researchers use the combination of several together to measure a variable. (5)

Mundane realism A type of external validity in which the experimental conditions appear to be real and very similar to settings or situations outside a lab setting. (8)

Mutually exclusive attributes The principle that response categories in a *scale* or other measure should be organized so that a person's responses fit into only one category (i.e., categories should not overlap). (5)

Narrative A type of writing and analysis in *field research* and *historical-comparative research* in which the writer attempts to "tell a story" by following chronological order, describing particular people and events, and focusing on colorful details. (13)

Naturalism The principle that researchers should examine events as they occur in natural, everyday ongoing social settings. (11)

Negative relationship An *association* between two variables such that as values on one variable increase, values on the other variable fall or decrease. (2)

Nominal-level measurement The lowest, least precise *level of measurement* for which there is only a difference in type among the categories of a variable. (5)

Nomothetic An approach based on laws or one that operates according to a system of laws. (2)

Nonlinear research path Research that proceeds in a circular, back-and-forth manner. It is more characteristic of a qualitative than a quantitative style to social research. (4)

Nonrandom sample A type of sample in which the sampling elements are selected using something other than a mathematically random process. (6)

Nonreactive Measures in which people being studied are unaware that they are in a study. (9)

Normal distribution A "bell-shaped" frequency polygon for a distribution of cases, with a peak in the center and identical curving slopes on either side of the center. It is the distribution of many naturally occurring phenomena and is a basis of much statistical theory. (10)

Normalize social research Techniques in *field research* used by researchers to make the people being studied feel more comfortable with the research process and to help them accept the researcher's presence. (11)

Null hypothesis A *hypothesis* that says there is no relationship or *association* between two variables, or no effect. (4)

One-shot case-study design An *experimental design* with only an *experimental group* and a *posttest,* no *pretest.* (8)

Open coding A first coding of *qualitative data* in which a researcher examines the data to condense them into preliminary analytic categories or codes for analyzing the data. (13)

Open-ended question A type of *survey research* question in which respondents are free to offer any answer they wish to the question. (7)

Operational definition The definition of a variable in terms of the specific activities to measure or indicate it with *empirical evidence.* (5)

Operationalization   The process of moving from the *conceptual definition* of a construct to a set of specific activities or measures that allow a researcher to observe it *empirically* (i.e., its *operational definition*). (5)

Oral history   A type of *recollection* in which a researcher interviews a person about the events, beliefs, or feelings in the past that were directly experienced. (12)

Order effects   An effect in *survey research* in which respondents hear some specific questions before others, and the earlier questions affect their answers to later questions. (7)

Ordinal-level measurement   A *level of measurement* that identifies a difference among categories of a variable and allows the categories to be rank-ordered. (5)

Orientation reading   At the start of *historical-comparative research*, reading several general but serious book-length works to acquire background knowledge about a specific era or culture. (12)

Overgeneralization   An error that people often make when using personal experience as an alternative to science for acquiring knowledge. It occurs when some evidence supports a belief, but a person falsely assumes that it applies to many other situations, too. (1)

Panel study   A powerful type of *longitudinal research* in which a researcher observes exactly the same people, group, or organization across multiple time points. (1)

Paradigm   A general organizing framework for *social theory* and *empirical* research. It includes basic *assumptions*, major questions to be answered, models of good research practice and theory, and methods for finding the answers to questions. (2)

Parameter   A characteristic of the entire *population* that is estimated from a *sample*. (6)

Paraphrasing   When a writer restates or rewords the ideas of another person, giving proper credit to the original source. (14)

Partially open question   A type of *survey research* question in which respondents are given a fixed set of answers to choose from, but in addition, an "other" category is offered so that they can specify a different answer. (7)

Partials   In *contingency tables* for three variables, tables that show the *association* between the *independent* and *dependent variables* for each category of a *control variable*. (10)

Percentile   A measure of dispersion for one variable that indicates the percentage of cases at or below a score or point. (10)

Pie chart   A display of numerical information on one variable that divides a circle into fractions by lines representing the proportion of cases in the variable's *attributes*. (10)

Placebo effect   A false *treatment* or one that has no effect in an experiment. It is sometimes called a "sugar pill" that a *subject* mistakes for a true *treatment*. (8)

Plagiarism   A type of unethical behavior in which one uses the writings or ideas of another without giving proper credit. It is "stealing ideas." (3) (14)

Population   The name for the large general group of many cases from which a researcher draws a *sample* and which is usually stated in theoretical terms. (6)

Positive relationship   An *association* between two variables such that as values on one increase, values on the other also increase. (2)

Possible code cleaning   Cleaning data using a computer in which the researcher looks for responses or answer categories that cannot have cases. (10)

Posttest   The measurement of the *dependent variable* in *experimental research* after the *treatment*. (8)

Praxis   An idea in critical social science that social theory and everyday practice interact or work together, mutually affecting one another. This interaction can promote social change. (2)

Prediction   A statement about something that is likely to occur in the future. (2)

Predictive validity   *Measurement validity* that relies on the occurrence of a future event or behavior that is logically consistent to verify the indicator of a construct. (5)

Preexperimental designs   *Experimental designs* that lack *random assignment* or use shortcuts and are much weaker than the *classical experimental design*. They may be substituted in situations where an experimenter cannot use all the features of a *classical experimental design*, but have weaker *internal validity*. (8)

Premature closure   An error that is often made when using personal experience as an alternative to science for acquiring knowledge. It occurs when a person feels he or she has the answers and does not

need to listen, seek information, or raise questions any longer. (1)

Prestige bias　A problem in *survey research* question writing that occurs when a highly respected group or individual is linked to one of the answers. (7)

Pretest　The measurement of the *dependent variable* of an experiment prior to the *treatment*. (8)

Prewriting　A very early step in the writing process, when one writes without worrying about word choice, spelling, or grammar, but tries to let "ideas flow" as quickly as possible to connect thinking processes with writing. (14)

Primary sources　*Qualitative data* or *quantitative data* used in historical research. It is evidence about past social life or events that was created and used by the persons who actually lived in the historical period. (12)

Principal investigator (PI)　The person who is primarily in charge of research on a project that is sponsored or funded by an organization. (14)

Principle of voluntary consent　An ethical principle of social research that people should never participate in research unless they first explicitly agree to do so. (3)

Probability proportionate to size (PPS)　An adjustment made in *cluster sampling* when each cluster does not have the same number of *sampling elements*. (6)

Probe　A follow-up question or action in *survey research* used by an interviewer to have a respondent clarify or elaborate on an incomplete or inappropriate answer. (7)

Proposition　A basic statement in social theory that two ideas or variables are related to one another. It can be true or false (e.g., most sex offenders were themselves sexually abused when growing up), conditional (e.g., if a foreign enemy threatens, then the people of a nation will feel much stronger social solidarity), and/or causal (e.g., poverty causes crime). (2)

Public sociology　Social science that seeks to enrich public debates over moral and political issues by infusing them with social theory and research and tries to generate a conversation between researchers and the public. Often uses *action research* and a *critical social science* approach with its main audience being nonexperts and practitioners. (3)

Purposive sampling　A type of *nonrandom sample* in which the researcher uses a wide range of methods to locate all possible cases of a highly specific and difficult-to-reach *population*. (6)

Qualitative data　Information in the form of words, pictures, sounds, visual images, or objects. (1)

Quantitative data　Information in the form of numbers. (1)

Quasi-experimental designs　*Experimental designs* that are stronger than *preexperimental designs*. They are variations on the *classical experimental design* that an experimenter uses in special situations or when an experimenter has limited control over the *independent variable*. (8)

Quasi-filter question　A type of *survey research* question including the answer choice "no opinion" or "don't know." (7)

Quota sampling　A type of *nonrandom sample* in which the researcher first identifies general categories into which cases or people will be selected, then he or she selects a predetermined number of cases in each category. (6)

Random assignment　Dividing research participants into groups at the beginning of *experimental research* using a random process, so the experimenter can treat the groups as equivalent. (8)

Random-digit dialing (RDD)　A method of randomly selecting cases for telephone interviews that uses all possible telephone numbers as a *sampling frame*. (6)

Random-number table　A list of numbers that has no pattern in them and that is used to create a random process for selecting cases and other randomization purposes. (6)

Random sample　A type of *sample* in which the researcher uses a *random number table* or similar mathematical random process so that each *sampling element* in the *population* will have an equal probability of being selected. (6)

Range　A measure of dispersion for one variable indicating the highest and lowest scores. (10)

Ratio-level measurement　The highest, most precise *level of measurement* for which variable *attributes* can be rank-ordered, the distance between the *attributes* precisely measured, and an absolute zero exists. (5)

Reactivity　The general threat to *external validity* that arises because research participants are aware that they are in an experiment and being studied. (8)

Recollections　The words or writings of people about their life experiences after some time has passed.

The writings are based on a memory of the past, but may be stimulated by a review of past objects, photos, personal notes, or belongings. (12)

Recording sheet   Pages on which a researcher writes down what is coded in *content analysis.* (9)

Reductionism   Something that appears to be a *causal explanation,* but is not, because of a confusion about *units of analysis.* A researcher has *empirical evidence* for an association at the level of individual behavior or very small-scale units, but *overgeneralizes* to make theoretical statements about very large-scale units. (4)

Reliability   The dependability or consistency of the measure of a variable. (5)

Replication   The principle that researchers must be able to repeat scientific findings in multiple studies to have a high level of confidence that the findings are true. (2)

Replication pattern   A pattern in the *elaboration paradigm* in which the *partials* show the same relationship as in a *bivariate contingency table* of the *independent* and *dependent variable* alone. (10)

Request for proposal's (RFP's)   An announcement by a funding organization that it is willing to fund research and it is soliciting written plans of research projects. (14)

Research fraud   A type of unethical behavior in which a researcher fakes or invents data that he or she did not really collect, or fails to honestly and fully report how he or she conducted a study. (3)

Response set   An effect in *survey research* when respondents tend to agree with every question in a series rather than thinking through their answer to each question. (7)

Revising   A step in the writing process that is part of *rewriting* in which a writer adds ideas or evidence, and deletes, rearranges, or changes ideas to improve clarity and better communicate meaning. (14)

Rewriting   A step in the writing process in which the writer goes over a previous draft to improve communication of ideas and clarity of expression. (14)

Running records   A special type of *existing statistics research* used in historical research because the files, records, or documents are maintained in a relatively consistent manner over a period of time. (12)

Sample   A smaller set of cases a researcher selects from a larger pool and generalizes to the *population.* (6)

Sampling distribution   A distribution created by drawing many *random samples* from the same *population.* (6)

Sampling element   The name for a case or single unit to be selected. (6)

Sampling error   How much a *sample* deviates from being representative of the *population.* (6)

Sampling frame   A list of cases in a *population,* or the best approximation of it. (6)

Sampling interval   The inverse of the *sampling ratio,* which is used in *systematic sampling* to select cases. (6)

Sampling ratio   The number of cases in the *sample* divided by the number of cases in the *population* or the *sampling frame,* or the proportion of the *population* in the *sample.* (6)

Scale   A type of *quantitative data* measure often used in *survey research* that captures the intensity, direction, level, or potency of a variable construct along a continuum. Most are at the *ordinal level* of measurement. (5)

Scattergram   A diagram to display the *statistical relationship* between two variables based on plotting each case's values for both of the variables. (10)

Scientific community   A collection of people who share a system of rules and attitudes that sustain the process of producing scientific knowledge. (1)

Scientific method   The process of creating new knowledge using the ideas, techniques, and rules of the *scientific community.* (1)

Scientific misconduct   When someone engages in *research fraud, plagiarism,* or other unethical conduct that significantly deviates from the accepted practice for conducting and reporting research within the *scientific community.* (3)

Secondary data analysis   A type of *existing statistics research* using data from a past study (1)

Secondary sources   *Qualitative data* and *quantitative data* used in historical research. Information about events or settings are documented or written later by historians or others who did not directly participate in the events or setting. (12)

Second-order interpretation   In qualitative research, what a researcher believes the people being studied feel and think. (4)

Selection bias   A threat to *internal validity* when groups in an experiment are not equivalent at the beginning of the experiment. (8)

Selective coding A last pass at coding *qualitative data* in which a researcher examines previous codes to identify and select illustrative data that will support the conceptual coding categories that he or she developed. (13)

Selective observation The tendency to take notice of certain people or events based on past experience or attitudes. (1)

Semantic differential A *scale* in which people are presented with a topic or object and a list of many polar opposite adjectives or adverbs. They are to indicate their feelings by marking one of several spaces between two adjectives or adverbs. (5)

Semantic relationship In *domain analysis,* a logical connection that links *included terms* in a domain to one another. (13)

Sequential sampling A type of *nonrandom sample* in which a researcher tries to find as many relevant cases as possible, until time, financial resources, or his or her energy are exhausted, or until there is no new information or diversity from the cases. (6)

Simple random sampling A type of *random sample* in which a researcher creates a *sampling frame* and uses a pure random process to select cases. Each *sampling element* in the *population* will have an equal probability of being selected. (6)

Skewed distribution A distribution of cases among the categories of a variable that is not *normal* (i.e., not a "bell shape"). Instead of an equal number of cases on both ends, more are at one of the extremes. (10)

Snowball sampling A type of *nonrandom sample* in which the researcher begins with one case, then, based on information about interrelationships from that case, identifies other cases, and then repeats the process again and again. (6)

Social desirability bias A bias in *survey research* in which respondents give a "normative" response or a socially acceptable answer rather than give a truthful answer. (7)

Social impact assessment study A type of *applied social research* in which a researcher estimates the likely consequences or outcome of a planned intervention or intentional change to occur in the future. (1)

Social research A process in which a researcher combines a set of principles, outlooks, and ideas with a collection of specific practices, techniques, and strategies to produce knowledge. (1)

Sociogram A diagram or "map" that shows the network of social relationships, influence patterns, or communication paths among a group of people or units. (6)

Solomon four-group design An *experimental design* in which research participants are randomly assigned to two *control groups* and two *experimental groups*. Only one *experimental group* and one *control group* receive a *pretest*. All four groups receive a posttest. (8)

Special populations People who lack the necessary cognitive competency to give real informed consent or people in a weak position who might comprise their freedom to refuse to participate in a study. (3)

Specification pattern A pattern in the *elaboration paradigm* in which the *bivariate contingency table* shows a relationship. One of the *partial tables* shows the relationship, but other tables do not. (10)

Spuriousness A statement that appears to be a *causal explanation,* but is not because of a hidden, unmeasured, or initially unseen variable. The unseen variable comes earlier in the temporal order, and it has a causal impact on what was initially posited to be the *independent variable* as well as the *dependent variable*. (4)

Standard deviation A measure of dispersion for one variable that indicates an average distance between the scores and the *mean*. (10)

Standard-format question A type of *survey research* question in which the answer categories fail to include "no opinion" or "don't know." (7)

Standardization The procedure to statistically adjust measures to permit making an honest comparison by giving a common basis to measures of different units. (5)

Static group comparison design An *experimental design* with two groups, no *random assignment,* and only a *posttest*. (8)

Statistic A numerical estimate of a *population parameter* computed from a *sample*. (6)

Statistical Abstract of the United States A U.S. government publication that appears annually and contains an extensive compilation of statistical tables and information. (9)

Statistical significance A way to discuss the likelihood that a finding or *statistical relationship* in a *sample* is due to the random factors rather than due to the existence of an actual relationship in the entire *population*. (10)

Stratified sampling A type of *random sample* in which the researcher first identifies a set of *mutually exclusive* and *exhaustive* categories, then uses a random selection method to select cases for each category. (6)

Structured observation A method of watching what is happening in a social setting that is highly organized and that follows systematic rules for observation and documentation. (9)

Subjects A name for the participants sometimes used in experimental research. (8)

Successive approximation A method of *qualitative data* analysis in which the researcher repeatedly moves back and forth between the *empirical data* and the abstract concepts, theories, or models. (13)

Suppressor variable pattern A pattern in the *elaboration paradigm* in which no relationship appears in a *bivariate contingency table*, but the *partials* show a relationship between the variables. (10)

Survey research Quantitative social research in which one systematically asks many people the same questions, then records and analyzes their answers. (1)

Systematic sampling A type of *random sample* in which a researcher selects every *k*th (e.g., 12th) case in the *sampling frame* using a *sampling interval*. (6)

Target population The name for the large general group of many cases from which a *sample* is drawn and which is specified in very concrete terms. (6)

Testing effect A threat to internal validity that occurs when the very process of measuring in the pretest can have an impact on the dependent variable. (8)

Text A general name for symbolic meaning within a communication medium measured in *content analysis*. (9)

Third-order interpretation In qualitative research, what a researcher tells the reader of a research report that the people he or she studied felt and thought. (4)

Threatening questions A type of *survey research* question in which respondents are likely to cover up or lie about their true behavior or beliefs because they fear a loss of self-image or that they may appear to be undesirable or deviant. (7)

Time-series study Any research that takes place over time, in which different people or cases may be looked at in each time point. (1)

Treatment What the *independent variable* in *experimental research* is called. (8)

Type I error The logical error of falsely rejecting the *null hypothesis*. (10)

Type II error The logical error of falsely accepting the *null hypothesis*. (10)

Unidimensionality The principle that when using *multiple indicators* to measure a construct, all the indicators should consistently fit together and indicate a single construct. (5)

Unit of analysis The kind of empirical case or unit that a researcher observes, measures, and analyzes in a study. (4)

Univariate statistics Statistical measures that deal with one variable only. (10)

Universe The broad class of units that are covered in a *hypothesis*. All the units to which the findings of a specific study might be generalized. (4)

Unobtrusive measures Another name for *nonreactive measures*. It emphasizes that the people being studied are not aware of it because the measures do not intrude. (9)

Validity A term meaning truth that can be applied to the logical tightness of *experimental design*, the ability to generalize findings outside a study, the quality of measurement, and the proper use of procedures. (5)

Variable A concept or its *empirical* measure that can take on multiple values. (4)

Verstehen A German word that translates as understanding; specifically, it means an empathic understanding of another's worldview. (2)

Whistle-blowing A person who sees ethical wrongdoing, tries to correct it internally but then informs an external audience, agency, or the media. (3)

Wording effects An effect that occurs when a specific term or word used in a *survey research* question affects how respondents answer the question. (7)

Zoom lens An organizational form often used by field researchers when writing reports that begin broadly then become narrow, focused, and specific. (14)

Z-score A way to locate a score in a distribution of scores by determining the number of *standard deviations* it is above or below the *mean* or arithmetic average. (10)

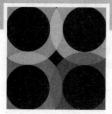

Abbott, Andrew. (1992). From causes to events. *Sociological Methods and Research,* 20:428–455.

Abrams, Philip. (1982). *Historical sociology.* Ithaca, NY: Cornell University Press.

Adams, Julia, Elisabeth Clemens, Ann Shola Orloff, and George Steinmetz, eds. (2005). *Remaking Modernity: Politics, History, and Sociology.* Durham, NC: Duke University Press.

Adams, Peter. (2004). "Gambling Impact Assessment." Centre for Gambling Studies, University of Auckland. www.waitakere.govt.nz/AbtCnl/pp/pdf/partoneintro.pdf, downloaded 08/15/05.

Adler, Patricia A., and Peter Adler. (1987). *Membership roles in field research.* Beverly Hills, CA: Sage.

Adler, Patricia A., and Peter Adler. (1993). Ethical issues in self-censorship. In *Research on sensitive topics,* edited by C. Renzetti and R. Lee, pp. 249–266. Thousand Oaks, CA: Sage.

Adler, Patricia A., and Peter Adler. (1994). Observational techniques. In *Handbook of qualitative research,* edited by N. Denzin and Y. Lincoln, pp. 377–392. Thousand Oaks, CA: Sage.

Agar, Michael. (1986). *Speaking of ethnography.* Beverly Hills, CA: Sage.

Alwin, Duane F., and Jon A. Krosnick. (1985). The measurement of values in surveys. *Public Opinion Quarterly,* 49:535–552.

American Sociological Association. (1997). *American Sociological Association style guide,* 2d ed. Washington, DC: Author.

Anderson, Barbara A., Brian D. Silver, and Paul R. Abramson. (1988). The effects of the race of interviewer on race-related attitudes of black respondents in SRC/CPS national election studies. *Public Opinion Quarterly,* 52:289–324.

Anderson, R. Bruce W. (1973). On the comparability of meaningful stimuli in cross-cultural research. In *Comparative research methods,* edited by D. Warwick and S. Osherson, pp. 149–186. Englewood Cliffs, NJ: Prentice-Hall.

Andren, Gunnar. (1981). Reliability and content analysis. In *Advances in content analysis,* edited by K. Rosengren, pp. 43–67. Beverly Hills, CA: Sage.

Aronson, Elliot, and J. Merrill Carlsmith. (1968). Experimentation in social psychology. In *The handbook of social psychology, Vol. 2: Research methods,* edited by G. Lindzey and E. Aronson, pp. 1–78. Reading, MA: Addison-Wesley.

Ayers, John W., C. Richard Hofstetter, Keith Schnakenberg, and Bohdan Kolody. (2009). Is immigration a racial issue?: Anglo attitudes on immigration policies in a border county. *Social Science Quarterly,* 90(3):593–610.

Babbie, Earl. (1989). *The practice of social research,* 5th ed. Belmont, CA: Wadsworth. (6th ed., 1992; 8th ed., 1998; 9th ed., 2001; 10th ed., 2004.)

Backstrom, Charles H., and Gerald Hursh-Cesar. (1981). *Survey research,* 2d ed. New York: Wiley.

Bailey, Kenneth D. (1987). *Methods of social research,* 3d ed. New York: Free Press.

Barzun, Jacques, and Henry F. Graff. (1970). *The modern researcher,* rev. ed. New York: Harcourt, Brace and World.

Bauer, Raymond, ed. (1966). *Social indicators.* Cambridge, MA: MIT Press.

Beck, Bernard. (1970). Cooking welfare stew. In *Pathways to data,* edited by R. W. Habenstein, pp. 7–29. Chicago: Aldine.

Beck, Richard A. (1995). Publishing evaluation research. *Contemporary Sociology,* 24:9–12.

Becker, Howard S., Blanche Geer, Everett C. Hughes, and Anselm Strauss. (1961). *Boys in white: Student culture in medical school.* Chicago: University of Chicago Press.

Ben-Yehuda, Nachman. (1983). History, selection and randomness—Towards an analysis of social historical explanations. *Quality and Quantity,* 17:347–367.

Bendix, Reinhard. (1963). Concepts and generalizations in comparative sociological studies. *American Sociological Review,* 28:91–116.

Bendix, Reinhard. (1978). *Kings or people: Power and the mandate to rule.* Berkeley: University of California Press.

Benediktsson, Mike Owen. (2010). The deviant organization and the bad apple CEO: ideology and accountability in media coverage of corporate scandals. *Social Forces* 88(5):2189–2216.

Bennett, Andrews, and Colin Elman. (2006). Qualitative research: Recent developments in case study methods. *Annual Review of Political Science* 9:455-78.

Best, Joel. (2001). *Damned lies and statistics: Untangling numbers from the media, politicians, and activists.* Berkeley: University of California Press.

Bischoping, Katherine, and Jennifer Dykema. (1999). Toward a social psychological programme for improving focus group methods of developing questionnaires. *Journal of Official Statistics,* 15:495–516.

Bishop, George F. (1987). Experiments with the middle response alternative in survey questions. *Public Opinion Quarterly,* 51:220–232.

Blee, Kathleen M. (1991). *Women of the Klan: Racism and gender in the 1920s.* Berkeley: University of California Press.

Block, Fred, and Gene A. Burns. (1986). Productivity as a social problem: The uses and misuses of social indicators. *American Sociological Review,* 51:767–780.

Blum, Debra E. (1989). Dean charged with plagiarizing a dissertation for his book on Muzak. *Chronicle of Higher Education,* 35:A17.

Blumberg, Stephen J., and Julian V. Luke. (2007). Coverage bias in traditional telephone surveys of low-income and young adults. *Public Opinion Quarterly,* 71(5):734–749.

Bogdan, Robert, and Steven J. Taylor. (1975). *Introduction to qualitative research methods: A phenomenological approach to the social sciences.* New York: Wiley.

Bonnell, Victoria E. (1980). The uses of theory, concepts and comparison in historical sociology. *Comparative Studies in Society and History,* 22:156–173.

Bradburn, Norman M. (1983). Response effects. In *Handbook of survey research,* edited by P. Rossi, J. Wright, and A. Anderson, pp. 289–328. Orlando, FL: Academic Press.

Bradburn, Norman M., and Seymour Sudman. (1980). *Improving interview method and questionnaire design.* San Francisco: Jossey-Bass.

Bradburn, Norman M., and Seymour Sudman. (1988). *Polls and surveys.* San Francisco: Jossey-Bass.

Brase, Gary L., and Jullian Richmond. (2004). The white-coat effect. *Journal of Applied Social Psychology,* 34:2469–2483.

Bratter, Jenifer L., and Rosalind B. King. 2008. 'But will it last?": Marital instability among interracial and same-race couples. *Family Relations,* 57(2):160–171.

Braudel, Fernand. (1980). *On history,* trans. Sarah Matthews. Chicago: University of Chicago Press.

Brenner, Michael, Jennifer Brown, and David Canter, eds. (1985). *The research interview: Uses and approaches.* Orlando, FL: Academic Press.

Briggs, Charles L. (1986). *Learning how to ask.* New York: Cambridge University Press.

Broad, W. J., and N. Wade. (1982). *Betrayers of the truth.* New York: Simon and Schuster.

Broadhead, Robert, and Ray Rist. (1976). Gatekeepers and the social control of social research. *Social Problems,* 23:325–336.

Brody, Charles J. (1986). Things are rarely black or white. *American Journal of Sociology,* 92:657–677.

Brown, Keith, Doris Hamner, Susan Foley, and Jonathan Woodring. (2009). Doing disability: Disability formations in the search for work. *Sociological Inquiry,* 79(1):3–24.

Brown, R. A. (2007). The Influence of personal and collective self-esteem on the interpersonal and inter-group evaluations of Japanese university students. *Bunkyo University Faculty of Informatics Research,* January 2007. http://www.bunkyo.ac.jp/faculty/lib/slib/kiyo/Inf/if36/if3601.pdf. Retrieved March 1, 2011.

Burawoy, Michael. (2004). Public sociologies. *Social Forces,* 82:1603–1618.

Burawoy, Michael. (2005). For public sociology. *American Sociological Review* 70:4–28.

Calhoun, Craig. (1996). The rise and domestication of historical sociology. In *The historical turn in the human sciences,* edited by T. J. McDonald, pp. 305–337. Ann Arbor: University of Michigan Press.

Callegaro, Mario, Allan L. McCutcheon, and Jack Ludwig. (2010). Who's calling?: The impact of caller ID on telephone survey. *Field Methods,* 22(2):175–191.

Cannell, Charles F., and Robert L. Kahn. (1968). Interviewing. In *Handbook of social psychology,* 2d ed., Vol. 2, edited by G. Lindzey and E. Aronson, pp. 526–595. Reading, MA: Addison-Wesley.

Cantor, Norman F., and Richard I. Schneider. (1967). *How to study history.* New York: Thomas Y. Crowell.

Carley, Michael. (1981). *Social measurement and social indicators.* London: Allen and Unwin.

Carr-Hill, Roy A. (1984). The political choice of social indicators. *Quality and Quantity,* 18:173–191.

Catania, Joseph, D. Dinson, J. Canahola, L. Pollack, W. Hauck, and T. Coates. (1996). Effects of interviewer gender, interviewer choice and item wording on responses to questions concerning sexual behavior. *Public Opinion Quarterly,* 60:345–375.

Chafetz, Janet Saltzman. (1978). *A primer on the construction and testing of theories in sociology.* Itasca, IL: Peacock.

Channels, Noreen L. (1993). Anticipating media coverage. In *Research on sensitive topics,* edited by C. Renzetti and R. Lee, pp. 267–280. Thousand Oaks, CA: Sage.

Chavez, Leo R. (2001). *Covering immigration.* Berkeley: University of California Press.

Chicago manual of style for authors, editors and copywriters, 13th ed., revised and expanded. (1982). Chicago: University of Chicago Press.

Church, Allan H. (1993). Estimating the effect of incentives on mail survey response rates: A meta analysis. *Public Opinion Quarterly,* 57:62–80.

Churchill, Gilbert A., Jr. (1983). *Marketing research,* 3d ed. New York: Dryden.

Clammer, John. (1984). Approaches to ethnographic research. In *Ethnographic research: A guide to general conduct,* edited by R. F. Ellen, pp. 63–85. Orlando: Academic Press.

Cogan, Johan, Judith Torney-Purta, and Douglas Anderson. (1988). Knowledge and attitudes toward global issues: Students in Japan and the United States. *Comparative Education Review,* 32:283–297.

Cole, Stephen, and Linda Perlman Gordon. (1995). *Making science.* Cambridge MA: Harvard University Press.

Converse, Jean M., and Stanley Presser. (1986). *Survey questions.* Beverly Hills, CA: Sage.

Converse, Jean M., and Howard Schuman. (1974). *Conversations at random.* New York: Wiley.

Cook, Thomas D., and Donald T. Campbell. (1979). *Quasi-experimentation.* Chicago: Rand McNally.

Cooper, Christopher A., and H. Gibbs Knotts. (2010). Declining Dixie: Regional identification in the modern American South. *Social Forces,* 88(3):1083–1101.

Corsaro, William. (1994). Discussion, debate, and friendship processes. *Sociology of Education,* 67:1–26.

Corsaro, William, and Luisa Molinari. (2000). Priming events and Italian children's transition from preschool to elementary school: Representations and action. *Social Psychology Quarterly,* 63:16–33.

Cotter, Patrick R., Jeffrey Cohen, and Philip B. Coulter. (1982). Race of interview effects in telephone interviews. *Public Opinion Quarterly,* 46:278–286.

Couper, Mick P. (2008). *Designing effective Web surveys.* Cambridge, UK: Cambridge University Press.

Couper, Mick P., Eleanor Singer, Richard A. Kula. (1998). Participation in the 1990 decennial census. *American Politics Quarterly,* 26:59–81.

Craib, Ian. (1984). *Modern social theory: From Parsons to Habermas.* New York: St. Martin's Press.

Crane, Diana. (1972). *Invisible colleges.* Chicago: University of Chicago Press.

Crozat, Matthew. (1998). Are the times a-changin'?: Assessing the acceptance of protest in Western democracies. In *The movement society,* edited by D. Meyer and S. Tarrow, pp. 59–81. Totowa, NJ: Rowman and Littlefield.

Dabbs, James M., Jr. (1982). Making things visible. In *Varieties of qualitative research,* edited by J. Van Maanen, J. Dabbs, Jr., and R. R. Faulkner, pp. 31–64. Beverly Hills, CA: Sage.

Dale, Angela, S. Arber, and Michael Procter. (1988). *Doing secondary analysis.* Boston: Unwin Hyman.

D'Antonio, William. (August 1989). Executive Office Report: Sociology on the move. *ASA Footnotes,* 17:2.

Davis, Darren W. (1997). The direction of race of interviewer effects among African-Americans: Donning the black mask. *American Journal of Political Science,* 41:309–322.

Davis, James A., and Tom W. Smith. (1992). *The NORC General Social Survey: A user's guide.* Newbury Park, CA: Sage.

Dean, John P., Robert L. Eichhorn, and Lois R. Dean. (1969). Fruitful informants for intensive interviewing. In *Issues in participant observation,* edited by G. McCall and J. L. Simmons, pp. 142–144. Reading, MA: Addison-Wesley.

DeAngelis, Tori (2003). Why we overestimate our competence. *Monitor on Psychology,* p. 60. Washington, DC: American Psychological Association. p. 60. http://www.apa.org/monitor/feb03/overestimate.aspx. Retrieved March 1, 2011.

De Heer, Wim. (1999). International response trends: Results from an international survey. *Journal of Official Statistics,* 15:129–142.

Denzin, Norman K. (1989). *The research act,* 3d ed. Englewood Cliffs, NJ: Prentice-Hall.

Diener, Edward, and Rick Crandall. (1978). *Ethics in social and behavioral research.* Chicago: University of Chicago Press.

Dijkstra, Wil, and Johannes van der Zouwen, eds. (1982). *Response behavior in the survey interview.* New York: Academic Press.

Dillman, Don A. (1978). *Mail and telephone surveys: The total design method.* New York: Wiley.

Dillman, Don A. (1983). Mail and other self-administered questionnaires. In *Handbook of survey research,* edited by P. Rossi, J. Wright, and A. Anderson, pp. 359–377. Orlando, FL: Academic Press.

Dillman, Don A. (2000). *Mail and Internet surveys,* 2d ed. New York: Wiley.

Dooley, David. (1984). *Social research methods.* Englewood Cliffs, NJ: Prentice-Hall.

Douglas, Jack D. (1976). *Investigative social research.* Beverly Hills, CA: Sage.

Douglas, Jack D. (1985). *Creative interviewing.* Beverly Hills, CA: Sage.

Draus, Paul J., Harvey Siegal, Robert Carlson, Russell Falck, and Jichuan Wang. (2005). Cracking in the heartland. *Sociological Quarterly,* 46:165–189.

Duncan, Otis Dudley. (1984). *Notes on social measurement.* New York: Russell Sage Foundation.

Duncan, Otis Dudley, and Magnus Stenbeck. (1988). No opinion or not sure? *Public Opinion Quarterly,* 52:513–525.

Duneier, Mitchell. (1999). *Sidewalk.* New York: Farrar, Straus and Giroux.

Dunning, David, Kerri Johnson, Joyce Ehrlinger, and Justin Kruger (2003). Why people fail to recognize their own incompetence. *Current Directions in Psychological Science,* 12(3):83–87.

Durkheim, Emile. (1951). *Suicide.* (Translated from original 1897 work by John A. Spalding and George Simpson). New York: Free Press.

Dykema, Jennifer, and Nora Cate Schaeffer. (2000). Events, instruments, and reporting errors. *American Sociological Review,* 65:619–629.

Edelman, Lauren, Sally R. Fuller, and Iona Mara-Drita. (2001). Diversity rhetoric and the managerialization of law. *American Journal of Sociology,* 106:1589–1641.

Eder, Donna. (1995). *School talk.* New Brunswick, NJ: Rutgers University Press.

Eder, Donna, and David Kinney. (1995). The effect of middle school extracurricular activities on adolescents' popularity and peer status. *Youth and Society,* 26:298–325.

Ehrlinger, Joy, and David Dunning (2003). How chronic self-views influence (and potentially mislead) estimates of performance. *Journal of Personality and Social Psychology,* 84(1):5–17.

Elder, Glen H., Jr., Eliza Pavalko, and Elizabeth Clipp. (1993). *Working with archival data.* Thousand Oaks, CA: Sage.

Elder, Joseph W. (1973). Problems of crosscultural methodology. In *Comparative social research,* edited by M. Armer and A. D. Grimshaw, pp. 119–144. New York: Wiley.

Eliasoph, Nina. (1998). *Avoiding politics.* New York: Cambridge University Press.

Emerson, Robert M. (1981). Observational field work. *Annual Review of Sociology,* 7:351–378.

Entwisle, Barbara, Katherine Faust, Ronald Rindfuss, and Toshiko Kaneda. (2007). Networks and contexts: Variation in the structure of social ties. *American Journal of Sociology,* 112(5):1495–1533.

Felson, Richard. (1991). Blame analysis. *American Sociologist,* 22:5–24.

Felson, Richard, and Stephen Felson. (1993). Predicaments of men and women. *Society,* 30:16–20.

Fetterman, David M. (1989). *Ethnography: Step by step.* Newbury Park, CA: Sage.

Finkel, Steven E., Thomas M. Guterbock, and Marian J. Borg. (1991). Race-of-interviewer effects in a pre-election poll: Virigina 1989. *Public Opinion Quarterly,* 55:313–330.

Finley, M. I. (Summer 1977). Progress in historiography. *Daedalus,* pp. 125–142.

Firebaugh, Glenn (2008). *Seven rules for social research.* Princeton, NJ: Princeton University Press.

Florida, Richard. (2002). *The rise of the creative class.* New York: Basic Books.

Florida, Richard. (2005). *Cities and the creative class.* New York: Routledge.

Foddy, William. (1993). *Constructing questions for interviews and questionnaires.* New York: Cambridge University Press.

Fowler, Floyd J., Jr. (1984). *Survey research methods.* Beverly Hills, CA: Sage.

Fowler, Floyd J., Jr. (1992). How unclear terms can affect survey data. *Public Opinion Quarterly,* 56:218–231.

Fox, Richard, Melvin R. Crask, and Jonghoon Kim. (1988). Mail survey response rate. *Public Opinion Quarterly,* 52:467–491.

Franke, Charles O. (1983). Ethnography. In *Contemporary field research,* edited by R. M. Emerson, pp. 60–67. Boston: Little, Brown.

Franke, Richard H., and James D. Kaul. (1978). The Hawthorne experiments. *American Sociological Review,* 43:623–643.

Freeman, Howard, and Peter H. Rossi. (1984). Furthering the applied side of sociology. *American Sociological Review,* 49:571–580.

Frey, James H. (1983). *Survey research by telephone.* Beverly Hills, CA: Sage.

Gallie, W. B. (1963). The historical understanding. *History and Theory,* 3:149–202.

Gamson, William A. (1992). *Talking politics.* Cambridge, UK: Cambridge University Press.

Gans, Herbert J. (1982). The participant observer as a human being: Observations on the personal aspects of fieldwork. In *Field research,* edited by R. G. Burgess, pp. 53–61. Boston: Allen and Unwin.

George, Alexander, and Andrew Bennett. (2005). *Case studies and theory development in the social sciences.* Cambridge, MA: MIT Press.

Georges, Robert A., and Michael O. Jones. (1980). *People studying people.* Berkeley: University of California Press.

Gibelman, Margaret. (2001). Learning from the mistakes of others. *Journal of Social Work Education,* 37:241–255.

Gillespie, Richard. (1988). The Hawthorne experiments and the politics of experimentation. In *The rise of experimentation in American psychology,* edited by J. Morawski, pp. 114–137. New Haven, CT: Yale University Press.

Gillespie, Richard. (1991). *Manufacturing knowledge.* New York: Cambridge University Press.

Goldner, Jesse A. (1998). The unending saga of legal controls over scientific misconduct. *American Journal of Law and Medicine,* 24:293–344.

Goldthorpe, John. (1977). The relevance of history to sociology. In *Sociological research methods,* edited by M. Bulmer, pp. 178–191. London: Macmillan.

Gonor, George. (1977). "Situation" versus "frame": The "interactionist" and the "structuralist" analysis of everyday life. *American Sociological Review,* 42:854–867.

Gorden, Raymond. (1980). *Interviewing: Strategy, techniques and tactics,* 3d ed. Homewood, IL: Dorsey Press.

Gordon, Phyllis, D. Feldman, J. Tantillo, and K. Perrone. (2004). Attitudes regarding interpersonal relationships with persons with mental illness and mental retardation. *Journal of Rehabilitation,* 70:50–56.

Gotham, Kevin Fox, and William G. Staples. (1996). Narrative analysis and the new historical sociology. *Sociological Quarterly,* 37:481–502.

Goyder, John C. (1982). Factors affecting response rates to mailed questionnaires. *American Sociological Review,* 47:550–554.

Graham, Sandra. (1992). Most of the subjects were white and middle class. *American Psychologist,* 47:629–639.

Griffin, Larry J. (1993). Narrative, event structure analysis and causal interpretation in historical sociology. *American Journal of Sociology,* 98:1094–1133.

Groves, Robert M., and Robert L. Kahn. (1979). *Surveys by telephone.* New York: Academic Press.

Groves, Robert M., and Nancy Mathiowetz. (1984). Computer assisted telephone interviewing: Effects on interviewers and respondents. *Public Opinion Quarterly,* 48:356–369.

Gurney, Joan Neff. (1985). Not one of the guys: The female researcher in a male-dominated setting. *Qualitative Sociology,* 8:42–62.

Hackworth, Jason. (2009). Normalizing 'solutions' to 'government failure': Media representations of Habitat for Humanity? *Environment and Planning,* 41:2686-2705.

Hage, Jerald. (1972). *Techniques and problems of theory construction in sociology.* New York: Wiley.

Hagstrom, Warren. (1965). *The scientific community.* New York: Basic Books.

Hammersley, Martyn, and Paul Atkinson. (1983). *Ethnography: Principles in practice.* London: Tavistock.

Harper, Douglas. (1982). *Good company.* Chicago: University of Chicago Press.

Harris, Sheldon H. (2002). *Factories of death.* New York: Taylor & Francis.

Hawkes, Daina, Charlene Senn, and Chantal Thorn. (2004). Factors that influence attitudes toward women with tattoos. *Sex Roles,* 50:593–604.

Hearnshaw, L. S. (1979). *Cyril Burt: Psychologist.* London: Holder and Stoughten.

Heberlein, Thomas A., and Robert Baumgartner. (1978). Factors affecting response rates to mailed questionnaires. *American Sociological Review,* 43:447–462.

Heberlein, Thomas A., and Robert Baumgartner. (1981). Is a questionnaire necessary in a second mailing? *Public Opinion Quarterly,* 45:102–107.

Hein, Jeremy, and Christopher Moore. (2009) Race relations stories: How Southeast Asian refugees interpret the ancestral narration of black and white peers. *Social Psychology Quarterly, 72*(1):9–23.

Herring, Lee, and Johanna Ebner. (May/June 2005). Sociologists' impact interpretation of federal welfare legislation. *American Sociological Association Footnotes,* 33:3.

Hill, Michael R. (1993). *Archival strategies and techniques.* Thousand Oaks, CA: Sage.

Hindess, Barry. (1973). *The use of official statistics in sociology: A critique of positivism and ethnomethodology.* New York: Macmillan.

Hippler, Hans J., and Norbert Schwartz. (1986). Not forbidding isn't allowing. *Public Opinion Quarterly,* 50:87–96.

Hirschman, Albert O. (1970). *Exit, voice, and loyalty: Response to decline in firms, organizations and states.* Cambridge, MA: Harvard University Press.

Holstein, James A., and Jaber F. Gubrium. (1994). Phenomenology, ethnomethodology and interpretative practice. In *Handbook of qualitative research,* edited by N. Denzin and Y. Lincoln, pp. 262–272. Thousand Oaks, CA: Sage.

Holsti, Ole R. (1968). Content analysis. In *Handbook of social psychology,* 2d ed., Vol. 2, edited by G. Lindzey and E. Aronson, pp. 596–692. Reading, MA: Addison-Wesley.

Holsti, Ole R. (1969). *Content analysis for the social sciences and humanities.* Reading, MA: Addison-Wesley.

Holt, Robert T., and John E. Turner. (1970). The methodology of comparative research. In *The methodology of comparative research,* edited by R. Holt and J. Turner, pp. 1–20. New York: Free Press.

Holy, Ladislav. (1984). Theory, methodology and the research process. In *Ethnographic research: A guide to general conduct,* edited by R. F. Ellen, pp. 13–34. Orlando: Academic Press.

Hoorens, Vera (1993). Self-enhancement and superiority biases in social comparison. *European Review of Social Psychology,* 4(1):113–139.

Horn, Robert V. (1993). *Statistical indicators for the economic and social sciences.* Cambridge, UK: Cambridge University Press.

Hubbard, Raymond, and Eldon Little. (1988). Promised contributions to charity and mail survey responses: Replication with extension. *Public Opinion Quarterly,* 52:223–230.

Humphreys, Laud. (1975). *Tearoom trade: Impersonal sex in public places.* Chicago: Aldine.

Hyman, Herbert H. (1975). *Interviewing in social research.* Chicago: University of Chicago Press.

Hyman, Herbert H. (1991). *Taking society's measure: A personal history of survey research.* New York: Russell Sage.

Jackson, Bruce. (1978). Killing time: Life in the Arkansas penitentiary. *Qualitative Sociology,* 1:21–32.

Jacobs, Harriet. (1987). *Incidents in the life of a slave girl, written by herself* (ed. Jean Fagan Yellin). Cambridge MA: Harvard University Press.

Johnson, John M. (1975). *Doing field research.* New York: Free Press.

Jones, J. H. (1981). *Bad blood: The Tuskegee syphilis experiment.* New York: Free Press.

Jones, Wesley H. (1979). Generalizing mail survey inducement methods: Populations' interactions with anonymity and sponsorship. *Public Opinion Quarterly,* 43:102–111.

Juster, F. Thomas, and Kenneth C. Land, eds. (1981). *Social accounting systems: Essays on the state of the art.* New York: Academic Press.

Kalmijn, Matthijus. (1991). Shifting boundaries: Trends in religious and educational homogamy. *American Sociological Review,* 56:786–801.

Kane, Emily W., and Laura J. MacAulay. (1993). Interview gender and gender attitudes. *Public Opinion Quarterly,* 57:1–28.

Kaplan, Abraham. (1964). *The conduct of inquiry: Methodology for behavioral science.* New York: Harper & Row.

Karweit, Nancy, and Edmund D. Meyers, Jr. (1983). Computers in survey research. In *Handbook of survey research,* edited by P. Rossi, J. Wright, and A. Anderson, pp. 379–414. Orlando, FL: Academic Press.

Katzer, Jeffrey, Kenneth H. Cook, and Wayne W. Crouch. (1982). *Evaluating information: A guide for users of social science research,* 2d ed. Reading, MA: Addison-Wesley.

Katzer, Jeffrey, Kenneth H. Cook, and Wayne W. Crouch. (1991). *Evaluating information: A guide for users of social science research,* 3d ed. New York: McGraw-Hill.

Keeter, Scott. (2006). The impact of cell phone non-coverage bias on polling in the 2004 presidential election. *Public Opinion Quarterly,* 70(1):88–98.

Keeter, Scott, et al. (2000). Consequences of reducing non-response in a national telephone survey. *Public Opinion Quarterly,* 64:125–148.

Keeter, Scott, Courtney Kennedy, April Clark, Trevor Tompson, and Mike Mokrzycki. (2007). What's missing from national landline RDD surveys: The impact of the growing cell-only population? *Public Opinion Quarterly,* 71(5):772–792.

Kelle, Helga. (2000). Gender and territoriality in games played by nine to twelve-year-old schoolchildren. *Journal of Contemporary Ethnography,* 29:164–197.

Kelman, Herbert. (1982). Ethical issues in different social science methods. In *Ethical issues in social science research,* edited by T. Beauchamp, R. Faden, R. J. Wallace, and L. Walters, pp. 40–99. Baltimore: Johns Hopkins University Press.

Kemp, Jeremy, and R. F. Ellen. (1984). Informants. In *Ethnographic research: A guide to general conduct,* edited by R. F. Ellen, pp. 224–236. Orlando, FL: Academic Press.

Kercher, Kyle. (1992). Quasi-experimental research designs. In *Encyclopedia of sociology,* Vol. 3, edited by E. and M. Borgatta, pp. 1595–1613. New York: Macmillan.

Kidder, Louise H., and Charles M. Judd. (1986). *Research methods in social relations,* 5th ed. New York: Holt, Rinehart and Winston.

Kiecolt, K. Jill, and Laura E. Nathan. (1985). *Secondary analysis of survey data.* Beverly Hills, CA: Sage.

Kirk, Jerome, and Marc L. Miller. (1986). *Reliability and validity in qualitative research.* Beverly Hills, CA: Sage.

Kissane, Rebecca Joyce. (2003). What's need got to do with it? *Journal of Sociology and Social Welfare,* 30:137–148.

Knäuper, Bärbel. (1999). The impact of age and education on response order effects in attitude measurement. *Public Opinion Quarterly,* 63:347–370.

Kohn, Melvin L. (1987). Cross-national research as an analytic strategy. *American Sociological Review,* 52:713–731.

Koretz, Daniel. (Summer 1988). Arriving in Lake Wobegon. *American Educator,* 12:8–15.

Kreuter, Frauke, Stanley Presser, and Roger Tourangeau. (2008). Social desirability bias in CATI, IVR, and web surveys: The effects of mode and question sensitivity. *Public Opinion Quarterly,* 72(5): 847–865.

Krippendorff, Klaus. (1980). *Content analysis: An introduction to its methodology.* Beverly Hills, CA: Sage.

Krosnick, Jon. (1992). The impact of cognitive sophistication and attitude importance on response-order and question-order effects. In *Context effects,* edited by N. Schwarz and Sudman, pp. 203–218. New York: Springer-Verlag.

Krosnick, Jon, and Duane Alwin. (1988). A test of the form-resistant correlation hypothesis: Ratings, rankings, and the measurement of values. *Public Opinion Quarterly,* 52:526–538.

Krueger, Richard A. (1988). *Focus groups: A practical guide for applied research.* Beverly Hills, CA: Sage.

Kruger, Justin, and David Dunning (1999). Unskilled and unaware of it: How difficulties in recognizing one's own incompetence lead to inflated self-assessments. *Journal of Personality and Social Psychology,* 77(6):1121–1134.

Kubrin, Charis E. (2005). Gangstas, Thugs, and Hustlas: Identity and the code of the street in rap music. *Social Problems,* 52(3):360-378.

Kusserow, Richard P. (March 1989). *Misconduct in scientific research.* Report of the Inspector General of the U.S. Department of Health and Human Services. Washington, DC: Department of Health and Human Services.

Labaw, Patricia J. (1980). *Advanced questionnaire design.* Cambridge, MA: Abt Books.

Lamont, Michèle. (2000). The rhetorics of racism and anti-racism in France and the United States. In *Rethinking comparative cultural sociology,* edited by M. Lamont and L. Thèvenot, pp. 25–55. New York: Cambridge University Press.

Land, Kenneth. (1992). Social indicators. In *Encyclopedia of sociology,* Vol. 4, edited by E. and M. Borgatta, pp. 1844–1850. New York: Macmillan.

Lang, Eric. (1992). Hawthorne effect. In *Encyclopedia of sociology,* Vol. 2, edited by E. and M. Borgatta, pp. 793–794. New York: Macmillan.

Lankenau, Stephen E. (1999). Stronger than dirt. *Journal of Contemporary Ethnography,* 28:288–318.

Lee-Gonyea, Jenifer A., Tammy Castle, and Nathan E. Gonyea. (2009). Laid to order: Male escorts advertising on the Internet. *Deviant Behavior,* 30:321–348.

LeMasters, E. E. (1975). *Blue collar aristocrats.* Madison: University of Wisconsin Press.

Lifton, Robert J. (1986). *Nazi doctors.* New York: Basic Books.

Link, Michael W., Michael P. Battaglia, Martin R. Frankel, Larry Osborn, and Ali H. Mokdad. (2007). Reaching the U.S. cell phone generation: Comparison of cell phone survey results with an ongoing landline telephone survey. *Public Opinion Quarterly,* 71(5):814–839.

Lofland, John. (1976). *Doing social life.* New York: Wiley.

Lofland, John, and Lyn H. Lofland. (1984). *Analyzing social settings*, 2d ed. Belmont, CA: Wadsworth.

Lofland, John, and Lyn H. Lofland. (1995). *Analyzing social settings*, 3d ed. Belmont, CA: Wadsworth.

Lofland, John, David Snow, Leon Anderson, and Lyn H. Lofland. (2006). *Analyzing social settings*, 4th ed. Belmont CA: Wadsworth.

Logan, John. (1991). Blaming the suburbs? *Social Science Quarterly*, 72:476–503.

Lowenthal, David. (1985). *The past is a foreign country.* New York: Cambridge University Press.

Luo, Michael. (January 25, 2011). N.R.A. stymies firearms research, scientists say. *New York Times.*

MacKeun, Michael B. (1984). Reality, the press and citizens' political agendas. In *Surveying subjective phenomena*, Vol. 2, edited by C. Turner and E. Martin, pp. 443–473. New York: Russell Sage Foundation.

Mahoney, James. (1999). Nominal, ordinal, and narrative appraisal in macrocausal analysis. *American Journal of Sociology*, 104:1154–1196.

Mahoney, James. (2003). Long-run development and the legacy of colonialism in Spanish America. *American Journal of Sociology*, 109:50–106.

Mahoney, James. (2004). Comparative-historical methodology. *Annual Review of Sociology*, 30:81–101.

Mahoney, James. (2008). Toward a unified theory of causality. *Comparative Political Studies*, 41(4/5):412–436.

Maier, Mark H. (1991). *The data game.* Armonk, NY: M. E. Sharpe.

Markoff, John, Gilbert Shapiro, and Sasha R. Weitman. (1974). Toward the integration of content analysis and general methodology. In *Sociological methodology, 1974*, edited by D. Heise, pp. 1–58. San Francisco: Jossey-Bass.

Martin, Elizabeth. (1999). Who knows who lives here? *Public Opinion Quarterly*, 63:200–236.

McDaniel, Timothy. (1978). Meaning and comparative concepts. *Theory and Society*, 6:93–118.

McKeown, Adam. (2001). *Chinese migrants' networks and cultural change.* Chicago: University of Chicago Press.

McLennan, Gregor. (1981). *Marxism and the methodologies of history.* London: Verso.

Merten, Don E. (1999). Enculturation into secrecy among junior high school girls. *Journal of Contemporary Ethnography*, 28:107–138.

Merton, Robert K. (1967). *On theoretical sociology.* New York: Free Press.

Merton, Robert K. (1973). *The sociology of science.* Chicago: University of Chicago Press.

Miles, Matthew B., and A. Michael Huberman. (1994). *Qualitative data analysis*, 2d ed. Thousand Oaks, CA: Sage.

Milgram, Stanley. (1963). Behavioral study of obedience. *Journal of Abnormal and Social Psychology*, 6:371–378.

Milgram, Stanley. (1965). Some conditions of obedience and disobedience to authority. *Human Relations*, 18:57–76.

Milgram, Stanley. (1974). *Obedience to authority.* New York: Harper & Row.

Mishler, Elliot G. (1986). *Research interviewing.* Cambridge, MA: Harvard University Press.

Mitchell, Alison. (May 17, 1997). Survivors of Tuskegee study get apology from Clinton. *New York Times*, 10.

Mitchell, Mark, and Janina Jolley. (1988). *Research design explained.* New York: Holt, Rinehart and Winston.

Monaghan, Peter. (April 7, 1993a). Facing jail, a sociologist raises question about a scholar's right to protect sources. *Chronicle of Higher Education*, p. A10.

Monaghan, Peter. (May 26, 1993b). Sociologist is jailed for refusing to testify about research subject. *Chronicle of Higher Education*, p. A10.

Monaghan, Peter. (September 1, 1993c). Sociologist jailed because he "wouldn't snitch" ponders the way research ought to be done. *Chronicle of Higher Education*, pp. A8–A9.

Morgan, David L. (1996). Focus groups. *Annual Review of Sociology*, 22:129–152.

Morgan, Kimberly J., and Monica Prasad. (2009). The origins of tax systems: A French–American comparison. *American Journal of Sociology*, 114(5):1350–1394.

Morse, Janice M. (1994). Designing funded qualitative research. In *Handbook of qualitative research*, edited by N. Denzin and Y. Lincoln, pp. 220–235. Thousand Oaks, CA: Sage.

Moser, C. A., and G. Kalton. (1972). *Survey methods in social investigation.* New York: Basic Books.

Mulkay, M. J. (1991). *Sociology of science.* Philadelphia: Open University Press.

Mullins, Nicholas C. (1971). *The art of theory: Construction and use.* New York: Harper & Row.

Murdock, George P. (1967). Ethnographic atlas. *Ethnology*, 6:109–236.

Murdock, George P. (1971). *Outline of cultural materials*, 4th ed. New Haven, CT: Human Relations Area Files.

Narayan, Sowmya, and John A. Krosnick. (1996). Education moderates some response effects in attitude measurement. *Public Opinion Quarterly*, 60:58–88.

Naroll, Raoul. (1968). Some thoughts on comparative method in cultural anthropology. In *Methodology in social research*, edited by H. Blalock and A. Blalock, pp. 236–277. New York: McGraw-Hill.

National Science Board. (2002). *Science and engineering indicators–2002* (NSB-02-1). Arlington, VA: National Science Foundation.

Neuman, W. Lawrence. (1992). Gender, race and age differences in student definitions of sexual harassment. *Wisconsin Sociologist*, 29:63–75.

Neuman, W. Lawrence. (2000). *Social research methods*, 4th ed. Boston: Allyn and Bacon.

Neuman, W. Lawrence. (2003). *Social research methods*, 5th ed. Boston: Allyn and Bacon.

Neuman, W. Lawrence. (2011). *Social research methods: Qualitative and quantitative approaches*, 7th ed. Allyn & Bacon.

Novick, Peter. (1988). *That noble dream*. New York: Cambridge University Press.

Oesterle, Sabrina, Monica Kirkpatrick Johnson, and Jeylan T. Mortimer. (2004). Volunteerism during the transition to adulthood. *Social Forces*, 82:1123–1149.

Olson, Kristen. (2010). An examination of questionnaire evaluation by expert reviewers. *Field Methods*, 22(4):295–318.

Ostrom, Thomas M., and Katherine M. Gannon. (1996). Exemplar generation. In *Answering questions*, edited by N. Schwarz and S. Sudman, pp. 293–318. San Francisco: Jossey-Bass.

Pager, Devah, and Lincoln Quillian. (2005). Walking the talk? *American Sociological Review*, 70:355–380.

Paige, Jeffrey M. (1975). *Agrarian revolution*. New York: Free Press.

Parcel, Toby L. (1992). Secondary data analysis and data archives. In *Encyclopedia of sociology*, Vol. 4, edited by E. and M. Borgatta, pp. 1720–1728. New York: Macmillan.

Patton, Michael Quinn. (2001). *Qualitative research and evaluation methods*, 3d ed. Thousand Oaks, CA: Sage.

Pearsall, Marion. (1970). Participant observation as role and method in behavioral research. In *Qualitative*

methodology, edited by W. J. Filstead, pp. 340–352. Chicago: Markham.

Phillips, Bernard. (1985). *Sociological research methods: An introduction*. Homewood, IL: Dorsey.

Piliavin, Irving M., J. Rodin, and Jane A. Piliavin. (1969). Good samaritanism: An underground phenomenon? *Journal of Personality and Social Psychology*, 13:289–299.

Pollner, Melvin, and Richard Adams. (1997). The effect of spouse presence on appraisals of emotional support and household strain. *Public Opinion Quarterly*, 61:615–626.

Porter, Stephen R., and Michael E Whitcomb. (2003). The impact of contact type on web survey response rates. *Public Opinion Quarterly*, 67(4):579–588.

Presser, Stanley. (1990). Measurement issues in the study of social change. *Social Forces*, 68:856–868.

Przeworski, Adam, and Henry Teune. (1970). *The logic of comparative inquiry*. New York: Wiley.

Punch, Maurice. (1986). *The politics and ethics of fieldwork*. Beverly Hills, CA: Sage.

Raento, Mika, Antti Oulasvirta, and Nathan Eagle. (2009). Smartphones: An emerging tool for social scientists. *Sociological Methods and Research* 37(3):426–454.

Ragin, Charles C. (1987). *The comparative method*. Berkeley: University of California Press.

Ragin, Charles C. (1992). Introduction: Cases of "what is a case?" In *What is a case?*, edited by C. Ragin and H. Becker, pp. 1–18. New York: Cambridge University Press.

Rampton, Sheldon, and John Stauber. (2001). *Trust us, we're experts*. New York: Putnam.

Rathje, William, and Cullen Murphy. (1992). *Rubbish: The archaeology of garbage*. New York: Vintage.

Reese, Stephen, W. Danielson, P. Shoemaker, T. Chang, and H. Hsu. (1986). Ethnicity of interview effects among Mexican Americans and Anglos. *Public Opinion Quarterly*, 50:563–572.

Reynolds, Paul Davidson. (1971). *A primer in theory construction*. Indianapolis, IN: Bobbs-Merrill.

Reynolds, Paul Davidson. (1979). *Ethical dilemmas and social science research*. San Francisco: Jossey-Bass.

Reynolds, Paul Davidson. (1982). *Ethics and social science research*. Englewood Cliffs, NJ: Prentice-Hall.

Rhomberg, Chris (2010). A signal juncture: The Detroit newspaper strike and post-accord labor relations in the United States. *American Journal of Sociology*, 115(6):1853–1894.

Rind, Bruce, and David Strohmetz. (1999). Effect on restaurant tipping of a helpful message written on the back of customers' checks. *Journal of Applied Social Psychology,* 29:139–144.

Ritchie, Donald A. (2003). *Doing oral history,* 2d ed. New York: Oxford University Press.

Roethlisberger, F. J., and W. J. Dickenson. (1939). *Management and the worker.* Cambridge, MA: Harvard University Press.

Roscigno, Vincent J., and William Danaher. (2001). Media and mobilization: The case of radio and southern textile worker insurgency, 1929–1934. *American Sociological Review,* 66:21–48.

Rosenberg, Morris. (1968). *The logic of survey analysis.* New York: Basic Books.

Rossi, Robert J., and Kevin J. Gilmartin. (1980). *The handbook of social indicators.* New York: Garland STPM Press.

Rueschemeyer, Dietrich, Evelyne Huber Stephens, and John D. Stephens. (1992). *Capitalist development and democracy.* Chicago: University of Chicago Press.

Runciman, W. G. (1980). Comparative sociology or narrative history. *European Journal of Sociology,* 21:162–178.

Saguy, Abigail C., and Kjerstin Gruys. (2010). Morality and health: News media constructions of overweight and eating disorders. *Social Problems,* 57(2):231–250.

Sanday, Peggy Reeves. (1983). The ethnographic paradigm(s). In *Qualitative methodology,* edited by J. Van Maanen, pp. 19–36. Beverly Hills, CA: Sage.

Sanjek, Roger. (1990). On ethnographic validity. In *Field notes,* edited by R. Sanjek, pp. 385–418. Ithaca, NY: Cornell University Press.

Schacter, Daniel L. (2001). *The seven deadly sins of memory.* Boston: Houghton Mifflin.

Schaffer, Nora Cate. (1980). Evaluating race-of-interviewer effects in a national survey. *Sociological Methods and Research,* 8:400–419.

Schatzman, Leonard, and Anselm L. Strauss. (1973). *Field research.* Englewood Cliffs, NJ: Prentice-Hall.

Schuman, Howard, and Jean M. Converse. (1971). Effects of black and white interviewers on black response in 1968. *Public Opinion Quarterly,* 65:44–68.

Schuman, Howard, and Stanley Presser. (1981). *Questions and answers in attitude surveys: Experiments on question form, wording and content.* New York: Academic Press.

Schwandt, Thomas A. (1994). Constructivist, interpretivist approaches to human inquiry. In *Handbook of qualitative research,* edited by N. Denzin and Y. Lincoln, pp. 118–137. Thousand Oaks, CA: Sage.

Sewell, William H., Jr. (1987). Theory of action, dialectic, and history. *American Journal of Sociology,* 93:166–171.

Shafer, Robert Jones. (1980). *A guide to historical method,* 3d ed. Homewood, IL: Dorsey.

Shaffir, William B., Robert A. Stebbins, and Allan Turowetz. (1980). Introduction. In *Fieldwork experience,* edited by W. B. Shaffir, R. Stebbins, and A. Turowetz, pp. 3–22. New York: St. Martin's Press.

Sharp, Elaine B., and Mark R. Joslyn. (2008). Culture, segregation, and tolerance in urban America. *Social Science Quarterly,* 89(3):573–591.

Shih, Tse-Hua, and Xitao Fan. (2008). Comparing response rates from Web and mail surveys: A meta-analysis. *Field Methods,* 20(3):249–271.

Singer, Eleanor. (1988). Surveys in the mass media. In *Surveying social life: Papers in honor of Herbert H. Hyman,* edited by H. O'Gorman, pp. 413–436. Middletown, CT: Wesleyan University Press.

Singleton, Royce, Jr., B. Straits, Margaret Straits, and Ronald McAllister. (1988). *Approaches to social research.* New York: Oxford University Press.

Skidmore, William. (1979). *Theoretical thinking in sociology,* 2d ed. New York: Cambridge University Press.

Smelser, Neil J. (1976). *Comparative methods in the social sciences.* Englewood Cliffs, NJ: Prentice-Hall.

Smith, Mary Lee, and Gene V. Glass. (1987). *Research and evaluation in education and the social sciences.* Englewood Cliffs, NJ: Prentice-Hall.

Smith, Tom W. (1987). That which we call welfare by any other name would smell sweeter. *Public Opinion Quarterly,* 51:75–83.

Smith, Tom W. (1995). Trends in non-response rates. *International Journal of Public Opinion Research,* 7:156–171.

Spector, Paul E. (1981). *Research designs.* Beverly Hills, CA: Sage.

Spradley, James P. (1979a). *The ethnographic interview.* New York: Holt, Rinehart and Winston.

Spradley, James P. (1979b). *Participant observation.* New York: Holt, Rinehart and Winston.

Stevenson, Richard W. (October 16, 1996). U.S. to revise its estimate of layoffs. *New York Times,* 5.

Stewart, David W. (1984). *Secondary research: Information sources and methods.* Beverly Hills, CA: Sage.

Stinchcombe, Arthur L. (1968). *Constructing social theories.* New York: Harcourt, Brace and World.

Stinchcombe, Arthur L. (1973). Theoretical domains and measurement, Part 1. *Acta Sociologica,* 16:3–12.

Stinchcombe, Arthur L. (1978). *Theoretical methods in social history.* New York: Academic Press.

Stone, Lawrence. (1987). *The past and present revisited.* Boston: Routledge and Kegan Paul.

Stone, Philip J., and Robert P. Weber. (1992). Content analysis. In *Encyclopedia of sociology,* Vol. 1, edited by E. and M. Borgatta, pp. 290–295. New York: Macmillan.

Strack, Fritz. (1992). "Order effects" in survey research. In *Context effects in social and psychological research,* edited by N. Schwarz and S. Sudman, pp. 23–24. New York: Springer-Verlag.

Strauss, Anselm, and Juliet Corbin. (1990). *Basics of qualitative research.* Newbury Park, CA: Sage.

Strauss, Anselm, and Juliet Corbin. (1994). Grounding theory methodology. In *Handbook of qualitative research,* edited by N. Denzin and Y. Lincoln, pp. 273–285. Thousand Oaks, CA: Sage.

Sudman, Seymour. (1976). Sample surveys. *Annual Review of Sociology,* 2:107–120.

Sudman, Seymour. (1983). Applied sampling. In *Handbook of survey research,* edited by P. Rossi, J. Wright, and A. Anderson, pp. 145–194. Orlando, FL: Academic Press.

Sudman, Seymour, and Norman M. Bradburn. (1983). *Asking questions.* San Francisco: Jossey-Bass.

Sudman, Seymour, Norman M. Bradburn, and Norbert Schwarz. (1996). *Thinking about answers.* San Francisco: Jossey-Bass.

Suls, Jerry M., and Ralph L. Rosnow. (1988). Concerns about artifacts in psychological experiments. In *The rise of experimentation in American psychology,* edited by J. Morawski, pp. 153–187. New Haven, CT: Yale University Press.

Sutton, John R. (2004). The political economy of imprisonment in affluent Western democracies, 1960–1990. *American Sociological Review,* 69:170–189.

Taylor, Steven. (1987). Observing abuse. *Qualitative Sociology,* 10:288–302.

Thorfason, Magnus Thor, and Paul Ingram. (2010). The global rise of democracy: A network account. *American Sociological Review,* 75:355–377.

Tourangeau, Roger, and Cong Ye. (2009). The framing of the survey request and panel attrition. *Public Opinion Quarterly,* 73(2):338-348.

Tourangeau, Roger, G. Shapiro, A. Kearney, and L. Ernst. (1997). Who lives here? *Journal of Official Statistics,* 13:1–18.

Tourangeau, Roger, Robert M. Groves, and Cleo D. Redline. (2010). Sensitive topics and reluctant respondents. *Public Opinion Quarterly,* 74(3):413–432.

Trinitapoli, Jenny (2007). I know this isn't PC, but ...": Religious exclusivism among U.S. adolescents. *Sociological Quarterly,* 48(3):451–483.

Tucker, Clyde, Michael Brick, and Brian Meekins. (2007). Household telephone service and usage patterns in the United States in 2004: Implications for telephone samples. *Public Opinion Quarterly,* 71(1):3–22.

Turner, Charles, and Elizabeth Martin, eds. (1984). *Surveying subjective phenomena,* Vol. 1. New York: Russell Sage Foundation.

Turner, Stephen P. (1980). *Sociological explanation as translation.* New York: Cambridge University Press.

Unnever, James, and Francis T. Cullen. (2007). The racial divide in support for the death penalty: Does white racism matter? Social Forces, 85(3):1281–1301.

Vallier, Ivan, ed. (1971a). *Comparative methods in sociology.* Berkeley: University of California Press.

Vallier, Ivan. (1971b). Empirical comparisons of social structure. In *Comparative methods in sociology,* edited by I. Vallier, pp. 203–263. Berkeley: University of California Press.

Van den Berg, Harry, and Cees Van der Veer. (1985). Measuring ideological frames of references. *Quality and Quantity,* 19:105–118.

Van Maanen, John. (1982). Fieldwork on the beat. In *Varieties of qualitative research,* edited by J. Van Maanen, J. Dabbs, Jr., and R. Faulkner, pp. 103–151. Beverly Hills, CA: Sage.

Van Maanen, John. (1988). *Tales of the field.* Chicago: University of Chicago Press.

Van Poppel, Frans, and L. Day. (1996). A test of Durkheim's theory of suicide—Without committing the "ecological fallacy." *American Sociological Review,* 61:500–507.

Vaquera, Elizabeth, and Grace Kao. (2005). Private and public displays of affection among interracial and intra-racial adolescent couples. *Social Science Quarterly,* 86:484–508.

Venkatesh, Sudhir. (2008*). Gang leader for a day: A rouge sociologist takes to the streets.* New York: Penguin.

Vidich, Arthur Joseph, and Joseph Bensman. (1968). *Small town in mass society,* rev. ed. Princeton, NJ: Princeton University Press.

Viterna, Jocelyn, and Kathleen M. Fallon. (2008). Democratization, women's movements, and gender-equitable states: A framework for comparison. *American Sociological Review,* 73:668–689.

Wade, Nicholas. (1976). IQ and heredity. *Science,* 194:916–919.

Wade, Nicholas. (August 11, 2010). Expert on morality is on leave after research inquiry. *New York Times.*

Walton, John. (1973). Standardized case comparison. In *Comparative social research,* edited by M. Armer and A. Grimshaw, pp. 173–191. New York: Wiley.

Wang, Jichuan, Russel S. Falck, Linna Li, Ahmmed Rahman, and Robert G. Carlson. (2007). Respondent-driven sampling in the recruitment of illicit stimulant drug users in a rural setting: Findings and technical issues. *Addictive Behaviors,* 32(5):924–937.

Warwick, Donald P. (1982). Types of harm in social science research. In *Ethical issues in social science research,* edited by T. Beauchamp, R. Faden, R. J. Wallace, and L. Walters, pp. 101–123. Baltimore: Johns Hopkins University Press.

Warwick, Donald P., and Charles A. Lininger. (1975). *The sample survey.* New York: McGraw-Hill.

Wax, Rosalie H. (1971). *Doing fieldwork: Warnings and advice.* Chicago: University of Chicago Press.

Webb, Eugene J., Donald T. Campbell, Richard D. Schwartz, Lee Sechrest, and Janet Belew Grove. (1981). *Nonreactive measures in the social sciences,* 2d ed. Boston: Houghton Mifflin.

Weber, Robert P. (1984). Computer assisted content analysis: A short primer. *Qualitative Sociology,* 7:126–149.

Weber, Robert P. (1985). *Basic content analysis.* Beverly Hills, CA: Sage.

Weeks, M. F., and R. P. Moore. (1981). Ethnicity of interviewer effects on ethnic respondents. *Public Opinion Quarterly,* 45:245–249.

Weinstein, Deena. (1979). Fraud in science. *Social Science Quarterly,* 59:639–652.

Weiss, Carol H. (1997). *Evaluation.* Englewood Cliffs, NJ: Prentice Hall.

Weiss, Janet A., and Judith E. Gruber. (1987). The managed irrelevance of educational statistics. In *The politics of numbers,* edited by W. Alonso and P. Starr, pp. 363–391. New York: Russell Sage Foundation.

Weitzman, Lenore, D. Eifler, E. Hokada, and C. Ross. (1972). Sex role socialization in picture books for preschool children. *American Journal of Sociology,* 77:1125–1150.

Whiting, John W. M. (1968). Methods and problems in cross-cultural research. In *The handbook of social psychology,* 2d ed., edited by G. Lindzey and E. Aronson, pp. 693–728. Reading, MA: Addison-Wesley.

Whyte, William Foote. (1955). *Street corner society: The social structure of an Italian slum,* 2d ed. Chicago: University of Chicago Press.

Whyte, William Foote. (1982). Interviewing in field research. In *Field research,* edited by R. G. Burgess, pp. 111–122. Boston: Allen and Unwin.

Whyte, William Foote. (1984). *Learning from the field.* Beverly Hills: Sage.

Willer, David, and Henry A. Walker. (2007a). *Building experiments, testing theory.* Stanford CA: Stanford University Press.

Willer, David, and Henry A. Walker. (2007b).Experiments and the science of sociology. In *Laboratory experiments in the social sciences,* edited by Murray Webster, Jr. and Jane Sell, pp. 25–54. New York: Academic Press.

Williams, Peter, and David Wallace. (1989). *Unit 731: Japan's secret biological warfare in World War II.* New York: Free Press.

Willimack, Diane K., Howard Schuman, Beth-Ellen Pennell, and James M. Lepkowski. (1995). Effects of prepaid non-monetary incentives on response rates and response quality in face-to-face survey. *Public Opinion Quarterly,* 59:78–92.

Wood, Elizabeth Anne. (2000). Working in the fantasy factory. *Journal of Contemporary Ethnography,* 29:5–32.

Yellin, Jean Fagan, ed. (2008). *The Harriet Jacobs Family Papers,* 2 vols. Chapel Hill: University of North Carolina Press.

Zane, Anne, and Euthemia Matsoukas. (1979). Different settings, different results?: A comparison of school and home responses. *Public Opinion Quarterly,* 43:550–557.

Ziman, John. (1999). Social rules of the game in doing science. *Nature,* 400:721.

Zimbardo, Philip G. (1972). Pathology of imprisonment. *Society,* 9:4–6.

Zimbardo, Philip G. (1973). On the ethics of intervention in human psychological research. *Cognition,* 2:243–256.

Zimbardo, Philip G., C. Haney, W.C. Banks, and D. Jaffe. (April 8, 1973). The mind is a formidable jailer. *New York Times Magazine,* 122:38–60.

Zimbardo, Philip G., C. Haney, W.C. Banks, and D. Jaffe. (1974). The psychology of imprisonment: Privation, power and pathology. In *Doing unto others,* edited by Z. Rubin. Englewood Cliffs, NJ: Prentice-Hall.

Name Index

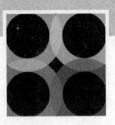

Subject Index

CREDITS

CHAPTER 2: EXAMPLE BOX 2.1, page 30, From Chafetz. *A Primer on the Construction and Testing of Theories in Sociology,* 1E. © 1978 Wadsworth, a part of Cengage Learning, Inc. Reproduced by permission. www.cengage.com/permissions

CHAPTER 4: EXPANSION BOX 4.2, page 82, Katzer, Jeffrey, et. al, *Evaluating Information: A Guide for Users of Social Science Research,* 4th edition, copyright © 1998 McGraw-Hill. Reproduced with permission of McGraw-Hill.

CHAPTER 5: Page 118, Sharp, E. B. and Joslyn, M. R. (2008), 'Culture, Segregation, and Tolerance in Urban America.' *Social Science Quarterly,* 89: 573–591. Used with permission; FIGURE 5.3, page 126, From Babbie, *The Practice of Social Research,* 4th edition © 1986 Wadsworth, a part of Cengage Learning, Inc. Reproduced by permission.

www.cengage.com/permissions; EXAMPLE BOX 5.4, page 138–139, Milton Kleg, Kaoru Yamamoto, *The Social Science Journal,* 1988. Elsevier Publishers. Reprinted with permissions; EXAMPLE BOX 5.5, page 141, Daina Hawkes *Sex Roles,* Vol. 50, No. 9; May 1, 2004. Springer Publishers. Reprinted with permission; EXAMPLE BOX 5.6, page 142, *The Social Movement Society: Contentious Politics for a New Century,* by Meyer, David S. Copyright 1998. Reproduced with permission of Rowman & Littlefield Publishing Group, Inc. in the format Textbook via Copyright Clearance Center.

CHAPTER 7: EXAMPLE BOX 7.1, page 176, Lloyd Jackson Fowler, Jr., 'How Unclear Terms Affect Survey Data.' *Public Opinion Quarterly,* (1992) 56(2): 218–231. Reprinted with permission.